P9-DGR-781

GREAT MINDS IN
MANAGEMENT

GREAT MINDS IN
MANAGEMENT

THE PROCESS OF
THEORY DEVELOPMENT

Edited by
KEN G. SMITH
and
MICHAEL A. HITT

WAGGONER LIBRARY
TREVECCA NAZARENE UNIVERSITY

WAGGONER LIBRARY
DISCARD

OXFORD
UNIVERSITY PRESS

OXFORD
UNIVERSITY PRESS

Great Clarendon Street. Oxford OX2 6DP

Oxford University Press is a department of the University of Oxford.
It furthers the University's objective of excellence in research, scholarship,
and education by publishing worldwide in

Oxford New York

Auckland Cape Town Dar es Salaam Hong Kong Karachi
Kuala Lumpur Madrid Melbourne Mexico City Nairobi
New Delhi Shanghai Taipei Toronto

With offices in

Argentina Austria Brazil Chile Czech Republic France Greece
Guatemala Hungary Italy Japan Poland Portugal Singapore
South Korea Switzerland Thailand Turkey Ukraine Vietnam

Oxford is a registered trade mark of Oxford University Press
in the UK and in certain other countries

Published in the United States
by Oxford University Press Inc., New York

© Oxford University Press 2005

The moral rights of the authors have been asserted
Database right Oxford University Press (maker)

First published 2005

All rights reserved. No part of this publication may be reproduced,
stored in a retrieval system, or transmitted, in any form or by any means,
without the prior permission in writing of Oxford University Press,
or as expressly permitted by law, or under terms agreed with the appropriate
reprographics rights organization. Enquiries concerning reproduction
outside the scope of the above should be sent to the Rights Department,
Oxford University Press, at the address above

You must not circulate this book in any other binding or cover
and you must impose the same condition on any acquirer

British Library Cataloguing in Publication Data

Data available

Library of Congress Cataloging in Publication Data

Data available

Typeset by SPI Publisher Services, Pondicherry, India
Printed in Great Britain on acid-free paper by
Biddles Ltd., King's Lynn, Norfolk

ISBN 0-19-927681-1   978-0-19-927681-3

1 3 5 7 9 10 8 6 4 2

Contents

List of Figures   ix
List of Tables   x
Acknowledgements   xi
List of Contributors   xii

1. Introduction: The Process of Developing Management Theory   1
   MICHAEL A. HITT AND KEN G. SMITH

PART I INDIVIDUALS AND THEIR ENVIRONMENT

2. The Evolution of Social Cognitive Theory   9
   ALBERT BANDURA

3. Image Theory   36
   LEE R. BEACH AND TERENCE R. MITCHELL

4. The Road to Fairness and Beyond   55
   ROBERT FOLGER

5. Grand Theories and Mid-Range Theories: Cultural Effects
   on Theorizing and the Attempt to Understand Active
   Approaches to Work   84
   MICHAEL FRESE

6. Upper Echelons Theory: Origins, Twists and Turns, and
   Lessons Learned   109
   DONALD C. HAMBRICK

7. Goal Setting Theory: Theory Building by Induction   128
   EDWIN A. LOCKE AND GARY P. LATHAM

8. How Job Characteristics Theory Happened   151
   GREG R. OLDHAM AND J. RICHARD HACKMAN

9. Do Employee Attitudes towards Organizations Matter?
   The Study of Employee Commitment to Organizations   171
   LYMAN W. PORTER, RICHARD M. STEERS AND RICHARD T. MOWDAY

10. Developing Psychological Contract Theory   190
    DENISE M. ROUSSEAU

11. The Escalation of Commitment: Steps toward an
    Organizational Theory   215
    BARRY M. STAW

12. On the Origins of Expectancy Theory   239
    VICTOR H. VROOM

PART II BEHAVIOR OF ORGANIZATIONS

13. Double-Loop Learning in Organizations: A Theory of Action
    Perspective   261
    CHRIS ARGYRIS

14. Where does Inequality Come from? The Personal and
    Intellectual Roots of Resource-Based Theory   280
    JAY B. BARNEY

15. Organizational Effectiveness: Its Demise and Re-emergence
    through Positive Organizational Scholarship   304
    KIM CAMERON

16. Managerial and Organizational Cognition: Islands of
    Coherence   331
    ANNE S. HUFF

17. Developing Theory about the Development of Theory   355
    HENRY MINTZBERG

18. Managing Organizational Knowledge: Theoretical and
    Methodological Foundations   373
    IKUJIRO NONAKA

19. The Experience of Theorizing: Sensemaking as Topic and Resource   394

KARL E. WEICK

PART III ENVIRONMENTAL CONTINGENCIES AND ORGANIZATIONS

20. The Development of Stakeholder Theory: An Idiosyncratic Approach   417

R. EDWARD FREEMAN

21. Developing Resource Dependence Theory: How Theory is Affected by its Environment   436

JEFFREY PFEFFER

22. Institutional Theory: Contributing to a Theoretical Research Program   460

W. RICHARD SCOTT

23. Transaction Cost Economics: The Process of Theory Development   485

OLIVER E. WILLIAMSON

24. Developing Evolutionary Theory for Economics and Management   509

SIDNEY G. WINTER

25. An Evolutionary Approach to Institutions and Social Construction: Process and Structure   547

LYNN G. ZUCKER AND MICHAEL R. DARBY

26. Epilogue: Learning to Develop Theory from the Masters   572

KEN G. SMITH AND MICHAEL A. HITT

Index   589

LIST OF FIGURES

5.1   Personal Initiative (PI): A concept of work for the twenty-first century 97

6.1   Strategic choice under bounded rationality: The executive's construed reality 113

8.1   The job characteristics model 153

11.1 A model of the commitment process 223

11.2 A temporal model of escalation 226

11.3 An aggregate model of escalation 229

13.1 Managerial and organizational learning 263

13.2 Model I: Unilateral control 264

13.3 Model II: Unilateral control 267

15.1 The competing values framework of organizational effectiveness 309

15.2 A continuum illustrating positive deviance 320

16.1 Individual cognition in a structuration framework 342

16.2 Stress and inertia influences on cognitive frameworks 344

18.1 The SECI process of knowledge creation and utilization 384

18.2 Underlying philosophical methodologies of SECI 385

25.1 Institutional theory approaches 550

25.2 Biotech firms are more successful if tied to star scientists or if linked to top-research-university faculty 558

25.3 Endowed supply of and demand for trust-producing social structure in scientific collaborations in physics 563

25.4 Cost conditions for total quantity of trust-producing social structure 564

25.5 Equilibrium social structures with different endowments of trust-producing social structure 565

25.6 Institutional tool kits: Mosaic pieces as illustration of inductive theorizing and formalization 567

26.1 The process of theory development 586

LIST OF TABLES

5.1   Facets of Personal Initiative (PI)   94

13.1 Examples of what subjects said and what they thought
      (but did not say)   269

15.1 The most well-known models of organizational effectiveness   308

22.1 Three pillars of institutions   465

25.1 Collaborating pairs for genetic discoveries   555

25.2 Relation of employment in new biotech firms to links to high science   560

26.1 Authors and their school of Ph.D.   578

Acknowledgements

The original idea for this book came from our discussions with Ed Locke and his concern about the current descriptions to theory published in AMJ and AMR and with existing prescriptions about theory building in the field. We thank Ed and all of our authors for their insights on how they developed their theories. We also thank Argie Butler and Sophia Marinova for their help with editing the book. We also want to thank our editor, David Musson, for his belief in the book and all of the Oxford University Press people for their support.

LIST OF CONTRIBUTORS

Chris Argyris	Harvard University, USA
Albert Bandura	Stanford University, USA
Jay B. Barney	Ohio State University, USA
Lee R. Beach	University of Arizona, USA
Kim Cameron	University of Michigan, USA
Michael R. Darby	University of California, Los Angeles, USA
Robert Folger	University of Central Florida, USA
R. Edward Freeman	University of Virginia, USA
Michael Frese	Giessen University, Germany
J. Richard Hackman	Harvard University, USA
Donald C. Hambrick	Pennsylvania State University, USA
Michael A. Hitt	Texas A&M University
Anne S. Huff	Technische Universität München, Germany
Gary P. Latham	University of Toronto, Canada
Edwin A. Locke	University of Maryland, USA
Henry Mintzberg	McGill University, Canada
Terrence R. Mitchell	University of Florida, USA
Richard T. Mowday	University of Oregon, USA
Ikujiro Nonaka	Hitotsubashi University, Japan
Greg R. Oldham	University of Illinois, Urbana Champaign, USA
Jeffrey Pfeffer	Stanford University, USA
Lyman W. Porter	University of California, Irvine, USA
Denise M. Rousseau	Carnegie-Mellon University, USA
W. Richard Scott	Stanford University, USA
Ken G. Smith	University of Maryland, USA
Barry M. Staw	University of California, Berkeley, USA
Richard M. Steers	University of Oregon, USA
Victor H. Vroom	Yale University, USA

Karl E. Weick	University of Michigan, USA
Oliver E. Williamson	University of California, Berkeley, USA
Sidney G. Winter	University of Pennsylvania, USA
Lynne G. Zucker	University of California, Los Angeles, USA

··

CHAPTER 1

INTRODUCTION

THE PROCESS OF DEVELOPING MANAGEMENT THEORY

··

MICHAEL A. HITT

KEN G. SMITH

Do not go where the path may lead, go instead where there is no path and leave a trail.

Ralph Waldo Emerson

THEORY provides the base for knowledge and understanding of important relationships in various disciplines. Theory development is highly important in the discipline of management and organizations as it is a relatively young field of study, in comparison to many other social science disciplines. As a young field of study, new theory provides important and unique insights that can advance the field's understanding of management phenomena. In fact, much of the theory used in management and organizational research has been derived from the social science disciplines of economics, psychology, and sociology; although new distinctive management theory has been developed, these theories are still in a developmental stage. Many of the most prominent theories used in the field of management and organizations are examined in this handbook.

Dubin (1969) was one of the first to address the importance of theory building to science. He argued that the focus of theory was the human mind, or that the need for theory building rests with the need for humans to order and make sense of reality. Sixty years ago, Kurt Lewin suggested that nothing is so practical as good theory and this was reemphasized by Andy Van de Ven (1989) forty-four years later. Good theory is practical to the extent that it advances science and knowledge development. Theory can advance science by providing cohesion, efficiency, and structure to our research questions and design (Kerlinger, 1973; Van de Ven, 1989). In a very practical sense, good theory helps identify *what* factors should be studied and *how* and *why* they are related. A high quality theory also states the conditions and boundaries of relationship (Dubin, 1969; Whetten, 1989). Thus, we advance our field by developing new theory.

Thanks to Dubin (1969) and others, we have a good sense of what theory is (or is not). However, we know much less about the process by which theory is developed. Our understanding of this process has been facilitated by two special issues in the *Academy of Management Review* (1989, 1999) and another in the *Administrative Science Quarterly* (1995). Even with these works, we know little about this process. Philosophers still disagree on how theory is best developed. Most seem to agree that deduction generally is a means for testing theory but not developing it. However, some agree with Popper (1959) that good theory is based on deductive falsification using conjecture and refutation. In other words, according to Popper, developing theory begins with the use of imagination and creativity, rather than induction. According to Ross (2003), such an approach allowed Einstein to "study the universe with no more than a piece of chalk." Yet, many others believe that theory can be, or indeed is, developed by induction based on observation (e.g., Glaser and Strauss, 1967). Adding to the "confusion" or difference in views, few management researchers have any significant experience and much less success in developing theory. Yet, to advance the field of management requires that we continue to build theory and to understand the phenomena operating in organizations.

The purpose of this book is to develop a better understanding about the process of developing theory. And, to further our understanding of the theory development process, we asked some "master" scholars who are pioneers in the development of new theory and/or contributed substantially to the development of an important theoretical paradigm in the management and organizations field to explain how they developed their contributions. While each author was asked to describe the theory that s/he contributed, the emphasis in each of their chapters is on the process by which the theory was developed. To guide their efforts, we posed the following guidelines for the discussion of their theory development journey.

• Explain their academic roots and the paths of their own development as a scholar.

- Describe the theory they developed, including key variables, relationships, the underlying logic and boundary assumptions.
- How did the process begin? Include a description of the problem and how they identified the opportunity to develop new theory. Was it an incremental process or "bolt of lightening" discovery?
- Explain the search process used to answer questions. Where did you look to find answers to the problems? What sources did you use? How were the various pieces of information integrated? Were there others who helped in this process? If so, how did they contribute? What were the steps in this process?
- Discuss how alternatives were developed. From where did the alternative solutions emerge? What process was used to identify them? How were the various alternatives evaluated?
- How were the pieces integrated to form a theory? Describe the process used to connect the variables, discover the order of relationships and the logic behind the theory.
- How was the theory refined? How has the theory changed over time?
- What advice would you give to scholars interested in developing new theory?

What follows are twenty-four chapters by outstanding and highly respected scholars describing the theories that they contributed to management and organizations literature and importantly the processes involved in their development. Most of these accounts involve highly personal and fascinating journeys. The styles used in the presentations vary as they are idiosyncratic to each of the authors; however, this variance adds value to the volume and heightens the interest in reading the separate chapters. The chapters communicate the personal challenges experienced by the scholars as they persevered in the development and refinement of their ideas. Many of them encountered serious barriers that had to be overcome to develop the theory and communicate it to a broad audience. Many of these authors invested a significant number of years into the development of the theory. For some, the ideas began germinating earlier in their lives before they entered the academic profession. Thus, for most of the scholars, there was a process, incremental in nature, that led to the development of the theory as we know it today. While some largely developed the theory on their own, most attributed some of the contributions in the theory development to several others (graduate students, colleagues, competitors, and even reviewers and editors).

The processes described show how imagination and creativity sometimes played a role in the theory development. For others, observation was most prominent. There was not one dominant approach as implied by some philosophers; indeed, in some cases, the processes involved different approaches at different stages of development and/or integration of several methods almost simultaneously. Explaining the processes involved was not easy for these scholars because some of the processes used were most assuredly tacit. Additionally, some of the theory development resulted from serendipitous events. Yet, the scholars had to be singularly attentive to their context in order to recognize the contribution of these events to their ideas.

We selected the authors because of the theories that they developed and because of the impact of their work. As our interest was in trying to better understand the process(es) they used to develop theory, we had no *a priori* organizing framework for the chapters. While there are recognizable patterns in the processes used by the authors in developing theory, their approaches usually integrate several behaviors and processes. Additionally, the theories developed by the authors are more recognizable than the processes they used to develop them. Thus, we offer a broad organizing framework based on the content of the theories for the presentation of these works in this Handbook. In the concluding chapter, we provide an analysis of the processes used and integrate them into a process framework that can be used by scholars to develop new theory. We organize the chapters into three broad categories: "Individuals and their Environment," "The Behavior of Organizations," and "Environmental Contingencies and Organizations."

In Part I, "Individuals and their Environment," the theories deal with how individuals behave within a personal environmental context. In some cases, the theories emphasize individuals' proactive behaviors (e.g., personal initiative—Frese; social cognitive theory—Bandura) while others focus on the interaction of the individuals and their environment (e.g., image theory—Beach and Mitchell; psychological contracts—Rousseau). Other theories help us understand how individuals react to their environments (e.g., organizational justice—Folger; organizational commitment—Porter, Steers, and Mowday) or how individuals essentially shape their environments by their actions (e.g., escalation of commitment—Staw; upper echelon theory—Hambrick). Finally, several of the theories explain the motivation that serves as a base for individuals' behaviors (e.g., expectancy theory—Vroom; goal setting theory—Locke and Latham; job enrichment—Oldham and Hackman).

In Part II, "The Behavior of Organizations," the theories help us to understand how organizations function and fulfill their purpose. For example, some theories explain how organizations interpret and give meaning to their internal system and external contexts (e.g., managerial and organizational cognition—Huff; organizational sensemaking—Weick). In fact, sensemaking resembles theorizing (Weick's chapter). Other theories help us to understand how organizations learn and create knowledge (e.g., organizational learning—Argyris; managing organizational knowledge—Nonaka), how they are structured and how managers organize their work in them (organizational structuring and the nature of managerial work—Mintzberg). Finally, the theories in this section help us to understand how they gain a competitive advantage and evaluate their degree of success (resource-based view—Barney; organizational effectiveness—Cameron).

Part III, "Environmental Contingencies and Organizations," includes theories that are more deterministic in orientation or at least explain how organizations act under specific environmental conditions. Prominent among these theories are those explaining the institutional environment in which organizations must gain legitimacy and exist (institutional theory—Scott; neo-institutional theory—Zucker and Darby). In addition, three theories that emerged during the "heyday" of organization theory and examine how organizations evolve, manage transactions, and obtain resources from their environments are discussed (evolutionary theory—Winter; transaction costs theory—Williamson; resource dependence theory—Pfeffer). Finally, while much of finance theory emphasizes the importance of shareholders, another perspective suggests that organizations must serve a variety of external groups in order to survive and succeed (stakeholder theory—Freeman).

In the concluding chapter, we attempt to identify, integrate, and codify the riches in the chapters from the "Master Theorists." Admittedly, any descriptions of the processes these scholars used to develop new theory are incomplete because, as we explain in the chapter, such processes are causally ambiguous, partially tacit, and thus non-codifiable. Yet, we were able to identify some common approaches, themes, and activities that we integrate into processes. In most of the chapters, the theory development process began with some form of tension, followed by search, elaboration and research, and proclamation or presentation. The processes described by these highly respected scholars involved passion, persistence, discipline, and ideation. There are multiple roles played by researchers that contribute to the theory development process. Some played all of the roles while others engaged in some but not all of them.

We elaborate on these systematic activities, ideas, and themes with the hope that other scholars can learn from and apply them in their own research. To publish research in the top scholarly journals requires that researchers develop and/or contribute new theoretical ideas. Thus, they need to learn how to develop theoretical notions that extend our knowledge. While the development of new major theories is an uncommon event, we can all add to knowledge in the field by identifying tensions and extending theoretical understanding. We hope that this book helps many of our colleagues, young and old, current and future to do just that. Therefore, we commend the following chapters to you; they present a collective wisdom from a group of major thinkers—i.e., "Great Minds"—from whom we can all learn. We believe you will find many of these chapters captivating, some even scintillating. Internalizing the knowledge that they offer may have a major effect on your professional contributions and career.

> Live out your imagination, not your history.
> Stephen Covey

References

DUBIN, R. (1969). *Theory Building.* New York: Free Press.

GLASER, B. G., and STRAUSS, A. L. (1967). *The Discovery of Grounded Theory.* New York: Aldine de Gruyter.

KERLINGER, F. N. (1973). *Foundations of Behavioral Research.* New York: Harcourt, Inc.

—— (1974). *Foundations of Behavioral Research.* New York: Holt Rinehart and Winston.

POPPER, K. R. (1959). *The Logic of Scientific Discovery.* New York: Basic Books.

ROSS, K. L. (2003). Sir Karl Popper (1902–1994). www.friesian.com/popper.htm.

VAN DE VEN, A. H. (1989). Nothing is so practical as a good theory. *Academy of Management Review,* 15: 486–489.

WHETTEN, D. A. (1989). What constitutes a theoretical contribution? *Academy of Management Review,* 13: 490–495.

PART I

INDIVIDUALS AND THEIR ENVIRONMENT

CHAPTER 2

THE EVOLUTION OF SOCIAL COGNITIVE THEORY

ALBERT BANDURA

THE present chapter documents the evolution of social cognitive theory. Before retracing this theoretical odyssey, I will describe briefly the key tenets on which this theory is founded. Social cognitive theory adopts an agentic perspective to self-development, adaptation, and change (Bandura, 2001). To be an agent is to influence intentionally one's functioning and life circumstances. In this view, people are self-organizing, proactive, self-regulating, and self-reflecting. They are contributors to their life circumstances not just products of them.

2.1 AGENTIC PERSPECTIVE OF SOCIAL COGNITIVE THEORY

There are several core features of human agency. One such feature is intentionality. People form intentions that include action plans and strategies for realizing them. The second feature involves the temporal extension of agency through forethought. This includes more than future-directed plans. People set themselves goals and anticipate likely outcomes of prospective actions to guide and motivate their efforts anticipatorily. A future cannot be a cause of current behavior because it has no material existence. But by being represented cognitively in the present, visualized futures serve as current guides and motivators of behavior.

Agents are not only planners and forethinkers. They are also self-regulators. They adopt personal standards, and monitor and regulate their actions by self-reactive influence. They do things that give them satisfaction and a sense of self-worth and refrain from actions that bring self-censure. People are not only agents of action. They are self-examiners of their own functioning. Through functional self-awareness they reflect on their personal efficacy, the soundness of their thoughts and actions, the meaning of their pursuits, and make corrective adjustments if necessary. Forethought and self-influence are part of a causal structure.

Human functioning is rooted in social systems. Therefore, personal agency operates within a broad network of sociostructural influences. In these agentic transactions, people create social systems to organize, guide, and regulate human activities. The practices of social systems, in turn, impose constraints and provide resources and opportunity structures for personal development and functioning. Given this dynamic bidirectionality of influence, social cognitive theory rejects a dualism between personal agency and a social structure disembodied from human activity.

2.2 CENTRALITY OF SOCIAL MODELING

Discontent with the adequacy of existing theoretical explanations provides the impetus to search for conceptual schemes that can offer better explanations and solutions to phenomena of import. Behaviorism was very much in vogue at the time I began my career. The process of learning occupied the central position in this form of theorizing. The prevailing analyses of learning focused almost entirely on learning through the effects of one's actions. The explanatory mechanisms were cast in terms of establishing connections between stimuli and responses at the peripheral level through reward and punish consequences. The behavioristic theorizing was discordant with the evident social reality that much of what we learn is through the power of social modeling. I found it difficult to imagine a culture in which its language, mores, familial customs and practices, occupational competencies, and educational, religious, and political practices were gradually shaped in each new member by rewarding and punishing consequences of their trial-and-error performances. This tedious and potentially hazardous process where errors are costly was shortcut by social modeling. In modeling, people pattern their styles of thinking and behaving after the functional ones exemplified by others.

The foremost proponents of behaviorism, Watson (1908) and Thorndike (1898), dismissed the existence of observational learning because, in their view, learning required performance of responses. The notion of learning by observation was too divergent to be given serious consideration. This was a durable legacy. Despite the centrality and pervasiveness of social modeling in everyday life, there was no research to speak of on modeling processes until the publication of *Social Learning and Imitation* by Miller and Dollard in 1941. They recognized modeling phenomena, but construed them as a special case of discrimination learning. A model provides a social cue, the observer performs a matching response, and its reinforcement strengthens the tendency to behave imitatively.

I found this conception seriously wanting on the determinants, mechanisms, and scope of observational learning. We launched a program of research on observational learning as it typically occurs in the absence of reinforced performance. We tested the determinants of observational learning and the mechanisms through which it works.

In a chapter entitled "Vicarious Processes: A Case of No-Trial Learning" (Bandura, 1965), I presented the findings of our studies showing that observational learning requires neither response enactment nor reinforcement. Social modeling operated through four cognitive subfunctions encompassing attentional, representational, enactive translational, and motivational processes (Bandura, 1971a). I came under heavy fire from operant conditioners for whom nonreinforced modeling posed a major problem for their explanatory system (Baer, Peterson, and Sherman, 1967). They contended that reinforcement of some matching responses would establish imitation as a conditioned reinforcer.

We conducted research demonstrating that generalized imitation is governed by social beliefs and outcome expectations rather than by infused reinforcement (Bandura and Barab, 1971). When the functional value of modeled behavior was systematically varied, children faithfully adopted the behavior of a female model who rewarded them for doing so, but quickly ignored the behavior of a male model when it brought them no rewards. When the discriminability of the rewarded modeled behavior was varied, children adopted discriminable rewarded motor responses, ceased imitating discriminable nonrewarded verbal responses, but imitated nonrewarded responses that lacked features that would make them easily discriminable from the other rewarded response classes.

On the occasions when children modeled discriminable behavior in the nonrewarded class, this tendency was very much under cognitive control. Some of the children believed that the model demanded it ("I supposed to"), others performed nonrewarded imitations on the mistaken hope that the nonrewarding model would become more beneficent ("I thought if I kept trying lots of times he might get used to it and start giving candy like the lady did"); and still others acted like seasoned scientists testing hypotheses about outcome contingencies by systematically varying their behavior and observing its outcomes ("Sometimes I'd do it and sometimes not to see if I'd get any candy"). So much for conditioned reinforcers.

Theorists tend to focus selectively on explaining either human cognition or human action. As a result, the mechanisms governing the translation of thought into proficient performance have received little attention. The dual knowledge system (Anderson, 1980)—combining declarative knowledge with procedural knowledge embodying decision rules for solving tasks—was widely adopted as the solution to the translation problem. Explaining the acquisition of competencies in terms of factual and procedural knowledge may be adequate for cognitive problem solving where the implementation actions are trivially simple. However, in developing proficiency in complex styles of behavior procedural knowledge is not enough. It requires enlistment of multifaceted self-regulative operations and corrective feedback systems through which knowledge structures are converted to proficient performances. For example, a novice given factual information on how to ski, a full set of procedural rules, and then launched from a mountain top would most likely end up in an orthopedic ward or in an intensive care unit of a local infirmary.

We devised a series of experiments to test the notion that the behavioral translation operates through a conception-matching process (Carroll and Bandura, 1982, 1985, 1987, 1990). Cognitive representations conveyed by modeling serve as guides for the production of skilled performances and as standards for making corrective adjustments in the development of behavioral proficiency. Skills are usually perfected by repeated corrective adjustments in conception-matching during behavior production. Monitored enactment with instructive feedback serves as the vehicle for converting conception to proficient performance. The feedback accompanying enactments provides the information for detecting and correcting mismatches between conception and action. The behavior is thus modified based on the comparative information to master the desired competencies. The findings of these experiments added to our understanding of how cognitive representations, monitored enactments, and instructive feedback operate in concert in the development of competencies.

The value of a psychological theory is judged not only by its explanatory and predictive power, but also ultimately by its operative power to promote changes in human functioning. Social cognitive theory lends itself readily to social applications because it specifies modifiable determinants and how they should be structured based on verified mechanisms through which they operate. Knowledge of modeling processes provided informative guides on how to enable people to effect personal, organizational, and social changes (Bandura, 1969, 1997; Bandura and Rosenthal, 1978).

2.3 CORRECTING MISCONCEPTIONS ABOUT THE NATURE AND SCOPE OF MODELING

There were a number of entrenched misconceptions about the nature and scope of modeling that put a damper on the research and social applications of this powerful mode of learning. Progress in this area, therefore, required research designed not only to elucidate the determinants and mechanisms of social modeling, but to put the misconceptions to rest.

One such misconception was that modeling, construed as "imitation," could produce only response mimicry. Exemplars usually differ in content and other details but embody the same underlying principle. To cite a simple example, the passive linguistic form may be embodied in any variety of utterances. Research on abstract modeling (Bandura, 1986; Rosenthal and Zimmerman, 1978) showed that social modeling involved abstracting the information conveyed by specific exemplars about the structure and the underlying principles governing the behavior, rather than simple response mimicry of specific exemplars. Once individuals learn the guiding principle, they can use it to generate new versions of the behavior that go beyond what they have seen or heard. They can tailor the behavior to suit changing circumstances. Thus, for example, generic managerial skills, developed through modeling and guided enactments with instructive feedback, improve managerial functioning that, in turn, reduces employee absentee and turnover rates, and raises the level of organizational productivity (Latham and Saari, 1979; Porras, et al., 1982).

Another misconception, requiring retirement, held that modeling is antithetical to creativity. We were able to show how innovation can emerge through modeling. When exposed to models who differ in their styles of thinking and behavior, observers rarely pattern their behavior exclusively after a single source. Nor do they adopt all the attributes even of preferred models. Rather, observers combine various features of different models into new amalgams that differ from the individual modeled sources (Bandura, Ross, and Ross, 1963). Thus, two observers can construct new forms of behavior entirely through modeling that differ from each other by selectively blending different features from the variant models.

Modeling was shown to promote creativity in two main ways. Modeled unconventional ways of thinking increases innovativeness in others (Harris and Evans, 1973; Gist, 1989). Creativity usually involves synthesizing existing knowledge into new ways of thinking and doing things (Bandura, 1986). Organizations engage in a great deal of selective modeling of what is found to be effective (Bolton, 1993). People are too perceptive and do not have the time and resources to keep reinventing the core characteristics of successful systems, services, and products. They adopt advantageous elements, improve upon them, synthesize them into new forms, and tailor them to their particular circumstances. These lines of research provided new insight into how selective modeling can, indeed, be the mother of innovation.

There was another oft-repeated misconception regarding the scope of modeling. Many activities involve cognitive skills on how to gain and use information for solving problems. Critics argued that modeling cannot build cognitive skills because thought processes are covert and are not adequately reflected in modeled actions, which are the end-products of the cognitive operations. This was a limitation of conceptual vision rather than an inherent limitation of modeling.

Meichenbaum (1984) showed that cognitive skills could be readily promoted by verbal modeling in which models verbalize aloud their reasoning strategies as they engage in problem-solving activities. The thoughts guiding their decisions and actions are, thus, made observable. During verbal modeling, the models verbalize their thought processes as they evaluate the problem, seek information relevant to it, generate alternative solutions, weigh the likely outcomes associated with each alternative, and select the best way of implementing the chosen solution. They also verbalize their strategies for handling difficulties, how to recover from errors and how to motivate themselves. Cognitive modeling proved to be more powerful in enhancing perceived self-efficacy and building innovative and other complex cognitive skills than the commonly used tutorial methods (Gist, 1989; Gist, Bavetta, and Stevens, 1990; Gist, Schwoerer, and Rosen, 1989; Debowski, Wood, and Bandura, 2001).

2.4 Power and Reach of Symbolic Modeling

A growing influential source of social learning is the varied and pervasive symbolic modeling through the electronic media. A major advantage of symbolic modeling is that it can transmit information of virtually limitless variety to vast populations simultaneously in widely dispersed locales. Extraordinary advances in the technology of communication are transforming the nature, reach, speed, and loci of human influence. These technological developments have radically altered the social diffusion process. Video systems feeding off telecommunications satellites have become the dominant means for disseminating symbolic environments. New ideas, values, and styles of conduct are now being rapidly spread worldwide in ways that foster a globally distributed consciousness. The Internet provides instant communicative access worldwide. This makes electronic modeling a powerful vehicle for transcultural and sociopolitical change (Bandura, 2002a; Braithwaite, 1994).

In this broadened function of social diffusion of innovation through symbolic modeling, I integrated sociocognitive theory with the knowledge from social network theory (Bandura, 1986, 2001; Rogers, 1995). Sociocognitive influences instruct people in new ideas and practices and motivate them to adopt them. Multilinked social networks provide the potential diffusion path through which they spread and are supported.

Through a collaborative partnership (Bandura, 2002c), the social cognitive approach combined three major components into a model for promoting society-wide changes. The first component is a *theoretical model*. It specifies the determinants of psychosocial change and the mechanisms through which they produce their effects. This knowledge provides the guiding principles. The second component is a *translational and implementation model*. It converts theoretical principles into an innovative operational model. It specifies the content, strategies of change and their mode of implementation.

Effective psychosocial models of change usually have limited social impact because of inadequate systems for their social diffusion. As a result, we do not profit from our successes. The third component is a *social diffusion model* on how to promote adoption of psychosocial programs in diverse cultural milieus. Each of these components serves a unique function requiring different types of expertise. The applications of social cognitive theory in Africa, Asia, and Latin America to alleviate some of the most urgent global problems document how these three competent functions evolved into a powerful model for social change (Bandura, 2002c).

Some forty years ago, I used modeling of novel physical and verbal styles of aggression toward a Bobo doll as the vehicle for studying the mechanisms of observational learning. The Bobo doll follows me wherever I go. The photographs are published in every introductory psychology text and virtually every undergraduate takes introductory psychology. I recently checked into a Washington hotel. The clerk at the desk asked, "Aren't you the psychologist who did the Bobo doll experiment?" I answered, "I am afraid that will be my legacy." He replied, "That deserves an upgrade. I will put you in a suite in the quiet part of the hotel." I recently was going through the Canadian customs in Vancouver. The customs' agent looked at the passport and asked, "Didn't you do the Bobo doll study?" She was a psych major at the University of British Columbia.

One morning I received a call from Miguel Sabido, a creative producer at Televisia in Mexico City. He explained that he was developing long-running serial dramas founded on the modeling principles to promote national literacy and family planning in Mexico (Sabido, 1981). These televised productions dramatize people's own everyday lives and the problems they have to manage. The enabling dramas help viewers to see a better life and provide them with the strategies and incentives that enable them to take the steps to achieve it.

Social cognitive theory provided the theoretical model. Sabido created the generic translational and implementational model. Based on the demonstrated success of this macrosocial approach, *Population Communication International*   in New York designed the social diffusion model (Poindexter, 2004). They provide the resources, enabling guidance, and technical assistance to media personnel in the host nations to create serial dramas appropriate to their culture and the problems with which they are struggling. These worldwide applications are promoting national literacy, family planning in countries with soaring population growth, raising the status of women in societies that marginalize or subjugate them, curtailing the spread of HIV/AIDS infection, fostering environmental conservation, and in other ways bettering people's lives (Bandura, 2005).

We often cite examples in the natural and biological sciences where knowledge pursued for its own sake has unforeseen human benefits. The knowledge gained from the early modeling experiments spawned, through interdisciplinary partnership, unimagined global applications forty years later to alleviate some of the most urgent global problems.

2.5 Exercise of Agency Through Self-Regulatory Capabilities

During this behavioristic era, learning was presumed to occur through classical and instrumental conditioning. In this conception, motivation was regulated by a crude functionalism grounded in rewarding and punishing consequences. This approach presented a truncated image of human nature given the self-regulatory capabilities of people to affect their thought processes, motivation, affective states, and actions through self-directed influence. As part of the development of the agentic theory of human behavior, I mounted a program of research aimed at elucidating the acquisition and function of self-regulatory capabilities (Bandura, 1971b, 1986). Before reviewing the development of this aspect of social cognitive theory, I will describe personal experiences that informed my theorizing and experimentation regarding self-regulatory mechanisms.

Theorists often get themselves into a disconcerting egocentric predicament. They exempt themselves from the theory they develop to explain how others behave. For example, Skinner argued that humans are shaped and controlled by environmental forces. As he put it, "Man does not act on the environment. The environment acts on him." But then he exhorted people to become agents of change and shape their society by dutifully applying his operant conditioning methods. It is amusing to see radical postmodernists arguing authoritatively for the correctness of their view that there is no one correct view. Physical eliminationists think, argue, and act agentically but characterize other folks as simply epiphenom-enal hosts of automata orchestrating their behavior under the illusion that they are personally influencing events.

The agentic theory of human self-development and functioning applies equally to the road I have traveled. I grew up in a tiny hamlet in northern Alberta, Canada. The one school in town was woefully short of educational resources. Because two teachers had to teach the entire high school curriculum, they were often poorly informed in key subject areas. We once pilfered the answer book for the trigonom-etry course and brought it to an abrupt halt. We had to take charge of our own learning. Self-directed learning was the means of academic self-development not a theoretical abstraction. The paucity of educational resources turned out to be an enabling factor that has served me well, rather than an insurmountable handicap-ping one. The content of courses is perishable, but self-regulatory skills have lasting functional value.

During summer vacations in high school, my parents, who had no formal schooling but placed a high value on education, encouraged me to seek experiences beyond the confines of this hamlet. I worked in a furniture manufacturing plant in Edmonton. The skills I acquired helped to support me through college in part-time work.

During another high school summer break, I ventured to the Yukon, where I worked in one of the base camps that maintained the Alaska highway from sinking into the muskeg. It contained an interesting mix of characters fleeing creditors, probationary officers, the military, and angry ex-wives demanding ali-mony payments. Alcohol was their main nutrient. They were brewing their own. One early morning they left jubilantly to distill their fermented mash only to return profoundly despondent. The grizzly bears had partied on their alcoholic mash. We were faced with animated grizzlies stumbling drunkenly in our camp. Fortunately, they were too uncoordinated to do much damage. Life amidst this frontier subculture of drinking and gambling elevated the survival value of personal resourcefulness and initiative. It provided me with a uniquely broad perspective on life.

In search of a benign climate, I enrolled in the University of British Columbia in Vancouver. Being short of the coin of the realm, I worked in a woodwork plant in the afternoons and took a heavy course load in the mornings to graduate early. I enrolled in the doctoral program at the University of Iowa. It was the center of Hullian learning theory, the dominant theoretical orientation in psychology at the time. Iowa equipped us with the values and tools to be productive scientists whatever future course our scholarly pursuits took. After I completed my doctoral study, I joined the faculty at Stanford University. I was blessed with illustrious colleagues, gifted students, and a university ethos that approaches scholarship, not as a matter of publish or perish, but with puzzlement that the pursuit of knowledge should require coercion. Stanford provided considerable freedom to go wherever one's curiosity might lead.

The exercise of personal agency over the direction one's life takes varies depending on the nature and modifiability of the environment. The environment is not a monolith bearing down on individuals unidirectionally. Operative environments take three different forms: those that are *imposed*, *selected*, and *created*. There is the physical and sociostructural environment that impinges on people whether they like it or not. They do not have much control over its presence, but they do have leeway in how they construe it and react to it.

For the most part, the environment is only a potentiality with affordances and impediments, and rewarding and punishing aspects. The environment does not come into being until it is selected and activated by appropriate action. This constitutes the selected environment. Which part of the potential environment becomes the actual experienced environment, thus, depends on what people make of it and recruit from it. Under the same potential environment, individuals whose sense of efficacy is raised focus on the opportunities it provides, whereas those whose self-efficacy is lowered dwell on problems and risks (Krueger and Dickson, 1993, 1994).

And finally, there is the environment that is created. It did not exist as a potentiality waiting to be selected and activated. Rather, people create the nature of their situations to serve their purposes. Gradations of environmental change-ability require increasing levels of personal agency, ranging from cognitive construal agency, to selection and activation agency, to constructional agency. People's beliefs in their personal and collective efficacy play an influential role in how they organize, create, and manage the life circumstances that affect the paths they take and what they become.

Given the meager educational resources and prevailing normative influences in this rural hamlet, the widely used psychological predictors would probably have me toiling in the fields in northern Alberta, playing pool, and drinking myself to oblivion in the local beer parlor, which was the main pastime. Viewed from a non-agentic perspective, I should not have gone to college, I should not have attained a doctoral degree, I should not be teaching amidst the balmy palms at Stanford University, and I should not be writing this chapter.

There is much that people do designedly to exercise some measure of control over their self-development and life circumstances. But there is a lot of fortuity in the courses lives take. Indeed, some of the most important determinants of life paths occur through the most trivial of circumstances. People are often inaugurated into new life trajectories, marital partnerships, occupational careers through fortuitous circumstances (Austin, 1978; Bandura, 1986; Stagner, 1981).

A chance event is an unintended meeting of persons unfamiliar with each other. Although the separate chains of events in a chance encounter have their own causal determinants, their intersection occurs fortuitously rather than by design (Nagel, 1961). A seemingly insignificant fortuitous event can set in motion constellations of influences that alter the course of lives. These branching processes alter the linearity, continuity, and gradualism of life-course trajectories. The profusion of separate chains of events in everyday life provides myriad opportunities for such fortuitous intersects. This complicates immensely the long-term prediction of human behavior.

Fortuitous events got me into psychology and my marital partnership. I initially planned to study the biological sciences. I was in a car pool with pre-meds and engineers who inrolled in classes at an unmercifully early hour. While waiting for my English class I flipped through a course catalogue that happened to be left on a table in the library. I noticed an introductory psychology course that would serve as an early time filler. I enrolled in the course and found my future profession. It was during my graduate school years at the University of Iowa that I met my wife through a fortuitous encounter. My friend and I were quite late getting to the golf course one Sunday. We were bumped to an afternoon starting time. There were two women ahead of us. They were slowing down. We were speeding up. Before long we became a genial foursome. I met my wife in a sand trap. Our lives would have taken entirely different courses had I showed up at the early scheduled time.

Some years ago I delivered a presidential address at the Western Psychological Convention on the psychology of chance encounters and life paths (Bandura, 1982). At the convention the following year, an editor of one of the publishing houses explained that he had entered the lecture hall as it was rapidly filling up and seized an empty chair near the entrance. In the coming week, he will be marrying the woman who happened to be seated next to him. With only a momentary change in time of entry, seating constellations would have altered and this intersect would not have occurred. A marital partnership was, thus, fortuitously formed at a talk devoted to fortuitous determinants of life paths!

Fortuitous influences are ignored in the causal structure of the social sciences even though they play an important role in life courses. Most fortuitous events leave people untouched, others have some lasting effects, and still others branch people into new trajectories of life. A science of psychology does not have much to say about the occurrence of fortuitous intersects, except that personal proclivities, the nature of the settings in which one moves, and the types of people who populate those settings make some types of intersects more probable than others. Fortuitous influences may be unforeseeable, but having occurred, they enter as contributing factors in causal chains in the same way as prearranged ones do. Psychology can gain the knowledge for predicting the nature, scope, and strength of the impact these encounters will have on human lives. I took the fortuitous character of life seriously, provided a preliminary conceptual scheme for predicting the psychosocial impact of such events, and specified ways in which people can capitalize agentically on fortuitous opportunities (Bandura, 1982, 1998).

Fortuity does not mean uncontrollability of its effects. People can make chance happen by pursuing an active life that increases the number and type of fortuitous encounters they will experience. Chance favors the inquisitive and venturesome, who go places, do things, and explore new activities. People also make chance work for them by cultivating their interests, enabling beliefs and competencies. These personal resources enable them to make the most of opportunities that arise unexpectedly. Pasteur put it well when he noted that, "Chance favors only the prepared mind." Self-development gives people a hand in shaping their life circumstances. These various proactive activities illustrate the agentic management of fortuity.

In our excursion into the nature of self-management, our laboratory studies explored the mechanisms of self-regulation. Our social applications translated theory into practice (Bandura, 1986, 1997). To exercise self-influence, individuals have to monitor their behavior, judge it in relation to a personal standard of merit, and react self-evaluatively to it. Some of the studies clarified how personal standards are constructed from the myriad of social influences. Others documented the regulatory power of self-reactive influences. Rational models of human behavior embraced the centrality of agency but they too, provided a truncated view of self-regulation rooted in the market metaphor. Behavior was said to be regulated by self-interest construed almost entirely in terms of material costs and benefits. We demonstrated that human motivation and performance attainments are governed not only by material incentives, but also by social incentives, and self-evaluative incentives linked to personal standards. People often settle for alternatives of marginal utility or even sacrifice material gain to preserve their positive self-regard. Some of our studies examined self-regulation under conflictual conditions where individuals are rewarded for behavior they devalue, or are punished for activities they personally value. Principled dissenters often find themselves in the latter predicament. Their sense of self-worth is so strongly invested in certain convictions that they will submit to maltreatment rather than accede to what they regard as unjust or immoral.

Operant conditioners defined self-regulation out of existence by rechristening it as "stimulus control" and locating it in the external environment (Catania, 1975). In rejoinders, I relocated self-management in the sentient agent and reviewed the growing body of evidence on the means by which individuals exercise self-directedness (Bandura, 1976).

This was not a hospitable time to present an agentic theory of human behavior. Psychodynamicists depicted behavior as driven unconsciously by impulses and complexes. Behaviorists depicted behavior as shaped and shepherded by environmental forces. The cognitive revolution was ushered in on a computer metaphor. This conception stripped humans of agentic capabilities, a functional consciousness, and a self-identity. The mind as a symbol manipulator in the likeness of a linear computer became the conceptual model for the times. It was not individuals, but their subpersonal parts that were orchestrating activities nonconsciously.

Control theories of motivation and self-regulation focused heavily on error correction driven by negative feedback loops in a machine metaphor of human functioning. However, self-regulation by negative discrepancy tells only half the story and not the more interesting half. Social cognitive theory posited dual control systems in self-regulation—a proactive discrepancy production system working in concert with a reactive discrepancy reduction system (Bandura, 1991c). In a series of studies, we demonstrated that people are aspiring and proactive organisms not just reactive ones. Their capacity to exercise forethought enables them to wield adoptive control anticipatorily rather than being simply reactive to the effects of their efforts. They are motivated and guided by foresight of goals not just hindsight of shortfalls.

In these studies, people motivated and guided themselves through proactive control by setting themselves challenging goals and performance standards that create negative discrepancies to be mastered. They then mobilized their effort and personal resources based on their anticipatory estimation of what it would take to fulfill those standards. Reactive feedback control came into play in subsequent adjustments of effort to achieve desired outcomes. After people attained the goals they have been pursuing, those of high perceived efficacy set a higher standard for themselves (Bandura and Cervone, 1986). The adoption of further challenges created new motivating discrepancies to be mastered.

A theory of self-regulation governed by forethought and affective self-reactions did not sit well with Powers (1991), the foremost advocate of control theory. In his view, the human organism is "nothing more than a connection between one set of physical quantities in the environment (input quantities) and another set of physical quantities in the environment (output quantities)" (Powers, 1978: 421). Cognitive and affective processes were dismissed as irrelevant because "we are not modeling the interior of the subject" (p. 432). We evaluated the adequacy of this austere mechanistic model, as well as the many control theories that take different forms depending on the mix of sociocognitive factors grafted on the negative feedback loop (Bandura, 1991b; Bandura and Locke, 2003).

The goal in theory building is to identify a small number of explanatory principles that can account for a wide range of phenomena. In the interest of comprehensive generality, social cognitive theory focuses on integrative principles that operate across differing spheres of functioning. The generality of the self-regulatory constituent in social cognitive theory was corroborated in the varied applications of this knowledge in educational development, health promotion, affect regulation, athletic performance, organizational functioning, and social change (Bandura, 1997; 2002a, 2004c; Frayne and Latham, 1987; Zimmerman, 1989).

The component subfunctions governing performance productivity were shown to operate similarly in the exercise of moral agency (Bandura, 1991a). After people adopt a standard of morality, their self-sanctions for actions that match or violate their personal standards serve as the regulatory self-influences. People do things that give them self-satisfaction and a sense of self-worth. They refrain from behaving in ways that violate their moral standards because it will bring self-disapproval.

Moral standards do not operate as fixed internal regulators of conduct, however. There are a number of psychosocial mechanisms by which moral self-sanctions are selectively disengaged from inhumane conduct. The disengagement may center on making harmful practices personally and socially acceptable by portraying them as serving worthy purposes, and by exonerating social comparison and sanitizing language. It may focus on obscuring personal agency by diffusion and displacement of responsibility so that perpetrators do not hold themselves accountable for the harm they cause. It may involve minimizing, distorting, or even disputing the harm that flows from detrimental actions. And the disengagement may include dehumanizing, and blaming the victims for bringing the maltreatment on themselves.

Our analyses of moral agency showed that selective moral disengagement operates at a social systems level, not just individually. Organizations often find themselves in moral predicaments where its members perform activities or produce products that bring them profits and other benefits at injurious costs to others. Self-exonerations are needed to neutralize self-censure and to preserve a sense of self-worth. We examined the form that moral disengagement takes and the justificatory exonerations and social arrangements that facilitate their use in different detrimental corporate practices (Bandura, 1999a, 2004a; Bandura, Caprara, and Zsolnai, 2002).

The generality of the self-regulatory aspect of social cognitive theory was further illustrated in applications of this knowledge to the psychosocial effects of dysfunctions in self-regulation. Depending on the sphere of coping, self-regulatory dysfunctions can give rise to transgressive conduct, substance abuse, eating disorders, and chronic depression (Bandura, 1976, 1997).

2.6 THEORETICAL EXTENSION WITH THE SELF-EFFICACY COMPONENT

Psychodynamic theory, especially the psychoanalytic form, reigned over the fields of personality, psychotherapy, and the pop culture when I entered the field of psychology. The mid-1950s witnessed growing disillusionment with this line of theorizing and its mode of treatment. The theory lacked predictive power, nor did it fare well in therapeutic effectiveness. During this time, I was examining the self-regulatory mechanisms by which people exercise control over their motivation, styles of thinking, and emotional life. As part of this line of research on the development and exercise of personal agency, we were devising new modes of treatment using mastery experiences as the principal vehicle of change. Talk alone will not cure intractable problems. Through guided mastery, we cultivated competences, coping skills, and self-beliefs that enabled people to exercise control over their perceived threats.

We initially tested the effectiveness of this enabling approach with severe snake phobics. When people avoid what they dread, they lose touch with the reality they shun. Guided mastery quickly restores reality testing in two ways. It provides disconfirming tests of phobic beliefs by convincing demonstrations that what the phobics dread is safe. Even more important, it provides confirmatory tests that phobics can exercise control over what they find threatening.

Intractable phobics, of course, are not about to do what they dread. We therefore, created environmental conditions that enabled phobics to succeed despite themselves. This was achieved by enlisting a variety of performance mastery aids (Bandura, Blanchard, and Ritter, 1969; Bandura, Jeffery, and Gajdos, 1975). Threatening activities were repeatedly modeled to demonstrate coping strategies and to disconfirm people's worst fears. Intimidating tasks were reduced to graduated subtasks of easily mastered steps. Treatment was conducted in this stepwise fashion until the most intimidating activities were mastered. Joint performance with the therapist enabled frightened people to do things they would refuse to do on their own. Another method for overcoming resistance was to have phobics perform the feared activity for only a short time. As they became bolder the length of engagement was extended. After bold functioning was fully restored, self-directed mastery activities were arranged in which clients manage different versions of the threat on their own under varying conditions.

This proved to be a powerful treatment. It instilled a robust sense of coping efficacy, transformed attitudes toward the phobic objects from abhorrence to liking, wiped out anxiety, biological stress reactions, and phobic behavior. The phobics were plagued by recurrent nightmares for some twenty or thirty years. Guided mastery transformed dream activity and wiped out chronic nightmares. As one woman gained mastery over her snake phobia, she dreamt that the boa constrictor befriended her and was helping her to wash the dishes. Reptiles soon faded from her dreams. The changes endured. Phobics who achieved only partial improvement with alternative modes of treatment achieved full recovery with the benefit of the guided mastery treatment regardless of the severity of their phobic dysfunctions (Bandura, Blanchard, and Ritter, 1969; Biran and Wilson, 1981; Thase and Moss, 1976).

The 1960s ushered in remarkable transformative changes in the explanation and modification of human functioning and change (Bandura, 2004b). *Causal analysis* shifted from unconscious psychic dynamics to transactional psychosocial dynamics. Human functioning was construed as the product of the dynamic interplay between personal, behavioral, and environmental influences. *Social labeling practices* regarding problems of living were changed. Problem behavior was viewed as divergent behavior rather than a symptom of a psychic disease. *Functional analysis* of human behavior replaced diagnostic labeling that categorized people into psychopathologic types with stigmatizing consequences. *Laboratory and controlled field studies* of the determinants of human behavior and the mechanisms through which they operate replaced content analyses of interviews. *Action oriented treatments* replaced interpretive interviews. The *modes of treatment* were altered in the content, locus, and agents of change.

Within a decade, the field was transformed by a major paradigm shift (Bandura, 2004b). New conceptual models and analytic methodologies were created. New sets of periodicals were launched for the rising stream of interest. New organizations were formed for the advancement of behaviorally oriented approaches. New professional conventions provided a forum for the exchange of ideas.

Psychodynamicists branded these new modes of treatment not only as superficial but dangerous. I was invited to present our program of research at the Langley Porter Clinic in San Francisco, a stronghold of psychodynamic adherents. The session began with a disparaging introduction to the effect that this young upstart will tell us seasoned analysts how to cure phobias! I explained that my host's "generous" introduction reminded me of a football contest between Iowa and Notre Dame in South Bend. Iowa scored a touchdown, which tied the score. As the player ran on the field to kick the extra point, coach Evashevski turned to his assistant coach and remarked, "Now there goes a brave soul, a Protestant attempting a conversion before 50,000 Catholics!"

Not all the critics of the psychodynamic model worshipped at the same theoretical altar. Some went the operant route as providing the best glimpse of the promised land. Others took the sociocognitive route. Vigorous battles were fought over cognitive determinants and their scientific legitimacy (Bandura, 1995, 1996). Operant analysts took the view that the only legitimate scientific enterprise is one that directly links observable environmental events to observable behavioral events (Skinner, 1977).

Scientific advances are promoted by two kinds of theories (Nagel, 1961). One form seeks relations between directly observable events but shies away from the mechanisms subserving the observable events. The second form focuses on the mechanisms that explain the functional relations between observable events. The fight over cognitive determinants was not about the legitimacy of inner causes, but about the types of inner determinants that are favored (Bandura, 1996). For example, operant analysts increasingly place the explanatory burden on determinants inside the organism, namely the implanted history of reinforcement. The implanted history is an inferred inner cause not a directly observable one. The dispute over internal determinants is not exclusively between behaviorists and cognitivists. There is a growing rift among operant analysts about the shift of emphasis within their own conceptual framework from models of environment-based control to organism-based control (Machado, 1993).

My entry into self-efficacy was serendipitous. In the development and evaluation of the guided mastery treatment, we focused on three fundamental processes: the power of the treatment to promote psychosocial changes; the generality or scope of the effected changes, and their durability or maintenance. Having demonstrated the power of this mode of treatment on each of these evaluative dimensions, I explored the possibility of a further function—the power of a treatment to build resilience to adverse experiences. The process of resiliency enhancement was based on the following rationale. The capacity of an aversive experience to reinstate dysfunctions depends, in large part, on the pattern of experiences in which it is embedded rather than solely on its properties. A lot of neutral or positive experiences can neutralize the negative impact of an aversive event and curtail the spread of negative effects. To test this notion, after functioning was fully restored, former phobics did or did not have the benefit of self-directed mastery experience with different versions of the threat.

In a follow-up assessment, the participants expressed deep gratitude to be rid of their phobia, but then explained that the treatment had a much more profound impact. Their lives had been debilitated socially, recreationally, and occupationally for twenty to thirty years. They were plagued by recurrent nightmares and perturbing ruminations. To overcome, within a few hours, a phobic dread that had constricted and tormented their lives was a transformational experience that radically altered their beliefs in their efficacy to exercise control over their lives. They were acting on their new self-efficacy belief and enjoying their successes, much to their surprise. These preliminary findings pointed to a common mechanism through which personal agency is exercised.

I mounted a multifaceted program of research to gain a deeper understanding of the nature and function of this belief system. To guide this new mission, the theory addressed the key aspects of perceived self-efficacy (Bandura, 1997). These include the origins of efficacy beliefs; their structure and function; their diverse effects; the processes through which they produce these effects, and the modes of influence by which efficacy beliefs can be created and strengthened for personal and social change. Diverse lines of research, conducted by a variety of investigators, provided new insights into the role of perceived self-efficacy in the fields of education, health promotion and disease prevention, clinical dysfunctions such as anxiety disorders, depression, eating disorders, substance abuse, personal and team athletic attainments, organizational functioning, and the efficacy of our social and political systems to make a difference in our lives (Bandura, 1995, 1997; Schwarzer, 1992; Maddux, 1995).

A major question in any theory of cognitive regulation of motivation, affect, and action concerns the issue of causality. A variety of experimental strategies were used to verify that beliefs of personal efficacy function as determinants of actions rather than being merely secondary reflections of them (Bandura, 1997; Bandura and Locke, 2003).

The field of personality is deeply entrenched in trait thinking that characterizes individuals in terms of clusters of habitual behaviors. These are measured by decontextualized behavioral descriptors in one-size-fits-all global measures. In this approach, behavioral taxonomy replaced self-referent structure, processes, and functions. Behavioral clusters get reified as personality determinants. In a chapter on a "Social Cognitive Theory of Personality," I argued that personality determinants reside in agentic self processes not in behavioral clusters (Bandura, 1999b).

I receive a steady flow of e-mails requesting my all-purpose measure of self-efficacy or a couple of trait-like items that could be inserted in an omnibus questionnaire. Thus, another entry in the research agenda was to differentiate an agentic model of personality from a trait model (Bandura, 1999b). It also required purging misconceptions of constructs. *Self-efficacy* as a judgment of personal capability is not *self-esteem*, which is a judgment of self-worth, nor is it *locus of control*, which is a belief about whether outcomes flow from behavior or from extraneous forces.

2.7 TRIADIC MODEL OF HUMAN AGENCY

The theorizing and research on human agency has centered almost exclusively on personal agency exercised individually. However, this is not the only way in which people bring their influence to bear on events that affect how they live their lives. Social cognitive theory distinguishes among three different modes of human agency: individual, proxy, and collective.

The preceding analyses centered on the nature of the direct personal agency and the cognitive, motivational, affective, and choice processes through which it is exercised to produce given effects. In many spheres of functioning, people do not have direct control over the social conditions and institutional practices that affect their everyday lives. Under these circumstances, they seek their well-being, security, and valued outcomes through the exercise of proxy agency. In this socially mediated mode of agency, people try by one means or another to get those who have access to resources or expertise or wield influence and power to act at their behest to secure the outcomes they desire.

People do not live their lives autonomously. Many of the things they seek are achievable only through socially interdependent effort. I extended the conception of human agency to collective agency rooted in people's shared belief in their joint capabilities to bring about changes in their lives by collective effort (Bandura, 2000, 2001). This made the theory generalizable to collectivistically-oriented cultures and activities. Self-efficacy theory (Bandura, 1997) distinguishes between the source of the data (i.e., the individual) and the level of the phenomenon being measured (i.e., personal efficacy or group efficacy). There is no group mind that believes. Perceived collective efficacy resides in the minds of members as beliefs in their group capability. All too often, because individual members are the source of the judgment of their group's efficacy, the assessment was misconstrued as the individual level of the measured phenomenon. It required clarification that appraisals of personal and group efficacy represent the different levels of collectivity, not the source of the judgment.

Contentious dualisms pervade our field pitting autonomy against interdependence, individualism against collectivism, and human agency against social structure reified as an entity disembodied from the behavior of individuals. It is widely claimed that Western theories lack generalizability to non-Western cultures. This prevailing claim had to be addressed empirically.

Most of our cultural psychology is based on territorial culturalism (Gjerde and Onishi, 2000). Nations are used as proxies for psychosocial orientations, which are then ascribed to the nations and its members as though they all thought and behaved alike. Residents of Japan get categorized as collectivists, those in the United States as individualists. Cultures are dynamic and internally diverse systems not static monoliths. There is a substantial diversity among societies placed in the same category (Kim, et al., 1994). There are large generational, educational, and socioeconomic differences among members of the same cultures (Matsumoto, Kudoh, and Takeuchi, 1996).

Analyses across activity domains and classes of social relationships revealed that people behave communally in some aspects of their lives and individualistically in many other aspects (Matsumoto, Kudoh, and Takeuchi, 1996). They express their cultural orientations conditionally rather than invariantly depending on incentive conditions (Yamagishi, 1988). Given the intracultural and interdomain variability, and changeability of cultural orientations as a function of incentive conditions, the categorical approach masks this extensive diversity. Much of the cross-cultural research relies on bi-cultural contrasts. Members of a single collectivist culture are typically compared to those of a single individual one. Given the notable diversity, the dichotomizing approach can spawn a lot of misleading generalizations.

Not only are cultures not monolithic entities, but they are no longer insular. Global connectivity is shrinking cross-cultural uniqueness. Moreover, people worldwide are becoming increasingly enmeshed in a cyberworld that transcends time, distance, place, and national borders. In addition, mass transnational influences are homogenizing some aspects of life, polarizing other aspects, and creating a lot of cultural hybridizations fusing elements from diverse cultures. These new realities call for a more dynamic approach to cultural effects and for broadening the scope of cross-cultural analyses. This is another area in which strongly held views placed a damper on research to test the scope of theoretical generalizability.

Social cognitive theory distinguishes between basic human capacities and how culture shapes these potentialities into diverse forms appropriate to different cultural milieus. For example, humans have evolved an advanced capacity for observational learning. It is essential for their self-development and functioning regardless of the culture in which people reside. Indeed, in many cultures, the word for "*teach*" is the same as the word for "*show*" (Reichard, 1938). Modeling is a universalized human capacity. But what is modeled, how modeling influences are socially structured, and the purposes they serve vary in different cultural milieus (Bandura and Walters, 1963).

I reviewed the findings of a growing number of studies that tested the structure and functional role of efficacy beliefs in diverse cultural milieus across a wide range of age levels, gender, and different spheres of functioning (Bandura, 2002*b*). The findings show that a strong sense of efficacy has generalized functional value regardless of the cultural conditions (Earley, 1993, 1994; Matsui and Onglatco, 1992; Park, et al., 2000). Being immobilized by self-doubt and perceived futility of effort has little evolutionary value. But how efficacy beliefs are developed and structured, the forms they take, the ways in which they are exercised, and the purposes to which they are put vary cross-culturally. In short, there is a commonality in basic agentic capabilities and mechanisms of operation, but diversity in the culturing of these inherent capacities.

2.8 PROCESS OF THEORY BUILDING

I would like to conclude with a few general remarks regarding the process of theory building and the advancement of knowledge. Theorists would have to be omniscient to provide an ultimate account of human behavior at the outset. They necessarily begin with an incomplete theory regarding the determinants of selected phenomena and the mechanisms through which those determinants operate. There are few, if any, psychosocial factors that produce effects nonconditionally. The plurality of determinants of human behavior, their intricate conditionality, and dynamic interactivity add complexity to the identification of functional relations. They are unravelable by intuitive analysis alone. Initial formulations prompt lines of experimentation that help to improve the theory. Successive theoretical refinements bring one closer to understanding the phenomena of interest.

The present chapter traced the evolution of social cognitive theory and the way in which it was expanded in scope, generality, and social application. The full exposition of the theory, which falls beyond the scope of this chapter, specifies how the key determinants and governing mechanisms operate in concert in human self-development, adaptation, and change (Bandura, 1986). Theory building is socially situated rather than proceeds isolatedly. Hence, I added the conceptual contexts within which social cognitive theory evolved as part of the chronicle.

There is a lot of idealization in the pronouncements of how science is conducted. A prominent group of social scientists was once brought to a mountain retreat to prepare a report on how they went about their theory building. After a couple of days of idealized show and tell they began to confess that they did not construct their theories by deductive formalism. A problem sparked their interest. They had some preliminary hunches that suggested experiments to test them. The findings from verification tests led to refinements of their conception that, in turn, pointed to further experiments that could provide additional insights into the determinants and mechanisms governing the phenomena of interest. Theory building is a long haul, not for the short winded. The formal version of the theory, that appears in print, is the distilled product of a lengthy interplay of empirically based inductive activity and conceptually based deductive activity.

Verification of deduced effects is central to experimental inquiry. The social sciences face major obstacles to the development of theoretical knowledge. Controlled experimental approaches are informative in verifying functional relations, but their scope is severely limited. They are precluded for phenomena that are not reproducible in laboratory situations because such phenomena require a lengthy period of development, are the products of complex constellations of influences by different social sources operating interactively, or are prohibited ethically.

Controlled field studies that systematically vary psychosocial factors under real-life conditions provide greater ecological validity, but they too are limited in scope. Finite resources, limits imposed by social systems on what types of interventions they permit, hard to control fluctuations in quality of implementation, and ethical considerations place constraints on controlled field interventions. Controlled experimentation must, therefore, be supplemented with investigation of naturally produced variations in psychosocial functioning linked to identifiable determinants (Nagel, 1961). The latter approach is indispensable in the social sciences.

Verification of functional relations requires converging evidence from different research strategies. Therefore, in the development of social cognitive theory, we have employed controlled laboratory studies, controlled field studies, longitudinal studies, behavior modification of human dysfunctions not producible on ethical grounds, and analyses of functional relations in naturally occurring phenomena. These studies have included populations of diverse sociodemographic characteristics, multiple analytic methodologies, applied across diverse spheres of functioning in diverse cultural milieus.

Empirical tests of a theory include the core theory, a set of auxiliary assumptions, operations presumed to create the relevant conditions, and the measures presumed to tap the key factors (Meehl, 1978). Therefore, it is not the core theory alone that is being put to the test. Evidence of discrepancy between the theorized and observed outcomes leaves ambiguity about what is at fault within this complex mix. Considering the causal complexity of human behavior, the severe constraints on controlled experimentation, and the coupling of the core theory with auxiliaries, conditions, and measures, that themselves have to be well founded, the notion that a single counterinstance falsifies the theory is a pretentious illusion. But these inherent difficulties are no cause for investigatory resignation and despondency. Psychological theories differ in their predictive and operative success. A scientific enterprise can improve a theory to predict human behavior and to promote improvements in the human condition. Weak theories are discarded not because they are falsified, but because they are withered by so many limiting conditions that they have little predictive or operative value. When better theoretical alternatives exist, there is little to be gained in pursuing the verity or falsity of a theory that can, at best, explain behavior under only a very narrow range of conditions and has little to say about how to effect psychosocial changes.

It is one thing to generate innovative ideas that hold promise for advancing knowledge, but another to get them published. The publication process, therefore, warrants brief comment from the trenches. Researchers have a lot of psychic scar tissue from inevitable skirmishes with journal reviewers. This presents special problems when there is conceptual inbreeding in editorial boards. The path to innovative accomplishments is strewn with publication hassles and rejections.

It is not uncommon for authors of scientific classics to experience repeated initial rejection of their work, often with hostile embellishments if it is too discordant with what is in vogue (Campanario, 1995). The intellectual contributions later become the mainstays of the field of study. For example, John Garcia, who eventually was honored for his fundamental psychological discoveries, was once told by a reviewer of his often-rejected manuscripts that one is no more likely to find the phenomenon he discovered than bird droppings in a cuckoo clock.

Gans and Shepherd (1994) asked leading economists, including Nobel Prize winners, to describe their experiences with the publication process. Their request brought a cathartic outpouring of accounts of publication troubles, even with seminal contributions. The publication hassles are an unavoidable but frustrating part of a research enterprise. The next time you have one of your ideas, prized projects, or manuscripts rejected, do not despair too much. Take comfort in the fact that those who have gone on to fame have had a rough time. In his delightful book *Rejection*, John White (1982) vividly documents that the prominent characteristic of people who achieve success in challenging pursuits is an unshakable sense of efficacy and a firm belief in the worth of what they are doing. This belief system provides the staying power in the face of failures, setbacks, and unmerciful rejections.

In an effort to raise the odds of making it through the publication gauntlet, authors are increasingly resorting to countless citations and tacking on constructs from different theories. All too often, the eclectic additive approach is passed off as integrative theorizing presumably combining the best of different approaches. It is difficult to find a coherent theory in the conceptual stew. To curb the rising proliferation of citations, a recent incoming editor of a flagship psychology journal has imposed a limit on the number of items that are cited in an article. Scientific progress is better achieved by encompassing more fully higher-order factors within a unified theoretical framework, than by creating conglomerate models with constructs picked from divergent theories with the attendant problems of redundancy, fractionation, and theoretical disconnectedness.

Theory building is not a vocation for the thin-skinned. Theorists must be prepared to see their conceptions and empirical findings challenged, misconstrued, or caricatured, sometimes with ad hominem embellishments. For example, I am often amused to see myself miscast as both an orthodox behaviorist and a dualistic mentalist! (Bandura and Bussey, 2004). Theorists differ in the extent to which they allow such events to intrude on their time. Eysenck rarely let critiques go unanswered. Skinner rarely responded to them. I try to resist the pull to respond unless it can advance understanding of the issues in question. This is difficult to do knowing that an unanswered mistaken critique will be read by many as conceding its correctness.

There is much talk about the validity of theories, but surprisingly little attention is devoted to their social utility. For example, if aeronautical scientists developed principles of aerodynamics in wind tunnel tests but were unable to build an aircraft that could fly the value of their theorizing would be called into question. Theories are predictive and operative tools. In the final analysis, the evaluation of a scientific enterprise in the social sciences will rest heavily on its social utility.

References

ANDERSON, J. R. (1980). *Cognitive Psychology and its Implications*. San Francisco: Freeman.

AUSTIN, J. H. (1978). *Chase, chance, and creativity: The lucky art of novelty*. New York: Columbia University Press.

BAER, D. M., PETERSON, R. F., and SHERMAN, J. A. (1967). The development of imitation by reinforcing behavioural similarity to a model. *Journal of the Experimental Analysis of Behaviour*, 10: 405–416.

BANDURA, A. (1965). Vicarious processes: A case of no-trial learning. In L. Berkowitz (ed.), *Advances in Experimental Social Psychology*. 2. 1–55. New York: Academic Press.

—— (1969). *Principles of Behavior Modification*. New York: Holt, Rinehart and Winston.

—— (ed.) (1971a). *Psychological Modeling: Conflicting theories*. New York: Aldine-Atherton.

—— (1971b). Vicarious and self-reinforcement processes. In R. Glaser (ed.), *The Nature of Reinforcement*: 228–278. New York: Academic Press.

—— (1976). Self-reinforcement: Theoretical and methodological considerations. *Behaviorism*, 4: 135–155.

—— (1982). The psychology of chance encounters and life paths. *American Psychologist*, 37: 747–755.

—— (1986). *Social Foundations of Thought and Action: A Social Cognitive Theory*. Englewood Cliffs: Prentice-Hall.

—— (1991a). Social cognitive theory of moral thought and action. In W. M. Kurtines and J. L. Gewirtz (eds.), *Handbook of Moral Behavior and Development*, vol. 1. Hillsdale, NJ: Erlbaum.

—— (1991b). Human agency: The rhetoric and the reality. *American Psychologist*, 46: 157–162.

—— (1991c). Self-regulation of motivation through anticipatory and self-reactive mechanisms. In R. A. Dienstbier (ed.), *Perspectives on Motivation: Nebraska Symposium on Motivation*: 38. 69–164. Lincoln: University of Nebraska Press.

—— (1995). Comments on the crusade against the causal efficacy of human thought. *Journal of Behavior Therapy and Experimental Psychiatry*, 26: 179–190.

—— (1996). Ontological and epistemological terrains revisited. *Journal of Behavior Therapy and Experimental Psychiatry*, 27: 323–345.

—— (1997). *Self-Efficacy: The Exercise of Control*. New York: Freeman.

—— (1998). Exploration of fortuitous determinants of life paths. *Psychological Inquiry*, 9: 95–99.

—— (1999a). Moral disengagement in the perpetration of inhumanities. *Personality and Social Psychology Review*, 3: 193–209.

—— (1999b). A social cognitive theory of personality. In L. Pervin and O. John (eds.), *Handbook of Personality*: 154–196. New York: Guilford Publications.

—— (2000). Exercise of human agency through collective efficacy. *Current Directions in Psychological Science*, 9: 75–78.

—— (2001). Social cognitive theory: An agentic perspective, *Annual Review of Psychology*, 52: 1–26. Palo Alto: Annual Reviews, Inc.

—— (2002a). Growing primacy of human agency in adaptation and change in the electronic era. *European Psychologist*, 7: 2–16.

—— (2002b). Social cognitive theory in cultural context. *Journal of Applied Psychology: An International Review*, 51: 269–290.

—— (2002c). Environmental sustainability by sociocognitive deceleration of population growth. In P. Schmuck, and W. Schultz (eds.). *The psychology of sustainable development*: 209–238). Dordrecht, the Netherlands: Kluwer.

—— (2004a). Selective exercise of moral agency. In T. A. Thorkildsen and H. J. Walberg (eds.), *Nurturing Morality*: 37–57. New York: Kluwer Academic.

—— (2004b). Swimming against the mainstream: The early years from chilly tributary to transformative mainstream. *Behavioral Research and Therapy*, 42: 613–630.

—— (2004c). Health Promotion by Social Cognitive Means. *Health Education and Behavior*, 31: 143–164.

—— (2005). Going global with social cognitive theory: From prospect to paydirt. In S. I. Donaldson, D. E. Berger, and K. Pezdek (eds.), *The Rise of Applied Psychology: New Frontiers and Rewarding Careers*. Mahwah: Lawrence Erlbaum Associates, Inc.

—— and BARAB, P. G. (1971). Conditions governing nonreinforced imitation. *Developmental Psychology*, 5: 244–255.

—— and BUSSEY, K. (2004). On broadening the cognitive, motivational, and sociostructural scope of theorizing about gender development and functioning. A reply to Martin, Ruble, and Szkrybalo. *Psychological Bulletin*, 130: 691–701.

—— BLANCHARD, E. B., and RITTER, B. (1969). Relative efficacy of desensitization and modeling approaches for inducing behavioral, affective, and attitudinal changes. *Journal of Personality and Social Psychology*, 13: 173–199.

—— CAPRARA, G. V., and ZSOLNAI, L. (2002). Corporate transgressions. In L. Zsolnai (ed.), *Ethics in the Economy: Handbook of Business Ethics*: 151–164. Oxford: Peter Lang.

—— and CERVONE, D. (1986). Differential engagement of self-reactive influences in cognitive motivation. *Organizational Behavior and Human Decision Processes*, 38: 92–113.

—— JEFFERY, R. W., and GAJDOS, E. (1975). Generalizing change through participant modeling with self-directed mastery. *Behaviour Research and Therapy*, 13: 141–152.

—— and LOCKE, E. (2003). Negative self-efficacy and goal effects revisited. *Journal of Applied Psychology*, 88: 87–99.

—— and ROSENTHAL, T. L. (1978). Psychological modeling: Theory and practice. In S. L. Garfield and A. E. Bergin (eds.), *Handbook of Psychotherapy and Behavior Change*: 621–658. New York: Wiley.

—— ROSS, D., and ROSS, S. A. (1963). A comparative test of the status envy, social power, and secondary reinforcement theories of identificatory learning. *Journal of Abnormal and Social Psychology*, 67: 527–534.

—— and WALTERS, R. H. (1963). *Social learning and personality development*. New York: Holt, Rinehart, and Winston.

BIRAN, M., and WILSON, G. T. (1981). Treatment of phobic disorders using cognitive and exposure methods: A self-efficacy analysis. *Journal of Counseling and Clinical Psychology*, 49: 886–899.

BOLTON, M. K. (1993). Imitation versus innovation: Lessons to be learned from the Japanese. *Organizational Dynamics*: 30–45.

BRAITHWAITE, J. (1994). A sociology of modeling and the politics of empowerment. *British Journal of Sociology*, 45: 445–479.

CAMPANARIO, J. M. (1995). On influential books and journal articles initially rejected because of negative referees' evaluations. *Science Communication* 16: 304–325.

CARROLL, W. R., and BANDURA, A. (1982). The role of visual monitoring in observational learning of action patterns: Making the unobservable observable. *Journal of Motor Behavior*, 14: 153–167.

—— —— (1985). Role of timing of visual monitoring and motor rehearsal in observational learning of action patterns. *Journal of Motor Behavior*, 17: 269–281.

—— —— (1987). Translating cognition into action: The role of visual guidance in observational learning. *Journal of Motor Behavior*, 19: 385–398.

—— —— (1990). Representational guidance of action production in observational learning: A causal analysis. *Journal of Motor Behavior*, 22: 85–97.

CATANIA, C. A. (1975). The myth of self-reinforcement. *Behaviorism*, 3: 192–199.

DEBOWSKI, S., WOOD, R. E., and BANDURA, A. (2001). Impact of guided exploration and enactive exploration on self-regulatory mechanisms and information acquisition through electronic search. *Journal of Applied Psychology*, 86: 1129–1141.

EARLEY, P. C. (1993). East meets West meets Mideast: Further explorations of collectivistic and individualistic work groups. *Academy of Management Journal*, 36: 319–348.

EARLEY, P. C. (1994). Self or group? Cultural effects of training on self-efficacy and performance. *Administrative Science Quarterly*, 39: 89–117.

FRAYNE, C. A., and LATHAM, G. P. (1987). Application of social learning theory to employee self-management of attendance. *Journal of Applied Psychology*, 72: 387–392.

GANS, J. S., and SHEPHERD, G. B. (1994). How are the mighty fallen: Rejected classic articles by leading economists. *Journal of Economic Perspectives*, 8: 165–179.

GIST, M. E. (1989). The influence of training method on self-efficacy and idea generation among managers. *Personnel Psychology*, 42: 787–805.

—— BAVETTA, A. G., and STEVENS, C. K. (1990). Transfer training method: Its influence on skill generalization, skill repetition, and performance level. *Personnel Psychology*, 43: 501–523.

—— SCHWOERER, C., and ROSEN, B. (1989). Effects of alternative training methods on self-efficacy and performance in computer software training. *Journal of Applied Psychology*, 74: 884–891.

GJERDE, P. F., and ONISHI, M. (2000). In search of theory: The study of "ethnic groups" in developmental psychology. *Journal of Research on Adolescence*, 10: 291–299.

HARRIS, M. B., and EVANS, R. C. (1973). Models and creativity. *Psychological Reports*, 33: 763–769.

KIM, U., TRIANDIS, H. D., KAĞITÇIBASI, C., CHOI, S., and YOON, G. (1994). *Individualism and Collectivism: Theory, Method, and Applications*. Thousand Oaks, Calif.: Sage.

KRUEGER, N. F., Jr., and DICKSON, P. R. (1993). Self-efficacy and perceptions of opportunities and threats. *Psychological Reports*, 72: 1235–1240.

—— —— (1994). How believing in ourselves increases risk taking: Perceived self-efficacy and opportunity recognition. *Decision Sciences*, 25: 385–400.

LATHAM, G. P., and SAARI, L. M. (1979). Application of social learning theory to training supervisors through behavioral modeling. *Journal of Applied Psychology* 64: 239–246.

MACHADO, A. (1993). Internal states: Necessary but not sufficient. *Journal of Experimental Analysis of Behavior*, 60: 469–472.

MADDUX, J. E. (1995). *Self-Efficacy, Adaptation, and Adjustment: Theory, Research and Application*. New York: Plenum Press.

MATSUI, T., and ONGLATCO, M. L. (1992). Career self-efficacy of the relation between occupational stress and strain. *Journal of Vocational Behavior*, 41: 79–88.

MATSUMOTO, D., KUDOH, T., and TAKEUCHI, S. (1996). Changing patterns of individualism and collectivism in the United States and Japan. *Culture and Psychology*, 2: 77–107.

MEEHL, P. (1978). Theoretical risks and tabular asterisks: Sir Karl, Sir Ronald, and the slow progress of soft psychology. *Journal of Consulting and Clinical Psychology*, 46: 806–834.

MEICHENBAUM, D. (1984). Teaching thinking: A cognitive-behavioral perspective. In R. Glaser and S. Chipman and J. Segal (eds.), *Thinking and Learning Skills: Research and Open Questions*: 2. 407–426. Hillsdale, NJ: Erlbaum.

MILLER, N. E., and DOLLARD, J. (1941). *Social Learning and Imitation*. New Haven: Yale University Press.

NAGEL, E. (1961). *The Structure of Science*. New York: Harcourt, Brace and World.

PARK, Y. S., KIM, U., CHUNG, K. S., LEE, S. M., KWON, H. H., and YANG, K. M. (2000). Causes and consequences of life-satisfaction among primary, junior high, and senior high school students. *Korean Journal of Health Psychology*, 5: 94–118.

POINDEXTER, D. O. (2004). A history of entertainment-education, 1958–2000. The origins of entertainment-education. In A. Singhal, M. J. Cody, E. M. Rogers, and M. Sabido (eds.), *Entertainment-Education and Social Change: History, Research, and Practice*: 21–38. Mahwah, NJ: Lawrence Erlbaum Associates.

PORRAS, J. I., HARGIS, K., PATTERSON, K. J., MAXFIELD, D. G., ROBERTS, N., and BIES, R. J. (1982). Modeling-based organizational development: A longitudinal assessment. *Journal of Applied Behavioral Science*, 18: 433–446.

POWERS, W. T. (1978). Quantitative analysis of purposive systems: Some spadework at the foundations of scientific psychology. *Psychological Review Monograph Supplements*, 85: 417–435.

—— (1991). Comment on Bandura's "human agency." *American Psychologist*, 46: 151–153.

REICHARD, G. A. (1938). Social Life. In F. Boas (ed.), *General Anthropology*: 409–486. Boston.

ROGERS, E. M. (1995). *Diffusion of Innovations*. New York: Free Press.

ROSENTHAL, T. L., and ZIMMERMAN, B. J. (1978). *Social Learning and Cognition*. New York: Academic Press.

SABIDO, M. (1981). *Towards the Social use of Soap Operas*. Paper presented at the Institute for Communication Research, Mexico City, Mexico.

SCHWARZER, R. (1992). *Self-Efficacy: Thought Control of Action*. Washington, DC: Hemisphere.

SKINNER, B. F. (1977). Why I am not a cognitive psychologist. *Behaviorism*, 5: 1–10.

STAGNER, R. (1981). Training and experiences of some distinguished industrial psychologists. *American Psychologist*, 36: 497–505.

THASE, M. E., and MOSS, M. K. (1976). The relative efficacy of covert modeling procedures and guided participant modeling on the reduction of avoidance behavior. *Journal of Behavior Therapy and Experimental Psychiatry*, 7: 7–12.

THORNDIKE, E. L. (1898). Animal intelligence: An experimental study of the associative processes in animals. *Psychological Review Monograph Supplements*, 2(4), Whole No. 8.

WATSON, J. B. (1908). Imitation in monkeys. *Psychological Bulletin*, 5: 169–178.

WHITE, J. (1982). *Rejection*. Reading, MA: Addition-Wesley.

YAMAGISHI, T. (1988). The provision of a sanctioning system in the United States and Japan. *Social Psychology Quarterly*, 51: 265–271.

ZIMMERMAN, B. J. (1989). A social cognitive view of self-regulated academic learning. *Journal of Educational Psychology*, 81: 329–339.

....

CHAPTER 3

IMAGE THEORY

....

LEE R. BEACH
TERENCE R. MITCHELL

In 1974, at the University of Washington, the two of us began a sixteen-year collaboration that possibly was the most productive period of our respective careers and that certainly was the most fun. The initial motive for collaborating was to meld our skills so we could broaden our research capability; Mitchell was skilled in field research and Beach was skilled in laboratory studies. The meld of skills was achieved, but the more important outcome of our collaboration was the melding of our respective substantive interests; Mitchell was interested in decisions made in organizations and Beach was interested in personal decisions. It was the process of working together to understand decision making in the broader sense that led us to Image Theory.

We began our collaboration by reviewing research on occupational preference and choice using Expectancy Theory (ET) and Subjective Expected Utility (SEU) theory (Mitchell and Beach, 1976). We concluded that both perspectives did a comparably good job of accounting for the data. This was not too surprising given that the two perspectives are conceptually and mathematically similar. Conceptually, they both hold that people choose the option (course of action) they believe will result in the greatest benefit to them, provided there is a good chance they actually can attain that benefit. Mathematically, they both are variations on the concept of expected value, which means that they both are linear equations. The equations prescribe how to combine evaluations of possible outcomes of an option with evaluations of the probabilities that the outcomes will in fact be attained

Portions of this chapter are taken from Beach and Mitchell (1996) and Beach (1990).

should the option be chosen. In both cases the theoretical prescription is to select the option with the maximum product sum of the attractiveness and probability evaluations, called "maximization." The research seemed to indicate that occupational preferences and choices conformed reasonably well to the predictions of the equations, implying that the conceptualization shared by the two viewpoints was plausible.

3.1 The Beginning of Doubt

After completing our review paper, we conducted research on a variety of topics using the ET/SEU framework and everything seemed fine. The problems began when Beach did some follow-up analyses of data from an earlier study (Townes et al., 1977). The study had been of married couples deciding whether to have a (or another) child. It used SEU as the theoretical model and the research involved having the couples evaluate the arguments for and against having the child as well as the probabilities that those arguments would eventuate if they in fact elected to have the child. The evaluations were put into the SEU equation to predict which couples would have children. At the group level the equation accounted for the couples' decisions rather well, where the criterion was having or not having a child in the two years following the initial phase of the study.

However, the follow-up analysis showed that evaluated probabilities played very little role in the birth-planning decisions. Moreover, an attempt to use the study's results to design a decision aid for counseling in a birth planning clinic revealed that people by and large had no idea what probability meant or how it applied to decisions about having a baby. The shock was that this major component of any variant of the expected value model, a component that had been the focus of a great deal of laboratory research, turned out not to be of much account in this important, real world decision.

The two of us talked about the follow-up and clinic results. Mitchell had no trouble believing that SEU theory was inadequate, because it had never fared very well in organizational studies, even though it had frequently appeared to be sufficient for personal decisions (Mitchell, 1974). He also knew that the various formulations of ET tended to have so many free parameters that data fitting was bound to be at least marginally acceptable, so its success was not as compelling as it sometimes appeared. Beach was a little harder to convince; at the time SEU was the only viable theory for personal decisions. Although studies showed that people's subjective probabilities did not conform to probability theory and that their evaluations of the utilities of options' features were fraught with difficulties, SEU was still widely accepted. We began to suspect that the successes of both ET and SEU meant that while they could be useful for prediction, especially for group data, they did not necessarily model the actual decision process very well.[1]

Quite aside from empirical problems with the equations, we also began to have doubts about the conceptual base of both ET and SEU. Both perspectives view decision making as analogous to gambling. Indeed, the entire expected value logic in decision making derives from the gamble analogy, beginning with Daniel Bernoulli's (1738) analysis of how to gamble and how to purchase insurance for risky ventures, through Von Neumann and Morgenstern's (1947) analysis of decisions as games against nature or against competitors, through Ward Edwards' (1954) discussion of economic logic as a tinplate for the psychology of decision making.

Basically, the gamble analogy holds that the decision maker evaluates the attractiveness of the potential outcomes of a bet (utilities) and the probabilities that those outcomes will occur if the bet is accepted, and then he or she either accepts or rejects the bet or accepts the best bet (maximum expected value) from an array of bets. By extension, all decisions involving risk (which is pretty much all decisions) are seen as decisions about gambles, and the logic devised by Bernoulli and his successors is seen as the proper way to make such decisions, called the *normative model*. ET logic is axiomatically and mathematically less rigorous than SEU logic, but it derives from this same historical line of thought about expected value maximization, diverging through Bentham and the Utilitarians and, thus, into the social sciences in general.

At about the time we were having our doubts, other researchers were having theirs. For example, Hershey and Shoemaker (1980) observed that decision maker's behavior seldom resembles maximization of expected value in process or prescription. Fischhoff, Goitein, and Shapira (1983) observed, "The story of behavioral decision theory has been the growing realization that SEU often does not describe the decision making process... The dramatic tension has been provided by SEU's remarkable ability to hang on despite mounting doubts about its descriptive competence" (p. 185).

Although these doubts were based to some degree upon experimental results, they were strongly reinforced by observations of professional decision makers making on-the-job decisions. For example, Mintzberg (1975) observed that most managerial decisions involved whether or not to go with a single option, seldom were they a choice among competing options. In either case, few decisions involved explicit balancing of costs and benefits, let alone explicit use of probability. Peters

---

[1] At the time in question, researchers were beginning to understand that linear equations (including both ET and SEU) are robust and frequently provide a reasonably good fit to data even when they are significantly incorrect, something that Dawes and Corrigan had tried to tell us in 1974.

(1979) confirmed these observations and, in addition, observed that the criterion for decisions seldom about pursuit of the maximum gain. Rather, it was, "Does this option contain the thrust we want to see?" (p. 166). Peters agreed with Selznick's (1957) conclusion that the decision making manager primarily acts as a promoter and protector of the organization's values rather than as a relentless seeker of maximal payoffs. In a similar vein, Donaldson and Lorsch's (1983) ambitious study of twelve major corporations found that corporate managers do not strive to increase shareholder wealth; their first priority is the survival of the corporation itself. Moreover, strategic decisions strongly reflect the managers' beliefs and their aspirations for their organizations, rather than just economic factors and analytic logic.

This state of affairs elicited two immediate responses from behavioral decision researchers. The first was to declare decision makers flawed and to insist that they learn to behave as the normative models prescribed. The impact of this response has been minimal; there is little or no evidence that training in decision theory or decision analytic methods makes one a better decision maker. The second response was to modify normative theory, usually by retaining the general maximization of expected value framework but adding psychological assumptions that make the theory more predictive of actual decision behavior. Kahneman and Tversky's Prospect Theory (1979, Tversky and Kahneman, 1992) is the prime example of this response. By taking into account various biases, the underlying logic of the normative model remained relatively unscathed.

Quite aside from whether observed decision making resembles a gambler behaving as normative theory prescribes, there are two very large logical problems with the gamble analogy itself. The first is that the expected value of a gamble is the amount that the gambler can expect to win, on average, if he or she plays the gamble repeatedly. However, it is not at all clear what expected value means for a single gamble; the gambler either wins or loses and the average is irrelevant. Thus, the gamble analogy may hold if a decision maker makes a series of highly similar decisions, but it probably does not hold for unique decisions. In fact, in laboratory studies, gamblers treat repeated and unique gambles very differently (Keren and Wagenaar, 1987). Because decision makers regard the bulk of their decisions as unique, it seems unlikely they would treat many of them like gambles, which makes the analogy inappropriate. A manager does not approach a major decision with the idea that he or she will get to do this repeatedly and all that matters is that he or she is successful, on average, over the long run.

The second problem with the gamble analogy is that real gamblers do not get to influence the outcomes of gambles; they place their bet and await the turn of the card or the spin of the wheel. In personal and organizational decision making, substantial time may elapse between the decision and its outcomes and most of us use this time to do our utmost to influence those outcomes. We acknowledge that risk abounds, but we do not accept the passive role of a gambler who patiently waits to see if he won or lost. This is why probabilities make so little sense to most people—they want to use probabilities to describe the overall riskiness of the decision task, but they do not want to attach probabilities to every attribute of each decision alternative. In fact, real world decision makers insist that they try to nullify risk (probability) by working hard to make sure that things come out well. Unlike gamblers, managers are paid specifically to be proactive interveners who strive to make events progress toward the desired state, or at least in the desired direction.[2] One consulting firm with which we were acquainted finally omitted probabilities from their analyses altogether, replacing it with a variable that reflected the overall riskiness of the decision task and having decision makers evaluate their disutility for the risk of making a "wrong" decision. Their clients were far more comfortable with this formulation.

3.1.1 The Doubt Thickens

At about the time our trust in expected value and the gamble analogy began to crumble, we performed the most embarrassing (if enlightening) experiment of our collaboration. Still clinging to the ET/SEU perspectives, we undertook a study of how decisions are made about where to site nuclear power plants. In the first phase, we used our colleagues from the University's various engineering departments as sources to construct an elaborate method to help planners evaluate the attributes of each potential site in order to choose the best (note that we had abandoned probabilities). In the second phase, we used planners from the local power company as subjects and asked them to use our system for a set of hypothetical sites. Our task was to use their evaluations to predict which site each planner would select.

Actually, the study worked out fairly well, although it never was finished. We could, in fact, predict choices of hypothetical sites for the few subjects we ever ran. However, soon after the second phase got underway, one of the planners remarked that all this rigmarole was very nice, but it really did not reflect how site decisions were made. He claimed that planners simply screened out all sites that violated federal, state, or company guidelines and then selected the cheapest of the surviving sites. His colleagues agreed with him. By relying too much on our theory, we had built a magnificent, but wholly irrelevant decision system. We did not publish.

[2] Although some ET formulations try to capture proactiveness in the idea of instrumentality, it is done in a very impoverished form. By the way, it should be noted that somewhat after the time under discussion it was demonstrated that the behavior of real gamblers in casinos does not reflect expected value (or SEU); which makes sense because the expected value for a gamble in a casino usually is negative so expected value would prescribe avoidance of the gamble in the first place. Gamblers rely on luck, which has no place in the expected value, ET or SEU equation (Wagenaar, 1988; Wagenaar and Keren, 1988).

On the other hand, we had learned something. Perhaps it would not have seemed profound to anyone other than us (and our fellow decision researchers) but we had learned that contrary to the theories to which we subscribed, there is more than one way to make decisions. Indeed, after this little epiphany, it took only a little introspection to identify the various decision strategies we used ourselves. We decided to pursue this insight and construct a model that reflected it.

3.1.2 The Strategy Selection Model

Both of us had a history of working with Fred Fiedler. Among the many contributions Fred has made to organizational theory, one of the most important is the concept of contingency theory. A contingency theory assumes that behavior is contingent upon the characteristics of the person, the characteristics of the task, and the characteristics of the environment in which the person and the task are embedded. The theoretical problem is to identify the components of each of these three classes of characteristics. The empirical problem is to see how the components of these classes of characteristics influence the behavior of interest.

So, based on our introspections about our own decision strategies and on our familiarity with the relevant literature, we began to write a contingency theory of decision strategy selection. We began with the idea that decision makers have repertories of strategies that range from aided analytic strategies, such as decision matrices and decision trees based on SEU, which usually require the help of a computer and/or a decision analyst; to unaided analytic strategies, such as Simon's (1957) "satisficing rule"; to simple nonanalytic strategies, such as a rule of thumb or asking a friend or consulting a fortune teller. The expenditure of effort (and, sometimes, money) required to use these strategies decreases from aided analytic to nonanalytic. Moreover, there are individual differences in the strategies decision makers have in their repertories.

The decision maker's characteristics are knowledge of strategies, ability to use them, and motivation. The latter is characterized as wanting to expend the least effort compatible with the demands of the decision task, whose characteristics are unfamiliarity, ambiguity, complexity, and instability. The decision maker and the task are embedded in a decision environment characterized by the irreversibility of the decision, significance, accountability for being correct, and time/money constraints. The strategy selection mechanism is driven by the decision maker's motivation: Select a strategy by balancing the effort of using it against its potential for producing a desirable outcome.

The debut publication of this theory fleshed out what is said above and added a few simple equations to suggest how the variables combined (Beach and Mitchell, 1978). Justly unsatisfied with our equations, Jay Christiensen-Szalanski (1978) formalized the theory and showed that the best strategy in the repertoire was the one with the highest SEU! He then did a series of studies demonstrating the viability of his formulation of our theory (1980). This was followed by research by Dan McAllister, Jim F. Smith, Bill Waller, and others, all of which generally supported the theory while correcting its errors and extending it.

In spite of the evidence, we were not all that happy about Jay's conclusions. After all, we had set out to explore alternative decision strategies and ended up right back at SEU. Moreover, we were uneasy about the fact that neither the model nor the research were wholly compatible with what our introspection and observation told us. Our uneasiness stemmed from three things.

First, almost nobody ever uses aided-analytic and unaided-analytic strategies for their own decisions, even people who are trained to use them. On those rare occasions when sophisticated people use them, they seldom accept results that run counter to their intuition (Isenberg, 1984). Moreover, even for very important decisions the formal strategies often seem too coldly intellectual (deciding to get married or to have a child). Instead, most times, most people, for most problems use some sort of simple, easy, rapid nonanalytic process.

Second, almost all choice strategies proposed by researchers are designed solely for identifying the "best" option in a set of plausible options—called the *choice set*. This left us with the question of how the choice set comes to exist in the first place. Clearly, the mechanism that governs admission to the set plays a major role in determining the eventual decision. Granting this, what are the implications when that mechanism admits only one option—does that option become the "best" by definition? If so, what if there is only one option to start with, as Mintzberg (1975) observed? Without an admission mechanism that single option would automatically be the "best" and be selected, which we know does not happen.

Third, we were concerned about frequency with which decision makers explain seemingly irrational decisions with, "I was trying to do the right thing." Decision makers often choose "right" options that clearly are not in their best interest and they often reject "wrong" options that an observer might think they would find most attractive. In short, decision making is strongly shaped by beliefs, morals, ethics, and social conventions; guiding imperatives that can be referred to collectively as *principles*. Social scientists appear to be embarrassed by the fact that they and others have principles that serve as standards against which they test their own behavior and the behavior of others. But, if you listen to even the most causal conversation, including your own, you will find it to be full of judgments and opinions that reflect the power and centrality of principles.

In light of our thinking about these three troubling issues, and in light of our doubts about the generality of the Strategy Selection Model, we actively tried to make ourselves think outside the accepted canon and lore about decision making. With the help of Kenneth Rediker, who was a graduate student at the time, we held weekly think-sessions in which we chased ideas. Slowly, we began to see a structure to what we were thinking, and we began to write small essays trying to pin down our ideas. These essays eventuated in our first attempt to go public (Mitchell, Rediker, and Beach, 1986).

After that first publication things got tough. American journal reviewers seemed particularly reluctant to publish our work, even the empirical studies. We did much better in Europe (e.g., Beach and Mitchell, 1987; Beach, et al., 1988; Beach and Strom, 1989). To get the word out, we decided to put our ideas, and our research, in a book, but no American publisher was interested. Finally, Britain's Wiley Ltd. took the risk, publishing *Image Theory: Decision Making in Personal and Organizational Contexts* in 1990. Although we do not believe many people read the book, its mere existence seemed to give the theory legitimacy and interest quickly grew.

3.2 IMAGE THEORY BRIEFLY

In the Image Theory view, the decision maker is an individual acting alone. Of course, most decisions are made in concert with others, be it a spouse, a friend, business colleagues, or whoever. But, even so, the decision maker has to make up his or her own mind and then differences of opinion must be resolved in some manner that depends upon the dynamic of the group. That is, Image Theory does not regard groups or organizations as capable of making decisions *per se*; they are the contexts within which individual members' decisions become consolidated through convincing others, negotiation and politics to form a group product (Beach, 1990; Beach and Mitchell, 1990; Davis, 1992). As a result, Image Theory focuses on the individual making up his or her own mind in the context[3] of a social relationship or an organization, with the presumption that the result may later prevail, be changed, or be overruled when presented to others.

Each decision maker is seen as possessing values that define for him or her how things *should* be and how people *ought* to behave. This involves such old-fashioned concepts as honor, morals, ethics, and ideals as well as standards of equality, justice, loyalty, stewardship, truth, beauty, and goodness, together with moral, civic, and religious precepts and responsibilities. Collectively these are called

---

[3] The social or organizational context includes knowledge about others' views, information about the issue requiring a decision and the values and meanings (culture) shared by members of the relationship or organization (Beach, 1993).

principles and they are "self-evident truths" about what the decision maker (or the group to which he or she belongs) stands for. They help determine the goals that are worthy of pursuit, and what are and what are not acceptable ways of pursuing those goals. Often these principles cannot be readily articulated, but they are powerful influences on decisions.

Whatever one's principles may be, they are the foundation of one's decisions: potential goals and actions must not be seriously incompatible (violate) with them or those goals and actions will be deemed unacceptable. Moreover, the utility of decision outcomes derives from the degree to which they conform to and satisfy the decision maker's values. That is, it is customary to think of decisions as involving the pursuit of desired outcomes, of maximization of something, of the attempt to end up better off after the decision is made than before it is made. Almost always the analysis begins with the potential contribution of the options' outcomes to attainment of this advancement in fortune; seldom is attention given to what really is being accomplished by such advancement. Our contention is that the motivation for profit, for gain, for advancement, and the values of outcomes that contribute to them derives from the degree to which those outcomes promote and comply with the decision maker's principles. It is this *compatibility* that is the key.

Indeed, as has frequently been observed, the most powerful motivation for action does not emerge from the profit-motive sort of thinking that is represented by normative decision theory. People often are personally altruistic and managers do not behave as single-minded maximizers of profit (Selznick, 1957). It takes a fair degree of logical contortion to make altruism and "suboptimality" fit the normative mold. But, such contortion is unnecessary because most people already know where the motivation for such behavior lies. It lies in the fact that getting things, doing things, making things happen gives intrinsic pleasure when it promotes and complies with one's principles. Introspection and observation provide clear evidence for the motivational nature of *autotelic* activity; that which is rewarding in and of itself (Csikszentmihalyi and Csikszentmihalyi, 1988). We submit that the intrinsic motivation for such actions, both the plans and the goals that they seek to attain, is provided by their compatibility with the decision maker's principles.

In addition to principles, the decision maker has an agenda of goals to achieve—some are dictated by his or her principles ("Because I believe in spiritual salvation, and because I am my brother's keeper, I must seek to convert unbelievers and, thereby, save their souls") and some are dictated by problems encountered in the environment—although principles still constrain how these problems are addressed ("Because my boss refuses to promote me, I must find a new job—but I still wouldn't feel right about leaving without giving proper notice"). Goals are desired alternative states of the world, each of which has an accompanying plan for its achievement, formulated at the time the goal is adopted or soon afterward (Tubbs and Ekeberg, 1991). A plan is a blueprint for goal achievement; tactics are behaviors in service of the plan and the logical implications of the plan's execution constitute a *forecast* of how the plan will work out. The various plans for the various goals must be interleaved in time and it must be possible to coordinate them so that they do not interfere with one another.

Decisions are about the adoption of goals and plans (and, more rarely for adults, principles) and about whether plan implementation is producing progress toward goal achievement. An *adoption* decision (adoption of a potential goal or plan) is based, first of all, on whether the goal or plan is compatible with other goals and plans and with relevant principles. If it is not wholly compatible with any of these, how incompatible is it? If it is not too incompatible, it might work out all right, but there is some point at which it is simply too incompatible and must be rejected. *Progress* decisions are about whether goal achievement will occur if the decision maker continues to implement the present plan. As long as progress is forecasted, implementation proceeds. If not, the plan must be revised or replaced, or its goal must be revised or abandoned.

Some goals may be adopted immediately, e.g., when assigned by one's employer or imposed by friends or family. However, when the decision maker is not, thus, constrained, adoption begins with screening out of incompatible goals. If this initial screening process involves only one goal and it is not judged to be too incompatible, it is adopted and the decision maker moves on to adopting a plan for accomplishing it. If the process involves multiple potential goals and only one survives screening, the situation is similar to starting with only one goal and having it survive screening—it is adopted. However, if more than one potential goal is involved and if more than one survives screening, something must be done to break the tie. This may involve raising the standard and re-screening until there is only a single survivor, or it may involve comparing the relative merits of the multiple survivors and choosing the best of them.

Adoption of a plan is similar to goal adoption except that it also involves imagining (forecasting) what might result if the plan were implemented; in particular, would it facilitate goal attainment? The ability to imagine what will happen as a result of plan implementation also serves to monitor the progress of implementation once the plan is adopted—"If I continue with this plan, do I foresee goal attainment?" If progress is not foreseen, the current plan must be revised or replaced. If a failing plan cannot be revised sufficiently, or if a promising replacement cannot be found, the goal itself must be altered or given up. Note that an individual's ability to make plausible forecasts plays an important role in his or her ability to make workable adoption and progress decisions—people who have difficulty thinking realistically about the future are prone to make short-sighted, disappointing decisions.

Of course, this all assumes that a decision has to be made at all. In familiar situations the decision maker may be able to call upon past experience to deal with whatever is demanded. That is, if he or she has encountered this situation (or one very like it), a variation on successful behavior that was used then can be used now—it becomes a policy for this sort of situation. If the past behavior was unsuccessful, it at least provides information about what not to do this time, and may even suggest alternatives that can then be considered for adoption through the decision process outlined above. The existence of policies reminds us that decisions are not made in a vacuum; they occur as points in an ongoing flow of experience. The decision maker usually knows about the events that led up to the present and has some grasp of the constraints upon what can be done. Without such contextual knowledge in which to embed decisions, they would not make sense at all. Moreover, this knowledge helps simplify the decision process by defining a subset of the decision maker's principles, goals, and plans as relevant to the current decision, called *framing* the decision. This reduces the cognitive effort that would be involved if everything the decision maker knows were brought to bear on every decision.

3.2.1 A Bit More Formality

To state all of this a bit more formally: Decision makers use their store of knowledge to set standards that guide decisions about goals to pursue and strategies for pursuing them. Potential goals and plans that are incompatible with (violate) the standards are quickly screened out and the best of the survivors is chosen. Subsequent implementation of the choice is monitored for progress toward goal achievement; lack of acceptable progress results in replacement or revision of the plan or adoption of a new goal.

Each decision maker possesses a store of knowledge that is far greater than needed for the decision at hand. That store can be conveniently partitioned into three categories, which are called images (Boulding, 1956; Miller, Galanter, and Pribram, 1960) because they are the decision maker's vision of what constitutes a desirable and proper state of events. The categories are labeled the value image (principles), the trajectory image (the agenda of goals), and the strategic image (the plans that are being implemented to achieve the goals).

The constituents of the three images can be further partitioned into those that are relevant to the decision at hand and those that are not. The relevant constituents define the decision's frame, which gives meaning to the context and provides the standards that constrain the decision.

There are two kinds of decisions, adoption decisions and progress decisions. Adoption decisions are about adding new principles, goals, or plans to the respective images. Progress decisions are about whether plan implementation is producing progress toward goal achievement.

There are two decision mechanisms, the compatibility test and the profitability test. The compatibility test screens candidate principles, goals, or plans on the basis of their quality. Actually, the focus is on lack of quality in that the candidate's compatibility decreases as a function of the weighted sum of the number of its violations of the relevant standards from the various images, where the weight reflects the importance of each violated standard. If a single candidate survives screening by the compatibility test, it is adopted as a constituent of its respective image. If there are multiple candidates and only one survives, it is adopted. If there are multiple candidates and more than one survives, the tie is broken by application of the profitability test. The profitability test focuses on quantity—choose the best candidate. The Christensen-Szalanski formalization of the Strategy Selection Model has been incorporated into Image Theory to account for the many ways in which the candidates in the choice set can be evaluated and the best of them chosen.

3.2.2 Research

Research began with a field study examining how potential plans are screened. Subjects were executives in successful sporting goods manufacturing companies with strong organizational cultures (which were taken as shared value images for the members of the organizations, Beach, 1993). It was found that rejection of plans could be predicted very well by their incompatibility with cultural standards.

This was followed by a series of laboratory studies on the nature of screening. For example, Beach and Strom (1989) demonstrated that rejection of hypothetical jobs occurred when an option violated three to four relevant decision standards and that screening was noncompensatory in that nonviolations had virtually no impact on acceptance or rejection. These results were replicated by Asare and Knechel (1995). Then Van Zee, Paluchowski, and Beach (1992) found that the information used in screening was not re-used in subsequent choice. It was as if decision makers regarded the earlier information as "used up" when it came time to make a choice. Beach and Frederickson (1989) applied Image Theory to screening of clients by audit firms and Asare (1996) empirically demonstrated that the application was appropriate.[4]

In 1990, Beach moved from the University of Washington to the University of Arizona, which made our close collaboration more difficult. Although we have continued to publish together, our research tended to go in rather different directions. We will review the work at Arizona first, and then the work at Washington.

---

[4] Sometime during all of this we wrote a paper (Mitchell and Beach, 1990) using Image Theory to account for intuitive and automatic decision making, which was fun to do even if it did not settle many philosophical questions about these two topics.

3.2.2.1 *Arizona Research*

Research at Arizona involved a series of collaborations with graduate students and faculty colleagues. Work with Richard Potter (Potter and Beach, 1994*a*) showed that when information about a relevant decision standard was unavailable for an option, decision makers treated the absence as though the option was in partial violation of that standard. Another study with Potter (Potter and Beach, 1994*b*) showed that when screening produces a set of survivors that later becomes unavailable, decision makers prefer to begin with a completely new set of options to screen rather than go back and select the best from among those they had previously rejected. If no new options can be obtained and a decision must be made, decision makers re-screen rejected options by raising their thresholds for rejection and downplaying the importance of the decision standards.

Work with colleagues Chris Puto and Susan Heckler and our students (Beach, et al., 1996) showed that the standards for a decision have differential weights and that assessed compatibility reflects those weights in the manner described by the theory (Beach, 1990; Beach and Mitchell, 1998). Work with Lehman Benson (Benson and Beach, 1996) showed that time constraints lead decision makers to speed up screening, but not to abbreviate the procedure. They save even more time by using very simple non-analytic strategies for choosing the best from among the survivors. Work with Lisa Ordóñez (Ordóñez, Benson, and Beach, 1999), showed that pre-choice processes more "naturally" focus on screening out bad options than on screening in good options. The latter agrees with the earlier finding (Beach and Strom, 1989) that nonviolations of decision standards do not contribute to an option passing into the choice set.

Work with Kris Weatherly (Weatherly, 1995; Weatherly and Beach, 1996), returned to organizational culture as a shared value image, demonstrating how culture influences organizational decisions. This work also contributed to a book that used Image Theory to account for organizational decision making (Beach, 1993).

Colleagues at Arizona and elsewhere used Image Theory as a framework for theoretical and empirical explorations of specific decision making domains. Cynthia Stevens (Stevens, 1996; Stevens and Beach, 1996) examined career decisions, job search, and job selection. Byron Bissell and Sandra Richmond (Bissell and Beach, 1996; Richmond, Bissell, and Beach, 1998) tested an Image Theory account of job dissatisfaction, hope for change, and turnover. Don Schepers (Schepers and Beach, 1998) studied the effects of differential framing on evaluations of compatibility in an occupational setting. Kenneth Walsh (1996) examined computer-supported group decisions. Kris Puto and Susan Heckler (1996) examined marketing and communications. Kim Nelson (1996) studied consumer decisions involving social responsibility. Stephen Gilliland and Lehman Benson (1998; Gilliland, Benson, and Schepers, 1998) demonstrated the difference between judgment and choice in social justice using Image Theory's compatibility test. Ken Dunegan and his colleagues (Dunegan, 1995; Dunegan, Duchon, and Ashmos, 1995) studied progress decisions and resource allocation decisions. Currently, Paul Falzer (personal communication) is examining clinical decision making within the Image Theory framework. Much of this work has been gathered in two anthologies, *Decision making in the workplace: A unified perspective* (Beach, 1996) and *Image Theory: Theoretical and empirical foundations* (Beach, 1998).

3.2.2.2 *Washington Research*

Mitchell began collaborative research with his faculty colleague Tom Lee soon after Beach left the University of Washington. Lee was interested in human resource topics like selection and turnover. So, they utilized Image Theory as a way of looking at how people made the decision to voluntarily leave an organization.

Turnover research had been characterized as having one rather dominant theoretical model: people became dissatisfied with their job, searched for alternatives and then engaged in an expected value type analysis to decide whether to go or stay. Research for years had elaborated on the many causes of dissatisfaction and the resulting search process but little had changed in the description of how the ultimate decision was made.

In 1994, Lee and Mitchell published their new theory of turnover, labeled the Unfolding Model (see also Lee, 1996). The central ideas were: (1) There were multiple ways (paths) that people left jobs; (2) These paths unfolded at different rates over time. Four paths were described and Image Theory played a role in three of these.

Path 1, which did not involve Image Theory, suggested that some event (called a shock to the system) triggers a preexisting script or plan and the person leaves.

In Path 2, a shock occurs, causing the person to use their value, trajectory, and strategic images to reassess their basic attachment, or commitment to their current organization. In other words, the person tries to fit the event (e.g., passed over for promotion, a fight with a co-worker) into their existing images. If there is a lack of fit (over some threshold) the person will either leave the organization or adjust their images. Note that for this path no search process is involved.

In Path 3, Image Theory enters the process twice. First, after the shock, the person does the same reassessment as in Path 2. If there is a lack of fit, the person has some relative dissatisfaction with their job, which prompts a search for alternatives. Once alternatives actually emerge, the person again utilizes their images to aid the judgment process. Initial screening determines whether one or more alternatives are seriously considered. This is the compatibility test. If one or more options survive, the person utilizes the profitability test to compare these options to each other and the current job. The option that is best is adopted, which may result in the person leaving their job.

In Path 4, accumulated job dissatisfaction, not shock, initiates the search process. Similar to Path 3, at this point the person screens alternatives using their images and engages in the compatibility and perhaps the profitability testing process.

This new approach to turnover provided a very different view of how the decision is made. It suggests new constructs and processes that are involved in this decision. Some of these ideas challenged longstanding conceptions about turnover but were unrelated to Image Theory. Mitchell and Lee (2001) provide a review and summary of these issues.

However, the Image Theory ideas were also central to the Unfolding Model and were tested empirically. In multiple studies using nurses, accountants, and bank employees, Lee and Mitchell assess the role of images in the leaving process. Using interviews in a qualitative study and questionnaires in a couple of other studies, they measured the fit process as a mechanism for producing job dissatisfaction (Paths 2 and 3) and as part of the compatibility and profitability tests involved in the decision whether to leave one's current job (Paths 3 and 4). These studies are reported in Lee, et al. (1996), Lee, et al. (1999) and Mitchell and Lee (2001) and provide substantial support for the use of Image Theory ideas on the decision to voluntarily leave an organization.

3.3 MAKING A SALE IN THE MARKETPLACE OF IDEAS

Research on Image Theory has been more concerned with the screening mechanism than with explicating the nature of images, although images are the heart of the theory. This is unfortunate, but frankly it was a strategic decision on our part. We knew that we could do more rigorous research on screening than we could on images, and that rigorous research on screening would be accepted by the decision research journals. Publication in these journals would in turn increase the likelihood that decision researchers would become interested in Image Theory. If we had begun with the necessarily less rigorous investigation of images, it is unlikely that our decision colleagues would ever have taken the theory very seriously.

The opposite strategy was used for the Unfolding Model. Because it addresses a specific class of decisions the relevant audience was sympathetic to examination of images and the research focused more on them than on the minute details of the decision mechanism.

In short, we tailored our research emphases to colleagues in two different, but related, disciplines. Decision researchers like equations and numbers, human resource researchers like interesting concepts. By couching our work in the appropriate terms we were able to arouse the interest of people in both disciplines. Of course, it would be nice if the world would beat a path to your door after you invent a better theory, but it really does not happen that way. There is a marketplace of ideas and marketing is as much a part of that marketplace as any other. Our research strategy was designed to address this marketing problem, and it has worked well enough, in that other people have taken up the cause and extended the theory in ways we could never have imagined. Moreover, this acceptance means we can now move on to examine a broader array of features of the theory.

REFERENCES

ASARE, S. K. (1996). Screening of clients by audit firms. In L. R. Beach (ed.), *Decision Making in the Workplace: A Unified Perspective*. Mahwah, NJ: Erlbaum.

—— and KNECHEL, R. (1995). Termination of information evaluation in auditing. *Journal of Behavioral Decision Making*, 8: 21–31.

BEACH, L. R. (1990). *Image Theory: Decision Making in Personal and Organizational Contexts*. Chichester, UK: Wiley.

—— (1993). *Making the Right Decision: Organizational Culture, Vision, and Planning*. Englewood Cliffs, NJ: Prentice Hall.

—— (ed.) (1996). *Decision Making in the Workplace: A Unified Perspective*. Mahwah, NJ: Erlbaum.

—— (ed.) (1998). *Image Theory: Theoretical and Empirical Foundations*. Mahwah, NJ: Erlbaum.

—— and FREDRICKSON, J. R. (1989). Image theory: An alternative description of audit decisions. *Accounting, Organizations and Society*, 14: 101–112.

—— and MITCHELL, T. R. (1978). A contingency model for the selection of decision strategies. *Academy of Management Review*, 3: 439–449.

—— —— (1987). Image theory: Principles, goals and plans. *Acta Psychological*, 66: 201–220.

—— —— (1990). Image theory. A Behavioral theory of decisions in organizations. In B. M. Staw and L. L. Cummings (eds.), *Research in Organizational Behavior*. 12. 1–41), Greenwich, Conn.: JAI Press.

—— —— (1996). Image theory, the unifying perspective. In Beach (1996: 1–20).

—— —— (1998). The basics of Image theory. In Beach (1998: 3–18).

—— SMITH, B., LUNDELL, J., and MITCHELL, T. R. (1988). Image theory: Descriptive sufficiency of a simple rule for the compatibility test. *Journal of Behavioral Decision Making*, 1: 17–28.

—— and STROM, E. (1989). A toadstool among the mushrooms: Screening decisions and image theory's compatibility test. *Acta Psychologica*, 72: 1–12.

BEACH, L. R., PUTO, C. P., HECKLER, S. E., NAYLOR, G., and MARBEL, T. A. (1996). Differential versus unit weighting of violations, framing, and the role of probability in image theory's compatibility test. *Organizational Behavior and Human Decision Processes*, 65: 77–82.

BENSON, L. III, and BEACH, L. R. (1996). The effects of time constraints on the pre-choice screening of decision options. *Organizational Behavior and Human Decision Processes*, 67: 222–228.

BERNOULLI, D. (1738). Specimen theoriae novae de mensura sortis. *Comentarii Academiae Scieniarum Imperiales Petropolitanae*, 5: 175–192.

BISSELL, B. L., and BEACH, L. R. (1996). Supervision and job satisfaction. In Beach (1996: 63–72).

BOULDING, K. E. (1956). *The Image*. Ann Arbor: University of Michigan Press.

CHRISTENSEN-SZALANSKI, J. J. J. (1978). Problem-solving strategies: A selection mechanism, some implications, and some data. *Organizational Behavior and Human Performance*, 22: 307–323.

—— (1980). A further examination of the selection of problem-solving strategies: The effects of deadlines and analytic aptitudes. *Organizational Behavior and Human Performance*, 25: 107–122.

CSIKSZENTMIHALYI, M., and CSIKSZENTMIHALYI, I. S. (1988). *Optimal Experience: Psychological Studies of Flow in Consciousness*. New York: Cambridge University Press.

DAVIS, J. H. (1992). Some compelling intuitions about group consensus decisions, theoretical and empirical research, and interpersonal aggregation phenomena: Selected examples. *Organizational Behavior and Human Decision Processes*, 52: 3–38.

DAWES, R. M., and CORRIGAN, B. (1974). Linear models in decision making. *Psychological Bulletin*, 81: 95–106.

DONALDSON, G., and LORSCH, J. W. (1983). *Decision Making at the Top: The Shaping of Strategic Direction*. New York: Basic Books.

DUNEGAN, K. J. (1995). Image theory: Testing the role of image compatibility in progress decisions. *Organizational Behavior and Human Decision Processes*, 62: 79–86.

—— DUCHON, D., and ASHMOS, D. (1995). Image compatibility and the use of problem space information in resource allocation decisions. Testing a moderating effects model. *Organizational Behavior and Human Decision Processes*, 64: 31–37.

EDWARDS, W. (1954). The theory of decision-making. *Psychological Bulletin*, 51: 380–417.

FISCHHOFF, B., GOITEIN, B., and SHAPIRA, Z. (1983). Subjective expected utility: A model of decision-making. In R. W. SCHOLZ (ed.), *Decision Making under Uncertainty*: 183–208. Amsterdam: North-Holland.

GILLILAND, S. W., and BENSON, L. III (1998). Differentiating between judgment and choice using image theory's compatibility test. In Beach (1998: 241–248).

—— —— and SCHEPERS, D. H. (1998). A rejection threshold in justice evaluations: Effects on judgment and decision making. *Organizational Behavior and Human Decision Processes*, 76: 113–131.

HERSHEY, J. C., and SHOEMAKER, P. G. H. (1980). Prospect Theory's reflection hypothesis: A critical examination. *Organizational Behavior and Human Performance*, 25: 395–418.

ISENBERG, D. J. (1984). How senior managers think. *Harvard Business Review* November/December: 81–90.

KAHNEMAN, D., and TVERSKY, A. (1979). Prospect theory: An analysis of decision under risk. *Econometrica*, 47: 263–291.

KEREN, G. B., and WAGENAAR, W. A. (1987). Violation of utility theory in unique and repeated gambles. *Journal of Experimental Psychology: Learning, Memory and Cognition*, 12: 387–396.

LEE, T. W. (1996). Why employees quit. In Beach (1996: 73–90).

—— and MITCHELL, T. R. (1994). An alternative approach: The unfolding model of voluntary employee turnover. *Academy of Management Review*, 19: 57–89.

—— —— WISE, L., and FIREMAN, S. (1996). An empirical examination of the unfolding model of voluntary employee turnover. *Academy of Management Journal*, 39: 5–36.

—— —— HOLTOM, B. C., McDANIEL, L., and HILL, J. W. (1999). A quantitative test of the unfolding model of voluntary turnover. *Academy of Management Journal*, 42: 450–462.

MILLER, G. A., GALANTER, E., and PRIBRAM, K. H. (1960). *Plans and the Structure of Behavior*. New York: Holt, Rinehart, and Winston.

MINTZBERG, H. (1975). The manager's job: Folklore and fact. *Harvard Business Review*, July/August: 49–61.

MITCHELL, T. R. (1974). Expectancy models of job satisfaction, occupational preference and effort: A theoretical, methodological and empirical appraisal. *Psychological Bulletin*, 82: 1053–1077.

—— and BEACH, L. R. (1976). A review of occupational preference and choice using expectancy theory and decision theory. *Journal of Occupational Psychology*, 99: 231–248.

—— —— (1990). "... Do I love thee? Let me count...". Toward an understanding of intuitive and automatic decision-making. *Organizational Behavior and Human Decision Processes*, 47: 1–20.

—— and LEE, T. W. (2001). The unfolding model of voluntary turnover and embeddedness: Foundations for a comprehensive theory of attachment. *Research in Organizational Behavior*, 23: 189–246.

—— REDIKER, K., and BEACH, L. R. (1986). Image Theory and its implications for policy and strategic decision-making. In H. P. Sims and D. A. Gioia (eds.), *The Thinking Organization*: 293–316. San Francisco: Jossey-Bass.

NELSON, K. A. (1996). Consumer decisions involving social responsibility. In Beach (1996: 165–180).

ORDÓÑEZ, L. D., BENSON, L. III, and BEACH, L. R. (1999). Testing the compatibility test: How instructions, accountability, and anticipated regret affect pre-choice screening of options. *Organizational Behavior and Human Decision Processes*, 78: 63–80.

PETERS, T. (1979). Leadership: Sad facts and silver linings. *Harvard Business Review*, November/December: 164–172.

POTTER, R. E., and BEACH, L. R. (1994a). Imperfect information in pre-choice screening of options. *Organizational Behavior and Human Decision Processes*, 59: 313–329.

—— —— (1994b). Decision making when the acceptable options become unavailable. *Organizational Behavior and Human Decision Processes*, 57: 468–483.

PUTO, C. P., and HECKLER, S. E. (1996). Designing marketing plans and communication strategies. In Beach (1996: 155–164).

RICHMOND, S. M., BISSELL, B. L., and BEACH, L. R. (1998). Image theory's compatibility test and evaluations of the status quo. *Organizational Behavior and Human Decision Processes*, 73: 39–53.

SCHEPERS, D. H., and BEACH, L. R. (1998). An image theory view of worker motivation. In Beach (1998: 125–131).

SELZNICK, P. (1957). *Leadership in administration*. Evanston, Ill.: Row, Peterson.

SIMON, H. A. (1957). *Models of man*. New York: John Wiley.

STEVENS, C. K. (1996). Career Decisions. In Beach (1996: 49–62).

—— and BEACH, L. R. (1996). Job search and job selection. In Beach (1996: 33–47).

TOWNES, B. D., BEACH, L. R., CAMPBELL, F. L., and MARTIN, D. C. (1977). Birth planning values and decisions: The prediction of fertility. *Journal of Applied Social Psychology*, 1: 73–88.

TVERSKY, A., and KAFIHNEMAN, D. (1992). Advances in prospect theory: Cumulative representation of uncertainty. *Journal of Risk and Uncertainty*, 5: 297–323.

TUBBS, M. E., and EKEBERG, S. E. (1991). The role of intentions in work motivation: Implications for goal setting theory and research. *Academy of Management Review*, 16: 180–199.

VAN ZEE, E. H., PALUCHOWSKI, T. F., and BEACH, L. R. (1992). The effects of screening and task partitioning upon evaluations of decision options. *Journal of Behavioral Decision Making*, 5: 1–23.

VON NEUMANN, J., and MORGENSTERN, O. (1947). *Theory of Games and Economic Behavior*. Princeton: Princeton University Press.

WAGENAAR, W. A. (1988). *Paradoxes of Gambling Behavior*. Hillsdale, NJ: Erlbaum.

—— and KEREN, G. B. (1988). Chance and luck are not the same. *Journal of Behavioral Decision Making*, 1: 65–75.

WALSH, K. R. (1996). Mitigating cultural constraints on group decisions. In Beach (1996: 133–142).

WEATHERLY, K. A. (1995). "The rapid assessment of organizational culture using the Organizational Culture Survey: Theory, research and application." Unpublished Ph.D. dissertation, University of Arizona, Tucson.

—— and BEACH, L. R. (1996). Organizational culture and decision-making. In Beach (1996: 117–132).

....

CHAPTER 4

THE ROAD TO
FAIRNESS AND
BEYOND

....

ROBERT FOLGER

LIKE the realtor's "location, location, location" mantra, surely "colleagues, colleagues, colleagues" is key to research and theory building. My debts of that kind are legion. Indeed, one of my concerns about this chronicle is that I might inadvertently omit some names among the friends, relatives, and colleagues who've helped me in intellectual quests. For that reason, this preface notes my apologies to those who remain unnoted.

The roots of my justice interests trace to a college course in experimental psychology. The course covered Helson's (e.g., 1967) *Adaptation Level* work, which captured the heart of a psychological perspective—namely that subjective experience can vary with identical stimuli (e.g., the perceived weight of an object can seem light or heavy depending on an immediate prior history of other objects lifted). Later I saw the same emphasis in work on relative deprivation and the *Comparison Level* concept in the classic Thibaut and Kelley (1959) text. Indeed, I pursued a social psychology Ph.D. at UNC-Chapel Hill from a desire to study such issues with Thibaut. On arriving in 1971, however, I found Thibaut studying psychology and the law with Laurens Walker, which led eventually to their 1974 book on procedural justice. That held no interest for me. Meanwhile, in reading Hal Kelley's (1967) seminal piece on attribution and finding it unsatisfying, I paid more attention to the next piece in the same *Nebraska Symposium on Motivation* volume (Pettigrew, 1967) about relative deprivation. It used the term *referent* throughout, and I borrowed that word as part of the title for my M.A. thesis the following year.

Then, as I began plans for a dissertation, I concluded that I'd want Thibaut to chair my committee. In preparation, I arranged to take a year-long readings course with him. I would read whatever interested me, and we would discuss the material on an every-other week basis. Still haunted by interests in relative deprivation, I gravitated toward the social comparison literature that had arisen since Festinger's (1954) original formulation. That led to finding work by Phil Brickman whom I greatly admired and that later played a role in my pursuing a post-doctorate with him at Northwestern University at Evanston.

The turning point in events that led to my dissertation's themes, however, came indirectly. At some point while perusing the social-comparison literature, I read the Adams (1965) chapter on inequity. Here was something I could sink my teeth into! Unlike ideas that seemed to go several directions at once, the Adams material had a focus that seemed promising. Also, I saw significant "holes" in the research. For one thing, Adams's own research stream had concentrated almost exclusively on the counterintuitive aspects of advantageous inequity ("overpay"), whereas I found the relative *deprivation* of disadvantageous inequity more interesting. I also thought the lack of systematic investigations into the latter left a large number of questions unanswered. Moreover, the Adams framework seemed well formulated in ways that would make useful operationalizations of the relevant constructs reasonably straightforward. The more I read, the more convinced I became that predictions about reactions to underpayment were problematic because of these unanswered questions. A series of early studies by Karl Weick (e.g., 1966) only confirmed this impression.

Then my wife, Pam, got a promotion at work. Having graduated from Wake Forest with a *cum laude* degree in biology, she could get hired (at the state's *Blue Cross/Blue Shield* headquarters) only as a secretary. Promoting women into advanced positions then took hold, and she became a manager. I was overjoyed—not only by her having finally achieved a position with some of the stature to which I thought she was entitled by dint of intelligence and qualifications, but also by the significant enhancement of our household income just after the birth of our first son, Marc. To my surprise, Pam expressed *increasing* resentment (cf. reactions as origins of the term, *relative deprivation* in Stouffer, et al., 1949). Here was a specific puzzle worth tackling.

Then a fellow graduate student gave me a dittoed copy of a working paper by Adams (a draft of what would become his chapter with Sarah Friedman in the volume of *Advances* dedicated exclusively to equity; Berkowitz and Walster, 1976). Delighted, I made an appointment to see him in his business-school office (although he had a joint appointment in psychology, I had only seen him once in our building during a colloquium). Disaster struck again. When I told him how excited I was to see him once again pursuing equity (after what I perceived as a hiatus on boundary-role research), he politely informed me that no, he was simply doing a favor for Walster and no longer had any plans on returning to any other equity-related efforts. Gentleman and scholar that he was, however, he graciously suggested that if other graduate students and me would like to meet with him informally over the summer, we could have a small seminar together on equity. My dissertation proposal grew out of those meetings.

I distinctly remember very uninformative feedback on one draft when Adams merely said that "it still needs something more" (a paraphrase). I thought my design had elegantly captured the antecedents of my wife's reaction—a sequence of improved outcomes would actually spark a more negative reaction than would unchanged outcomes. A chance conversation with Alan Lind, then also a graduate student, reminded me about procedural justice research by him with Thibaut, Walker, and other students. Also, I'd run across the Hirschman (1970) book on *Exit, Voice and Loyalty* while browsing the bookstore. Discussion with Alan prompted a procedural component as the "something more" in my design, and Hirschman's book prompted my referring to *voice* rather than *process control* (the Thibaut–Walker term).

Why *voice* rather than *process control*? The latter implies an explanation involving perceived control or indirect influence. I felt that the nature of such mechanisms should be left open to investigation because prejudging the relevant mechanism might preclude thinking about other possible causes. Ever since, I've tried to use terminology I consider more neutral and less likely to foreclose issues (e.g., *voice* simply names what's happening, rather than addressing why certain effects might result).

Second, I thought it useful to have a situation in which the same term, *voice*, could readily do double-duty as either a predictor (independent variable) or criterion (dependent variable). In Hirschman's theorizing, voice plays the role of dependent variable; that is, he focused on situations of decline or disappointment as indicated when the response to such situations might take various forms (viz., in particular, as either the *exit* strategy of withdrawing from the situation or the *voice* strategy of staying engaged and trying to work toward improvements in conditions). In my dissertation, on the other hand, I manipulated levels of voice (i.e., voice versus what I called *mute*, or the absence of an opportunity to voice one's opinions and preferences) as an independent variable. This usage illustrates a research-and-theorizing tactic I've found useful ever since, in addition to the idea of choosing terms with neutral, purely descriptive features: Look to mechanisms with broad applicability. For example, Hirschman referred to voice as "political process, *par excellence*" (Hirschman, 1970: 16), whereas the operationalizations of *process control* in the Thibaut–Walker paradigms seemed to imply a much more narrowly circumscribed realm of applicability chiefly aimed at instances in which third parties exercised control of settling conflict-resolution matters. Eventually, such thoughts led to other heuristics I've found useful for generating theory and research, which I outline below before continuing about the origins of referent cognitions theory.

4.1 TOWARD A THEORY OF THEORY BUILDING

A "Huh? Aha!" model of the theory-building process (cf. Folger and Turillo, 1999) essentially captures features that I've found useful in my own work or have noted from others. "Huh?" refers to a puzzling phenomenon; "Aha!" refers to mechanisms or processes postulated as its potential explanation. Proceeding along the Huh-Aha path has an internal logic (known by philosophers as *abduction* or *retroduction*) but does not necessarily follow steps in the order I describe.

4.1.1 Think Before Reading—Reflect on Experience

When I describe this approach to doctoral students, I begin by noting Simonton's (2003) claim that breakthrough developments in science ordinarily take about ten years. I then note that (*a*) they do not have ten years to finish a dissertation, and (*b*) many academic institutions require tenure decisions in less than ten years. What is a student to do? I tell them to call upon an equivalent body of expertise, namely the last ten years of their life experiences.

I also convey the "don't read . . . think" dictum that John Thibaut told me had come from Kurt Lewin (see Nisbett, 1990). Lewin recommended to avoid literature immersion before first reflecting on some preliminary "conclusion," even if only as questions and puzzles identified. Thinking in advance about what's interesting, and why, alters the way literatures get read afterward—as, of course, they must. First, prior reflection can help preclude taking a literature's conclusions for granted or accepting them without question. Thus, parts of a literature's conventional wisdom might no longer seem to convey obvious truth or "the final word."

Second, prior introspection creates a frame of reference for a wider variety of reactions to what gets read thereafter. The more typical process of jumping into the literature first often involves simply assimilating information rather than active questioning. With prior personal reflection as a frame of reference, however, some of the information read subsequently will seem contrary to those pre-formed impressions—which provides a great opportunity for questions about why (*a*) I had one kind of idea in advance, but (*b*) this article seems to imply otherwise. In other words, this sequence can bring about occasions for seeing two possibilities as worthy of pitting against one another. Of course, the literature can also seem to confirm prior impressions. Again, that can prove instructive. When prior reflection led to speculating that a particular type of phenomenon might occur (perhaps along with some rudimentary sense of when and why), and the literature verifies that occurrence, what types of explanations apply? Do your own speculations about this occurrence match, at least roughly, the explanatory accounts provided in the literature? Still, one's own ideas about the exact nature of explanatory antecedents might differ from the literature's account—perhaps only subtly, yet in ways worth considering.

I've also adopted a related habit when reading research articles or reviewing submitted manuscripts. Rather than moving linearly through the paper, I try first to find only as much information as necessary for getting some sense of how to read the data as presented in tables or figures, which usually means that I start in the methods section. There I try not so much to comprehend the relevant constructs as expressed theoretically but instead to concentrate on details of operationalization (e.g., What did the instructions actually say? How were questionnaire items worded?). Then I scrutinize the results to judge for myself what patterns seem evident (e.g., ignoring indications of "statistically significant"). I try to interrogate the data myself before seeing what the authors say. Similarly, when first hearing about a study or an idea for one, I try to make my own predictions before learning what someone hypothesizes. I think such habits can facilitate theory building.

4.1.2 Start with the Dependent Variable

My next recommendation also runs against the grain of common practice. Most students not only start by reading the literature but also by trying to identify the existence of one or more relevant theoretical models in it. They assume that theory should drive the development of hypotheses they aim to investigate, so they try to find an apt theory from which to deduce yet-untested predictions. That approach can have at least two kinds of potentially problematic consequences. First, it generates the experience of learning how to do incremental research but may preclude originality. Existing approaches do not always provide the best source for genuinely new theoretical insight. Moreover, current theories must of necessity trace back to an earlier time when no theory existed. Someone at the outside had to "start from scratch," and I think the skills for that type of competency need encouragement.

Second, exclusive reliance on deductions from existing theory runs the risk of an incestuousness that can lead the researcher farther and farther from actual phenomena. Theories deal in abstractions somewhat removed from reality. Constructs become reified and interpreted as if their conceptual definitions adequately represent all one needs to know about a phenomenon. In short, I find that later stages of research within a well-developed theoretical tradition can too often involve studying esoterica: The methodology for assessing what has remained untested at that point, or for assessing a key aspect of the theory in more rigorous and highly refined ways, tends to bore into artificially contrived minutia. My recommendation of "start with the dependent variable" seeks to head off such dangers. I tell students to make sure they have in mind a genuine *phenomenon* for investigation, which dovetails with the earlier recommendation of starting with one's own prior experience (including vicarious experience and the kinds of universal phenomena that comedians use for their best material).

I recommend a variation on Flanagan's (1954) *critical incident technique* in this regard. As I explain it to students, an ABC acronym—in terms of Antecedents, Behavior, and Consequences—summarizes the key elements. Beginning in reverse order, however, I stress that zeroing-in on a phenomenon needs a linkage with potential interest and relevance to others; that is, phenomena whose *consequences* should "matter." When students tell me they want to study X, for example, I ask why it interests them—the point being to help them find ways of articulating why other people might also want to learn something new about X.

Drawing attention to the *antecedent* and *behavior* aspects of an incident simply provides a means for disciplining one's description of events. When I began to formulate ideas about my dissertation, for example, the incident in question involved my wife's having expressed herself negatively (in ways I thought sounded resentful) just after being promoted from a secretarial position into management. The antecedent elements, therefore, surrounded the promotion itself. Her apparent resentment constituted the behavioral phenomenon I wanted to understand. To me, it seemed consequential because (*a*) it had an anomalous, counterintuitive quality, and (*b*) companies who promote people might fail to expect such reactions and, thus, fail to "manage" them in mutually constructive ways.

4.1.3 Which Incidents? Which Phenomena?

Above all, I stress to students that they should try to generate at least one such incident where something about the antecedent–behavior–consequence set does not lend itself to straightforward explanation—at least in their eyes, even though the initial impressions of other people might not find it particularly surprising or puzzling. My illustration for the Huh/Aha approach comes from the preface to

Festinger's (1957) book on dissonance theory. Festinger actually began "on assign-ment," having agreed to a piece for a compendium of social-science findings. Based on Festinger's work regarding informal social communication, the compendium editor asked Festinger to focus on communication findings. The vastness of that subject matter reminds me of what students sometimes express as their interests (e.g., saying "I'm interested in organizational communication" because it often seems problematic). Festinger knew better, however, and concentrated on phenomena associated with rumors.

In this case, the critical incident did not involve Festinger's own direct or vicarious experience but the conjunction of two actual events that occurred in a particular province of India: (*a*) an earthquake, and (*b*) wild rumors in the province (e.g., "The end of the world is at hand"; "A great tidal wave is coming") immediately after the earthquake. I argue that the keys to his theorizing could *in principle* have been made available to Festinger and his colleagues from any of a variety of possible descriptions of rumor-transmission incidents, including their own introspections about personal prior experiences. Indeed, the idea of wild rumors spreading seems relatively commonplace. Even the combination of a major catastrophe (e.g., earthquake) and subsequent rumors probably would not strike most people as signifying anything particularly out of the ordinary. In that regard, I stress to students that the "Huh?" of the Huh/Aha process need not involve something inherently mysterious or initially unfathomable. Rather, part of Festinger's insightfulness involved taking what others might shrug off ("ho hum, yes those things happen") and instead *framing* it as problematic vis-à-vis straight-forward explanation. Specifically, Festinger's reasoning began by juxtaposing (*a*) the scariness of these rumors' content, with (*b*) the taken-for-granted assumption of commonsense psychologizing that people seek pleasure and avoid pain. Why, then, would the rumor originators and transmitters deliberately engage in an activity that surely had an adverse pain-to-pleasure ratio?

Put that way, the question generates the "Huh?" of consequence, worth trying to understand and explain. I also describe this as an $A \rightarrow X$ versus $A \rightarrow Y$ juxtapos-ition of alternative cause–effects. The initially presumed causal antecedent in both cases, A, refers to the pleasure–pain assumption that ordinarily might get taken for granted as self-evidently true. As the premise in a deductively structured argument chain, however, we can refer to it as a stipulated initial condition: "Given that people seek pleasure and avoid pain..." (i.e., take that assumption as a given). Take X as referring to behaviors regarded as consistent with such an assumption (e.g., "people will be reluctant to place their hands onto very hot objects"). It might seem to follow from implicit additional premises (e.g., that expecting disaster causes discomfort), therefore, that rumors causing people to expect disasters will have a *low* likelihood of occurrence: the $A \rightarrow X$ causal sequence predicted on the basis of this "common sense" reasoning. Now take Y as the presence of wildly distressful rumors such as actually occurred, thereby representing a phenomenon seemingly at odds with commonsense expectations. What makes this *Y* surprising, anomalous, and puzzling, therefore, depends on the set of background assumptions (theoretic premises, whether scientifically formulated or drawn from everyday reasoning). Put another way, expecting the absence of something (no rumors) makes its presence need explanation; similarly, expecting one thing (simple, ordinary, mildly evocative rumors) makes the appearance of their opposite or substantially divergent (wildly alarming rumors) in need of explanation.

No such anomalies will prove explainable by means of applying the same rote procedure in each instance; rather, part of the creativity of theorizing comes from finding clever ways to sort among the possibilities. In the earthquake-rumor case, for example, (*a*) common sense might be wrong; (*b*) the commonsense pleasure–pain principle might not apply as directly in this case as first assumed; (*c*) perhaps the rumors did not really cause much discomfort after all; and so on. One way of addressing the quandary from confronting such a plethora of possibilities, however, might tend to prove useful more often than not: Try to accumulate examples of the surprising phenomenon in question (more than one "critical incident") along with examples of otherwise parallel situations in which the originally presumed, non-surprising effect instead obtains (viz., in this case, situations that involve an earthquake *without* wild rumors afterward).

Luckily for Festinger, available evidence provided just such a comparison case, namely from a different province at the same time of the earthquake. In fact, the province where the rumors had occurred was located at the outer reaches of the earthquake's impact, whereas evidence from the province located at the earthquake's epicenter revealed the virtual *absence* of rumors. Festinger then considered the difference in the pattern of the dependent variable (rumor vs. no rumor) in light of the difference in the setting (at the earthquake's periphery vs. at its center). Notably, buildings crashed and people died at the epicenter, whereas nothing especially calamitous took place in the peripheral province that felt only the earthquake's aftershocks.

This fact led Festinger to reframe his initial characterization of the dependent-variable phenomenon itself. He conceptualized this particular instance of rumor-spreading not as an anxiety-*provoking* event but as anxiety-*relieving* (or in a broader sense, as tension-reducing). The clue came from that absence of calamity in the peripheral province. Festinger concluded that in that rumor-filled area, residents had (*a*) experienced an agitated state of distressful arousal and anxiety, but (*b*) found little if anything thereafter congruent with such a reaction (no deaths, destruction). Imagine, for example, being rudely shaken for several moments by the ground's buckling and heaving, then having everything return to normal. Although now all seems calm, no doubt the surge of adrenaline and arousal of the sympathetic nervous system would leave you still in an agitated state.

Festinger reasoned that the mind likes to view the world in terms that make experiences interpretable. Incongruent experiences, which lack a straightforward connection with other experiences and assumptions at first blush, spur people to seek and to "create," if need be, some underlying reasons for what happened—as a way of post hoc sense-making (i.e., rationalization). In the outlying province where the ground shook for awhile and then returned to normal without devastation, yet leaving people anxious, they would want to "find" and "invent" a way to explain their anxiety. If future disasters loom immanently, feeling anxious becomes a reasonable and sensible reaction rather than something stupid or foolish. Hence the rumors acted as rationalizations or dissonance-reducing "cognitive elements" that served to interpret the otherwise uninterpretable. Out of this observation grew the concept of *cognitive dissonance* and the roots of Festinger's theory by that name.

Festinger's chain of reasoning thus illustrates a Huh?/Aha! pathway from a seemingly anomalous phenomenon to a hypothesized antecedent as presumed cause. This logic need not seem shrouded in mystery about how intuition works to reverse-engineer a plausible answer (the "aha!") for questions concerning the kinds of mechanisms and processes that might account for apparent anomalies (the "huh?"). Indeed, C. S. Peirce translated Aristotle as having given the label of *abductive logic* (also "abduction" or "retroduction") to this form of reasoning. Basically, it involves working backwards from an unexplained effect to its putative cause as hypothesized antecedent. Contemporary philosophy of science calls this reasoning to the best explanation.

4.2 ORIGINS OF REFERENT-COGNITIONS THEORY (RCT)

After the seeds of my justice interests had taken root and received nourishment from friends, relatives, and colleagues, an NSF fellowship allowed me to take a sabbatical/post-doctorate year at Northwestern in 1978–1979. I planned to study with Phil Brickman but found equally attractive the prospects for contact with others also there (e.g., Don Campbell, Tom Cook, Camille Wortman—all of whom had done work related to relative deprivation).

One small glitch occurred: Brickman moved to the University of Michigan at mid-year. We had initiated a "micro–macro justice" project (Brickman, et al., 1981), but its incomplete status led him to suggest a short visit to Ann Arbor. An added attraction was the Katz–Newcomb ceremonies that annually honored a distinguished psychologist. A departure from custom, however, scheduled presentations by two people—Danny Kahneman and Amos Tversky. I remember after hearing Danny's talk on "The Psychology of Possible Worlds" telling Phil that if the Nobel committee got around to giving another behavioral scientist like Herb Simon the economics prize again, it would surely be one, the other, or both of these two guys.

4.2.1 The Simulation Heuristic as the Generator of Referent Cognitions

I drove back to Evanston thinking "the answer's in there somewhere" for (*a*) the puzzle that had drawn me to Northwestern, and (*b*) relevant ideas in Danny's talk. Beyond my dissertation, this occasion represented a second major puzzle-solving issue as the spark for an original idea. The puzzle stemmed from seemingly contradictory reasoning and conflicting results in work by Tom Cook, Karen Hennigan (a student working with Cook on relative deprivation), and Faye Crosby: (*a*) on the one hand, future prospects of improved outcomes sometimes instigate feelings of relative deprivation and resentment—Crosby's (1976) review, for example, quoted de Tocqueville that although marginalized populations might remain passive during extended deprivation, rebellion might occur with the onset of improvements (as in my dissertation); (*b*) alternatively, improvements might instead pacify and placate.

After Danny's talk, I realized that superior outcomes can seem "feasible" in either of two ways: (*a*) in the sense that "good times lie just around the corner" (e.g., a bad quiz grade might not alarm the student aware of several further tests plus having the lowest grade dropped); (*b*) as cause for feeling deprived if the salience of better alternatives comes not from anticipated *future* improvements but because something in the *present or past* makes obtained outcomes seem worse by comparison— something as "realistic" as the results actually experienced, even though that sense of realism doesn't come from access to those superior outcomes. Both sources of "realism" relate to states of affairs not appearing far-fetched (i.e., mechanisms or processes capable of producing such states seem plausible). I distinguished between them as *likelihood* expectations, which extrapolate outcome trends into the future, versus *referent* cognitions, which instead contrast current outcomes with *counterfactual*-outcomes (e.g., what might have happened "if only…").

Some of Danny's Michigan talk became a chapter (Kahneman and Tversky, 1982) on the *simulation heuristic*. Such heuristics more generally involve short-cut ways in which impressions of circumstances get created. The simulation heuristic relates to counterfactuals deemed plausible ("realistic"). It operates via the ease with which alternative "constructions of reality" (imaginable conditions) come to mind. The 1982 chapter includes the example of Mr. Tees and Mr. Crane sharing a cab to the airport. They're traveling to different points on different flights that have the same departure time. Because of heavy traffic, they arrive thirty minutes late. Crane learns that his flight departed on time. Tees instead hears that his flight had a delayed departure and took off just five minutes before he arrived. When asked who's more upset, virtually all respondents indicated Tees.

Tees's knowledge about the delayed flight made a *counterfactual* event (i.e., being aboard the plane) nonetheless seem "real" because it "almost happened." Presumably the counterfactual of making it on board the scheduled flight would come readily to mind in juxtaposition with Tees's actual outcome, relative to the identical missed-flight outcome for Crane. Tees's barely missing his flight makes his deprivation seem relatively worse than Crane's. This example makes tractable the classic problem of "the" comparison-other that has confounded students of relative deprivation and inequity. Most approaches assume the centrality of social comparison (e.g., co-worker pay; industry average). Alternatively, people might develop expectations from their own past experience. The Tees–Crane example, however, portrays emotions susceptible to moment-by-moment fluctuation as the result of "online" processing; aspects of the immediate environment can override the influence of otherwise stable sources of comparison. This conceptualization obviates the necessity of determining how idiosyncratic influences (e.g., differences in personal history) shape each person's own unique frame of reference. Instead, we can look to ways in which the situation induces a given counterfactual.

Counterfactuals extend beyond social comparison and expectancy. Both Tees and Crane had identical sources of social comparison and expectancy, yet their reactions plausibly might differ substantially. Both, by the time they arrived at the airport, expected to miss their flights. Which types of "comparison other" would each tend to use? Consider the comparison to those better off, namely passengers en route to the destinations desired by Tees and Crane, respectively. Both men, making such a comparison, should feel equally deprived. On the other hand, they each knew of one other person who missed his flight (Tees = Crane; Crane = Tees), so any such source of comfort on misery-loves-company grounds became equally available to both. This example, thus, illustrates instigations from current events contrasting with "simulated" counterfactuals such as those that "almost" took place (e.g., the winning lottery ticket differs from yours by a single digit). Among instigations to counterfactual processing, note the *ideological* (e.g., Folger, 1987) as also beyond social comparison and expectations. Political ideals, for example, might reflect utopian dreams rather than conditions ever actually experienced, but a convincing rationale for such ideals might make existing conditions seem dissatisfying.

4.2.2 Procedures Again: In and Out of the Picture

My thinking remained outcome-focused, and the role of a procedural justice manipulation in my dissertation (voice) still seemed tangential, but I still suspected that counterfactual referents yielded only a simplified account. Specifically, it bothered me that two people who felt equally deprived might respond in entirely different ways—such that both might have similar "if only" instigations to a better alternative that "almost was," yet perhaps only one of the two might become hostile based on that sense of deprivation. I imagined feeling dissatisfied with a cheap watch when seeing expensive watches displayed. I doubted I'd feel resentful. Some disparities *have a legitimate basis in prior events* (not being able to afford a better watch is my own fault). I could start thinking about ways to obtain one of those nicer watches *now*, without having to wait until I can make enough money. The images of how to satisfy such cravings without imposing delayed gratification, however, start to seem "unrealistic" in a key way. Thinking about how to steal a watch might cross my mind, for example, but wouldn't cause obsessive rumination. Thus, I saw a gap that failed to address the perceived *legitimacy* of deprivations. The thought experiment convinced me that "you deserve the watch you've got—you're not yet entitled to one of those better ones" addressed legitimacy. Thinking "yes, you could steal one—but what would you think of yourself," however, made me treat legitimacy as something beyond the input-based-entitlement of equity theory.

These ideas led to *referent cognitions theory*, or RCT (Folger, 1986a, 1986b, 1987), which depicted relative deprivation in terms of *referent outcomes* (counterfactually alternatives compared to obtained outcomes). Dissatisfaction with received outcomes need not entail feeling resentful about them, however, nor resentment toward those with better watches. Given a referent outcome better than a current outcome, resentment hinges on perceived legitimacy. Here, I want to note some features of this *justification* component that went beyond outcomes in distinguishing dissatisfaction from resentment. First, I did not have in mind an invariant sequence such as (*a*) outcome seems negative, so (*b*) investigate legitimacy of outcome determinants. I've always thought it entirely possible for the sequence to run in the reverse direction at least on some occasions. A candidate denied a job, for example, might not initially react with much angst (e.g., perhaps other job prospects seem to loom favorably) but might rethink grounds for dissatisfaction *after* discovering something that seems illegitimately unjustified about the hiring process (e.g., discrimination).

Second, I used the term *justification* broadly. On the one hand, journal article publications (e.g., Folger, Rosenfield, and Robinson, 1983) drew a direct parallel between (*a*) referent outcomes and a distributive or outcome-focused perspective, as with (*b*) referent justification and a procedural justice perspective. On the other hand, at that time I was still resisting a "conversion" into being a "procedural justice researcher," so my notions about the construct of *justification* (/legitimacy) had led me to think of it as conceptually broader than procedures *per se*.

Paying attention to Tom Tyler and Bob Bies gradually led me to acknowledge procedural matters as more significant than I had thought. Even before their substantial influence, however, my intellectual debts began in collaboration with

David Rosenfield, a junior colleague at SMU. Ed Deci's (1976) book on intrinsic motivation had addressed another fairness-related issue puzzling me. Ed noted that the Adams (1965) account of equity theory left the door open for competing predictions about either overpay or underpay because inequity-resolution methods can take either cognitive routes or those seeking actual change. The former fits professors who, feeling underpaid, think how much they love their work, get to deal with young minds, have great autonomy, and so on. Such a person might actually work *harder* than someone who instead thinks of revenge against an employer—thereby perhaps working *less* diligently.

David and I examined this puzzle in studies (Folger, Rosenfield, and Hays, 1978; Folger, et al., 1978) focused on *choice* as a key moderator confirmed by interactions in our data. High-choice plus underpayment, for example, generated enhanced effort and task enjoyment, whereas underpayment under no-choice conditions generated a dislike for the task and less effort. The published versions emphasized procedural justice (*choice* differentiating two types of procedures), although I confess that it represented more the "marketing" of a relevance to existing concepts than a theoretical commitment to procedural justice.

One of many coincidences began to change all that. While at Northwestern, I had a revise-and-resubmit for the *Journal of Personality and Social Psychology* (Folger, et al., 1979). I discovered some shared interests with a new Ph.D. from UCLA then just starting at Northwestern—Tom Tyler. Hal Kelley had been one of his professors, whose connection with John Thibaut made Tom aware of the work on procedural justice. Tom focused on political psychology and the legitimacy of authority. I found out about his background and asked for comments on my revision. Then, after he collected survey data on citizens' reactions to encounters with the police, he asked me for advice in writing it up, which led to our co-authorship on that paper (Tyler and Folger, 1980).

At the time, the mainstream journals reacted negatively to the presentation of results from those surveys in terms of procedural justice because the items referred not to choice or voice but to the demeanor and conduct of the police. Having been influenced by Leventhal's (1980) approach to procedural variables, however, Tom conceived of procedures more inclusively. Hindsight indicates we had addressed what Bob Bies later termed interactional justice (e.g., treating people with dignity and respect), but his writings on that topic had not yet appeared in print.

Bob became the next source for my recognizing the incompleteness of outcome-dominated thinking because of the frequency with which people care as much or more "how" things transpire as they do "what" they receive as tangible benefits. The evolution of my thinking did not move in a linear fashion; various side-ways investigations also occurred (e.g., Folger and Konovksy, 1989; Folger, Konovsky, and Cropanzano, 1992). I only realized gradually that traditionally conceived "outcomes" (e.g., pay amounts) often fail to have the psychic and symbolic impact of interpersonal misconduct that demeans (e.g., publicly insulting subordinates in front of their peers).

Work by Bies influenced me in several ways. His notion of interactional justice had a lasting impact not only on me but also on organizational science. He also stressed social accounts, however, in ways that linger at least as much in my case. Here, I saw that my RCT manipulations of "procedural" factors (e.g., Folger, Rosenfield, and Robinson, 1983; Folger and Martin, 1986) did not actually manipulate the structural aspects of procedures but instead applied social accounts to influence the participants' perceptions of procedures. Bob's, having made that explicit, led to a follow-up study (Cropanzano and Folger, 1989) showing that the effects of both accounts and structural elements nonetheless paralleled one another. Bies also reinforced my thinking that notions regarding legitimacy stretched beyond the structural design features of formal procedures *per se*—the very intuition that had guided me in using *justification* as the key non-outcome element in RCT rather than procedures or procedural justice. In addition, I saw this beyond-structure impact as coming from social *conduct*, such as choices of how, when, and what to communicate (the accounts emphasis) but also including a range of interpersonal behaviors whether explicitly linked with communication efforts or not (such as giving someone the "cold shoulder," deliberately ignoring someone or taking pains to have nothing to do with them; e.g., Folger, 1993).

Having given an historical background on RCT, I turn now to *Fairness Theory* as an outgrowth from that line of thought.

4.3 Fairness Theory

Fairness Theory or FT (e.g., Folger and Cropanzano, 1998, 2001; Folger, Cropanzano, and Goldman, forthcoming), herein reflects as yet unpublished developments in that model. It stresses the theme of *accountability* impressions (not necessarily from conscious, deliberative thought—at least for some instances of initial reactions to events and persons) in relation to counterfactuals. Accountability regarding blameworthiness can, in principle, reflect a continuum but in practice tends towards such poles as innocence versus guilt, blame versus credit, merit versus demerit. FT posits that the motives and intentions presumed to underlie a person's mode of conduct can influence impressions about unfairness when the person seems at fault for wrongdoing.

The relevant counterfactuals—*Would, Could,* and *Should*—align roughly with elements from Schlenker's (e.g., 1997) triangle model of moral accountability as three interlocked components. FT treats unfairness (holding someone accountable and blameworthy) as derived from a conjunction among these three facets relevant to impressions about human conduct. Blame for unfairness amounts to a negative impression concerning each facet: What actually happened appears detrimental vis-à-vis three *counterfactual* representations (what did *not* happen) that each, in some sense, seem positive by comparison.

Pain contrasts negatively with pleasure as its (implicit) counterfactual, for example, just as guilt contrasts negatively with innocence. Perceived unfairness metaphorically mirrors the "pain" associated with a perceiver's impressions about an incident (e.g., one person scathingly belittles another) that *Would* NOT have generated concern "if only" the incident had never taken place. Blame also constitutes a negative (e.g., disapproving) impression related to at-least implicitly activated counterfactual representations concerning how the blamed person did *not* behave but *Could* and *Should* have behaved.

An example of an employee treating a customer in a rudely unfair manner (adapted from McColl-Kennedy and Sparks, 2003) illustrates these abstractions. The rudely treated customer perceives unfairness with regard to the following conjunction of counterfactual standards or referents: "what *could* have occurred (being served with a smile), what *should* have occurred (being treated politely), and how it *would* have felt had an alternative action been taken (feeling happier)" (McColl-Kennedy and Sparks, 2003, 254). Similarly, a third-party observer might consider the rudeness unfair and blame the employee for it if that perceiver's impressions include the sense that (*a*) the employee *Could* have smiled (e.g., did not have his or her mouth wired shut), (*b*) the employee *Should* have had more respect for the customer (e.g., by virtue of service-employees' duly assigned responsibilities and obligations toward customers in general), and (*c*) the situation *Would* not have aroused any concern on the observer's part in the absence of the kind of incident that occurred.

4.3.1 Key Variables and the Logic of Their Relationships

My ideas regarding justice differ from other approaches in how to characterize the primary dependent variable of interest. Much of the organizational justice literature looks at how unfairness perceptions might influence various kinds of reactions from people who feel unfairly mistreated. My interests focus explicitly on a particular *target* of those reactions—a social *agent* (presumed or suspected of some kind of contributory association with an unwarrantedly detrimental *state of affairs*). I first give a brief overview of the *agent* component (subsequently returning to it under the heading of *Conduct*) and then turn to *conditions*.

4.3.1.1 *Agency and Focal Agents*

Stated simply, humans act as agents contributing to conditions experienced by other humans. Perceivers *attribute* agency (making inferences about possible social as well as non-social or inanimate influences, such as the weather) in ways that sometimes take into account how one or more humans might have played a contributing role. The scientific understanding of lay inferences and attributions continues apace (e.g., Alicke, 2000), and many details remain incompletely formulated. My key interests lie with (*a*) how perceivers who deem conditions unjust associate those conditions with one or more other people in a "he or she/they seem potentially accountable" fashion, and (*b*) how those accountably associated agents (e.g., by reason of suspicion if not confirmation) become targeted by condition-perceivers as foci for negative attitudes and behavioral reactions to the agent-condition connection.

Agents eventually deemed blameworthy (culpably accountable) might first pass through stages not unlike when the law initially treats someone as a "person of interest," then a suspect, then a defendant indicted, convicted, and punished. For convenience consider these collapsed into the category of *culprit*, thereby emphasizing culpability. Various issues follow in relation to putative misdeeds: Whose untoward conduct do we deem wrongfully unfair—and in light of the conclusion we reach as an answer to that question, how might we feel inclined to react vis-à-vis that person? More concretely, if a subordinate considers a supervisor's conduct as "beyond the pale" in some sense, what attitudes toward that supervisor (and what concomitant action proclivities) might result?

4.3.2 Conditions: Beyond the Merely Detrimental

FT treats reactions to culprits based on *agency* considerations (e.g., moral-responsibility attributions). Put another way, implicit/tacit or explicitly considered issues concerning personal agency and accountability will govern fluctuations in the criterion variable (culprit-oriented reactions). Especially after hearing Danny Kahneman's talk about the psychology of possible worlds (cf. the simulation heuristic as described in Kahneman and Tversky, 1982), I had already begun thinking along those lines in generating RCT. Along the way, I came to treat as absolutely essential the differentiation between *mere dissatisfaction* and *resentment*, discussed separately as follows.

4.3.2.1 *Mere Dissatisfaction*

Stimuli have objective properties that humans process in subjective terms. Stimuli can possess a measurable temperature, for example, but responses to a hot object's pressure against human skin can vary (e.g., reduced sensitivity after nerve damage).

A scorched area of skin also can have negative implications for the burned person (e.g., possible infection). Scorched skin has objective properties, too, just as with the measurable temperature of the burning object that caused it; untreated, for example, scorched skin might cause infection. In such situations, hedonic negativity (e.g., dissatisfaction) can stem from objective conditions in more than one way: (*a*) more or less automatically, without much if any need for sustained deliberation, as when your hand's contact against a burning object causes you to pull it back immediately, scream "ouch," etc.; (*b*) by virtue of its processing from within some frame of reference, as when a 20-pound weight might seem subjectively "light" after bench-pressing a 200-pound barbell but would seem subjectively "heavy" when instead following immediately after a considerable time spent lifting paper clips.

Beginning with the RCT formulation based on the Kahneman and Tversky (1982) simulation of counterfactual emotions framework, I wrote about the experience of dissatisfaction (or "mere discontent," etc.) as if it entailed the latter, frame-of-reference basis for reactions. Although I still find notions about counterfactuals and the simulation heuristic helpful (e.g., *norm theory*; Kahneman and Miller, 1986; cf. Folger and Kass, 2000), I no longer think about processing that generates dissatisfaction as literally requiring some counterfactual-like simulation—at least not as a matter of conscious, deliberative rumination as a prerequisite. You do not have to cogitate about how much better you'd feel if your skin weren't burning in order to feel pain, withdraw your hand, yell "ouch," and so on.

Your processing of discomfort from contact with a burning object will nonetheless amount to a "virtual" counterfactual ("this is bad...I've known better"). Fairness Theory identifies such experiences as comprising a *Would* counterfactual: Your awareness of pain, for example, registers negatively not only in some absolute sense ("This hurts!") but also, even if only in a tacit way at least perhaps sometimes beyond conscious awareness, in a frame-of-reference sense as *worse* than other kinds of experiences (e.g., "This *Would* feel better otherwise"; or "Given a choice between this pain and many other experiences with which I'm familiar, I gladly *Would* rather have almost any of them"). The latter, frame-of-reference representation of feeling pain from touching a hot stove certainly can occur readily and quite soon *after* you've removed your hand, as you start to feel just how much it hurts (viz., recognizable by conscious awareness as worse than you felt immediately before touching the stove, worse than you feel most of the time, etc.). Thus, it follows that (*a*) the *Would* counterfactual does not have to entail conscious processing and awareness of specific, alternatively imaginable conditions as referent states; and (*b*), nevertheless, the virtual or as-if result at least implicitly corresponds to something along the lines of "Hmm, condition *A* or *B* both exemplify things easily brought to mind. *B*'s what I'm actually experiencing. Gee, *B* sure *Would* be better."

4.3.2.2 *How* Would *can become Associated with Impressions about Unfair Outcomes*

Recall from the RCT description of referents that they can come in more than one version. Thus far, I have mentioned only those that function in a manner not unlike sensation in general, as illustrated by Helson's *adaptation level* effects. Consider an emotionally toned experience such as pain, for example. You might size-up the nature of that pain in various ways. Perhaps you feel in pain but realize that on other occasions, having suffered a similar type of pain-causing injury, you felt much worse (or not nearly as bad). In that case, you have used a *past experience* referent (moreover, drawn from your own personal history rather than based vicariously on knowledge of someone else's past). Alternatively, you might find yourself involved in making various sorts of social comparisons, such as to states or conditions presently experienced by friends, neighbors, co-workers, casual acquaintances, or people often in the news. In addition, some comparisons might pertain to what we could call *ideological* referents—that is, to states or conditions envisioned according to "ideals" about possible or desirable state–condition experiences, such as according to various kinds of social, political, or economic philosophies. Indeed, the popularization of such ideas can lead to uprisings and social movements, as encouraged by circulated pamphlets, or can simply become part of common knowledge, as in the case of notions such as *utopia*.

Described as merely one other type of referent, these ideologically based counterfactuals (clearly not *actual* in the case of utopian visions) seem simply like one other way in which affect can vary hedonically as a function of the frame of reference brought to bear on experience. Numerous streams of research as well as common introspection, however, suggest otherwise: Ideological referents can have a *normative* (and morally toned) impact that extends beyond the mere realm of *evaluative description*. Being injured can cause pain, but that statement (*a*) simply describes factually that something has occurred (the injury) and (*b*) describes hedonically the type of experience created. Both say what *is* without necessary implications regarding what *ought* to be—the realm of the *morally normative* (e.g., encouraged by ideological referents) that extends beyond the evaluative that is merely descriptive.

Moral ideologies can introduce one or both of two evaluative standards, classically categorized by ethicists as pertaining to the *good* and the *right*, respectively. Standards regarding the good, as I use that term here, refer to states of well-being (most often vis-à-vis humans, but sometimes extended to other organisms as well as perhaps to the inanimate realm in general, which might include such notions as "the good of planet Earth"). Standards regarding *right*, on the other hand, refer to intrinsic value apart from consequences that have a direct bearing on welfare. Specifically, the valence in this case—positive or negative—stems from assigning human agents *moral accountability* for their *discretionary conduct*. Moral tenets can designate some forms of conduct as *wrong* and others as *right*.

In short, *good* and *right* referents pertain to *consequences* and *conduct*, respectively. An example will help clarify this distinction. Consider Robinson Crusoe's situation before Friday arrives, isolated on a remote island. Crusoe needs food, so he plants a garden and diligently tends it. Hail destroys his crops. For Crusoe, this devastating result constitutes a detriment to his welfare that will surely feel unpleasant (i.e., negatively valenced vis-à-vis the counterfactual of how much more pleasure a bumper crop *Would* have given him). Does a standard also exist regarding his moral state? The answer to that question involves considering *fairness* on some basis other than what Crusoe might deem applicable merely out of pure self-interest for his own personal welfare. To the extent that fairness transcends self-interest (or else why have a concept such as fairness), it calls for impressions formed on grounds more impartial than those Crusoe alone might develop—consistent with the philosophical position in ethics that moral principles should have the kind of universal applicability that rises above idiosyncrasy of egoistically biased, personal wants. In other words, fairness standards establish grounds for impressions apart from those of a given target person in question (e.g., Crusoe), which entails the perspective of more neutral and relatively "disinterested" (non-biased) or impartial third-party observers of the state experienced by that person.

The reader of the story can play that third-party role by reflecting on why Crusoe's condition seems unfair because of the hail-damaged crops. Note in particular an implicit counterfactual contrast regarding Crusoe's conduct: He worked diligently in doing his best to grow the crops, but circumstances beyond his control now jeopardize his welfare. When we seek to know whether we have grounds for holding him morally accountable for his detrimental state, this implicit contrast deems him innocent of any wrongful conduct. Instead, he has suffered without just cause—that is, in the absence of wrongdoing imputed to him. Impressions about the *distributive injustice* of his deprived state thus hinge on taking his prior conduct into account.

This first variation on Crusoe's plight illustrates why I have come to think that although distributive-justice standards such as implicated by equity theory (Adams, 1965) seem only to involve *Would*-like referents involving actual and counterfactual outcomes, the nature of human impressions about fairness instead entails considerations that at least implicitly invoke moral standards of accountability regarding conduct as *agency*—that is, impressions about how a given person might have contributed to the consequences in question. Put differently, *Would* impressions about damaged or jeopardized welfare entail only variation with regard to a target person's own pleasure–displeasure, satisfaction–dissatisfaction, and the like, whereas *Should* impressions point toward the role of humans as *discretionary agents held accountable according to moral standards of conduct.*

4.3.3 Conduct: *Should* and *Could* as Beyond the Merely Causal

Holding people morally accountable for their conduct requires considerations that extend beyond the mere cause and effect connection of *agentic means* leading to some current *consequential ends* (e.g., state or conditions such as in terms of implications for the personal welfare of one or more persons). A comprehensive portrayal of moral accountability would take us deeply into a morass of issues still unresolved in complex literatures such as those regarding attribution of responsibility and legal culpability, as mentioned during my earlier discussion in the *Agency and Focal Agents* section (see 4.3.1.1). Moral accountability, thus, engages a host of considerations (re *Should* counterfactuals) beyond the merely factual analysis of causal antecedents in an instrumental, means-ends chain of events (*Could* related).

4.3.3.1 Should *and* Could *Counterfactual Referents*

Moral accountability—like beauty—resides "in the eye of the beholder" because people form impressions about other persons' conduct on a subjective basis that goes beyond the objective facts. Certainly many types of biases might color such impressions, which can mean the absence of a *fair* and *impartial* assessment. Once again, therefore, we can think about the need for impartiality by addressing the perspective of third-party observers. Jurors, of course, represent a paradigmatic example. Given legal considerations as an outgrowth of public morality, therefore, we can examine the relevant foci of counterfactuals by thinking about how a public would want jurors to conduct themselves as they form impressions concerning a suspect's guilt or innocence (i.e., extent of moral culpability). Indeed, Tetlock (2002) has portrayed such impressions in a similar fashion in referring to accountability attributions from the standpoint of a person acting as *intuitive prosecutor*.

Fairness theory adopts a simplistic—but, I think, intuitively compelling—perspective by referring to the use of *Could* and *Should* counterfactuals (again, not necessarily as outputs from conscious deliberation). Essentially the common-sense basis for this distinction corresponds to grounds on which holding people morally accountable constitute a *reasonable* (cf. fair-minded, commendable) basis for doing so. As an illustration, think about making an impossible action a moral obligation, such as by saying "To avoid running into other people, you must flap your arms hard enough to levitate above them." Humans cannot fly that way, making it unreasonable to demand that they do so. In short, stipulating what people *Should* have done under a given set of circumstances incorporates considerations about what they *Could* have done.

What makes these into standards relevant to moral accountability on a counterfactual basis? First, regarding *Could*, a third-party observer at least implicitly takes into account the *discretionary* aspects of a person's conduct based on something not unlike the "reasonable person" standard applied in legal settings: What else

Could someone else have had available as conduct options, given impressions about the feasibility and desirability of such options from the vantage point of normally prudent people with physical and cognitive capabilities typical for human beings? Those suffering from severe mental deficiencies or having an age too immature for them to distinguish right from wrong properly, for example, compare to that standard in ways that encourage finding them non-culpable because they *Could* not have "stood in for" someone with the requisite prudence and capabilities.

Given the impression that someone *Could* reasonably have chosen to conduct himself or herself in a matter other than how he or she in fact acted, circumstances warrant the applicability of an associated co-requirement of moral accountability—considerations about how people *Should* act in the light of widely held socio-moral standards regarding human conduct. Fleshing out what that means can make contact with two concepts central in today's organizational justice literature: *procedural* and *interactional* justice.

Morally accountable conduct can relate to procedural justice during at least two distinct points in time: (*a*) at the time of a procedure's codification, and (*b*) during periods of its administration and implementation (when a pre-codified procedure applies). Relating procedural justice to *Should* per codification refers to the *ex ante* design or structural features of procedural regulations, their architectural blueprint as it were. Not unlike looking at a blueprint for a building and seeing it as wrongly conceived (e.g., likely to collapse), impressions about procedures can connote something morally objectionable about them. Imagine, for example, a legal procedure whose designed-in-advance features included no opportunity for defendants (or someone acting on their behalf) to address charges made against them.

Impressions about the fairness of procedures can form not only on an *ex ante* basis, such as considering them wrong in principle because they omit consideration of defendants' rights or fail by comparison with a (counterfactual) check-and-balance criterion to provide other important kinds of safeguards, but also on the *ex post* basis of how they happen to function in action. Indeed, *Should* counterfactuals might instigate impressions of unfairness quite readily when people see administrator–implementer officials exhibiting "they don't practice what they preach" forms of misconduct whereby they flaunt on-the-books regulations that *do* have rights-safeguarding protections.

In contrast with procedural justice impressions regarding formal regulations as designed and as implemented, interactional justice impressions introduce *Should* considerations of a different sort—namely on the basis of moral standards for interpersonal conduct as it plays out spontaneously within ordinary interactions among people. Consider, as the basis for this distinction, that procedural regulations typically apply to the formal process of decision making (e.g., procedural guidelines or regulations for governing the process for conducting 360-degree feedback). I've suggested that many pertinent features of such decision-making contexts prove capable of advance specification (i.e., stipulating designed-in-advance structural features, such as provision for filing complaints about the results of a decision). On the other hand, (*a*) no set of regulations can specify in advance every detail conceivably pertinent to a given instance in which a decision will get made, and (*b*) not all conduct among members of workplace organizations involves the handing down of decisions and implementation of their consequences. Moral tenets regarding interpersonal conduct among human beings in general, therefore, capture the sense of what I mean by *interactional justice*.

Because *Could* and *Should* counterfactuals govern impressions about human conduct from a morally accountable perspective, I need only point out their relevance to procedural and interactional justice by indicating how they can call attention to any of three roles in organizational contexts: (*a*) the role of rule makers such as top executives who establish policies and procedures in advance; (*b*) the role of rule implementers who carry out the practice of administering decisions; and (*c*) the world of human beings at large, whereby standards of interpersonal conduct independent of particular roles. By virtue of a procedure's designed-in-advance features, third-party observers can form impressions of whether that structural blueprint for governing relations among interacting parties sufficiently safeguards the dignity and respect each deserves. By virtue of the conduct exhibited among decision makers and implementers, third-party observers can form impressions how such conduct compares to standards of propriety for treating others with dignity and respect. And regardless of role or circumstance, third-party observers can form impressions about interpersonal conduct based on dignity–respect standards.

4.4 Limitations, Boundary Conditions, Conclusion

Recently my ideas about applicable standards for morally accountable conduct have taken what I call a *deontic* direction, which I treat separately in a later section. For now I will instead simply conclude this section with a few more brief statements about Fairness Theory as construed above. I begin by mentioning some potential limitations and boundary conditions. Despite the success of RCT and its FT reincarnation, both have constituted rather generic models and, hence, have certain limitations of scope. Here, I address only FT. At the conclusion of this section I will also point toward further developments.

Although not an explicit limitation *per se*, thus far FT has focused exclusively on negative states of affairs and anger-like emotions directed toward an agent because of impressions about that person's unfairness. Nothing about the theory, however, requires that restriction. In principle, the same kinds of counterfactuals apply to positive events, with directions reversed. Presumably some instances of over-benefit will arouse guilt rather than anger, for example, in much the same fashion as described by equity theory. Also, *Would, Could,* and *Should* clearly have the status of place-holder concepts at present, and fleshing them out will take further theory development. I have not attempted, for example, to incorporate all the developments seen in continuing work on the principles by which counterfactuals function. Such developments may allow for further elaborations about *Could* in particular, related specifically to causal attributions as part of imputing moral accountability and blame.

Some issues related to moral accountability have also become the basis for my recent work on a related perspective I call *deonance* (a term whose interpretation I postpone until a further section below), which relates directly to further elaborations on the concept of *Should*. FT emphasizes the role of humans as moral agents held accountable for their conduct. Rather than restricting attention to *what* might seem unfair, FT focuses on *who* might have acted unfairly. Equity theory, in contrast, considers pairs of outcome/input ratios as indicating an unfair condition (when unbalanced) but ignores the agency-related issues of blame that determined how those ratios became unbalanced in the first place. Put another way, equity theory avoids addressing accountability because it takes "inputs" as a given, rather than asking about the appropriateness of the conduct of those who "put in" their labor or other kinds of investments in exchange for expected returns. From the perspective of FT, accusing one person of inequitably compensating another only makes sense in light of the conduct of the parties on both sides.

Unfortunately, I have not clarified this point in my prior writings on the topic of justice. I now think that FT has as a boundary condition the limitation of addressing only cases where accusations of blame or fault apply. Some everyday usage of words such as fairness and justice, however, extend beyond situations involving blame. A given political or socio-economic ideology, for example, might deem some situations as inherently unfair simply if the overall distribution of some important good or goods seems disproportionately skewed, with the result that some people have much more than others. FT remains silent on such cases (that is, where questions of blame do not come up or are hopelessly indeterminate). Its only applicability in such cases consists of proposing that presumably the conduct of the deprived parties seems to have made them "innocent," or that their deprived condition has come about despite the absence of any unworthy conduct by them in ways that would have made them deserve deprivation.

It may surprise some to learn that I do not consider the *would/could/should* construction of Fairness Theory as necessarily its most distinctive or potentially useful feature. Instead, I regard those three concepts merely as convenient, short-hand terms for pointing toward the kinds of things people take into account when they form impressions about fairness. In no way do I mean to imply that anything like a full-blown, consciously deliberate assessment of a set of reasoned judgments concerning all three has to take place whenever people form fairness impressions. Nor do I believe that they need occur in any particular order. For example, someone examining the stipulated-in-advance features designed to regulate the process of making up-or-out tenure decisions might conclude that policies at a given university unfairly jeopardize the chances of junior faculty—or simply constitute a demeaning way of conducting such decision-making events.

4.5 THE DEONTIC OUTLOOK: TOWARD A THEORY OF DEONANCE

Currently, I'm working on *deonance theory* (from the Greek root *deon*, for duty) to model a broader range of phenomena than those concerning only the sense of injustice. Deonance Theory (DT) will aim to address various moral emotions in general (e.g., shame, indignation, and remorse) rather than isolating only reactions to specific forms of unfairness—although interactional injustice of the belittling, demeaning variety remains prototypical. Space considerations allow only the briefest of introductions (see Cropanzano, Goldman, and Folger, 2003; Folger, 1998, 2001, 2004; Folger and Butz, 2004).

The "Huh?" puzzle in this case comes from a series of studies (Turillo, et al., 2002) in which up to 75 percent of our participants made a financial sacrifice to punish someone without any corresponding return—that is, they accomplished no self-interested gain. Jim Lavelle posed the puzzle by saying that if self-interest could not account for the results, what would? I came to see that existing approaches to fairness presupposed various forms of self-interest, either as a return on investment (distributive justice as equity) or in the interest of selfish concerns about being well regarded by others (called a "relational" perspective but inherently wrapped up with needing, wanting, and feeling entitled to respect from others for the sake of self-worth assurance). Our punishers acted from a third-party awareness of an unknown stranger's conduct toward yet another unknown person, with anonymity devoid of personal relevance. In some studies, our participants punished a stranger—a person who merely attempted (and failed) to take advantage of someone else—by denying that miscreant any money. In another, they similarly chose to withhold funds from an unnamed company's unidentified supervisor who had ridiculed subordinates. Both results involved scenarios in which the miscreant would never learn that he or she had been punished (i.e., simply not receiving any part of a sum that, unknown to this person, would otherwise have gone to him or her). Thus, the designs precluded accomplishing self-beneficial results such as the deterrence of evil or others' praise for acting virtuously.

The essence of deonance, or a deontic perspective, consists of recognizing that people sometimes react to events based on their perceptions of an applicable moral duty (e.g., "Do not risk wrongfully hurting people"; cf. Murphy, 2003) even though the restrictions thereby placed on personal freedom may seem burdensome rather than desirable. Heider (1958) described an *ought force* in terms calling for obedience, allegiance, and commitment; similarly I refer to moral imperatives issuing from an impersonal Deontic Regime that places the greatest emphasis on "ought nots" of interpersonal misconduct. The fairness and organizational justice literatures always assume some exchange-like context or one involving decision makers, administrators, and the like; whereas I conceptualize the Deontic Regime's prohibitions as forbidding *categories of intention-inspired action* that more generally apply, relatively independent of context and circumstance. As third-party deontic "spectators," therefore, ordinary humans possess a capacity to render such judgments as "that's plain *wrong*" about acts themselves, without needing any personal connection to a wrongdoer or the target of a wrongful act. Similarly, writers of fiction such as the screen plays for movies have no trouble portraying a completely fictional character as villainous (e.g., Darth Vader's very image itself can elicit a negative emotional reaction toward him).

Part of this capacity, I suggest, lies at the heart of an answer to Lavelle's question, namely that forces of natural selection have evolutionarily provided the human viscera and neuro-cognitive architecture with processes and mechanisms for rapid categorizations of persons, places, things, and events in an emotion-laden way (e.g., as potential friend or foe). Consistent with the survival and reproduction logic of evolution, negative phenomena demand more immediate attention and mobilize available resources more urgently than do positive phenomena. An evolutionary trajectory especially within mammalian species, therefore, may account for the depth of feeling associated with allegiance to the mandate for forbidding certain generic classes of human conduct as impermissibly wrong. Of course, the exact nature of liability for culpable wrongdoing can vary according to mitigating versus aggravating features of a given event. As philosophers speak of such matters, deontic prohibitions connote acts forbidden *prima facie* (or *ceteris paribus*), but accused wrongdoers can offer rebuttal on excusing or justifying grounds—as can independent witnesses. The greater the strength of deontic forcefulness and demandingness associated with a prohibition, however, the greater the burden of proof on the would-be rebutter (which can relate to social accounts offered).

Loosely described, DT aims to combine some parallels to reactance theory with a reformulated integration concerning the metaphors of persons as intuitive politicians, prosecutors, and (moral) theologians in Tetlock (2002). Whereas, the third of those metaphors looks to what Tetlock calls *sacred values*, DT combines that orientation with the prosecutorial metaphor whereby both act in defense and protection of the Deontic Regime and deontic prohibitions.

DT assigns a central role to deontic prohibitions, rather than singling out sacred values, in reference to proscriptions about morally impermissible human actions. In a rough fashion akin to reactance-like tendencies that accompany what people experience when they fell their personal "free behaviors" attacked or at risk, I conceptualize the reactions of third parties, victims, and culprits as oriented in regard to "ought nots" as widely shared tenets of a Deontic Regime (i.e., morally authoritative precepts concerning wrongful conduct). Thus, unlike reactance, DT applies not just to violations of one's own personal liberty (cf. Gaus, 1999). Deontic prohibitions demand committed allegiance from all—at least provisionally. Culprits thus not only arrogate and abuse power (Folger and Butz, 2004) by placing others at risk of hardship (which includes such psychological belittling as cruel insults and the like) but also by acting confrontationally toward a sovereign authority vested in the Deontic Regime's edicts.

DT seeks to address multiple puzzles concerning moral sentiments and concomitant behavioral tendencies. Tetlock's (2002) metaphor of the intuitive politician refers chiefly to face-saving defensiveness by accused culprits, for example, whereas DT translates this into the following puzzle in search of moderators: What prompts defensiveness as a priority over, say, confession, remorse, apology, and various reconciliation-related efforts (e.g., begging forgiveness, offering compensation, trying to facilitate reconciliation)? Some headway on this front appears elsewhere (e.g., Folger and Pugh, 2002; Folger and Skarlicki, 1998), but much work remains. Moreover, DT seeks a unified conception of third-party reactions to violated deontic prohibitions as requirements of self-governed moral restraint vis-à-vis externalizing one's own costs by transferring them to others (cf. the economists' notions of *externalities*). Thus, DT also looks for moderators as determinants of when and why people seem more willing to impose the risk of hardship on others, and what kinds of excuses or justifications they are most likely to offer when confronted/accused accordingly. Finally, DT postulates that people mainly make right-versus-wrong assessments in terms of categories of behavior as intentionally pursued courses of action—rather than by making evaluations solely, or even primarily, in terms of criteria for results (e.g., attempted but failed murder still qualifies as blameworthy). In current research with Elizabeth Umphress, Ramona Bobocel, and colleagues on what we call the "Kemosabe effect" (named for a joke in which the Lone Ranger learns that this term conveys insult), for example, we find that a third party finds communications blameworthy when intended derogatorily, even when the target of those remarks actually takes them as a compliment! I'm happy to say that enough puzzles lie within those borders to keep me busy for quite some time, and I hope others will join in trying their own hand at such puzzle-solving activities.

REFERENCES

ADAMS, J. S. (1965). Inequity in social exchange. In I. Berkowitz (ed.), *Advances in Experimental Social Psychology*: 267–299. New York: Academic Press.

ALICKE, M. D. (2000). Culpable control and the psychology of blame. *Psychological Bulletin*, 126: 556–574. American Psychological Association.

BERKOWITZ, L., and WALSTER, E. (1976). *Advances in experimental social psychology*, vol. 9, *Equity Theory: Toward a General Theory of Social Interaction*. New York: Academic Press.

BRICKMAN, P., FOLGER, R., GOODE, E., and SCHUL, Y. (1981). Micro and macro justice. In M. J. Lerner and S. C. Lerner (eds.), *The Justice Motive in Social Behavior: Adapting to Times of Scarcity and Change*: 173–202. New York: Plenum.

CROPANZANO, R., and FOLGER, R. (1989). Referent cognitions and task decision autonomy: Beyond equity theory. *Journal of Applied Psychology*, 74: 293–299. American Psychological Association.

—— GOLDMAN, B., and FOLGER, R. (2003). Deontic justice: The role of moral principles in workplace fairness. *Journal of Organizational Behavior*, 24: 1019–1024.

CROSBY, F. (1976). Model of egotistical relative deprivation. *Psychological Review*, 83(2): 85–113.

DECI, E. L. (1976). *Intrinsic Motivation*. New York: Plenum Press.

FESTINGER, L. (1954). A theory of social comparison. *Human Relations*, 7: 117–140.

—— (1957). *A Theory of Cognitive Dissonance*. Stanford, Calif.: Stanford University Press.

FLANAGAN, J. C. (1954). The critical incident technique. *Psychological Bulletin*, 51: 327–358.

FOLGER, R. (1986a). A referent cognitions theory of relative deprivation. In J. M. Olson, C. P. Herman, and M. P. Zanna (eds.), *Social Comparison and Relative Deprivation: The Ontario Symposium*, vol. 4: 33–55. Hillsdale, NJ: Lawrence Erlbaum Associates.

—— (1986b). Rethinking equity theory: A referent cognitions model. In H. W. Bierhoff, R. C. Cohen, and J. Greenberg (eds.), *Justice in Social Relations*: 146–162. New York: Plenum.

—— (1987). Reformulating the preconditions of resentment: A referent cognitions model. In J. C. Masters and W. P. Smith (eds.), *Social Comparison, Justice, and Relative Deprivation: Theoretical, Empirical, and Policy Perspectives*: 183–215. Hillsdale, NJ: Lawrence Erlbaum Associates.

—— (1993). Reactions to mistreatment at work. In K. Murnighan (ed.), *Social Psychology in Organizations: Advances in Theory and Research*: 161–183. Englewood Cliffs, NJ: Prentice-Hall.

—— (1998). Fairness as a moral virtue. In M. Schminke (ed.), *Managerial Ethics: Morally Managing People and Processes*: 13–34. Mahwah, NJ: Lawrence Erlbaum Associates.

—— (2001). Fairness as deonance. In S. W. Gilliland, D. D. Steiner, and D. P. Skarlicki (eds.), *Research in Social Issues in Management*: 3–31: Information Age Publishers.

—— (2004). Justice and employment: Moral retribution as a contra-subjugation tendency. In J. A.-M. Coyle-Shapiro, L. M. Shore, M. S. Taylor, and L. E. Tetrick (eds.), *The Employment Relationship: Examining Psychological and Contextual Perspectives*. Oxford, UK: Oxford University Press.

—— and BUTZ, R. (2004). Relational Models, "deonance," and moral antipathy toward the powerfully unjust. In N. Haslam (ed.), *Relational Models Theory: A Contemporary Overview*. Mahwah, NJ: Lawrence Erlbaum Associates.

—— and CROPANZANO, R. (1998). *Organizational Justice and Human Resource Management*. Thousand Oaks, Calif.: Sage.

FOLGER, R. and CROPANZANO, R. (2001). Fairness theory: Justice as accountability. In J. Greenberg and R. Cropanzano (eds.), *Advances in Organizational Justice*: 1–55. Stanford: Stanford University Press.

—— —— and GOLDMAN, B. (forthcoming). What is the role of accountability in perceptions of organizational justice? In J. Greenberg and J. A. Colquitt (eds.), *Handbook of Organizational Justice*. Mahwah, NJ: Lawrence Erlbaum Associates.

—— and KASS, E. (2000). Social comparison and fairness: A counterfactual simulations perspective. In J. Suls and L. Wheeler (eds.), *Handbook of Social Comparison: Theory and Research*: 423–441. New York: Kluwer Academic/Plenum.

—— and KONOVSKY, M. A. (1989). Effects of procedural and distributive justice on reactions to pay raise decisions. *Academy of Management Journal*, 32(1): 115.

—— —— and CROPANZANO, R. (1992). A due process metaphor for performance appraisal. *Research in Organizational Behavior*, 14: 129.

—— and MARTIN, C. (1986). Relative deprivation and referent cognitions: Distributive and procedural justice effects. *Journal of Experimental Social Psychology*, 22: 531 546.

—— and PUGH, S. D. (2002). The just world and Winston Churchill: An approach/avoidance conflict about psychological distance when harming victims. In M. Ross and D. T. Miller (eds.), *The Justice Motive in Social Life: Essays in Honor of Melvin Lerner*: 168–186. Cambridge: Cambridge University Press.

—— ROSENFIELD, D., GROVE, J., and CORKRAN, L. (1979). Effects of "voice" and peer opinions on responses to inequity. *Journal of Personality and Social Psychology*, 37: 2243–2261.

—— —— and HAYS, R. P. (1978). Equity and intrinsic motivation: The role of choice. *Journal of Personality and Social Psychology*, 36: 556–564.

—— —— —— and GROVE, R. (1978). Justice versus justification effects on productivity: Reconciling equity and dissonance findings. *Organizational Behavior and Human Performance*, 22: 465–478.

—— —— and ROBINSON, T. (1983). Relative deprivation and procedural justifications. *Journal of Personality and Social Psychology*, 45: 268–273.

—— and SKARLICKI, D. P. (1998). When tough times make tough bosses: Managerial distancing as a function of layoff blame. *Academy of Management Journal*, vol. 41: 79: Academy of Management.

—— and TURILLO, C. J. (1999). Theorizing as the thickness of thin abstraction, *Academy of Management Review*, 24: 742: Academy of Management.

GAUS, G. F. (1999). *Social Philosophy*. New York: M. E. Sharpe.

HEIDER, F. (1958). *The Psychology of Interpersonal Relations*. New York: Wiley.

HELSON, H. (1967). *Adaptation-Level Theory: An Experimental and Systematic Approach to Behavior*. Harper and Row.

HIRSCHMAN, A. O. (1970). *Exit, Voice, and Loyalty: Responses to Decline in Firms, Organizations, and States*. Cambridge, Mass.: Harvard University Press.

KAHNEMAN, D., and MILLER, D. T. (1986). Norm theory: Comparing reality to its alternatives. *Psychological Review*, 93(2): 136–153.

—— SCHKADE, D., and SUNSTEIN, D. R. (1998). Shared outrage and erratic awards: The psychology of punitive damages. *Journal of Risk and Uncertainty*, 16: 49–86.

—— and TVERSKY, A. (1982). The simulation heuristic. In D. Kahneman, P. Slovic and A. Tversky (eds.), *Judgment under Uncertainty: Heuristics and Biases*: 201–208. New York: Cambridge University Press.

KELLEY, H. H. (1967). Attribution theory in social psychology, *Nebraska Symposium on Motivation*, 15: 192–238: University of Nebraska Press.

LEVENTHAL, G. S. (1980). What should be done with equity theory? New approaches to the study of fairness in social relationships. In K. Gergen, M. Greenberg, and R. Willis (eds.), *Social Exchange: Advances in Theory and Research*: 27–55. New York: Plenum Press.

LIND, E. A., and TYLER, T. R. (1988). *The Social Psychology of Procedural Justice.* New York: Plenum Press.

McCOLL-KENNEDY, J. R., and SPARKS, B. A. (2003). Application of fairness theory to service failures and service recovery. *Journal of Service Research*, 5(3): 251–266.

MURPHY, J. G. (2003). *Getting Even.* New York: Oxford University Press.

NISBETT, R. E. (1990). The anticreativity letters: Advice from a senior tempter to a junior tempter, *American Psychologist*, 45: 1078–1082: American Psychological Association.

PETTIGREW, T. F. (1967). Social evaluation theory: Convergences and applications. *Nebraska Symposium on Motivation*, 15: 241–311.

SCHLENKER, B. R. (1997). Personal responsibility: Applications of the triangle model. In L. L. Cummings and B. M. Staw (eds.), *Research in Organizational Behavior*, 19: 241–301.

SIMONTON, D. K. (2003). Scientific creativity as constrained stochastic behavior: The integration of product, person, and process perspectives. *Psychological Bulletin*, 129(4): 475–494.

STOUFFER, S. A., SUCHMAN, E. A., DeVINNEY, L. C., STAR, S. A., and WILLIAMS, R. M., Jr. (1949). *The American Soldier: Adjustment During Army Life* (vol. 1). Princeton, NJ: Princeton University Press.

TETLOCK, P. E. (2002). Social functionalist frameworks for judgment and choice: Intuitive politicians, theologians, and prosecutors., *Psychological Review*, 109: 451–471: American Psychological Association.

THIBAUT, J. W., and KELLEY, H. H. (1959). *The Social Psychology of Groups.* John Wiley.

TURILLO, C. J., FOLGER, R., LAVELLE, J. J., UMPHRESS, E. E., and GEE, J. O. (2002). Is virtue its own reward? Self-sacrificial decisions for the sake of fairness., *Organizational Behavior and Human Decision Processes*, 89: 839: Academic Press Inc.

TYLER, T. R., and FOLGER, R. (1980). Distributional and procedural aspects of satisfaction with citizen–police encounters. *Basic and Applied Social Psychology*, 1: 281: Lawrence Erlbaum Associates.

WEICK, K. (1966). The concept of equity in the perception of pay. *Administrative Science Quarterly*, 11(3): 414–439.

....

CHAPTER 5

GRAND THEORIES AND MID-RANGE THEORIES

CULTURAL EFFECTS ON THEORIZING AND THE ATTEMPT TO UNDERSTAND ACTIVE APPROACHES TO WORK

....

MICHAEL FRESE

As is true of all human behavior, theory building is based on environmental forces and on person factors. It has been my curse and my blessing to be overactive. My overactive nature led me to believe that it was good to be active and to be in control of things. Therefore, I quickly embraced theories that seemed to correspond with this prejudice. The three theories that seemed to encompass what I stood for were Rotter's cognitive behaviorist theory (Rotter, Chance, and Phares, 1972), Seligman's learned helplessness theory (Seligman, 1975), and Hacker's action (regulation) theory (Hacker, 1973; Volpert, 1974). Both Rotter's as well as Hacker's theories were indirectly related to a common source: Lewin's influence in Germany and in the U.S. All my research centered around the themes of an active approach to work-life (the opposite of helplessness): Thus, I became interested in personal initiative as one such instance of an active approach. Since an active approach means to explore, I also became interested in errors and how one can learn from errors.

My environment helped me tremendously. I had the good fortune to be socialized as a scientist both in Germany and in the U.S. In Germany, I worked with Walter Volpert at the Technical University of Berlin who proposed a combination of Marx and action theory to understand "work actions" (I did my Ph.D. with him in 1978); others who influenced me during this time were Norbert Semmer, Siegfried Greif, and Eberhard Ulich. In the U.S. I had my first important job (as associate professor at the University of Pennsylvania). Whenever people move from one culture to the other, they become much more conscious of how they are doing things—routines are no longer effective and need to be (re-)intellectualized (this is what action theory would propose). It was eye-opening for me, how quickly American scientists started to do empirical work and how seriously and deeply they thought about specific phenomena. While Germans like to think of themselves to be theoretically driven, they are often more interested in large, all-encompassing theories (often excessively complex). Hofstede (1991) has argued convincingly, that one way how cultures cope with high uncertainty avoidance is to develop "grand" theories because understanding the "complete" picture is uncertainty-reducing. Germany is one of the most uncertainty avoidant countries in the world (Brodbeck, Frese, and Javidan, 2002). This may be one of the factors that makes German scientific culture skeptical towards simplicity. Germans assume routinely that a certain amount of theoretical complexity is needed to mirror the complexity of the world. One often hears in discussions, "this is too easy," as if Occam's razor (the dictum that a theory should only have as many concepts as absolutely necessary and that more parsimonious theories with fewer variables are superior) had never made it to Germany.[1] In contrast, the environment of University of Pennsylvania's psychology department endorsed a high degree of interest in specific phenomena with precise middle-range theorizing (and precise experimentation). While the interest in phenomena was probably more pronounced at the University of Pennsylvania psychology department than at other departments, the interest in developing mid-range theories is common within the Anglo-Saxon tradition, which is more pragmatic than the German tradition. A mid-range theory consists of a limited number of variables, they are in between a working hypothesis and an all-inclusive effort of a unified grand theory, and they have limited assumptions, and high problem specification (Weick, 1989). Weick argued that for effective problem solving science needs to move towards mid-range theories. In contrast, grand theories are all-encompassing and, therefore, less precise.

---

[1] Germany is rapidly changing and becoming more Americanized; this includes a keener interest to publish in international journals and to develop more middle range theories. However, there is still interest in complex theoretical thinking.

Since more variables are involved and since the relationship cannot be developed with the same precision, falsifiability decreases. Examples of grand theories in this German tradition are Freud's psychoanalysis; Marx's theory of history, society, and organizations; Lewin's field theory; or Gestalt theory. No wonder that as psychology students in Germany we were much more enthused about these grand theories than about the typical article in *Psychological Review*. Stereotype has it that Germany is a conformist country. However, there is a high degree of intellectual autonomy (Schwartz, 1999). People are fiercely independent up to the point of attempting to constantly differentiate themselves from other scientists (or their mentors). This makes the evolution of common approaches more difficult and scholarly work is less oriented towards a common mainstream than in the U.S.:[2] German professors tend to build little kingdoms around them and there is little cooperation between them.

I found this cultural difference fascinating and through socialization into these two cultures, I tried to synthesize the two approaches: Take a grand all-encompassing theory as a general guideline—and I have found action theory to be such a theory—this was my German heritage (Frese and Sabini, 1985; Frese and Zapf, 1994); but combine this with a keen interest to develop theories of middle range that have a phenomenological approach—these were the lessons learnt from colleagues such as Martin Seligman, John Sabini, Henry Gleitman, Rob DeRubeis, and Paul Rozin at the University of Pennsylvania.

From this dual cultural experience I took the following message: I continued to be interested in a somewhat simplified (i.e., Americanized) version of action theory (Frese and Zapf, 1994); in addition, I started my research in each case by first studying a specific phenomenon in real life through observation, qualitative approaches, thinking about the phenomenon, and introspecting (or at least I encourage graduate students to do that). I usually choose phenomena to study and to theorize about that I find to be under-researched (or at least inadequately researched). Let me be very honest and clear: I do not usually read the literature and then come to one particularly important issue that has been neglected in the literature; nor do I read the literature and examine it for contradictions between theories and evidence. To the contrary, I often started my research with little knowledge of the literature but with a general idea of what I wanted to study (don't get me wrong, I am also an avid reader of science, but this is not where I get my research ideas from—rather they resonate in the background). This approach gave me a chance to make contributions to the literature and, in some cases, to start new trends. The phenomena were often culturally influenced, as will become clear in the following.

---

[2] Thanks to Johannes Rank who suggested this idea.

5.1 THE STUDY OF ERRORS: ERROR MANAGEMENT

When I came back to Germany from the U.S. in 1984, I noticed how much Germans were afraid of new technology. When I observed people working with computers, I noticed, how difficult it was for them to deal with errors. The German government financed large projects on errors in human–computer interaction and so I was set to explore the phenomenon of errors with a number of researchers (most notably with Felix Brodbeck, Jochen Prümper, and Dieter Zapf).

Then I did not yet know what I know now from a reanalysis of the GLOBE study (House, et al., 2004): Germans are highly intolerant of errors—only Singapore has a higher intolerance for errors among the sixty-one GLOBE countries.[3] Thus, the problem of dealing with errors caught my eye and fitted well with my interest in action theory (which emphasizes the importance of negative feedback: an error is a special form of negative feedback). With a group of students, I developed a new kind of training that would produce an active error orientation and would promote use of errors actively—quite the opposite of what I saw people doing and how I saw trainers teaching computer skills.

This was my approach: I observed something of general interest that I then married with my general psychological theory (action theory). I then attempted to do empirical research that produced (theoretical) advance in the understanding of this specific phenomenon. The resulting middle-range theory became a building block for my general approach to a theory of work actions. In this way, I use an American approach to produce a well-developed middle-range theory but I am true to my German heritage of keeping a grand theory alive.

5.1.1 Error Management Training

Our phenomenological orientation towards errors allowed us to make a discovery: When people are permitted and encouraged to make errors during training and are instructed to learn from errors, they perform better after training than when they are hindered from making errors. This was surprising because most software trainers and a lot of theorists (e.g., Skinner and Bandura) had suggested otherwise: They favored the avoidance errors because they considered errors were too frustrating and inefficient for the learner, and that people would simply learn the

---

[3] Thanks to Paul Hanges who has provided me with this reanalysis of the relevant item of the GLOBE.

wrong things. Our so-called error training (later called error management training) proved to be superior to other methods of training people in computer skills (Heimbeck, et al., 2003; Ivancic and Hesketh, 2000; Keith and Frese, forthcoming).

Action theory argues that negative feedback is useful (Miller, Galanter, and Pribram, 1960): Action implies a goal (some set point that needs to be achieved). Until one has achieved the goal, a person receives information that there is a discrepancy between the present situation and the set point (achievement of the goal, e.g., a person wants to travel to Rome and acknowledges that he or she is 500 miles away). Thus, negative feedback presents information on what we have not yet achieved and it provides guidance to action. Errors provide negative feedback but with a specific twist: An error implies that the actor should have known better. It is the latter that produces the problems of blaming people—both oneself and others.

Therefore, we developed a training procedure (error management training) which gave participants explicit instructions to use errors as a learning device and not to blame themselves. Participants are supposed to explore a system with minimal information provided; in contrast to exploratory training, error management training tasks are difficult right from the start, thereby exposing participants to many errors. Error management training explicitly informs the participants of the positive function of errors; these so-called error management instructions are brief statements (we often called them heuristics because they allow us to deal with the error problem) designed to reduce potential frustrations in the face of errors: "Errors are a natural part of the learning processes!" "I have made an error, great! Because now I can learn!" While participants work on the training tasks, the trainer provides no further assistance but reminds the participants of the error management instructions. When comparing error management training with a training procedure that does not allow errors, error management training proved to be more effective across diverse groups of participants (university students as well as employees), training contents (e.g., computer training, driving simulator training), and training durations (1-hour training to 3-day training sessions), with medium to large effect sizes (Frese 1995).

Once we had established empirically that we were dealing with a consistent phenomenon of the usefulness of this training procedure, we developed more detailed theoretical ideas on the potentially mediating mechanisms of error management training. In the beginning, I was somewhat naive: I actually thought, the more errors a trainee makes, the more chances he or she has to learn. This is definitely not so. We learnt in experiments that the number of errors did not positively predict learning (Van der Linden, et al., 2001): We should have thought a bit harder, because action theory does not suggest that any feedback has positive value—rather, only feedback that leads to new understanding; and this occurs only when participants use a systematic approach to dealing with errors (Van der Linden, et al., 2001).

It became apparent that the error management instructions were crucial. Error management training without these instructions was as inefficient as "error-avoidant" training (Heimbeck, et al., 2003). Cognitive activities are instigated by error management training, for example, errors encourage exploration and meta-cognitive activities. Meta-cognitive activities imply that participants develop cognitive activities, using skills of planning, monitoring, and evaluation of their progress towards their goals (Schmidt and Ford, 2003). These meta-cognitive activities are encouraged because errors prompt participants to stop and think about the causes of the error, to come up with new solutions, to implement them and to test their effectiveness (Ivancic and Hesketh, 2000). Meta-cognitive activities help to focus participants' attention on task-relevant system features during training, and they enable trainees to later master new tasks on their own and meta-cognitive activity explains how error management training produces positive performance effects (Keith and Frese, forthcoming).

Error management instructions should also decrease emotionally negative effects (e.g. frustrations) because they help trainees to frame errors positively. This is, indeed, one of the explanations for the efficacy of error management training (Keith and Frese, forthcoming).

5.1.2 The Function of Error Culture in Organizations

I usually attempt to develop some knowledge about the boundary conditions of my theories. Thus, with time, I attempt to develop hypotheses that are more risky. I agree with Popper (1972) that scientists need to be interested in risky hypotheses because risky hypotheses advance science by producing interesting thoughts and potential falsifications of theories (of course, personally, we always strive for verification—we love our theories after all; but we should be ready to falsify them as well).[4]

To test a more risky hypothesis, some students and I combined the ideas of control, of action orientation and of an active approach to errors to study the organizational culture of error management (Van Dyck, et al., forthcoming). We argued and showed empirically that a positive error management culture leads to higher profitability.

We do not know yet exactly how this works, but our theorizing on error management and error prevention leads us to a few ideas. Any organization should use both error prevention *and* error management to optimize the chance to reduce the negative consequences of errors. We argue that errors are ubiquitous. If human

---

[4] I disagree with Popper's idea (1972) that the process of developing new ideas is beyond science. As a matter of fact, I think this is the most important part of science to come up with interesting and new ideas.

errors *per se* can never be completely prevented, it is necessary to ask the question of what can be done *after* an error has occurred (Frese, 1995)—the issue of error management. The fallibility of human reasoning is the flipside of the advantages of the human cognitive apparatus characterized by fast processing in uncertain environments (Reason, 1990) and bounded rationality (March and Simon, 1958). A pure error prevention approach cannot adequately deal with the fact that errors are ubiquitous. Therefore, error management is a second line of defense for quality and safety after error prevention has failed.

The error management approach distinguishes between errors and their consequences. While error prevention aims at avoiding negative consequences of error by avoiding the error altogether, error management focuses on reducing the negative consequences of error and on increasing the potentially positive consequences. The error management approach attempts to ensure that errors are reported and detected quickly in an organization, that negative error consequences are effectively handled and minimized, that errors are discussed and communicated, and that learning occurs. Dealing with errors includes secondary error prevention (i.e., learning from errors so that the same ones do not recur). Examples of employing an error management approach can be found in software systems (e.g., UNDO capability is a good error management device), physical set-ups (e.g., the containment egg around nuclear power plants), and organizational practices. Organizational error management practices relate to using errors as information for improving work procedures, to communicating about errors, and to helping in error situations. If people talk openly about errors, people in the organization can detect them and deal with those errors quickly. Innovations are inherently risky and, therefore, chances of failure always exist. For this reason, an organization's innovativeness is higher when people are confident they will not be blamed or ridiculed when errors occur (Edmondson, 1999). Quick error detection, effective and coordinated error handling, higher task orientation, innovativeness, and secondary error prevention make it possible to improve product or service quality.

5.2 PERSONAL INITIATIVE BY EMPLOYEES AND ACTIVE PLANNING IN ENTREPRENEURSHIP

Our research on errors has led us from a problem that we observed in a specific environment (Germany) to a general recommendation of how organizations should deal with errors to enhance profitability. The approach to errors is based on the idea that it is necessary to explore the environment and that making errors is particularly prevalent when we are active. An active approach was a theme that occupied me in my study of personal initiative in East Germany. Again, the trigger was a socio-political problem and event: German (re-)unification happened in 1990 and journalists came back from East Germany lamenting about the lack of personal initiative there.

5.2.1 Personal Initiative (PI) of Employees

One of the basic tenets of action theory is that people are active in the approach to their environment. This helped us to understand a "real" phenomenon: Personal initiative (PI) implies that people behave actively—often changing the environment instead of just reacting to it. Studying personal initiative also allowed me to worry more about my nagging suspicion that work and organizational psychology follows a performance model which is too "reactive." This performance model assumes that people perform well, when they do what they were told to do ("do a task well"). In contrast, personal initiative implies that people perform well when they go beyond what they are told to do (add tasks). The tasks of a job are not fixed — every job contains emergent elements (Ilgen and Hollenbeck, 1991). For example, if a person initiates improvement of productivity, his or her job is changed and control and complexity are increased. Work then becomes more interesting and more controllable, and one is further encouraged to change it by developing better work procedures (i.e., by exhibiting PI). Superiors may be involved in this process. A secretary might have been hired originally as a typist; if she or he takes over more and more tasks within the organization or the group, the superior will rely on him or her, and in this way, the secretary's control and the complexity of her or his job increase.

I am interested in questioning two assumptions that are often found in traditional performance models: first, that the pathway from an outside task to the acceptance of the task is direct and not problematic. Action theory argues that this is not so and assumes that a "redefinition" process takes place that often modifies what the employee perceives to be his or her task (Hacker, 1973). A full performance concept needs to take this "redefinition" into account. The second assumption is that the influence of the employee on the work situation is minimal, and that the work situation is not modified by the employee's actions. I believe that people change their jobs appreciably via PI (also discussed as job crafting by Wrzesniewski and Dutton, 2001).

East Germany at the time of reunification provided a lot of examples of *not* using PI. Bureaucratic socialism in East Germany had given the employees incentives, *not* to show initiative and to become reactive. Initiative was negatively sanctioned, work was organized tightly with a high degree of supervision and little control. Interestingly, East Germany has Taylorized jobs to a larger extent than capitalist countries—at least more than in West Germany (Fay and Lange, 1997; Frese, et al., 1996).

However, I did not want to stick to just documenting this, but wanted to find out how personal initiative develops and how it can be changed. Therefore, we did a large-scale longitudinal study in East Germany to study the antecedents and consequences of personal initiative and to develop a training program.

5.2.1.1 *The Concept of Personal Initiative (PI)*

Personal initiative (PI) is self-starting work behavior, proactive, and overcomes difficulties (Frese, et al., 1996). One consequence of such an active approach is that the environment is changed (if ever so slightly). This distinguishes it from a reactive approach characterized by the following features: doing what one is told to do, giving up in the face of difficulties, not developing plans to deal with future difficulties, and reacting to environmental demands.

5.2.1.2 *The Three Aspects of PI: Self-Starting, Proactive, and Persistent*

Self-starting implies that a person does something without being told, without getting an explicit instruction, or without an explicit role requirement. Thus, PI is the pursuit of self-set goals in contrast to assigned goals. An example is a blue-collar worker who attempts to fix a broken machine even though this is not part of his or her job description.

Originally, we had conceptual problems in applying this definition to entrepreneurs because they are often required to show initiative and PI is part of their "job description." Can we still speak of self-starting, if the chief executive officer initiates many process and product innovations? Is he or she then just "doing his or her job" or showing initiative? After lengthy deliberations, we now define self-starting as being characterized by a deviation from the "normal" or obvious path (Frese and Fay, 2001). If something is not obvious, if one needs a certain degree of mental anticipation to recognize its importance, it is PI. If a high-ranking manager takes up an innovation that is "in the air," that other managers have already put into practice, and that has been discussed in professional magazines for some time, it is not PI.

Proactivity relates to having a long-term focus on opportunities and problems and not waiting until one *must* respond to a demand. The long-term focus on work enables the individual to anticipate things (new demands, new or recurring problems, emerging opportunities) *and* to do something proactively about them.

When taking initiative, *persistence*—in the sense of overcoming barriers—is usually necessary to reach one's goal. Whenever things get changed, there are difficulties to overcome because one does not possess all the required skills and knowledge; moreover other people (supervisors and colleagues) may not like the changes and develop resistance that needs to be overcome.

The three aspects of PI—self-starting, proactive, and persistent—reinforce each other. A proactive stance is required to self-start actions, because a proactive orientation toward the future makes it more likely to develop goals that go beyond what one is expected to do. Self-started goals lead to the need to overcome barriers (persistent) because of the changes inherent in their implementation. Finally, self-starting makes it often necessary to think of future issues, and, therefore, there is a higher degree of proactivity. Thus, there is a tendency for these three aspects of PI to co-occur (Frese, et al., 1997).

PI in employees is not always welcomed by supervisors or colleagues. Often high-PI people are perceived by their colleagues as being tiring and too strenuous. Every initiative "rocks the boat" and makes changes. Since people tend not to like changes, they often greet initiatives with skepticism. Supervisors may even think of high-PI employees as being rebellious and as a "pain in the butt." In the short run, PI is not always appreciated, although in the long run, it is crucial for organizational health and survival.

5.2.1.3 *Facets of PI*

The facets of PI can be described using the action sequence perspective of action theory (Frese and Fay, 2001; Frese and Zapf, 1994), consisting of goal development, collecting information and prognosis, planning, monitoring the action, and feedback. After a goal is established, a person looks for information needed to accomplish this goal and, when dealing with dynamic systems, makes some kind of prognosis of future states of the action environment. This information is used to develop plans that are executed and monitored. During monitoring concurrent feedback is used to adjust actions and outcome feedback is similarly used. This sounds like a logical sequence in which an action unfolds. However, we do not assume that this sequence is immutable; for example, people may jump from a goal directly to planning and then go back to get more information. Each part of this action sequence can be related to the three aspects of PI self-starting, proactive, and overcoming barriers (as described in Table 5.1; cf. for more details Frese and Fay, 2001).

5.2.1.4 *Antecedents and Consequences of PI*

The general model of antecedents and consequences of PI is shown in Figure 5.1. The following points are important for understanding this figure: First, PI is conceptualized as behavior. Second, we differentiate between proximal and distal causes (Kanfer, 1992). Personality along with knowledge, skills, and abilities (KSA) are distal causes; orientations are proximal causes (environmental supports are a

Table 5.1 Facets of Personal Initiative (PI)

Action sequence	Self-starting	Proactive	Overcome barriers
Goals / redefinition of tasks	– Active goal, redefinition	– Anticipate future problems and opportunities and convert into a goal	– Protect goals when frustrated or taxed by complexity
Information collection and prognosis	– Active search, i.e., exploration, active scanning	– Consider potential problem areas and opportunities before they occur – Develop knowledge on alternatives routes of action	– Maintain search in spite of complexity and negative emotions
Plan and execution	– Active plan	– Back-up plans – Have action plans for opportunities ready	– Overcome barriers – Return to plan quickly when disturbed
Monitoring and feedback	– Self-developed feedback and active search for feedback	– Develop pre-signals for potential problems and opportunities	– Protect feedback search

Source: Frese and Fay (2001: 144) (copyright 2001, reprinted with permission from Elsevier)

mixture of distal and proximal causes). Orientations are of medium specificity; they are more specific, more action-oriented, and closer to PI behavior than the distal causes. Third, environmental support, knowledge, skills and abilities, and personality variables influence orientations, which, in turn, influence PI. Initiative exerts an influence on individual and organizational level performance. In the following, we shall briefly walk through the figure, starting with orientations because they take a central place in the model (details in Frese and Fay, 2001).

Orientations. In line with Rotter, et al. (1972), we think that all inter-individual difference concepts can be distinguished along the dimension of generality, and that the generality of the concept should fit the research question. The term orientation signifies a concept of medium specificity. An orientation is neither a highly specific attitude (e.g., toward one task) nor a general personality trait. The orientations motivate PI, because they make people believe that showing PI is possible and that potentially negative consequences can be dealt with. The orientations center around control/mastery (control appraisals, self-efficacy, and control and responsibility aspirations) and dealing with potentially negative effects of personal initiative, mainly change, stress, and errors. Control beliefs can appear in two areas, namely, the areas of control over outcomes (control appraisal) and control over one's actions (self-efficacy). *Control and responsibility aspirations* are the opposite of learned helplessness (Seligman, 1975). Helplessness leads to negative motivational consequences because the organism stops trying to control the environment when it does not expect any positive outcomes (Seligman, 1975). One aspires for control only if one also accepts the responsibilities associated with control. These three control orientations—control appraisal, self-efficacy, and control aspiration—affect PI (Frese, Garst, and Fay, 2005). The second set of orientations that influence PI relate to potentially negative consequences of personal initiative: The themes of change, stress, and errors. People who perceive changes as negative, who have a negative orientation to errors, and who are not sure whether they can deal with stressors actively are less likely to exhibit PI behavior.

Personality Factors. Personality factors are more general than orientations, less changeable and more distal causes. Need for achievement (McClelland, 1987), action control Kuhl, 1992), need for cognition (Cacioppo and Petty, 1982), proactive personality (Crant, 1995), and psychological conservatism (Wilson, 1973) are such personality factors that should predict PI but should also be distinguishable from PI. Many of these concepts (such as need for achievement and action control) do not imply self-starting, others are quite similar to PI, such as proactive personality but constitute a general personality variable and not behavior.

The issue of personality, particularly proactive personality haunted me for a while. Since I came from action theory, I naively assumed that everyone else should also understand that PI was a behavioral concept and not a personality dimension (we measured it with an interview that carefully looked at self-starting behaviors, proactive behaviors, and behaviors to overcome barriers). When we attempted to publish our papers in international (mainly U.S.) journals, however, I noticed that the misunderstanding that PI is a personality dimension was running deep. We ourselves were also muddled in our thinking but in the opposite direction: We thought at first that our questionnaire measure of PI was just an imperfect version of the interview until we noticed that it was very similar to the proactive personality scale. We did not become aware of the concept of proactive personality originally proposed by Bateman and Crant (1993) until some time after we started our research on PI in 1990. Once we compared Bateman and Crant's (1993) proactive personality scale with our PI personality questionnaire measure, we found a very high correlation, suggesting that these two scales essentially measure the same thing (Frese and Fay, 2001).

Knowledge, Skills, Ability (KSA). PI can develop better if a person is good at his or her work and is able to learn quickly. Therefore, high knowledge, skills, and ability (KSA) are antecedents of PI. Indeed, a longitudinal study (Fay and Sonnentag, 2002) provided evidence that cognitive ability affected PI. Similarly, qualifications (as a summary measure of job knowledge and skills) were also related to PI (Frese and Hilligloh, 1994).

Environmental Supports. Environmental supports are job and organizational conditions that make it easier to show PI. Two of the most important supports for PI are control and complexity at work affecting the orientations of control aspirations, control appraisal, and self-efficacy, which, in turn, lead to higher PI. Personal initiative, in turn, leads to long-term higher control and complexity of work (Frese, Garst, and Fay, 2005). Figure 5.1 argues that stressors should have a positive relationship to PI. At first sight, this may seem counterintuitive. However, the argument is that stressors are signs that something is wrong. Therefore, stressors activate employees to deal with the negative situation in order to improve it (Fay and Sonnentag, 1998)—again changing the environment. This may be one of the few positive functions of stressors. An important influence is probably the general climate or culture of a company as well as top management support for PI (Morrison and Phelps, 1999).

5.2.1.5 *The Effects of PI on the Environment*

Active behavior impacts on the environment. PI should eventually exert an influence on work characteristics. Two mechanisms may play a role here: First, people with high PI may generate some added complexity and control in given jobs. The person who takes the initiative to develop and implement a good, long-term solution for the company's homepage adds complexity to her job. Simultaneously, she increases her job control, because she needs to make decisions and she takes responsibility for something that is not part of her normal role. Increased control and complexity can be transitory (until she has finished the design of the homepage), or permanent (when she decides to take care of the homepage in the long term in order to keep it up to date). Work then becomes more interesting and more controllable—this might lead to further increases of PI. Superiors can play a role in this process: If the supervisor observes that a certain team member takes care of neglected issues and works self-reliantly, the supervisor may feel that this is a reliable team member who can be assigned tasks that involve more responsibility and control.

A second mechanism involves job change. People with higher PI may leave one job to obtain more challenging work. People with higher PI may also be more successful in finding challenging jobs because they give others the impression that they will do a job well (Frese, et al., 1997). These effects only work in the long range: Each of the above mechanisms requires a certain amount of time to unfold.

5.2.1.6 *PI and Individual and Organizational Performance*

The more people deviate from a prescribed or conventional path, the more they show personal initiative. PI also implies the task is performed effectively even when the person does not follow the normal and prescribed approach. Otherwise, deviations from the prescribed path would be due to inefficiency or mistakes. Actions that lack a pro-company orientation do not signify PI.

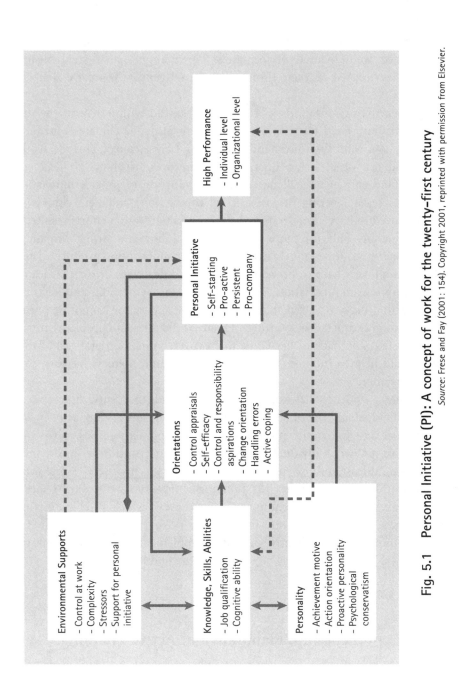

Fig. 5.1   Personal Initiative (PI): A concept of work for the twenty-first century

Source: Frese and Fay (2001: 154). Copyright 2001, reprinted with permission from Elsevier.

Unemployed people with a high degree of PI are able to find a job faster than those with low PI (Frese, et al., 1997). Personal initiative is related to developing clear career plans and to executing them (Frese, et al., 1997). Personal initiative is also related to individual performance: For example, small-scale business owners' PI was related to their firms' success in Uganda (Koop, De Reu, and Frese, 2000).

PI also benefits organizations when it is widespread within a company. In a sample of medium-sized German companies, pro-initiative climate contributed substantially to a company's profitability (Baer and Frese, 2003). This means that a widespread use of PI in an organization improves its ability to deal with challenges. One particular challenge is the introduction of process innovations (e.g., process re-engineering or just-in-time production) and here climate for initiative proved to have a moderator effect: Process innovation efforts resulted in higher profitability only for those companies that showed a strong climate for initiative (Baer and Frese, 2003). Reasons are that innovations produce disruptions, and employees have to prevent problems and deal with errors that lead to serious disruptions in production (pro-activity). Moreover, actions and ideas that help production need to be self-started because the supervisor cannot be present all the time to give orders (self-starting). Finally, difficulties and problems are met with a persistent approach to overcome them (overcoming barriers). All of these factors should help to increase smooth production and, thereby, increase company performance.

Thus, there is evidence that exhibiting initiative leads to positive outcomes for both the individual and the organization, because PI means dealing actively with organizational and individual problems and applying active goals, plans, and feedback. This furthers individual self-development and contributes to organizational success. At least in those environments in which it is necessary to deal with a changing world, PI is important. My thinking is now moving toward issues of developing an entrepreneurial culture in companies of which PI-climate is one essential aspect. Moreover, I am now interested in looking more closely at the issue of PI and innovation (particularly innovation implementation) and I think that increasing personal initiative may be one aspect of good leadership.

5.2.2 Entrepreneurship: Elaborate and Active Planning

Once I had studied PI, I became interested in those people who show the highest degree of personal initiative: The entrepreneurs. Again, I was interested in this area because I thought this was an important societal issue. First, Germany shows a rather low degree of entrepreneurship in comparison to other countries—and this is particularly true for East Germany (Sternberg, 2000; Sternberg and Bergmann,

2003). Moreover, I had taught a few weeks per year for a number of years in Zimbabwe and I noticed that without entrepreneurship (also from the informal sector—the one not regulated by government), people would die from starvation and there would be no development in low income countries. As a matter of fact, I started to get convinced that small business was of particular importance in developing countries because small and medium-sized businesses are the principle source of the creation of employment (and wealth) in these countries (Mead and Liedholm, 1998). About 17 to 27 percent of the working population in five African countries are involved in small-scale enterprises outside agriculture (Mead and Liedholm, 1998)—this percentage is twice as high as those employed by large companies or the public sector and it is growing in contrast to large companies. Small firms are also able to react flexibly to global competition and service the local small markets adequately and with adequate technology. Finally, civil society can only develop if a middle class grows in developing countries—again related to building up small and medium-sized businesses. I wanted to contribute as a scientist to the success of small and medium business. I am convinced that psychological factors need to be studied in this area (cf. Baum, Frese, and Baron, forthcoming) and that the nearly exclusive orientation on economic and legal factors shown by governments, development agencies, and worldbank is a mistake. I, therefore, started to work on research in entrepreneurship in East and West Germany (Frese, 1998) and in Africa (Frese, 2000).

Again, I turned to action theory and noticed that there was one factor developed in action theory that was of particularly importance for business people: Planning. It took me a while to notice that planning was really the opposite of a reactive approach (which we already described as the opposite of PI). To show an active orientation in entrepreneurship implies a higher degree of planning. Planning may be more important for entrepreneurs than for employees. For employees, there are always supervisors (and organizational routines) that structure their activities— the organizational hierarchy, the organizational context, etc. This is not the case for business owners: Their plans are more important because they often provide the only structure that exists in the small firm.

For action theory, a plan has a central theoretical function because it is a bridge between goals (intention) and action (Miller, et al., 1960). Plans can take the form of conscious or of non-conscious (automatized or routinized) plans. Plans are routinized and automatized when they are repeatedly used in a redundant environment. We chose to look at conscious plans because they refer to new and important situations. These plans are steps towards important goals to be reached within a few months or a year, for example, buying a new machine or building a roof for an open-air repair shop in Africa. From an action theory perspective, conscious plans are mental simulations of actions (Probehandlung) that regulate actions to achieve goals; plans make it possible to anticipate the action environment and action parameters; planning requires a certain analysis of the situation and decisions on how to proceed to achieve a goal (Hacker, 1992). Experimental research has demonstrated that specific plans on the when and where of actions convert goals into actions (Gollwitzer, 1996).

Planning may cover very different time spans—planning may be a matter of a few minutes, hours, one day, one month, one year, or twenty years. Planning does not require people to write plans down or to develop elaborate business plans— individuals may just think of action steps before starting an action and even during the action stream.

Planning can be conceptualized as a dimension with one side being characterized by a high degree of planning which is elaborate, detailed, and specific and which may include precise timing, thoughts about circumstances, and back-up plans in case something goes wrong. The opposite side of this dimension implies that actions are not regulated by elaborate plans but only by a very general idea of how to act; the actions need to be regulated on the spot during the course of action. Therefore, they rely more strongly on external conditions and obvious signals, which determine the action to a much higher extent than when there is a well-developed plan of action; thus, people react to the situation rather than act upon the situation. Hence, this end of the dimension is called "reactive." Owners with reactive approaches are driven by the immediate situational demands; they are dependent on others which may mean that they copy their competitors' products, that they follow a consultant's advice word by word, or that they wait for their suppliers, customers, or distributors to tell them what to do next. At the level of the firm, reactive companies reach the market too late (Lieberman and Montgomery, 1998). Empirically, a reactive approach contributes to failure (Van Gelderen, et al., 2000).

Planning is related to PI. An active plan requires a long-term focus on potential opportunities or threats; this long-term focus makes it possible to prepare (plan) now to enhance those opportunities and to prevent those threats. A long-term focus is a prerequisite of an active plan, but people who are focused on the long term also develop more elaborate plans. Action theory argues that very good employees (from blue collar worker to software developers) show higher performance if they produce active and elaborate plans (Hacker, 1992). Elaborate plans produce broad and deep mental models of the work to be done which includes a large inventory of potential signals (Hacker, 1992). Some of these signals are developed by the owners themselves. Signals tell the actor whether it is useful to implement a plan, and they also indicate future difficulties and opportunities. For example, the owner anticipates potential errors and, therefore, develops backup plans in case something goes wrong. Elaborate planning does *not* mean, however, that *all* important parameters are pre-planned in detail; rather it implies that several important parameters of reaching the goal are considered, at least briefly. However, elaborate planning also entails costs. Planning takes time, and the psychological investments in planning may increase the tendency to stick to plans developed earlier even if they are no longer adequate.

Action theory suggests that elaborate and active planning should help owners to be successful, to increase the likelihood that people get started by translating their goals into actions and to mobilize extra effort (Gollwitzer, 1996), to amplify persistence or decrease distraction (Diefendorff and Lord, 2004), to produce better knowledge on contingency conditions and time allocation to tasks, and to lead to a clearer focus on priorities (Tripoli, 1998), to reduce load during actions because some parts of the actions have been planned beforehand (actions will, therefore, run more smoothly), to motivate the owners to deal with additional problems, and to prepare them to have a ready-made answer if something goes wrong. Elaborate and active planning allows the person to cope with the inherent insecurities of being a business owner by making good use of scarce resources. Planning helps a person to stay on track and ensures that the goal is not lost or forgotten (Locke and Latham, 1990) and makes the premature triggering of an action less likely. In addition, the activeness of the plan increases exploration and allows the person to learn better (Bruner, 1960), which improves the mental model of the situation and one's own action possibilities. An active plan allows the owners to explore new strategies and to quickly retract if things do not work out; consequently, knowledge of boundary conditions of their explanatory concepts is enhanced; this improves problem solving because business owners receive more and better feedback than from a reactive and passive approach.

In a number of studies, we showed that an active and planning approach to the firm by the firm owners was related to a higher degree of success for the firm—in Europe (Van Gelderen, Frese, and Thurik, 2000) and in Africa (Frese, 2000; Frese, et al., 2004). The study by Van Gelderen, et al. (2000) was a longitudinal study which also showed that planning changed with success (it became more elaborate) and that success led to planning and planning led to success (or a reactive approach led to failure and failure led to more reactive approaches).

5.2.3 Changing Personal Initiative: Developing a Training Program

I would not have been satisfied simply to document and theorize about personal initiative: I also wanted to be able to improve PI. Most recently, I have concentrated on training programs that change PI and on demonstrating that such programs have positive effects for unemployed, for employees, and for business owners. None of these articles have yet been published (except a small study in German: Frese, et al., 2002), but most of the studies that we have done are quite encouraging.

Our training for business owners is, for example, based on the following facets: (1) Understanding PI situations; (2) proactive planning; (3) proactive goal setting;

(4) innovating; (5) emotion regulation of difficult barriers to success; and 6) time management (Frese, Friedrich, and Hass, 2005; Glaub, et al., 2005).

Understanding PI situations implies that a person understands PI itself and reviews situations in which he or she could have shown a higher degree of initiative. Case studies of owners using different strategies were distributed. Each group had to discuss, whether the owner described in their study used a reactive strategy or a planning strategy. Within this discussion, participants developed a list of learning principles for active planning.

Proactive goal setting focuses on maximizing the positive effect of goals by developing specific, time-bound, and challenging goals to which the participants feel highly committed: For example, in a first step, the participants were asked to write down their current business goals, in a second step they were to compare these goals to highly motivating goals.

Proactive planning: To improve both goal setting and planning, we utilized the concept of personal project (McGregor and Little, 1998). Participants were asked to develop a personal business project and to plan to implement it within two months to a year. To be action-oriented, we requested the participants to focus on the first step which they would implement within the next week (this short-term goal was already developed in the goal setting module). To strengthen commitment and to receive feedback, this first step was presented to another participant who was also called after two weeks. In addition, the participants trained the translation of short-term goals into actions by having to implement a self-developed goal in the training room right on the spot.

Innovation as a training module was to convince the participants to invest more time and effort into producing innovative solutions and to teach them methods and techniques to be more creative and innovative.

Emotion regulation was based on Ellis's (1962) approach to dealing with one's emotions in a difficult environment, for example, to learn not to become discouraged and not to become angry if things are not working out.

Time management is related to one aspect of planning—planning of time and coping with lack of time. Owners of small businesses have to deal with high time pressure. Using time management, owners actively identify important tasks, set priorities and plan their daily business according to the importance of tasks—thus, there is also some relation to PI. Here, we used principles from traditional time management training with a few modifications.

Together with students, we have done about ten of these training sessions so far, and we have found that they lead to higher PI, better strategies and planning, higher motivation, and to the use of novel approaches. Moreover, indicators such as growing the firm in terms of number of employees and sales growth are higher in those business people who participated in the training than in comparison groups (Frese, Friedrich, and Hass, 2005; Glaub, et al., 2005).

5.3 CONCLUSION

What have I learnt from my journey as a scientist who contributed both to a grand theory as well as to middle range theories? The most important issue seems to me to have an open mind to the quirks and difficulties, as well as to beautiful coping strategies that people show in their environment—I think that curiosity and being able to wonder and be surprised are the hallmark of good science. I am very interested in concrete phenomena and I suggest one should become intensively involved in real life phenomena (these may also be laboratory phenomena but I, personally, have been more interested in those that constitute important issues in society—not necessarily in my own society). It helps to cultivate contacts across cultures and maintain contacts with various strata in society—varied experiences support the process of being surprised, stumbling across interesting phenomena, and of developing a wider net of theoretical ideas and methodological approaches.

Good research questions often start with wonderment and surprise. We then have to work on understanding experiences and phenomena theoretically. For this it is helpful to look at the world like a theory machine that attempts to understand all sorts of phenomena with theoretical concepts. I remember that as students and young researchers my friends and I used to apply theories like a 2-year-old takes a hammer: We continuously attempted to use it to explain every phenomenon possible—in this way we quickly stumbled across the limits of the usefulness of these theories and, at the same time, we started to understand the theories better.

In terms of the development of competencies, the most important competence (aside from thinking clearly and methodological competence) was to go back and forth between the concrete and the abstract from the concrete phenomenon to the abstract concepts and back again. Many students seem to think of theories as something to learn by heart and then reproduce them on demand. I think of them, however, as something that should kick in, when we sit alone in a bar and observe other people or organizations, e.g., a competent bartender mixing a drink, a couple flirting, another one arguing, and an individual stumbling under the influence of alcohol—we should be able to understand all of these phenomena with the help of our theories (or grand theory). This is, by the way, the most important message of Lewin—many of his theories and experiments came from watching people with his students in cafes (e.g., the Zeigarnik effect) (Marrow, 2002). In other words, theories are instruments for understanding the world—functional tools that make our lives more interesting and sometimes easier to comprehend. Obviously, we then want to bring this use of theories into the scientific realm by systematically examining our hypotheses.

For me, it was important to have a grand theory. The following are the most important reasons: First, a grand theory makes it easier to accumulate knowledge in various areas of research. Plucking the middle-range theories into the grand theory, makes it possible to combine knowledge. Second, I chose action theory because I am convinced that one basic category of humans is that they act (and interact). Humans are not contemplating beings who sit in a chair and think about the world—they are acting beings who are constantly swirling and twirling and in interaction with the environment. Moreover, the basic building block of work and organizational psychology needs to be work actions—that is the start of all development of humankind (just think of how much we have changed our environment because we are working—we sit in offices at the computer, work in large offices, go home into house, in clothes, etc.—all of these are materialized results of work-actions). And we are doing these work-actions within a social context—we are actively organizing work-actions. Thus, it makes sense to start with a grand theory that focuses on actions. Third, whenever, I am approaching a new area, my general grand theory gives me a first set of hypotheses. For example, when I started to be interested in emotions at work, my grand theory (or my prejudice) gave me an idea of how to approach emotion, although action theory is silent on emotions. Action theory suggested that emotions have something to do with actions, emotions keep people actionable because they provide motivation to overcome or deal with barriers; and certain actions results in certain emotions (e.g., shame or pride) (Pekrun and Frese, 1992). Thus, a grand theory does not always suggest the right questions and certainly does not always provide the right answers (these should exist within the realm of a middle-range theory); however, the grand theory gives a starting point and structures our approach to theorizing.

But there are also disadvantages. I have chosen to publish articles in international journals and American journals are dominant. Since every article is a cultural communication, it is sometimes difficult to make this interplay between grand theory and middle-range theory understandable. I have usually been asked to cut the (loose) references to action theory and to stick to the middle-range theory. Thus, I have done little to describe in my articles the relationship between middle-range theory and grand theory. Moreover, I sometimes had difficulties with some theoretical terms. For example, all my American friends and reviewers advised me that I should not use the term "heuristic" for "error management instructions," even though I wanted to use precisely this term because it is an old term used within the tradition of action theory to mean a general approach to solving problems (Duncker, 1935).

In terms of methodology, I have come to rely more and more on a combination of qualitative and quantitative approaches. I use structured interviews because differential anchor points are particularly problematic in any questionnaire research: What is high planning for one owner may be complete chaos for another one. Structured interviews are useful, not only because they showed excellent validity in meta-analytic research (Hunter and Schmidt, 1996), but also because interviews gave me a chance to probe owners' answers and to understand precisely what they mean. Questionnaires sometimes "lead" participants to certain answers.

For example, it would have been "leading" to ask directly for planning and activity within the questionnaire survey. This is particularly true for cultural contexts in which it is improper to contradict others and where there is a tendency to create harmony (as in Africa). All of this speaks for interviews. At the same time, I want to have quantitative data to test hypotheses and to confirm and falsify them— therefore it is necessary to use coding procedures (I use very robust ones—not complicated content analyses).

I should warn you, however. Not all of this writing immediately gets translated into academic success. As a matter of fact, it is my observation that some of the empirical articles that I am most proud of (probably because they are dearest to my theoretical approach), have been the most difficult to publish. My hunch is that they break with the typical approach to doing things and, therefore, invite criticism that reviewers are only too glad to provide. On the other hand, those articles, that I am most proud of, are also often the ones that have the highest impact. And that is after all what we are interested in. We should never want to publish something just because we need another publication (well . . . at least never after we get tenure . . .). I usually was driven to work hard on publications by the fact that I wanted to communicate something that I found to be important. We should all want to shape and influence the development of science and knowledge rather than just be a smoothly functioning particle of a scientific machine.

REFERENCES

BAER, M., and FRESE, M. (2003). Innovation is not enough: Climates for initiative and psychological safety, process innovations, and firm performance. *Journal of Organizational Behavior*, 24: 45–68.

BATEMAN, T. S., and CRANT, J. M. (1993). The pro-active component of organizational behavior: A measure and correlates. *Journal of Organizational Behavior*, 14: 103–118.

BAUM, J. R., FRESE, M., and BARON, R. A. (eds.) (forthcoming). *The Psychology of Entrepreneurship*. Hillsdale, NJ: Lawrence Erlbaum Publishers.

BRODBECK, F. C., FRESE, M., and JAVIDAN, M. (2002). Leadership made in Germany: Low on compassion, high on performance. *Academy of Management Executive*, 16(1): 16–29.

BRUNER, J. S. (1960). *The Process of Education*. Cambridge, Mass.: Harvard University Press.

CACIOPPO, J. T., and PETTY, R. E. (1982). The need for cognition. *Journal of Personality and Social Psychology*, 42: 116–131.

CRANT, J. M. (1995). The proactive personality scale and objective job performance among real estate agents. *Journal of Applied Psychology*, 80: 532–537.

DIEFENDORFF, J. M., and LORD, R. G. (2004). The volitional and strategic effects of planning on task performance and goal commitment. *Human Performance*, 16: 365–387.

DUNCKER, K. (1935). *Zuer Psychologie des produktiven Denkens*. Berlin: Springer.

EDMONDSON, A. (1999). Psychological safety and learning behavior in work teams. *Administrative Science Quarterly*, 44: 350–383.

ELLIS, A. (1962). *Reason and Emotion in Psychotherapy*. New York: Lyle Stuart.

FAY, D., and LANGE, I. (1997). Westdeutsche Unternehmen in den Neuen Bundesländern: Garant für bessere Arbeitsgestaltung? *Zeitschrift für Arbeits- und Organisationspsychologie*, 41: 82–86.

—— and SONNENTAG, S. (1998). *Stressors and Personal Inititative: A Longitudinal Study on Organizational Behavior* (manuscript submitted for publication).

—— (2002). Rethinking the effects of stressors: A longitudinal study on personal initiative. *Journal of Occupational Health Psychology*, 7: 221–234.

FRESE, M. (1995). Error management in training: Conceptual and empirical results. In C. ZUCCHERMAGLIO, S. BAGNARA, and S. U. STUCKY (eds.), *Organizational Learning and Technological Change*: 112–124. Berlin: Springer.

—— (ed.) (1998). *Erfolgreiche Unternehmensgründer: Psychologische Analysen und praktische Anleitung für Unternehmer in Ost- und Westdeutschland*. Göttingen: Angewandter Psychologie Verlag.

—— (ed.) (2000). *Success and Failure of Microbusiness Owners in Africa: A Psychological Approach*. Westport, Conn.: Quorum Books.

—— and FAY, D. (2001). Personal Initiative (PI): A concept for work in the 21st century. *Research in Organizational Behavior*, 23: 133–188.

—— FRIEDRICH, C., and HASS, L. (2005). Training entrepreneurs for higher efficiency and effectiveness: A psychological training study. University of Giessen: Report.

—— GARMAN, G., GARMEISTER, K., HALEMBA, K., HORTIG, A., PULWITT, T., et al. (2002). Training zur Erhöhung der Eigeninitiative bei Arbeitslosen: Bericht über einen Pilotversuch (Training to increase personal initiative in unemployed: a pilot study). *Zeitschrift für Arbeits- und Organisationspsychology*.

—— GARST, H., and FAY, D. (2005). Making Things Happen: Reciprocal Relationships between Work Characteristics and Personal Initiative (PI) in a Four-Wave Longitudinal Structural Equation Model. University of Giessen (forthcoming).

—— and HILLIGLOH, S. (1994). Eigeninitiative am Arbeitsplatz im Osten und Westen Deutschlands: Ergebnisse einer empirischen Untersuchung. In G. Trommsdorf (ed.), *Psychologische Aspekte des sozio-politischen Wandels in Ostdeutschland*: 200–215. Berlin: Walter de Gruyter.

—— KRAUSS, S., ESCHER, S., GRABARKIEWICZ, R., FRIEDRICH, C., and KEITH, N. (2004). *Micro Business Owners Characteristics and their Success: The Role of Psychological Action Strategy Characteristics in an African Environment*. Giessen: Dept. of Psychology (submitted for publication).

—— KRING, W., SOOSE, A., and ZEMPEL, J. (1996). Personal Initiative at work: Differences between East and West Germany. *Academy of Management Journal*, 39(1): 37–63.

—— FAY, D., HILBURGER, T., LENG, K., and TAG, A. (1997). The concept of personal initiative: Operationalization, reliability and validity in two German samples. *Journal of Organizational and Occupational Psychology*, 70: 139–161.

—— and SABINI, J. (eds.) (1985). *Goal Directed Behavior: The Concept of Action in Psychology*. Hillsdale: Erlbaum.

—— and ZAPF, D. (1994). Action as the core of work psychology: A German approach. In H. C. Triandis, M. D. Dunnette, and L. Hough (eds.), *Handbook of Industrial and Organizational Psychology*: 4. 271–340. Palo Alto, Calif.: Consulting Psychologists Press.

GLAUB, M., GRAMBERG, K., FRIEDRICH, C., and FRESE, M. (2005). *Personal Initiative Training for Small Business Owners in South Africa: Evaluation Study of a 3-day-Training Program*. Giessen: Univ of Giessen.

GOLLWITZER, P. M. (1996). The volitional benefits of planning. In P. M. Gollwitzer and J. A. Bargh (eds.), *The Psychological of Action*: 287–312. New York: The Guilford Press.

HACKER, W. (1973). *Allgemeine Arbeits-und Ingenieurpsychologie*. Berlin: VEB Deutscher Verlag der Wissenschaften.

—— (1992). *Expertenkönnen. Erkennen und Vermitteln*. Göttingen: Hogrefe.

HEIMBECK, D., FRESE, M., SONNENTAG, S., and KEITH, N. (2003). Integrating Errors into the Training Process: The Function of Error Management Instructions and the Role of Goal Orientation. *Personnel Psychology*, 56: 333–362.

HOFSTEDE, G. (1991). *Cultures and Organizations*. London: McGraw-Hill.

HOUSE, R. J., HANGES, P. J., JAVIDAN, M., DORFMAN, P. W., and GUPTA, V. (eds.) (2004). *Cultures, Leadership and Organizations: A 62 Nation GLOBE Study*. Thousand Oaks, Calif.: Sage.

HUNTER, J. E., and SCHMIDT, F. L. (1996). Cumulative research knowledge and social policy formulation: the critical role of meta-analysis. *Psychology, Public Policy, and Law*, 2: 324–347.

ILGEN, D. R., and HOLLENBECK, J. R. (1991). The structure of work: Job design and roles. In M. D. Dunnette and L. M. Hough (eds.), *Handbook of Industrial and Organizational Psychology*: 2. 165–208. Palo Alto, Calif.: Consulting Psychologists Press.

IVANCIC, K., and HESKETH, B. (2000). Learning from errors in a driving simulation: Effects on driving skill and self-confidence. *Ergonomics*, 43: 1966–1984.

KANFER, R. (1992). Work motivation: New directions in theory and research. In C. L. COOPER and I. T. ROBERTSON (eds.), *International Review of Industrial and Organizational Psychology, 1992*: 7. 1–54. Chichester: Wiley.

KEITH, N., and FRESE, M. (forthcoming). Self-regulation in error management training: Emotion control and metacognition as mediators of performance effects. *Journal of Applied Psychology*.

KOOP, S., DE REU, T., and FRESE, M. (2000). Sociodemographic factors, entrepreneurial orientation, personal initiative, and environmental problems in Uganda. In M. Frese (ed.), *Success and Failure of Microbusiness Owners in Africa: A Psychological Approach*: 55–76. Westport, Conn.: Quorum.

KUHL, J. (1992). A theory of self-regulation: Action vs. state orientation, self-discrimination, and some applications. *Applied Psychology: An International Review*, 41: 97–129.

LIEBERMAN, M. B., and MONTGOMERY, D. B. (1998). First mover (dis-)advantages: Retrospective and links with the resource-based view. *Strategic Management Journal*, 19: 1111–1125.

LOCKE, E. A., and LATHAM, G. P. (1990). *A Theory of Goal Setting and Task Performance*. Englewood Cliffs, NJ: Prentice-Hall.

McCLELLAND, D. C. (1987). *Human Motivation*. Cambridge: Cambridge University Press.

McGREGOR, I., and LITTLE, B. R. (1998). Personal projects, happiness, and meaning on doing well and being yourself. *Journal of Personality and Social Psychology*, 74: 494–512.

MARCH, J., and SIMON, H. A. (1958). *Organisations*. New York: Wiley.

MARROW, A. J. (2002). *The Practical Theorist: The Life and Work of Kurt Lewin*. German edn.: Klette-Cotta.

MEAD, D. C., and LIEDHOLM, C. (1998). The dynamics of micro and small enterprises in developing countries. *World Development*, 26: 61–74.

MILLER, G. A., GALANTER, E., and PRIBRAM, K. H. (1960). *Plans and the Structure of Behavior*. London: Holt.

MORRISON, E. W., and PHELPS, C. C. (1999). Taking charge at work: Extrarole efforts to initiative workplace change. *Academy of Management Journal*, 42: 403–419.

PEKRUN, R., and FRESE, M. (1992). Emotions at work and achievement. In C. L. Cooper and I. T. Robertson (eds.), *International Review of Industrial and Organizational Psychology 1992*: 7. 153–200. Chichester: Wiley.

POPPER, K. R. (1972). *Objective Knowledge: An Evolutionary Approach*. Oxford: Oxford University Press.

REASON, J. (1990). *Human Error*. New York: Cambridge University Press.

ROTTER, J. B., CHANCE, J. E., and PHARES, E. J. (1972). An introduction to social learning theory. In J. B. Rotter, J. E. Chance, and E. J. Phares (eds.), *Applications of a Social Learning Theory of Personality*: 1–44. New York: Holt.

SCHMIDT, A. M., and FORD, J. K. (2003). Learning within a learner control training environment: The interactive effects of goal orientation and metacognitive instruction on learning outcomes. *Personnel Psychology*, 56: 405–429.

SCHWARTZ, S. H. (1999). A theory of cultural values and some implications for work. *Applied Psychology: An International Review*, 48: 23–48.

SELIGMAN, M. (1975). *Helplessness: On depression, development and death*. San Francisco: Freeman.

STERNBERG, R. (2000). *Entrepreneurship in Deutschland*. Berlin: edition sigma.

—— and BERGMANN, H. (2003). *Global entrepreneurship monitor: Länderbericht 2002*. Cologne: Institute of economic and social geography, University of Cologne.

TRIPOLI, A. M. (1998). Planning and allocating: Strategies for managing priorities in complex jobs. *European Journal of Work and Organizational Psychology*, 7: 455–475.

VAN DER LINDEN, D., SONNENTAG, S., FRESE, M., and VAN DYCK, C. (2001). Exploration strategies, performance, and error consequences when learning a complex computer task. *Behaviour and Information Technology*, 20: 189–198.

VAN DYCK, C., FRESE, M., BAER, M., and SONNENTAG, S. (forthcoming). Organizational error management culture and its impact on performance: A two-study replication. *Journal of Applied Psychology*.

VAN GELDEREN, M., FRESE, M., and THURIK, R. (2000). Strategies, uncertainty and performance of small business startups. *Small Business Economics*, 15: 165–181.

VOLPERT, W. (1974). *Handlungsstrukturanalyse als Beitrag zur Qualifikationsforschung*. Cologne: Pahl-Rugenstein.

WEICK, K. E. (1989). Theory construction as disciplined imagination. *Academy of Management Review*, 14: 516–531.

WILSON, G. D. (1973). *The psychology of conservatism*. New York: Academic Press.

WRZESNIEWSKI, A., and DUTTON, J. E. (2001). Crafting a job: Revisioning employees as active crafters of their work. *Academy of Management Review*, 26: 179–201.

....

CHAPTER 6

UPPER ECHELONS THEORY

ORIGINS, TWISTS AND TURNS, AND LESSONS LEARNED

....

DONALD C. HAMBRICK

THE central idea of upper echelons theory is that executives act on the basis of their highly personalized interpretations of the situations and options they face. That is, executives inject a great deal of themselves—their experiences, personalities, and values—into their behaviors. To the extent those behaviors are of consequence, say in shaping strategy or influencing the actions of others, organizations then become reflections of their top managers.

6.1 ORIGINS OF UPPER ECHELONS THEORY

....

The genesis of my work on the upper echelons perspectives was a term paper I wrote in my first semester as a doctoral student at Penn State, for a strategy seminar taught

I want to thank Craig Crossland for helpful suggestions on an earlier draft.

by Max Richards. It was 1975, the heyday of formal planning systems, elaborate strategy development processes, and management science. As a student with deep interest in strategy and policy, these were the things I craved to learn about and expected to study in Max's course. I was eager to learn about the science of strategy.

But it was not to be. The first readings on the syllabus were from "the Carnegie School": Simon (1945), March and Simon (1958), and Cyert and March (1963). Here I was, all set to learn about grand plans and brilliant strategies, only to be abruptly confronted with the human realities of executive work—bounded rationality, limited search, information overload, and coalitional dynamics. Once I recovered from my initial disorientation, these ideas greatly resonated with me. For, in my own bit of managerial work, I had personally experienced what the Carnegie theorists had described. I had held low-level administrative jobs in which I had been confronted with far more complexity, stimuli, and options than I could possibly consider. I had taken short-cuts, tuned-out lots of things, played to my strengths, and prayed that my weaknesses wouldn't be too crippling. Now, here in Max's classroom, it became eminently clear to me that, if I had acted exactly the way that Carnegie theorists described, then executives who were responsible for far bigger, more complicated domains would succumb to their human limitations as well.

About the time I owed Max an outline of my proposed paper, I happened upon a *Fortune* article that gave a listing and statistical profile of the CEOs of the Fortune 500 companies, complete with information about their ages, tenures, functional backgrounds, educational institutions and fields of study, religions, and hometowns. My initial reaction was to wonder why we should care about the backgrounds of these people. But I quickly realized it's because they matter. These executives, who shape what happens to their companies, see the world through the lenses of their personal histories, knowledge, values, and other biases. I became mesmerized by the *Fortune* listings and even started playing around with some primitive analyses, in which I constructed little subsamples of the youngest and oldest CEOs, those with the most and least formal education, and so on; then I went to *Moody's* to study the recent performance and actions of their companies. I don't remember any stark patterns emerging; and, in any event, my unrefined investigative methods would have made it nearly impossible to detect or make sense of any such patterns. But still I thought I was onto something.

The paper I wrote for Max's course represented the intersection of my interests in the Carnegie School on the one hand and executive dispositions and biases on the other. In the paper, I proposed that executives' background characteristics (such as tenure, education, and functional backgrounds) serve to filter and distort the stimuli that the executives confront, and that, in turn, those background characteristics could be used to predict executives' strategic choices. Max gave me an A for the paper but clearly lacked enthusiasm for my ideas. (Actually, over the years, it dawned on me that Max, a cigar-smoking curmudgeon—to whom, nonetheless, I owe a great deal—was rarely effusive about anything, and he may have liked the paper more than he let on.) Deflated, I set the paper aside, and it lay dormant for several years.

6.2 The Initial Presentation

In early 1983, I was having an informal discussion with a doctoral student at Columbia, where I was then teaching. Phyllis Mason and I were talking about whether managers who have MBAs act and perform any differently than those who don't. It was a casual, frivolous discussion, probably prompted by a momentary despondency I was feeling about whether I was having any enduring effect on my MBA students; it certainly didn't start out as a talk about theory or research. But the discussion became animated and fun, and before long it reminded me of the paper I had written for Max at the beginning of my doctoral studies eight years before.

Somehow, I was able to locate the earlier paper. I re-read it, both cringing at its naivety and relishing its promise. I remembered how excited I was by these ideas. I asked Phyllis if she wanted to team up on a major revision, updating, and extension of the paper. Within a few months we had what we thought was a credible manuscript, and we submitted it to the *Academy of Management Review*. For the first and only time in my career, the paper was accepted outright, and it was published in April 1984 under the title, "Upper Echelons: The Organization as a Reflection of Its Top Managers" (Hambrick and Mason, 1984). This paper then launched what has come to be known as "upper echelons theory."

Looking back on the Hambrick and Mason paper, it seems we were trying to make three major points. First, top managers act on the basis of their personal biases, experiences, and values. If we want to understand why organizations do the things they do, or why they perform the way they do, we need to understand the people at the top. Second, the characteristics of the entire top management team (TMT) will be far more predictive of organizational outcomes than will those of the individual top executive (CEO) alone. For example, we will be able to make far more reliable predictions if we know that the average age of the TMT is 62 than if we know only that the CEO is 62. And, third, we argued that demographic variables may serve as useful, albeit muddy and imprecise, proxies for executive cognitions and values. Confronted with the practical difficulties of obtaining psychometric data from large samples of executives, scholars might profitably rely on demographic data as a fallback.

One of the major refinements Phyllis and I brought to our *AMR* paper, compared to the earlier version I had written as a student, was that we attempted to specify the operative mechanisms by which executives' biases become manifested in their choices. This refinement was an essential component to our claim of a new theory. After all, in order to establish a theory it is not sufficient simply to propose that X leads to Y; rather, there must be a description of *why* the association exists, or a portrayal of the operative mechanism at work (Dubin, 1969).

To us, the mechanism that converted executive biases into behaviors was an information filtering process. Thus, upper echelons theory is, ultimately, an information processing theory, offering a way to systematically explain how executives act under conditions of bounded rationality. We developed a schematic of the process we envisioned, which Syd Finkelstein and I later refined in our book on strategic leadership (Finkelstein and Hambrick 1996), and which I further adapt here as Figure 6.1.

On the far left side of the figure is the "strategic situation" confronting an executive, or the myriad events, trends, and conditions that exist inside and outside the organization; this situation consists of far more phenomena than the executive can comprehend. Confronting this situation is the "executive's orientation," comprised of an interwoven set of psychological characteristics (including values and personality) and observable experiences (such as age and functional background). This executive orientation, then, serves as the basis by which the executive engages in a three-step information filtering process which eventually yields a highly personalized "construed reality."

As the first step in the filtering process, the executive's orientation affects his or her *field of vision*—those sectors to which attention is directed. Namely, a manager, or even an entire team of managers, cannot scan every aspect of the environment and the organization. Second, the manager's perceptions are further limited because he or she will *selectively perceive* only some of the phenomena that lie within the field of vision. That is, an executive sees or notices only a subset of what is on the radar screen. As the third step in the sequential filtering process, the executive then *interprets*, or attaches meaning, to the stimuli that have been noticed. As an example of this three-step process, we can imagine (1) a manager (or TMT) intently scanning the technological environment, but not the customer environment (restricted field of vision); (2) then, among all the technological information the manager has accessed, he only notices or comprehends a subset (selective perception); (3) then, the manager weighs the implications of what he has noticed—in terms of opportunity vs. risk, probabilities of occurrence, and so on (interpretation). As a result of this three-step filtering process, an executive's ultimate reading of the strategic situation, or "construed reality," may bear only a faint correspondence to the overall objective situation. Or, put another way, two executives who have very different personal orientations will arrive at very different construals of a given situation.

The elaboration of this three-step information filtering process amounted to a considerable advance in theoretical precision, compared to the primitive ideas I had set forth in my paper for Max Richards several years prior. To some extent, this increased sophistication was due to my overall maturation as a scholar, and

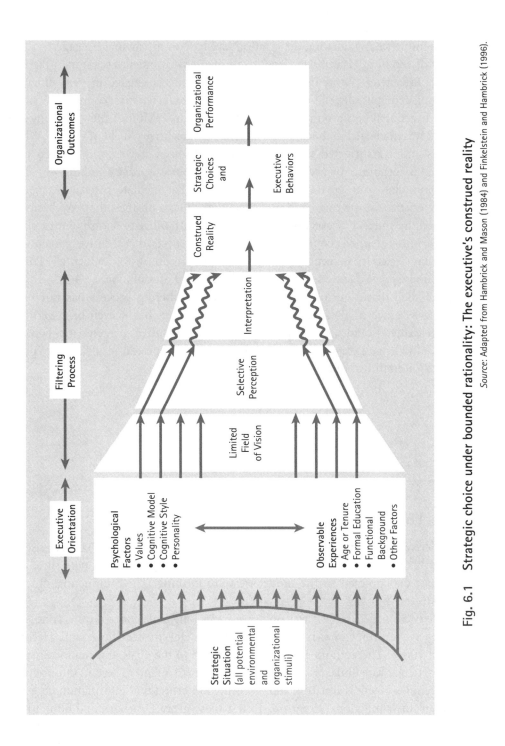

Fig. 6.1 Strategic choice under bounded rationality: The executive's construed reality

Source: Adapted from Hambrick and Mason (1984) and Finkelstein and Hambrick (1996).

particularly my increased ability to think carefully about causal processes. But to an even greater degree, the specification of the information filtering process was due to the influence my doctoral dissertation had had on my mental baggage.

My dissertation (Hambrick, 1979) examined environmental scanning practices of top executives. I was interested in how executives engage in very different scanning activities, depending on their industry characteristics, competitive strategies, functional backgrounds, and current positions. Without then invoking the term, I was interested in the factors that affect an executive's "field of vision." When Phyllis and I resurrected the upper-echelons project, it was only natural that I would incorporate my accumulated insights about executive scanning—or field of vision—into our portrayal of the processes that mediate between executive characteristics on the one hand and executive choices on the other. We basically married the concept of executive field of vision with other previously introduced, but variously-defined, concepts that described aspects of executive perception, including "selective perception" (Dearborn and Simon, 1958), "noticing" (Porter and Roberts, 1976), and "sensemaking" (Kiesler and Sproull, 1982).

As I shall discuss below, this highly-specified filtering process has not been studied as much as it needs to be; nor, to be honest, has it even been verified. But, at least, it provided a coherent logic as to how executive characteristics become reflected in organizational outcomes. And, when it appeared in 1984, it provided license for empirical research to proceed.

6.3 EMPIRICAL EVIDENCE

6.3.1 Foundational Evidence

The derivation of upper echelons theory was not simply an armchair exercise in scholarly reflection. Phyllis Mason and I were stimulated by preliminary shreds of evidence that pointed to the model we were forming. Three influential studies come to mind.

One was a little study (it was only five pages long and reported on a sample of merely twenty-three managers) conducted by DeWitt Dearborn and Herbert Simon (1958). The authors argued that exposure to the goals and reinforcements of a particular functional area will cause managers to attend to certain information in a complex business situation and, in turn, to interpret that information in terms that suit their functional expertise. To test these ideas, Dearborn and Simon had middle managers from a single company read a 10,000-word business case that presented a large number of facts with virtually no structure or interpretation.

The managers were then asked to identify the major problem facing the company. As the researchers expected, the managers tended to gravitate to interpretations that mirrored their functional backgrounds. For example, sales executives mentioned more sales-related problems than did executives from other functional areas. This study, then, reported the first systematic evidence that managers see the world through lenses created by their experiences.

The second study, by Miller, Kets de Vries, and Toulouse (1982) examined the influence of a CEO's locus of control—a personality factor that captures whether individuals believe that events in their lives are within their control ("internals") versus outside their control, stemming from luck, fate, or destiny ("externals"). With a sample of Canadian executives, Miller, et al. found that firms led by internals were more innovative and more likely to be in dynamic environments than were firms led by externals. The authors concluded: "Managers who believe that their destiny lies in their own hands are more likely to try to control it actively" (p. 245). In a supplementary analysis, the authors found that the relationships between executive locus of control and organizational innovation and environmental dynamism were far stronger in cases of long CEO tenures than of short ones, prompting the researchers to further conclude that executive personality shapes strategy, rather than the other way around.

We became aware of the third study only while our *AMR* paper was in press, so we couldn't acknowledge it; but nonetheless it was reinforcing and encouraging. Gupta and Govindarajan (1984) conducted a systematic study of division general managers, finding that certain managerial characteristics were associated with performance of businesses that were pursuing "build" strategies (in pursuit of market share), while a very different set of managerial characteristics were associated with performance of businesses that were pursuing "harvest" strategies (in pursuit of cash flow). In particular, the most successful "growth" businesses had general managers with considerable experience in marketing/sales and who had high tolerance for ambiguity. In contrast, the most successful "harvest" businesses had managers with little or no marketing/sales experience (who presumably instead had extensive experience in operations or accounting/finance) and who had low tolerance for ambiguity. Although this study did not directly explore the central tenet of upper echelons theory—that executives characteristics are manifested in their choices—it certainly reinforced the general premise of the theory by showing that alignment of business strategy and executive characteristics is beneficial for performance.

6.3.2 Reinforcing Evidence

From the time we wrote our *AMR* paper, evidence in support of upper echelons theory mounted quickly and steadily. Several projects were undertaken as doctoral dissertations by students at Columbia, all focusing on the top management team as the unit of analysis. Ricardo Barbosa (1985) found that TMT characteristics were strongly predictive of innovation strategies and firm performance in the forest products industry. Richard D'Aveni was able to document the deterioration of TMT qualities that occur when a firm is sliding toward bankruptcy (D'Aveni, 1990; Hambrick and D'Aveni, 1992). Syd Finkelstein studied how TMT tenure is predictive of strategic persistence and conformity to industry norms (Finkelstein, 1988; Finkelstein and Hambrick, 1990). Bert Cannella (Cannella, 1991; Cannella and Hambrick, 1993; Hambrick and Cannella, 1993) examined the factors that cause executives in an acquired company to depart, as well as the performance implications of such departures. Sylvia Black (1997) found support for her expectation that the international experiences and exposures of TMTs would be associated with the subsequent internationalization of their firms' strategies as well as the performance from such international initiatives. Marta Geletkanycz found striking evidence regarding the influence of executives' external ties on company strategy (Geletkanycz, 1994; Geletkanycz and Hambrick, 1997). Specifically, she found that the greater the executives' intra-industry ties, the more that the firm would pursue strategies that conformed to the industry's central tendencies; in contrast, the greater the extra-industry ties, the more the firm would pursue strategies that deviated from their industry's prevailing approach.

More recently, Theresa Cho (1999) examined how managerial attention patterns mediate between TMT composition and strategic outcomes. Using automated text analysis of letters to shareholders as a way to gauge managerial attention, she found that, following deregulation, airlines that changed the composition of their TMTs the most exhibited the greatest and fastest changes in their attention patterns; in turn, they changed their strategies the most to deal with the newly deregulated regime. And most recently, Kristin Stucker (2001) conducted a very intriguing study of executive profiles associated with success (and failure) of corporate spinoffs—companies that abruptly face the opportunities and perils of independence. Again, all these empirical projects helped to reinforce the basic logic of upper echelons theory.

My doctoral students obviously played a major role in advancing upper-echelons theory. Through their creative energies and astute empirical executions, we were able to generate considerable supportive evidence on a wide array of fronts—far more evidence, far faster than would have been possible without such exceptional young collaborators. I never cease to feel great gratitude for the role that doctoral students have played in my intellectual development and ongoing invigoration.[1]

---

[1] Over the years, I've supervised the dissertations of several other very talented doctoral students who studied strategy topics outside of the upper echelons vein—including Jorge Vasconcellos é Sa, Diana Day, John Michel, Mat Hayward, and Eric Jackson.

Research in the upper echelons vein was being done outside the walls of Columbia as well. Some scholars were examining the influence of various psychological and personality factors on executive behavior. For example, Day and Lord (1992) found that the cognitive structures of executives in machine tool companies were related to their organizations' strategies. In particular, executives whose firms had the widest arrays of product or service offerings tended to draw the finest distinctions between different types of strategic problems (in an experimental setting). Whether these results indicate that cognitively complex executives had chosen complex business strategies, or that their cognitions had been influenced by their strategies, cannot be discerned from the data. Miller and Droge (1986) examined the influence of CEO personality, specifically need for achievement, on the firm's degree of structural centralization. Wally and Baum (1994) studied the effect of executive tolerance for risk on speed of decision making. Numerous other studies of the associations between executive psychological characteristics and firm outcomes were undertaken as well.

Some scholars relied on demographic descriptors of executives, as we had encouraged in our *AMR* paper. For example, a series of studies examined the associations between the functional backgrounds of CEOs and business strategy, particularly by applying Miles and Snow's (1978) strategic typology. In a study of major tobacco companies, Chaganti and Sambharya (1987) found that the top executive ranks of the Prospector company they examined (Philip Morris) had proportionately more executives with marketing and R&D backgrounds and fewer with finance backgrounds than the Analyzer (R. J. Reynolds) and Defender (American Brands) companies. Thomas, Litschert, and Ramaswamy (1991) examined the functional backgrounds of the CEOs of computer companies and found similar results. Of the Prospector companies studied, 77 percent of their CEOs had experience primarily in "output-oriented" functions (i.e., marketing, sales, and R&D), as compared to only 10 percent of the CEOs in the Defender companies. Conversely, 90 percent of the Defenders' CEOs were primarily from "throughput-oriented functions" (manufacturing, accounting, finance, administration), compared to 23 percent of the Prospector CEOs.

Similarly, several studies examined the link between the education level of senior executives and the amount of innovation in their organizations. Kimberly and Evanisko (1981) were among the first to document this pattern, finding that the amount of formal education of hospital chief administrators was positively associated with the adoption of both technological and administrative innovations in hospitals. Similar positive associations between executives' education levels and organization innovation were subsequently observed in samples of commercial banks (Bantel and Jackson 1989), forest product companies (Barbosa 1985), and computer companies (Thomas, Litschert, and Ramaswamy 1991). Relatedly, Norburn and Birley (1988) found that amount of formal education of top executives was positively associated with company growth in three of five industries studied.

Finally, Wiersema and Bantel (1992) found that education levels of top executives were positively associated with strategic portfolio changes in a large sample of diversified firms. Thus, the effects of executive education levels on organizational innovation, change, and growth were widely documented.

In their recent analysis of upper echelons research, Carpenter, Geletkanycz, and Sanders (forthcoming) identify several additional topics that have received particularly heavy attention in the upper echelons arena. These include the effects of TMT heterogeneity on strategic processes, strategic behavior, and performance; the effects of TMT tenure on firm behavior and performance; and the influence of executive characteristics in shaping the degree and form of international strategy pursued by firms.

In the twenty years following the presentation of upper echelons theory in *AMR*, dozens, and possibly hundreds, of studies have examined, tested, or refined some aspect of the theory. As I write this, in mid-2004, the Hambrick and Mason article has been cited 568 times, according to the Social Science Citation Index. Obviously, not all these citations were contained within empirical projects. Overall, however, substantial evidence has accumulated to indicate that executives act, in part, on the basis of their personal characteristics; in turn, organizations become reflections of their top managers.

6.4 THEORETICAL REFINEMENTS

Over the years, I have proposed two major refinements to upper echelons theory, which I thought would enhance its predictive power. The first, the introduction of "managerial discretion" as a moderator in the upper echelons model, has stimulated a great deal of research and has proven to be a worthwhile contribution. The second, the introduction of the idea that the collective characteristics of TMTs will only affect organizational outcomes to the extent that the TMTs act as teams rather than as collections of solo operators, has had far less impact.

6.4.1 Managerial Discretion

My early work on managerial discretion was done with Syd Finkelstein, starting with our 1987 chapter in *Research in Organization Behavior*, "Managerial Discretion: A Bridge Between Polar Views of Organizational Outcomes." This paper attempted to reconcile two then antagonistic, polar views: managers don't matter very much to organizational outcomes vs. managers matter immensely. Our idea was that sometimes managers matter a great deal, sometimes not at all, and often somewhere in between, depending on how much discretion—or latitude of action—they possess. Discretion exists when there is an absence of constraint and when means–ends ambiguity is great, that is, when there are multiple plausible alternatives. Discretion, we argued, emanates from the environment, the organization, and from the executive himself or herself.

We proposed that executive discretion can be expected to affect a variety of phenomena of interest to organizational scholars. For example, in situations of low discretion, the following could be expected: older CEOs promoted from within (to fulfill largely figurehead roles), low executive compensation, little use of incentive executive compensation, low involuntary turnover of CEOs, stable strategy, and changes in organizational performance tied closely to changes in the task environment. Situations of high discretion would tend to result in opposite effects.

As important, however, Syd and I proposed that discretion serves to enhance the relationship between executive characteristics (values, experiences, and so on) and organizational outcomes. Namely, if high discretion exists, executive orientations become reflected in organizational outcomes; if low discretion exists, they do not. On this matter, subsequent research support has been clear and consistent. For example, Finkelstein and Hambrick (1990) found that executive tenure was positively related to strategic persistence and strategic conformity to industry central tendencies (reflecting presumably risk-averse and imitative tendencies of long-tenure executives) in high-discretion industries but not in low-discretion industries. We also found that when organizational conditions allowed top managers significant latitude—as indicated by abundant slack and small company size—the firm's strategic choices were more likely to reflect the tenure of the top executives than when slack was limited or the company was large. That is, when discretion is low—either because of industry or organizational conditions—executives' characteristics don't vividly show up in their choices, primarily because there are few or no genuine choices to be made.

Several studies have supported Hambrick and Finkelstein's ideas that discretion affects executive compensation arrangements, particularly by showing that executives in low-discretion situations receive relatively low amounts of pay and little incentive pay. For example, Rajagopalan and Finkelstein (1992) studied the electric utility industry from 1978 to 1987, a period of steadily increasing deregulation and hence, increasing discretion. They found that executive compensation (for the CEO and top team) and the use of performance-contingent compensation increased over time, as environmental discretion increased. Balkin and Gomez-Mejia (1987) found that high-technology firms, which tend to confer greater levels of managerial discretion (Hambrick and Abrahamson 1995), use incentive pay plans more than other firms do. Napier and Smith (1987) found that the proportion of corporate managers' incentive pay was significantly greater in more diversified (and hence, higher discretion) firms. Further, Jensen and Murphy (1990) found that the relative amount of incentive compensation of CEOs was much greater in small firms than in large firms, prompting the authors to conclude: "Higher pay-performance sensitivities for small firms could reflect that CEOs are more influential in small companies" (p. 260).

I should note that Syd and I hit upon the concept of managerial discretion in a roundabout way. We were actually studying CEO compensation, searching for an explanation as to why executives in different industries are paid such wildly different amounts. For instance, after controlling for company size and profitability, CEOs in fashion, cosmetics, entertainment, and high-tech are paid a lot, whereas (at least when we were doing our research) CEOs in insurance, utilities, and commodity industries are paid much less. Our first explanation—that some industries are simply more flamboyant than others—was not very conceptually appealing. Upon thinking more about it, and by looking more carefully at the characteristics of the industries that had very high and very low executive pay, we eventually identified the concept of discretion as the underlying driver: In some industries, managers are frequently allowed to make very big choices, and the difference in performance between the best managers and the worst managers is huge; in these industries, boards and shareholders will be inclined to pay handsomely in an effort to get one of the golden managers. In other industries, where managers are more constrained and hemmed-in, the difference in results between the best and worst managers is not so great, and boards can be more sparing in what they pay. Syd and I didn't set out to study managerial discretion, but instead stumbled upon it, thus illustrating how concepts and theories can emerge from the most unexpected of places, sometimes even serendipitously—a theme I will revisit below.

6.4.2 Behavioral Integration

While doing field research in the early 1990s, interviewing CEOs about their top management teams (TMTs), an unsettling fact become clear: Many, many top management teams have few "team" properties. They consist primarily of solo operators who are largely allowed to run their own shows, who interact minimally, sometimes rarely seeing each other. Such a condition poses a problem for upper echelons theory, or at least for that aspect that deals with how TMT characteristics affect firm outcomes. For, if TMTs are highly fragmented, then team characteristics will matter very little to firm outcomes. Instead, firm outcomes are the outgrowth of a host of narrow, specialized choices made by various individual executives (Hambrick, 1994).

These observations lead me to develop and elaborate on the concept of "behavioral integration" within TMTs. Behavioral integration is the degree to which mutual and collective interaction exists within a group, and it has three main elements or manifestations: information exchange, collaborative behavior, and joint decision making. That is, a behaviorally integrated TMT shares information, shares resources, and shares decisions. In its focus on substantive interaction, behavioral integration is related to, but distinct from, "social integration," a concept that places more emphasis on members' sense of group pride or team spirit (Shaw, 1981).

In my initial presentation of behavioral integration, I proposed an array of factors that will determine the degree of behavioral integration that will exist in a given TMT. These factors included environmental factors, organizational factors, and the CEO's own personality or performance. Recently, Simsek, et al. (forthcoming) collected data on TMTs in 402 small- and mid-sized companies, verifying some of the key predictors of TMT behavioral integration. In particular, they found that behavioral integration was positively related to the CEO's own collectivist orientation and tenure, and negatively related to TMT size and several types of TMT diversity.

Initially, I took an agnostic stance about the general merits of behavioral integration in TMTs. As someone who believes in the importance of individual accountability and entrepreneurial initiative, I was resistant to the idea that behavioral integration is necessarily a good thing. Over time, however, I saw in my field research and consulting more and more instances of companies paying a big price because their TMTs were fragmented, or lacking in behavioral integration. Therefore, in 1998, I wrote on the prevailing merits of behavioral integration, or conversely, the costs of an absence of behavioral integration (Hambrick, 1998). These costs include the following: (1) potential economies of scope go unrealized; (2) brands and market positions of different businesses are poorly coordinated; (3) business units fail to exchange key learnings and intelligence; and (4) the company is slow to formulate company-wide strategic changes in response to major environmental shifts. In that same paper, I laid out the major initiatives CEOs can take to enhance the behavioral integration of their TMTs.

Again, behavioral integration has not been rigorously examined or applied to the extent I would have wished. Obviously, doing so will require in-depth data from a substantial number of TMTs, which is a difficult undertaking. However, I am heartened by the work of Simsek and colleagues, and I have work underway with J. T. Li in which we rigorously measure and apply the concept of behavioral integration in a large-sample study of joint venture management teams (Li and Hambrick, forthcoming). Even with this bit of progress, however, we still have not addressed the idea that potentially makes behavioral integration so centrally important to upper echelons theory: TMT characteristics will predict organizational outcomes only in proportion to the degree that TMT behavioral integration exists. That is, behavioral integration is a key moderator of the basic upper echelons relationships. Again, this central idea still awaits scholarly investigation.

6.5 FRUSTRATIONS

Even though upper echelons theory has made its mark on the organizational sciences, I have some lingering disappointments about our shortcomings in testing and verifying the theory. Foremost, I am disappointed that we have not done a better job of directly examining the psychological and social processes that stand between executive characteristics on the one hand and executive behavior on the other. Namely, we have done a poor job of getting inside "the black box" (Lawrence, 1997; Markoczy, 1997). For example, when we observe that long-tenured executives engage in strategic persistence, why is that? Are they committed to the status quo? Risk-averse? Tired? or What? Even examination of executive psychological properties is not exempt from such questions. So, for example, when we find that executives who have a high tolerance for ambiguity perform well when they pursue growth-oriented strategies (as opposed to harvest-oriented strategies) (Gupta and Govindarajan, 1984), why is that? What's going on? How does tolerance for ambiguity affect executive behaviors? Even though we have talked for a long time about the need to get inside the black box (to the point that it has become a cliché to express the need), we still have made exceedingly little progress in doing so.

In this same vein, we have little evidence that executives filter the information they confront in any way that resembles the three-stage process depicted here as Figure 6.1. For example, do executives with technology backgrounds scan more technology-oriented information sources than those who don't have technology backgrounds? Do they notice, or perceive, more of the technology information they scan? Do they require fewer pieces of information to form an opinion about a technology trend? In short, there is a pressing need to gather data on the actual information-processing behaviors of individuals (and teams) in strategic decision-making situations. Pursuing this perspective will certainly require laboratory-type or experimental research designs, as well as the tools and concepts of the psychologist.

A related disappointment is that we have done an inadequate job of disentangling causality in upper echelons studies. Do executives make strategic choices that follow from their own experiences, personalities, and biases, as posited by the theory? Or do certain organizational characteristics lead to certain kinds of executive profiles? Over time, a reinforcing spiral probably occurs: managers select strategies that follow from their beliefs and preferences; successors are then selected according to how well *their* qualities suit that strategy; and so on. Thus far, relatively few upper echelons studies have been designed in ways as to allow convincing conclusions about causal direction.

I want to note yet one more frustration. Some critics claim that upper-echelons theory puts too much weight on the importance of executives, and, thus, contributes to the glorification and hero-worship of elites. These critics go on to say that there are many people throughout organizations who affect results, and they are all worthy of scholarly attention. I have never disputed this latter point, and I have always hoped and assumed that researchers would maintain interest in human endeavor at all organizational levels. But the criticism about glorifying executives is ironic in the extreme. For, upper echelons theory is entirely premised on the flaws and human limits of executives. The theory pokes holes in the mythology of the all-knowing economic optimizer at the top of the firm. This is the antithesis of glorification.

Interestingly, when I present my research results to executives—say from my study of CEO hubris (Hayward and Hambrick, 1997) or my work on the seasons of a CEO's tenure (Hambrick and Fukutomi, 1991)—they certainly don't feel glorified. In fact, they often react by saying they are smarter, more level-headed, more utterly capable than I give them credit for. So, I get it from both sides.

No, upper echelons theory does not glorify executives at all. But neither does it demean them. Being an executive is exceedingly demanding. I greatly admire those who do it well, and I'm deeply troubled by those who don't. Part of our job as management scholars is to develop insights that will improve executive effectiveness. But no matter how clever our insights, we will not be able to surmount or escape the fact that executives have the same human foibles as the rest of us.

6.6 NOTES TO THE ASPIRING THEORIST

The editors of this volume have asked the contributors to provide advice to scholars who might be interested in developing new theory. I will attempt to do so, but only reluctantly, even sheepishly. For—and this is my key point here—I don't see how you can will yourself to develop a theory. You can't just sit down one day and resolve, "I'm going to work up a theory." Theories emerge, arise, take form, but they are not engineered. Theories are rarely a product of an intentional effort to "theorize"—at least in my experience.

So, how do theories emerge? My sense is that those who have a knack for developing theories are astute observers of phenomena; they detect puzzles in those phenomena; and they then start thinking about ways to solve the puzzles. The phenomena and puzzles that trigger theory development, or more simply concept development, can take any of a number of forms. In my case, for instance, upper echelons theory was stimulated in great part by one kind of puzzle: Why would a reputable magazine like *Fortune* devote a lot of space to detailing the demographic characteristics of 500 CEOs? The concept of managerial discretion arose out of a very different kind of puzzle: Why does executive compensation differ so much between industries? And the concept of behavioral integration was triggered by yet another type of puzzle that came out of my interviews with CEOs: Why do a lot of TMTs not have many "team" properties? And what are the implications of that for upper echelons theory and firm behavior?

I am pretty sure about where theories *don't* come from. They don't come from scholars struggling to find holes in the literature. Young academics, especially doctoral students, become so immersed in the extant theory and research in a field that they become overtaken by it. They often come to believe that the written word is their entire intellectual armament; and they then become riveted on finding ways to patch, reconcile, or fill holes in the literature. I don't think you can read your way to developing a theory. It is far better to start with a real-life, interesting puzzle; then develop a preliminary set of ideas for solving the puzzle; and *then* turn to the literature for guidance and insight.

References

BALKIN, D. B., and GOMEZ-MEJIA, L. R. (1987). Toward a contingency theory of compensation strategy. *Strategic Management Journal*, 8: 169–182.

BANTEL, K. A., and JACKSON, S. E. (1989). Top management and innovations in banking: Does the composition of the top team make a difference? *Strategic Management Journal*, 10: 107–124.

BARBOSA, R. R. (1985). Innovation in a mature industry. Unpublished Ph.D. dissertation, Columbia University.

BLACK, S. S. (1997). Top management team characteristics: A study of their impact on the magnitude of international operations and international performance. Unpublished Ph.D. dissertation, Columbia University.

CANNELLA, A. A. (1991). Executive departures from acquired firms: Antecedents and performance implications. Unpublished Ph.D. dissertation, Columbia University.

—— and HAMBRICK, D. C. (1993). Effects of executive departures on the performance of acquired firms. *Strategic Management Journal*, 14 (special issue): 137–152.

CARPENTER, M. A., GELETKANYCZ, M. A., and SANDERS, W. G. (forthcoming). Upper echelons research revisited: antecedents, elements, and consequences of top management team composition. *Journal of Management*.

CHAGANTI, R., and SAMBHARYA, R. (1987). Strategic orientation and characteristics of upper management. *Strategic Management Journal*, 8(4): 393–401.

CHO, T. (1999). The effects of increased managerial discretion on top executive team composition, compensation and attention: The implications for strategic change and performance. Unpublished Ph.D. dissertation, Columbia University.

CYERT, R. M., and MARCH, J. G. (1963). *A Behaviorial Theory of the Firm*. Englewood Cliffs, NJ, Prentice-Hall.

D'AVENI, R. A. (1990). Top managerial prestige and organizational bankruptcy. *Organization Science*, 1: 121–142.

DAY, D. V., and LORD, R. G. (1992). Expertise and problem categorization: The role of expert processing in organizational sensemaking. *Journal of Management Studies*, 29(1): 35–47.

DEARBORN, D. C., and SIMON, H. A. (1958). Selective perception: A note on the departmental affiliations of executives. *Sociometry*, 21: 144–150.

DUBIN, R. (1969). *Theory Building*. New York: Free Press.

FINKELSTEIN, S. (1988). Managerial orientations and organizational outcomes: The moderating roles of managerial discretion and power. Unpublished Ph.D. dissertation, Columbia University.

—— and HAMBRICK, D. C. (1990). Top management team tenure and organizational outcomes: The moderating role of managerial discretion. *Administrative Science Quarterly*, 35: 484–503.

—— —— (1996). *Strategic Leadership: Top Executives and their Effects on Organizations*. Minneapolis/St. Paul, West Pub. Co.

GELETKANYCZ, M. A. (1994). The external networks of senior executives: Implications for strategic innovation and imitation. Unpublished Ph.D. dissertation, Columbia University.

—— and HAMBRICK, D. C. (1997). The external ties of top executives: Implications for strategic choice and performance. *Administrative Science Quarterly*, 42(4): 654–682.

GUPTA, A. K., and GOVINDARAJAN, V. (1984). Business unit strategy, managerial characteristics, and business unit effectiveness at strategy implementation. *Academy of Management Journal*, 27: 25–41.

HAMBRICK, D. C. (1979). Environmental scanning, organizational strategy, and executive roles: A study in three industries. Unpublished Ph.D. dissertation, The Pennsylvania State University.

—— (1994). Top management groups: A conceptual integration and reconsideration of the "team" label. In B. M. Staw and L. L. Cummings (eds.), *Research in Organizational Behavior*: 171–214. Greenwich, Conn.: JAI Press.

—— (1998). Corporate coherence and the top management team. In D. C. Hambrick, D. A. Nadler, and M. L. Tushman (eds.), *Navigating Change: How CEOs, Top Teams, and Boards Steer Transformation*: 123–140. Boston: Harvard Business School Press.

—— and ABRAHAMSON, E. (1995). Assessing managerial discretion across industries: A multimethod approach. *Academy of Management Journal*, 38(5): 1427–1441.

—— and CANNELLA, A. A. (1993). Relative standing: A framework for understanding departures of acquired executives. *Academy of Management Journal*, 36: 733–762.

—— and D'AVENI, R. A. (1992). Top team deterioration as part of the downward spiral of large corporate bankruptcies. *Management Science*, 38: 1445–1466.

—— and FINKELSTEIN, S. (1987). Managerial discretion: A bridge between polar views of organizational outcomes. In L. L. Cummings and B. M. Staw (eds.), *Research in Organizational Behavior*: 9: 369–406. Greenwich, Conn.: JAI Press.

HAMBRICK, D. C. and FUKUTOMI, G. (1991). The seasons of a CEO's tenure. *Academy of Management Review*, 16(4): 719–743.

—— and MASON, P. (1984). Upper echelons: The organization as a reflection of its top managers. *Academy of Management Review*, 9(2): 193–206.

HAYWARD, M. L. A., and HAMBRICK, D. C. (1997). Explaining the premiums paid for large acquisitions: Evidence of CEO hubris. *Administrative Science Quarterly*, 42(1): 103–128.

JENSEN, M. C., and MURPHY, K. J. (1990). Performance pay and top management incentives. *Journal of Political Economy*, 98: 225–264.

KIESLER, C. A., and SPROULL, L. S. (1982). Managerial responses to changing environments: Perspectives on problem sensing from social cognition. *Administrative Science Quarterly*, 27: 548–570.

KIMBERLY, J. R., and EVANISKO, M. J. (1981). Organizational innovation: The influence of individual, organizational, and contextual factors on hospital adoption of technological and administrative innovations. *Academy of Management Journal*, 24(4): 689–713.

LAWRENCE, B. S. (1997). The black box of organizational demography. *Organization Science*, 8: 1–22.

LI, J. T. and HAMBRICK, D. C. (forthcoming). Demographic faultlines and disintegration in factional groups: The case of joint venture management teams. *Academy of Management Journal*.

MARCH, J. C., and SIMON, H. A. (1958). *Organizations*. New York: Wiley.

MARKOCZY, L. (1997). Measuring beliefs: Accept no substitutes. *Academy of Management Journal*, 40: 1228–1242.

MILES, R. H., and SNOW, C. C. (1978). *Organizational Strategy, Structure, and Process*. New York: McGraw-Hill.

MILLER, D., and DROGE, C. (1986). Psychological and traditional determinants of structure. *Administrative Science Quarterly*, 31: 539–560.

—— KETS DE VRIES, M. F. R., and TOULOUSE, J. M. (1982). Top executive locus of control and its relationship to strategy-making, structure, and environment. *Academy of Management Journal*, 25: 221–235.

NAPIER, N. K., and SMITH, M. (1987). Product diversification, performance criteria and compensation at the corporate level. *Strategic Management Journal*, 8: 195–201.

NORBURN, D., and BIRLEY, S. (1988). The top management team and corporate performance. *Strategic Management Journal*, 9: 225–237.

PORTER, L. W., and ROBERTS, K. H. (1976). Communication in organizations. In M. F. Dunnette (ed.), *Handbook of Industrial and Organizational Psychology*: 1553–1589. Chicago, Ill.: Rand McNally.

RAJAGOPALAN, N., and FINKELSTEIN, S. (1992). Effects of strategic orientation and environmental change on senior management reward systems. *Strategic Management Journal*, 13: 127–142.

SHAW, M. E. (1981). *Group Dynamics*. New York: McGraw-Hill.

SIMON, H. A. (1945). *Administrative Behavior*. New York: Free Press.

SIMSEK, Z., VEIGA, J. F., LUBATKIN, M. H., and DINO, R. N. (forthcoming). Modeling the multilevel determinants of top management team behavioral integration. *Academy of Management Journal*.

STUCKER, K. A. (2001). Does break up lead to break down? Effects of parent and industry influences on spinoff firms. Unpublished Ph.D. dissertation, Columbia University.

THOMAS, A. S., LITSCHERT, R. J., and RAMASWAMY, K. (1991). The performance impact of strategy–manager coalignment: An empirical examination. *Strategic Management Journal*, 12: 509–522.

WALLY, S., and BAUM, J. R. (1994). Personal and structural determinants of the pace of strategic decision making. *Academy of Management Journal*, 37(4): 932–956.

WIERSEMA, M. F., and BANTEL, K. A. (1992). Top management team demography and corporate strategic change. *Academy of Management Journal*, 35: 91–121.

CHAPTER 7

GOAL SETTING THEORY

THEORY BUILDING BY INDUCTION

EDWIN A. LOCKE

GARY P. LATHAM

7.1 THE THEORY

LIFE is a process of goal-directed action. This applies both to the vegetative level (e.g., one's internal organs) and to the level of purposeful choice (Locke and Latham, 1990). The conscious mind is the active part of one's psychology; one has the power to volitionally focus one's mind at the conceptual level (Binswanger, 1991; Peikoff, 1991). Volition gives one the power to consciously regulate one's thinking and thereby one's actions. Goal setting theory (Locke and Latham, 1990, 2002) rests on the premise that goal-directedness is an essential attribute of human action and that conscious self-regulation of action, though volitional, is the norm.

We do not deny the existence of the subconscious nor its power to affect action. In fact, the subconscious is essential to survival in that only about seven separate elements can be held in focus awareness at the same time. The subconscious operates automatically and serves to store knowledge and skills which are needed in everyday action. The subconscious is routinely activated by our conscious purposes and also determines our emotional responses (Locke, 1976).

As organizational psychologists, we were concerned mainly with how well people perform work tasks, so that has been the focus of our research. We also chose to focus on conscious performance goals, on the assumption that most human action at work is consciously directed.

1. *Core findings.* The core of goal setting theory asserts that performance goals lead to the highest level of performance when they are both clear (specific) and difficult. Specific, hard goals lead to higher performance than easy or vague goals, such as trying to "do your best."

2. *Mediators of goal effects.* Goal effects are mediated most directly by three relatively automatized mechanisms: (1) focus of attention on the desired end state to the exclusion of other goals, (2) regulation of physical as well as cognitive effort (Wegge and Dibbelt, 2000) in proportion to what is required to attain the goal, and (3) persistence of effort through time until the goal is attained. The role of a fourth mediator, task knowledge or skill, is more complex (Locke, 2000). A goal cannot be attained unless the individual knows how to do so. We will have more to say about this later.

3. *Moderators.* Goal effects are moderated by at least four factors. First, people need feedback regarding their progress in order to see if they are "on target." This not only allows adjustments in level of effort, it may imply the need for modifying their task strategy. Second, for goals to be effective, people must be committed to them (Seijts and Latham, 2000); they must be "real" goals. Commitment is especially important when goals are difficult. This is because hard goals require great effort, and failure and discouragement are more likely than is the case when easy goals are set. Commitment is highest when people have confidence in being able to reach their goal and believe the goal to be important or appropriate. These two factors also affect goal choice.

   There are numerous ways to generate goal commitment, e.g., assignment and supportiveness by a respected leader (Latham and Saari, 1979b), affirming the goal in public so as to make it a test of integrity, clarifying outcome expectancies, incentives, etc. (Latham, 2001; Locke and Latham, 1990, 2002). Participation in goal setting was once thought to be a powerful determinant of goal commitment, but as shown below, this is not true.

   Third, the beneficial effects of goal setting are stronger with simple, straightforward tasks than with tasks that are complex for people. On the latter tasks, some people may not perform well despite having high goals because they lack the needed knowledge, though such knowledge may be acquired. Fourth, goal attainment is adversely affected by situational constraints.

4. *Satisfaction.* Goals are at the same time outcomes to attain and standards for judging one's accomplishments. Thus, people are more satisfied when they

attain their goals or make meaningful progress toward them, than when they fail, or make little or no progress. Failure is more likely when goals are hard than when they are easy; so, on average, people are less likely to be satisfied with their performance when their goals are quite difficult. Nevertheless, they work harder for such goals as we explain below.

5. *Goals (and self-efficacy)* may serve as mediators of external incentives and personality. Since performance goals are task and hence situationally specific, it follows that goals are more immediate determinants of performance than are indirect or general determinants. For example, self-set goals, along with self-efficacy (Bandura, 1997), have been found to mediate the effects of assigned goals, feedback, participation, monetary incentives, job enrichment, leadership, and personality variables, particularly conscientiousness, on performance (Locke, 2001). This is not to suggest that conscious goals mediate all incentives; some incentives or traits may operate through one's subconscious (e.g., McClelland's achievement motive; Collins, Hanges, and Locke, 2004).

6. *Levels of analysis.* Goals have been found to affect performance at the individual, group, organizational unit, and organizational levels (Baum, Locke, and Smith, 2001; Latham and Locke, 1975; Locke and Latham, 2002; O'Leary-Kelly, Martoccio, and Frink, 1994; Rogers and Hunter, 1991).

7. *Time.* Our research on goal setting theory has spanned a period of over forty years. The issue of time spent in theory building is an important one that we will return to later in this chapter.

8. *Generality.* Goal setting effects have been found using more than 100 different tasks; in laboratory, simulated and field settings; using time spans ranging from one minute to twenty-five years; using experimental, quasi-experimental and correlational designs; using goals that are assigned, self-set, and set participatively; using over 40,000 participants in eight countries; using sundry dependent variables including quantity, quality, time spent, costs, job behavior of scientists, sales, student grades, and professors' publications. Goal setting is effective on any task where the person has control over his or her performance. A recent evaluation by Miner (2003), based on the assessments of OB scholars, rated goal setting theory first in importance among seventy-three management theories. So—how was this accomplished?

7.2 GENESIS: EDWIN LOCKE

In college, I majored in psychology. My first course in motivation was taught by David McClelland (1961), well known for his work on the achievement motive which he alleged to be subconscious. He measured motivation with the TAT (Thematic Apperception Test) which requires respondents to write stories in responses to pictures. The stories are then coded for achievement imagery. I was not enamored by projective tests, but the course did arouse my interest in the topic of human motivation. My undergraduate advisor was Richard Herrnstein (later to co-author the controversial book, *The Bell Curve*). I told him I did not want to work with rats and pigeons, and that, because of my father's business experience, I had an interest in business, though I did not want to pursue it as a career. He suggested I combine psychology and business by studying industrial psychology, a field that I had never heard of.

I took his advice and entered graduate school at Cornell in 1960. My first textbook was Art Ryan's and Pat Smith's *Principles of Industrial Psychology*, published in 1954. In it was a report, originally published in 1935, of studies on goal setting conducted in the United Kingdom by C. A. Mace. Even though Mace did not do any statistical analyses, his results, which included a comparison of the effects of specific to "do best" goals, fascinated me.

My assessment was reinforced by Art Ryan who was, at the time, working on a book, *Intentional Behavior* (Ryan, 1970). He argued that the best way to explain human action was to start with its immediate conscious determinants such as intentions and build "backwards" from there.

In that time period, the field of psychology was dominated by behaviorism. Its basic tenets are that: (1) human action is controlled by the environment and can be understood without reference to consciousness–consciousness is not causal but simply an epiphenomenon of brain activity and environmental conditioning; and (2) consciousness falls outside the realm of science (i.e., it involves dealing with mystical phenomena). This behaviorist *zeitgeist* was an intimidating one, and many scholars who did not agree with behaviorism remained silent.

In the 1970s, behaviorism collapsed as the dominant paradigm in psychology, because it could not explain human action (e.g., see Bandura, 1977*a*, 1977*b*, 1986). Fortunately, I believed from the outset, as did my mentors, Ryan and Smith, that the behaviorists were wrong. First, one can refute behaviorism through introspection (i.e., we can observe that our ideas affect how we act). Second, Ayn Rand, whose philosophy of Objectivism I had been studying (see Peikoff, 1991, for the essentials of her philosophy), demonstrated that consciousness is an irrefutable and irreducible axiom. She also showed, as did other philosophers, that psychological determinism—the denial of free will—is a self-contradiction (Binswanger, 1991). Determinists make a claim of knowledge, implying that they are free to look at the evidence and draw logical conclusions from it, while at the same time claiming that they are mindless individuals who make word sounds as a sole result of conditioned responses. In logic, this is called the fallacy of self-exclusion.

Thus, I proceeded to do my doctoral dissertation on the topic of goal setting confident that it was scientifically appropriate to study conscious goals. I wanted to see if goal setting could be shown to be effective when analyzed statistically. It could. My first job subsequent to leaving Cornell was at the American Institutes for Research (AIR).

At that point in time, I was unsure how to build a theory. I did have a negative exemplar—an example of what *not* to do. My exemplar was Frederick Herzberg, who with Mausner and Snyderman, published their famous motivator-hygiene theory in 1959, based mainly on two interview studies. My initial skepticism was that two studies are not a sufficient basis for building a theory. I also had doubts, shared by many, about his exclusive reliance on the critical incident technique to elicit the causes of job satisfaction and dissatisfaction.

Herzberg had participated in an APA symposium on his theory while I was in graduate school. Frank Friedlander, Lyman Porter, and Victor Vroom were on the panel. Herzberg reacted angrily to what seemed to be valid criticisms of his theory and/or method. I realized that this was an inappropriate approach to theory building, because it meant putting "ego" ahead of reality (defending one's position in defiance of the facts).

Herzberg's theory was eventually rejected, at least in the form that he initially proposed it (Locke, 1976). Furthermore, his theory remained static. For example, he never used other methods to test this theory and never did a subsequent critical incident study asking for the causes of high and low performance. Nevertheless, to his credit, his work focused the field on the importance of the job itself on a person's job satisfaction (e.g., see Hackman and Oldham, 1980).

I concluded that the first axiom of theory building had to be: "reality first." This was reinforced by Ayn Rand's philosophy, specifically her concept of the "primacy of existence" (Peikoff, 1991) which specifies the proper relationship between two of her three philosophical axioms: existence (existence exists) and consciousness. Existence is primary and the function of consciousness is to perceive it. Facts are what they are regardless of whether one likes them or not.[1]

Thus, I began my work at AIR convinced that I had to do many experiments using a variety of methodologies before I could make any claim to a theory, and that I had to accept the results—and take into account criticisms of my work. After conducting a number of experiments, I published an article in 1968 entitled "Toward a Theory of Task Motivation and Incentives." I deliberately chose the word "toward," because I did not believe there were sufficient data to develop a theory.

Furthermore, there were criticisms of my work. The main one at that time was: "How do you know your findings are not just a laboratory phenomenon with no generalizability to the world of work?" (e.g., Hinrichs, 1970). I had no answer. But fortunately, Gary Latham soon discovered my laboratory results.

---

[1] Ayn Rand recognized the existence of man-made facts resulting from human choice (the Empire State building). But man-made facts must recognize the metaphysically given (e.g., the laws of nature) or disaster will be the result, e.g., a skyscraper build on a foundation of sand will collapse.

7.3 Gary Latham

Similar to Locke, I majored in experimental psychology. Dalhousie University, where I was an undergraduate student, was a bastion of behaviorism in Canada during the 1960s. My mentor was a clinical psychologist, Dr. H. D. Beach, whose specialty included behavior modification. Unlike Ed, I initially embraced behaviorism because of its emphasis on the careful specification and measurement of action and the proven ability of rewards to affect action.

I was very much influenced in life by my father, whom I loved. Nevertheless, he did not influence my career as such. From my earliest recollections, he would look me in the eye and say, "Son, do your best." Had he assigned me a specific high goal, I undoubtedly would have progressed in my field at a much faster rate!

Similar to Locke, it was my professor, Dr. Beach, who suggested that I pursue graduate studies in I/O psychology, knowing that my interests were in the application of psychology. Like Ed, I had never before heard of this area of psychology.

Georgia Tech, where I obtained my MS degree, embraced the scientist/practitioner model. The faculty there opposed the hypothetico-deductive method. The lifelong—and convoluted—efforts of psychologists such as Clark Hull to develop a theory before gathering data led me to favor induction. My mentor at Tech was Bill Ronan who had studied under John Flanagan, who had developed the critical incident technique (CIT). I used it to identify the behaviors that impact an employee's productivity.

In 1968, the American Pulpwood Association requested Dr. Ronan to help them identify ways to improve the productivity of pulpwood crews in the southern United States. I worked as his assistant. Dr. Ronan advocated induction for categorizing critical incidents whereby similar incidents are grouped together. The pattern of data that I collected revealed that a critical behavior that differentiates the productive from the unproductive pulpwood producer was goal setting.

Upon receiving my MS, I was hired by the American Pulpwood Association as their first staff psychologist. One day I returned to the Tech library to peruse the *Psychological Abstracts* for ways to improve the productivity of pulpwood crews. Soon I was reading a series of abstracts of laboratory experiments which showed that a person who sets a specific high goal performs better on laboratory tasks than do people who are urged to do their best. I quickly called Dr. Ronan. In a factor analysis of our survey data, we too had found that pulpwood crews who set specific high goals have higher productivity than those who don't (Ronan, Latham, and Kinne, 1973). Yet, our previous findings had not captured our attention until that day I was in the library. "Dr. Ronan," I said excitedly, "Locke says . . ."

In reading the journals, I repeatedly encountered two other names, Gary Yukl and Ken Wexley. Recognizing that my knowledge was limited, I decided to return to school for my Ph.D. and entered the University of Akron in 1971.

Not much older than I, Yukl and Wexley shared and enhanced my love of application as well as the need for empirical research. Within the year, I devoured the work of Rensis Likert and Ed Lawler and the newly published book by Campbell, et al. (1970). But most of all, I continued to read everything published by Ed Locke.

In 1973, while I was still a doctoral student, the Weyerhaeuser Company hired me as their first staff psychologist and gave me the resources to do my doctoral dissertation. Impressed by the goal setting results I had obtained with uneducated, independent loggers in the South who were paid piece rate (Latham and Kinne, 1974), they wanted to see if I could obtain similar results using goal setting with educated unionized hourly paid loggers in the West. I did (Latham and Baldes, 1975).

Similar to Locke, I too had an exemplar for conducting research, but my exemplar was positive. My lasting "take-away" from my exemplar, however, was the same as Locke's. Ed Fleishman, Locke's first boss, thrilled me by accepting an invitation to speak on the subject of leadership to the Weyerhaeuser Company. As the President of Division 14 (I/O Psychology) and as Editor of the *Journal of Applied Psychology*, Fleishman gave me invaluable advice: "Give your manuscript to your 'enemies' before you submit it to a journal; whereas your friends will tell you how good it is, your 'enemies' will gladly point out its weaknesses." In short, don't be defensive and do look at all the relevant facts. To this day, I heed his advice.

At the end of a 1974 symposium I participated in at the American Psychological Association, Ed Locke came up and introduced himself. At that convention, we became close friends and colleagues, a relationship that has lasted for more than thirty years. This has occurred for a number of reasons.

First, although I have not been influenced by Ayn Rand's philosophy, like Locke, I am influenced by facts, facts derived from rigorous methodological discipline and empirical testing that allow generalizable solutions. 1977 was a watershed year for me. Albert Bandura sent me a preprint of his paper that would soon appear in the *Psychological Review* (1977a) as well as a book (1977b). His work shattered any remaining beliefs regarding the validity of behaviorism as a philosophy of science. Bandura and I have been citing one another's work to the present day.

Second, Locke and I immediately saw how our strengths complimented one another. On the scientist–practitioner continuum, Locke places himself on the scientist end. I, on the other hand, view myself on the practitioner side of the continuum. We found that we stimulated one another intellectually, and this has led to an enduring collaborative relationship. Locke and I both believe in programmatic research in which there is no conflict between theory and practice. Goal setting studies drove theory, theory drove practice that, in turn, drove the theory. By working together, as scientists and as practitioners, Locke and I were able to build a theory that works in organizations.

7.4 BUILDING THE THEORY

How did we build the theory? Basically by doing many experiments over a long period of time; by showing that our experiments worked and thereby getting other researchers interested in goal setting research; by coming at the subject of goal setting from many different angles; by examining failures and trying to identify their causes; by resolving contradictions and paradoxes; by integrating valid ideas from other developing theories; by responding to criticisms that seemed to have merit and refuting those that did not; by asking ourselves critical questions; by differentiating the various elements of the theory; and finally by tying them together into a whole when we believed that there was sufficient evidence to do so.

We did not have a grand plan since we did not know at the outset how to actually build a theory, but each study (many of which were done by others) had a purpose, and each outcome led to new knowledge and additional questions. Various aspects of our theory building process can be grouped into a number of categories.

7.4.1 Replicating the Original Laboratory Findings

After leaving graduate school, the first author wanted to replicate the findings from his dissertation regarding the superiority of specific, hard goals to "do best" and easy goals, but with variation. For example, for my dissertation I used tasks that involved generating uses for objects; one of the early experiments done at AIR examined goal setting effects on a complex psychomotor task (Locke and Bryan, 1966).

7.4.2 Conducting Field Studies

Logging crews were matched and randomly assigned by Latham to one of two conditions, specific, high goals as to number of trees to cut down, or "do best" goals. All crews were paid by piece rate. Both productivity and job attendance were significantly higher in the high goal condition (Latham and Kinne, 1974). Challenging goals had provided loggers with excitement. They gave meaning and purpose to what had previously been viewed by them as a relatively meaningless task.

7.4.3 Differentiation of Goal Attributes

People kept saying that goals needed to be specific without mentioning difficulty. We differentiated the effects of goal difficulty from those of goal specificity, by showing that specificity alone affected performance variance (Locke, et al., 1989), whereas difficulty affected performance level (but most effectively if goals were also specific).

7.4.4 Conflict

We realized that goals could sometimes be in conflict. We found that intra-individual goal conflict undermined performance (Locke, et al., 1994). We also recognized that team members' personal goal(s) could be in conflict with those of a work team. Latham's field observations formed the basis for a laboratory simulation where students working in teams were put in a dilemma by being able to allocate money to a personal account or the group account (Seijts and Latham, 2000). High personal goals that were compatible with the group's goal of maximizing performance enhanced group performance, but personal goals that conflicted with group goals had a detrimental effect on the group's performance.

7.4.5 Understanding the Role of Feedback

The first author conducted a series of studies to examine feedback in relation to goal setting (Locke and Latham, 1990). I found that feedback (knowledge of score) was a mediator of performance; it led to improved performance only to the extent that it led to the setting of goals (e.g., Locke and Bryan, 1968). Years later, Erez (1977) examined feedback from the opposite angle. She discovered that goals which were not accompanied by feedback do not lead to an improvement in performance. Thus, we came to understand that if you start with feedback alone, goals are a mediator of its effects, but if you start with goals alone, feedback is a moderator of its effects. Goals and feedback consistently work better together than either one do alone.

7.4.6 Discovering Goal Mechanisms

We documented the directive effect of goals by showing that when feedback is given for multiple performance dimensions, performance only improves on those dimensions for which goals are set (Locke and Bryan, 1969). The effort dimension was validated implicitly by showing that people with hard goals work harder, and later others did studies involving direct ratings of effort. LaPorte and Nath (1976) and Latham and Locke (1975) showed that goals affect persistence. Direction, intensity and persistence, of course, are the three aspects of motivated action. Each of these mechanisms is easily verifiable by introspection. Knowledge is another goal mechanism; this is discussed in Section 7.4.11.

7.4.7 Resolving Conflict over how to Get Goal Commitment

We recognized early on, again by introspection, that goal commitment is critical to goal effectiveness. We, like everyone else, knew that most New Year's resolutions are abandoned. Lofty sounding intentions do not necessarily indicate commitment to specific goals.

The question was: How do you get goal commitment? Our initial belief was: through participation. Participation in decision making (pdm) was a popular topic of study following World War II. Locke (1968) predicted that participation would enhance goal commitment. We did not pursue this matter for some time; then, starting in the 1970s, there was chaos in the literature on this topic. The reason was largely political (Wagner and Gooding, 1987). For many scholars participation was viewed not only as a potentially useful managerial technique, but as a "moral imperative." Because it was considered a "democratic" practice and an antidote to fascism, the results simply *had* to be supportive of the former ideology.

Locke and Schweiger (1979) conducted a literature review. They discovered that the interpretation of many pdm studies had been distorted to make the results appear supportive. When the data were interpreted objectively, pdm only had a minimal effect on performance. Strongly worded arguments on this issue went back and forth in the literature for years; heated debates took place at professional meetings.

Latham and I, however, stuck to our core principle: "reality (facts) first." We had no "moral" bias either for or against pdm. As noted, we both initially *expected* pdm to lead to higher goal commitment, because the positive effects of pdm had been touted so much in the earlier literature.

The thrill of inductive, programmatic research is akin to that of being a detective. Latham's doctoral dissertation involving logging crews revealed that productivity was highest in those who were randomly assigned to the participatively set goal condition and less educated (Latham and Yukl, 1975). This supported the value of pdm—but there was a confound. It turned out that goal difficulty was also significantly higher in that condition. The same result was obtained in a field experiment (Latham, Mitchell and Dossett, 1978). Then a series of laboratory experiments showed that when goal difficulty was held constant, participation in goal setting had no effect on goal commitment or performance (Latham and

Marshall, 1982; Latham and Saari, 1979a; Latham and Steele, 1983). All this seemed to indicate that the initial pdm effects had simply been goal effects. The issue of pdm was momentarily settled.

Soon, however, a series of studies by Miriam Erez and her colleagues appeared (e.g., Earley and Kanfer, 1985; Erez, Earley and Hulin, 1985). The results of this work can be summarized in a single sentence: Latham is wrong; participatively set goals work better than assigned goals. Instead of attacking Erez, Latham posed the question: why the differences?

When competent researchers obtain contradictory findings, the explanation may lie in differences in methodology. We decided to resolve the conflict in a revolutionary way. Latham and Erez would design experiments with Locke, who was a close and respected friend of both parties, agreeing to serve as a helper and a mediator between us. The result was a series of experiments jointly designed by the three of us.

It turned out that the main cause of the differences in results was how goals were set in the assigned and pdm conditions. Latham gave a rationale for the assigned goal (e.g., Weyerhaeuser needs ideas on ways to increase log exports to Asia), the goals were described as attainable, and the assignments were given in a supportive manner. In Erez's studies, the goals were assigned tersely (e.g., "do this") with no rationale and no implication that they could be attained. Also, only Erez's pdm subjects were given efficacy enhancing instructions. When all these factors were controlled, pdm had no advantage over assigned goals.

This was the first paper in psychology that was based on the collaboration of two antagonists who worked with a neutral party to resolve their differences. It won a best paper award from the Academy of Management OB division (Latham, Erez, and Locke, 1988).

But the story did not end there. Pdm might yet be beneficial in a nonmotivational way—through cognition. This hypothesis originated in part from Latham observing quality circles at Weyerhaeuser where the objective is to generate ways to "work smarter rather than harder." Consequently, Latham, Winters, and Locke (1994) randomly assigned people to an assigned or a participative goal condition in which people worked in a group (pdm) or alone on a task that was complex for them. No main effect was obtained for goal setting as the two conditions were yoked. But, there was a main effect for decision making with performance significantly higher in the pdm than in the individual decision making condition. The pdm subjects gave each other useful task strategy information. This main effect of pdm on performance was completely mediated by self-efficacy and task strategy.

In 1997, Locke, Alavi, and Wagner reviewed all the reviews and controversies regarding pdm. They concluded that pdm is more fruitfully conceived as a method of information exchange or information sharing rather than as a method of gaining goal commitment. Since that time, the controversy over pdm has died down.

Meanwhile, researchers were discovering other factors that affected goal commitment. We were able to classify most of the factors into those that made the goal important vs. those that increased confidence in being able to reach the goal (Locke and Latham, 1990).

Hollenbeck, Williams, and Klein (1989) developed a useful measure of goal commitment, which they have subsequently refined. They and others found that goal commitment was most important when goals are difficult. This suggests that commitment acts in two different ways: as a moderator when there is a range of goal difficulty, and as a main effect when goal level is held constant at a high level.

7.4.8 Reconciling "Conflicting" Theories about Expectancy and Performance

Atkinson (1958), a student of McClelland, predicted that one's motivation is highest when task (goals were not part of his model) difficulty is .50. This suggested a possible curvilinear (inverted-U) relationship between goal difficulty and performance.

In contrast, expectancy theory (Vroom, 1964) states that the force to act is a multiplicative function of valence, instrumentality, and effort–performance expectancy. Holding the first two factors constant, the theory predicts a positive, linear association between expectancy and performance. However, difficult goals are harder to attain than easy goals, thus we had found a negative linear relationship between expectancy of success (high expectancy meant easy goals) and performance (Locke, 1968).

All three theories could not be correct. Aided by an insight by Howard Garland, Locke, Motowidlo, and Bobko (1986) resolved the puzzle. When goal level is held constant, that is, *within* any given goal group, the positive linear relationship asserted by expectancy theory is correct. Between groups, when goal level is varied, the relationship is negative. This does not contradict expectancy theory, because expectancy theory assumes that the referent is fixed. When Bandura's self-efficacy measure is used (which averages a person's confidence estimates *across* multiple performance outcome levels) both the within and between group associations are positive. The curvilinear relationship between expectancy, or goal difficulty, and performance as suggested by Atkinson replicates only when there are a substantial number of people in the hard goal condition who reject their goals (Erez and Zidon, 1984; Locke and Latham, 1990).

Measures of expectancy (except as a correlate of goal difficulty) and self-efficacy were not initially a part of goal setting theory. We incorporated self-efficacy into our theorizing after recognizing the importance of the concept (Bandura, 1986).

People with high self-efficacy are more likely to be committed to difficult goals when goals are assigned, to set high goals when goals are self set, to respond with renewed effort when feedback shows that they are not attaining their goals, and to develop effective strategies for goal attainment (Latham and Seijts, 1999; Locke and Latham, 2002; Locke, et al., 1984; Seijts and Latham 2001).

7.4.9 Puzzling over Satisfaction

It came as no surprise that goal success led to satisfaction, but we were at first baffled by repeated findings (the first from Howard Garland) that, despite the positive effects of goals on performance, valence (anticipated performance satisfaction in expectancy theory) was lower at every level of performance for people with high goals than for people with low goals. We finally realized that the reason high goals are more effective than low goals is that people set the bar for their satisfaction higher. Thus, people who have high goals must do more to be pleased with their performance.

This raised another question: If anticipated performance satisfaction for high goals is less, why do people set high goals? We discovered the answer in another experiment (reported in Mento, Locke, and Klein, 1992). People expect more practical and psychological benefits from trying for high goals. For example, when undergraduate students consider attaining high grade goals, they expect to experience more pride in their performance than from low grades and also expect to attain better academic outcomes (admission to a graduate school), better job offers and more career success. Ambitious people are willing to set the bar high, both because they feel pride in leaping over the bar and because practical life benefits typically accrue to those who try for more rather than less.

7.4.10 Dealing with Failures

A relatively unique feature of our 1990 book was the analysis of *every single goal setting study which we could find that failed to obtain the predicted results.* If a study fails, either the theory is wrong or incomplete, or the study itself was not conducted properly. Thus, we tried to determine the causes of each failure by references to goal theory tenets. Because these analyses were after the fact, we could not prove that our explanations were correct. However, any or all the studies can now be repeated with the hypothesized flaws corrected as a means of validating our interpretation. Some of the studies even suggested new theoretical ideas.

7.4.11 Discovering the Need for Knowledge, Skill, or Task Strategies

The goal setting studies we conducted in the early years either used simple tasks (e.g., giving uses for objects) that everyone knew how to do or somewhat more complex tasks that people also knew how to do based on their previous experience (e.g., addition). We knew that the effect size of goals was smaller on complex tasks than on simple tasks (Wood, Mento, and Locke, 1987). This implied that on some complex tasks, some people lacked the requisite skill or knowledge. Goal effects are often delayed on such tasks, because learning is required. The passage of time, however, does not guarantee that everyone will learn how to perform a task effectively.

The results of studies which assessed knowledge or ability were puzzling. Some showed direct effects of both goals and ability. Others showed knowledge to be a moderator of goal effects, with the highest performance being shown by people with high task knowledge and high goals. Still others showed that knowledge mediated goal effects. Sorting this out was complicated. Task knowledge is stored in the subconscious (tacit knowledge), it is also held consciously; some is brought to the experiment and some is learned during the experiment itself. In some experiments, knowledge is provided directly by the experimenter. Furthermore, the knowledge acquisition is dynamic in that new learning may be occurring continuously. This makes measurement of knowledge difficult, especially the part that is held subconsciously.

Ten years after our 1990 book was published, the first author tried to integrate these results (Locke, 2000). My conclusion was that *all* goal effects are mediated by task knowledge. Motivation without cognition is useless. Motivation may energize a person, but such an individual will not be able to get anything done unless the person knows how to do so. Conversely, cognition in the absence of motivation is also useless because the individual will have no desire to act on what is known. I suggested that the inconsistent results in the literature were a result of either not measuring all the relevant knowledge or of people acting on their knowledge motivated by factors other than their task goals.

7.4.11.1 *Learning Goals*

On tasks that are complex, people often have to acquire the requisite knowledge on their own. Latham puzzled as to how people could be helped to do this. Several studies had shown that specific hard goals not only fail to enhance performance in comparison to "do best" goals, they may make it worse (e.g., Earley, Connolly, and Ekegren, 1989.) In do best conditions, people often took the time to systematically test different task strategies, whereas those with difficult outcome goals frantically switched from one strategy to another without being systematic.

Latham hypothesized that when tasks are new and difficult for people, the best idea is not to set performance goals but rather to set learning goals. To test this hypothesis, Winters and Latham (1996) used a complex class scheduling task developed by Chris Earley. Consistent with the findings of Kanfer and Ackerman, there was a decrease in performance when a specific high outcome goal was set regarding the number of schedules to be produced relative to simply urging people to do their best. But, when a high learning goal was set in terms of discovering a specific number of ways to solve the task, performance was significantly higher in this condition than it was when people were either urged to do their best or had set an outcome goal. Higher performance is not always the result of greater effort, but rather, of greater understanding (Frese and Zapf, 1994; Latham and Saari, 1979b).

7.4.11.2 *Proximal Goals*

Among the biggest impediments to the usual positive benefits of goal setting is environmental uncertainty (Locke and Latham, 1990). The information required to set goals may be unavailable or may become obsolete due to rapid changes in the environment. Thus, as uncertainty increases, it becomes increasingly difficult to set and commit to a long-term outcome goal. Latham and Seijts (1999) used a business game in which students were paid to make toys, and the dollar amounts paid for the toys changed continuously without warning. Setting specific, difficult outcome goals resulted in profits that were significantly worse than urging the students to do their best. But when proximal outcome goals were set in addition to the distal outcome goals, self-efficacy as well as profits were significantly higher than in the other two conditions. This is because in highly dynamic situations, it is important to actively search for feedback and react quickly to it (Frese and Zapf, 1994). In addition, Dorner (1991) has found that performance errors on a dynamic task are often due to deficient decomposition of a distal goal into proximal goals.

In a follow-up study, Seijts and Latham (2001) examined the effect of setting proximal goals in conjunction with either a distal learning or a distal outcome goal on a task that required new. Setting proximal, learning goals resulted in the greatest number of strategies generated. The number of task relevant strategies, in turn, correlated positively with performance.

7.4.12 Protecting Goal Theory from Materialists

In the 1970s, behaviorists attempted to incorporate goal setting into their domain by relabeling the goal setting process. Thus, goals were labeled as "controlling" or "discriminative" stimuli, and feedback was alleged to be a "reinforcer." They denied that how goals function depends on mental processes. They unsuccessfully attempted to externalize what is, in reality, internal (Locke, 1977).

In the 1980s, control theory, a neo-behavioristic theory derived from cybernetic engineering (e.g., physical systems with feedback loops), became popular. The theory relabels goal concepts in the language of machinery. Thus goals are called "reference standards." Goal failures are called "deviations." A person who acts to attain the goal is called an "effector." Commitment is "error sensitivity." Decision making is done by a "selector."

The problem with this relabeling is that the goal concepts are no longer cognitive processes when they are debased by machine terminology. A thermostat setting (a reference standard) has nothing in common with a consciously held goal. This relabeling fosters the illusion of reductionism. Control theorists, based on the concept of a negative feedback loop, state that people seek only to eliminate goal-performance discrepancies. People are not thermostats (Binswanger 1991, see n. 1). Human life involves the constant creation of discrepancies, that is, the setting of new goals. Goal directed action is required for survival.

Some control theorists also deny the causal role of self-efficacy in human action. We have responded vigorously to attempts to evade the axiom of consciousness, and thereby deny its causal efficacy (e.g., Bandura and Locke, 2003; Locke and Latham, 1990).

7.5 IMPLICATIONS FOR THEORY BUILDING

Our approach to theory building effort is *inductive*. Induction means going from the particular to the general. This is in contrast to the "hypothetico-deductive" method. The latter view stems from a long line of philosophical skeptics, from Hume to Kant to Popper to Kuhn. The core premise of this view is that knowledge of reality is impossible. Popper, believed that because theories are not based on observations of reality, they can start, arbitrarily, from anywhere. Thus, theories cannot be proven, they can only be falsified by testing deductions from them. Even falsification, Popper asserted, never gets at truth. Induction is rejected. If Popper were correct, scientific discovery would be impossible. But history refutes this view.

The history of science is the history of discoveries made by observations of reality, and integrated into laws and principles. Subsequent discoveries do not necessarily invalidate previous ones, unless errors of observation or context-dropping were made. They simply add to knowledge. Mankind did not get from the swamps to the stars by eschewing the search for knowledge and seeking only to disprove arbitrary hypotheses.

Galileo, for example, did numerous experiments with freely falling objects, objects rolling down inclined planes, swinging pendulums, and trajectories of objects and induced the law of intertia, the constancy of gravity, and the laws governing horizontal and vertical motion. He also invented an improved telescope and discovered four moons of Jupiter. He proved that Venus orbits the sun—giving further credence to Copernicus's heliocentric theory. Newton discovered that white light is composed of different colors by doing experiments with prisms. He drew upon the observations of Kepler and Galileo to discover the laws of motion. Especially revolutionary was the idea that all bodies are attracted to one another by a force (gravity) whose magnitude is proportional to the masses of the bodies, and inversely proportional to the square of the distance separating them. With this knowledge, including his invention of calculus, he was able to explain the actions not only of the planets but of the tides. Both Galileo and Newton used observation to gather data, conduct experiments, and then integrated their observations into a theory.

Einstein agreed: "Turning to the subject of the theory of [special] relativity, I want to emphasize that this theory has no speculative origin, it rather owes its discovery only to the desire to adapt theoretical physics to observable facts as closely as possible" (Einstein, 2002: 238).

Contrast Galileo, Newton, and Einstein to Descartes who argued that one can deduce the components of matter, the nature of the planets, moons, and comets, the cause of movement, the formation of the solar system, the nature of light and of sunspots, the formation of the stars, the explanation of tides and earthquakes, the formation of mountains, magnetism, the nature of static electricity and chemical interactions—all from what he claimed were innate ideas discovered intuitively. Not surprisingly, every single one of his theories was wrong.[2]

Of course, theory building does include deduction. But, the major premises that form the beginning of any syllogism (e.g., "all men are mortal") have to be established by induction, or else the conclusion, even if valid in "form," will be false.

What then does induction involve?

7.5.1 Data Gathering

Accumulating facts related to some issue or question—based on observations of reality. In our case, this meant conducting studies, including laboratory and

[2] The comments about Galileo, Newton, and Descartes were based on portions of a forthcoming book by David Harriman. These portions were published in *The Intellectual Activist*, vol. 14, nos. 3–5 (2000) and vol. 16, no. 11 (2002). The authors are indebted also to Stephen Speicher for providing the information on Einstein.

field experiments. (We were very fortunate that many other researchers conducted goal setting experiments as well.) However, in the case of theories which are psychological in nature, using introspection is also critical. In fact, we have argued that it should be acknowledged candidly by scientists building theories of motivation (Locke and Latham, 2004). No psychological concept can be grasped without the use of introspection, and it was clearly an aid to our thinking.

7.5.2 Differentiating

Proper differentiation begins with a clear definition of the concept(s) in question (e.g., a goal is the object or aim of an action; Locke and Latham, 1990). Definitions tie concepts to reality and distinguish them from other concepts (Locke, 2003; Rand, 1990). Data also have to be differentiated before they can be integrated. For example we had to differentiate the various goal attributes (specificity and difficulty) and the various elements from one another (e.g., mediators, moderators), and we had to differentiate within each of these categories. (e.g., direction, effort, feedback, commitment). We also had to differentiate goal theory from other theories (expectancy theory, behavior modification, control theory). Differentiation is a key step involved in organizing data.

7.5.3 Integrating

To make an inductive theory, the differentiated data have to be integrated into an organized whole. A key law of logic involved in integration is Aristotle's law of contradiction. A thing cannot be A and non-A at the same time and in the same respect. If two or more theories are contradictory, at least one of them must be wrong. If data contradict a theory, then either the data or the theory, or both, must be wrong. Hegelian mumbo-jumbo aside, contradictions cannot be integrated; they have to be resolved. For example, the conflict over the importance of participation in setting a goal between Latham and Erez noted earlier was resolved by discovering that the two types of studies used somewhat different methodologies, and by verifying that these differences made a difference by means of a new set of experiments. The conflict between goal and expectancy theories was resolved by distinguishing between within vs. between goal conditions. We have also attempted to integrate goal theory with other theories of motivation (Locke, 1997; Latham, Locke, and Fassina, 2002).

7.5.4 Identifying Causal Relationships

Integration, if it is to be useful, must lead to the establishment of laws or general principles. Identifying generalizable principles requires identifying *causal* relationships. Induction is more than enumeration (counting). It is more than meta-analysis, which is enumeration that includes mean effect sizes. When using enumeration alone, there is no answer to the skeptics' query: "How do you know that the relationship will come out the next time?"

This was an issue we did not fully understand when developing goal theory. We thought that the more types of tasks, subjects, settings, performance measures used, etc., the better—that is, the more confidence one could have in the theory. Although variation in conditions is beneficial (e.g., to discover moderators), we did not see that *identifying causal relationships* (which we subsequently did identify) *was the fundamental issue*. For example, we can have confidence that goals work when we know the means by which they work (mediators) and the relevant context factors (moderators). Similarly, by understanding that emotions were implicit value judgments (Locke, 1976; Locke and Latham, 1990) and that a goal is a specific type of value, we now understand why goal success causes satisfaction.

7.5.5 Taking Time

Inductive theory building takes time, especially when starting from scratch. It is much harder than deduction. The present authors worked for twenty-five years before we were ready to claim we had a theory. We had to integrate the results of several hundred studies conducted by ourselves and others. We had to resolve many contradictions and paradoxes. We had to relate many different parts to the whole. And we had to understand many causal relationships. There is no law that says twenty-five years is the "right" amount of time. But, that was the time taken for us to have something substantial before we could make claims for a meaningful theory.

7.5.6 Keeping Theories Open-Ended

Although we presented our theory in 1990, after twenty-five years of research, we did not close the theory to further development. Today, some forty years after we started, we are still accumulating knowledge about goal setting. For example, since publication of the 1990 book, we have learned about the benefits of learning goals (Winters and Latham, 1996) as noted earlier; we have found that goals affect small venture growth over two and six year periods (Baum, Locke, and Smith, 2001; Baum and Locke, 2004)—the first macro level studies; we have studied the effects of goals on risk-taking (Knight, Durham, and Locke, 2001), and we have discovered an interactive relationship between subconsciously primed and consciously assigned goals (Stajkovic, Locke and Blair, 2004; see also Locke and Latham, 2004). We have also learned that goals may tempt some people to cheat (Schweitzer, Ordóñez, and Douma, 2004). These discoveries do not contradict earlier findings; they add knowledge.

Our advice for scholars who want to build a theory: Do it inductively and be prepared to spend years doing it. We also believe that both the history of science and our own success has implications for the *Academy of Management Review*. We encourage the editorial staff to discourage hypothetico-deductive theorizing and to promote more inductive theorizing.

References

ATKINSON, J. (1958). Towards experimental analysis of human motivation in terms of motives, expectancies and incentives. In J. W. Atkinson (ed.), *Motives in Fantasy, Action and Society*. Princeton: Van Nostrand.

BANDURA, A. (1977a). Self-efficacy: Toward a unifying theory of behavioral change. *Psychological Review*, 84: 191–215.

—— (1977b). *Social Learning Theory*. Englewood Cliffs, NJ: Prentice-Hall.

—— (1986). *Social Foundations of Thought and Action: A Social-Cognitive Theory*. Englewood Cliffs, NJ: Prentice Hall.

—— (1997). *Self-Efficacy: The Exercise of Control*. New York: Freeman.

—— and LOCKE, E. A. (2003). Negative self-efficacy and goal effects revisited. *Journal of Applied Psychology*, 88: 87–99.

BAUM, R. J., LOCKE, E. A., and SMITH, K. G. (2001). A multi-dimensional model of venture growth. *Academy of Management Journal*, 44: 292–303.

—— —— (2004). The relationship of entrepreneurial traits, skill, and motivation to subsequent venture growth. *Journal of Applied Psychology*, 89: 587–598.

BINSWANGER, H. (1991). Volition as cognitive self-regulation. *Organizational Behavior and Human Decision Processes*, 50: 154–178.

CAMPBELL, J. P., DUNNETTE, M. D., LAWLER, E. E., and WEICK, K. E. (1970). *Managerial Behavior, Performance, and Effectiveness*. NY: McGraw-Hill.

COLLINS, C., HANGES, P., and LOCKE, E. (2004). The relationship of achievement motivation to entrepreneurial behavior: A meta-analysis. *Human Performance*, 17: 95–117.

DORNER, D. (1991). The investigation of action regulation in uncertain and complex situations. In J. Rasmussen and B. Brehmer (eds.), *Distributed Decision Making: Cognitive Models for Cooperative Work*: 349–354. Oxford: Wiley.

EARLEY, P. C., CONNOLLY, T., and EKEGREN, G. (1989). Goals, strategy development and task performance: Some limits on the efficacy of goal setting. *Journal of Applied Psychology*, 74: 24–33.

—— and Kanfer, R. (1985). The influence of component participation and role models on goal acceptance, goal satisfaction, and performance. *Organizational Behavior and Human Decision Processes*, 36: 378–390.

Einstein, A. (2002). King Albert College lecture, June 13, 1921. In *The Collected Papers of Albert Einstein: The Berlin years: Writings 1918–1921*, vol. 7, doc. 58.

Erez, M. (1977). Feedback: A necessary condition for the goal-performance relationship. *Journal of Applied Psychology*, 62: 624–627.

—— Earley, C. P., and Hulin, C. L. (1985). The impact of participation on goal acceptance and performance: A two-step model. *Academy of Management Journal*, 28: 50–66.

—— and Zidon, I. (1984). Effects of goal acceptance on the relationship of goal setting and task performance. *Journal of Applied Psychology*, 69: 69–78.

Frese, M., and Zapf, D. (1994). Action as the core of work psychology: A German approach. In H. C. Triandis and M. D. Dunnette (eds.), *Handbook of Industrial and Organizational Psychology*: 4. 271–340. Palo Alto, Calif.: Consulting Psychologists Press.

Hackman, J., and Oldham, G. (1980). *Work Redesign*, Reading, Mass.: Addison-Wesley.

Herzberg, F., Mausner, B., and Snyderman, B. (1959). *The Motivation to Work*. New York: Wiley.

Hinrichs, J. R. (1970). Psychology of men at work. *Annual Review of Psychology*, 21: 519–554.

Hollenbeck, J. R., Williams, C. R., and Klein, H. J. (1989). An empirical examination of the antecedents of commitment to difficult goals. *Journal of Applied Psychology*, 74: 18–23.

Knight, D., Durham, C., and Locke, E. A. (2001). The relationship of team goals, incentives, and efficacy to strategic risk, tactical implementation, and performance. *Academy of Management Journal*, 44: 326–338.

LaPorte, R. E., and Nath, R. (1976). Role of performance goals in prose learning. *Journal of Educational Psychology*, 68: 260–264.

Latham, G. P. (2001). The importance of understanding and changing employee outcome expectancies for gaining commitment to an organizational goal. *Personnel Psychology*, 54: 707–716.

—— and Baldes, J. J. (1975). The "practical significance" of Locke's theory of goal setting. *Journal of Applied Psychology*, 60: 122–124.

—— Erez, M., and Locke, E. A. (1988). Resolving scientific disputes by the joint design of crucial experiments by the antagonists: Application to the Erez-Latham dispute regarding participation in goal setting. *Journal of Applied Psychology*, 73: 753–772.

—— and Kinne, S. B. (1974). Improving job performance through training in goal setting. *Journal of Applied Psychology*, 59: 187–191.

—— and Locke, E. A. (1975). Increasing productivity with decreasing time limits: A field replication of Parkinson's law. *Journal of Applied Psychology*, 60: 524–526.

—— —— and Fassina, N. E. (2002). The high performance cycle: Standing the test of time. In S. Sonnentag (ed.), *The Psychological Management of Individual Performance. A Handbook in the Psychology of Management in Organizations*: 201–228. Chichester, UK: Wiley.

—— and Marshall, H. A. (1982). The effects of self set, participatively set, and assigned goals on the performance of government employees. *Personnel Psychology*, 35: 399–404.

—— Mitchell, T. R., and Dossett, D. L. (1978). The importance of participative goal setting and anticipated rewards on goal difficulty and job performance. *Journal of Applied Psychology*, 63: 163–171.

—— and SAARI, L. M. (1979*a*). The effects of holding goal difficulty constant on assigned and participatively set goals. *Academy of Management Journal*, 22: 163–168.

—— —— (1979*b*). The importance of supportive relationships in goal setting. *Journal of Applied Psychology*, 64, 151–156.

—— and SEIJTS, G. H. (1999). The effects of proximal and distal goals on performance on a moderately complex task. *Journal of Organizational Behavior*, 20: 1–429.

—— and STEELE, T. P. (1983). The motivational effects of participation versus goal setting on performance. *Academy of Management Journal*, 26: 406–417.

—— —— and SAARI, L. M. (1982). The effects of participation and goal difficulty on performance. *Personnel Psychology*, 35: 677–686.

—— WINTERS, D. C., and LOCKE, E. A. (1994). Cognitive and motivational effects of participation: A mediator study. *Journal of Organizational Behavior*, 15: 49–63.

—— and YUKL, G. A. (1975). Assigned versus participative goal setting with educated and uneducated woods workers. *Journal of Applied Psychology*, 60: 299–302.

LOCKE, E. A. (1968). Toward a theory of task motivation and incentives. *Organizational Behavior and Human Performance*, 3: 157–189.

—— (1976). The nature and causes of job satisfaction. In M. Dunnette (ed.), *Handbook of Industrial and Organizational Psychology*. Chicago: Rand-McNally.

—— (1977). The myths of behavior mod in organizations. *Academy of Management Review*, 2: 543–553.

—— (1997). The motivation to work: What we know. In M. Maehr and P. Pintrich (eds.), *Advances in Motivation and Achievement*, vol. 10. Greenwich, Conn.: JAI Press.

—— (2000). Motivation, cognition and action: An analysis of studies of task goals and knowledge. *Applied Psychology: An International Review*, 49: 408–429.

—— (2001). Self-set goals and self-efficacy as mediators of incentives and personality. In M. Erez, U. Kleinbeck, and H. Thierry (eds.), *Work Motivation in the Context of a Globalizing Economy*. Mahwah, NJ: L. Erlbaum.

—— (2003). Good definitions: The epistemological foundation of scientific progress. In J. Greenberg (ed.), *Organizational Behavior: The State of the Science*. Mahwah, NJ: L. Erlbaum.

—— ALAVI, M. and WAGNER, J. (1997). Participation in decision making: An information exchange perspective. In G. Ferris (ed.), *Research in Personnel and Human Resource Management*, vol. 15. Greenwich, Conn.: JAI Press.

—— and BRYAN, J. F. (1966). Cognitive aspects of psychomotor performance. *Journal of Applied Psychology*, 50: 286–291.

—— —— (1968). Goal setting as a determinant of the effect of knowledge of score on performance. *American Journal of Psychology*, 81: 398–407.

—— —— (1969). The directing function of goals in task performance. *Organizational Behavior and Human Performance*, 4: 35–42.

—— CHAH, D. O., HARRISON, S., and LUSTGARTEN, N. (1989). Separating the effects of goal specificity from goal level. *Organizational Behavior and Human Performance*, 43: 270–287.

—— FREDERICK, E., LEE, C., and BOBKO, P. (1984). The effects of self-efficacy, goals and task strategies on task performance. *Journal of Applied Psychology*, 69: 241–251.

—— and LATHAM, G. (1990). *A theory of goal setting and task performance*. Englewood Cliffs, NJ: Prentice Hall.

—— —— (2002). Building a practically useful theory of goal setting and task motivation: A 35-year odyssey. *American Psychologist*, 57: 705–717.

LOCKE, E. A., and LATHAM, G. (2004). What should we do about motivation theory? Six recommendations for the twenty-first century. *Academy of Management Review*, 29: 388–403.

—— MOTOWIDLO, S., and BOBKO, P. (1986). Using self-efficacy theory to resolve the conflict between goal setting theory and expectancy theory in organizational behavior and industrial/organizational psychology. *Journal of Social and Clinical Psychology*, 4: 328–338.

—— and SCHWEIGER, D. M. (1979). Participation in decision-making: One more look. In B. M. Staw (ed.), *Research in Organizational Behavior*. Greenwich, Conn.: JAI Press.

—— SMITH, K. G., EREZ, M., CHAH, D. O., and SCHAFFER, A. (1994). The effects of intraindividual goal conflict on performance. *Journal of Management*, 20: 67–91.

MACE, C. A. (1935). Incentives: Some experimental studies (Report No. 72). London: *Industrial Health Research Board*.

McCLELLAND, D. C. (1961). *The Achieving Society*. Princeton: D. Van Nostrand.

MENTO, A. LOCKE, E. A., and KLEIN, H. (1992). Relationship of goal level to valence and instrumentality. *Journal of Applied Psychology*, 77: 395–405.

MINER, J. B. (2003). The rated importance, scientific validity, and practical usefulness of organizational behavior theories. *Academy of Management Learning and Education*, 2: 250–268.

O'LEARY-KELLY, A., MARTOCCHIO, J., and FRINK, D. (1994). A review of the influence of group goals on group performance. *Academy of Management Journal*, 37: 1285–1301.

PEIKOFF, L. (1991). *Objectivism: The Philosophy of Ayn Rand*. New York: Dutton.

RAND, A. (1990). *Introduction of Objectivist Epistemology*. New York: NAL.

ROGERS, R., and HUNTER, J. (1991). Impact of management by objectives on organizational productivity. *Journal of Applied Psychology*, 76: 322–336.

RONAN, W. W., LATHAM, G. P., and KINNE, S. B. (1973). The effects of goal setting and supervision on worker behavior in an industrial situation. *Journal of Applied Psychology*, 58: 302–307.

RYAN, T. A. (1970). *Intentional Behavior*. New York: Ronald.

—— and SMITH, P. C. (1954). *Principles of Industrial Psychology*. New York: Ronald.

SEIJTS, G. H., and LATHAM, G. P. (2000). The construct of goal commitment: Measurement and relationships with task performance. In R. Goffin and E. Helmes (eds.), *Problems and Solutions in Human Assessment*. Dordrecht: Kluwer Academic.

—— —— (2001). The effect of learning, outcome, and proximal goals on a moderately complex task. *Journal of Organizational Behavior*, 22: 291–307.

SCHWEITZER, M. E., ORDÓÑEZ, L., and DOUMA, B. (2004). Goal setting as a motivator of unethical behavior. *Academy of Management Journal*, 47: 422–432.

STAJKOVIC, A. D., LOCKE, E. A., and BLAIR, E. S. (2004). A first examination of the relationship between subconscious (primed) goals, time delay, conscious goals and task performance. Ms. under review.

VROOM, V. H. (1964). *Work and Motivation*. New York: Wiley.

WAGNER, J., and GOODING, R. (1987). Effects of social trends on participation research. *Administrative Science Quarterly*, 32: 241–262.

WEGGE, J., and DIBBELT, S. (2000). Zur wirkung von Zielsetzungen auf die Informationsverarbeitung bei Buchstabenvergleichsaufgaben [Effects of goal setting on information processing in letter-matching tasks]. *Zeitschrift für Experimentelle Psychologie*, 47: 89–114.

WINTERS, D., and LATHAM, G. P. (1996). The effect of learning versus outcome goals on a simple versus a complex task. *Group and Organization Management*, 21: 236–250.

WOOD, R. E., MENTO, A. J., and LOCKE, E. A. (1987). Task complexity as a moderator of goal effects. *Journal of Applied Psychology*, 17: 416–425.

....

CHAPTER 8

HOW JOB CHARACTERISTICS THEORY HAPPENED

....

GREG R. OLDHAM

J. RICHARD HACKMAN

ONE afternoon in 1971, Greg Oldham, then a doctoral student at Yale, walked into Richard Hackman's faculty office and announced that we had a relationship problem. Richard was taken aback because he thought the relationship was excellent. In his view, Greg was well-launched on his own research trajectory, having recently completed a fine pre-dissertation project on leadership and goal setting. It was just the kind of mentoring relationship Richard most valued: Greg autonomously had developed a research question about a phenomenon that interested him and, with only modest coaching, had designed, executed, and written up an excellent empirical study. Richard thought that Greg was now well positioned to develop a dissertation proposal that would significantly advance understanding of his phenomenon.

The conversation, as best as we can reconstruct it more than three decades later, unfolded as follows:

G: Are you aware that I've now been here more than two years and we have not yet collaborated on a single research project?

R: Yes, isn't that wonderful? You're well on your way, and I couldn't be happier.

G: Well, *I'm* not happy. Sure, our personal relationship is great. We spend all this time in your boat fishing and talking about just everything, including research and theory. Don't you think it's a little strange that all those conversations have not resulted in a single research study, or even a review paper?

R: But that's how it's supposed to be. My job is to help you develop your own research ideas and directions. You're not my research assistant, and you're not an apprentice. The worst thing that could happen to you would be to graduate from this program looking like a carbon copy of me [note that this conversation happened back when there *were* carbon copies].

G: I don't want to be a carbon copy of anybody, but I know I'd learn a lot if we did some research together. Besides, it would be fun. Why do you have a problem with this?

R: Okay, look, Bob Janson and Ken Purdy from the Roy Walters and Associates consulting firm are coming to visit in a couple of weeks. They specialize in consulting about job enrichment, and they read my paper with Ed Lawler on job characteristics (Hackman and Lawler, 1971). They want to see if there are some uses they might make of those findings, or maybe some ways we might collaborate with them. How about you sit in on that meeting? Maybe something will develop.

Something did. Bob and Ken brought extensive experience with the design of jobs in complex organizations and a clear focus on implementation challenges. We had begun to erect a reasonably sturdy conceptual and empirical platform from which to examine task influences on attitudes and behavior. Together, we refined our emerging theory of work redesign (Hackman and Oldham, 1976, 1980) and developed a set of implementing principles for enriching jobs in organizational settings (Hackman, et al., 1975).

In this chapter, we first provide a brief description of the theory itself—material that readers who have some familiarity with the theory surely will want to skip. Then we describe the personal, social, and contextual conditions that, in our retrospective reconstruction, shaped the development of the theory. Finally, we discuss what happened after the theory was published and came to be noticed—sometimes sympathetically, sometimes with great skepticism—by other organizational behavior scholars and by practitioners.

8.1 JOB CHARACTERISTICS THEORY: AN OVERVIEW

The primary aspirations of Job Characteristics Theory (JCT) were to explain how properties of the organizational tasks people perform affect their work attitudes and behavior, and to identify the conditions under which these effects are likely to be strongest. Because the theory is situated at the boundary between basic knowledge and organizational applications, we also were able to suggest a number of specific strategies for redesigning or enriching the properties of jobs intended to enhance both jobholders' performance and their own well-being.

The original version of the theory (Hackman and Oldham, 1975, 1976) is shown in Figure 8.1. As is seen in the figure, the theory posits that five characteristics of the work itself affect a variety of personal and work outcomes via their effects on three psychological states of employees. In addition, the theory argues that these core characteristics have their strongest effects when employees have high Growth Need Strength (i.e., when they have a strong desire for growth and personal development at work).

The conceptual core of the theory is the set of three psychological states that mediate between job attributes and outcomes. They are:

- Experienced Meaningfulness. The degree to which the jobholder experiences the work as inherently meaningful, as something that "counts" in his or her own system of values.

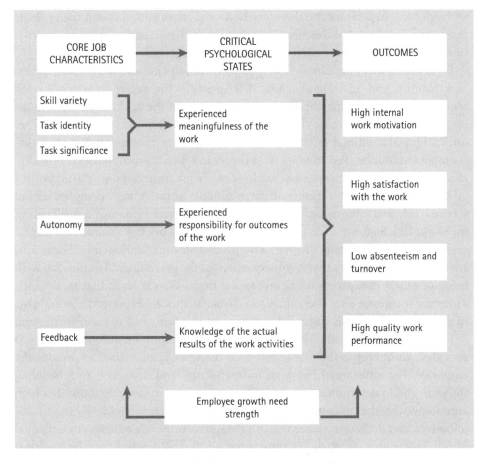

Fig. 8.1   The job characteristics model

- Experienced Responsibility. The degree to which the jobholder feels personally accountable and responsible for the results of the work he or she does.
- Knowledge of Results. The degree to which the jobholder has confident knowledge about how well he or she is performing.

JCT posits that the simultaneous presence of the three psychological states results in a number of favorable personal and work outcomes. Specifically, the jobholder should (1) be internally motivated at work (i.e., feel good when performing well, and feel bad or unhappy when performing poorly), (2) be satisfied both with the opportunities for personal growth and development at work and with the job in general, (3) produce work that is of high quality, and (4) exhibit generally low absenteeism and turnover. However, if one or more of the psychological states is absent or at very low level, fewer of these desirable outcomes should emerge.

The three psychological states are internal to individuals and, therefore, do not represent properties of the work itself that might be changed or manipulated. JCT identifies five characteristics of jobs that, when present, increase the chances that a jobholder will experience the three psychological states and, through them, shape the personal and work outcomes. The specific job characteristics that are expected to most strongly influence each of the psychological states are as follows.

Experienced Meaningfulness is shaped by three job characteristics: Skill Variety, Task Identity, and Task Significance. Skill Variety is the degree to which the job requires a number of different activities in carrying out the work, which involve the use of a number of different skills and talents of the jobholder. Work that stretches one's skills and abilities invariably is experienced as more meaningful than work that is simple and routine. Task Identity is the degree to which the job requires completion of a whole and identifiable piece of work—doing a job from beginning to end with a visible outcome. Putting together an entire product or providing a complete unit of service is inherently more meaningful than being responsible for only a small part of the work. Task Significance is the degree to which the work has a substantial impact on the lives of other people, whether in the immediate organization or in the external environment. An activity that is consequential for the psychological or physical well-being of others is experienced as more meaningful than is work that makes little difference to anyone else. These three job characteristics are expected to be additive, in that meaningfulness is enhanced to the extent that any or all of them are present.

Experienced Responsibility is shaped by the amount of autonomy the job provides. Autonomy is the degree to which the work is structured to provide the employee with substantial freedom, independence, and discretion in scheduling the work and in determining the procedures to be used in carrying it out. For high autonomy jobs, the outcomes of the work depend on the jobholder's own efforts, initiatives, and decisions, rather than on the instructions of a manager or a manual of job procedures. In such circumstances, the jobholder feels greater personal responsibility for his or her own successes and failures at work.

Knowledge of Results is shaped by the degree to which carrying out job-specified work activities provide the jobholder with direct and clear information about the effectiveness of his or her performance. When someone receives information about his or her performance from the work itself (e.g., when a salesperson closes a deal and receives payment from a customer), that feedback is direct and immediate and, therefore, contributes substantially to his or her overall knowledge of results about work outcomes.

The degree to which a job has an overall high standing on the five characteristics described above, and, therefore, is likely to prompt favorable personal and work outcomes, is summarized by an index called the Motivating Potential Score (MPS). To engender all three of the psychological states, a job must have a high standing on one or more of the three characteristics that boost meaningfulness, and be high on both autonomy and feedback as well. The MPS score indicates the degree to which that is the case through the following formula:

$$\text{MPS} = (\text{Skill Variety} + \text{Task Identity} + \text{Task SignifiCANCE})/3 \times \text{Autonomy} \times \text{Feedback}$$

Thus, a low score on either Autonomy or Feedback will substantially reduce a job's MPS, since both Experienced Responsibility and Knowledge of Results must be present for personal and work outcomes to be high, and those two job attributes produce the corresponding two psychological states. Conversely, a low score on one of the three job characteristics expected to foster Experienced Meaningfulness may not necessarily compromise a job's MPS, since the absence of any one of those three attributes can be compensated for by the strong presence of the others.

As is seen in Figure 8.1, the original version of the theory identifies one individual difference characteristic: Growth Need Strength (GNS), as a moderator of the impact of the core job characteristics on an employee's responses (two additional moderators were added in our 1980 revision of the theory; Hackman and Oldham, 1980). GNS is the strength of a person's need for personal accomplishment, learning, and development. The theory posits that jobholders who have strong growth needs value the opportunities for accomplishment and self-direction provided by jobs high on the five core characteristics and, as a result, respond positively to them. Low GNS jobholders, by contrast, place less value on the opportunities provided by high MPS jobs and therefore respond less positively to them.

Simultaneous with the development of the theory, we created two research instruments for assessing theory-specified constructs—the Job Diagnostic Survey (JDS) and the Job Rating Form (JRF) (Hackman and Oldham, 1975, 1980). The JDS assesses jobholders' perceptions of the five core job characteristics, their experienced psychological states, their growth need strength, and affective outcomes including internal motivation, job satisfaction, and satisfaction with several aspects of the work context. The JRF is used to obtain the assessments of external observers, such as supervisors or researchers, of the core job characteristics. This instrument provides measures of job characteristics that are assumed to be more objective than those provided by jobholders, since observers' perceptions are not influenced by the experience of actually performing the work. The JRF does not provide measures of the experienced psychological states or of affective reactions to the work, and neither the JDS nor the JRF assesses jobholder work effectiveness, absenteeism, or turnover.

8.2 CONDITIONS THAT SHAPED DEVELOPMENT OF THE THEORY

As we reflected back on the process of developing Job Characteristics Theory in preparation for writing this chapter, we discovered that we have forgotten many details of what we did, when, and how. Worse, we suspect that some of what we *did* recall was heavily influenced by retrospective reconstruction. Any blow-by-blow account of the process of theory development, therefore, would certainly be riddled with omissions and distortions. What is clearer to us, and perhaps more useful to readers engaged in their own theory-making work, are the personal and organizational conditions that were in place at the time we did our conceptual work. We summarize those conditions next and suggest how they may have influenced— whether for better or for worse—the content and shape of our model.

8.2.1 Relevant Preparation

When we began having serious discussions about Job Characteristics Theory in 1971–1972, we both were affiliated with the Department of Administrative Sciences at Yale University. Greg was a 24-year-old second year doctoral student in the Organizational Behavior program. Richard was a 31-year-old associate professor and Greg's academic advisor.

Our backgrounds and interests back then were quite different and, as we will discuss later, it is likely that these differences contributed substantially to the development of the theory. Greg grew up in the suburbs of Southern California, and had arrived at Yale with an undergraduate degree in sociology from the University of California at Irvine and a year of graduate work in the Industrial

Relations program at Purdue University. He had held a number of summer jobs including service station attendant, cabinet assembler, and meat packer. These jobs ranged in motivating potential from repetitive, machine-paced work to relatively complex assembly jobs that permitted the completion of an entire piece of work from beginning to end.

Although those jobs had exposed Greg to the importance of the work itself, his interests in graduate school had nothing to do with job design. He had read early work in that area by authors such as Herzberg (1966) and Blauner (1964), but his background in sociology at Irvine and his coursework in organizational behavior at Purdue and Yale had sparked an interest in research and writing about leadership and about the social context of organizations. He found these topics much more stimulating than anything he had read about either motivation or job design.

Richard grew up in a very small town in central Illinois. He earned his undergraduate degree in mathematics from MacMurray College and a doctorate in social psychology from the University of Illinois at Urbana-Champaign. His limited work experience included some jobs that he found quite engaging (such as being custodian of his local Methodist church, running a service station for a small-town oil distributor, and serving as acting Director of Public Relations at his undergraduate college) and others that he did not (e.g., working on a state road crew, and refinishing furniture for the oil distributor when the service station closed). That these two sets of jobs differed radically on the job characteristics that turned out to be central to our model entirely escaped his notice.

In his application essay for graduate school, Richard said he intended to study the effects of mass communications on social attitudes—a topic he promptly and permanently forgot about once he began work as a research assistant in Fred Fiedler's Group Effectiveness Research Laboratory. Being in groups had always been discomfiting to Richard, and studying them, first with Fred and subsequently with Joe McGrath, appeared to offer an opportunity to understand why. But it was the power of group *tasks* that caught Richard's interest, initially in his master's thesis, which showed unexpectedly strong task effects on group products (Hackman, Jones, and McGrath, 1967), and subsequently in his dissertation. The dissertation research, conducted jointly with Tony Morris (it was the first and may still be the only joint dissertation in psychology ever done at the University of Illinois), affirmed that group task characteristics powerfully affect both group process (Morris, 1966) and group performance (Hackman, 1968).

When Richard joined the Yale faculty, he had no knowledge about organizational behavior (he had taken but a single seminar at Illinois on the topic and found it both uninteresting and uninformative) and no experience whatever in field research. So when his new colleague Ed Lawler suggested that it might be a good idea to see if task attributes made as big a difference in organizations as they did in the experimental laboratory, he jumped at the chance. Although the study Richard and Ed carried out at a local telephone company was exclusively about individual rather than team tasks (Hackman and Lawler, 1971), it sparked a line of research that took on a life of its own—and that, a couple of years later, provided the opportunity for a research collaboration with Greg.

8.2.2 Robust Relationship

Scholars interested in teams that produce creative work have long noted the importance of differences in members' backgrounds and work styles (Milliken, Bartel, and Kurtzberg, 2003), a conclusion that is entirely consistent with our attempt to develop an original model of how job characteristics affect people and performance. Our work was greatly facilitated by the fact that our intellectual backgrounds and previous experiences, as well as our characteristic work styles, were so different. Richard was much more knowledgeable than Greg about psychological theory and research methodology, and tended to be something of a conceptual optimist: Any roadblock we encountered in our conceptual work, he felt, could either be solved or circumvented. Greg was more familiar with the organizational behavior literature, more sensitive to the role of extra-organizational contexts (to such an extent that Richard once announced to a group of colleagues that there was a sociologist in our midst), and tended to be the conceptual critic: No proposition we developed was ever clear enough or convincing enough to completely satisfy him.

Yet, our differences were not so large or deeply ingrained that we had trouble understanding and building on one another's ideas. And we had good chemistry, both intellectually and personally. That chemistry made it possible for us to actively exchange, critique, and modify ideas as they emerged and evolved—activities that are critical steps in any creative process. Because our relationship was solid, we were completely comfortable disagreeing with one another and critiquing one another's ideas in meetings when discussing features of the model we were developing. We never held back out of worry that a comment might offend or damage the other; indeed, our exchanges often were as heated as they were productive. The climate of our working meetings, then, were psychologically safe for both of us—and psychological safety has turned out to be key to learning in interpersonal settings because it provides the latitude to experiment and make the mistakes that learning requires (Edmondson, 1999).

Our psychologically safe climate was entwined with, and actually may have developed from, the personal relationship we began to establish soon after Greg arrived at Yale. We had few times more enjoyable than those we spent in Richard's boat on Lake Lillinonah—purportedly fishing, but more importantly just getting to know one another, discussing ideas, and becoming comfortable with each other's perspectives and styles. One of the things we learned in these discussions was that initially neither of us had much interest in job design, or much knowledge about the topic. Perversely, that also may have facilitated our theory development activities because it ensured that we were at essentially no risk of being trapped or constrained by preexisting and generally accepted ways of thinking about the design of work in organizations.

By the end of 1971, even though we still had not yet collaborated on a research project, we were ready—both intellectually and interpersonally—to do something in the area of job design. What was needed was something to kick us into gear.

8.2.3 External Impetus

Scholars of creativity have shown that identification of a problem or an opportunity is the first step in the creative process (the others being gathering information or resources, generating ideas, and evaluating, modifying, and communicating ideas) (Amabile, 1996; Stein, 1967). That opportunity came when Bob Janson and Ken Purdy, from the Roy Walters and Associates consulting firm, showed up at Yale a few weeks after Greg's confrontation of Richard about the fact that we had done no collaborative research.

Specifically, Bob and Ken were interested in the effects of job enrichment interventions on employees' performance and satisfaction. Our initial discussions with them were extremely engaging and informative, and led to a series of meetings at which we explored possible avenues for cross-organization collaboration. They had special interest in two topics: (1) linking the "implementing concepts" that their firm had developed and were using in job enrichment consultations to our emerging job characteristics model and (2) developing a theory-based instrument that could be used both to diagnose existing jobs and to assess the effects of job redesign interventions. We found both possibilities intriguing. Our preliminary thinking about work design, prompted by the Hackman–Lawler study of the motivational properties of jobs, had viewed jobs essentially as static entities, and our thinking was greatly enriched by our discussions with Bob and Ken about strategies for actually changing jobs in ways that enhanced both performance motivation and employee satisfaction. Moreover, we would need some kind of instrument for assessing theory-specified concepts if we were to empirically test our ideas in the field.

Our meetings with Bob and Ken were enormously helpful both in clarifying our thinking about job characteristics and work redesign, and in providing us the opportunity to test our ideas on smart consultants whose daily work and main business was redesigning jobs. Bob and Ken also offered us the opportunity to refine our diagnostic instrument and empirically assess our model at their clients' organizations. Moreover, they offered to pay all research expenses, to help us recruit as many organizations and research participants as we required, and to ensure that we could obtain all available information about employees' job behaviors from organizational records and supervisory staff. We realized that the arrangement Bob and Ken suggested was an incredible research opportunity, and we jumped at the chance to work with them.

Any relationship between scholars and consultants is almost certain to generate tensions, because the two groups operate in different worlds that have different values. Our quartet was no exception. Commercial considerations, for example, were of little interest to us but central to Bob and Ken's motivation for working with us. When it came time to name the diagnostic instrument we had developed, we first proposed the "Yale Job Inventory." Both Bob and Ken had a very favorable reaction to this name. They explained that having the word "Yale" in the title would help a great deal in marketing both the instrument and their services—a view that made sense to us but not to university officials with whom we checked. So the instrument was renamed the "Job Diagnostic Survey," which pleased us and which Bob and Ken at least could accept.

Another tension had to do with rights to publish the results of research we conducted with our instrument in their client organizations. Following standard practice, we agreed to give Bob, Ken, or their designated associates the opportunity to comment on a draft of any article that was based on data from their clients, but we insisted that we have full autonomy in deciding whether, where, and what to publish. This arrangement generally worked quite well until Richard and master's student Linda Frank [now Rodman] published an article unfortunately titled "A failure of job enrichment: The case of the change that wasn't" (Frank and Hackman, 1975), which showed that job enrichment sometimes can appear to fail simply because the intervention did not generate much change in the actual structure of the target jobs. Our failure to thoroughly vet this article, including the title, with Bob and Ken resulted in a crisis so severe that it threatened the foundations of our relationship with them.

We all survived that and other small crises, and our relationship with Bob, Ken, and their colleagues at the Roy Walters firm continued to be productive for many years—indeed, into the 1980s when our own evolving research interests and activities gradually took us in new directions. We learned as much from Bob and Ken as with even the most stimulating of our scholarly colleagues—and, in retrospect, we realize that absent our engagement with them it is quite unlikely that we ever would have become involved in field research on job design.

8.2.4 Supportive Context

Although some accounts of conceptual advances depict a scholar working all alone and, eventually, coming up with a wholly original understanding of some phenomenon, our experience was nearly the opposite. The Department of

Administrative Sciences at Yale in the 1970s was something of a hotbed of intellectual activity and exchange, with organizational behavior scholars such as Clay Alderfer, Chris Argyris, Tim Hall, Ed Lawler, Ben Schneider, and several other colleagues providing a level of stimulation and support for our thinking that neither of us had experienced before and have not experienced since. There was always someone around with whom to try out an idea and who, as often as not, came up with a perspective or possibility that we had not even considered. Had we been working anywhere else, our job characteristics model might never have been completed—and if it had been, it certainly would have turned out to be far less robust and provocative of empirical research.

Partly at the urging of our colleagues, we finally got serious about studying relevant research literatures. Our point of departure, of course, was the recently published study of the motivational properties of jobs by Richard and Ed Lawler (Hackman and Lawler, 1971) which, in turn, was based on Lawler's highly original use of the expectancy theory of work motivation to explain why some jobs are inherently more motivating than others (Lawler, 1969). We also gained much by studying the classic literature in work psychology and organizational behavior, especially books by Walker and Guest (1952), Blauner (1964), Argyris (1964), and Turner and Lawrence (1965). Once we had talked extensively with our Yale colleagues and done our homework with the existing research literature, our emerging model seemed a bit less fresh and original than we had thought it to be—a sentiment nicely captured by psychologist Don Dulany in introducing a new theory of his own: "Suffice it to say that I have borrowed along the way, and the occasional sense of originality has faded on a little better scholarship" (Dulany, 1968: 342).

8.2.5 Endless Iteration

We suspect that no theory, and certainly not ours, emerges all at once in a flash of insight. Instead, theory development can seem as if it is an endless iterative process, moving back and forth between choice of variables and specification of the links among them, hoping that eventually the small, grudgingly achieved advances will outnumber the forced retreats. In the paragraphs that follow, we discuss some of the choices that most occupied us as we developed Job Characteristics Theory. We discuss them in an orderly, organized fashion, beginning with outcome variables, and then moving, in turn, through the mediating psychological states, the core job characteristics, and the individual difference moderator. That is not how it actually happened. Instead, the process of crafting the theory involved cyclic movement among the several sets of variables until a reasonably simple and internally coherent model gradually began to emerge from the chaos of too many variables and too many links among them.

8.2.5.1 *Outcome Variables*

Our reading of the research literature on the consequences of work (e.g., Blauner, 1964; Walker and Guest, 1952) suggested that how work is designed could have consequences both for the affective well-being of jobholders and their likelihood of withdrawal from the workplace. So we included satisfaction, absenteeism, and turnover as outcomes of interest in the initial model. Hackman and Lawler (1971) also had assessed internal motivation and found the concept to be quite useful in interpreting their findings about job effects. So we included the concept in our model, although we did not give it as central a role as we would if we were revising the model today.

8.2.5.2 *Psychological States*

We drew upon cognitive motivation theory, as well as the writings of Chris Argyris, Ed Lawler, and Lyman Porter in identifying the psychological states that, when present, increase the likelihood of favorable outcomes (Argyris, 1964; Lawler, 1969; Porter and Lawler, 1968). Experienced Meaningfulness, Experienced Responsibility, and Knowledge of Results were not new discoveries by any stretch of the imagination, but they had not yet been systematically assessed in empirical research, nor had it been shown that all three were necessary to produce favorable outcomes. We sought to redress these oversights.

8.2.5.3 *Core Job Characteristics*

Earlier research by Turner and Lawrence (1965) and Hackman and Lawler (1971) suggested that four job characteristics—autonomy, variety, identity, and feedback—were likely to foster several favorable outcomes, including attendance, satisfaction, and work performance. Since it was obvious that these job attributes should be included in the model, our conceptual task was to explicate the connections between them and the psychological states. Most of this was straightforward—Feedback certainly was likely to have its strongest effect on Knowledge of Results, and Autonomy should engender Experienced Responsibility. Moreover, conceptual arguments by Argyris (1964) and Hackman and Lawler (1971) suggested that Task Identity and Variety were likely to contribute directly to Experienced Meaningfulness. But Greg's work experience suggested that there might be yet another contributor to meaningfulness. He recalled that he experienced meaningfulness even when working on an assembly line job because he knew that if he failed to complete his part of the work process others down the line would be adversely affected. We generalized from Greg's experience to develop the concept of Task Significance, which was posited as a third route to Experienced Meaningfulness.

8.2.5.4 *Individual Differences*

Previous research suggested that enriched jobs are far more engaging to some people than to others (e.g., Hackman and Lawler, 1971; Hulin and Blood, 1968; Turner and Lawrence, 1965). For example, some researchers (including Hulin and Blood, and Turner and Lawrence) argued that only individuals with certain cultural backgrounds (i.e., employees from organizations located in small towns) would respond positively to a job that had a high standing on the core job characteristics. But Hackman and Lawler had suggested that individuals' need states might be a more appropriate way to capture this phenomenon, since cultural background assumed greater homogeneity of employee characteristics than might typically be the case. That observation, coupled with work by Alderfer (1972) on human needs, led us to conclude that it would be preferable to focus on differences in individual needs rather than cultural background. Specifically, we posited that individuals with strong needs for growth and development at work would be more likely to value the opportunities for personal accomplishment provided by jobs high in motivating potential, and respond most positively when those opportunities were present—a position consistent with the expectancy theory of motivation as articulated by Vroom (1964). So, we opted for the concept of Growth Need Strength as an individual difference moderator of the impact of the core job characteristics.

8.2.5.5 *Subsequent Developments*

We continued to revise and refine the model during the period between when we initially published it (Hackman and Oldham, 1975, 1976) and the completion of our book on work redesign (Hackman and Oldham, 1980). The most substantial change was a greater emphasis on Internal Work Motivation as the pivotal outcome variable in the model. That prompted us to incorporate two additional moderating variables—knowledge and skill, and context satisfaction—into the model, and to reduce the centrality in the model of absenteeism and turnover as outcomes of well-designed work.

Internally motivated employees feel good when they perform well and feel bad when they perform poorly. Jobholders who have ample talent and skill, therefore, will predominantly experience positive affect, and those who do not will experience negative affect, as they work. The model, we concluded, should take explicit account of that reality. Greg proposed the addition of context satisfaction after he visited an organization to discuss with managers and employees the possibility of conducting a work-redesign intervention. Employees told him that they might indeed be interested in having their jobs redesigned, but only after several problems with the work context—such as over-controlling supervisors and an unsatisfactory compensation system—were addressed. Greg realized that the model ignored properties of the organizational context that could significantly moderate how jobholders reacted to their work. After we empirically documented that context satisfaction does moderate the impact of work design on employee reactions (Oldham, 1976; Oldham, Hackman, and Pearce, 1976), we incorporated it into the final version of the model presented in the *Work Redesign* book.

8.3 IMPACT OF THE THEORY

8.3.1 Early Success

Once published, Job Characteristics Theory attracted a great deal of attention. Our supply of reprints was quickly exhausted, and we received a seemingly never-ending stream of requests for copies of the Job Diagnostic Survey from colleagues who wished to test or apply the model. The instrument has been adapted for use with several special populations, such as students and teachers, and it has been translated into numerous foreign languages. By the mid-1980s, all or portions of the theory had been tested in more than 200 empirical investigations (Fried and Ferris, 1987), and there have been many more tests in the years since then. Citation Classics reported that our three main publications about the model and the instrument (Hackman and Oldham, 1975, 1976, 1980) were among the most frequently cited publications in the entire field of organizational behavior. Even today, the model continues to be prominently discussed in textbooks on organizational behavior, industrial/organizational psychology, and management.

Why did the model catch on so quickly, become so prominent, and have the scholarly equivalent of a long shelf life? We suggest four reasons.

1. The phenomenon addressed by the model–that is, the effects of work on people and performance–is important. Almost all adults perform work of some kind, and are powerfully affected by their work experiences. Moreover, the decisions managers make about how work is structured is consequential not just for those who perform it but also for organizational outcomes.

2. The model makes sense to people. Readers of our *Work Redesign* book repeatedly have told us that what we say fits well both with their own organizational experiences and with how they construe the world of work. Such reactions are, for us, as worrisome as they are reassuring: Did we somehow wind up generating a model that became popular merely because it compactly captures everyday experiences? Did we miss the opportunity to develop a more subtle and original way of understanding work that would have required people to fundamentally reframe how they construe the impact of work on those who perform it? Even three decades later these questions nag at us.

3. The model is readily testable and applicable. One does not have to do much conceptual work to use the model either in empirical research or in practical applications. Although the model is sufficiently complex that it defies test or application in a single step, its many specific propositions are quite straight-forward and relatively easy to test or apply. It is, therefore, attractive both to scholars who are looking for a ready-made research question and to practi-tioners who seek guidance about how a job might be better designed. Many doctoral students, in particular, have found Job Characteristics Theory to be an inviting topic for their dissertation research. And several consulting firms—not just Roy Walters and Associates—have drawn heavily on the model in working with clients who are experiencing problems with employee motivation or performance. Indeed, one consultant made a few minor modifications of the model and the accompanying diagnostic instrument, copyrighted his revision, and then published it as entirely his own—thereby providing perverse but compelling testimony to the model's attractiveness and seeming usefulness.

4. We provided an instrument, the Job Diagnostic Survey (JDS), that directly measures jobholders' perceptions of the work and their reactions to it. There is, we suspect, no more efficient way to garner many citations in the literature than to publish an instrument that others can adopt or adapt for their own purposes. The popularity of the JDS has been gratifying to us, but also has prompted serious concerns about the thoughtlessness with which the instru-ment sometimes has been used. Especially worrisome to us are what we call "no variance" studies that purport to test Job Characteristics Theory. That is, the JDS is administered to some large but homogeneous group of employees who are performing essentially the same job (think of 100 clerks in the back room of an insurance company, all of whom perform the same job of review-ing claim forms for accuracy and completeness). Then correlations are com-puted to see if there is support for various model-specified propositions. The problem, of course, is that proper test of those propositions requires that there be *variance* both in the job characteristics studied and in the talents, needs, or context satisfaction of jobholders—an essential condition that is not met in far too many of the research uses the JDS. The easy availability of a ready-made research instrument brings many advantages, such as the possibility of accu-mulating a solid body of normative data. But it also can invite uses of the instrument that are more expedient than thoughtful.

8.3.2 Controversy Later

When it became clear that Job Characteristics Theory was becoming popular, Richard issued a warning to Greg. "Let me tell you what is going to happen," he said. "We're going to enjoy a good deal of acclaim for a while. But then the backlash is sure to come. Everything about our model is going to be questioned, and we're going to take some major hits." And that is just what happened, in both the applied and the scholarly domains.

Although, as noted, many consultants and managers embraced Job Characteristics Theory and used it in their work, practitioner acceptance was far from universal. Those whose practices relied on Fred Herzberg's well-known two-factor model of work motivation (Herzberg, 1966) were especially skeptical of a new model that implicitly called into question orthodox job enrichment theory. Even Herzberg himself took us on, most pointedly in a letter to his friend and colleague Roy Walters, the founder of the consulting firm with which we had collaborated in developing our model. Roy had sent Herzberg a copy of the paper "A New Strategy for Job Enrichment," co-authored with our collaborators from his firm (Hackman, et al., 1975). Herzberg responded in a letter to Roy that reads, in part, as follows:

> at this stage of the game in the field, I don't believe you can afford third rate theorizing in such a blatant, self-serving paper. I think you can now afford to go first class and forget this kind of stuff. I agree that there is always a market at the fourth echelon but you are better than that. Some major reports are forthcoming and I hate to see this type of paper listed in your credentials with the five and dime people that have entered into a very serious area...

The five and dime people to which Herzberg referred, lest there be any question, were Richard and Greg.

The opening salvo on the scholarly side was fired by Gerry Salancik and Jeff Pfeffer in an important and influential *Administrative Science Quarterly* article critiquing theories, including our own, that give a prominent role to human needs (Salancik and Pfeffer, 1978). Other critiques soon followed, especially regarding three aspects of our model: (1) the degree to which job perceptions may be more powerfully shaped by social cues than any "objective" properties of the work itself, (2) the role of individual differences in moderating reactions to work, and (3) the shaky psychometric status of our summary Motivating Potential Score.

8.3.2.1 *Job Perceptions*

In developing the model, we gave considerable attention to the objectivity of job characteristics, a significant worry given that the JDS relied on employee descriptions of job attributes. Although we believed at the time that people were able to provide generally accurate assessments of the properties of their jobs, we also recognized that we needed to demonstrate this empirically by assessing the degree to which employee reports converged with assessments made by external observers. We developed the Job Rating Form (JRF) specifically to allow test of our assumption about the accuracy of jobholder reports. Once we found that JDS and JRF assessments were, in fact, reasonably well correlated, we felt comfortable continuing to rely on the JDS for our measures of job characteristics.

That was a mistake, and one that prompted Richard to give some decidedly poor advice to Jone Pearce, then a doctoral student at Yale. Jone thought it might be interesting and informative to systematically study the relation between objective job properties and jobholders' perceptions of those properties. "That's not really necessary," Richard responded. "We've already shown that there is a strong relation between objective properties and employee perceptions." Shortly thereafter, numerous studies appeared in the literature assessing precisely that relation, unfortunately not including work by Jone, who had been dissuaded from proceeding by Richard's poor advice.

Many of the studies of job perceptions that were conducted had the character of horse races, in that our position (that objective job properties matter most) was put in competition with that of Salancik and Pfeffer (that social cues matter more). Predictably, scholars who were *a priori* sympathetic to us tended to find support for our position, whereas those who were more attuned to our critics tended to find support for theirs. Research horse races never can be definitively won, although we do believe that two studies are particularly informative—one by Griffin (1983) that included data both from the field and from the experimental laboratory and that provides a reasonably convincing demonstration of relative power of objective and social influences on job perceptions under varying conditions, and another by Weiss and Shaw (1979) that shows how different individuals are differentially responsive to objective properties and social cues.

8.3.2.2 *Individual Differences*

Questions about the role of the individual difference moderators in Job Characteristics Theory, on the other hand, remain unresolved—and probably will continue to be for a seemingly mundane practical reason. As noted earlier, properly testing how individual differences moderate reactions to job characteristics requires that there be ample variance in both sets of variables. But the realities of organizational life make it nearly impossible to meet that condition. There tends to be considerable homogeneity among the people who hold any given job, because of attraction and selection processes certainly, but also because job experiences gradually but inexorably shape both jobholders' needs and their capabilities. Only if one could randomly assign people from a heterogeneous population to jobs that vary widely in motivating potential would it be possible to definitively assess the robustness of the individual difference moderators posited by the model—and that, clearly, is a practical impossibility. Moreover, our 1980 version of Job Characteristics Theory specifies that Growth Need Strength, Context Satisfaction, and Knowledge and Skill *all* should be present if high motivating potential jobs are to have positive effects. No study has simultaneously considered these three moderators, which also may help account for the inconsistent results obtained for the individual difference moderators in the model (Oldham, 1996).

8.3.2.3 *Motivating Potential*

Empirical findings clearly show that our summary indicator of the motivational properties of jobs—the Motivating Potential Score (MPS)—is *not* more predictive of outcomes than a simpler index computed by merely adding up scores on the five core job characteristics (Fried and Ferris, 1987). We blush as we acknowledge this, because Richard's graduate school minor was psychological measurement and he, therefore, should have known that the psychometric properties of the JDS do not allow for the multiplication of variables specified in the formula for the MPS score. MPS does indeed make conceptual sense, but it is a psychometric disaster.

8.3.3 Theories (and Instruments) Never Die

It has been three decades since we published our first paper on Job Characteristics Theory, and nearly every week we still receive letters, phone calls, and e-mails asking about the latest research on the model, requesting reprints that are no longer available, and seeking permission and technical advice about the use of the Job Diagnostic Survey. It is a bit awkward to have to acknowledge that we really do not know much about what is going on with the theory these days. In fact, Richard stopped his research on issues related to our theory in 1980, as soon as the *Work Redesign* book was published, and returned to his first love—the study of small groups. Greg lasted a little longer, but once he had satisfied himself that he had a good enough understanding of contextual factors that affect work design, he too moved on to other interests (e.g., the effects of personal and contextual conditions on employee creativity).

Yet, even now, we continue to be reasonably well pleased with the model we developed, as well as with all the lessons we learned from each other and from our academic colleagues and students during the time that we were developing and testing it. For all its flaws, the theory did stimulate the thinking of others and prompt a great deal of research that turned out to help clarify how the design of work shapes both personal and organizational outcomes. And we would be disingenuous to claim that we did not enjoy the recognition that we received from having developed the theory, or that we do not appreciate the opportunities the theory provided for us to conduct field research even on topics quite remote from work redesign.

Two things can go wrong when you develop a theory. One, nobody notices. Two, everybody notices and you never get free of it. Of the two, the latter clearly is the more agreeable, and we would not have had it any other way.

REFERENCES

ALDERFER, C. P. (1972). *Existence, Relatedness, and Growth.* New York: Free Press.

AMABILE, T. M. (1996). *Creativity in Context.* Boulder, Colo.: Westview.

ARGYRIS, C. (1964). *Integrating the Individual and the Organization.* New York: Wiley.

BLAUNER, R. (1964). *Alienation and Freedom.* Chicago: University of Chicago Press.

DULANY, D. E. (1968). Awareness, rules, and propositional control: A confrontation with S-R behavior theory. In T. Dixon and D. Horton (eds.), *Verbal Behavior and General Behavior Theory:* 340–387. Englewood Cliffs, NJ: Prentice-Hall.

EDMONDSON, A. C. (1999). Psychological safety and learning behavior in work teams. *Administrative Science Quarterly,* 44: 350–383.

FRANK, L. L., and HACKMAN, J. R. (1975). A failure of job enrichment: The case of the change that wasn't. *Journal of Applied Behavioral Science,* 11: 413–436.

FRIED, Y., and FERRIS, G. R. (1987). The validity of the job characteristics model: A review and meta-analysis. *Personnel Psychology,* 40: 287–322.

GRIFFIN, R. W. (1983). Objective and social sources of information in task redesign: A field experiment. *Administrative Science Quarterly,* 28: 184–200.

HACKMAN, J. R. (1968). Effects of task characteristics on group products. *Journal of Experimental Social Psychology,* 4: 162–187.

—— JONES, L. E., and MCGRATH, J. E. (1967). A set of dimensions for describing the general properties of group-generated written passages. *Psychological Bulletin,* 67: 379–390.

—— and LAWLER, E. E. (1971). Employee reactions to job characteristics. *Journal of Applied Psychology,* 55: 259–286.

—— and OLDHAM, G. R. (1975). Development of the Job Diagnostic Survey. *Journal of Applied Psychology,* 60: 159–170.

—— —— (1976). Motivation through the design of work: Test of a theory. *Organizational Behavior and Human Performance,* 16: 250–279.

—— —— (1980). *Work Redesign.* Reading, Mass.: Addison-Wesley.

—— —— JANSON, R., and PURDY, K. (1975). A new strategy for job enrichment. *California Management Review,* 17: 57–71.

HERZBERG, F. (1966). *Work and the Nature of Man.* Cleveland: World Publishing.

HULIN, C. L., and BLOOD, M. R. (1968). Job enlargement, individual differences, and worker responses. *Psychological Bulletin,* 69: 41–55.

LAWLER, E. E. (1969). Job design and employee motivation. *Personnel Psychology,* 22: 426–435.

MILLIKEN, F. J., BARTEL, C. A., and KURTZBERG, T. (2003). Diversity and creativity in work groups: A dynamic perspective on the affective and cognitive processes that link diversity and performance. In P. Paulus and B. Nijstad (eds.), *Group Creativity:* 32–62. New York: Oxford University Press.

MORRIS, C. G. (1966). Task effects on group interaction. *Journal of Personality and Social Psychology,* 4: 545–554.

OLDHAM, G. R. (1976). Job characteristics and internal motivation: The moderating effects of interpersonal and individual variables. *Human Relations,* 29: 559–569.

—— (1996). Job design. In C. Cooper and I. Robertson (eds.), *International Review of Industrial and Organizational Psychology:* 11. 33–60. New York: Wiley.

OLDHAM, G. R., HACKMAN, J. R., and PEARCE, J. L. (1976). Conditions under which employees respond positively to enriched work. *Journal of Applied Psychology*, 61: 395–403.

PORTER, L. W., and LAWLER, E. E. (1968). *Managerial Attitudes and Performance*. Homewood, Ill.: Irwin.

SALANCIK, G. R., and PFEFFER, J. (1978). An examination of need-satisfaction models of job attitudes. *Administrative Science Quarterly*, 22: 427–456.

STEIN, M. I. (1967). Creativity and culture. In R. Mooney and T. Razik (eds.), *Explorations in Creativity*: 109–119. New York: Harper.

TURNER, A. N., and LAWRENCE, P. R. (1965). *Industrial Jobs and the Worker*. Boston: Harvard Graduate School of Business Administration.

VROOM, V. (1964). *Work and Motivation*. New York: Wiley.

WALKER, C. R., and GUEST, C. H. (1952). *The Man on the Assembly Line*. Cambridge, Mass.: Harvard University Press.

WEISS, H. M., and SHAW, J. B. (1979). Social influences on judgments about tasks. *Organizational Behavior and Human Performance*. 24: 126–140.

....

CHAPTER 9

DO EMPLOYEE ATTITUDES TOWARDS ORGANIZATIONS MATTER?

THE STUDY OF EMPLOYEE COMMITMENT TO ORGANIZATIONS

....

LYMAN W. PORTER

RICHARD M. STEERS

RICHARD T. MOWDAY

9.1 INTRODUCTION

....

THE late 1960s and early 1970s in the United States were both turbulent and tranquil. Campus unrest over the war in Vietnam and civil rights wreaked havoc across many college campuses as students, and sometimes faculty, picketed, struck, and otherwise protested situations that they thought were both unjust and unfair. Occasionally, the demonstrations turned violent and at its peak collective action was sufficiently strong and vocal to bring down a sitting U.S. president. At the same time, however, most major U.S. companies remained bastions of relative tranquility as blue- and white-collar employees went to work every day and worked hard for a better life. The "organization man" described in William H. Whyte's classic 1952 book of the same name was alive and well. Managers (almost exclusively male) wore business suits and downsizing was not yet on the corporate radar screen. People typically worked for one company throughout their career and retired at age 65. While college campuses may have been in crisis, everything was "normal" in Corporate America.

These two contrasting pictures, one of strife and turmoil and one of stability and tranquility, puzzled many social observers of the time. Exactly what was going on here? Why were some employees, be they university professors or corporate managers, highly committed to their organizations, while others were indifferent or even antagonistic? What caused some employees to form emotional bonds and strategic attachments to their organizations, while others quit as soon as they had a chance? And throughout it all, how could organizations entice their best employees to remain with them for the duration? These issues intrigued social scientists of the time because they forced organizations—and to some extent societies—to grapple with fundamental questions about the legitimate role of employees in work organizations. Scholars began asking questions about the nature of employee commitment to organizations, as well as how commitment developed or failed to develop over time. How did employers and employees define their mutual dependencies and how did they negotiate and implement psychological contracts? From a research standpoint, the search was on for what became known as the causes and consequences of organizational commitment.

9.2 EARLY RESEARCH ON ORGANIZATIONAL COMMITMENT

If contemporary researchers stepped back to the late 1960s and reviewed the scholarly literature on the topic of organizational commitment at the time, they would find very little guidance. While there was some literature on this topic, it was certainly not abundant. Indeed, there were fewer than a dozen solid pieces of research (Becker, 1960; Brown, 1969; Etzioni, 1961; A. W. Gouldner, 1958; H. P. Gouldner, 1960; Grusky, 1966; Kanter, 1968). While much of this research was excellent, virtually all of it took the macro (i.e., group or societal) perspective of the sociologists who generated it. There was no systematic input from social or industrial-organizational psychologists focusing on the micro (or individual) level of analysis.

Clearly, one of the major contributions of the time was Alvin Gouldner's distinction between "cosmopolitan" and "local" members of organizations. Drawing on previous work by Merton (1957), Gouldner (1958: 278) postulated that, "in addition to their manifest identities, members of formal organizations may have two latent social identities." Cosmopolitans were described as "low on loyalty to the employing organization, high on commitment to specialized role skills, and likely to use an outer reference group orientation," while locals were "high on loyalty to the employing organization, low on commitment to specialized role skills, and likely to use an inner reference group orientation" (1958: 290). This distinction seemed to resonate with social scientists of the time. One could easily think about faculty members who were so strongly identified with their academic specialty on a national or international level that they had little time or interest in the local challenges facing their home universities, while other faculty members exhibited precisely the opposite pattern of behavior. Likewise, one could see many corporate employees who seemed so bound up with their own particular organization that they appeared to give little attention to their own status or recognition in their external professional or specialty areas; their total focus seemed to be on loyally supporting their company. Yet, there were other corporate members who showed a stronger outward than inward orientation, caring more for their professional associations than their particular employer.

It is important to point out that one issue that was largely neglected in the formulation of the cosmopolitan–local dichotomy was whether these two types represented opposite ends of a single dimension or constituted relatively independent dimensions. In other words, if an employee is strongly cosmopolitan (in Gouldner's terminology), could that person also be strongly local? Or, does being strongly cosmopolitan mean that by definition one could not also be local? Gouldner (1958: 291) obviously felt that the two dimensions were polar opposites, arguing that "loyalty to the organization often implies . . . (1) a willingness to limit or relinquish the commitment to a specialized professional task and (2) a dominant career orientation to the employing organization as a reference group." However, everyday observation of people in organizations suggests that some people are both highly visible cosmopolitans and influential locals. Others seem to be relatively indifferent to both the welfare of their own local organization and their outside reference groups. This suggests that a two-dimension formulation is viable, and that any given organization member can be a high-high, a low-low, a low-high, or a high-low. If this is correct, an individual could be committed both to his or her organization and to an external entity such as a profession. Being committed to one does not necessarily exclude the other.

The other signal contribution from this era came from Amatai Etzioni in his classic 1961 book, *A Comparative Analysis of Complex Organizations*. Etzioni presented a typology of patterns of member involvement in organizations that, in turn, are related to the kinds of power that organizations can wield to induce compliance with their directives. Three types of member involvement were identified: moral, calculative, and alienative. The first of these, moral involvement, refers to a strong, positive relationship with an organization in which an individual believes in and internalizes the values and objectives of the organization. With this type of involvement, organizations can utilize normative power and allocate symbolic rewards that are highly salient to members. By contrast, calculative involvement, as the name implies, involves a relationship based on an individual's rational decision to give something to the organization—work effort in the case of employing organizations—in return for some kind of specific reward from the organization, such as salary and benefits. This is a clear exchange type of relationship, which March and Simon (1958) called an inducements–contributions approach. The organization exercises power by granting or withholding various levels and types of remuneration. The more such remuneration is desired and obtained, the stronger and more positive will be the bond between the member and the organization. The third type of involvement, alienative, exists where a member has a negative attitude toward the organization, often exacerbated when he or she feels severely constrained by it. A good example here is correctional institutions, where physical restraints substitute for goal internalization or reciprocity. The type of power exercised by the organization in this set of circumstances is that of coercion and force.

The critical elements of Etzioni's typology from the standpoint of organizational commitment comes from the first two types of involvement he identified—normative and calculative. These two types are relevant to the modern world of work and are often found in organizations, whether they are industrial, commercial, governmental, or educational. These types of involvement are not only common, but they can also exist independently of each other. That is, even though most organizations rely to some form on calculative involvement and the exchange of inducements for contributions, many of these same organizations also try to promote normative involvement. Thus, following Etzioni, it is possible to consider organizational commitment (involvement, in his terms) as composed of separable elements, normative and calculative. Indeed, both Meyer and Allen (1997) and Cappelli (1999) built upon Etzioni's basic concept in their recent research on commitment in the workplace. Finally, in addition to his basic typology, Etzioni also contributed to our thinking about commitment by emphasizing the degree or intensity of each type of involvement. Etzioni stressed that the degree or amount of each type of involvement matters. That is, in one organization, normative commitment can be low, intermediate and high, and so too can be calculative involvement. From this follow a series of predictions about behavior at work.

9.2.1 UCI Individual–Organization Linkages Project

Beginning in the late 1960s, a small group of researchers at the University of California, Irvine, determined to explore this topic further. The effort, headed by Lyman W. Porter and Robert Dubin, was called the "Individual–Organization Linkages" project and was funded by a series of research grants from the U.S. Office of Naval Research. A number of graduate students joined the project, including John Van Maanen, Joseph Champoux, William Crampon, Richard Steers, Richard Mowday, and Harold Angle. Work continued over a ten-year period.

While the early work of Gouldner and Etzioni clearly influenced our initial thinking about the nature of organizational commitment, we chose to approach the topic from a more psychological orientation. At the time, psychologists were focusing their research attention on job satisfaction and job involvement, ignoring organization-wide attitudes like commitment. In our view, the reason for this resulted from a decades-long emphasis in industrial-organizational psychology on individuals' reaction to jobs and on factors affecting job performance. The organization *per se* was not a principal object of research attention. Attitudes toward jobs had been extensively studied, but attitudes toward the organization had not. Thus, in our view, this was an under-researched area of psychology worthy of attention.

The combination of all of these factors—social turmoil during the 1960s, influential scholarship and theoretical paradigms in the field of sociology, and an absence of systematic research on employee attitudes toward their employer—motivated our own thinking and research addressed to the topic of organizational commitment.

9.2.2 Towards a Definition of Organizational Commitment

To initiate a systematic approach to studying organizational commitment, we first examined existing definitions in the literature and found a general lack of agreement on the topic. For example, Becker (1960: 32) defined commitment as the result of "a consistent line of activity," suggesting that "commitments come into being when a person, by making a side-bet, links extraneous interests with a consistent line of activity." H. P. Gouldner (1960: 469) focused on constraints in the commitment process, arguing that commitment "refers to those kinds of constraints which are generated by the actor's own motivation, orientation, and behaviors." A. W. Gouldner (1958: 290), though not directly defining organizational commitment, emphasized "loyalty to the organization" as a distinguishing characteristic of "local." Kanter (1968: 499) stressed voluntary actions by individuals; that is, "the willingness of social actors to give their energy and loyalty to social systems, the attachment of personality systems to social relations which are seen as self-expressive." Finally, Grusky (1966: 489) viewed commitment as "the nature of the relationship of the member to the system as a whole."

Clearly, there was a lack of consensus among scholars regarding what the term organizational commitment meant. As a result, we were faced with the task of developing our own definition, being guided by an analysis of the issues, as well as the array of existing definitions and the larger body of scholarly work on the topic. To build our definition, we chose to emphasize three key ideas: First, we focused on commitment *to the organization*, defining organization largely as a place of employment. Second, we were interested in commitment to the organization as an *attitude* held by members or employees. And third, we took the view that the intrinsic nature of commitment had to mean *something deeper and more intensive than simple passive loyalty* to an organization. Using these three stipulations as our conceptual foundation, we proceeded to develop a definition of organizational commitment as "the relative strength of an individual's identification with, and involvement in, a particular organization" (Mowday, Porter, and Steers, 1982: 27). We further postulated that organizational commitment is characterized by at least three factors: (*a*) a strong belief in and acceptance of the organization's goals and values; (*b*) a willingness to exert considerable effort on behalf of the organization; and (*c*) a strong desire to maintain membership in the organization (Porter, et al., 1974; Porter, Crampon and Smith, 1976; Mowday, et al., 1982; Steers, 1977). In essence, our definition emphasized an individual's "active relationship with the organization such that [they] are willing to give something of themselves in order to contribute to the organization's well-being" (Mowday, et al., 1982: 27).

Two aspects of this definition deserve additional comment. First, it is important to note that our definition was anchored in the attitudes of members or employees. It refers to what people want to do voluntarily, as well as what they choose to believe with regard to the organization, not necessarily what a person actually does or is compelled to do. In subsequent research by ourselves and others, this definition came to be labeled as "affective commitment," a term which emphasizes the feelings that a person has toward his or her organization. An attitudinal or affective approach to defining organizational commitment is obviously different from one based on behavior. For example, the fact that an individual leaves an organization tells us very little about whether he or she actually wanted to leave, only that he or she left. Similarly, seeing an individual exerting extra effort on behalf of the organization does not necessarily mean that he or she wanted to do this; rather, it could have been behavior that was compelled in some way. As we have noted elsewhere, "attitudinal commitment focuses on the process by which people come to think about their relationship with the organization... [whereas] behavioral commitment, on the other hand, relates to the process by which individuals become locked into a certain organization and how they deal with that problem" (Mowday, et al., 1982: 26).

Second, our definition does not preclude an individual from being committed to other social objects, such as a professional organization, a union, a political party, or a religious group. Multiple commitments are often a fact of organizational life in today's increasingly complex world of work.

9.2.3 Organizational Commitment Questionnaire

Defining a construct is only a first step in research. We must also have a way of measuring it and determining its relative strength in various situations. At the time we began our studies, we found no satisfactory measure of organizational commitment we deemed suitable for empirical study. Most existing measures consisted of ad hoc scales consisting of two, three, or four scale items with little or no supporting data on reliability and validity. Our goal was to develop an improved research instrument with the capacity to tap the three components of our definition, as well as provide an overall score for organizational commitment. Our intent was not to develop the definitive instrument, but rather to create a reasonably valid and easy-to-administer instrument that could be used in a number of different organizations among a wide variety of employees or members. As a result, a fifteen-item instrument called the Organizational Commitment Questionnaire (OCQ) was constructed and administered to diverse samples of employees in several studies conducted over the following decade.

Details on the psychometric properties of the OCQ and evidence on its convergent, discriminant, and predictive validity were published in both article and book form (Mowday, Steers, and Porter, 1979; Mowday, et al., 1982). Taken together, these studies indicated that the OCQ exhibits good internal and test–retest reliabilities, as well as reasonable patterns of correlations with other appropriate variables such as independent supervisor ratings of employees' commitment and voluntary employee turnover. Even so, developing the OCQ was not our end objective; rather, our intent was to use this instrument to explore the antecedents and consequences of organizational commitment.

9.2.4 Development of Organizational Commitment

We have always believed that "the commitment of employees to organizations is . . . best characterized as a process that unfolds over time" (Mowday, et al., 1982: 45). In the literature, two major conceptual approaches have been identified to explain the process by which commitment to organizations is developed. The first views commitment as an independent variable predicting various hypothesized job-related behaviors, such as reduced absenteeism or turnover (Mowday, et al., 1979; Steers, 1977). The second views commitment as a dependent variable representing a set of attitudes consistent with prior decisions to engage in freely chosen behaviors. Thus, a person might conclude that since he or she had chosen to take on some unpleasant tasks, he or she must be committed to the organization (Salancik, 1977). Thus, one approach posits an attitude-to-behavior sequence, and the other a behavior-to-attitude sequence. Rather than viewing these two approaches as mutually exclusive, our position was that attitudinal commitments, on the one hand, and behavioral commitments, on the other, are reciprocally related over time. Where the process begins—with attitudes or behaviors—is not as important as the probability, as we hypothesized, that the development of commitment involves the reciprocal interplay of attitudes and behaviors in repetitive cycles over time. We, thus, posited that each influences the other in recurring fashion.

9.2.4.1 *Anticipation Stage*

In our research, we proposed that the process of development of organizational commitment moved through three stages that we labeled anticipation, initiation, and entrenchment. The first of these stages, anticipation, refers to the pre-entry stage of employment with an organization. We proposed that in this stage there are at least three important sets of factors—personal characteristics, expectations about the organization, and situational circumstances surrounding the decision to join— that can interact to determine a given level of organizational commitment *before* the new member has even begun work. It is important to point out, however, that such commitment will not necessarily be high. These factors may combine to produce a medium or even decidedly low level of pre-commitment. The actual level will be determined by the specific nature and strength of each of the variables involved.

One set of factors that can influence the initial development of commitment at this pre-joining stage is the prospective member's personal characteristics in the form of values, beliefs, and personality characteristics. Some individuals are, in essence, "hard-wired" or predisposed to be committed to an employing organization by virtue of prior socialization and/or beliefs about the worth of organized activity and organizations in general. Another variable likely to have an impact on attitudinal commitment even before a person joins an organization is his or her expectations. Typically, an individual does not join a particular work organization without at least some prior knowledge and image about it, however ill informed these preconceptions may be. Such expectations about a particular organization can come about from a variety of sources, including the past use of the organization's products or services, information from media stories or advertisements, and communication with current or former employees. In other words, the specific organization to be joined is usually not a tabula rasa. As a result, views held by a member-to-be prior to joining can have an impact on how fast and how strong organizational commitment develops.

An additional possible influential variable in the anticipation phase is the set of situational circumstances surrounding an individual's decision to join a particular organization. If a new member has made an organizational choice that is voluntary, explicit, public, and perceived as difficult to change (at least in the short run), it would be assumed in line with cognitive dissonance theory that the person will be more likely to find reasons to justify their decision to join and, thus, more likely to express attitudinal commitment to the organization.

9.2.4.2 *Initiation Stage*

The proposed second stage of development of organizational commitment is the early employment period, or what we call the initiation stage. In contrast to the pre-entry or anticipation stage, a new organizational member will now start to have actual experiences rather than simply untested expectations as a significant source of attitudes about the organization. In fact, it is in this initiation stage where prior attitudes will confront reality. Since this is a period in which experiences are likely to be quite vivid for the entering employee, those events can be assumed to exert a powerful influence. The first time a new member encounters his or her supervisor, for example, is likely to have a much greater impact than the 35th or 135th time he or she interacts with that same supervisor.

Some of the more likely sources of influence on organizational commitment in this second stage include the nature of job activities and task assignments (especially the degree of felt responsibility of the work assignments—see Salancik, 1977), the immediate supervisor, the work group, and overall organizational policies and procedures. We hypothesize that the more salient or critical a particular source is for the individual, the greater its effect on organizational commitment. Thus, we would expect that job responsibilities and supervisor interactions would likely have more impact than the work group or general organizational policies and practices. Furthermore, we would expect that the more favorable a member's experiences in encountering each source, the more positive would be the impact on resulting commitment.

In addition to organizational sources of influence during this early encounter period, there could also be non-organizational factors that could affect a new member's commitment to the organization, including the attitudes of family members or other salient members of the individual's social role set. A spouse who is unhappy with the type of work the new member is doing on the job, for example, is not likely to cause an increase in that person's commitment to her or his organization. A different kind of external factor that could prove to be powerful during this period would be the existence of alternative job offers. The availability of attractive job alternatives outside the organization could serve to weaken organizational commitment, although employees who don't take advantage of attractive job alternatives may actually increase their commitment as a result of psychologically justifying their decision.

9.2.4.3 *Entrenchment Stage*

Following the stages of pre-entry and early employment, a member who has not left the organization tends to settle into an extended employment period that we have called entrenchment. It is a stage in which factors from the prior initiation stage can still be prominent, such as changing job duties, a new supervisor, revised organizational policies, and the like. However, this third stage of continuing tenure in the organization also brings into play factors not present in the preceding stage. In this regard, we note that there is a fairly consistent body of evidence that indicates that, on average, longer-tenure employees are more likely to express higher levels of commitment.

Why might this be the case? Several variables can be proposed as critical in the continued employment period. One is simply that a longer-term employee has a higher probability of engaging in job tasks of a more challenging and satisfying nature than do most new hires. Another factor is that a person who has maintained membership over time in an employing organization is likely to have made psychological investments—spent emotional capital—on behalf of the organization. Moreover, the longer a person remains in an organization the more likely he or she is to have significant invested social capital in building friendships and relationships. Still another factor is that of opportunity costs, in which the member may over time have sacrificed other job alternatives or potential attainments to continue with the organization and eventually comes to justify this by increasing her or his level of commitment.

Taken together, there are a number of possible variables that appear to have the effect of increasing organizational commitment with increasing length of tenure in the organization. However, as several researchers have noted, it is difficult to interpret the cause–effect form of the relationship—and, therefore, its practical significance—because other variables may co-vary with tenure. Nevertheless, the existence of such a relationship seems well established.

9.3 CONSEQUENCES OF ORGANIZATIONAL COMMITMENT: THEORY AND RESEARCH

In the preceding paragraphs, we reviewed our three-stage model of the development of organizational commitment across time beginning with the period before a person joins an organization and continuing when that individual is well along in organizational tenure. In so doing, we postulated a set of antecedents (e.g., personal characteristics, interactions with supervisor) that can operate in particular stages to either enhance or diminish its presence. However, for organizational commitment to be an important variable in the study of workplace behavior, it should also logically be associated with important consequences in that workplace, not just antecedents. In this regard, we view commitment as an intervening variable: certain factors cause organizational commitment, which, in turn, has consequences for workplace attitudes and behavior. Four possible consequences can be identified from both theory and research on commitment: job performance, employee turnover, employee absenteeism, and extra-role behavior. Each of these variables is discussed below.

In the years since the concept was first introduced to the field of management, organizational commitment has been extensively studied. Two major reviews of research on organizational commitment (Mathieu and Zajac, 1990; Meyer and Allen, 1997) allow some conclusions to be drawn concerning its important behavioral consequences. A more recent meta-analysis of research on organizational commitment (Meyer, et al., 2002) was limited to studies using Meyer and Allen's (1997) measure of affective commitment. The results of that review will be considered here because, as Meyer and Allen (1997) have noted, there is a high degree of conceptual overlap between their measure of affective attachment and the organizational commitment questionnaire discussed earlier. Even so, the quantitative results presented below were taken from the Mathieu and Zajac (1990) review because it largely focused on studies using the organizational commitment questionnaire.

9.3.1 Job Performance

In theory, it is possible that higher levels of organizational commitment would lead to higher job performance. However, as we have argued, a careful reading of the theory suggests that this relationship would typically be relatively weak. The potential impact of commitment on performance comes from the presumed effect that it could have on the voluntary level of effort that a person exerts in a job situation. A person with higher commitment levels might want to try to work harder on behalf of the organization, but since effort, albeit important, is only one determinant of job performance, commitment's effect on overall performance would likely be constrained. Other major determinants of performance, such as abilities and skills and one's training and education, are unlikely to be affected by organizational commitment. Hence, we would expect low but positive correlations between commitment and job performance. In this regard, commitment may be an energizer to job performance, but this alone does not guarantee actual follow-through.

If we look at the empirical research on this relationship, although a number of studies have reported positive and significant relationships between commitment and performance, a meta-analysis of these studies found that the mean weighted correlation corrected for attenuation between commitment and performance was $r_t = .135$ when performance was measured by supervisory ratings and $r_t = .054$ when performance was measured by output. This pattern of results was very similar to those reported by Meyer, et al. (2002), although they found that affective commitment was more strongly related to supervisory ratings of performance than self-ratings.

Mathieu and Zajac (1990: 184) concluded that, "the present findings suggest that commitment has relatively little direct influence on performance in most instances." The fact that this same meta-analysis found strong positive relationships between commitment and measures of overall and internal motivation ($r_t = .563$ and .668, respectively) suggests that the relationship between commitment and job performance may be far more complex than a simple direct relationship. Several contextual reasons why attitudes like commitment may not always translate into higher performance are well known, including the fact that employee performance is often constrained by factors such as employee skills and access to resources. In addition, employees may not have adequate control over performance outcomes in the workplace. Thus, although there is strong evidence linking commitment to motivation (effort), motivation may not always be translated into improved performance at the individual level of analysis. At present, we do not have a complete understanding of those situations in which commitment is likely to have a relatively strong relationship to performance versus situations in which the relationship is likely to be weaker or nonexistent.

Past research attention has been primarily directed at the relationship of commitment to performance at the individual level of analysis. However, several studies have found that commitment aggregated at the sub-unit and organizational levels of analysis is related to organizational performance (Mowday, Porter and Dubin, 1974; Ostroff, 1992). Moreover, research on high commitment human resource management systems has found intriguing relationships between the nature of the relationship between employees and employers, and organizational outcomes (Arthur, 1994; Huselid, 1995; MacDuffie, 1995). Mowday (1998) speculated that the relationship between high commitment human resource management practices and organizational outcomes may be mediated by employee commitment. Tsui, et al. (1997) found that the highest levels of individual performance were found in work environments characterized by a relationship between the employer and employee of high mutual investment, which would be likely to result in high levels of employee commitment. Unfortunately, given its design, this study did not include performance measures at the organizational level of analysis. Although there is no consensus on a definition of what constitutes high commitment human resource management practices, Pfeffer (1998) emphasized employment security, selective hiring, self-managed teams and decentralized decision making, comparatively high compensation contingent on organizational performance, training opportunities, reduced status distinctions between levels of the organization, and extensive information sharing.

9.3.2 Employee Turnover

The theory underlying organizational commitment clearly indicates that it should have a strong negative influence on employee turnover. This is because we assume that turnover has a strong volitional component. That is, an individual's decision to leave an organization is often not highly constrained and represents a deliberate choice to make a job change that will presumably provide a greater level of need fulfillment and satisfaction. Thus, if a person is highly committed to a particular organization, we would predict that he or she would be unlikely to leave, even if job dissatisfaction is high. This leads us to predict a stronger relationship between commitment and turnover than between commitment and job performance.

Mathieu and Zajac's (1990) meta-analysis confirmed this prediction, as did Meyer, et al.'s (2002) review. Mathieu and Zajac (1990) found that the mean weighted correlation between these two variables was $r_t = -.277$. Stronger relationships were found between commitment and behavioral intentions to search for a job and to leave ($r_t = -.59$ and $-.46$, respectively), suggesting that behavioral intentions may mediate the relationship between commitment and turnover. This is not entirely surprising since behavioral intentions are more proximal to overall attitudes toward the organization than are actual behaviors.

9.3.3 Employee Absenteeism

The situation with employee absenteeism is similar to that of turnover: a moderately strong relationship with organizational commitment would be predicted in large part because employees typically have a degree of choice to decide whether or not to come to work on a given day (Steers and Rhodes, 1978). As with turnover, however, this choice is not wholly unconstrained. Illness or a pressing family or transportation problems, for example, can cause an absence despite a person's strong motivation to be present. In fact, if absenteeism statistics were refined sufficiently to exclude instances of clear inability to come to work, we would expect a very strong relation between commitment and absenteeism. However, since obtaining such precise data is highly problematic, the prediction is that studies of commitment's impact on absenteeism will be only moderate—but positive.

Although this prediction has been borne out by subsequent research, the magnitude of the relationship has been relatively weak. Mathieu and Zajac (1990) found mean weighted correlations of $r_t = .102$ and $-.116$ for attendance and lateness, respectively. A marginally stronger relationship was found by Meyer, et al. (2002) between affective commitment and attendance. As is the case with both job performance and turnover, commitment may be only one of many variables that influence attendance behaviors and, thus, it is probably not reasonable to expect strong relationships. Moreover, these relationships may be mediated and/or moderated by a variety of work-related variables.

9.3.4 Extra-Role Behavior

The fourth potential work performance consequence that could be affected by organizational commitment is extra-role behavior on behalf of the organization. Often referred to in the literature as "organizational citizenship behavior," extra-role behavior is presumed to be highly volitional on the part of employees. In fact, since this behavior is "extra-role" it is behavior that by definition is not required by the organization as part of assigned job duties. It represents contributions to the organization above and beyond what it could ordinarily expect of a given employee in a given job situation. Consequently, we would hypothesize that among the four work-related consequences discussed here, extra-role behavior would have the strongest relationship with organizational commitment. If commitment can be assumed to have any impact at all, it should, at the very least, be on this type of behavior. Indeed, it would be very surprising if it were otherwise.

This expectation has been supported by research using both self-reports and independent assessments of extra-role behaviors. A meta-analysis by Organ and Ryan (1995) found that commitment was related to two forms of extra-role behavior, altruistic acts ($r = .226$) and behavior consistent with norms and rules ($r = .296$). Although Mathieu and Zajac (1990) did not include organizational citizenship behaviors in their review, Meyer, et al. (2002) found that affective commitment was significantly related to these behaviors.

9.4 The Road Ahead

This program of research began with the straightforward idea that employee attitudes toward their employing organization, in addition to their attitudes toward their job, have behavioral relevance. In the thirty years or so since work on the concept of organizational commitment first began, numerous studies have been conducted that shed light on the relevance of employee attitudes toward the overall organization. In general, the predictions made as a result of our initial work concerning performance, turnover, attendance, and extra-role behavior have been supported. This support comes from several meta-analyses of hundreds of studies and the results are robust with respect to the different measures of affective commitment that have been used. In addition, although the number of studies conducted outside North America remains limited, Meyer, et al. (2002) found that the pattern of relationships between affective commitment and other variables is very similar across national boundaries.

The weight of the evidence suggests that employee attitudes toward the organization are behaviorally relevant. However, the magnitude of these relationships reported in the literature suggests that organizational commitment, while important, is obviously not the only attitude that influences behaviors in the workplace. Rather, the determinants of employee behavior in the workplace are complex and involve attitudes toward multiple features of work (e.g., the job and the organization), behavioral intentions, and contextual factors that facilitate or inhibit employees from acting on their intentions. Given that this line of research on organizational commitment was motivated to redress the imbalance in research on job satisfaction and other job-focused attitudes that existed at the time, it seems reasonable to conclude that subsequent research has demonstrated that a broader array of attitudes are important to understanding behavior at work.

Even so, the world of work has changed dramatically since our initial research on organizational commitment in the 1970s and 1980s. Downsizing and minimum wage jobs have become a strategy of choice for many firms in order to meet intense competitive pressures, while employees who retain their jobs are under increasing pressure for increased productivity and efficiency. Working hours, including both voluntary and involuntary overtime, as well as stress levels, are on the increase. Increased globalization pressures have led to a marked expansion of overseas manufacturing and outsourcing, even among white-collar and professional employees. Meanwhile, younger employees of both genders are becoming increasingly vocal about securing a suitable work–family balance just at the time when such a balance may be the more difficult to achieve. Above all, gone are the days when most young high school and college graduates sought a career and a company for the long term.

In this regard, Peter Capelli (1999: ix) has noted that "[T]he older, internalized employment practices, with their long-term commitments and assumptions, buffered the employment relationship from market pressures, but they are giving way to a negotiated relationship where the power shifts back and forth from employer to employee based on conditions in the labor market." Even so, Capelli acknowledges that most contemporary firms still require some form of employee commitment to meet their goals. To accomplish this, he observes that many companies have tried to refocus employee commitment away from the company as a whole and towards specific aspects of the company, such as work teams. "For many jobs, commitment to the corporation as a whole is largely irrelevant as long as the employees feel commitment to their team or project" (p. 11). At the same time, he points out that in recent years "voluntary turnover has been less of a problem for the corporate world because virtually all corporations have been downsizing at the same time, creating a big surplus of talent on the market and also restricting those who quit voluntarily" (p. 6).

The trends in the workplace and economy noted by Capelli (1999) raise serious questions about the extent to which employee attitudes, like organizational commitment, really matter in today's temporary society. Others who have observed the same trends, however, have come to very different conclusions with respect to the relevance of commitment. Pfeffer (1998) strongly advocates that organizations need to implement high commitment work practices, including providing employment security, as a way to achieve long-term competitive advantage and profitability. He believes that organizations that effectively implement such practices will benefit in several ways, including having employees who work harder and smarter.

More recently, Collins (2001) reported a study of companies that had made the transition from being good companies to great companies. One of the defining characteristics of the companies he identified as making this transition was a tendency to emphasize hiring the right people and providing long-term employment. For Collins (2001), the key to success in great companies was not necessarily vision, strategy, or implementation. These things were important, but the principal key to success was having a committed and talented management team. In his view, once you have the right people in the right places, decisions about strategy and how to implement the strategy can be more effectively made.

Building organizational capacity, with its concomitant need for a stable and committed workforce, advocated by Pfeffer (1998) and Collins (2001) may seem, at least on the surface, to be at odds with the need to manage financial performance and costs. However, two of the most successful firms in one of the most highly competitive industries have managed to both build organizational capacity and control costs in achieving superior financial performance. Both Southwest Airlines and JetBlue are leaders in the highly competitive airlines industry, in part because they have placed employees first and emphasized employee commitment. Even so, their approaches to human resource management have been somewhat different. While both Southwest and JetBlue place considerable emphasis on hiring the right people, Southwest takes a fairly traditional approach to developing employment relationships emphasizing internalized employment practices and job security, while JetBlue recognizes that not all employees wish to work in the airline industry for the long term. Instead, JetBlue offers special contracts to college students, for example, who seek the excitement and adventure of travel and living in Manhattan for one to five years. Employees wishing to achieve a greater balance between work and family responsibilities are offered the opportunity to job share or to work from home as reservation agents. Although this may not produce the long-term employee–employer relationship commonly associated with high commitment work systems, it produces high levels of employee commitment over the period of time the relationship lasts. At both Southwest and JetBlue, costs are controlled by having highly committed employees who are willing to work harder and take more personal responsibility. Overall employment costs are managed because fewer managers and employees are needed compared to other airlines.

It can be argued that highly committed employees can be a source of competitive advantage and, thus, a good thing for organizations. It is important to also ask, however, whether high levels of commitment are beneficial for employees. Mowday, et al. (1982) noted there are both advantages and disadvantages associated with organizational commitment from an employee perspective. It seems likely that high levels of commitment provide a sense of meaning, direction, and accomplishment for some—but not all—employees. In addition, Meyer, et al. (2002) reported that affective commitment has been found to negatively correlate with both work stress and work–family conflict. Clearly, employees who are committed to an organization may incur opportunity costs and may be exploited by companies that are less committed to their employees. Nevertheless, employee commitment to organizations has the potential to have positive implications for an employee, both in the short and long term.

As we noted above, the world is a dramatically different place than it was in the late 1960s when our program of research on employee commitment to organizations first began. It may be presumptuous to suggest that a concept that was viewed as relevant back then would still be relevant today. In our opinion, however, attitudes employees hold toward their organizations, as well as towards their jobs, continue to matter both to organizations and to individual employees. As a result, the concept of employee commitment to organizations and the human resource management practices designed by organizations to enhance such commitment continue to be worthy of serious research attention and study.

References

ARTHUR, J. B. (1994). Effects of human resource systems on manufacturing performance and turnover. *Academy of Management Journal*, 37: 670–687.

BECKER, H. S. (1960). Notes on the concept of commitment. *American Journal of Sociology*, 66: 32–42.

BROWN, M. E. (1969). Identification and some conditions of organizational involvement. *Administrative Science Quarterly*, 14: 346–355.

CAPELLI, P. (1999). *The New Deal at Work*. Boston: Harvard Business School Press.

COLLINS, J. (2001). *Good to Great*. New York: Harper Business.

ETZIONI, A. (1961). *A Comparative Analysis of Complex Organizations.* New York: Free Press.

GOULDNER, A. W. (1958). Cosmopolitans and locals: Toward an analysis of latent social roles—I. *Administrative Science Quarterly,* 2: 281–306.

GOULDNER, H. P. (1960). Dimensions of organizational commitment. *Administrative Science Quarterly,* 4: 468–490.

GRUSKY, O. (1966). Career mobility and organizational commitment. *Administrative Science Quarterly,* 10: 488–503.

HUSELID, M. A. (1995). The impact of human resource management practices on turnover, productivity, and corporate financial performance. *Academy of Management Journal,* 38: 635–672.

KANTER, R. M. (1968). Commitment and social organization: a study of commitment mechanisms in utopian communities. *American Sociological Review,* 33: 499–517.

MACDUFFIE, J. P. (1995). Human resource bundles and manufacturing performance: Organizational logic and flexible production systems in the world auto industry. *Industrial and Labor Relations Review,* 48: 197–221.

MARCH, J. G., and SIMON, H. A. (1958). *Organizations.* New York: Wiley.

MATHIEU, J. E., and ZAJAC, D. M. (1990). A review and meta-analysis of the antecedents, correlates, and consequence of organizational commitment. *Psychological Bulletin,* 108: 171–194.

MERTON, R. K. (1957). *Social Theory and Social Structure.* Glencoe, Ill.: Free Press.

MEYER, J. P., and ALLEN, N. J. 1997. *Commitment in the Workplace: Theory, Research, and Application.* Thousand Oaks, Calif.: Sage.

—— STANLEY, D. J., HERSCOVITCH, L., and TOPOLNYTSKY, L. (2002). Affective, continuance, and normative commitment to the organization: A meta-analysis of antecedents, correlates, and consequences. *Journal of Vocational Behavior,* 61: 20–52.

MOWDAY, R. T. (1998). Reflections on the study and relevance of organizational commitment. *Human Resource Management Review,* 8: 387–401.

—— PORTER, L. W., and DUBIN, R. (1974). Unit performance, situational factors, and employee attitudes. *Organizational Behavior and Human Performance,* 12: 231–248.

—— —— and STEERS, R. M. (1982). *Employee–Organization Linkages: The Psychology of Commitment, Absenteeism, and Turnover.* New York: Academic Press.

—— STEERS, R. M., and PORTER, L. W. (1979). The measurement of organizational commitment. *Journal of Vocational Behavior,* 14: 224–247.

ORGAN, D. W., and RYAN, K. (1995). Meta-analytic review of attitudinal and dispositional predictors of organizational citizenship behavior. *Personnel Psychology,* 48: 775–802.

OSTROFF, C. (1992). The relationship between satisfaction, attitudes, and performance: An organization level analysis. *Journal of Applied Psychology,* 77: 963–974.

PFEFFER, J. (1998). *The Human Equation.* Boston: Harvard Business School Press.

PORTER, L. W., CRAMPON, W., and SMITH, F. (1976). Organizational commitment and managerial turnover: A longitudinal study. *Organizational Behavior and Human Performance,* 15: 87–98.

—— STEERS, R. M., MOWDAY, R. T., and BOULIAN, P. (1974). Organizational commitment, job satisfaction, and turnover among psychiatric technicians. *Journal of Applied Psychology,* 59: 603–609.

SALANCIK, G. (1977). Commitment and control or organizational behavior and belief. In B. Staw and G. Salancik (eds.), *New Directions in Organizational Behavior.* Chicago: St Clair Press.

STEERS, R. M. (1977). Antecedents and consequences of organizational commitment. *Administrative Science Quarterly*, 22: 46–56.

—— and RHODES, S. R. (1978). Major influences on employee attendance: A process model. *Journal of Applied Psychology*, 63: 391–407.

TSUI, A. S., PEARCE, J. L., PORTER, L. W., and TRIPOLI, A. M. (1997). Alternative approaches to the employee–organization relationship: Does investment in employees pay off? *Academy of Management Journal*, 40: 1089–1121.

WHYTE, W. (1952). *The Organization Man*. Garden City, NY: Doubleday.

CHAPTER 10

··

DEVELOPING PSYCHOLOGICAL CONTRACT THEORY

··

DENISE M. ROUSSEAU

10.1 Developing Psychological Contract Theory

··

THIS chapter opens with a disclaimer: My recollections of how my own contributions to psychological contract theory came about cannot be completely accurate. The biases of recall, availability, and attribution are impossible to cull completely. I started actively working on the psychological contract twenty years ago in 1985. What I recall is undoubtedly weighted in the direction of my own motives and experiences, hence I might not do justice to other factors that operated too. One such factor may have been the zeitgeist of the late 1980s with its disruptions of employment via downsizing, buyouts, and restructurings. Nonetheless, I have tried to be reflective and balance the personal and the situational to describe the process whereby my contributions to psychological contract theory came about. Though the zeitgeist undoubtedly played a part, by making it easier to gather certain kinds of data on broken contracts, it is my belief that its role was peripheral. Broken contracts have never been a major focus for me—their actual fulfillment and how to make contracts that are fulfilling to the people who create them are much more intriguing.

Given that disclaimer, this chapter needs a method section to describe how I have tried to provide an accurate account. I began writing this chapter by reviewing files, marginalia, jottings to myself, notes from others, old reviews of early psychological contract manuscripts I submitted (most of which were rejected), scraps of old tables and sketches of models that led to a published product, etc. For the most part, I find that what I actually recall is relatively accurate, but I had forgotten the role certain people played and failed to appreciate how extensively others had contributed until I reread my old files. Also, I see that some "new" ideas (i.e. what I am working on now) waft through my old files' dusty strata. Ideas related to *ex ante* and *ex post* contracts (Rousseau, 2005) and person-specific employment deals (Rousseau, 2004) are scribbled all over these old notes. The process this chapter portrays is still on-going.

10.1.1 Roots

Valery (1938, 1958) said, "There is no theory that is not a fragment, carefully prepared of some autobiography." In my case, family background is as powerful as my academic training in laying the ground work for investigating the dynamics of employment relations. My father hated his job. He probably should have been a high school history teacher or basketball coach. Instead of going to college or pursuing work that interested him, with a large number of brothers and sisters to support, and after serving in the U.S. Navy during World War II, he went to work for the telephone company first as a lineman and then a cable splicer, ultimately working there for thirty-six years. Though the work was physically somewhat hard, it was the political and abusive behavior from telephone company foremen and managers that my father talked about at dinner. (Later as an adult, I did some genealogical research and found out that during the late 1880s my French-Canadian great-grandfather had been a telephone company *supervisor*. Dad was aghast.) My father's dissatisfaction with his job and career led me to focus on the work lives of workers, and especially of *employees*, those who work for somebody aside from themselves. In hindsight, it seems natural that I became an industrial psychologist.

The first course I took in the field as an undergraduate at Berkeley, from Milt Blood, was an eye opener. I learned how work environments were shaped by the people in them. I was fascinated by how situational factors, rewards, goals, norms, etc., also shaped why managers behave as they do. I learned about concepts like attribution bias: In effect, people judge themselves by their intentions and others by their behavior. When I came home at Christmas break and picked my dad up from work, I described Milt Blood's class. I still remember my dad's reply: "There has to be a way to keep work from grinding men down, grinding men down, grinding men down." I was hooked and I knew (more or less) what I would do if I could get accepted into a graduate program in industrial psychology. I began wondering how employers could be helped to anticipate the impact of their actions on workers, and what workers might do on their own behalf. It took me another fifteen years or so, after admission to the Ph.D. program at Berkeley and a decade as a professor, to see that studying the concept of a psychological contract would let me act more fully upon this initial motivation. It was if something inside me said "Finally."

Of course academic training gives a focus and a method to tackling theoretical and practical questions. Industrial psychology is grounded in the theory of psychological measurement, and Ed Ghiselli's (1964) book on the topic was a core part of my training. Essentially, industrial psychologists define the construct(s) under study, identify the nomological system or network of concepts in which the construct is embedded, and then put the ideas to empirical test. There are two kinds of models I learned to work with: composition models that specify the building blocks of a construct, and content models explicating the causal relations one construct has to others. Psychological contract requires a well-specified composition model because it is a distinctive part of more commonly studied concepts such as expectations and beliefs associated with an exchange relationship (more later). In my last year in the doctoral program at Berkeley, I was privileged to work with Karlene Roberts and Chuck Hulin on *Developing an Interdisciplinary Science of Organizations*, a book that dealt with the modeling requirements critical to understanding organizational phenomena. One of the book's themes, the need to span levels to understand organizational phenomena, has shaped my subsequent thinking and research. In the case of psychological contracts, a multilevel view entails attention to an individual's biological and psychological processes, his or her interactions with others (dyads and networks), the social standing of individuals within the work group and organizations influencing their contributions and entitlements, and the norms and practices groups and organizations manifest that shape and are shaped by individual actions and psychological contract beliefs.

Another important part of my early academic training was an unexpected event: the shutdown of Berkeley's doctoral program toward the end of my first year in graduate school. Two of the three junior faculty members who constituted the I/O program's faculty failed to receive tenure. Doctoral students already in the program were grandfathered in and told that if they wanted to stay they needed to build relationships with other faculty in and outside of psychology. After the announcement of the program's closing, I walked down the hall to the professor I TA'ed for, psychometrician Bill Meredith. Breathlessly I told him my program was being closed and I needed to get faculty to agree to serve on my orals and dissertation committees (assuming I got to that point). Without missing a beat, Dr. Meredith (I never could call him anything else) said, "Sure." Within a week, I made my way over to the two other areas at Berkeley where I knew organizations were studied: the business school where a relatively new area, Organizational Behavior, had been started with faculty trained in management, industrial relations, and sociology;

and the industrial engineering department's sociotechnical systems program whose faculty had been involved in Tavistock-based clinical interventions, work systems design, and human factors research. These two programs treated me to an array of disciplinary points of view regarding organizational research.

In retrospect, I am struck that rather than being stressed by the upheaval in the doctoral program, I was more caught up in learning these areas and figuring out how they were interconnected. While the questions I was interested in remained fundamentally psychological, I began to see what might be termed a consilience (cf. Wilson, 1999) of employment relations as studied in industrial psychology with sociology, industrial relations, economics, and clinical psychology. Sociology heightened my sense of how social status and socioeconomic forces shape work relations. Industrial relations made salient the limited influence workers as individuals often have over their employment conditions. Clinical psychology with its focus on mental models and person–object relations stimulated attention to employment relations as rooted in cognitive schemas and interpersonal attachment. Lastly, economics, with its tendency to assume mutual agreement (ignoring asymmetry of power and information) and that workers shirk while the firm does not, seemed out of keeping with both my experience and existing research in I/O Psychology, providing a counterpoint to what I came to understand about the dynamics of psychological contracts. Each of these areas would prove relevant to understanding the role that psychological contracts play in employment.

10.2 PSYCHOLOGICAL CONTRACT THEORY IN A NUTSHELL

Psychological contract comprises the beliefs an individual holds regarding an exchange agreement to which he or she is party, typically between an individual and an employer (Rousseau, 1995). These beliefs are largely based upon promises implied or explicit, which over time take the form of a relatively stable mental model or schema. A major feature of a psychological contract is the individual's belief that an agreement exists that is mutual; in effect, his or her beliefs in the existence of a common understanding with another that binds each party to a particular course of action. Since individuals rely upon their understanding of this agreement in the subsequent choices and efforts they take, they anticipate benefits from fulfilled commitments and incur losses if another fails to live up to theirs, whatever the individual interprets another's commitments to be.

Psychological contract theory is construct-driven. The features of this construct, particularly its schematic nature, give rise to its dynamic properties. These dynamics are central to its distinctive consequences, antecedents, and boundary conditions. A central dimension of this construct is incompleteness, in that the full array of obligations associated with the exchange are typically not known or knowable at an exchange relationship's outset; requiring the contract to be fleshed out over time. Incomplete contracts are completed, updated, and revised through processes that affect both the degree of actual agreement between the exchange parties as well as the psychological contract's flexibility in the face of change (cf. Rousseau, 2001). As a form of schema or mental model, psychological contracts become more durable as they move toward a high level of completeness, wherein they enable prediction of future actions by contract parties and effectively guide individual action. This durability also poses difficulty in response to changing circumstances. Sources of information used in developing and completing the psychological contract include the agents of the firm (e.g., managers and human resource representatives) as well as the social influence of peers and mentors, along with administrative signals (e.g., human resource practices) and structural cues (e.g., informal network position) to which individuals are exposed (Rousseau, 1995; Dabos and Rousseau, 2004b).

Perceived mutuality is another feature of the psychological contract. When an individual believes another shares his or her understanding of commitments each has made, reliance upon these commitments shapes the future. Actual agreement between the parties has been found to benefit each while producing higher performance for both individual and organization (Dabos and Rousseau, 2004a). Mutuality in psychological contract can offer an essential material benefit to the parties involved, and by implications to society generally, by engendering cooperation and trust under conditions of incomplete information and uncertainty. Numerous social mechanisms support promise-keeping (e.g., reputation effects) and constitute broader organizing principles that go beyond the isolated obligations between any two parties to create patterns of reciprocity and shared beliefs characterizing well-functioning work groups and larger social units.

The key boundary assumption of psychological contract theory is individual choice whereby the parties freely participate in the exchange and voluntarily agree to bind themselves to a course of action (Rousseau, 1995). The individual is the primary actor in the theory with no isomorphism assumed at group or organizational levels (though functional isomorphism might exist as in the case of individual and group-level contracts, e.g., Klein and Koszlowski, 2001). I have been hesitant to employ the concept of psychological contract across societies since property rights and individual freedom are inherent in the modeling of voluntary agreement. This agnosticism regarding the existence and dynamics of psychological contracts across societies ultimately motivated the creation of an international team to investigate the question (Rousseau and Schalk, 2000).

10.2.1 The Beginning

I began by trying to understand what people believed to be the obligations firms had to the workers they employed. The notion of a psychological contract, where commitments exchanged shape how employers and workers act toward each other, had been on my mind for sometime. In graduate school, I had read the Ur-texts by Chris Argyris, Chester Barnard, Harry Levinson, all of whom had written about a psychological contract. Because the concept of a psychological contract already had people intrigued when I took it up, its existence gave the theory legs. It was not a conscious decision on my part to capitalize on that fact but in retrospect it was an advantage in capturing interest in and legitimating the study of beliefs regarding the employment relationship. The first formal question I asked was do people have a mental model (which I labeled a psychological contract) regarding the obligations employers have toward workers?

To explore this question, I read and read. Soon after it came into print, I marked up the definitional section that in Nicholson and Johns's (1985: 398) article described the concept of psychological contracts as unwritten reciprocal expectations between an individual employee and the organization. As this article put it, the psychological contract is the essence of individual–organizational linkage. When I turned my attention to the notion of a psychological contract, I began by playing with what seemed to me to be the bases of this linkage—promises, obligations, implied commitments, etc. Looking up these terms in the host of textbooks my colleagues and I had around the office, I found that nothing was listed in any text on social psychology, organizational behavior, or human resource management regarding these terms. This struck me as odd, since commitments about the future are central to most forms of employment and indeed to exchange generally, from year-end bonuses to seniority systems. The role of promises is addressed by Orbell, Van de Kragt, and Dawes (1988) in their study of discussion-induced cooperation, but social psychology texts as yet haven't keyed on that aspect of cooperation. I also learned from my colleague Jim Anderson that marketing researchers used the notion of pledges in business-to-business channels, but that was pretty much it (e.g., E. Anderson and Weitz, 1992). Only later, after a systematic search of the psychological literature for promise and contract-related writings, would I discover the important work of Frederick Kanfer and his colleagues on promises and commitment in behavior modification (e.g., Kanfer and Karoly, 1972; Kanfer, et al., 1974). An example of how a field can lose track of essential work, psychological texts seem to have overlooked Kanfer's behavioral studies of contract. I found these invaluable as a behavioral basis for the formation and consequences of a psychological contract.

By this time, I was a professor at the Kellogg School at Northwestern. When it dawned on me that the notion of a psychological contract might be an important way to capture both the employee's experience at work as well as a dynamic in the employment relationship, I spent about a year and a half reading everything I could find on contracts, employment relations, and mental models, and talking with local colleagues. Having done a literature search, I knew that Ian Macneil at Northwestern's Law School in downtown Chicago had written on relational contracts, a concept that sounded a lot like psychological contracts to me. I made an appointment to meet Professor Macneil. He was generous with his time and ultimately came to the Evanston campus to give a presentation at Kellogg and meet with those of us interested in this work. In his office, he gave me copies of his own articles and sent me off to the law library to read two seminal books on contract, one by Corbin (1952) and the other by Farnsworth (1982). From the moment I opened up these books, I realized that legal scholars sounded like psychologists when they wrote about contracts. For instance, Corbin (1952) described how silence serves as a mode of acceptance: when a party accepts services knowing others have a certain belief about obligations incurred, it can be legally binding. Inferring commitments from behavior (or its absence) was part and parcel of how I thought psychological contracts might function. Reading legal theory on contracts while sitting amid the leather-bond books of the law library, I was in heaven.

Looking over the marginalia on the Xerox copies in my files I can provide a picture of how my own thinking on psychological contracts came about. For instance here are the notes and circled sections from Ian Macneil (1985):

P. 496 describes the promise-centered scholarship that takes promise as central focus of contract. "This focus does not, of course, mean that non-promissory aspects are omitted—that would be impossible—nor even that promise may not in the end be swamped by nonpromissory aspects, although it may mean that."

P. 497 Macneil's position: "all contract is relational."

But Macneil argues a promise centered approach is inherently limited as means to explain a relational contract. (p. 508, "I am, however, morally certain that global promise-centered theories of this kind create mind-sets virtually guaranteeing that we will not understand highly relational contractual behavior, and that view I shall press at every opportunity.")

P. 519 obligation takes over when promise gives out.

I had also underlined words like "voluntarily," "reasonably fair" (elements in definition of a contract) and written in the margins, "voluntariness is linked to contract enforcement," "the possibility of real voluntariness, actual and realistic." I marked footnotes indicating where the courts compensated people not for promise unfulfilled but for their actual damages incurred by trusting other party. Another note highlighted that people are expected to take responsibility for those with whom they interact.

I began working on a composition model for the psychological contract that incorporated notions of promise, payment, and reliance (upon promises another has made), where these psychological contract elements become elaborated over course of employment. Working through this model led me to read Patrick

S. Atiyah (1981) with his basic theme that moral rules regarding promising represent many of the features underlying contract law. My old notes on Atiyah emphasize his focus on promise and role of consideration as defining features in society's view of contract:

p. 10 obligation to keep promises derives from a duty not to cause harm in early contract law.

p. 18 perceived obligations are not proper basis for a binding promise else only honest men would be bound by contracts.

p. 21 reciprocity is important element determining if promise is binding.

p. 25 common law interprets promise to mean what "reasonable third party" believes it to be, not what parties intend.

p. 32–33 makes strong distinction between promises and expectations. A disappointed expectation is an evil but principle of free choice gives weight to promises since these are voluntary, positive acts. Pure expectations aren't deserving of high protections.

Societal effects: notes that (p. 140) in UK and US there is toleration of contract breaking (e.g., clauses specify that payments are due if contract is breeched).

Treating promises as fact that if stated makes it true and therefore binding on the speaker. Implied promises come from words and conduct.

The moral basis of promises have changed over time from freedom of contract in 19th century to paternalism in 20th. What of today? What is basis?

The next important step in the development of psychological contract research came out of a lunchtime conversation with a colleague at Kellogg, Max Bazerman, a well-known experimentalist. I knew I needed to pick Max's brain because of his work on cognition and judgment. Over a Chinese lunch, I described for him my efforts to operationalize the psychological contract concept. Max told me to try policy capturing, a methodology for examining how people make judgments. If people faced with scenarios describing employment situations made judgments that conformed to a theory of psychological contracts that would be evidence that people used such mental models. I knew of this methodology from graduate school where I had seen it used to examine how performance raters made their judgments, but had never thought of it in the context of psychological contracts. Max helped me reframe my thinking to recognize that psychological contracts provided a basis for judgments that themselves could be studied experimentally.

Over the next couple of years, I conducted a series of policy capturing studies with doctoral students Ron Anton and Karl Aquino, using MBA and executive program participants, which demonstrated how third parties evaluated the employer's obligation to workers. The studies provided consistent evidence that seniority created a perceived obligation to retain people, as did continuing good performance (Rousseau and Anton, 1988, 1991; Rousseau and Aquino, 1993). These obligations were not reduced by advance notice or severe economic conditions, though the latter were more closely tied to beliefs regarding fairness. These studies also demonstrated that the judgments made regarding obligations were related to but distinct from fairness. Armed with evidence of both convergent and discriminant validity regarding the psychological contract, I felt we were on to something.

10.2.2 The Search for Answers

I suspect my approach in pursuing a new organizational research topic is fairly typical: Observe and listen to people in the workplace, do lots of reading, and talk with other colleagues to figure out the way forward. The idea of "pointer knowledge" is used to describe how information searches tend to start with the people we think are likely to know where an answer might lie, even if they don't know the answer themselves. I have been extremely fortunate to have been aided by a number of people "who know who knows what." Though I was fairly deliberate in seeking out colleagues whose work seemed relevant, I was privileged to be in a university that gave me firsthand access to smart, generous people. Here is a list of the people who were influential in helping me get started, the pointer knowledge they provided, and resources they shared with me. A sign that proximity does indeed matter to both knowledge sharing and influence, all were at Northwestern at the time unless otherwise indicated.

1. Ian Macneil—contracts and law—general encouragement that the topic of psychological contract was worth pursuing.
2. Max Bazerman—how to actually operationalize psychological contract-related beliefs, methodological help, wrote Joel Brockner to get me papers on survivor effects. Max also pointed me to question existing full information theories of labor (where a firm offers a contract and workers accept it as evidenced from studies of compensation). We agreed this was unrealistic.
3. Mike Roloff—a walking archive of the social psychology and communications research on relationships, taking Mike to lunch at Northwestern's University Center was the easiest, most enjoyable way to get full access to the literature in the shortest amount of time. Mike provided a lot of ideas in his 1987 chapter describing dimensions of exchange (e.g. time until payment or return, non-contingency, etc.). He pointed me to the secret tests that couples can use to evaluate the health of their relationship (with resultant dysfunctional consequences), and that relationships can undergo a change in frame over time (e.g., from friends to family). Conversations with Mike led me to many of the ideas I later studied with regard to organizational change and its relationship with psychological contract.
4. Tom Tyler—justice and legalistic thinking. Tom helped me to see how both field and laboratory methods could be used to study psychological contracts, and to

appreciate the role of group and organizational identification in how people think about justice.

5. Bob Bies—violation and the hot feelings which result from it, calculative justice where paying back a shortage in money differs from interactive justice where explanations are given to reduce hot feelings.

6. Ed Zajac—agency theory and transaction cost economics. Through conversations with Ed, it became clearer to me that these particular economic theories made assumptions regarding information availability and worker/employer motives that differ from the dynamics I saw underlying psychological contracts. As psychological contract theory begins to be applied in labor market research, conversations with Ed have proven invaluable in recognizing the contradictions and challenges economic and psychological models of employment pose for each other.

7. Larry Cummings—encouraged me to publish a conceptual paper on psychological contract, read its multiple (rejected) versions, and provided the opportunity to write a chapter for *Research on Organizational Behavior.*

8. Jim Anderson—power/marketing channels, a regular lunch buddy who helped me see contracts through the lens of business partnerships and business-to-business channels.

9. David Messick—exchange norms and types of resources exchanges involve.

10. Don Prentiss—unconscious processes in relationships, marriage contracting literature. Don pointed me to the work of Sager (1976) on marriage contracts and couples therapy. We discussed how parties can have a single common non-verbal, interaction-based contract along with their own personal views. His conversations with me helped me think through many of the problems that mutuality entails.

11. Judi Maclean Parks (Iowa, Minnesota)—exchange norms, resources, and neat illustrations of how contracts are made. Judi sent me an example of a contract making device: The front cover of Ashton Tate dBase III Plus software. Its shrink-wrapped package was marked: "IMPORTANT NOTICE PLEASE READ BEFORE OPENING." The package itself was a licensing agreement, created if it were opened. Judi could always be counted on to provide a wealth of psychological contract examples from the Stone Age to Silicon Valley.

12. Margaret Clark (Carnegie Mellon)—corresponded with me regarding types of exchange (with strangers or friends, transaction-based or relational). Peggy's work focused on context, friendship, non-friends and meaning of delayed repayment (not significant for friendships, but more so for strangers) and the nature of the exchange (the more similar the resources, the more the parties see it as repayment).

13. Doctoral students—throughout the process of working on psychological contracts, I have been incredibly fortunate to have teamed up with wonderful doctoral students, including Ron Anton, Karl Aquino, Matt Kraatz, Sandra

Robinson, Kathy Tinsley, and Kim Wade-Benzoni at Kellogg and Guillermo Dabos, Violet Ho, Tai Gyu Kim, and Snehal Tijoriwala at Carnegie Mellon, who provided provocative ideas, connected me to new literatures, figured out how to execute new statistical techniques, and made the research process fun.

14. Journal reviewers—consistently in the early days of trying to break into the literature, they raised issues of how psychological contracts were distinct from expectations (answer: the former are commonly promised-based, the latter not necessarily so), implied and normative agreements different from psychological ones (trickier to disentangle until we hit on distinguishing them via frame of reference and level of analysis).

Since I was located close to Chicago at the time, I made appointments with people whom I knew had gone through various kinds of recent organizational changes, having met them through my executive courses. I talked with them about their relationship with their employer, what obligations they felt party to, whether commitments were kept, etc. Aside from tapping the people I knew and reading whatever I could get my hands on, following submission of the initial policy capturing study to a journal (Rousseau and Anton, 1988), I began working on a conceptual paper trying to articulate the distinctiveness of psychological contract as a concept in employment. I needed this task to begin organizing my thinking. Despite help from supportive colleagues, in particular Larry Cummings who read drafts of this paper, I had great difficulty laying out my ideas effectively. I struggled with the first conceptual paper (Rousseau, 1989), which was under review at *Academy of Management Review*, starting in 1986. In retrospect, I see the paper to be burdened by my fascination with all the different forms of contract (implied, implicit, psychological, relational). I needed to have spent more time focusing on what was new—how psychological contracts of individuals resulted from reciprocal exchanges...etc. Today when I read it, I see how much carpentry and refinement it needed. The paper specified constructs (i.e., built a composition model) but provided no content model specifying postulates or underlying causal mechanisms. I learned from this process how important it is to lay an empirical foundation where there are fundamental disputes such as the distinction between psychological contract and expectations and a clear set of testable postulates. After several rounds at *AMR*, the paper was rejected. I felt deeply the compassion colleagues could provide as Larry Cummings was as disappointed about this rejection as I was. Ultimately, a revision was published by a new journal at that time *Employee Rights and Responsibilities Journal*. I have been asked why I went with a new journal rather than trying to publish in another more established outlet. I don't think I gave the decision a lot of thought at the time: I wanted to get the paper out (i.e., published), declare victory (!), and move on. I was relieved when *ERRJ* took the paper so that I had something to cite in the introduction of the empirical papers I was now trying to publish. The need to legitimate the study of the psychological contract was something I keenly felt, and absent an early hit in an established journal, I pursued an incremental strategy. This is a case of loving the goals you are near when you aren't near the goals you love.

Meanwhile, as the policy capturing work continued, I began the first wave in a longitudinal study of the graduating Kellogg MBA class of 1987 (Rousseau, 1990; Robinson and Rousseau, 1994; Robinson, Kraatz, and Rousseau, 1994) as part of a course I taught on Human Resource Management. With students participating in the design and implementation of a survey to be administered to the graduating class, this project was intended to investigate the types of obligations new recruits formed with their employer. Ultimately, this project investigated whether psychological contract obligations took stable forms over time, whether individual motives of recruits such as careerism shaped their initial psychological contract with their employer, and the factors that influenced any change in psychological contract terms over time. In designing these studies, the fact that I regularly taught executives at Kellogg's Allen Center was a great help. Every week I had access to people who actually did recruiting for their employer. They provided me with insights into the types of commitments their firms tended to make to newly minted MBAs. This information formed the basis of the initial assessments we made of the psychological contract terms employers offer. Admittedly, this assessment was not theory-based, but rather was a representative set of the commitments gleaned from interviews with managers and executives who actually did recruiting.

The first field study had two important findings. First, two factors accounted for the employment obligations terms, which, in turn, appeared to resemble the transactional and relational distinction Macneil (1985) had made. Second, careerism, that is, the individual intention to move from employer to employer during the course of a career rather than remain with one, was positively related to the transactional contract and negatively related to the relational one.

The follow-up studies conducted with Sandra Robinson and Matt Kraatz beginning in 1990 revealed the role of micro processes, such as interaction with one's manager as a source of psychological contract with the whole firm. In responses to open-ended questions in the second wave of the MBA survey, we found that violations often occurred when promises had been made by a recruiter or boss who subsequently left—without telling anyone of the commitments made. Such data suggest that full information models of employment are not realistic since workers incorrectly assume that promises agents have made to them are known to and supported by their employer.

A side payoff of the two-wave, follow-up study was that we finally were able to put to rest the recurring challenge that psychological contracts were no different from expectations. We had submitted a paper to *Academy of Management Journal* and its editor, Mike Hitt, indicated that we should go get some additional data to see whether expectations and promise-based obligations function differently.

Sandra Robinson, by this time a very productive assistant professor at NYU, gathered some data on her students showing that psychological-contract based beliefs engendered more negative reactions than expectations did when violated, and that objection was countered. The overlap of expectations with psychological contracts had been raised by reviewers in previous manuscript submissions, and now we were in a position to nip this objection in the bud with subsequent reviewers.

10.2.3 Developing Alternatives

By accident, the development of psychological contracts theory took a new twist in 1990 when Sandra Robinson and I were creating the second wave of the MBA survey. We were interested in whether the recruits hired in 1987 would view their psychological contracts as having been fulfilled by their employers. On the second survey, we first asked the question "... please indicate how well, overall, your *first* employer has fulfilled the promised obligations they *owed you*." This measure was intended to operationalize Psychological Contract Fulfillment, the study's (intended) primary dependent variable. To gather data on what might have happened when the contract was not fulfilled, we asked some open-ended questions about what workers had experienced, preceded by a single item which read "Has or had your employer ever failed to meet the obligation(s) that were promised you," followed by "If yes, please explain..." As one of our questionnaire respondents noted "I think you worded the question wrong it's the same as number xxx." The second Yes/No question was intended only as a transition to the open-ended questions. Serendipity was at work: It became our most important indicator. When I realized from the respondent's comment we had asked the same question twice, but differently, we ran a correlation and a cross-tabulation. Though the two measures correlated at .53 ($p < .001$), violation and fulfillment appeared to be distinct constructs and not ends of the same continuum because the cross-tabs revealed some unexpected patterns. First, employees who reported no violation on the dichotomous measure included 28 percent who reported their employer had only "somewhat fulfilled" its commitments. In the opposite end, employees who reported their employer had violated its commitments included 22 percent who reported at least "somewhat fulfilled" obligations. I was always interested in the fulfillment side of contracts, and less so their violation. But this finding was intriguing since it suggested that even the absence of violation might not be enough to create fulfillment. Moreover, violation need not mean that a psychological contract was not also fulfilled.

Sandra Robinson has pursued the violation aspect of psychological contracts, her work prompting a large body of research, perhaps the hottest topic to date in this area. (At a recent meeting of psychological contracts researchers, Sandra was dubbed Breach Girl!) We published our findings using the above two measures as alternative indicators of contract violation (Robinson and Rousseau, 1994.) Thus, the differential wording of two questions bore fruit, creating a new branch of research on the psychological contracts tree. What has fascinated me throughout is the possibility that broken contracts might be remedied and renegotiated. Insights regarding how violation can turn into fulfillment appear in more recent work on individually negotiated employment deals (Rousseau, 2005).

Violation is an essential issue in the dynamics of psychological contract. As Edmund O. Wilson has stated so well, "Contractual agreement so thoroughly pervades human social behavior, virtually like the air we breathe, that it attracts no special notice—until it goes bad" (Wilson, 1999: 186). Not surprising then, cheater detection appears to be hard wired not only in human beings but in the great apes (Cosmides and Tooby, 1992) and is an important dynamic in the creation of trust in exchange relations (Fichman, 2003). Moreover, the original work done by Kanfer (e.g. Kanfer and Karoly, 1972) addressed conditions under which violation is likely to occur. He linked contracts made between subjects and researchers to self control, using the reminder of promises made to continue despite painful situations. Kanfer and Karoly further suggest that attention be given to the state prior to execution of self control where promises, intentions, performance criteria are developed since these can determine exercise of self control later. They report that promise is less powerful than rewards attached to fulfillment of it (e.g. a prize for keeping one's word, the competing incentives associated with promise keeping and its violation). The behavioral and attitudinal implications of violations connect psychological contract research to other psychological research and reveal the power psychological contracts can wield over individuals and organizations. The question I myself turned to involved the nature and underpinnings of the psychological contract itself and the conditions affecting its formation and functionality.

10.2.4 Putting the Pieces Together

Four sets of activities helped me elaborate on the mechanisms underlying the psychological contract and identify its antecedents and consequences. The first was spending a lot of time in organizations, with working people, managers, and executives talking and observing. The second and third were book projects and the fourth a set of recent productive research activities where two doctoral students, Violet Ho and Guillermo Dabos, each took the lead in blazing the trail.

Starting in 1984, I spent at least part of each week working with managers in executive education activities, or in field settings such as hospitals or insurance offices. Being in contact with organizations and observing their human resource practices helped ground the conceptual work I was doing. Pursuing an understanding of the psychological contract, I came across virtually no circumstances in which people weren't cognizant of exchanging, making, or receiving promises in employment. Despite the popular press where executives were quoted as saying that workers were promised nothing, this was inconsistent with the day-to-day work experiences I observed and documented. Promises, covenants, and oaths have been described as the bonds of society (John Locke, p. 265 in Wilson, 1999).

I decided to write a book to give me a format for wrestling with what seemed to be the key issues regarding promise making in organizations. I felt I needed the freedom to develop the psychological contract construct and its implications that a book offered. Whereas the journal review process is largely about weeding out inconsistencies, sharpening and deepening a set of hypotheses or postulates, I wanted to both drill down into the psychological contract while conveying its scope in everyday organizational life. The book also let me more fully integrate work earlier researchers had done to build a case for the explanatory power and pervasiveness of psychological contracts. An old friend in the publishing business, Bill Hicks, told me the book I proposed looked like I wanted to "put a stake in the ground." He was right but I was also keen to have the luxury of a book project so that so I could figure out the phenomenon of psychological contract for myself. Originally it was entitled "Promises in Action," but my editor, Harry Briggs, talked me into changing it to *Psychological Contracts in Organizations* to make it easier for interested readers to identify. (I remembered that Freeman and Rogers' seminal book on transfer of knowledge, *Diffusion of Innovation*, was initially classified under Chemistry by the Library of Congress and I didn't want my book to end up in Political Science.)

The pieces I hoped to fit together involved basic issues like the evidence for a link between promises and beliefs regarding a psychological contract, why promises were made and kept, and what happened if conditions changed. I wanted to understand and then explain how people could restore a relationship where trust was violated. Writing this book was one of the most enjoyable times of my life. It was a chance to map out a new territory and discover connections to early work others had done that hadn't received its due. To get time to work on it, in the spirit of Frederick Kanfer, I created a contract with myself. I would take a day a week where I did no executive education and didn't go into the office. Instead I *bought* myself the day (as I thought about it at the time) and stayed home to work on the book to frame the psychological contract construct into a theory. Trying to avoid the mistakes I had made in the first conceptual paper, I tried to put a boundary on what the book would focus.

I needed to make clear to myself as much as to a reader what a psychological contract was and what it was not (i.e., differentiating it from normative, implied, and social contracts). This led to the first of the 2 × 2 tables, a heuristic that helped me organize my thinking. Sometimes I think I may be the world's oldest poster child for attention deficit disorder, but I get so caught up in the many sides of an issue, playing so much with its details that I cannot convey the ideas to anyone else. I have learned some heuristics to help me structure my thoughts so they can be conveyed more clearly to others. The anthropologist Lévi-Strauss claimed that human beings have a binary instinct (e.g., male/female; relational/transactional). Dichotomies provide a sort of heuristic for organizing ideas. But the concepts involved in employment relations are more complicated than a simple dichotomy, so I started to play with 2 × 2 tables to organize and express ideas. (One reviewer of my book later referred to "yet another" 2 × 2 table so it's possible I overdid it.)

While writing the book, I spent a lot of time reading and re-reading law, social psychology, economics, industrial relations, and started everyday by reading the *New York Times* with scissors in my hand in case I found a good blurb to highlight a point I wanted to make. (As soon as I heard the *NYT* hit the front door each morning I was up. I was literally addicted (no pun intended) to seeing what psychological contract manifestation the newspaper might have that day.) Several times a week, I found an article illustrating the workings of the psychological contract (e.g., a memorable one described how the Queen of England reduced her household expenses by no longer letting servants take home her special soap or the liquor left over from her dinner parties. That she offered them extra money in their paychecks instead was viewed as a poor substitute for the changes introduced into their employment relationship).

Psychological contract has been a satisfying topic to work on because it cuts across a host of settings, is interdisciplinary in its implications as well as influenced by multilevel factors. All this makes it possible to find writings in other areas that can be useful in explicating psychological contract issues. Not being limited to my own research in developing every aspect of the book's domain made it possible to cast a broad net. I basically worked from definitions (what a psychological contract is) to a composition model (what underlies it) to a content model (what its antecedents and consequences are), and on to broader issues of context. In the process, I felt that it became a sort of self-assembling framework that linked readily to other models (e.g., Miles and Snow's discussion of HR strategy, Clark and Reis's exchange models, Hirschman's responses to dissatisfaction/violation, etc.). My recollection is of moving pretty quickly through stages, though it was most definitely an incremental process. By the Society for Industrial Organizational Psychology meetings in April 1993 where I conducted a workshop on psychological contracts, I felt I had a good understanding of the construct of psychological contract and much of the broader network of ideas to which it was tied. In 1996 the book, dedicated to my father, won the best book award from the Academy of Management. I was proud and honored. Giving the book to my father for his 70th birthday was the highpoint.

Among many issues that the book raised but didn't resolve was the role of society as a context for individual beliefs regarding employment relationships. Atiyah (1989) has argued that freedom of contract is always a matter of degree. For many citizens the contracts they are party to have terms that are imposed on them (e.g., we don't negotiate with the power company what we will pay for electricity). Moreover, European governments in the last hundred years have in many cases discarded the doctrine of mutuality which underpins employment contracts, maintaining instead that firms with too much freedom to fire would engender anti-social conditions (Glendon, Gordon, and Osakwe, 1985). Government statute can dominate employment relations giving individuals and employers less room to create agreements based upon individual or employer choice. It seemed appropriate to examine employment, including promise-making cross-nationally.

Rene Schalk, a Dutch colleague I had met at the Academy of Management meetings in 1995, and I decided to build a team of researchers from a variety of countries, and learn together what might be the areas of convergence and difference in the dynamics of psychological contract across societies. With occasional face-to-face meetings with parts of the team (in Tilburg and at Academy meetings), we coordinated via e-mail to produce perspectives on psychological contracts across thirteen countries, an anthology entitled *Psychological Contracts in Employment: Cross-national Perspectives*. Across all countries, our scholars found evidence of psychological contract dynamics. This was not surprising; perhaps, because each country was a stable democracy. But there were differences in the level at which the employment relationship tended to be instantiated (e.g., work group versus individual), and considerable difference in how much local flexibility employers and individuals had in shaping the terms and conditions of employment.

One idea that came out of this book has been particularly influential on my current work. The zone of negotiability refers to the extent to which an individual can bargain for conditions of employment, how much influence individuals have, and the scope of resources subject to negotiation. A country such as France, for example, has many constraints on what individuals can bargain for because of the strong role played by the government, particularly via statues specifying conditions of employment (Cadin, 2000). In contrast, New Zealand (Peel and Inkson, 2000), United Kingdom (Millward and Herriot, 2000), and the United States (Rousseau, 2000b) provide few standardized conditions *a priori* and leave more terms subject to individual–employer bargaining. The notion that individuals in societies differ in the zone in which they can or need to bargain, raises the issue of how much variability there is *within* a society in the leverage workers have to bargain for themselves. The idea that some aspects of the psychological contract may be unique to the individual had been around for a while, and certainly in my early thinking I had the notion of person-specific components of the psychological contract. (There are scribbles regarding "person-specific" terms in the margins of my old Xeroxes.) But there was one other stray idea that the notion of individual bargaining linked up with.

In my own research in American settings, I had been finding that psychological contract obligations had substantial within-work group variation. Thus, workers in the same firm supervised by the same boss had somewhat different beliefs regarding their obligations (e.g., Rousseau and Tijoriwala, 1999). These factors were not accounted for by demographic differences, including time on the job, so the finding was puzzling. I began wondering whether individual bargaining might play a role, at least in the United States, where labor laws are relatively weak and few if any of the workers I had studied were unionized. The concept of idiosyncratic deals (Rousseau, 2004, 2005; Rousseau, Ho, and Greenberg, forthcoming), where individuals negotiate for terms and conditions of employment that differ from their peers, came about from this process.

Violet Ho and I began looking into the role of resources exchanged in employment as a way to understand the nature of the psychological contracts workers develop. Violet led the way on this in examining the role of social networks in shaping beliefs about employer commitments. She developed theory to specify how individuals use social cues regarding organization-wide, person-specific, contingent and non-contingent rewards in interpreting psychological contract fulfillment (Ho, 2002, 2005).

Guillermo Dabos took the idea of differential individual psychological contracts in another direction by asking the question whether position in the social structure influences what workers believe the employer owes them. Guillermo successfully combined approaches he learned from David Krackhardt, my colleague at Carnegie Mellon, with psychological contract theory, to identify how psychological contract beliefs are shaped by the people with whom workers interact regularly and by their position in the larger social structure. Results suggest that people in high network centrality positions viewed themselves as owed more by the organization than less central counterparts, controlling for demographics and positional factors (Dabos and Rousseau, 2004b).

Both Violet and Guillermo initiated these streams of psychological contract research while I, along with colleagues at Carnegie Mellon, have played more the role of supporter and kibitzer. From a psychological contract perspective, this work suggests that micro processes such as friendship ties and local contributions workers make can shape their beliefs regarding reciprocal obligations on the part of their employer. Recent work with Violet and Tai Gyu Kim further suggests that workers who successfully bargain for particular resources such as developmental opportunity can develop distinctive psychological contracts (Rousseau and Kim, 2005; Rousseau, Ho, and Kim, 2005).

I came to recognize that the type of resources its terms involve, and the particular resources exchanged matter to the meaning and nature of the contract. Judi Maclean Parks had turned me on to the work of Foa and Foa (1975). I had wanted to work that theory into psychological contract theory in some way but couldn't quite figure out how. It finally hit me when working with Guillermo, Violet, and Tai that the resources exchanged are a signal as to the nature of the psychological contract. By raising the issue of negotiability in employment relations, the work of the international team had pointed the way to the role played by resources and individual negotiations in the emergence of psychological contract terms.

10.3 REFRAMING THEORY: EMERGING AND FUTURE DEVELOPMENTS

....

As psychological contract theory has evolved, more research examines the mechanisms underlying formation of worker beliefs regarding obligations and factors shaping the experience of both fulfillment and violation. Consistent with the theory building process David Whetton (2001) has described, if we place psychological contract concept in the center of a page, we can see an expansion of constructs, linkages, and empirical evidence to its left (antecedents) and to its right (consequences).

The major feature I am concerned with is mutuality, that is, actual agreement between worker and employer (or agent thereof). Taking advantage of recently developed methodologies for studying congruence (Edwards, 1994), Guillermo Dabos and I were able to operationalize agreement and test its effects on outcomes of interest to both worker and employer. Results demonstrate strong positive effects (Dabos and Rousseau, 2004a) while raising the question of why divergent beliefs exist between the parties.

Consistent with Whetton's (2001) notion that all theory building requires boundaries specifying its limits, the boundary conditions need attention. The modeling of psychological contracts has ruled out general expectations because their effects when unmet do not have the same intense responses that unmet obligations and promised-based beliefs have. Yet, I wonder how much *ex-ante* promises matter in relation to *ex-post* reliance. Considering that people are expected to have adverse reactions to losses, is failing to meet an *ex-ante* promise significant to worker responses if they haven't relied upon that promise? I wonder how much of the effects of psychological contracts come from reliance as opposed to promises *per se*. Another boundary condition is the sources of meaning of promise and obligation in other countries as well as the evolving status of contracts and contract making. I suspect that in non-Western societies, the operative level for employment obligations may be the work group rather than the individual. A host of unresolved issues remain, many of which surround employment-related obligations across levels, including normative contracts.

Another fertile area for theory building and research is the varying tendency of individuals to believe they are bound to keep an obligation or promise. Early experiences gleaned from my executive teaching suggested that while most people believe their firm has an obligation to honor commitments made at the time of hire, others do not see it that way. Anecdotally, this difference seems to be experience-related such that chief executives and finance officers are less inclined to see the obligations recognized by their counterparts at other levels and functions. Ranging further afield, I think that we will someday see work into the biological and genetic bases in promise making and keeping, since there is reason to believe that there is a material process that promotes the making and keeping of promises in human beings (see Wilson, 1999).

10.4 ADVICE FOR DEVELOPING NEW THEORY

I worry a bit about generalizing too much from my own experience. This account plays up my personal and professional circumstances and the fact that I have focused a long time on the same research domain. Not every interesting problem is anchored in a scholar's life history. The problem can be created by need, opportunity, or circumstance. I also doubt that a good theory requires a single dominant theme in one's research over time. Monad and Jacob managed to discover how gene functioning could be switched on and off and win a Nobel Prize, without having any apparent personal angle to the problem, and each went on to study a variety of other things. The best advice implicit in my experience is to experiment with ways of working that help you learn and seek out others to help and learn with you. Here are some ways of working that I found useful.

Figuring out the right question to ask has to be the hardest part. A good question can guide discovery because even if the answer proves it wrong, you move forward (Wilson, 1999). The question "Do people think in psychological contract-like ways?" arose from talking with Max Bazerman. Formulating that question was important since it had the possibility of disconfirmation, and the potential to establish convergent and discriminant validity. Good questions also call attention to mediating processes that underlie causal relationships. It is not enough to know that something is related to something else. Why and how are what matter.

Talking to smart people who think differently than we do helps in identifying important questions. I was fairly systematic in meeting with colleagues at Northwestern, in the Business School, Psychology, Communications, and Law to see what suggestions they might have for exploring the notion of a psychological contract. Being at a good research university with a diverse faculty is a great asset. I used these conversations to get pointer knowledge about what to read and whom else to talk with. I learned from their answers to the query, "What do you think would be a good question to ask about X (psychological contract, employment relationships, agreements between workers and employers, etc.)? Trying to explain what I thought a psychological contract was and why it mattered invited informed and useful criticism, even if some of my colleagues might refer to it as the "so-called 'psychological contract'." Talking with others made it easier to place the construct of a psychological contract into a theoretical framework. The construct became clearer and more concrete to me while becoming more nuanced and differentiated from look-alike notions of expectations with which the field was already very familiar. I also learned a lot from taking the theory on the road and doing colloquia. (NB: This may work better if you aren't looking for a job.)

Being exposed to real people in real organizations demonstrates a phenomenon's reality and scope. It is incredibly exhilarating to recognize a concept you are trying to tease out in the words or behavior of someone you encounter in a field setting. The words of an MBA with a violated contract, "I am in the process of negotiating with higher mgt for some logic. I do have places to go with my concerns and have never felt the need to remain silent," helped me realize that violation need not be fatal to a psychological contract. Another person describing how he complained when a promise went unmet, "They said the situation was out of their hands and gave me a substantial salary increase," helped me see that idiosyncratic deals can come out of remedies employers offer for violations. The statement, "The recruiter who brought me in left his position and had not communicated our agreements ... I had to start over from ground zero with no negotiating leverage," is ripe with the notion that power plays a role in determining the terms of the psychological contract, and whether it is kept. I never leave a workplace I have visited without a new idea and some intriguing nuances regarding old ones.

My own understanding of the psychological contract has been fed by helping doctoral students to do their *own* work, rather than mine. Though I have had a variety of students help me with my own projects, I spend a fair amount of time helping students conduct research they initiate based on their own questions, preferred field settings, and methodologies. In this way students with good ideas take ownership and the lead in their research, taking it in gratifying directions I couldn't have foreseen. Sometimes this work goes in the direction of psychological contract issues, sometimes not. When psychological contract issues are involved, they often spring up apparently on their own behest—honest. The result of being an advisor on a student's own project has been that I have learned things I wouldn't have found out otherwise.

Lastly, though this may be quirky to me, heuristics can be a precursor to theory development. In the form of diagrams, continua, NxN tables, etc., heuristics can help organize thinking and probe what we know and/or need to know. Sometimes, I get flooded with all the details and nuances relevant to a concept or behavioral process. Taking dimensions that seem to characterize the data or observations and juxtaposing them can help reveal sensible patterns that can be used to provide more nuanced, richer, yet accessible descriptions. This is how the four quadrants representing psychological contract forms came about, which has helped to frame psychological contract description, operationalization, and theory building (Rousseau, 1995; Hui, et al., 2004). Though heuristics don't always lead to an "ah ha," they can spur thinking in new directions and make the path easier to explain to others.

10.5 CONCLUSION

Herb Simon, a wonderful colleague and awe-inspiring scholar, was once asked whether his work had had the kind of impact he had hoped. "No," he said, "I never had apostles." It is hard for me to imagine what our field would look like without Herb Simon's work and legacy, but his comment is a reminder that if any theory has real impact it's only because a lot of people make it so. (This will be immediately evident to readers who check out the citation to Shore, et al., 2004, in this chapter's reference section.) I think Herb was saying that many unresolved issues remained in his work; and, until they are addressed, the impact he hoped for is not fully realized. That I can appreciate because there remain so many important unanswered questions pertaining to the psychological contracts of workers and employers. Thus, my hope is that future theory builders and testers enjoy the same fascination with the psychological contract that I do.

REFERENCES

ANDERSON, E., and WEITZ, B. (1992). The uses of pledges to sustain commitment in distribution channels. *Journal of Marketing Research*, 29: 18–34.

ARGYRIS, C. (1962). *Understanding Organizational Behavior*. Homewood, Ill.: Dorsey.

ATIYAH, P. S. (1981). *An Introduction to the Law of Contract*. 4th edn., Oxford: Clarendon Press.

BARNARD, C. I. (1938). *Functions of the Executive*. Cambridge, Mass.: Harvard University Press.

CADIN, L. (2000). Does psychological contract theory work in France? In Rousseau and Schalk (2000, pp. 67–86).

CLARK, M. S., and REIS, H. T. (1988). Interpersonal processes in close relationships. *Annual Review of Psychology*, 39: 609–672.

CORBIN, A. K. (1952). *Corbin on Contracts*. St. Paul, Minn.: West Publishing.

COSMIDES, L., and TOOBY, J. (1989). Evolutionary psychology and the generation of culture: II. Case study: A computational theory of social exchange. *Ethology and Sociobiology*, 10: 51–97.

—— —— (1992). Cognitive adaptations for social exchange. In *The Adapted Mind: Evolutionary Psychology and the Generation of Culture*: 163–228. London: Oxford University Press.

DABOS, G., and ROUSSEAU, D. M. (2004a). Mutuality and reciprocity in the psychological contracts of employee and employer, *Journal of Applied Psychology*, 89: 52–72.

—— —— (2004b). Social interaction patterns shaping employee psychological contracts: Network-wide and local effects. *Proceedings of the Academy of Management Meetings*, New Orleans.

EDWARDS, J. R. (1994). The study of congruence in organizational behavior research: Critique and a proposed alternative. *Organizational Behavior and Human Decision Processes*, 58: 51–100.

FARNSWORTH, E. A. (1982). *Contracts.* Boston: Little, Brown.

FOA, U. G., and FOA, E. B. (1975). *Societal Structures of the Mind.* Springfield, Ill.: Charles C. Thomas.

FICHMAN, M. (2003). Straining toward trust: Some constraints on studying trust in organizations. *Journal of Organizational Behavior,* 24: 133–157.

GHISELLI, E. (1964). *Theory of Psychological Measurement.* New York: McGraw Hill.

GLENDON, M. A., GORDON, M. W., and OSAKWE, C. (1985). *Comparative Legal Traditions: Text, Materials, and Cases on the Civil Law, Common Law, and Socialist Law Traditions, with Special Reference to French, West German, English, and Soviet Law.* St. Paul, Minn.: West.

HIRSCHMAN, A. O. (1970). *Exit, Voice, and Loyalty.* Cambridge, Mass.: Harvard University Press.

HO, V. T. (2002). Evaluation of psychological contract fulfillment: A social network perspective. Carnegie Mellon University Dissertation, Pittsburgh, Pa.

—— (2005). Social influence on evaluations of psychological contract fulfillment. *Academy of Management Review,* 30: 113–128.

HUI, C., LEE, C., and ROUSSEAU, D. M. (2004). Psychological contracts in China: Investigating instrumentality and generalizability. *Journal of Applied Psychology,* 89: 311–321.

KANFER, F. H., and KAROLY, P. (1972). Self-regulation and its clinical applications: Some additional considerations. In R. C. Johnson, P. R. Dokecki, and O. H. Mowrer (eds.), *Conscience, Control, and Social Reality.* New York: Holt, Rinehart and Winston.

—— Cox, L. E., GREINER, J. M., and KAROLY, P. (1974). Contracts, demand characteristics, and self-control. *Journal of Personality and Social Psychology,* 30: 605–619.

KLEIN, K. J., and KOZLOWSKI, S. W. J. (2001). *Multilevel Theory, Research, and Methods in Organizations: Foundations, Extensions, and New Directions.* San Francisco: Jossey-Bass.

LEVINSON, H., PRICE, C., MUNDEN, K., MANDL, H., and SOLLEY, C. (1962). *Men, Management, and Mental Health.* Cambridge, Mass.: Harvard University Press.

MACNEIL, I. R. (1985). Relational contract: What we do and do not know. *Wisconsin Law Review:* 483–525.

MILES, R. E., and SNOW, C. C. (1980). Designing strategic human resource systems. *Organizatonal Dynamics:* 36–52.

MILLWARD, L., and HERRIOT, P. (2000). The psychological contract in the United Kingdom. In Rousseau and Schalk (2000: 231–249).

NICHOLSON, N., and JOHNS, G. (1985). The absence culture and the psychological contract: Who's in control of absence? *Academy of Management Review,* 10: 397–407.

ORBELL, J. M., VAN DE KRAGT, A. J. C., and DAWES, R. M. (1988). Explaining discussion-induced cooperation. *Journal of Personality and Social Psychology,* 54: 811–819.

PEEL, S., and INKSON, K. (2000). Economic deregulation and psychological contracts: The New Zealand experience. In Rousseau and Schalk (2000: 192–212).

ROBERTS, K. H., HULIN, C. L., and ROUSSEAU, D. M. (1978). *Developing an Interdisciplinary Science of Organizations.* San Francisco: Jossey-Bass.

ROBINSON, S. L., and ROUSSEAU, D. M. (1994). Violating the psychological contract: Not the exception but the norm. *Journal of Organizational Behavior,* 15: 245–259.

—— KRAATZ, M. S., and ROUSSEAU, D. M. (1994). Changing obligations and the psychological contract: A longitudinal study. *Academy of Management Journal,* 37: 137–152.

ROLOFF, M. (1987). Communication and reciprocity in intimate relationships. In M. E. Roloff and G. R. Miller (eds.), *Interpersonal Processes:* 11–38. Newbury Park, Calif.: Sage.

Rousseau, D. M. (1989). Psychological and implied contracts in organizations. *The Employee Rights and Responsibilities Journal*, 2: 121–139.

—— (1990). New hire perceptions of their own and their employer's obligations: A study of psychological contracts. *Journal of Organizational Behavior*, 11: 389–400.

—— (1995). *Psychological Contract in Organizations: Understanding Written and Unwritten Agreements*. Newbury Park, Calif.: Sage.

—— (1996). Keeping the deal while changing the people. *Academy of Management Executive*, 10: 50–61.

—— (2000a). LMX meets the psychological contract: Looking inside the black box of leader-member exchange. In F. Dansereau and F. Yammarino (eds.), *Leadership: The Multilevel Approaches*, Greenwich, Conn.: JAI Press.

—— (2000b). Psychological contracts in the United States: Diversity, individualism, associability in the market place. In Rousseau and Schalk (2000a: 250–282).

—— (2001). Schema, promises, and mutuality: The psychology of the psychological contract. *Journal of Organizational and Occupational Psychology*, 24: 511–541.

—— (2004). Under the table deals: Idiosyncratic, preferential or unauthorized? In R. Griffin and A. O'Leary-Kelly (eds.), *The Dark Side of Organizational Behavior*: 262–290. San Francisco: Jossey-Bass.

—— (2005). *Idiosyncratic Deals: When Employees Bargain for Themselves*. New York: M. E. Sharpe.

—— and Anton, R. J. (1988). Fairness and implied contract obligations in terminations: A policy-capturing study. *Human Performance*, 1: 273–289.

—— —— (1991). Fairness and obligations in termination decisions: The role of contributions, promises, and performance. *Journal of Organizational Behavior*, 12: 287–299.

—— and Aquino, K. (1993). Fairness and implied contract obligations in job termination: The role of remedies, social accounts, and procedural justice. *Human Performance*, 6: 135–149.

—— Ho. V. T., and Greenberg, J. (forthcoming). Idiosyncratic deals: Theoretical implications of workers' bargaining as individuals. *Academy of Management Review*.

—— Ho, V. T., and Kim, T. G. (2005). Idiosyncratic deals and the psychological contract. Unpublished manuscript, Carnegie Mellon University, Pittsburgh, Pa.

—— and Kim, T. G. (2005). Idiosyncratic deals workers bargain for themselves. Unpublished manuscript, Carnegie Mellon University, Pittsburgh, Pa.

—— and Maclean Parks, J. M. (1993). The contracts of individuals and organizations. In L. L. Cummings and B. M. Staw (eds.), *Research in Organizational Behavior*: 15. 1–43. Greenwich, Conn.: JAI Press.

—— and Schalk, R. (2000). *Psychological Contract in Employment: Cross-national Perspectives*. Newbury Park, Calif.: Sage.

—— and Tijoriwala, S. A. (1999). What's a good reason to change? Motivated reasoning and social accounts in promoting organizational change. *Journal of Applied Psychology*. 84: 514–528.

Sager, C. J. (1976). *Marriage Contracts and Couple Therapy: Hidden Forces in Intimate Relationships*. Oxford: Brunner/Mazel.

Shore, L. M., Tetrick, L. E., Taylor, S., Coyle Shapiro, J. A.-M., Liden, R., McLean Parks, J., Wolfe Morrison, E., Porter, L. W., Robinson, S. L., Roehling, M., Rousseau, D. M., Schalk, R., Tsui, A., and Van Dyne, L. (2004). The employee–organization relationship: A timely concept in a period of transition. J. Martucchio (ed.), *Research in Personnel and Human Resource Management*, vol. 23. Elsevier.

VALERY, P. (1938, 1958): See A. Bedeian, 2004, The gift of professional maturity. *Academy of Management Learning and Education*, 3, 92–98.

WHETTON, D. A. (2001). Modeling-as-theorizing: A methodology for theory development. In D. Partington (ed.), *Essential Skills for Management Research*. Newbury Park, Calif.: Sage.

WILSON, E. O. (1999). *Consilience: The Unity of Knowledge*. New York: Vintage.

....

CHAPTER 11

THE ESCALATION OF COMMITMENT

STEPS TOWARD AN ORGANIZATIONAL THEORY

....

BARRY M. STAW

In this chapter, I will describe the evolution of my research on the escalation of commitment—how it began, how it changed, and where the stream of research now stands, at least from my perspective. It is my hope that some insights may be gained from the way this theory and research developed over time, moving from the test of a relatively narrow hypothesis to the broader investigation of an organizational phenomenon. With luck, this narrative will also provide some lessons, both good and bad, for future researchers seeking to explain a variety of organizational issues.

11.1 ORIGINS OF A THEORY

....

It was the summer of 1973 and I had just completed my first year as a faculty member at the University of Illinois. I had never worked so hard, having taught a large introductory course on behavioral science and a couple of electives on organizational behavior—all without any prior teaching experience. I had also launched several research projects, the most notable being a series of studies with Bobby J. Calder on the effects of extrinsic rewards on intrinsic motivation. Thus, by the end of the school year, I was ready to spend some time away from Urbana-Champaign.

My wife had been lobbying to spend the summer in France, hoping to refresh her language skills and to renew some old friendships. She held a Ph.D. in French literature and needed to reconnect with the mother culture. Not knowing any French, I, naturally, had some trepidation, but thought it would be a delightful experience to rent an apartment in Paris for the summer months. So off we went during the summer of 1973. I had visions of sitting in a Parisian café writing an important theoretical article that would someday be remembered. However, this is not exactly what happened during those summer months.

In preparing for the trip, I realized that it would be difficult to do any writing that depended on data analyses or extensive library resources. Therefore, I came to Paris with a collection of articles on intrinsic motivation, prepared to write a conceptual piece on the effects of intrinsic and extrinsic rewards. But the distractions were too many and varied. I took language classes. I saw the sights. I sat in cafés. As a result, I was making little or no progress on the planned theoretical article. My guilt started to build, especially after receiving a postcard from a senior faculty member at Illinois, Ken Rowland, who remarked casually at the bottom of the card, "I do hope you are getting something done over there in Paris."

What I did get done at those Parisian cafés was an initial mapping of the study of escalation. This was prompted, not by my planned literature review of intrinsic motivation, but by daily reading in the *New York Herald Tribune* about the difficulties the U.S. was having in extricating itself from the Vietnam War. It was also prompted by my prior research and personal experiences during graduate school. As a consequence, I looked at U.S. involvement in Vietnam in a way that was a bit different from others who shared my generation's social values. Let me elaborate.

I had spent much of my graduate student days trying to avoid being drafted, since I was classified "1A" ("available for service") for nearly three years. Therefore, when I was asked to design a study for my research methods course in psychology, I proposed (with my colleague, Bill Notz) a study of the effect of draft lottery numbers on students' attitudes toward the Vietnam War (Notz, Staw, and Cook, 1971; Staw, Notz, and Cook, 1974). Even my dissertation (Staw, 1974) was designed to capitalize on the draft lottery as a naturally randomized treatment. The dissertation was about what happed to young men who joined ROTC in order to avoid being drafted, only to learn later that they had received a high lottery number, thereby making them safe from the draft. The most interesting part of the thesis was the role that commitment played in people's adjustment to changes in organizational inducements. If young men had recently joined ROTC, they could withdraw from the organization when they received a high draft number (and they often did just that). However, for young men who had already signed a binding military contract, receiving a high draft number meant that they would have to stay in ROTC, even though the organization would not be providing any rewards such as draft avoidance. For those who were bound by their previous commitment, receiving a high number was like a dissonance-arousing treatment. It exposed their membership in ROTC as a serious mistake. Although they had joined to avoid the draft, and the organization no longer provided draft avoidance, they could not withdraw. As a consequence, these young men tended to change their attitudes toward ROTC, saying that the drills were more interesting, the uniform was more handsome to wear, and the educational benefits were more desirable. Compared to those who received lower draft numbers, young men with high numbers held more positive attitudes toward ROTC and scored somewhat higher in their performance ratings.

Armed with this dissertation experience, I looked at U.S. involvement in Vietnam as a series of commitments that were hard to break. Early participation in the war (primarily during the Kennedy administration) was marked by setbacks that were interpreted, not as a signal to withdraw, but as a sign that greater involvement was necessary to get the job done. When Lyndon Johnson assumed office, he apparently had doubts about the war effort, but soon became ensnared in the same dilemma as Kennedy. Withdrawal was feared more for its potential damage to the reputation of the United States (which might be seen as weak and its commitments not to be trusted by other nations) than for the particular consequences facing Vietnam. As a result, the Johnson administration chose to dramatically increase the number of U.S. troops in Vietnam and soon became closely identified with the fate of the war. When Johnson decided not to run for re-election in 1968, many thought the U.S. would quickly withdraw its troops from Vietnam. But, again, the exit was painfully slow. As a candidate, Richard Nixon promised that he had a plan for ending the war, yet as President, he too became trapped by its consequences. Therefore, by the summer of 1973, the *International Herald Tribune* was filled with articles about difficulties the U.S. faced in ending its costly participation in the Vietnam War. And it was at one of those Parisian cafes, with newspaper in hand, that I began to ponder whether the escalation of commitment to the Vietnam War was indicative of a more general decision process.

From some initial sketches (probably on a napkin or two), I was able to design my first study of the escalation of commitment. I initially conceived of the problem as an application of dissonance theory (Festinger, 1957), where individuals would be likely to keep investing in a losing course of action in order to avoid admitting a mistake. Prior dissonance research, like my dissertation, had examined how people's attitudes toward a task might be affected by self-justification (e.g., Festinger and Carlsmith, 1959; Weick, 1964). Perhaps, this same logic might also apply to an investment situation where people put money or effort into a course of action, only to find out that the consequences are negative. Like the Vietnam War effort, people may invest in stocks, careers, or even marriages, and when these investments do not pay off, they may not necessarily withdraw from the situation. Instead, people may actually invest further so as to turn the situation around—to prove that their prior decision was indeed an accurate or appropriate one.

Given the basic idea that escalation may be due to an effort to justify or rationalize a course of action, I thought through some options for testing the hypothesis. I knew that I needed to demonstrate more than continued investment following negative feedback, since this could be interpreted as a rational effort to recoup losses rather than a result of self-justification. That is, individuals may choose to redouble efforts to save an investment because it is simply the strategy of greatest economic gain, making it impossible to separate economic and psychological processes. Therefore, after some consideration, I came up with a design that compared the actions of decision makers who faced differing consequences (gains and losses) and levels of responsibility for those consequences. I predicted a general tendency for decision makers to invest greater resources when a course of action was not succeeding. I also predicted that those who were responsible for initiating the course of action would be more likely to invest further resources in it. More important, however, was the prediction of an interaction between responsibility and consequences. When those who originated a course of action also suffered a setback, they would be especially likely to reinvest in the losing course of action, since they would be particularly motivated to justify or rationalize their behavior.

11.1.1 Initial Research Findings

At the end of our stay in Paris, I returned to Illinois with detailed notes about how to conduct a study of escalation. Soon I hired a research assistant (William Brighton) who helped develop some of the initial materials used in a decision case. The case was a fairly straightforward outline of a large firm facing a decision to allocate R&D funds among various product lines. We opted for an initial decision to allocate monies to consumer versus industrial products so that subjects would not base their decisions on knowledge of particular products or technology (e.g., computers or electronics). We also decided to conduct the study as a role-playing exercise so that business school students could play the part of a practicing manager. Though the decision making would be simulated, we thought this would provide more external validity than an exercise in which students make small gambles or financial choices using nominal amounts of money.

The results of this first investigation were highly supportive of the original hypotheses about escalation and were published in a paper called "Knee-Deep in the Big Muddy: A Study of Escalating Commitment Toward a Chosen Course of Action" (Staw, 1976). Although responses to the paper were generally positive, few anticipated that the paper would be the start of a larger theory. Basically, the paper was viewed as a clever demonstration of the escalation phenomenon, with the title of the paper gaining almost as much attention as the research itself. I had succeeded in isolating a behavioral effect, something that social psychologists were trained to do. The research was interpreted as a useful application of social psychological theory to an organizational problem, not as the beginning of a separate, organizationally based theory.

Sometime after the completion of the "Big Muddy" paper, I realized that I was not alone in discovering the escalation effect. Joel Brockner and Jeffrey Rubin had been studying a similar phenomenon they called "entrapment," using various games to demonstrate how people will invest additional time and effort toward an elusive goal (for a review, see Brockner and Rubin, 1985). Allen Tegar (1980) was also investigating a similar effect using numerous variations of the Dollar Auction Game (Shubik, 1971). In these auctions, subjects placed bids on various denominations of money (usually $1.00 or $5.00), with the winning bid gaining the currency but the second highest bidder also having to pay for the prize (without ever receiving the money). Results showed that the auctions generally started low, but did not often end until participants paid much greater than face value for the currency (e.g., more than $1.00 for the sale of a dollar), as both parties bid to avoid finishing in second place.

When I first discovered these competing studies, I was a bit crestfallen. My efforts were not unique and I would have to share any glories to be garnered. There may even be some squabbling over who did what, and during what time period, as with many scientific quests. Fortunately, these worries were soon overtaken by the more positive thought that three separate and independent investigations had found essentially the same thing. None of us knew about the others' work when we designed our studies and we all used different methods and procedures. Still, we all found a similar tendency for individuals to increase their investment in a losing course of action.

To avoid any rivalries over this literature, Joel Brockner and I made an explicit pact to mention each other's studies whenever we were questioned about the subject in academic or popular forums. However, over the years, the designation of "escalation of commitment" seemed to take hold in the organizational literature, probably because most of the early work in our field used this terminology. Brockner and Rubin's labeling of "entrapment" was more predominant in the social psychological literature, no doubt because most of their studies were published for that audience. Tegar's "too much invested to quit" designation tended to be confined to the conflict literature, since his studies (collected in book form) were primarily concerned with interpersonal and international disputes.

11.1.2 Subsequent Research

Often when a phenomenon is isolated (such as the "over-justification" and "by-stander" effects), an initial demonstration study is quickly followed by a series of research papers that seek to condition or limit the effect. A number of third variables are identified that may interact with the original treatment, showing that the effect only occurs under certain specified conditions. After a group of moderators are found, the original effect may be reinterpreted as a somewhat rare, even trivial, phenomenon. Then, researchers move on to other, seemingly robust main effects, only to begin the "process of limitation" all over again.

By the late 1970s, the search for conditions limiting escalation effects had begun, probably fueled in part by my own follow-up studies on escalation. After completing the "Big Muddy" paper, I attempted to document other conditions that might facilitate or inhibit escalation. One study (Staw and Fox, 1977) manipulated the efficacy of adding resources to a course of action by providing subjects with information about the management of units receiving the funds (the Consumer or Industrial Products divisions in the original Adams and Smith Case). Another study examined the consequences of prior failure as well as the likely cause of that failure, showing that commitment was highest when prior failure could be attributed to an exogenous cause that was not likely to persist (Staw and Ross, 1978). Other limiting conditions were soon isolated by other authors as well (e.g., Conlon and Wolf, 1980; McCain, 1986; Northcraft and Wolf, 1984).

With the number of potential moderators rapidly mounting during the 1980s, I presented an Academy of Management paper strongly criticizing this incremental search for third variables. To discourage more piecemeal bites out of the original escalation effect, I even passed out a "mock listing" of possible moderators. Although I had intended to discourage the search for moderators, I discovered on a visit to another university that this same list was posted on a faculty member's wall, heralding the many opportunities for future research on escalation.

Fearing the eventual demise of the escalation effect, I sought to demonstrate that the phenomenon was more than a simple decision bias that may occur under some limited conditions. I had originally been attracted to the concept of escalation because of the frequency that leaders seemed to fall into this trap. Yet, my initial studies were devoid of either interpersonal or organizational mechanisms. They appeared, on the surface, to be more grounded than either the Brockner or Tegar streams of research, largely because I had asked business students to work on a somewhat realistic case rather than having used a more artificial game or bargaining task. Nonetheless, I somehow left out key social and political determinants of how escalation arises in organizational contexts.

The first study designed to capture some of these contextual elements was the "Trapped Administrator" experiment (Fox and Staw, 1979). In this study, we demonstrated that administrators often increase their commitment to a losing course of action, not because they want to rationalize or justify a decision to themselves, but because their credibility is threatened by other organizational actors. Unlike the cognitive dissonance (or self-justification) literature in which individuals seek to prove to *themselves* that they are rational or competent decision makers, we thought the effort to demonstrate competence may be more externally based. Therefore, in the Fox and Staw (1979) experiment, we showed that when decision makers faced job insecurity and resistance to their decision making (by a board of directors), they tended to increase their investment in the previously chosen (and losing) course of action. The results demonstrated that administrators may try to save losing courses of action so as to avoid being criticized, demoted, or even fired.

The Fox and Staw (1979) study helped move escalation from a process that is strictly cognitive (such as a decision bias) to one that is more socially based. Another experiment (Staw and Ross, 1980) pushed that logic further by showing how escalation is often bound to a culture's prevailing stereotype of leadership. The idea for this leadership study came from observations of the presidency of Jimmy Carter. At the time, Carter's leadership was under fire, and a Gallop Poll noted that perceived inconsistency was one of the main faults people found with his leadership style. Interestingly, of those who disapproved of Carter's leadership, business and professional workers were most disturbed by his apparent inconsistency. Although one might think business and professional groups would be more tolerant of complexity (c.f., Tetlock, 1981), these data pointed to the existence of a strong norm for consistency. The same conclusion might also be drawn from the 2004 presidential campaign. George Bush's re-election committee worked hard (largely through television advertising) to characterize John Kerry as a "flip-flopper," and the effort is thought to have contributed to the Bush victory. It therefore seems, at least in the American culture, that leaders are rewarded for appearing to be consistent, even if such consistency means remaining committed to a losing course of action.

To test for norms of consistency, Staw and Ross (1980) asked people to read about the behavior of a state administrator trying to cope with a housing crisis. The administrator had appointed a blue ribbon commission to recommend ways of improving housing in his state. In the *experimenting* condition, he chose the first recommended course of action and waited for the results. When he saw no improvement in housing data, he switched to the second recommended policy. Then, when there was again no improvement, the administrator moved to the third policy option. In the *consistent* condition, the administrator was described as persisting with the initial policy recommendation, regardless of the lack of progress reflected by the housing data.

In addition to the style of leadership, Staw and Ross (1980) also manipulated the ultimate fate of the chosen policy. Some administrators were described as being ultimately successful in their actions, since the housing data finally improved over time. Some administrators were described as continuing to fail, because the housing data showed no upturn at all. As predicted, the results of the study showed main effects of both consistency and success on the perception of leadership. Those who were consistent or successful were rated by subjects as being higher in leadership qualities. More importantly, the ratings also showed a significant inter-action of consistency and consequences. Special praise and approval was reserved for those who were both persistent *and* successful. They were the heroes who were lauded for "sticking to their guns" in the face of seemingly bleak odds, only to have their patience and "insight" rewarded in the end.

11.2 TOWARD AN ORGANIZATIONAL THEORY OF ESCALATION

In 1981, I published an article that reviewed the literature on escalation and outlined what I thought was a reasonable model of the escalation process. Al-though the paper (Staw, 1981) is still often cited as a summary of escalation theory, I now think its model (Figure 11.1) contains a fairly limited view of the escalation process. As shown in the figure, commitment to a course of action is a function of three major determinants: motivation to justify previous decisions, norms for consistency, and expected value calculations. Stated in process terms, there is retrospective rationality (based primarily on needs to justify behavior to oneself and others), modeling (based on adherence to cultural and organizational norms for consistency), and prospective rationality (based on perceived probability of outcomes and the utility of those outcomes). Thus, at its core, the model shows three separate and competing determinants of commitment to a course of action.

There are also a few subtleties inherent in the 1981 escalation model (illustrated by the dotted lines in Figure 11.1). Motives to justify a course of action are predicted to cause individuals to overstate the efficacy of future expenditures and also to lead one to underestimate the persistence of the cause of a setback. Justification is likewise expected to lead individuals to alter the value of future outcomes, since the value of outcomes may become more intense after experiencing a loss. Finally, it is possible that a need to justify prior decisions may heighten norms for consistency, and that consistency may itself lead to the perception of more likely outcomes. To my knowledge, none of these linkages has been researched, except for the predic-tion that the experience of losses may influence the valuation of subsequent outcomes (e.g., Kahneman and Tversky, 1982). Nor has there been much concern for how commitment is derived from conflicting processes, as is often the case with prospective and retrospective rationality.

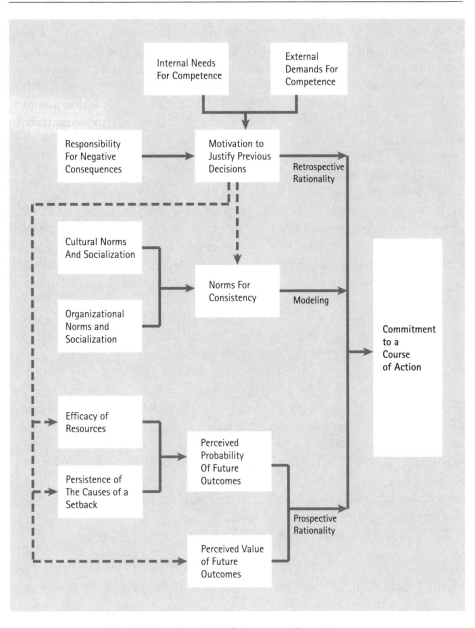

Fig. 11.1   A model of the commitment process

Source: Staw (1981)

Major improvements in escalation theory (or at least my interpretation of it) did not come until Jerry Ross and I embarked on a case study of the world's fair, Expo 86 (Ross and Staw, 1986). Jerry Ross was teaching at Simon Fraser University while the Canadian Province of British Columbia constructed Expo. He was a nearby witness to what was widely viewed as a planning disaster, and the situation seemed to fit the classic pattern of escalating commitment to a losing course of action. When British Columbia first proposed hosting the world's fair (in 1978), the project was projected to cost $78 million, with a "worst-case" deficit of $6 million. As events transpired, however, the project grew to a $1.5 billion project with a projected deficit of $311 million, far beyond what any decision maker would have approved at the outset of the course of action. Still, there was no backing down from the Province's commitment to the fair. As things continued to worsen, expenditures were continually increased in order to complete the project before its scheduled opening date.

Jerry Ross collected an enormous amount of background material on Expo (e.g., prior newspaper articles, documents, press releases) and conducted a number of interviews with reporters and Expo staff members. Our joint task was to learn from this vast amount of material about escalation as it transpired in the field. Thus, instead of formulating experimental scenarios that might tap escalation processes, we examined how escalation played out in a real organizational and political context.

After sifting through the materials, it appeared that there were several key forces at work in the Expo case. The project was initiated with overly optimistic estimations about costs and revenues. But, as the financial situation worsened, a great deal of defensiveness and justification was exhibited by the Premier of British Columbia in discounting the warnings of budget analysts and critics. And, the Premier's defense of Expo seemed to become heightened as his political career and the fate of his party became increasingly staked to Expo. Finally, as other groups and organizations started to be linked economically to the fair, the project appeared to gain a wide range of advocates throughout the public and private sectors. Thus, over time, the commitment to host the 1986 world's fair seemed to grow from a limited decision based on (often faulty) economic expectations to one that was governed by a host of behavioral processes.

The Expo case forced us to move away from the prevailing debate about whether escalation of commitment was an economic or behavioral question. It was clearly both. Economic projections were not only part of the initial planning process, but played a key role throughout the ongoing saga of the project. And, economic projections were something more than a cold estimation based on objective facts. They were political ammunition for efforts to convince various constituencies that Expo was the right or wrong course of action, and, as such, they were regularly slanted and misrepresented to the public. Nonetheless, when Expo's financial situation became absolutely dire, even the most ardent adversaries had to recognize the economic realities. Unfortunately, one of those realities was that Expo needed to proceed to completion once a certain level of expenditures had already been made, since opening the fair was the only way to bring forward some, albeit smaller than expected, revenues. Thus, it made little sense in the case of Expo to say that escalation was a purely rational or irrational process. It was both.

The Expo case also forced us to confront the multiplicity of variables that may be important in escalation situations. Because of Expo's complexity, we were compelled to place all the possible causes into some logical order. We did this by sorting the various causes into broader categories, such as psychological, social, and organizational determinants. We also tried to reduce the complexity by thinking about whether a more limited set of factors might be important at certain points in the escalation cycle. Such a temporal ordering did seem to characterize the Expo case, since commitment to the fair appeared to be especially determined by particular forces at different stages of the project.

Over the years, Jerry Ross and I have articulated several variations of a temporal model of escalation, breaking the process into three or four distinct stages (Ross and Staw, 1986; Staw and Ross, 1987, 1989). As shown in Figure 11.2, the decision to begin a course of action generally starts with some projection of gains and losses. As demonstrated by many researchers (e.g., Buehler, Griffen, and Ross, 1994; Shapira, 1995) initial projections are likely to be overly optimistic. People tend to underestimate (or not see) the difficulty of implementing a new policy or product, and the political dynamics of firms may actually encourage managers to overstate the facts. As in a "winners curse" experiment (Samuelson and Bazerman, 1985), administrators who succeed in getting funding for their projects may be precisely the ones who make the most rosy (and unrealistic) projections.

If results from a course of action are clear-cut, and are extremely negative, there may be an early exit from the line of behavior. In contrast, when initial results are somewhat ambiguous, or at least not so negative that one can still see hope for the future, the process of escalation may begin. As shown in Figure 11.2, psychological and social forces may start to act as a counterweight to more objective economic data. Motivation to justify a course of action, both to oneself and others, may lead decision makers to discount economic warnings or to assume that success is just around the corner. And, as results get worse, exit can be prevented as other behavioral forces build up over time to form a defense of the course of action. Various stakeholders may start to depend on the continued viability of a project for their own political power and livelihood. Careers may be staked to the project. Departmental budgets may depend on continuation of the course of action. At the extreme, a losing project or product can become so institutionalized in an organization that it becomes almost impossible to eliminate. A classic case is the now defunct Pan American Airlines. When the airline was losing a tremendous amount of money on its air travel routes, the organization responded by selling its profitable real estate, catering, and hotel businesses, using the funds to offset losses incurred by the ailing airline business. A wiser choice would have been to sell the money-losing airline and invest the proceeds in its more economically viable units.

Figure 11.2 explains why some organizations persist with losing ventures all the way until bankruptcy. The figure also explains why some organizations are able to

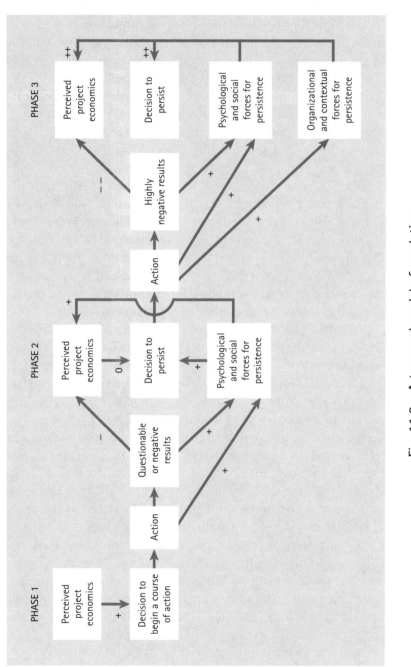

Fig. 11.2   A temporal model of escalation

Source: Staw and Ross (1989)

exit a losing course of action without going through so much protracted pain. As depicted in the model, behavioral variables (e.g., needs for justification and norms of consistency) are not absolute determinants of commitment, where commitment is *guaranteed* under high levels of these variables. Behavioral determinants are simply portrayed as hurdles that perceived project economics (i.e., expectations of gain and loss) must surmount. Therefore, if losses occur rapidly after implementing a course of action—before other behavioral determinants have had a chance to take hold—then economic feedback is less likely to be biased and projections are less likely to be slanted by decision makers. When losses come early and are highly negative (e.g., a fast food chain implementing an undesirable menu item), they will generally swamp any behavioral variables. In contrast, more dangerous cycles of escalation are created when results are initially clouded by extenuating circumstances (e.g., delays in advertising, implementation problems) and when prospects for the future worsen slowly over time. In such cases, behavioral sources of commitment can build up to the point where they will outweigh the influence of negative economic data. Also, especially prone to escalation are projects in which nearly all the economic costs are committed up-front, with revenues not expected until a later date. Once ground is broken and significant monies expended for a construction project, for example, there may be economic as well as behavioral reasons for staying with the project until its completion.

11.2.1 Modifications to the Theory

Once we had derived the temporal model of escalation, Jerry Ross and I sought to apply the theory to another rather extreme example of escalation. The Long Island Lighting Corporation had initially proposed the construction of the Shoreham nuclear power plant in the mid-1960s. It was originally forecasted to cost $65–70 million and to be completed by 1973. However, a series of cost overruns and delays, some caused by exogenous circumstances (e.g., the Three Mile Island accident and the Chernobyl disaster), forced project costs to balloon exponentially to $5.5 billion and for the plant not to be completed until 1989. The plant was never operated commercially and was ultimately sold to the State of New York for $1.00 (for subsequent dismantlement).

An historical analysis of the Shoreham case demonstrated some overall support for the temporal model of escalation (Ross and Staw, 1993). However, the exact ordering of the processes shown in Figure 11.2 was not upheld. Organizational determinants, such as political support and institutionalization, occurred somewhat earlier than we had anticipated. We also underestimated the importance of the sheer size of the project on its likelihood of survival. Because management had "bet the company" on the project, there was little alternative (other than bankruptcy) to persistence in the course of action. Finally, we did not anticipate the role of contextual influences on the project's longevity, since external political groups seemed to be almost as influential as the organization's management in determining commitment to the power plant.

Though Shoreham was not an exact fit to Figure 11.2, it did uphold many of the model's general principles. It was clear from an analysis of the project that commitment was a joint function of behavioral and economic forces. It was also clear that the relative strength of particular forces depended to a great extent upon the time period of the project. As predicted, the Shoreham project started with feedback that was ambiguous enough to allow psychological, social, and organizational forces to take hold. Therefore, by the time results were clearly negative, countervailing forces were sufficiently strong to maintain commitment to the course of action. Finally, the Shoreham case (like Expo) illustrated how commitment can be sustained by the economic facts of the situation during the late stages of an escalation cycle. At a certain point in an escalation situation, there may be no turning back, because ending a project will also mean the demise of the organization itself.

11.2.2 Is the Theory of Escalation Falsifiable?

Although the temporal model of escalation has been applied to some real-world cases, it would be naive to expect that the model will exactly predict any particular episode of escalation. There is just too much uniqueness in most organizational situations to prescribe an exact blueprint for how events will unfold over time. Therefore, one should consider Figure 11.2 less as a strict template and more as a guideline for what to expect in escalation situations. In other words, the temporal model probably represents a prototype, around which individual cases will no doubt vary.

Does the above logic mean that the temporal model of escalation is non-falsifiable? Not at all. Our model may be reversed or thrown out entirely by future empirical studies, especially if they are conducted by scholars not associated with the original theory. My guess is that future theories of escalation will differentiate into specific subtypes, where escalation episodes can be expected to differ depending on the type of project undertaken (e.g., construction, new product development, existing division of a business). It is also possible that future models will become more specific as to the location of particular influences, such as those stemming from the actions of leaders versus other constituents inside and outside the organization.

If the temporal aspect of our escalation model does not hold up to empirical tests, then the resulting theory may look something like the aggregate model in

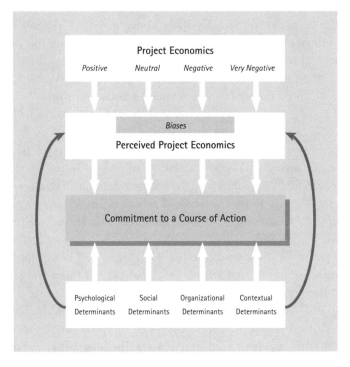

Fig. 11.3   An aggregate model of escalation
Source: Staw (1997)

Figure 11.3. This is a fall-back position (or more rudimentary theory) in which various behavioral and economic determinants vie for influence in an ongoing process of commitment. The model aggregates the various behavioral influences rather than attempts to separate them over time (Staw, 1997). The emphasis is upon continual ebb and flow of commitment to a course of action. The crucial assumption is that behavioral forces must match or exceed the strength of any negative economic data in order to hold organizations (and their decision makers) in a losing course of action. However, there is less concern with the exact ordering of the effects or when particular forces take hold over time in this aggregate model.

11.2.3 From Lab to Field

In many ways, the empirical literature on escalation has been far behind the theoretical reasoning. Most of the research has consisted of experimental tests in which a small number of variables have been isolated as causes of investment decisions. The majority of this research has also been based on a single point in time (see Golz, 1992, 1993 for exceptions). Such a research strategy is understandable, given that the literature has largely been concerned with demonstrating (and debating) the simple existence of behavioral as opposed to economic determinants of commitment. However, owing to the complexity of most field situations, there is no guarantee that the variables manipulated in the laboratory have captured the reality of escalation as it occurs in actual organizations over time.

In light of these uncertainties, I expect that the major advances will come from both additional case studies and quantitative field studies. The later mode of research is perhaps the most challenging, since it is necessary to find situations that have the key ingredients of an escalation situation. To test escalation in the field, one needs to find a situation with the following characteristics: (1) an ongoing rather than one-shot decision; (2) feedback which is ambiguous or negative; and (3) an opportunity to commit additional resources over time. Two recent studies have met these qualifications.

In our first archival study on escalation, Ha Hoang and I examined the investment of time and money in professional basketball players (Staw and Hoang, 1995). Using at least five years of data for each member of the NBA, we found that the size of teams' original investment in players (measured by how highly they were drafted) determined how much time they were granted on the court. We also found that the more highly drafted were players, the longer they remained on the teams that originally drafted them, and the longer they survived in the league. On the surface, these findings might seem rather obvious given that the most highly drafted players would be expected to become the best future performers on the floor (thus meriting more playing time and greater longevity on the team). However, these indicators of commitment were significant after each player's performance was statistically controlled. Thus, regardless of players' actual performance, the commitment of teams to their players was determined, at least in part, by the size of their original investment. These data illustrated that sunk costs can be an important component of personnel decisions, where continued investment in team members can determine the success or failure of the organization.

In a second archival study, Sigal Barsade, Ken Koput, and I analyzed how 132 California banks coped with their bad loans (Staw, Barsade, and Koput, 1997). Using banks' financial data over a nine-year period of time, we predicted that turnover of senior bank managers would lead to a de-escalation of commitment to problem loans. Managerial turnover was used as a proxy for changes in personal responsibility, since it could be assumed that new bank officers would have less responsibility for prior losses (and therefore less need to justify their previous decisions about these loans). The results were fairly straightforward. Turnover of banks' top executives (CEOs, chairmen) as well as other senior managers (vice-presidents, chief financial officers, controllers) predicted subsequent provisions for loan losses and the write-off of bad loans. Neither provisions for loan losses nor write-offs predicted subsequent turnover. These longitudinal analyses, therefore, validated one of the key hypotheses from escalation research, namely that responsibility for prior losses will influence commitment to a costly course of action.

11.2.4 Alternative Paths to Understanding the Phenomenon

The two archival studies demonstrated that it is possible to isolate escalation determinants that will hold up over time and in the midst of complicated social situations. These demonstrations do not, of course, explain all the mechanisms and processes involved in escalation situations. For such a detailed understanding, one might go back to the laboratory in an effort to untangle the interactions. The rationale behind this cycling of research is that causal relationships can be established in the controlled setting of a laboratory (or simulation exercise), while generalizability will be provided by field research. The sequence can go either from lab to field or from field to lab, with the product being knowledge that has both internal and external validity.

Unfortunately, such a traditional sequence of laboratory and field tests usually contains some questionable assumptions. One typical assumption is that greater understanding requires increasingly detailed knowledge of a phenomenon. The objective is to break a complex phenomenon into its constituent parts, with the goal of showing how a particular tendency of individuals (e.g., a cognitive bias) may underlie large-scale effects. As an advocate of such an approach, I started investigating escalation with the idea that understanding psychological processes would be necessary (and perhaps even sufficient) to explain an organization's commitment to a course of action. I believed that strong individual-level effects might manifest themselves in many organizational actions. This might happen through the biases leaders bring to the organization or via the aggregation of individual tendencies in interpersonal settings. Although the logic seemed reasonable and could be defended to others (e.g., Staw, 1991; Staw and Sutton, 1993), I started to appreciate the difficulties of generalizing individual effects to organizational phenomenon as my studies of escalation became more contextually based. I started to realize that, even though psychological effects might be manifested in an organizational setting, they may also set in motion other, more macro processes. Therefore, the dynamics of escalation may be a truly multilevel process that necessitates much more interdisciplinary thinking than most researchers (including me) have been comfortable with.

It is certainly possible to learn something about escalation from laboratory research, especially if a lab study is designed to capture processes observed from real-life episodes of escalation. This may often require materials that are contextually based (such as in-basket exercises) and experiments that run over multiple periods of time. Yet, understanding the dynamics of escalation—how multiple variables interact over time—is very difficult with experimental research. These dynamics are also hard to see with field studies that are designed to illustrate the power of a few determinants over time (such as our NBA and bank studies). Missing from such inquiries is a representation of how variables at different levels of analysis influence organizational decisions regarding a course of action. It is especially difficult to discern how individual tendencies translate (perhaps indirectly) into departmental and organizational actions. Such inquiries usually require softer studies that shed light on a phenomenon *as a whole* rather than only its constituent parts.

Given these research difficulties, I believe an understanding of escalation processes will require a great deal of flexibility in method. By defining escalation as an organizational rather than an individual problem, the research must necessarily be interdisciplinary. It will require modes of inquiry that isolate more than a small slice of the phenomenon, and will necessitate many case studies as well as more traditional quantitative research. However, that is the beauty of this particular area of research. The study of escalation may be especially valuable as a point of contact between micro and macro styles of inquiry—perhaps as a test case for whether multilevel theorizing is even possible in the field of organizational behavior.

11.2.5 Learning from Controversy

Although I have tried to make the case for multilevel research on escalation, the simple demonstration of individual-level effects was, for a long time, considered to be a controversial finding. This was especially true in the 1970s and 1980s before decision biases were widely accepted in the behavioral sciences. Arguments that investment decisions might be determined by behavioral tendencies rather than more traditional economic (or expected value) calculations were especially suspect in the eyes of business school faculty. Consider, for example, the following story. In the mid-1970s, I presented some of my early escalation research as a job talk at one (unnamed) business school. After the presentation, I was assured by a senior member of the faculty that I would soon receive a job offer. However, when nothing transpired over the next several weeks, I asked this same colleague what had happened. He promised to tell all, but only after a few drinks at a future Academy of Management meeting. Apparently, following my talk (and after I had discussed how people can behave somewhat irrationally in escalation situations), two senior economists visited their dean's office. They assured the dean that they would resign if I were ever hired by their school.

Though advocating behavioral rather than economic determinants is no longer considered heresy, there are still some controversial issues that have not been resolved. For example, a few authors have demonstrated that behavioral effects can be overridden by an economic calculus if costs and benefits are made sufficiently clear (e.g., Northcraft and Neale, 1986). Bowen (1987) and Whyte (1986) similarly criticized escalation studies for presenting subjects with an uncertain course of action instead of alternatives with specified outcomes and known probabilities. In a sense, these researchers would like escalation situations to be converted from states of uncertainty (where probabilities cannot be specified) to questions of risk and reward. They would like to convert complicated but realistic situations into contexts where straightforward calculations and decision rules can be applied. Unfortunately, escalation may occur precisely in those situations where the facts are vague and where the observation of events can be colored by prior commitment to a course of action.

A related, but broader, theoretical issue concerns the possible conversion of various psychological and social determinants into some form of common calculus. For example, it can be argued that self-justification effects are essentially the result of expected pain or embarrassment associated with having to admit a mistake to oneself or others (Aronson, 1972). Likewise, when consistency in action leads to approval by others and inconsistency is associated with censure, this can be interpreted as bringing reputational gains and losses to an organizational leader. Similar reputational consequences can be incurred by an organization having to sever contracts and obligations associated with the closure of a product line or operating division of a company. Thus, when various behavioral mechanisms are evaluated in terms of their impact on commitment to a course of action, it is possible to view each mechanism as bringing some change to an overall cost–benefit ratio.

The problem with such cost–benefit reasoning, of course, is whether anything new is learned by distilling all forms of psychological and sociological effects into the logic of subjective utility. If we focus too much on the calculus, we may miss the reasons why a psychological or social mechanism is brought to the fore by a particular situation. Nonetheless, by emphasizing an expanded set of expected gains and losses, it may be possible to develop a common metric for aggregating various forces in an escalation situation. Such a metric might, for example, allow us to predict what will happen when there are three moderate forces for commitment and one very strong force for withdrawal. This would be impossible with current models (e.g., Figures 11.2 and 11.3), since they are better at pointing out the existence of conflicting forces than at predicting their exact consequences.

11.3 SOME POSSIBLE ADVICE

In advising young scholars interested in developing new theory, I would offer the following tips from escalation research:

First, I would consider the events of the world (from business, government, and politics) to be as rich a source of ideas as any academic literature. One's own personal and family experiences can also be mined for interesting research ideas. In the case of escalation, I was not only prompted to the research idea by observing the U.S. involvement in Vietnam, these observations took on particular meaning given my prior experiences with the military draft. In addition, when I derived my specific hypotheses on self-justification, I drew on some vivid personal recollections. Once, on vacation from college, my father asked me to look over some financial statements to see whether he should buy a particular retail store. When I studied the numbers (with my recently acquired knowledge of introductory accounting) and pronounced the purchase to be a waste of money, my father drew a line through both the revenue and cost figures. He said that the financial forecasts were far too conservative. When I protested, he admitted that it really didn't matter since he had already purchased the store a few weeks earlier! Experiences such as these can be an invaluable tool for constructing theory, since they have more depth and meaning than any perusal of the research literature.

Although I tout experience over literature reviews, I still think it is important to confront a potential research question with as broad a theoretical arsenal as possible. Certainly my initial studies of escalation were shaped in large part by my earlier dissertation. I also believe that the theory's transformation from a psychological to a more interdisciplinary model may have been aided by prior academic training. At the time of my graduate work at Northwestern University, the doctoral program in organization research was almost entirely sociological. Though I was greatly influenced by social psychologists such as Thomas D. Cook and Donald T. Campbell, most of my colleagues and faculty advisors were interested in macro or sociological questions. Therefore, it was probably easier for me than other psychologists interested in escalation to make the transition from a largely individually-oriented theory to one that is also based on social and organizational forces.

A third piece of advice from work on escalation would be to approach research questions with as much methodological flexibility as possible. As I have noted, my research started with a series of laboratory experiments designed to show that, under certain conditions, people may throw good money after bad. Unfortunately, my own theoretical reasoning did not really broaden until I had worked on some case studies of escalation. Only then did I realize that escalation was an interdisciplinary problem with multilevel forces at work. As a result of this experience, I am now a firm believer in the power of grounded research, at least as a means of theory formulation. Such investigations need not come in the form of publishable case studies. They can also result from in-depth examinations of organizational events or from interviews with key actors in a social situation. Regardless, grounded observations will likely enrich your hypotheses and broaden your understanding of an organizational phenomenon.

A fourth tip might concern the orchestration or sequencing of research studies. When I entered academia, I had the naive impression that discoveries would be followed by press conferences and then a flurry of follow-up research. Forget the press conferences and be satisfied with a few colleagues (and relatives) reading a paper. Also forget the flurry of follow-up studies, if you are not willing to do them yourself. Rarely does a single study ignite enough interest to start a genuine stream of research. So be prepared to carry on alone for a while. And, even when others have been brought into a line of research, do not expect them to pursue the issue in exactly the way you might prefer. That is why I initiated case studies and archival research on escalation. Without some intervention, I feared that escalation research might stagnate and eventually die in the laboratory.

My fifth and final tip relates to the process of theory formulation itself. The field of organizational behavior is fond of summary models using a series of boxes and arrows. I too have found them to be helpful devices in illustrating a theoretical process or set of mechanisms. My complaint is that much of our field equates the graphical listing of variables with theoretical formulation. Therefore, we need to be constantly reminded that the goal of theory is to answer the question of "why" (Kaplan, 1964; Merton, 1967). Strong theory delves into the connections underlying a phenomenon. It is a story about why acts and events occur, with a set of convincing and logically interconnected arguments (Sutton and Staw, 1995). Hence, my advice for young scholars is to use diagrams as an aid to theoretical reasoning, but not as an end in itself. With luck, your models will have implications that cannot be seen with the naked (or theoretically unassisted) eye, and may have implications that run counter to common sense. If successful, the product may even satisfy Weick's (1989) dictum that good theory will explain, predict, and delight.

11.4 FINAL THOUGHTS

I have tried in this chapter to trace the origins of my research on escalation, and to show how this research progressed into an organizational theory. As I have illustrated, the theory was not evident until the research was well underway, and even then the theoretical formulation took many unexpected turns. Although external events had prompted the original set of hypotheses and empirical tests, these ideas did not grow into a broader theory until many years (and several studies) had transpired. Even now, with escalation research having matured over nearly three decades, one can still consider the theory to be an unfinished product.

Its future form will no doubt be determined by scholars who can see events and processes more clearly than I have been able to do.

REFERENCES

ARONSON, E. (1972). *The Social Animal.* San Francisco: W. H. Freeman.

BOWEN, M. G. (1987). The escalation phenomenon reconsidered. Decision dilemmas or decision errors? *Academy of Management Review,* 12: 52–66.

BROCKNER, J., and RUBIN, J. Z. (1985). *Entrapment in Escalating Conflicts: A Social Psychological Analysis.* New York: Springer-Verlag.

BUEHLER, R., GRIFFEN, D., and Ross, M. (1994). Exploring the "Planning Fallacy": Why people underestimate their task completion times. *Journal of Personality and Social Psychology,* 67: 366–381.

CONLON, E. J., and WOLF, G. (1980). The moderating effects of strategy, visibility, and involvement on allocation behavior. *Organizational Behavior and Human Performance,* 26: 172–192.

FESTINGER, L. (1957). *A Theory of Cognitive Dissonance.* Stanford, Calif.: Stanford University Press.

—— and CARLSMITH, J. M. (1959). Cognitive consequences of forced compliance. *Journal of Abnormal and Social Psychology,* 58: 203–210.

Fox, F. V., and STAW, B. M. (1979). The trapped administrator: Effects of job insecurity and policy resistance upon commitment to a course of action. *Administrative Science Quarterly,* 24: 449–471.

GOLTZ, S. M. (1992). A sequential analysis of continued investments of organizational resources in non-performing courses of action. *Journal of Applied Behavior Analysis,* 25: 561–574.

—— (1993). Examining the joint roles of responsibility and reinforcement history in recommitment. *Decision Sciences,* 24: 977–994.

KAHNEMAN, D., and TVERSKY, A. (1982). Psychology of preferences. *Scientific American,* 246: 161–173.

KAPLAN, A. (1964). *The Conduct of Inquiry.* New York: Harper and Row.

McCAIN, B. E. (1986). Continuing investment under conditions of failure: A laboratory study of the limits to escalation. *Journal of Applied Psychology,* 71: 280–284.

MERTON, R. K. (1967). *On Theoretical Sociology.* New York: Free Press.

NORTHCRAFT, G., and NEALE, M. A. (1986). Opportunity costs and the framing of resource allocation decisions. *Organizational Behavior and Human Decision Processes,* 37: 348–356.

—— and WOLF, G. (1984). Dollars, sense, and sunk costs: A life-cycle model of resource allocation decisions. *Academy of Management Review,* 9: 225–234.

NOTZ, W. W., STAW, B. M., and COOK, T. D. (1971). Attitude toward troop withdrawal from Indochina as a function of draft number: Dissonance or self-interest. *Journal of Personality and Social Psychology,* 20: 118–126.

Ross, J. and STAW, B. M. (1986). Expo 86: An escalation prototype. *Administrative Science Quarterly,* 32, 274–297.

—— —— (1993). Organizational escalation and exit: The case of the Shoreham nuclear power plant. *Academy of Management Journal*, 36: 701–732.

SAMUELSON, W. F., and BAZERMAN, M. H. (1985). The winner's curse in bilateral negotiations. In V. Shubik (ed.), *Research in Experimental Economics*: 3. 105–137. Greenwich, Conn.: JAI Press.

SHAPIRA, Z. (1995). *Risk Taking: A Managerial Perspective*. New York: Russell Sage Foundation.

SHUBIK, M. (1971). The dollar auction game: A paradox in noncooperative behavior and escalation. *Journal of Conflict Resolution*, 15: 109–111.

STAW, B. M. (1974). The attitudinal and behavioral consequences of changing a major organizational reward: A natural field experiment. *Journal of Personality and Social Psychology*, 1974, 29: 742–751.

—— (1976). Knee-deep in the big muddy: A study of escalating commitment to a chosen course of action. *Organizational Behavior and Human Performance*, 16: 27–44.

—— (1981). The escalation of commitment: A review and analysis. *Academy of Management Review*, 6: 577–587.

—— (1991). Dressing up like an organization: When psychological theories can explain organizational action. *Journal of Management*, 17: 805–819.

—— (1997). The escalation of commitment: An update and appraisal. In Z. Shapira (ed.) *Organizational Decision Making*: 191–215. Cambridge: Cambridge University Press.

—— BARSADE, S. G., and KOPUT, K. W. (1997). Escalation at the credit window: A longitudinal study of bank executives' recognition and write-off of problem loans. *Journal of Applied Psychology*, 82: 130–142.

—— and FOX, F. (1977). Escalation: Some determinants to a previously chosen course of action. *Human Relations*, 30: 431–450.

—— and HOANG, H. (1995). Sunk costs in the NBA: A behavioral determinant of playing time and survival in professional basketball. *Administrative Science Quarterly*, 40: 474–494.

—— NOTZ, W. W., and COOK, T. D. (1974). Vulnerability to the draft and attitudes toward troop withdrawal from Indochina: A replication and refinement, *Psychological Reports*, 34: 407–417.

—— and ROSS, J. (1978). Commitment to a policy decision: A multi-theoretical perspective, *Administrative Science Quarterly*, 23: 40–64.

—— —— (1980). Commitment in an experimenting society: An experiment on the attribution of leadership from administrative scenarios. *Journal of Applied Psychology*, 65: 249–260.

—— —— (1987). Understanding escalation situation: Antecedent, prototypes, and solution. In B. M. Staw and L. L. Cummings (eds.), *Research in Organization Behavior*: 9. 39–78. Greenwich, Conn.: JAI Press.

—— —— (1989). Understanding behavior in escalation situations. *Science*, 246: 216–220.

—— and SUTTON, R. (1993). Macro-organizational psychology. In J. K. Murnighan (ed.), *Handbook of Organizational Psychology in Organizations*: 350–384. Englewood Cliffs, NJ: Prentice-Hall.

SUTTON, R. I., and STAW, B. M. (1995). What theory is *not*. *Administrative Science Quarterly*, 40: 371–384.

TEGEAR, A. (1980). *Too Much Invested to Quit*. New York: Wiley.

TETLOCK, P. (1981). Pre-to postelection shifts in presidential rhetoric: Impression management or cognitive adjustment? *Journal of Personality and Social Psychology*, 41: 207–212.

WEICK, K. E. (1964). Reduction of cognitive dissonance through task enhancement and effort expenditure. *Journal of Abnormal and Social Psychology*, 68: 533–539.

—— (1989). Theory construction as disciplined imagination. *Academy of Management Review*, 14: 516–531.

WHYTE, G. (1986). Escalating commitment to a course of action: A reinterpretation. *Academy of Management Review*, 11: 311–321.

C H A P T E R   1 2

ON THE ORIGINS OF EXPECTANCY THEORY

VICTOR H. VROOM

12.1 INTRODUCTION

THIS chapter deals with a psychological theory variously referred to as expectancy theory or VIE theory. It first saw the light of day in a book, which I wrote in 1964 entitled *Work and Motivation*. Expectancy theory was the organizing focus of this book which attempted to create order among previously disparate findings about why people choose the kinds of work they do, the satisfaction that they derive from that work, and the quality of their work performance. Expectancy theory is sufficiently general to be applied to other behavior in other domains, but due to its initial connection with *Work and Motivation*, it has almost exclusively been applied to work behavior.

Reduced to its simplest terms, the theory argues that people have preferences among outcomes or states of nature. Outcomes, which are strongly preferred, are positively valent while those to be avoided have negative valence. These valences have their roots in relatively stable motives, or needs, the strengths of which vary both within and across persons. Some outcomes have valence because of their inherent properties whereas others derive their valence because of their perceived instrumentality for the attainment of other outcomes. Valent outcomes have no impact on behavior unless accompanied by an expectancy that actions have some likelihood of attaining a positively valent outcome or avoiding a negatively valent one.

As in other chapters in this volume, our purpose here is to attempt to shed light on the process within the author, which resulted in the creation of the theory, the impact of the theory on the author, and of the author's current appraisal of the theory. Since expectancy theory is a psychological theory, I will begin with my earliest experiences studying psychology as an undergraduate. It was during this period in my life that I developed an intense interest in psychological theory, particularly theories that cut across the boundaries of basic and applied psychology.

12.2 ACADEMIC ROOTS

My first serious connection with the field of psychology came when I was an entering freshman at George Williams College in my hometown of Montreal, Canada. Like all new entrants into the school, I was given a battery of tests designed to measure my aptitudes, abilities, and vocational interests. The results were given to me as part of a one-hour interview with a counselor. The only findings, which I can recall, were my very high scores on two scales on the Strong Vocational Interest Test. The first of these—"Musician" did not surprise me since I had been studying and playing saxophone and clarinet for the previous five years. It was my love of music, particularly jazz, that had convinced me years earlier to forgo the college education that my two older brothers had received in favor of pursuing a job with a big band such as Tommy Dorsey, Stan Kenton, or Duke Ellington. When I graduated from high school and discovered that none of the bandleaders was about to offer me a job, it was the income that I had saved up from my musical career that enabled me to pay the modest tuition at Sir George Williams College.

The second of these two scales was "Psychologist," a field to which I had only the vaguest of associations. It was clear to me that the counselor clearly preferred the psychologist option. He, himself, was working for an advanced degree in the field. He also argued that jazz music was a very uncertain career against which there was a social stigma, based on the wild, unfettered lives enjoyed by many prominent jazz artists. (I must admit that it was this latter quality that was a part of my attraction to the field.)

I resolved to learn more about this field called psychology, but Sir George Williams College was not the ideal setting. It was a small school then located on the third floor of the YMCA building in the middle of downtown Montreal. (It has since joined with Loyola College and is now called Concordia University.) The school's only psychology professor was on leave, and his course was normally taken in one's junior or senior year.

For a variety of reasons including the absence of an opportunity to learn more about psychology, I applied to transfer to McGill University at the conclusion of my freshman year. McGill was just a few blocks away but light years ahead of Sir George in terms of academic opportunity. For the next three years, I took every psychology course offered and, in my junior year, I entered a special "honors program" in psychology, which gave me and the other four people in that program educational opportunities often restricted to graduate students. One of these was the opportunity to have a weekly lunch with Donald Hebb, the chairman of the department. Hebb had recently written a very important book entitled *The Organization of Behavior* (Hebb, 1949). The book was pioneering in its day as it sought to organize the disparate fields of psychology in terms of a simple set of theoretical constructs residing in neural and physiological processes. I grew to admire Hebb greatly, both for his modest unassuming persona and for the power of his intellect. While I was not convinced that a reductionist theory was the course for me to follow, I left McGill and the honors program firmly committed to becoming a psychologist and, hopefully, a psychological theorist. Music would remain a part of my life but a secondary part.

12.2.1 Becoming an Industrial Psychologist

My one hesitation about becoming a theorist was my desire to have a positive impact on the real world, not just the world of academe. I had read about the Hawthorne experiments (Roethlisberger and Dickson, 1939), been exposed to the writings of Kurt Lewin and his often quoted phrase "that there is nothing as practical as a good theory," and even read the recently published Harwood (Coch and French, 1948) experiments by some of Lewin's disciples. Perhaps one need not choose between relevance to the real world and academic respectability. But where could I find a field in which psychological theory could be readily applied?

At that time, McGill was developing a new graduate program in industrial psychology. Headed by Professor Edward Webster, it led to either a Master or Doctoral degree in Psychological Science. An integral part of the program was the requirement of internships in local firms applying psychological concepts and methods to real problems. This sounded exactly like what I was looking for and it was right in my hometown. I applied to the two-year Masters Program and was accepted.

My first internship was in the employment department of Canadair Ltd. Ed Webster had developed a consulting relationship with Canadair which was attempting to modernize its methods of selecting hourly workers manufacturing F-86 fighter planes. My task was to develop a method of scoring information contained on application forms to predict employee turnover. The task was a boring one, sifting through old records to find information on employment application forms that might discriminate between those who left the company shortly after employment and those who remained for five years or more. The only respite from the boredom came when I discovered unorthodox responses by the French Canadian applicant pool, some of whom misunderstood the information that was being requested. For example, a request for the applicant's sex was occasionally met with responses such as "jamais" (never) or "deux fois par semaine" (two times a week).

After sorting hundreds of applications and comparing the information with longevity of employment, I found discriminating items and developed methods of scoring application forms. Then, I began the process of cross-validating the scoring system. It all seemed so mindless and mechanical. Why were people resigning from the company? Why did one need separate scoring keys for assembly fitters and for riveters? What did all of this have to do with psychology?

Industrial psychology was emerging in my mind as a set of methods and techniques that were obviously of value in rationalizing employment decisions but of little relevance in understanding or explaining behavior. I could not see any connection between what I was doing at Canadair and what I had learned in my courses in experimental and social psychology. Were the processes underlying behavior at work really different from those being studied by psychologists in the laboratory, in the clinic, or in schools?

The possibility of reconciling industrial psychology with the psychology that I had known as an undergraduate in the honors program was given new life by my attendance at the International Congress of Applied Psychology, which was conveniently held in Montreal in 1955. There I met Carroll Shartle and learned about the Ohio State Leadership studies. I also met Rensis Likert and Daniel Katz, who helped me to learn about the Human Relations in Industry research program in the Survey Research Center at Michigan. There was an air of excitement and discovery. People were studying how and why people behaved as they did and how work could be made more satisfying and more productive. Perhaps applied and basic psychology could be connected after all. Perhaps connections could even be made between theories of perception, motivation, and learning, and how people perceived, were motivated, and learned in work settings.

My course was clear. It was time to cross the border into the United States. This time it was not to pursue a career in jazz music but rather to pursue a Ph.D. in psychology. Of the possible universities, I chose the University of Michigan, largely because of the Survey Research Center.

Michigan was a great place for me. Here, I studied motivation with Jack Atkinson, attitude structure with Helen Peak, group dynamics with Jack French and Doc Cartwright, and social psychology with Ted Newcomb. The closest thing to an industrial psychologist was Norman Maier whose textbook *Psychology in Industry* (Maier, 1955) and whose background as a distinguished experimental psychologist attested to his commitment to using psychological constructs and processes to account for behavior at work.

While I was at Michigan, Lee Cronbach published his APA presidential address in the *American Psychologist* on the two disciplines of psychology (Cronbach, 1957). One of these disciplines concerned the structure of individual differences. It was labeled R-R psychology since its core methods involved correlating responses among different psychological tests or between tests and criteria of performance. R-R psychology was the source of most of the practical applications of psychology but very little theory. The second discipline (S-R psychology) was concerned with the effects of situations on behavior. Its methods were largely experimental and it was the heart of both experimental and social psychology. Cronbach argued that S-R psychology was the source of most psychological theory but that the practical applications were slower to develop.

Cronbach's distinction made great sense to me and helped me to explain my difficulty in reconciling industrial psychology (which exemplified the R-R tradition) with my experimental training. But Cronbach's influence went beyond that by arguing for an integration of these two disciplines, exploring the distinctive role of each as well as their joint effects or interactions. The key seemed to me to find a way of characterizing individual differences in ways that could be linked theoretically to their situational counterparts. My attempt to resolve this dilemma would ultimately lead me to expectancy theory.

One of the greatest things about Michigan in the late 1950s was the opportunity provided by the Survey Research Center to design and execute field projects in large organizations such as Detroit Edison, Texas Instruments, and United Parcel Service. Through working on projects in each of these companies, I was able to test the applicability of some of my ideas to explaining behavior in organizations. It was my doctoral dissertation that gave me the first opportunity to follow Cronbach's lead and to incorporate personality variables and the study of situational effects in the same investigation.

In searching for a dissertation topic, I read a detailed account of the experiment by Lewin, Lippitt, and White (1939) on the effects of leadership style on the behavior of 8-year-old boys. I came across a description of one boy who displayed a strong preference for the autocratic style rather than the democratic style preferred by virtually all others. He was described as the son of an army officer, which may or may not have had a bearing on his preference. Following Cronbach's cry for integration of situational and dispositional sources of variance, it occurred to me that it might be possible to measure one or more personality variables that would interact with participation in decision making in influencing not only work satisfaction but also work performance.

At the time, I was designing a survey to be conducted at the United Parcel Service on the effects of the leadership style of supervisors on those who worked for them. I included two personality variables which I thought had a reasonable probability of interacting with participation. One was a motivational measure called need for independence adapted from a study by Tannenbaum and Allport (1956); the second was a measure of authoritarianism called the F-scale (Adorno, et. al., 1950). To my delight, both measures worked perfectly and they were uncorrelated with one another. The correlation between participation and job satisfaction ranged from +.73 for those high in need for independence and low in authoritarianism, to +.04 for those low in need for independence and high in authoritarianism. Similar results were obtained for job performance. My hunch was correct. Participation appeared to have beneficial effects on some workers but not others. Furthermore, it was possible to predict in advance who would be affected positively and who would not.

The combination of these striking results and the hubris of a newly minted Ph.D. caused me to view my study as a prototype for a new approach to studying behavior at work. This new approach would include both situational and dispositional variables with the expectation that they would be likely to interact with one another. In the final chapter of my dissertation (Vroom 1960: 71–74), I speculated that similar interactions between personality characteristics and situational variables might be found in moderating the effects of other situational variables such as the job content, reward systems, and work group characteristics. Anticipating expectancy theory, I speculated that the most useful way of conceptualizing personality was in terms of motive strength. Similarly, work situations could be conceptionalized in terms of their "instrumentality for the satisfaction of each motive" and/or in terms of their potential for arousing motives by creating an "expectancy that actions will lead to the attainment of the incentives" (Vroom 1960: 72). Expectancy theory was yet to see the light of day but, in 1957, it was beginning to take shape in my mind.

My training at McGill, particularly as an undergraduate, helped me to complete my doctoral work in a short two and a half years. But it was not yet time to leave Michigan. I had married another doctoral student in psychology during my first year in Ann Arbor. She would not finish her studies in clinical psychology for another two years. Rather than it being a wasted two years for my scholarly development, exactly the opposite occurred. I was hired as a lecturer in the psychology department and as a study director in the Survey Research Center. In the former, I taught courses called "Industrial Social Psychology" and "Attitudes and Motivation." In the latter, I became part of a research team working on a new research program on Mental Health in Organizations. The opportunity to work closely with Robert Kahn, Stan Seashore, Doc Cartright, and Jack French in developing a theoretical framework for this program was a very important learning experience. My role was to direct a study on the effects of shift work. Not surprisingly, I approached this design of the study with a bias that much of the variance would reside in interactions between personality dispositions and shift-work properties.

Shift work could be perceived as highly satisfying by some and as a source of great frustration by others, depending on the sources of their satisfaction and enjoyment. Shift work would be satisfying if it increased the likelihood that a person could do what he or she liked to do. On the other hand, it would have deleterious effects if it made it more difficult for a person to perform activities that were a source of enjoyment.

To test this idea, I proposed describing people in terms of the valence to them of each of a set of non-work activities, e.g., playing golf, drinking with friends, playing with their children, etc. Each activity would then be described in terms of its unique time pattern (the times of the day within which it could be performed). Anticipating the concept of Person/Environment fit, I introduced a new term the "concordance/discordance" of a specific shift for a person. I even formulated my theory in mathematical terms. The valence of a particular shift for each person would be a monotonically increasing function of the valence of each activity multiplied by its concordance/discordance. Although the term "instrumentality" was never explicitly used, the conceptual structure underlying the shift-work study was a special case of the expectancy theory just around the corner.

12.2.2 Onward to Penn

The empirical test of my shift-work model never saw the light of day. Early in 1960, I received an attractive offer from the Psychology Department at the University of Pennsylvania. However, there were a couple of complications that delayed my acceptance. The most severe of these was my exchange visitor status, which obliged me to return to Canada for at least two years after Michigan. The second was my wife's dissertation. When would she be able to finish her dissertation? With a little luck and a lot of hard work, both obstacles were resolved and, in the summer of 1960, we were off to the University of Pennsylvania.

Penn was different from Michigan. Michigan was very cohesive, friendly, and collegial. Penn seemed filled with resentments, politics, and distrust. The only industrial psychologist was Maurice Viteles, who divided his time between teaching at Penn and a job at the Philadelphia Electric Company. The Department Chair was Robert Bush, a mathematical psychologist who had brought in Duncan Luce and Gene Galanter, each in the forefront of a movement for mathematizing psychological theory. Their views were less than appreciated by the older guard and by newer people who represented the softer areas of psychology.

At Penn, faculty kept pretty much to themselves. This was fine with me since I was on a mission. Just before leaving Michigan, I had written my manifesto. It was the first chapter in what was to be a 150-page monograph tentatively entitled *Work and Motivation.* The monograph was intended to be a critical appraisal of what is known about the motivational aspects of people and the work they do. The monograph would also organize the field around my emerging theory of motivation, which could both integrate what was known and point to the questions that remained unanswered.

When I now look back at that proposed monograph, I see it as amazingly presumptuous. I was 28 years old, a neophyte in the field, just about to assume my first real teaching job, planning to write a major opus purporting to integrate a broad and disconnected literature on work motivation. Substantively, I can see Hebb's influence on me in my desire to find a basic structure, which could integrate previously disparate fields of study and methods of inquiry. I can also see the influence of Lee Cronbach, Jack Atkinson, and Helen Peak, as well as the disciples of Kurt Lewin. But where did the chutzpah come from? Where did the belief (i.e., expectancy) spring from such that I could attempt anything as broad as the integration of the field contemplated in my manifesto.

Part of this confidence may have stemmed from an opportunity that came my way in 1959. Norman Maier had agreed to write the chapter in the forthcoming *Annual Review of Psychology* entitled "Industrial Social Psychology" (Vroom and Maier, 1961). Subsequent to his acceptance, he had agreed to go to the University of Ghent in Belgium for the year. He asked me if I would write a first draft of the chapter for his review on his return. I did so and he accepted it without changing a single word!

I suspect that another part of the answer came from encouragement from the Ford Foundation. My dissertation "Some Personality Determinants of the Effects of Participation" was one of five dissertations in the social sciences picked in their first dissertation competition designed to upgrade the role of research in business schools. This brought with it many accolades. The dissertation was published as a book by Prentice Hall (Vroom, 1960). I received phone calls from many of my heroes including Donald Taylor of Yale, William Foote White of Cornell, and Douglas McGregor of MIT. Also the General Electric Foundation offered an unsolicited research grant to cover any research or writing expenses that I might have over the next three years.

Reflecting back on these events after more than forty years, I have to believe that receiving the Ford Foundation award and the events that followed had a great deal to do with giving me the necessary confidence to undertake the writing of *Work and Motivation* and the formulation of expectancy theory which was its organizing framework.

12.3 Motivation and Expectancy Theory

One of my early assignments at Penn was to teach a Ph.D course on motivation. I had to become familiar with the many ways in which that topic had been dealt with in psychology. In searching for a theory to integrate the literature on such topics as to why people choose the job or occupations they do, the satisfaction they have with these jobs, and their effectiveness in performing them, motivation seemed to be a natural focus. As I discussed in Chapter 2 of *Work and Motivation*, the study of motivation has historically addressed two problems. The first was the issue of arousal of behavior. What events start a pattern of activity, determine its duration, and finally, its cessation? The second was the issue of choice. Once aroused, what determines the direction of behavior, including the choices that are made among different actions?

In formulating the theory, I chose to focus on the latter, arguing that for the psychologist it was the more important of the two (Vroom, 1964: 9). In so doing, I set aside issues of goal setting and intentionality, which will be covered by Professor Locke in another chapter in this volume.

I defined motivation as the explanation of choices made among different behaviors that are under central or voluntary control. Therefore, I ruled out reflexes, behaviors regulated by the autonomic nervous system, and behaviors that are expressive of emotional states. Motivation was the process underlying choices that were hypothesized to be influenced by their expected consequences.

Early in my Michigan studies, I had taken a course with a visiting professor, Gustav Bergmann, using his book on the philosophy of science (Bergmann, 1957). Bergmann had participated in the Vienna Circle discussions of logical positivism before moving to the University of Iowa at the invitation of Kurt Lewin. He sought an ideal language whose semantic features would reflect the fundamental structure of reality. Bergmann expressed support for Kurt Lewin's field theory, which asserted that behavior was the result of a field of forces operating at a particular point in time.

This course strengthened my interest in understanding the basic structure of phenomena as had my early exposure to the work of Donald Hebb. It also strengthened my conviction that causation is best understood ahistorically. Earlier events clearly have effects but they do so in terms of their manifestations in the present. Kurt Lewin's dictum that behavior is a function of person and environment was a clear example of an ahistorical explanation, as would be my version of expectancy theory.

Expectancy theory has often been treated as though it were an original creation. On the contrary, it has its roots in the writings of many of my mentors during my graduate studies. In *Work and Motivation*, I pay homage to Lewin (1938), Rotter (1955), Peak (1955), Davidson, Suppes, and Siegel (1957), Atkinson (1957, 1958), and Tolman (1959). My formulation was identical to none of these theorists but has some similarities to each. The similarity is undoubtedly greatest to that of Kurt Lewin, whom I never met and whose work I knew only through his writings and those of his colleagues at the Research Center for Group Dynamics at Michigan.

From Lewin, I borrowed the concept of force. Employing a spatial or geographical metaphor, I saw the choices made by a person as the result of a field of forces, each of which has both direction and magnitude. In Lewin's theory, the force operating on a person to move in a particular direction was assumed to be a function of the valence of a region in the life space and of the psychological distance of that region from the person. I also borrowed the term valence from Lewin, although I attached it to outcomes while eschewing the concepts of both region and life space.

I did not know how to deal with the concept of psychological distance which never seemed clear to me in Lewin's writings. Was it the effort required to reach the valent outcome? Was it the number of regions to be traversed to reach the goal or was it the subjective probability that the outcome could be attained? Of these, I chose to focus on subjective probability, using the term expectancy, previously employed by both Atkinson and Tolman. In one of my two central propositions, the force on a person to perform an action was equal to the product of the expectancy that the act will be followed by an outcome and the valence of that outcome. By multiplying the two terms together, I could represent my belief that expectancies would have no effect on behavior unless valence was different from zero and that valence would have no effect unless there was some expectancy that one's actions could affect its attainment.

The second proposition in expectancy theory formalizes the observation that not all positively valent outcomes are desired because of their inherent properties. Outcomes can also acquire valence because of their perceived instrumental connection to other valent outcomes. Thus, "people may join groups because they believe that their membership will enhance their status in the community, and they may desire to perform their jobs effectively because they expect it will lead to a promotion" (Vroom, 1964: 18).

In articulating this proposition, I was most influenced by Helen Peak, one of my Michigan professors, who hypothesized that an attitude, or effective orientation toward an object, is related to both its perceived instrumentality for the obtainment of other objects and to the intensity and direction of the effect attached to each object (Peak, 1955). While obviously related to the proposition concerning force, it seemed to be that the underlying mechanism would be important for predicting the valence of occupations, jobs, or careers to their aspirants as well as the degree of satisfaction of current occupations of those currently performing their work roles. The proposition states that the valence of an outcome is equal to the product of the instrumentality of the outcome for the obtainment of another outcome and the valence of that other outcome.

These two propositions are stated here in words rather than in the formal mathematical language in which they were presented in *Work and Motivation*. These mathematical formulations say more about the mathematical culture of the Penn environment at that time than they do about their ultimate usefulness or testability. The only function, which they have served is to point to the many outcomes that might be relevant for determining forces and valences and to the possibility that each may simultaneously possess both positive and negative components.

In *Work and Motivation*, I used a figure (Vroom, 1964: fig. 2.1) to show the central proposition of expectancy theory along with the variety of measures, manipulations, and behaviors that have been or could be used to test the proposition. Without these empirical coordinates, the model is untestable. It is only through linking these internal states to their empirical representations that the model can make verifiable predictions about behavior. I believed that much of the empirical literature on choice behavior was encompassed by the relationships between the situational manipulations and behavioral measures shown in the figure.

It would remain to be seen whether the model would serve the unique functions of making sense out of the diverse literature on the relationship between people and the work they do and of pointing the way to new problems and research. From my personal standpoint, this was the goal underlying these formulations of expectancy theory. Could a theory, which had its roots in experimental psychology, find a home in the emerging field of organizational psychology?

12.3.1 Fitting the Theory to the Data

The reader will recall my preoccupation with merging the psychology of individual differences with the psychology of experimental and social psychology. Lewin's proposition that behavior is a function of Person and Environment subsumed the individual differences under Person and the more transient situational variables under Environment. But how can we position the concepts of valence, expectancy, and instrumentality to dispositional and situational effects?

The assumption that I made was convenient although oversimplified. Expectancies and instrumentalities were situational. For people working in jobs, the means–ends relationships would be learned, perhaps imperfectly by experience with actual contingencies. One could learn through experience whether one's effort led to higher performance and, similarly, whether high performance would lead to higher income. Yet, in applying the theory to occupational choice, I could not assume such a close correspondence. People undoubtedly had beliefs about what work would be like in different careers. But their information would not be based on actual experience and could be seriously in error.

On the other hand, the valence of outcomes was related to motives or needs. These were fairly stable dispositions learned early in life and would be consistent across situations. Motives were simple aggregates of the valences of similar outcomes such as achievement, affiliation, or power.

This oversimplification led to an interesting revelation. Studies of occupational choice almost exclusively dealt with dispositional factors. There were very few attempts to assess people's perceptions of occupations and of the ease and cost of getting in to them. However, in the few studies in which such factors were measured, the accuracy of predictions increased substantially (Vroom, 1964).

On the other hand, studies of job satisfaction and the motivation for effective performance largely ignored individual differences and relied instead on measures of situational factors such as pay, supervision, work group properties, or job content. In the few studies in which motivation dispositions were measured, the accuracy of predictions also increased (Vroom, 1964).

The extensive literature review in *Work and Motivation* had identified a strange anomaly. Studies of the fit between the motives of people and the work roles they perform must, of necessity, consider both properties of persons and work roles. Why is it that those concerned with occupational choice only concern themselves with properties of persons while those concerned with satisfaction and performance within work roles only concern themselves with work role properties? Expectancy theory not only predicts that both must be involved but also shows a specific way in which they interact. If one of the functions of expectancy theory were to point to gaps in existing research and to new directions, it seemed to have performed that function.

Of the three areas in which expectancy theory was applied (occupational choice, job satisfaction, and job performance), it is the latter which has achieved the greatest attention. While it has yet to be tested systematically, expectancy theory could identify a list of four variables affecting the strength of individual's motivation to do his or her own job effectively. They are: (1) Expectancy that increased effort will lead to high performance; (2) Valence of high performance (independent of its instrumentality); (3) Instrumentality of high performance for other rewards; and (4) Valence of these other rewards.

Each of these leads to a different kind of intervention to increase performance. The first of these can be increased by training interventions designed to increase employee confidence in their ability. See for example Eden's extensive work on the Pygmalion effect (Eden, 1990). The second could be enhanced by job redesign

(Hackman and Oldham, 1980) and both the third and fourth would be achieved by changing reward contingencies or by substituting rewards that are more valued by employees (Lawler, 1981).

In addition, expectancy theory posits that there are interactions among several of these components. For example, increasing an individual's belief that he or she is capable of higher performance with greater effort should have no effect on motivation if the individual does not value the rewards offered by the organization for high performance and/or if such performance has no intrinsic value to the person.

Similarly, the theory posits that the introduction of an incentive compensation plan will have greater motivating effect on individuals placing a high value on money. I know of no experimental test of all of these predictions but know many managers who find the framework of great value in identifying and solving problems of low motivation.

12.3.2 Expectancy Theory: A Self Analysis

Let me digress from a presentation of the formal derivations from the theory to a more personal topic. Does the theory help me to describe or make sense of my own behavior surrounding its development? How do I now make sense of my own choices using the expectancy theory framework?

It is now very clear that I was very highly motivated to complete *Work and Motivation*. On many nights, I was still working in the university library when it closed at midnight, and I was asked to leave. Developing a theory which made sense out of otherwise disparate findings was something that was "Hebb like," albeit in a totally different domain. Furthermore, it represented a tangible effort at integrating the two disciplines of psychology, which Cronbach had advocated. Finally, it united theory and application in a manner which might have received Kurt Lewin's blessing. For these and probably many other reasons, writing *Work and Motivation* was something that I had to do. At times, it felt like a labor of love and, at other times, a neurotic compulsion. It was a completely positively valent endeavor.

It was also clear that this strong desire was intrinsic and not based on a well-conceived career strategy. My colleagues at Penn kept telling me that what I was doing was the province of those with tenure and that empirically based articles were a far safer course for those on a three-year contract. If they were correct, I was jeopardizing my chances of getting promoted, at least at Penn by doing what I was doing.

Complementing this positive valence was a reasonable expectancy that I was capable of "pulling it off." I have previously alluded to the many sources of support and encouragement I had received during my early academic years. These served to sustain my belief that I was capable of the task at hand and made it possible to ignore the voices pointing to the peril that could lie ahead. I also received support from my doctoral students at Penn who read the chapters as they were produced and made many helpful suggestions. Prior to leaving Penn, I had met Gordon Ierardi, then editor of a highly prestigious Wiley psychology series. Gordon asked to review my almost completed manuscript on *Work and Motivation* and subsequently extended a contract.

Further evidence of the intrinsic rather than extrinsic motivational forces surrounding this project is represented by the fact that my work on expectancy theory ceased totally with completion and submission of the final manuscript! While it has stimulated a great deal of research on the part of others, for me the task was done. I have published a substantial amount since 1964, but none of it deals with or even mentions valence, expectancy, or instrumentality.[1]

I now believe that this fact points to a motivational phenomenon, which was given short shrift in expectancy theory and will be examined later in this chapter. I had assumed that the valence of outcomes, like their underlying motives, were relatively stable dispositions and varied across persons but not within them. But now as soon as the ink was dry and the pen put down, my interest went on to other things. In deciding to focus on choice rather than arousal, I had ignored an aspect of motivation that was to be demonstrated so vividly in my own behavior—the starting and stopping of behavior!

12.3.3 The Aftermath of Work and Motivation

I wish that it were not so, but my colleagues' advice, while not particularly helpful, was correct. During my third year at Penn, I submitted my draft chapters to my review committee. After suitable deliberation, the committee asked me to meet with them. While reappointment as an assistant professor was not explicitly eliminated, I was encouraged to pursue other alternatives.

Fortunately, these other options were not lacking. The most appealing of them were at what was then called the Department of Industrial Administration at Yale and at the Graduate School of Industrial Administration at Carnegie Tech, later to become Carnegie Mellon. Both offered a promotion to associate professor. I chose Carnegie which seemed, at that time, to be Mecca for the emerging discipline of organizational behavior. I was reluctant to leave the familiar home of a psychology

---

[1] Two articles written after the publication of *Work and Motivation* (Vroom, 1966 and Deci and Vroom, 1971) used attitude measures, which required prospective managers to rate their goals and the perceived instrumentality of a job for attaining them. However, the focus of both articles was testing theories of post-decision dissonance (Festinger, 1957).

department, but neither of these two seemed to be business schools in the traditional sense and both appeared to value my brand of scholarship.

12.3.4 Expectancy Theory: A Reprise

In this, the final section of this chapter, I will describe how, with the benefit of hindsight combined with forty years of reading and doing research on human behavior, I now view my expectancy theory. I will also try to be a Monday-morning quarterback and describe the changes that I would make in the theory today if I were to rewrite the book. In so doing, I will rely in part on a preface for a reissue of *Work and Motivation* published in 1995 by John Wiley.

Since 1964, expectancy theory has arguably become one of the dominant theories of work motivation. The essential concepts have been incorporated with minor modifications into the theories of others such as Lawler (1973) and to a lesser degree Naylor, Pritchard, and Ilgen (1980). It has also stimulated many empirical investigations; a large proportion of which I have been asked to referee or review prior to journal submission. Many of these were intended to "test" expectancy theory. Questionnaire measures of expectancy, instrumentality, and valence, were multiplied and summed over outcomes with total disregard for the limitations of the scales used. These were aggregates used to predict job choices, job preferences, or work performance. In general, the theory predicted job choices and job satisfaction better than it did job effort or job performance. Also, its predictions were more likely to be confirmed when the more appropriate methodology of within-subject designs was used (Kanfer, 1990).

I would be less than candid if I were to say that I have not been gratified by the attention given to the theory and for the frequent and continuing references to it. A decade or more after its publication, *Work and Motivation* was selected as a Citation Classic by the Committee on Scientific Information. It continues to be referenced in texts in organizational psychology, organizational behavior, and management. More than forty years after inception, it is still rated the most important motivation theory, according to a recent survey of ninety-five organization/management experts (Miner, 2003: 252).

Even more gratifying has been an increased recognition of the importance of linking psychological theory with industrial and organizational psychology. It is my belief that there is substantially more acceptance of the need for general theories to guide research in the field than there was in the 1950s and 1960s. I made the following observation in the introduction to the revised or classic edition of *Work and Motivation* in 1995.

The changes in the field are well documented in the most recent *Handbook of Industrial and Organization Psychology* (Dunnette and Hough, 1990). Chapters on motivation theory, learning theory, judgment, and decision-making theory make up a large part of the first volume. Each chapter makes extensive use of general psychological concepts and processes in an attempt to explain behavior in the workplace. Furthermore, the relevant bodies of theory are described with much greater rigor than in prior work, including the previous editions of the Handbook (Dunnette, 1976). No longer is work behavior explained by a different set of processes than behavior in other settings. Industrial and organizational psychology is now integrated into the discipline of psychology. (Vroom, 1995: xvii)

The possibility that my expectancy theory may have contributed to this development was immensely gratifying. For me, it meant that the emerging fields of industrial and organizational psychology could capitalize on the theoretically relevant developments in other parts of our science and, perhaps of even greater importance, that new theoretical developments could be informed by knowledge gleaned from the real world, not just from the laboratory.

While I am proud of any positive impact that expectancy theory might have had, I would make changes if I were to revise it today. First and foremost, I would certainly eliminate the mathematization and formalization of the theory. I was probably unduly influenced by the mathematical zeitgeist at Penn at the time. Unfortunately, I believe that my mathematical formulation contributed to many ill-advised attempts to test the theory using measures lacking the ratio/scale properties necessary. Eliminating the formalization might have helped to convey my belief that the theory should be used for its heuristic value in providing a language for formulating questions about the role of beliefs and motives in work performance.

I also regret an identification of the motivational factors in work performance solely with amount of activity (effort) rather than type of activity. To be sure, people make choices about the amount of time they put into their work and the persistence with which they pursue these tasks. However, they also make decisions about how they go about the tasks they are assigned. Professors make decisions about whether to emphasize research, teaching, or citizenship; managers make choices about whether to follow existing practices or to search for new and more effective ones; and leaders make choices about the form and degree to which to involve their team members in decision making. If behavior is, in fact, controlled by people's beliefs or expectancies and the goals that they seek to obtain, then these choices too should be predictable from measures of VIE constructs and changeable by altering one or more of the components. I note with embarrassment that even my own work on leadership styles, while demonstrating the situational variability of these choices, has not examined the manner in which different expectancies are evoked by different situations (Vroom and Yetton, 1973; Vroom and Jago, 1988; Vroom, 2003).

A decade ago, I noted this difficulty in the following language: "It is unfortunate that expectancy theory has become fixed on the amount rather than on the direction of effort. Such a prediction restricts motivation for effective performance for a directionless behavior reminiscent of Hull's (1951) concept of drive, and it relegates all of the residual to a rather vague concept of ability. I believe that the theory can do better if given a chance" (Vroom, 1995: xxii).

My revised expectancy theory would also pay much more attention to the question of arousal—the starting and stopping of behavior—which I forsook in favor of a focus on choice. I have previously alluded to this in my attempt to account for my own feeling of closure after completion of the book and theory. It was time to move on to another goal. In Lewin's language, the tension system which gave rise to the valence was dissipated. Both casual and more systematic observation of behavior of persons and organizations as well reveals a similar pattern. They attend to goals sequentially. A fire elevates safety concerns, quality defects stimulate a search for causes and remedies, interrupted tasks perpetuate tension systems, completion reduces the tension. A more complete description of the dynamics of valence would recognize its variability within, as well as between, persons.

My desire to equate valence and higher level concepts of motive came from a need to stress the ways in which these affective orientations vary among people, not within a person. Such an emphasis provided me with a link to the individual difference component identified by Cronbach as one of his two disciplines of psychology. Valence became almost equivalent to utility, which is typically treated to be relatively stable over choice situations.

Apart from these modifications, a new expectancy theory would have to ac-knowledge a "cognitive revolution" which has taken place in the field of psychology during the last several decades. I first became aware of an information-processing perspective to cognition through discussions with Herb Simon on my move to Carnegie in the 1960s. Verbal protocols of human subjects solving algebra word problems and playing chess revealed people actively searching for alternatives not just choosing among them as I had postulated. To use Simon's language, they "satisficed," rather than optimized, searching until an alternative reaching a level of aspiration was found. Furthermore, they evaluated alternatives sequentially and at a relatively slow speed with no suggestion of the exhaustive multiplication over all outcomes built into my propositions. These cognitive limits on rationality did not seem to pose a great problem for simple choices such as choosing among effort levels in a performance task but were integral to occupational and career choice as well as to possible attempts to apply expectancy theory to problem solving at work.

The development of prospect theory (Kahneman, Slovic, and Tversky, 1982) also exposed limitations of expectancy theory even in the realm of choice behavior. Human choices are led astray from subjective rationality by a number of identifi-able heuristics and biases, including the manner in which the alternatives have been framed.

But such is the way of science. Theories seldom meet the test of time. At best, they are reasonably consistent with an existing body of evidence but invite and guide the collection of additional evidence necessary to refute or extend them. Expectancy theory was a useful first approximation to our effort to understand and explain behavior in and around the workplace. But, there is much more to be done.

12.4   EPILOGUE

At least once a week, I receive an e-mail from a student somewhere around the globe asking for my current thoughts on expectancy theory. The specific requests vary. The student has been asked to write a paper or make a presentation on a theorist and has chosen me. Would I explain the theory to them in simple terms or tell them how I came up with the theory or reveal some anecdote about my personal life that would add "punch" to their presentation? I am typically in a quandary about how to respond. Seldom do I have the time to do justice to the request. Now that this chapter will be available, I have something to which to refer them that might answer their questions.

But my quandary is more than that. The truth is that I have difficulty jumping "back into the skin" of a 25 year old on a mission. Even writing this chapter was not easy. Fortunately, I had the aid of notes of previous reminiscences to make the task easier. Expectancy theory was a chapter in my life, not my whole life. Subsequent events have produced marked changes in my personal agenda. Some say that I am still "driven" but with different priorities. In the 1950s and early 1960s, I wore psychology "on my sleeve." It was the only path to my personal truth. Business schools and schools of management were, in my mind, lower-class institutions uninitiated in the scientific method.

Perhaps, it was the nine years at Carnegie Mellon or subsequently the thirty plus at Yale helping to found and then teach in their new School of Management that has produced a different frame of mind. Or, perhaps, it is simply the passage of time that has dimmed the single-minded idealism of youth and replaced it with a more balanced and societal anchored quest. Forty years of attempting to make the behavioral sciences relevant to present and future managers has made me highly sympathetic to their needs. Furthering the science of psychology is no longer my primary goal but is rather a means to the goal of helping managers to better understand themselves, those with whom they work, and the organizations they serve. I like to think that I have not abandoned the scientific method. Instead, I have tried to use it in ways to help managers deal with the complexities in their world (Vroom and Yetton, 1973; Vroom and Jago, 1988; Vroom, 2003).

Along with this changed role of science in my life has come an increased impatience with the trappings of formal science. Often the postulates, assumptions, derivations, and formal mathematical models of my youth seem like a premature attempt to mimic the physical sciences and do little to advance the state of our knowledge, particularly knowledge that is actionable. Furthermore, I no longer seek one lens or theory that will explain or unify it all. Pluralism and the interplay of conflicting modes of sense-making have replaced my need for order and convention. Perhaps the jazz musician and the psychologist have finally come together!

REFERENCES

ADORNO, T., FRENKEL-BRUNSWICK, E., LEVINSON, D. J., and SANFORD, R. N. (1950). *The Authoritarian Personality.* New York, Harper.

ATKINSON, J. W. (1957). Motivational determinants of risk-taking behavior. *Psychological Review,* 64: 359–372.

—— (1958). *Motives in Fantasy, Action, and Society.* New York: Van Nostrand Reinhold, 288–305.

BERGMANN, G. (1957). *Philosophy of Science.* Wisconsin: University of Wisconsin Press.

COCH, L., and FRENCH, J. R. P. JR. (1948). Overcoming resistance to change. *Human Relations,* 1: 512–532.

CRONBACH, L. J. (1957). Two disciplines of scientific psychology. *American Psychologist,* 12: 671–684.

DAVIDSON, P. E., SUPPES, P., and SIEGEL, S. (1957). *Decision Making: An Experimental Approach.* Stanford, Calif.: Stanford University Press.

DECI, E. L., and VROOM, V. H. (1971). The stability of post-decision dissonance: A follow-up study of the job attitudes of business school graduates. *Organizational Behavior and Human Performance,* 6: 36–49.

DUNNETTE, M. D. (1976). *Handbook of Industrial and Organizational Psychology.* Skokie, Ill.: Rand McNally.

—— and HOUGH, L. M. (eds.) (1990). *Handbook of Industrial and Organizational Psychology,* vol. 1. Palo Alto, Calif.: California Consulting Psychologists Press.

EDEN, D. (1990). *Pygmalion in Management: Productivity as a Self-fulfilling Prophecy.* Lexington, Mass.: Lexington Books.

FESTINGER, L. A. (1957). *A Theory of Cognitive Dissonance.* Stanford, Calif.: Stanford University Press.

HACKMAN, J. R. and OLDHAM, G. R. (1980). *Work Redesign.* Reading, Mass.: Addison Wesley.

HEBB, D. O. (1949). *The Organization of Behavior.* New York: Wiley.

HULL, C. L. (1951). *Essentials of Behavior.* New Haven: Yale University Press.

KAHNEMAN, D., SLOVIC, P., and TVERSKY, A. (eds.) (1982). *Judgment Under Uncertainty: Heuristics and Biases.* New York: Cambridge University Press.

KANFER, R. (1990). Motivation theory and industrial and organizational psychology. In Dunnette and Hough (1990: 1. 75–170).

LAWLER, E. E., III (1973). *Motivation in Work Organizations.* Pacific Grove, Calif.: Brooks/Cole.

—— (1981). *Pay and Organization Development.* Reading, Mass.: Addison Wesley.

LEWIN, K. (1938). The conceptual representation and measurement of psychological forces. *Contributions to Psychological Theory,* 4: 247.

—— LIPPITT, R., and WHITE, R. K. (1939). Patterns of aggressive behavior in experimentally created social climates. *Journal of Social Psychology,* 10: 271–299.

MAIER, N. R. F. JR. (1955). *Psychology in Industry.* Boston, Mass.: Houghton Mifflin.

MINER, J. B. (2003). The rated importance, scientific validity, and practical usefulness of organizational behavior theories: A quantitative review. *Academy of Management Learning and Education,* 2: 250–268.

NAYLOR, J. C., PRITCHARD, R. D., and ILGEN, D. R. (1980). *A Theory of Behavior in Organizations.* New York: Academic Press.

PEAK, H. (1955). Attitude and motivation. In M. R. Jones (ed.), *Nebraska Symposium on Motivation*: 149–188. Lincoln, Neb.: University of Nebraska Press.

ROETHLISBERGER, F. J., and DICKSON, W. J. (1939). *Management and the Worker*. Cambridge, Mass.: Harvard University Press.

ROTTER, J. B. (1955). The role of the psychological situation in determining the direction of human behavior. In M. R. Jones (ed.), *Nebraska Symposium on Motivation*: 245–268. Lincoln, Neb.: University of Nebraska Press.

TANNENBAUM, A., and ALLPORT, F. H. (1956). Personality structure and group structure: an interpretative study of their relationship through an event-structure hypothesis. *Journal of Abnormal Social Psychology*, 53: 272–280.

TOLMAN, E. C. (1959). Principles of purposive behavior. In S. Koch (ed.), *Psychology: A Study of a Science*: 2. 92–157. New York: McGraw-Hill.

VROOM, V. H. (1960). *Some Personality Determinants of the Effects of Participation*. Englewood Cliffs, NJ: Prentice Hall.

—— (1966). Organizational choice: A study of pre- and postdecision processes. *Organizational Behavior and Human Performance*, 1: 212–225.

—— (1995). *Work and Motivation* (rev. edn.) San Francisco, Calif.: Jossey-Bass.

—— (2003). Educating managers in decision making and leadership. *Management Decision*, 41(10): 968–978.

—— and MAIER, N. R. F. (1961). Industrial Social Psychology. *Annual Review of Psychology*: 12. 413–446. Palo Alto, Calif.: Annual Reviews.

—— and JAGO, A. G. (1988). *The New Leadership*, Englewood-Cliffs, NJ: Prentice Hall.

—— and YETTON, P. W. (1973). *Leadership and Decision Making*. Pittsburgh: University of Pittsburgh Press.

PART II

BEHAVIOR OF ORGANIZATIONS

DOUBLE-LOOP LEARNING IN ORGANIZATIONS

A THEORY OF ACTION PERSPECTIVE

CHRIS ARGYRIS

I BEGAN my work on organizational behavior by observing several puzzles. The first was that human beings created policies and practices that inhibited the effectiveness of their organizations. Why did human beings create and maintain these policies and practices that they judged to be counterproductive?

The second puzzle, human beings reported a sense of helplessness about changing these policies and activities because they were the victims of organizational pressures not to change them? How did human beings create organizational pressures that inhibited them from changing the phenomena they saw as counterproductive? Is it possible to help individuals and organizations to free themselves from this apparent self imposed enslavement? I begin my inquiry with an examination of how action is produced be it productive or counterproductive. I then examine the role of learning focusing on learning that challenges the existing routines and the status quo. Next, I present a model of a theory of action that explains the puzzles described above. This is followed by a description of a theory of action that can be used to resolve these puzzles. Next, is a description of intervention processes that are derivable from the theory that can be used to get from here to there. This is followed with discussions of some implications for scholars in developing theory and conducting empirical research that leads to actionable knowledge. I close with some personal observations of my tribulations over the years while building the theory and conducting research.

13.1 How is Action Produced?

Human beings produce action by activating designs stored in their heads (mind/brain) that when activated produce the actions that are necessary to implement their intentions. Human beings also develop designs to assess the degree to which they achieve what they intended to produce. If they achieve what they intended, there is a match between intentions and actions. If they do not achieve what they intended there is a mismatch. In order to make valid evaluations of their effectiveness, human beings must detect mismatches and correct them. At the core of acting effectively is learning. Learning also occurs if actions produce a new outcome for the first time. I will focus heavily on the detection and correction of error in order to understand the causes of the puzzles described at the outset. I will then focus on producing new matches when I describe the interventions required to produce the new models of effective actions.

13.1.1 Single and Double-loop Learning

Organizations create designs for action that they teach individuals to produce skillfully in order to achieve the organization's goals effectively. The designs are part of a master program that defines and frames organizational effectiveness. The master programs act as guides to action because human beings cannot act *de novo* every time they encounter a problem. To do so runs the risk of losing the opportunity to act in a timely manner. The master programs are the basis for the routines that make organizational life manageable. Every master program specifies the behavioral strategies and the consequences that will follow if it is implemented correctly. In addition, the master program identifies the values that govern the actions and the intentions.

Single-loop learning occurs when errors are detected and corrected without altering the governing values of the master program. Double-loop learning occurs

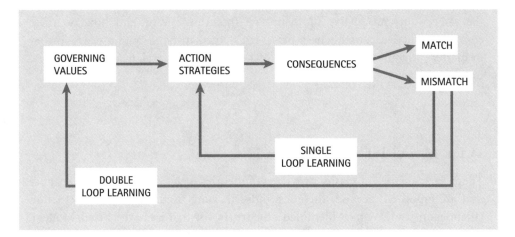

Fig. 13.1   Managerial and organizational learning

when, in order to correct an error, it is necessary to alter the governing values of the master programs.

An example of single-loop learning would be to correct an error in an existing strategy without altering the underlying governing variables of that strategy. Double-loop learning would occur if, in order to correct and error, it is necessary to change the underlying assumptions and values that govern the actions in the strategy. A thermostat is a single-loop learner. It is programmed to turn the heat up or down depending upon the temperature. A thermostat would be a double-loop learner if it questioned the existing program that is should measure heat.

The premise of this approach is that all actions (behavior with intentions) are produced as matches with the designs stored in our heads that we activate. These designs are developed by human beings as they strive to become skillful in whatever actions they intend. But, what about actions considered to be counter-productive? Do we have designs that when activated produce counterproductive consequences? There is a puzzle. Human beings cannot knowingly design and produce errors because when they produce any action it is a match and matches are not errors. Human beings are unaware when they are producing consequences that are errors.

But, if unawareness is behavior then it too must be designed. How is this possible? One way is for human beings to hold a micro theory of effectiveness that makes it possible for them or produce actions that they do not intend and that they are unaware that they are doing so. Thus we have skilled incompetence. The puzzle deepens a bit because if unawareness is behavior then it too must be designed. Hence skilled incompetence is combined with skilled unawareness.

These puzzles are at the heart of the problem of double-loop learning. Recall, the questions raised at the outset; why do human beings create and maintain actions that are counterproductive to their own intentions? Why and how do these counterproductive consequences persevere? I turn to describing a micro theory or master program for effective action that can help us to explain and correct these puzzles.

13.1.2 Model I Theory-in-Use

There are two types of master programs of theories of action. First, there are those that are espoused. Second, there are those that are used to produce the action (theories-in-use). We have identified a theory–in-use that we have labeled, Model I. Model I is said to be dominant because we have found it to be used regardless of gender, race, education, social status, wealth, type, age, and size of organization as well as culture (Argyris, 1982, 1985, 1990, 1993, 2000, 2004; Argyris, Putnam, and Smith, 1985, Argyris and Schön, 1996). The governing values or variables of Model I are (*a*) be in unilateral control, (*b*) maximize winning and minimize losing, (*c*) suppress negative feelings, and (*d*) be rational.

The three most prevalent action strategies are, advocate ideas and positions, evaluate performance, and make attributions about causes of the actions of self and others. Action strategies are implemented in ways that are consistent with the governing values, which means inquiry into them is not encouraged nor is testing

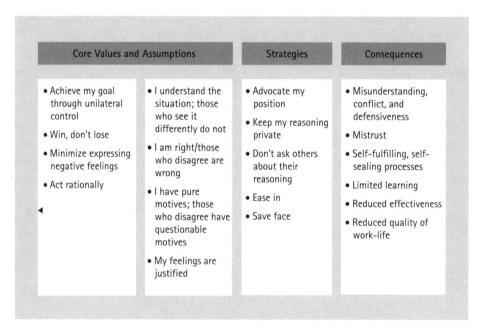

Core Values and Assumptions		Strategies	Consequences
• Achieve my goal through unilateral control • Win, don't lose • Minimize expressing negative feelings • Act rationally	• I understand the situation; those who see it differently do not • I am right/those who disagree are wrong • I have pure motives; those who disagree have questionable motives • My feelings are justified	• Advocate my position • Keep my reasoning private • Don't ask others about their reasoning • Ease in • Save face	• Misunderstanding, conflict, and defensiveness • Mistrust • Self-fulfilling, self-sealing processes • Limited learning • Reduced effectiveness • Reduced quality of work-life

Fig. 13.2   Model I: Unilateral control

of claims such as the conclusions are self-seeking. Testing is based upon the use of self-referential logic. The logic used to generate a claim is the same logic used to test the claim (e.g., trust me, my conclusion is valid because I know the organization, group, or individual).

The consequences of Model I action strategies include misunderstanding and escalating error, self-fulfilling prophecies, and self-fueling processes. These feed back to reinforce the governing values and the action strategies. The use of Model I produces a defensive reasoning mind-set. Premises and inferences are implicit and minimally transparent. The purpose of testing claims or conclusions is self-protective. A self-protective mind-set generates skills that produce consequences that are counterproductive to valid learning and systematic denial that this is the case. The incompetence and unawareness or denial are skilled. They have to be. Otherwise, they would not exist as theory-in-use designs in the human mind to produce the actions observed.

Model I theory-in-use and defensive reasoning mind-set combine to produce organizational defensive routines. Organizational defensive routines are any actions or policies intended to protect individuals, groups, inter-groups, or organizations as a whole from embarrassment or threat and do so in ways that prevent getting at the causes of the embarrassment or threat. Organizational defensive routines are anti-learning and overprotective. For example, organizations exhibit mixed messages. The theory-in-use to produce them is (1) state a message that is mixed; (2) act as if it is not mixed; (3) make (1) and (2) undiscussable; and (4) make the undiscussability undiscussable.

Defensive routines feed back to reinforce Model I, and the defensive reasoning mind-set. There is a tightly integrated relationship between individual theory-in-use and group, inter-group and organizational factors. The result is an ultra-stable, self-fueling, and self-sealing state. Under these conditions, it is difficult to call any factor (individual, group, inter-group, and organizational) the primary cause. They are highly interrelated. We arrive at these conclusions by observing the actions of the actors. But if we focus on how the subjects *create* the patterns then we must get at the designs in their heads. Our research suggests they are consistent with Model I theory-in-use. If so, then we may predict that if we give human beings a genuine opportunity to help others and themselves to create double-loop learning, they will fail to do so and be unaware of their failure, even if the conditions are ideal for double-loop learning. For example, thirty-eight CEOs came together in a seminar to learn more about effective leadership (Argyris, 2000). They were asked to help "Andy" who sought advice as to how to overcome the blindness and incompetence that he admits he exhibited in the way he leads. Thus the CEOs are embedded in a context where Andy seeks help, where the credibility of the leadership of the CEOs is not in jeopardy, where they do not come together with an organizational history and culture that contains organizational defensive routines. Moreover the context is not hierarchical and unilaterally controlling of their actions, and where the pressures of everyday work life to act are not required to behave consistently with Model I, to use a defensive reasoning mind-set, and to create organizational defensive routines. Yet they produced all of these consequences. Indeed, the actions they produced were consistent with those documented to exist in many different types of organizations (Argyris, 1990, 1993, 2003, 2004; Argyris and Schön, 1996).

13.1.3 Overcoming the Dysfunctionality of Model I and Organizational Defensive Routines

As stated earlier, learning means the detection and correction of error. In order to correct the dysfunctional features of Model I for double-loop learning, it is necessary to have a model that does so and a theory of how to get from here to there. First I should like to describe the model. Model II theory-in-use specifies how the counterproductive factors to learning and effective action can be reduced as well as inhibited from developing in the first place. Model II has the same conceptual structure of a theory of action. It contains governing values, action strategies, and consequences. The governing values of Model II are valid information, free and informed choice, and internal commitment to the choice. Model II values are not the opposite of Model I values, an error made during the early days of experiential learning and T-groups.

The action strategies are the same but implemented in the service of Model II governing values. The emphasis is upon illustrating one's claims, encouraging inquiry into them and testing them as robustly as possible. Self-referential logic in the service self-protection is discouraged. The consequences are the reduction of self-fulfilling, self-sealing, error escalating processes and effective problem solving and action. These consequences feed back to reinforce the Model II governing values and action strategies. We have a self-fueling, self-reinforcing set of activities that are now in the service of learning. This, in turn, produces organizational Model II behavioral systems that encourage, reinforce learning, especially around potentially difficult, rationally embarrassing, or threatening situations.

Model II theory-in-use encourages a productive reasoning mind-set. Premises are made explicit, inferences are made transparent, and conclusions are crafted in ways that are subject to robust independent tests. Models I and II make causal claims about the relationships between governing values, actions strategies and consequences. The consequences for each model should follow as claimed. For example, one should not be able to observe some combination of Model I values and action strategies that produce Model II consequences.

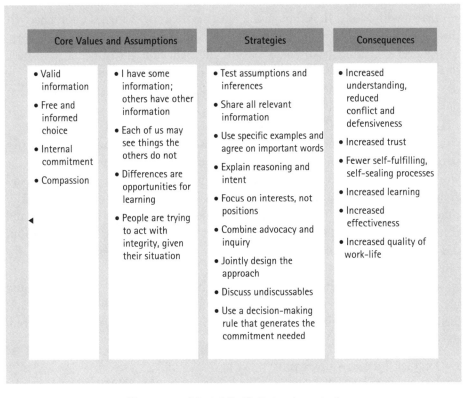

Core Values and Assumptions		Strategies	Consequences
• Valid information • Free and informed choice • Internal commitment • Compassion	• I have some information; others have other information • Each of us may see things the others do not • Differences are opportunities for learning • People are trying to act with integrity, given their situation	• Test assumptions and inferences • Share all relevant information • Use specific examples and agree on important words • Explain reasoning and intent • Focus on interests, not positions • Combine advocacy and inquiry • Jointly design the approach • Discuss undiscussables • Use a decision-making rule that generates the commitment needed	• Increased understanding, reduced conflict and defensiveness • Increased trust • Fewer self-fulfilling, self-sealing processes • Increased learning • Increased effectiveness • Increased quality of work-life

Fig. 13.3   Model II: Unilateral control

13.2 GOING FROM HERE TO THERE

Moving toward Model II, productive reasoning mind-set, and organizational behavioral systems that encourage the good dialectic and double-loop learning, requires double-loop learning. The nature and design of the educational experience have been described at length elsewhere (Argyris, 1982, 1984, 1990, 1993, 2000, 2004; Argyris and Schön, 1974, 1996). Very briefly, they are designed and implemented as follows.

13.2.1 Provide the Participants with an Opportunity to Diagnose Accurately their Theory-in-Use

This means that if variances exist in actions and consequences, they will be within Model I. Regardless of the variance, it should not include actions and consequences consistent with Model II. Although the ultimate focus of change is upon relatively directly observable behavior, the change is accomplished by changing the theory-in-use and the mind-set used to inform the behavior. Instruments have been developed to generate such data in economical and meaningful ways. They are designed in ways that the participants cannot hold others responsible for what they have written or how they have acted.

For example: We ask individuals, by the use of a case method, to describe a challenging, non-routine problem that they wish to solve. They are then asked, in a paragraph, to describe how they would go about solving it, if they could design the world as they wish. Next, they divide their paper into a left-hand and right-hand column. In the right-hand column they describe the dialogue that they had with others (or would have if the incident has not yet occurred). In the left-hand column they describe any thoughts or feelings that they had (or would have) but did (or would) not express. They do not have to explain the reasons for the self-censorship.

Since 1974, we estimate that over ten thousand such cases have been written and used to design and execute many learning seminars. As we shall see, the talk and feelings vary widely but their causes do not. I focus on the left-hand column. Examples are:

1. Don't let these guys upset you.
2. This is not going well. Wrap it up and wait for another chance.
3. He is clearly defensive.
4. He is playing hardball because he is afraid of losing power.
5. This guy is unbelievable.
6. You are nowhere as good as you think you are.
7. I am losing her, so I have to go in for the kill.
8. Great, try patronizing me. That won't get you far. Since he cares about trust, talk about trust.

This list contains feelings and thoughts that are evaluations of the others' actions and attributions about their motives. These actions are kept secret. Their validity is not tested. One reason not to test is that the writers' honestly believe that their views are valid. If there is a problem of validity it resides outside of them. The second reason is that to test their views could, in their opinion, open up a can of worms and not much will be accomplished that is constructive. Indeed they are right. The left-hand columns are loaded with potential for defensive dialogue. What do they do? They spin. Table 13.1 gives some examples of the left-hand column combined with their right-hand column counterparts.

Human beings appear to have a skillful and systematic strategy when dealing with difficult problems that are potentially or actually embarrassing, upsetting and in some cases, threatening. This sense making strategy includes the following rules:

Table 13.1 Examples of what subjects said and what they thought (but did not say)

Left-hand column	Right-hand column
(1) I am going to get attacked, straight out of the box.	(1) I'm so happy to meet you and get to know you. I think we will have a great working relationship and can learn a lot from each other.
(2) What a bunch of crap. I don't want to get drawn into this discussion.	(2) I'd like you to know that I believe in open, direct communication.
(3) Did he say *our* plan? He must have meant his plan. Doesn't he know I disagree with his decision?	(3) No problem, it seems like we are at a crucial point.
(4) Winning the Nobel Prize will not help the company. Perhaps it is time to expand the development stuff and downsize the research stuff.	(5) I am sure that you all realize that we work in a for-profit industry and must be realistically oriented.

1. Make evaluations and attributions required to make sense of what is going on.
2. When these evaluations and attributions are problematic hide them but act as if you are not hiding them.
3. In the name of concern for not upsetting others as well as getting on with the task at hand, test the validity of the evaluations and attributions privately and by using self-referential logic. (The logic used to test is the same as the logic used to evaluate and attribute). Hide that you are doing so.

The irony of this sense making process is that it blocks the learning required to check the effectiveness of the sense making and the action taken. The additional irony is that the others involved use the same sense making strategy. They too spin and cover up. We now have a systematic self-reinforcing behavioral pattern of increasing defensiveness and error.

The findings described above that come from various seminars and workshops are not disconfirmed by research in field settings. The theory used to design the organizational research is the one just described. The primary research methods are observations of actual events, tape recordings of meetings in organizations, and interviews with employers and employees. Details of these methodologies may be found in several publications (Argyris, 1982, 1985, 1990, 1993, 2000, 2004; Argyris, Putnam, and Smith, 1985; Argyris and Schön, 1996). In all of these studies the hypotheses and predictions derived from our theory were not disconfirmed.

The findings below have been replicated in the field studies. These studies include:

1. The study of top management decision making and strategy development over a period of eleven years. The interactions among the top executives and their

immediate reports were informed by Model I theory-in-use. This led to mis-understanding, miscommunications, mistrust, especially around double-loop issues. These were covered up and the cover-up was covered up. We were able to implement a change program that was heavily based on the case methodology described above. This led to a reduction of the Model I consequences and an increase in Model II consequences. The degree of reduction varied and their variance became the basis for continued learning (Argyris, 1982).

2. A second study of a consulting firm began with the same methodology. It went beyond, by focusing on a greater proportion of the organization. More import-antly, it focused on developing new products and services as well as more effective relationships with their clients (Argyris, 1993).

3. A series of studies were conducted on assessing the internal dynamics of case teams in various consulting firms. The focus was on the Model I relationships and how these prevented the consultants from implementing their new meth-odologies of more powerful strategy formulation and implementation with their clients (Argyris, 1985).

4. Over a period of several years we studied professional departments such as finance, accounting, and IT and their effectiveness with line management. For example, in a study of IT we were able to describe the self-fueling, self-sealing, counter-productive processes between top line management and IT organiza-tions. For example, the IT groups viewed the top management as illiterate and ignorant of the positive impact IT could have on the organization's abilities for more effective knowledge management. The line management saw the IT group as self-serving "Teckies" who were blind to the legitimate challenges of the organization as a whole (Argyris and Schön, 1996).

5. We conducted several field studies of change and organizational development professionals. All had more than five years experience with the mode about twelve years. All designed and executed various change and organizational development programs in their respected organizations. The programs focused on diagnosis Model I theories-in-use and organizational defensive routines. We were able to document through tape recording of their actions that, although they espoused Model II, their theory-in-use was Model I. They were unaware of the discrepancy. Not surprisingly when they got into difficult conversations with their clients they behaved in precisely the manner that they were advising the line managers not to use (Argyris, 2000).

13.2.2 Using the Case Data to Diagnose

I now turn to describing features of the intervention approach that was guided by the theory of action, described earlier. Each individual case is discussed by the group members who act as consultants to help the writer of the case become aware of gaps and inconsistencies that were produced and that were counterproductive to his or her intentions. These conversations are tape recorded so that the actions of the consultants are also subject to inquiry and to test. Each case discussion typically requires two hours.

Interestingly, although writers typically exhibit skilled incompetence and skilled unawareness, the same individuals are more accurate in diagnosing the others' cases. However, they return to Model I, and defensive reasoning mind-set when they actually converse with others in order to help them.

Another important consequence is that individuals often defend their defensive reasoning and actions by blaming the organizational defensive routines. They claim that they are being realistic; that they are victims. Thus the intimate relationship with supra-individual factors, such as organizational defensive routines, develops as predicted by the theory.

The next question is, do the participants wish to change their Model I theory-in-use and defensive reasoning mind-set? If they decide that they wish to continue their learning, exercises are available to help them do so. For example, each individual selects several of hers or his Model I conversations in the case they had written, and redesigns these more consistently with Model II. Each takes five or so minutes to rewrite the conversation. Each then shares the new conversation with the group members for their evaluation. Of course, the members' conversations are subject to inquiry. Thus the members not only have an opportunity to redesign their talk but to help others to do the same.

Typically, at the end of the seminar most members begin to see how they can craft Model II conversations. It is possible for them to continue their learning by periodically studying their actions back home. If they are not part of an organic group, they often communicate with each other through e-mail or tape recording. Some groups have chosen to meet every three to six months to get helpful advice from each other.

The learning is neither simple nor linear. Individuals proceed by developing hybrids, some Model II and some Model I. As their competence increases they are able to produce Model II conversations or, at least, identify at the outset that they are having trouble doing so. In our experience, it takes most individuals as much time to become relatively competent as it does to learn to play a very middling game of tennis. By the way, human beings do not forget their Model I competencies. They now have two degrees of freedom.

Double-loop learning is not likely to persevere if it does not lead to changes in the organizational context. The participants spend much time in diagnosing, for example, organizational defensive routines in order to reduce them. This leads them to examine critically organizational policies and practices that reinforce anti-double-loop learning. For example, they examine their actions when they develop competitive strategies, use new accounting procedures, design new IT architecture, alter marketing strategies, and develop new governance procedures (Argyris, 1982, 1990, 1993, 2002, 2004; Argyris and Schön, 1996). One of the future challenges is how to genuinely integrate managerial disciplines with effective implementation of double-loop learning in such a way that the new changes persevere.

13.3 Advice to Scholars

It is important that scholars take more initiatives in building theories and in conducting empirical research that questions the status quo. The first reason is that it makes it less likely that scholars will become, unintentionally, servants of the status quo. The second reason is that identifying possible inconsistencies and inner contradictions is a powerful way to examine our own inconsistencies and inner contradictions. For example, we espouse that we should describe the universe (that we construct) as accurately and completely as possible. This means that we should include research on how the universe would act if it was being threatened. In order to conduct such research we require empirical research on how the existing status quo inhibits learning and produces inner contradictions. This, in turn, requires the development of testable theories about new and rare universes, which, if implemented, would threaten the status quo.

The long-term commitment to describing the universe as it is inhibits the study of new universes that would encourage liberating alternatives and double-loop learning. For example, the core concepts of the behavioral theory of firms include the existence of competing coalition rivalries and limited learning. The limited learning is partially caused by the limited information processing capacity of the human mind. This claim is, in my opinion, valid. Another claim that may also be valid is that the competing coalitions (and other organizational defensive routines) may also limit learning. To my knowledge, scholars have not tested this claim. More importantly, they appear not to do so because they (e.g., March) express doubts that such factors as mistrust produced by competitiveness can be reduced (see Argyris, 1996). Burgelman also doubts that organizational defensive routines can be reduced. He also acknowledges that not testing this claim could have anti-learning and self-sealing consequences (see Argyris, 2004).

Similar questions may be raised about the rules and norms of conducting rigorous empirical research. For example, the theory-in-use (not espoused theory) of rigorous research is consistent with Model I. It is the researchers who are in unilateral control. The result is that the empirical propositions when *implemented* create a world consistent with Model I (Argyris, 1980, 1993). For example, studies on communication to generate trust advise that, when communicating to "smart" people, offer them several views. When communicating to "those judged to be less smart," offer one view. Implementing this advice requires that the implementer cover up the reasoning behind it. It also requires that the implementer covers up the cover-up. None of these consequences are explored by the researchers. Yet, all of them are consistent with Model I theory-in-use; a theory-in-use that facilitates mistrust.

Studies on frustration and regression conclude that mild frustration actually produces creative reactions. After a certain frustration threshold is passed, the predicted regression results (Argyris, 1980, 1993). Let us assume that a leader wishes to generate the creativity predicted during the early stages. This would mean that she would have to create low to moderate frustration. It also is likely that she cannot tell the "subjects" of her intention because doing so could lead the subordinates to react negatively to what they may interpret as her manipulation. If some do not react negatively then she would have created sub-groups that conflict with each other. In short, the leader would have to cover up that she is covering up. If there are members of the group who believe that she is covering up, they too may cover up their attributions. They would place these thoughts and feelings in their left-hand column. The multilevel cover-up will make it more difficult to assess the arrival of the threshold point beyond which regressions would appear.

All of these issues arise when attempts are made to implement the knowledge produced in the original experiments. These conclusions appear to hold for humanities research intended to bypass the Model I theory-in-use. Indeed the same appears to be true for interpretive research where testing stories is a primary methodology (Argyris, 2004).

These and other similar observations (Argyris, 1997) raise doubts that our theories and our research methods are neutral to normative features of everyday life. The theories and empirical research methodologies are highly influenced by Model I and organizational defensive routines. They are not neutral whenever social scientists create theories limited to Model I and use research method whose theory-in-use is Model I. Moreover they get rewarded for doing so by the norms of their scholarly community, they become skillfully unaware of the limits of their claims, especially about neutrality and the promise of a scientific enterprise that does not limit truth-seeking (Miner and Meziac, 1996).

13.4 THE ROLE OF INTERVENTION

Intervention is the most effective methodology for empirical research, related to double-loop learning. Interventions are social experiments where understanding and explanation are in the service of valid implementation intended to be of help. It is difficult for an interventionist to obtain permission and request cooperation from "subjects" on the claim that the research may be helpful and then stop before providing such help. The "subjects" would feel betrayed because the promise to be of help includes implementation (Argyris, 2003). These feelings of betrayal are being built up within society—including congressmen and foundations—by researchers who have promised that they are committed to producing valid and actionable knowledge but who fail to fulfill their promises (Argyris, 1993; Argyris and Schön, 1996; Johnson, 1993).

Interventions require skills for producing internal and external validity. Such skills can be developed and taught. Interventionists also need to develop Model II skills if they choose to give implementable validity equal status. Implementable validity has its own internal and external features. Internal implementable validity is established by the degree to which the claims in the proposition actually lead to the specified consequences. For example, it is claimed that Model I theory-in-use is an important cause of organizational defensive routines. This causal claim can be tested through observations. External implementable validity is assessed by the extent to which specified organizational defensive routines are reduced when human beings become skilled at Model II theories-in-use. The former prediction is internal as long as it is not implemented. The moment we implement the claim the validity of the implementation is external.

For the most part, social scientists are taught to be concerned about internal implementations because the credibility of their theories depends upon their predictions not being disconfirmed (Popper, 1959). But, as we have seen, the predictions are limited to the status quo conditions of the existing universe. The moment predictions are made that cannot be tested, because human beings do not have the rare skills required and because they work in a context that does not encourage them to act in these rare ways, external implementable validity becomes crucial not only to the success of the interventions but also to the successful testing of the theory.

Ackoff (1999) has proposed a structural theory of organization that, if implemented effectively, should reduce the organizational defensive routines against learning. Attempts by him, and colleagues, have shown that the results are positive, but limited. One important cause of the limits is that the new theory requires Model II actions. The executives who are to implement this "democratic hierarchy" do not have the requisite skills. Even when the champion of the new hierarchy is the chairman of the board and CEO, even when his immediate reports agree with purpose and validity of the ideas, they have great difficulty in doing so (Argyris, 2004).

13.5 SOME PERSONAL REFLECTIONS

I should like to divide my research into an early period and a later period. The early period of my work was informed by the then rules of normal science. I cannot recall any unusual frustrations except one, my focus on interdisciplinary research. Senior mentors warned me to focus on one discipline in depth. This politically correct advice frustrated me because double-loop problems did not come packaged or organized by academic disciplines.

My frustration accelerated non-trivially when one of my mentors told me that I was compounding the felony of seeking changes in the status quo by using intervention as my preferred method for empirical research. To endanger my career even more, I sought to produce valid knowledge that was generalizable and applicable in the individual case. I did believe, following Lewin (1933), that it made little scholarly sense to have one theory for the "many" and another for the individual case if social scientists aspired to produce knowledge that practitioners could implement in their everyday affairs. Unfortunately, this advice is still a powerful source of fear by younger scholars who believe that they would harm their careers if they took such a path (Argyris, 2004).

There is another anxiety embedded in this perspective. Social scientists who strive to conduct research on double-loop issues and who seek to be interventionist will find that they have to face the likelihood that they too use Model I theory-in-use in their everyday lives as well as in their scholarly efforts. On double-loop issues they too are likely to be skillfully incompetent and skillfully unaware of their incompetence. Moreover, they are likely to live in a world where Model II may be espoused but Model I reigns supreme as the theory-in-use. The defensive routines of their communities of practice (e.g., describe the universe as is, focus on internal and external validity to the exclusion of implementable validity) protect them from having to face these issues just as practitioners in organization build organizational defensive routines to protect themselves from similar awareness.

I recall my shock many years ago, when I discovered features of my skilled incompetence and skilled unawareness as an officer in charge of nearly 300 employees in a Signal Corps depot. My first reaction was to blame the employees for not only hiding their true feelings, about me as their leader, but covering up by giving me a gift that described me as a humane and wonderful officer. When I was able to inquire why they withheld their true feelings, the employees who presented the gift explained their actions by saying that they had to go through the charade for all the officers as they were discharged. In their view, they too were victims (Argyris, 2003).

The experience remained at the forefront of my awareness. It guided me to be concerned about the impact I may be having upon those with whom I was trying to help to become more effective at creating liberating alternatives. After giving an extended feedback to the senior executives on the defensive routines of their organization, they responded that they found the presentation interesting. They hoped it would help me get promoted. It did not help them to produce liberating alternatives. Their problem was that I provided little knowledge on implementing the recommendations (Argyris, 2003).

13.5.1 Early Sources of Knowledge

In the early days of my career there was little research on interventions that were related to double-loop issues. I found the work of Kurt Lewin and William F. Whyte was most helpful.

My biggest learning came from the seminars and workshops that we designed to help the attendees to become more effective double-loop learners. As the faculty, we had to develop the cognitive and experiential content as we went along because there was little available literature. I recall the many discussions into the early mornings and before and during the seminars; as well as in planning and executing the interventions and that we conducted in organizations.

If I had to start my research all over again, I would still focus on observing everyday life and on implementing seminars and workshops whose thrust was double-loop learning. I would place a much greater emphasis on connecting with the managerial functions such as accounting, economics, finance, strategy, and information technology. Doctoral students and younger faculty who are able to integrate several of these disciplines will be more effective in producing double-loop changes because they are able to integrate the requirements of the managerial functions with the requirements of double-loop learning.

Recent work, for example Snyder and Lopez's *Handbook of Positive Psychology*, shows a developing emphasis upon "positive research" in organizations. This is an important trend that I hope continues and is extended to include double-loop learning and liberating alternatives in organizations. The book illustrates that there are social scientists interested in solving double-loop problems (e.g., reducing violence, use of drugs). Many use interventions where implementable validity is important. Unfortunately, the sections on organizations contain no interventions related to double-loop learning (Snyder and Lopez, 2002).

13.6 CONCLUDING COMMENTS

If we examine the cases of Enron, Arthur Anderson, Shell, the Catholic Church, FBI, CIA, *New York Times*, *USA Today*, UN oil-for-food programs, we will find that these different organizations have two fundamental characteristics in common. First, they covered up their dishonesty and covered up that they covered up. Second, when caught, the players denied personal responsibility and proclaimed that they were victims of the system.

Our society responds to these problems in two ways. First, commissions are appointed to establish the causes. New policies, new structures, the injunction to tighten things up, coupled with the admonition that the players take on more personal responsibility are recommended. These actions do result in progress but it is limited. We do not seem to be aware of the limitations. For example, recall that the Challenger tragedy was examined carefully and thoroughly. Corrections of all sorts were instituted to assure us that the errors would not be repeated. Several years later the Columbia disaster occurred in spite of these rules, policies, and structures.

The second strategy is to place a greater emphasis on culture. After Columbia, NASA promised to change its culture. How good are we at changing culture? The literature is full of claims that we are pretty good. Again, this is true but this claim is also limited. Recall ABB. It was touted for several years as an illustration of successful cultural change that turned the company around. The new culture emphasized openness, initiatives, trust, risk taking, and personal responsibility. A few years ago, the *Financial Times* interviewed the new CEO of ABB. He reported that the biggest challenge he faced was to create a new culture that emphasized openness, initiative, trust, risk taking, and personal responsibility. These were the same features the previous CEO had been acclaimed for creating (Argyris, 2004).

3M was a corporation acknowledged, for several decades, as a company that rewarded innovation. Last year, the new CEO told a *Wall Street Journal* reporter that his biggest challenge was to recreate a culture of innovation that had been lost. How do innovative cultures get lost? Why are these causes not foreseen (Argyris, 2004)?

One way to begin to explain all these puzzles is to realize that in all organizations there are managerial components that are above ground and underground. The above ground in organizations is managed by productive reasoning, transparency, and tough testing of performance. Truth (with a small "t") is a good idea. The underground organization is dominated by defensive reasoning where the objective is to protect the players from embarrassment or threat. It rewards skilled denial and personal responsibility. Truth is a good idea, when it is not troublesome. If it is, massage it, spin it, and cover up.

The underground organization has several fascinating features. It develops even though it violates the current concepts of effective management. It survives even though there are no courses taught to executives how to help it to survive. It flourishes by engaging the rules and regulations intended to smother it. It is a major cause for individuals using defensive mind-sets protected by organizational defensive routines that guarantee its survival.

These self-sealing processes are counter-productive to a productive reasoning mind-set. They make it difficult to produce trust, openness, transparency, and testing of ideas, all features that I suggest will be increasingly required for the future design of organizations and their management.

REFERENCES

ACKOFF, R. L. (1999). *Re-creating the Organization.* New York: Oxford University Press.
ARGYRIS, C. (1980). *Inner Contradictions of Rigorous Research.* San Diego, Calif.: Academic Press.
—— (1982). *Reasoning, Learning, and Action: Individual and Organizational.* San Francisco: Jossey-Bass.
—— (1985). *Strategy, Change and Defensive Routines.* New York: Harper Business.
—— (1990). *Overcoming Organizational Defenses.* Needham, Mass.: Allyn Bacon.
—— (1993). *Knowledge for Action: A Guide to Overcoming Barriers to Organizational Change.* San Francisco: Jossey-Bass.
—— (1996). Unrecognized defense of scholars' impact on theory and research. *Organization Science,* 7(1): 77–85.
—— (1997). Field theory as a basis for scholarly research-consulting. *Journal of Social Issues,* 53(4): 809–824.
—— (2000). *Flawed Advice and the Management Trap, How Managers Can Know When They're Getting Good Advice and When They're Not.* New York: Oxford University Press.
—— (2002). Double loop learning, teaching, and research. *Academy of Management Learning and Education,* 1(2): 206–219.
—— (2003). A life full of learning. *Organizational Studies,* 24(7): 1178–1192.
—— (2004). *Reasons and Rationalizations: The Limits to Organizational Knowledge.* Oxford: Oxford University Press.
—— PUTNAM, R., and SMITH, D. (1985). *Action Science.* San Francisco: Jossey-Bass.
—— and SCHÖN, D. (1974). *Theory in Practice: Increasing Professional Effectiveness.* San Francisco: Jossey-Bass.
—— —— (1996). *Organizational Learning II.* Reading, Mass.: Addison-Wesley.
JOHNSON, D. (1993). Psychology in Washington: Measurement to improve scientific productivity: A reflection on the Brown Report. *Psychological Science,* 4(2): 67–69.
LEWIN, K. (1933). *A Dynamic Theory of Personality.* New York: McGraw-Hill.

MINER, A. S., and MEZIAC, S. J. (1996). Ugly ducking no more: Pasts and futures of organizational learning research. *Organization Science*, 7(1): 88–99.

POPPER, K. (1959). *The Logic of Scientific Inquiry.* New York: Basic Books.

SNYDER, C. R., and LOPEZ, S. J. (2002). *Handbook of Positive Psychology.* Oxford: Oxford University Press.

CHAPTER 14

WHERE DOES INEQUALITY COME FROM?

THE PERSONAL AND INTELLECTUAL ROOTS OF RESOURCE-BASED THEORY

JAY B. BARNEY

IT has been said that all writing is autobiographical. If true, then one's research—because it is such an intense and focused form of writing—must be a particularly intimate form of autobiography. In this sense, all scholarship is self-revelatory. It is as if there is embedded, within the body of one's published work, a hidden Rorschach test that reveals more than even the author sometimes knows.

The most influential scholars, I think, embrace the self-revelatory nature of research. They understand that the "search for truth" is conditioned by our personal experiences, and that the definition of what constitutes an "interesting question" is only partly a matter of logic and epistemology. After all, from among all the "interesting questions" one could pose, why is a particular question asked?

I appreciate comments from Sharon Alvarez, Mike Hitt, Michael Leiblein, and Ken Smith on earlier versions of this chapter.

For me, this "interesting question" has been: Why do some firms outperform other firms? At first, this seems like a very narrow question, a question that would only interest business managers and scholars, hardly one that would engage a broader audience in society. However, understanding why some firms outperform others is, to me, just a special case of a much broader question, a question that has been at the center of discourse and debate in the social sciences, in philosophy, and in politics for centuries and a question that has been of concern to me for as long as I can remember. That broader question is: What are the causes and consequences of inequality in society?

Growing up in the 1960s in the San Francisco Bay area, I was confronted with two very different "theories" about inequality in society. On the one hand, the popular mood of the day seemed to be that inequality was, at its core, bad for society. This view argued that any society that tolerated, or celebrated, inequality in any form was on shaky moral grounds and would not stand. On the other hand, this egalitarian view seemed to be inconsistent with my personal experiences— experiences that suggested to me that not only was inequality in society inevitable, that sometimes it was a good thing, that sometimes it created incentives for creativity and innovation by rewarding these accomplishments.

I remember, for example, this kid in my high school—we called him Posy. (I don't remember ever knowing his real name.) Posy was the most intuitive mathematician I have ever known. He had a way of thinking about math problems that, frankly, never occurred to me. His solutions were inevitably correct, and subtle, and elegant, and creative. But Posy had no inter-personal skills. He wasn't an athlete. And his academic skills in other high school classes were average, at best. Even in high school, I recognized that we—both Posy and I—were better off acknowledging our differences and excelling in our own spheres. So, I let Posy be Posy, and I decided that rather than being a mediocre Posy, I would try to be an excellent me.

Posy was just one of numerous examples in my daily life where differences between people inevitably led to differences in outcomes and that sometimes these outcomes were unequal, even grossly unequal. But since I could never be like Posy, and since he could never be like me, pretending that the inequality between Posy and I was a bad thing seemed, frankly, silly.[1] Moreover, by each of us focusing on excelling in our own spheres of endeavor, a natural division of labor could develop, a division of labor that promised more progress for each of us personally, and for society as a whole, than would be the case if everyone tried to be the same.

The conflict between these two ideologies of inequality came into stark relief during my senior year in high school. During that year, I was part of an experimental "school within a school" that allowed me to define my own curriculum and

---

[1] Even as I write this, I am struck by the parallel between my experiences with Posy and resource-based theories of why some firms outperform other firms.

engage in independent research and learning. During my semester in this program, I developed and executed a series of projects on a variety of topics. As far as I could tell, while I was working, most of my classmates in this program just "hung out." Then, one week before the end of the semester, my classmates began working at a fever pitch to complete the projects they had committed to previously. There was no doubt in my mind that the quality of my work and the work of my classmates was significantly different, that is, unequal. However, in the end, we all got the same grades.

In retrospect, this outcome should not have surprised me. The mythology of equality was so entrenched among those that administered this educational program that they actually lacked the ability to recognize differences among the students. Giving everyone the same grade was simply their way of making sure "no one got left behind." Of course, in this Lake Wobegone world where all students are above average, there is also no room for excellence, no room for uniqueness, and no room for distinction. And, as it turned out, no room for me. I left the program after one semester.

Thus, to me, questions about the "rightness and wrongness" of inequality have always been central. Indeed, in many ways, my academic career—and certainly my efforts in helping to develop resource-based theory in the field of strategic management—can be understood as an effort to understand the relationship between these two "theories" of inequality in society—that it is morally bad and that it is both inevitable and can be good. That I have chosen to confront these issues in the context of business firms is at least partially a matter of chance and good fortune. I could have chosen to confront these same issues in a very different context, say in the context of the ideological struggle between socialism and capitalism. Whether we study "Why do some firms outperform others" or "Why do some economic systems outperform others," at some level, these are both questions about the causes and consequences of inequality.[2]

Indeed, my initial academic choices were not focused on studying inequality among firms at all, but on studying inequality in society, more generally. This is the main reason why, when it came time for me to choose an academic major in college, I chose sociology. It was in my study of sociology that I began to assemble the intellectual tools I would use in helping the development of resource-based theory.

---

[2] My interest was in understanding the causes and consequences in the inequality of outcomes. In high school, I was less interested in inequality in opportunities since—in my white, middle class high school—inequality in opportunities was not likely to be much of a problem. However, in retrospect, it seems to me that my high school teachers adopted the same logic that I will describe among SCP scholars—that any heterogeneity in outcomes must reflect heterogeneity in opportunity. This conclusion only makes sense if people/firms are perfectly homogeneous.

14.1 ASSEMBLING THE TOOLS

Of course, my understanding of the relationship between my beliefs about the causes and consequences of inequality in society and resource-based theory emerged only after years of study and work. The specific intellectual paths that led to this thing called resource-based theory began as an undergraduate sociology major at Brigham Young University, in Provo, Utah. I was a student at BYU from September 1972 to December 1975.

In retrospect, I can identify four classes at BYU that were particularly important to my intellectual journey: Two classes on sociological theory taught by Genevieve DeHoyos and James Duke, a class on the philosophy of the social sciences taught by Don Sorenson, and a class on organizational sociology taught by Phillip Kunz. Each of these classes added specific tools to my intellectual tool chest that would later find use in developing resource-based theory.[3]

From my sociological theory classes I learned to appreciate theory and the theory development process. The concept of theory for theory's sake was foreign to my middle-class upbringing. The thought of intellectuals sitting around a room and trading quips about how society operates would amuse and confuse most of my friends and family.[4] But I found great joy in creating and extending these abstractions. While I have always recognized the importance of empirical work, both for developing and testing theory, I have also always been drawn to the purity of theoretical thought. I first discovered that purity in my sociological theory classes.

We did "high theory" in those sociology classes—Durkheim, Parsons, Marx, Weber. These scholars asked the biggest of questions about society and its institutions—"What is social reality?", "How does the organization of society affect individuals and institutions?", "What is a moral basis for organizing society?", and "Can the organization of society be studied?" And it didn't matter to me that the answers these great thinkers developed were often obscure and abstract— the act of asking seemed like a worthwhile endeavor by itself. After all, if one only asks little questions, then one can only develop little answers. If one asks big questions, there is at least a chance that some bigger answers might emerge.

In my philosophy of social science class, I was introduced to a different kind of theory—a theory about theories. If theory development was pure, then philosophy

---

[3] I doubt any of these professors, all of whom have long since retired, remember me. But I remember them. It has always been my secret desire to have the same kind of effect on at least some students that these professors had on me.

[4] But not my father who was something of a frustrated academic. In 1947, he had to choose between continuing a career as a middle manager in the Pacific Telephone Company and accepting a scholarship to Stanford to study industrial psychology. Having lived through the great depression, he chose the relative security of Pac Bell—a decision I think he continues to regret today. I became the professor my father always wanted to be.

was the purist of all. However, I soon recognized that the "dependent variable" in a theory about theories was quite elusive, and for that reason, most of the philosophical debates I entered into in that course had been raging, literally, for centuries. It was unlikely that I would be able to make much of a contribution to these debates.

However, it was during this course that I was introduced to, and convinced by, reductionism. While I had been weaned on the god Emile Durkheim and his concept of social facts, I came to believe that, in the end, people make decisions, people act, and people are the ultimate unit of analysis in the social sciences. This does not deny the importance of studying aggregate phenomena like firms and markets. However, it does reaffirm that firms and markets are aggregates of people, and the decisions people make, not things in their own right.

In my organizational sociology class, I was introduced to Mancur Olson's little book, *The Logic of Collective Action*. In this book, Olson takes a simple concept—collective goods—and sews together an impressive theoretical quilt, explaining everything from small group behavior, to the behavior of labor unions, to the evolution of class conflict in society. Olson's book defined my ideal in theory development: A simple idea with powerful, broad ranging, and counter-intuitive implications. My academic dream was to develop such a theory. That Olson's theory also focused on inequality in society was simply a bonus.

At some point during my junior year at BYU, I discovered two things about college: I liked it and I was good at it. So, I decided to never leave. Changing my plans, I decided to apply, not to law school, but instead to Ph.D. programs in sociology. I applied to several schools and ultimately went to Yale—because they offered me the most money. So, pulling a little U-Haul trailer with our total earthly possessions across the country, me, my wife, and our 3-month-old daughter moved to New Haven, Connecticut. I brought with me an ambition to write "elegant theory" and a desire to understand the causes and consequences of inequality in society. I did not understand that this broad ambition required considerable honing before it would turn into a viable research question.

14.2 DISCOVERING MY QUESTION

For me, graduate school was something of a mixed experience. On the one hand, I rapidly became disillusioned with the discipline of sociology. Where my work as an undergraduate had focused on "high theory," the sociologists at Yale had taken Merton's (1949) call for "theories of the middle range" to an extreme. In fact,

I concluded that—at Yale, at least—there was no sociological theory, only a loosely connected set of ideas that were applied to studying a wide variety of disconnected phenomena—the sociology of medicine, the sociology of sport, the sociology of religion. Sociology had become applied statistics.

A simple story makes this point. The Ph.D. students in the Sociology Department decided to form a softball team for the graduate school softball tournament. At the organizing meeting, we had to choose a name for our team. Here we were, fifteen Ph.D. students in sociology and we couldn't come up with a single uniquely sociological concept which we could use to name our team. In the end, we decided to call ourselves the "Chi Squares"—we gave up on sociological theory as a source of inspiration and fell back on statistics![5]

I also found that the notion that inequality in society was inevitable and can be good—beliefs that were reasonably common, even among sociologists, at BYU— were completely unacceptable among my peers at Yale, where the 1960s assumptions of egalitarianism were taken to an extreme. In the sociology department at Yale, I could not debate alternative views of the morality of inequality in society since, in the view of most of my peers, there were not two legitimate perspectives on this question. In their view, socialism had won and capitalism was in the process of dying.

I know now that my initial conclusions about sociology were probably overly harsh. Indeed, the sociologists I now know the best—organizational sociologists— have made very significant contributions to the field of strategic management and to my understanding of why some firms outperform others. But in 1977, I did not see it.

On the other hand, in my early days in the Sociology Department, I did begin working with one of the best-known social network scholars of that time—Scott Boorman. From him I learned all about block modeling, social network theory, and a variety of related topics. It seemed that Scott had read everything that had ever been written and contributed to most of it. I admired his theoretical and mathematical skills, although I also concluded that social network theory—with the exception of Grannovetter's (1973) distinction between strong and weak ties—was really "social network method," a descriptive approach that was difficult to use to either develop or test theory. Indeed, it took almost twenty years for sociologists such as Brian Uzzi, Ranjay Gulati, Toby Stewart, and Ed Zajac to move beyond the descriptive power of the network metaphor, to use it to develop and test new theory.

In the midst of my sociology program, it became necessary for me to choose a second area of emphasis—besides network theory. The seminars being offered in the Sociology Department that semester did not interest me. So, I walked across the street to the brand new Yale School of Organization and Management (SOM),

---

[5] I personally liked the name proposed by a child of one of my fellow students—"The Swords!"

where I took a Ph.D. seminar from Bob Miles on organization theory. I remember three things about Bob's class: First, he had the longest reading list I had ever seen; second, he required two term papers, not just one; and third, he was among the most prolific scholars I had ever met. Bob Miles introduced me, in a real sense, to the serious study of organizations.

I quickly recognized two important differences between my experiences in the Sociology Department and SOM. First, from a methodological point of view, there was little doubt that the Sociology Department was much more rigorous than SOM, or at least the part of SOM where I was studying. In sociology, I had been exposed to the absolute state-of-the-art, both in statistical analysis and network methodology. My SOM colleagues had received reasonable training in the first area, but virtually no training in the second. However, I also discovered that SOM students—and especially the professional students in SOM (at the time, Yale's equivalent to MBA students)—were less ideologically bound than the sociology students. Indeed, at least some SOM students acknowledged the possibility that inequality in outcomes among people in society might be inevitable and could be good for society. For this reason, I felt more at home in SOM than I did sociology.

Ultimately, I was able to pursue the one and only joint degree between the Administrative Sciences and Sociology Departments at Yale.[6] I took most of my methods and social networks classes from the Sociology Department and most of my theory classes from Administrative Sciences. After Bob Miles's seminar, I took another seminar on organization theory from John Kimberly. I also took two seminars on the social psychology of organizations—one from Rosabeth Kanter (who had a joint appointment between the Sociology and Administrative Sciences Departments) and one from Clay Alderfer. Although these classes both had the title "The Social Psychology of Organizations," they could not have been more different. I also took a class on managing organizational change from Clay Alderfer.

As part of my joint degree program, I took three days of general exams—one day on network sociology, one day on research methods, and one day on organization theory. I was well prepared for all three days, but my reactions to the examination process varied dramatically by day. With respect to network sociology, I concluded that there were limited opportunities to develop the kinds of theory I wanted to develop using the tools that were available at that time. While I went on to complete my dissertation in network sociology, I did not see this as an area where I would ultimately make much of a contribution.

---

[6] The departments in the graduate school where I arranged for the joint degree were Sociology and Administrative Sciences. The Administrative Sciences department, in turn, provided faculty to teach in the School of Organization and Management. Students in SOM received a professional degree called a Masters of Public and Private Management, or MPPM. It was my interaction with these professional students—both as a teaching assistant and as a classmate when we took classes together—that led me to rethink my exclusive association with the Department of Sociology.

With respect to research methods, I felt competent, but did not want to become the resident "quant jock" in a department. So while I knew I would always want to remain current in research methods and statistics—to this day, I still surprise my colleagues by making reasonably coherent comments about statistics in research seminars—I also knew that this was not where I wanted to make a contribution.

That left organizational sociology or, as it is known today, organization theory. Here, my response to the general exam was very disturbing. After writing about organization theory for some eight hours, I concluded that there really wasn't much to this field. Keep in mind the time—I took my exams in 1978. The only coherent theoretical perspective in organization theory at the time was, I think, resource-dependence theory. This was before population ecology—Hannan and Freeman (1977) published their first paper just after I took my exams—before institutional theory, and certainly before the new institutional economics became well known in management departments.

My main problem with the organizational theories of the day was that they did not meet the theoretical standard that Mancur Olson had set in his book *The Logic of Collective Action*. They were, in my Ph.D. student mind, not terribly elegant. They did not generate interesting counter-intuitive predictions. They did not have implications for a wide range of phenomena. And while I recognized that resource-dependence theory did have some implications for the study of inequality in society, I did not think those ideas were as sophisticated and interesting as some of the work I had already seen in sociology.

Of course, organization theory has progressed significantly since the mid-1970s. Some of the theories developed by organization theorists—especially population ecology theory—are, in my view, elegant and have implications for a reasonably broad range of phenomena. But the literature I had read in preparing for my qualifying exams did not meet the standard I aspired to for my own work. I was deeply concerned about my academic career—what would I study?

Then Bill Ouchi came to give a talk at Yale. He presented a talk on an early draft of a paper that later was published in *Administrative Sciences Quarterly* titled "Market, Bureaucracies, and Clans." I loved three things about his presentation. First, Bill was very articulate—he moved from first principles, to theory development, to implications in a very clear and logical way. His paper demonstrated great care in theory development, something I had not seen much during my time in graduate school. Second, it was clear to me that Bill was discussing an approach to organization that was entirely new to me. While Sid Winter and Dick Nelson were both on the faculty at Yale at that time, I had not been exposed to their thinking or the thinking of any of the economists at Yale. So, when Bill talked of market failures and the "theory of the firm," I truly had not heard of these ideas previously. Finally, and most importantly, I didn't understand what Bill was talking about. This was good news to me because it suggested that, in fact, I had a great deal left to learn about studying organizations. Maybe there was something for me to study after all!

After his talk, I asked Bill what else I should read to understand his paper. He told me to read Williamson's (1975), *Markets and Hierarchies*. So, I went to the library, borrowed a copy, and read about transactions cost economics for the first time. I found the book incomprehensible. In the first chapter of *Markets and Hierarchies*, Williamson summarizes his perspective—a summary that made no sense to me. At the end of that chapter, he provides a couple of examples of applying his framework. I remember saying to myself, "Well, I might not understand his summary, but I will be able to see how he applies the theory in his examples." After reading the examples, I was more confused than ever.

All this was very exciting to me! Obviously, this was "high theory" of the type I had seen as an undergraduate. And while I did not understand much of his argument, my intuition was that Williamson was addressing an important question. It was also clear that he felt that his argument had broad implications—the examples in the first chapter were very wide ranging. And while I didn't see, at that time, how Williamson's argument could be extended to understanding inequality in society, it did seem at least possible—what with Williamson's discussions of markets and hierarchies. So, based on the confusion created in my mind after hearing Ouchi's talk and reading Williamson's book, I decided that transactions cost economics was an area that I wanted to study more.[7]

While I was completing my dissertation—an exercise in mathematical network analysis and applied statistics from which I learned very little about organizations—I went on the job market. One of the places where I interviewed was UCLA—where Bill Ouchi had gone when he left Stanford. Again, my intuition told me that if I was going to learn about this new "institutional economics" UCLA might be a good place to go. I was excited when they gave me a job offer and me, my wife, and now two children flew across the country to start a career in Los Angeles.

UCLA was paradise for a budding theoretician. The list of people either in the Graduate School of Management or part of the greater UCLA community from whom I could learn was remarkable. My direct faculty colleagues included, at various times, Bill Ouchi, Bill McKelvey, Dick Rumelt, Barbara Lawrence, Connie Gersick (a close friend from our days at Yale), J. C. Spender, and Steve Postrel, to name just a few. Tom Copeland, Dick Roll, and Sheridan Titman were finance colleagues right down the hall. The economics department turned out to include a "Who's Who" in the new institutional economics: Armen Alchian, Harold Demsetz, Ben Klein, and Jack Hirshleifer. And Lynne Zucker was in the Sociology

[7] The one experience in "high theory" I did have in graduate school, before transactions cost economics, was when I read John Rawls's *A Theory of Justice* (1971). Interestingly, I had the same initial response to this work as I did to transactions cost economics: At first, I did not understand it, but my intuition was that it was important and widely applicable. Rawls also develops a theory which defines the conditions under which inequality in society is beneficial. However, the very abstract philosophical nature of his argument led me to conclude that it would be difficult to build a research career in the social sciences based on this work. That said, Rawls's argument continues to influence much of my thinking about inequality.

Department. Bill Ouchi's close relationship with Oliver Williamson and David Teece meant that these two scholars visited UCLA with some frequency. And some of our Ph.D. students—including Kate Conner, Todd Zenger, Bill Hesterly, Julia Liebeskind, and Jim Robbins, to name just a few—were just amazing.

I remember a conference that Bill Ouchi organized—sponsored by the consulting firm Booze, Allen, Hamilton—on the new institutional economics. I was on a panel with Armen Alchian, Dick Rumelt, and Oliver Williamson. In retrospect, I think of that panel—with me, a brand new Assistant Professor, sitting with this group—and the old Sesame Street song "Which of These Things is Not Like the Others?" comes to mind.

For me, the early 1980s was a time of intense education. I read more, debated more, and wrote more during those first few years then I had ever done previously. I taught myself what little micro-economics I've ever understood during that time period. Indeed, I actually got to the point where not only did I understand Williamson, I could apply his theory, I could explain it to others, and I could even make contributions to it—or at least I thought I could.

It turned out, of course, that transactions cost economics does have a nice explanation of at least one type of inequality in society: When transaction specific investments are required to complete an economic exchange, parties to that exchange will find it in their self interest to have their exchange monitored by a third party—the boss. By assigning residual rights of control to the boss, hierarchy enables people who cannot anticipate all the ways that an exchange could evolve to still engage in exchanges, exchanges that are mediated by a hierarchy over time.[8] So, transactions cost economics explains the existence of organizational hierarchies, where some people tell other people—within pre-specified ranges—what to do. It also explains why this type of inequality in society is efficient and can benefit all members of society in the long run.

A second, wholly unanticipated event, also took place during this time period: Bill Ouchi's book, *Theory Z*, suddenly became the first book written by a business school professor to become a best seller. Bill had had an active consulting practice before the popularity of *Theory Z*. After *Theory Z*, he had more consulting opportunities than he could possibly accept. In the beginning, Bill took me along—sort of as a highly paid apprentice—on these consulting trips. Later I began to do some of this work on my own.

Consulting had a profound impact on me. While I was becoming very well versed in the new institutional economics and the theory of the firm in my academic life, I found that most of the issues we were dealing with in our consulting had less to do with the kind of inequality studied by transactions cost theorists—the inequality created by hierarchical governance—and much more to

---

[8] Ironically, there are some interesting parallels between Williamson's logic and Rawls's logic which, I think, have not yet been explored in the literature.

do with the inequality between firms—that some firms were able to outperform other firms. While it was possible to extend transactions cost logic to study differences in firm performance, this was not the original purpose of the theory, and the extensions seemed somewhat artificial. I did not know it then, but my consulting experience had actually led me to the question that was to organize my intellectual life for the next twenty years—why do some firms outperform others? I was in the process of discovering my question.[9]

Beyond my general education in the new institutional economics, four things I read gave me the specific tools—and the motivation—I needed to begin my work in what became known as the resource-based view of the firm. The first of these was Jensen and Meckling's (1976) *Journal of Financial Economics* paper on Agency Theory. From this paper I learned about the concept of efficient capital markets and that it was very difficult for managers to "fool" efficient markets and thereby earn superior economic profits.

The second was an obscure paper by Dick Rumelt and Robin Wensley, published only in the 1982 *Academy of Management "Best Paper" Proceedings*, titled "In Search of the Market Share Effect." From this paper, I learned about rational expectations and that the competitive dynamics in one market can be affected by the competitive dynamics in a prior market. Rational expectations markets essentially extend the concept of efficient markets temporally.

The third of these four papers provided very valuable insights to me. Written by Harold Demsetz and published in the *Journal of Law and Economics* in 1973, "Industry Structure, Market Rivalry, and Public Policy" showed that unequal outcomes in firm performance and market share, far from being unusual or inconsistent with social welfare, were likely to be common and could be quite consistent with social welfare. Demsetz's argument was that firms might vary systematically in their ability to meet customer needs, that these differences may not diffuse rapidly among a firm's competitors, and thus that different firms in an industry may have different levels of performance—all without resorting to anti-competitive tactics. Moreover, Demsetz argued—in this remarkably rich nine-page article—that far from being inconsistent with social welfare, when firms maximize their performance, given their differential ability to meet customer needs, any resulting heterogeneity in performance was actually perfectly consistent with social welfare.

It was with these three articles in mind that I first read the fourth piece that influenced my thinking: Michael Porter's (1980) book, *Competitive Strategy*. I did not react positively to Porter's arguments. The margins in my copy of his book are filled with not very flattering characterizations of his arguments. My first reaction to those arguments was that Porter was ignoring the ideas about efficient markets,

---

[9] Initially, I did not anticipate that consulting would have such a profound effect on my theory development work. Since those early days, I have come to expect that consulting will often generate unanticipated insights about the theories I am trying to develop or refine.

rational expectations markets, and firm skill differences I had culled from my own study. I believed this put his arguments on shaky theoretical ground.

In retrospect, I think what I was really responding to in Porter's book was the theoretical framework upon which his argument was based. That theoretical framework—known as the Structure–Conduct–Performance paradigm—in its simplest, and most extreme, form asserts that any deviations from homogeneous firm performance in an industry must reflect anti-competitive actions by firms that destroy social welfare. This was the old egalitarian philosophy—although dressed up nicely in some apparently rigorous economic logic—that I had seen in high school and that had been part of my disillusionment with sociology. And here it was again—denying differences between firms, denying that those differences might naturally lead to unequal outcomes, denying that those unequal outcomes might actually benefit society in some settings.

Of course, my initial reactions to Porter's work were overstated—I was young and passionate and thus prone to overstatement and exaggeration. But even today, while acknowledging that SCP logic can apply in some settings, my strong theoretical preference is to presume that markets are reasonably competitive, that firms can systematically differ in their capabilities, that these differences can lead to heterogeneous performance outcomes in even the most competitive settings, and that such outcomes are perfectly consistent with social welfare. In the battle between Bain and Demsetz, I sided with Demsetz. And, whereas, the implications of Bain's argument for managers had been described by Porter, no one had yet done the same for Demsetz's argument.

I had my question.

14.3 DEVELOPING THE RESOURCE-BASED VIEW

I wrote the first draft of an outline for my first resource-based paper in 1983 on a subway in Tokyo, Japan. That paper was ultimately published in 1991 when I became an Associate Editor at the *Journal of Management* and accepted my own paper.

It wasn't as if I wasn't working hard during this eight-year time span. I usually was writing or re-writing no fewer than four or five papers at a time. Some of these were transactions cost/agency theory papers, but the bulk of them focused on developing a theory of why some firms outperformed others that was consistent with market efficiency and consistent with the notion that heterogeneity in firm performance could be good for society. But I was having limited success publishing any of this work.

In 1982, I published an article in *AMR* (with Dave Ulrich) that integrated three types of theoretical models within the field of organization theory. I published my next paper in a competitive journal in 1986—four years later. In 1986, I published two papers in *AMR* (one that examined whether or not organizational culture could be a source of sustained competitive advantage (Barney, 1986*a*) and one that examined three kinds of competition in strategic management theory (Barney, 1986*b*)), one paper in *Management Science* (a paper that introduced the notion strategic factor markets to the literature (Barney, 1986*c*)), and a book (with Bill Ouchi called *Organizational Economics* (1986).)

Each of these papers had a torturous history. However, none exemplified the challenges associated with developing this new theoretical approach more than my *Management Science* paper. The first version of the paper received decidedly mixed reviews—reviewer #1 thought it did not say anything new and should be rejected, reviewer #2 thought it was too abstract and should be rejected, and reviewer #3 thought it was one of the most important papers he/she had ever read in strategy. Arie Lewin was the Associate Editor for that paper and I will always be grateful to him that he invited it for a revise and resubmit. After several rounds of revision—I think it says four rounds in the published version of the paper—all three reviewers maintained their original position: Reviewer #1 was even more clear why he thought there was nothing new in the paper, reviewer #2 was even more convinced that it was too abstract for the field of strategic management, and reviewer #3 was even more convinced of its importance.

Despite these mixed reviews, Arie Lewin accepted the paper. Arie has always understood that good editing is not simply accounting—counting up the number of yes and no votes about whether or not a paper should be published. Good editing always involves exercising editorial judgment. Arie concluded that any paper that created so much controversy among reviewers must be worthy of publication.

So, in 1986, some of my first work on what became known as the resource-based view was published. Of course, these articles were not the first in this area of work to be published. The first papers published by strategy scholars were Dick Rumelt's 1984 book chapter "Toward a Strategic Theory of the Firm" and Birger Wernerfelt's 1984 *SMJ* article "A Resource-based View of the Firm." Also, work by others, including Penrose (1959) and Demsetz (1973), had pre-dated all these strategy publications. However, I do believe that the work I published in 1986, especially the *AMR* article on organizational culture and the *Management Science* article on strategic factor markets, helped set the ground work for what came to be known as resource-based theory.

Of course, after all this hard work, the publication of all these papers and a book in 1986 led to—absolutely nothing. The field of strategic management was completely dominated by the Porter framework and by research based on the SCP paradigm that underpinned the Porter framework. Scholars were studying industry structure, strategic groups, and generic strategies, and had little interest in firm-specific resources and capabilities, especially when the most important of those resources and capabilities were likely to be intangible in nature.

By 1986, I had moved from UCLA to Texas A&M University. When I was deciding whether or not to stay at UCLA and come up for tenure, I still had only my 1982 *AMR* publication. It seemed prudent for me to move, although within two months of accepting an offer from Texas A&M, I had three papers accepted for publication, and a book published. But moving to Texas A&M was a good thing to do for a variety of reasons, not the least of which was I did not want to raise my now three children in Southern California. I was very attracted by the small town college life that Texas A&M promised. And so, me, my wife, and our three children packed our belongings and moved to Texas.[10]

A&M turned out to be good for me for several reasons that would have been difficult for me to anticipate. For example, the strategy faculty and students at UCLA had been rather isolated intellectually. We felt no compulsion to contribute to the Academy of Management meetings, to become involved in the governance of what at the time was the BPP division.[11] Thus, while at UCLA, I had little idea about how important the Academy could be for popularizing a new theoretical point of view. The faculty at Texas A&M—including Mike Hitt, Bob Hoskisson, Tom Turk, Barry Baysinger, Gerry Keim, Javier Gimeno, and Bert Canella—were experts on the Academy of Management and its role in diffusing new research. I had much to learn from them about these issues.

Also, while I was at A&M, Ricky Griffin—an organizational behavior colleague in the Management Department—was appointed as the editor for the *Journal of Management*. Ricky asked me if I would be willing to become the Associate Editor for the journal. Shortly after accepting this responsibility, I suggested to Ricky that I edit a special research forum on something called "The Resource-based View." He said yes.

There were several events that led to my decision to edit this special theory forum. First, the junior faculty at Wharton had organized in the late 1980s two conferences on the New Jersey shore to which I was invited. That was the first time I met Connie Helfat and Margie Peteraf. I also got to know, among others, Cynthia Montgomery and Raffi Amit much better at those conferences. These conferences were the first time I presented what became my 1991 *Journal of Management* paper in public. The ideas in that paper seemed to go over reasonably well at the conference. Raffi Amit and I still talk of the long walk on the beach we took

---

[10] At the time, I also had an offer to move to the Wharton School at the University of Pennsylvania. I put the options—Texas A&M and Wharton—to my family for a discussion. My son, then about 7 years old, asked me "Where will you travel more, Texas or Philadelphia?" I said that I would probably travel more if we moved to Philadelphia—anticipating the consulting opportunities that would probably exist at Wharton. He replied, "Then we should move to Texas!" That is remarkable wisdom from a 7 year old!

[11] BPP stood for: Business Policy and Planning.

where I argued—for well over an hour—with him about the theoretical underpinnings of resource-based logic.

Based on that experience, Margie Peteraf and I organized a symposium at the Academy of Management in 1990, the year it was held in San Francisco. Panel members included me, Margie, Raffi Amit, David Teece, and Garth Saloner. I presented what later became the 1991 *Journal of Management* paper, Raffi presented what later became his very influential *SMJ* paper (Amit and Schoemaker, 1993), Margie presented an early version of her influential—and award winning—*SMJ* paper (Peteraf, 1993), David presented what later became his award winning *SMJ* paper (Teece, Pisano, and Shuen, 1977), and Garth presented a rousing and quite humorous defense of game theory. This session, to say the least, was electric.

After my experiences at the shore conferences and at the Academy, I became convinced that there was a new theory of competitive advantage here, and that a forum was required to publish these new and innovative ideas. And, since I was now an Associate Editor, I was in a position to create such a forum.

Ultimately, some of the papers published in that 1991 *Journal of Management* special issue have become among the most cited of all papers in the field of strategic management. In fact, that special issue could have had an even more substantial impact if I had accepted Margie Peteraf's (1993) paper on the "Cornerstones of Competitive Advantage" and Teece, Pisano, and Shuen's (1997) paper on "Dynamic Capabilities"—both of which were submitted to the *Journal of Management* special issue and later published in *SMJ*. But I was facing some space and time constraints and did not push for these papers to be accepted as much as I should have. It was a huge mistake!

Of course, publishing this special issue also gave me an opportunity to publish my own paper—first conceived of in Japan, rejected twice by *AMR* and once by *SMJ*. However, beyond any contributions that individual papers in this special research forum made, these papers also called attention to the papers—by Wernerfelt, Rumelt, and myself—that had originally been published in 1984 and 1986. This body of work—from the mid-1980s and the early 1990s—became much of the central core of what has come to be known as resource-based theory.

14.4 RETROSPECTION AND GENERALIZATION

In hindsight, I have often wondered if my work over the last twenty-five years or so met the standards I set for myself as an undergraduate sociology student at BYU.

At one level, those standards were so high as to be unattainable by anyone. This is not surprising. It is usually the case that the standards set by young scholars for their own, and others', work are unrealistically ambitious. This is why almost no papers are ever accepted for publication by Ph.D. student reviewers.

However, given more reasonable expectations about what one might accomplish as a scholar, I feel satisfied about how resource-based theory has developed and evolved and how it has been applied. Resource-based theory is simple. It rests on just a few, what appear to be very reasonable, assumptions. Whether or not it is elegant is really a matter of personal taste, so I won't judge its elegance here.

It certainly has had broad ranging implications—well beyond anything I was thinking about when I began this work. For example, while Dick Rumelt first talked about a new theory of the firm based on resource-based logic in his 1984 book chapter, Kate Conner (in her 1991 *Journal of Management* paper) and Kate and C. K. Prahalad (in their *Organization Science* paper) have made theory of the firm issues central to work in the resource-based view. I did not anticipate this development when I was working on my 1986 and 1991 papers. Within strategic management, the logic has been applied to understand firm versus industry effects, the performance effects of specific resources and capabilities, business and corporate strategies, international strategies, and strategic alliances.[12]

Resource-based logic has also been applied outside the field of strategic management (Barney and Arikan, 2002). For example, resource-based logic has become a centerpiece in strategic human resource management research (see, for example, Huselid, 1995). It also has had an impact on the management information science literature (see, e.g., Ray, Barney, and Muhanna, 2004), the marketing literature (see, e.g., Ghingold and Johnson, 1997), the entrepreneurship literature, (see, e.g., Alvarez and Busenitz, 2001), the operations management literature (see, e.g., Powell, 1995), and the technology and innovation management literature (see, e.g., Stuart and Podolny, 1996).

And, what is personally satisfying is that resource-based theory really is a theory about inequality in society. While acknowledging that sometimes inequality in outcomes can be inefficient, even evil, resource-based theory's core message is: heterogeneity in outcomes in society is common and natural and is often good for all of us, those who are advantaged as well as those who are disadvantaged. If firms are "better off" because they are more skilled at addressing customer needs, then this inequality in outcomes is perfectly consistent with maximizing social welfare in society.

I have also wondered about how generalizable my experiences in being part of the development of resource-based theory are. No doubt, much of this experience has been—to use the language of resource-based logic—idiosyncratic and path dependent. However, I also think that there may be some patterns within my own

---

[12] See Barney and Arikan (2002) for a review.

experience that may have implications for others seeking to generate new theory. It would be way too ambitious to call these observations a "theory of how to generate theory." More modestly, I would characterize them as some hypotheses about the theory development process derived from my own experience.[13]

14.4.1 The Role of Literature in Theory Development

Obviously, a prerequisite for good theory development is to know the literature. By this, I do not mean that a scholar must know every paper that has ever been written on a subject—only Joe Mahoney can do that. But it is important to know the major theoretical issues in the literature, how they are related, and especially what is missing in the literature.

I remember meeting with a new Ph.D. student who had arrived on campus early and was interested in getting a head start on his reading. He came to my office and asked me what he should read. Following the example of Bill Ouchi, I suggested that he read Williamson's *Markets and Hierarchies* and come back in a few weeks to talk about it. The student came back with a forty-page summary of Williamson's arguments that he wanted to give to me. I thanked him, but declined. My response to him was, "I know you have read the book and can summarize what's in it. My only question for you now is—what is missing from the book?" That was a question this new Ph.D. student had not considered. A week later, we got together again and had a rousing discussion of what Williamson's book did not cover.

For me, personally, if I had not had an in-depth understanding of the new institutional economics, it would have been very difficult for me to contribute to the development of resource-based theory. This is the case, even though the connections between these sets of ideas are subtle and complex.[14] Institutional economics provided me with the tools, but more importantly, a way of thinking about problems, that was instrumental in my resource-based work. But it was what was missing in institutional economics—a rigorous theory of inequality among competing firms—that led me to think more about resource-based logic.

This said, once one understands the literature, the essential task is to learn to ignore that which you have learned. Prior literature is both a guide and a blinder. I have found in my own case that knowing the literature too well can actually prevent me from generating new insights.

---

[13] This, then, represents my limited effort at developing "grounded theory."

[14] Indeed, the connection between, say, transactions cost economics and resource-based theory continues to be discussed today. See, for example, Lieblein and Miller (2003).

I recall, for example, meeting with Mark Hansen when he was a Ph.D. student at Texas A&M.[15] Mark had written a paper that argued—albeit in an incomplete way—that trust was not just an "efficient governance device"—as described by Williamson and others—but that it could also be a source of competitive advantage. However, I had spent years putting transactions cost blinders firmly in front of my eyes. It took several years, and Mark's undying persistence, before I understood his argument and before we could write our *SMJ* paper (Barney and Hansen, 1994) on trustworthiness and sustained competitive advantage.

My own sense is that if Ph.D. students have a consistent limitation in doing good theory work it is that they rely too much on the received literature. If all one does is answer questions defined by the received literature, it will rarely be possible to go beyond that literature. Only by ignoring parts of the received literature is it possible to set aside its blinders to do theoretically creative work.

14.4.2 The Role of Empirical Research in Theory Development

The field of strategic management has become enamored with what I call the "norm of completeness." This norm suggests that a single paper can develop a new theory, derive specific testable hypotheses from this theory, develop appropriate data and methods to test these hypotheses, report results, and discuss the theoretical implications of these results—all within thirty-two manuscript pages. This is insane.

Writing papers that meet the norm of completeness generally means that authors have to compromise on some aspect of their paper. In general, for most of our journals, the part of the paper that gets short shrift is the theory section. For most empirical work, theory means: Show how your research question is related to a body of previous literature and develop some new hypotheses that typically require no more than a paragraph of justification. Indeed, it is not too much of an overstatement to say that there is almost no new theory in most empirical papers.

Look at the seminal theoretical papers and books in strategy. As Bill Ouchi used to say, "The only numbers in these seminal contributions are page numbers."[16] Moving too quickly to traditional empirical tests of theory can doom creative efforts.

I remember, for example, giving a transactions cost paper at the Academy of Management meetings sometime in the early 1980s. After presenting what

---

[15] Mark is currently on the faculty of the Marriott School of Management at Brigham Young University.

[16] The one exception to this assertion may be Kogut's (1991) paper on real options that developed new and very interesting theory but also had empirical tests.

I thought was a nice little argument, someone in the back of the room raised his hand and said, "I really like your argument and its implications. I have only one question—how do you measure transactions costs?" I now know that that was the wrong question. Even if one could measure transactions costs—and if they were easy to measure, would they really be transactions costs?—the purpose of this theory was to inform the analysis of a broad range of empirical phenomena, many of which could be studied with traditional empirical methods.

I have run into this problem with the framework presented in my 1991 *Journal of Management* paper. Ph.D. students have frequently asked me how to measure value, rarity, imitability, and substitutability. I laugh and respond that what they are really asking is how to measure these variables easily. The answer is, of course, that this framework was never designed to be tested directly, with measures of value, rarity, imitability, and substitutability as independent variables and firm performance as a dependent variable. Rather, I always thought that the purpose of this framework was to lead scholars to think about the attributes of resources that made them valuable, rare, costly to imitate, and non-substitutable, and that through that effort, empirical implications of resource-based logic could be developed and examined. If I had felt compelled to include an empirical test for every theoretical paper I have written, there would have been not much theory developed.

So, if you want to focus on developing theory, avoid moving too quickly to traditional empirical research. On the other hand, my own experience was that it was very important for me to immerse myself in real organizational phenomena. In this sense, I believe that I would not have come to the question "Why do some firms outperform other firms" as quickly as I did without my consulting experiences. Consulting gave me an opportunity to discover what I now call "theory opportunities."

A theory opportunity is any actual business phenomenon that is apparently inconsistent with received theory. In such settings, there are only two possible explanations: First, that you didn't really understand the phenomenon, and with this greater understanding, there really isn't a conflict with received theory, or second, that received theory is either wrong or has to be extended in new ways to deal with these phenomena. Significant learning is associated with either outcome.

I have done very little traditional empirical research in my career. Instead, consulting has been my empirical research. By trying to understand why a theory does not apply in a given setting, I have learned a great deal more about that theory and, sometimes, have been forced to develop new theory.[17]

---

[17] Of course, scholars can use other mechanisms to embed themselves in real organizational phenomena, including in-depth case studies. However, I am personally somewhat skeptical about the ability of scholars to discover many theory opportunities by exclusively studying large secondary data sets. Becoming "embedded in a data set" is, to me, not the same as becoming "embedded in organizational reality."

14.4.3 Management Practice and Theory Development

In this era of best-selling business books, it seems that many strategic management scholars believe that it is possible to develop good theory by solving managerial problems. That has not been my experience. My experience is that the best theory is developed by trying to solve problems derived from theory, not from practice. Scholars solve theory problems not the problems of practicing managers.

At first, this principle seems to contradict the role that consulting has played in my own theory development process. It is true that when one is hired as a consultant, there is an expectation that one is trying to help managers solve a problem. The process of solving a managerial problem—like any good empirical work—might help develop new theory. However, for me, the purpose of developing this new theory is primarily to solve some theoretical problems and only secondarily to solve practical problems.

Of course, I am not appalled if the theories we develop happen to have implications for managers and firms. Indeed, it is not uncommon that the theories developed by strategy scholars have broad managerial implications. I consider this a "happy accident." The reason I develop theory is to solve theory problems, not to solve managerial problems.

I recognize that this perspective contradicts some widely held beliefs about the relationship between business scholars and practitioners. One of those beliefs is that practitioners typically lead scholars—that the best scholarship describes the actions of practitioners and rationalizes these actions relative to theory. And, it is certainly the case that empirical research assumes that managers have been behaving in ways consistent with a particular theory in order to generate data consistent with theoretical expectations.

However, in my career, I have met very few managers that are also good theorists. In fact, they are usually quite bad at it. For example, ask any successful entrepreneur why they are successful, and they will give some version of the following answer: "I worked hard, I took risks, and I surrounded myself with good people." Go to a failed entrepreneur and ask what happened, and they will say, "I don't know. I worked hard, I took risks, and I surrounded myself with good people." Theory suggests that working hard, taking risks, and surrounding yourself with good people are not sufficient for entrepreneurial success. Indeed, given the role of luck in entrepreneurial endeavors, such attributes may not even be necessary for entrepreneurial success. However, few entrepreneurs have broad enough experiences to be able to develop this general theory.

There is a division of labor in society between those that practice and those that theorize about practice. Just as managers are—and should be—skeptical about a theoretician's ability to manage a real company, theoreticians should be skeptical about a manager's ability to generate theory.

14.4.4 Developing a Body of Theoretical Work

Finally, I think those who are really interested in developing theory must learn to ask big theoretical questions, one paper at a time. It is important to ask big questions in order to link your particular area of research to broader areas of discourse in the social sciences. Interesting as the question "Why do some firms outperform others" is in the business community, it becomes, in my mind, an even more interesting question when we recognize that we are actually about trying to understand inequality in society. To the extent that strategic management scholars can say something that is relevant to this, and other, of the fundamental issues in society, I think our impact as scholars will be substantially enhanced.

However, from a more practical point of view, it is very hard to answer "big questions" in a single paper. This is the case even if that paper is a pure theoretical contribution. Answers to "big questions" in a single paper are generally so abstract and obscure that they are very hard to understand and are almost never published. All this suggests that those interested in attacking "big questions" must learn to carve their analysis into small components, each of which is addressed in a separate paper.

For example, there was a point in my work on the resource-based view where it became clear that, in order to present the entire model, I would have to write and publish something like eight papers. I realized this shortly after the 1991 *Journal of Management* paper was published. For the next three years, I set about writing those papers and revising them so that they would be published. When I finished those papers, I was confident that the essential arguments in resource-based theory were now in the literature.

14.4.5 Colleagues and Friends in Theory Development

Beyond these observations about how to create new theory, I think the most important thing I have learned over the last twenty-five years has had to do with the role of colleagues and friends in the intellectual process. I began my career assuming that other professors were competitors. It was almost as if I had a "zero-sum" mentality about the publication process—if they published a paper, I would not be able to publish a paper. This, of course, is nonsense.

In fact, your colleagues can be your friends, and they can provide significant support in what is, in fact, a very lonely intellectual journey. Moreover, these colleagues and friends can be the source of new ideas and insights. I think that as I have shifted my perspective from one where I was competing with other professors to one where I was learning from my colleagues, the quality of my theoretical contributions has improved.

Of course, I am not suggesting that there have not been wild disagreements between me and my colleagues. This is both good and natural—part of the inevitable inequality in outcomes that has so fascinated me in life. These debates have enriched my arguments and strengthened my theoretical choices. But these are debates and disagreements among friends designed to enhance the understanding of all parties, not debates with zero-sum outcomes—I win you lose!

14.5 CONCLUSIONS

In the end, my own experience is consistent with the view that all writing, and especially research, is self-revelatory in nature. Writing this chapter has given me the unique opportunity to reflect on the central issues underlying my own work. In the process, I have had a chance to rediscover the influences that have molded me into what I have become, and what I have done.

Questions about inequality—its existence, its justice, its broader implications—are at the core of all the work I have done. That I have examined these questions in the context of business firms is a matter of chance—after all, SOM at Yale was right across the street from the Sociology Department—and personal preference. That I have taken largely an economic perspective in my approach reflects my early dissatisfaction with organizational sociology, and my fascination—preceded by initial confusion—with transactions cost and the new institutional economics. While, strictly speaking, resource-based theory is not an example of this new institutional economics, there is a common approach to thinking about economic questions that underlies both these theories.

It is my hope that I will be able to extend my interest in inequality between organizations to the study of inequality in society, more generally. This would be a return to my intellectual, and personal, roots. And, perhaps, from these roots will spring some new ideas—perhaps ideas about the relationship between firms and the broader society within which they operate.

REFERENCES

ALVAREZ, S. A., and BUSENITZ, L. W. (2001). The entrepreneurship of resource-based theory. *Journal of Management*, 27: 755–775.

AMIT, R., and SCHOEMAKER, P. (1993). Strategic assets and organizational rent. *Strategic Management Journal*, 14: 33–46.

BARNEY, J. B. (1986a). Organizational culture: Can it be a source of sustained competitive advantage? *Academy of Management Review*, 11(3): 656–665.

—— (1986b). Types of competition and the theory of strategy: Toward an integrative framework. *Academy of Management Review*, 11(4): 791–800.

—— (1986c). Strategic factor markets: Expectations, luck, and business strategy. *Management Science*, 32: 1231–1241.

—— and ARIKAN, A. (2002). The resource-based view: Origins and implications. In M. A. Hitt, R. E. Freeman, and J. S. Harrison, *The Blackwell Handbook of Strategic Management*: 124–188. Malden, Mass.: Blackwell.

—— and HANSEN, M. H. (1994). Trustworthiness as a source of competitive advantage. *Strategic Management Journal*, 15: 175–190.

—— and OUCHI, W. (1986). *Organizational Economics: Toward a New Paradigm for Studying and Understanding Organizations*. San Francisco: Jossey-Bass.

CONNER, K. (1991). An historical comparison of resource-based theory and five schools of thought within industrial organization economics: Do we have a new theory of the firm here? *Journal of Management*, 17(1): 121–154.

DEMSETZ, H. (1973). Industry structure, market rivalry, and public policy. *Journal of Law and Economics*, 16: 1–9.

GHINGOLD, M., and JOHNSON, B. (1997). Technical knowledge as value added in business markets. *Industrial Marketing Management*, 26(3): 271–280.

GRANNOVETTER, M. (1973). The strength of weak ties. *American Journal of Sociology*, 78: 1360–1380.

HANNAN, M. T., and FREEMAN, J. (1977). The population ecology of organizations. *American Journal of Sociology*, 82(5): 929–964.

HUSELID, M. (1995). The impact of human resource management practices on turnover, productivity, and corporate financial performance. *Academy of Management Journal*, 38: 635–672.

JENSEN, M. C., and MECKLING, W. H. (1976). Theory of the firm: managerial behavior, agency costs and ownership structure. *Journal of Financial Economics*, 3: 305–360.

KOGUT, B. (1991). Joint ventures and the option to expand and acquire. *Management Science*, 37(1): 19–33.

LIEBLEIN, M. J., and MILLER, D. J. (2003). An empirical examination of transaction- and firm-level influences on the vertical boundaries of the firm. *Strategic Management Journal*, 24: 839–859.

MERTON, R. K. (1949). *Social Theory and Social Structure*. New York: The Free Press.

PENROSE, E. T. (1959). *The theory of the growth of the firm*. New York: Wiley.

PETERAF, M. (1993). The cornerstones of competitive advantage: A resource-based view. *Strategic Management Journal*, 14(3): 179–192.

PORTER, M. E. (1980). Generic competitive strategies. *Competitive Strategy*. New York: Free Press, 34–46.

POWELL, T. C. (1995). Total quality management as competitive advantage: A review and empirical study. *Strategic Management Journal*, 16: 15–37.

RAWLS, J. (1971). *A Theory of Justice*. Cambridge, Mass.: Harvard.

RAY, G., BARNEY, J. B., and MUHANNA, W. A. (2004). Capabilities, business processes, and competitive advantage: Choosing the dependent variable in empirical tests of the resource-based view. *Strategic Management Journal*, 25(1): 23–38.

RUMELT, R. (1984). Toward a strategic theory of the firm. In R. Lamb (ed.), *Competitive Strategic Management*: 556–570. Englewood Cliffs, NJ: Prentice-Hall.

STUART, T. E., and PODOLNY, J. M. (1996). Local search and the evolution of technological capabilities. *Strategic Management Journal*, 17: 21–38.

TEECE, D. J, PISANO, G., and SHUEN, A. (1997). Dynamic capabilities and strategic management. *Strategic Management Journal*, 18(7): 509–533.

WERNERFELT, B. (1984). A resource-based view of the firm. *Strategic Management Journal*, 5: 171–180.

WILLIAMSON, O. (1975). *Markets and Hierarchies*. NY: Free Press.

CHAPTER 15

....

ORGANIZATIONAL EFFECTIVENESS

ITS DEMISE AND RE-EMERGENCE THROUGH POSITIVE ORGANIZATIONAL SCHOLARSHIP

....

KIM CAMERON

A FUNDAMENTAL shift has occurred over the last two decades in the organizational studies literature. Whereas the concept of organizational effectiveness was once the dominant dependent variable in organizational studies and lay at the center of discussions about organizational success, it gradually lost favor and has largely been replaced by an emphasis on single indicators of outcomes such as share price, productivity, financial ratios, error rates, or customer loyalty (Cameron and Whetten, 1996). One well-known effectiveness scholar concluded, in fact, that organizational effectiveness as a topic of study is dead (Whetten, 2004). It was killed by the "validity police" (Hirsch and Levin, 1999), who tend to discard nonuseful and unmeasurable concepts. It was abandoned as uninteresting and unfruitful in understanding the performance of organizations.

Because effectiveness is a "construct" (i.e., its meaning is mentally constructed, and no inherent indicators exist for effectiveness), other more straightforward and quantifiable concepts have largely replaced it in the organizational studies literature. It is ironic that a casual review of *Amazon.com* reveals more than 650 books with "organizational effectiveness" in the title, yet only about twenty have appeared in the last ten years. Moreover, a search of *Proquest* using the term "organizational effectiveness" generated thirty-six academic journal articles appearing in the last five years, yet none appeared in the most visible organizational studies journals (e.g., *AMJ, AMR, ASQ, Organizational Science, ROB*). In virtually none of these recent references, moreover, is organizational effectiveness carefully and precisely defined as a construct or treated as a central variable in the investigation. Instead, effectiveness is used as a general indicator of success, and it is most frequently employed as a unidimensional outcome variable.

The purpose of this chapter is to identify the scholarly development of the concept of organizational effectiveness—its emergence and its waning in organizational studies literature—and to introduce a recently emerging approach that promises to revitalize interest in the topic. The first section reviews the major theoretical approaches to organizations from which emerged five key models of organizational effectiveness. These models guided the bulk of organizational effectiveness literature for several decades and were integrated, finally, by one overarching framework. The next section highlights methodological issues associated with empirical research on effectiveness to illustrate an additional reason why effectiveness research almost disappeared. The final section of the chapter introduces a newly emerging approach to effectiveness that supplements, and promises to renew interest in, the general topic of organizational effectiveness. This new approach focuses on positive organizational scholarship—i.e., positive deviance and extraordinary performance—that stretch beyond the traditional levels of performance labeled as effective in the past. A brief overview of this new approach to effectiveness is presented, and suggestions for future research directions are offered by way of conclusion.

15.1 FOUNDATIONS OF ORGANIZATIONAL EFFECTIVENESS

The earliest models of organizational effectiveness emphasized "ideal types," that is, forms of organization that maximized certain attributes. Weber's (1947) characterization of bureaucracies is the most obvious and well-known example. This "rational–legal" form of organization was based on rules, equal treatment of all employees, separation of position from person, staffing and promotion based on skills and expertise, specific work standards, and documented work performance. These principles were translated into dimensions of bureaucracy, including formalization of procedures, specialization of work, standardized practices, and centralization of decision making (Perrow, 1986).

Early applications of the bureaucratic model to the topic of effectiveness proposed that efficiency was the appropriate measure of performance—i.e., avoidance of uncoordinated, wasteful, ambiguous activities. That is, the more nearly an organization approached the ideal bureaucratic characteristics, the more effective (i.e., efficient) it was. The more specialized, formalized, standardized, and centralized, the better.

Subsequent scholars challenged these assumptions, however, suggesting that the most effective organizations are actually non-bureaucratic. Barnard (1938), for example, argued that organizations are cooperative systems at their core. An effective organization, therefore, channels and directs cooperative processes to accomplish productive outcomes, primarily through institutionalized goals and decision making processes. Barnard's work led to three additional ideal type approaches to organization—Selznick's (1948) institutional school, Simon's (1956) decision making school, and Roethlisberger and Dickson's (1947) human relations school. Each of these schools of thought represents an ideal to which organizations should aspire—e.g., shared goals and values, systematic decision processes, or collaborative practices. Whereas devotees disagreed over what the ideal standard must be for judging effectiveness, all agreed that effectiveness should be measured against an ideal standard represented by the criteria.

Over the years, ideal types proliferated, including goal accomplishment (Price, 1982), congruence (Nadler and Tushman, 1980), social equity (Keeley, 1978), and interpretation systems (Weick and Daft, 1983). However, mounting frustration over the conflicting claims of ideal type advocates gave rise to a "contingency model" of organizational effectiveness. This perspective argued that effectiveness is not a function of the extent to which an organization reflects qualities of an ideal profile but, instead, depends on the match between an organization's attributes and its environmental conditions.

Burns and Stalker's (1961) differentiation between organic and mechanistic organizational types represents an early bridge from ideal type to contingency models. These authors argued that mechanistic organizations (e.g., those reflecting Weber's bureaucratic dimensions) are best suited to highly stable and relatively simple environments. In contrast, organic organizations (e.g., those reflecting Barnard's cooperative dimensions) are better suited to rapidly changing, highly complex situations. This idea spawned several significant research programs, all based on a contingency view of effectiveness—Lawrence and Lorsch's (1967) study of multiple industries in which differentiation and integration were predictive of effectiveness, the Aston studies in England (Pugh, Hickson, and Hinings, 1969) in which structural arrangements were predictive of effectiveness, and Van de Ven and

Ferry's (1980) development of the *Organizational Assessment Survey* in which different processes and design features were predictive of effectiveness. All these studies concluded that evaluations of effectiveness differed depending on environmental circumstances. Complex and changing environments give rise to different appropriate effectiveness criteria than do stable and undemanding environments.

A third shift occurred in the conception of organizations as economists and organizational theorists became interested in accounting for transactions across organizational boundaries and their interactions with multiple constituencies. This emphasis highlighted the relevance of multiple stakeholders in accounting for an organization's performance (e.g., Williamson, 1983; Connolly, Conlon, and Deutsch, 1980; Zammuto, 1984). Effective organizations were viewed as those which had accurate information about the demands and expectations of strategically critical stakeholders and, as a result, adapted internal organizational activities, goals, and strategies to match those demands and expectations. This viewpoint held that organizations are elastic entities operating in a dynamic force field which pulls the organization's shape and practices in different directions—i.e., molding the organization to the demands of powerful interest groups including stockholders, unions, regulators, competitors, customers, and so forth. Effectiveness, therefore, is a function of qualities such as learning, adaptability, strategic intent, and responsiveness.

15.2 MODELS OF ORGANIZATIONAL EFFECTIVENESS

From these various viewpoints about the nature of organizations, their relevant features and dimensions, and their key effectiveness criteria, multiple models of organizational effectiveness naturally arose. Debates about which approach was best, which model was most predictive, and which criteria were most appropriate to measure were typical of the organizational studies literature in the 1970s and 1980s.

Five models, in particular, became representative of the best known and most widely used in scientific investigations. Price (1982) and Bluedorn (1980), for example, argued that the *goal model* was the most appropriate model of choice—i.e., organizations are effective to the extent to which they accomplish their stated goals. Seashore and Yuchtman (1967) and Pfeffer and Salancik (1978) argued for a *resource dependence model*—i.e., organizations are effective to the extent to which they acquire needed resources. Nadler and Tushman (1980) and Lewin and Minton

(1986) proposed an *internal congruence model*, i.e., organizations are effective to the extent to which their internal functioning is consistent, efficiently organized, and without strain. Connolly, Conlon, and Deutsch (1980) and Tsui (1990) maintained that a *strategic constituencies model* was best, i.e., organizations are effective to the extent to which they satisfy their dominant stakeholders or strategic constituencies. Likert (1961) and Argyris (1960) championed the *human relations model*, arguing that organizations are effective to the extent to which they engage members and provide a collaborative climate. Several other less well-known models have appeared periodically as well (e.g., legitimacy models, fault-driven models), but Table 15.1 summarizes the five most recognized models of organizational effectiveness available during this period of time. The conditions under which each is most useful are also pointed out.

One framework that helped integrate these different models, and has taken into account their different assumptions, is the Competing Values Framework (Quinn and Rohrbaugh, 1981; Cameron, 1986; Cameron and Quinn, 1999). This framework was developed empirically after submitting a comprehensive list of the criteria— which had been used in assessments of organizational effectiveness up to 1980—to a multidimensional scaling procedure. Those effectiveness criteria clustered together into four groupings, divided by a vertical dimension and a horizontal dimension (see Figure 15.1). These clusters of criteria indicated that some organizations are effective if they demonstrate flexibility, change, and adaptability. Other organizations are effective if they demonstrate stability, order, and control. This vertical dimension is anchored on one end by effectiveness criteria emphasizing predictability, steadiness, and mechanistic processes and on the other end by criteria emphasizing dynamism, adjustment, and organic processes. In addition,

Table 15.1 The most well-known models of organizational effectiveness

Model	Definition	Appropriateness
	Organization effective if:	Model preferred when:
Goal	It accomplishes stated goals.	Goals are clear, overt, consensual, time bound, and measurable.
System resource	It acquires needed resources.	Resources and outputs are clearly connected.
Internal processes	It has smooth functioning and an absence of strain.	Processes and outcomes are clearly connected.
Strategic constituencies	All constituencies are at least minimally satisfied.	Constituencies have power over or in the organization.
Human relations	Members are satisfied and collaboration occurs.	Coordinated effort and harmony are directly attached to results.

Source: Adapted from Cameron, 1984.

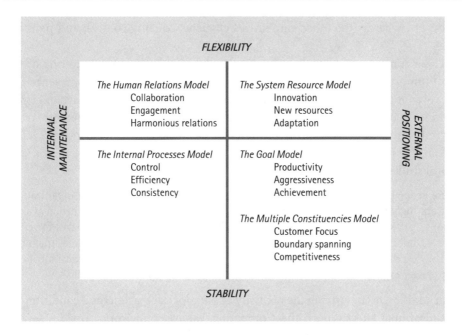

Fig. 15.1   The competing values framework of organizational effectiveness: An integration of the five well-known models (with key areas of emphasis)

some organizations are effective if they maintain efficient internal processes and congruence, whereas others are effective if they maintain competitive external positioning and aggressiveness relative to stakeholders. This horizontal dimension is anchored on one end by criteria emphasizing internal maintenance and on the other end by criteria emphasizing external positioning. The competing or conflicting emphases represented by each end of the two dimensions constitute the rudiments of the Competing Values Framework.

The resulting four quadrants into which the criteria clustered represent opposite or competing models of effectiveness. Specifically, the key effectiveness criteria in diagonal quadrants are opposite to one another. The upper left quadrant, for example, is consistent with the *human relations model*—i.e., emphasizing cohesion, harmony, collaboration, and coordination criteria. The lower right quadrant, on the other hand, is consistent with the *goal achievement* and *external constituencies models*—i.e., emphasizing productivity, outcome achievement, competition, and profitability criteria. One quadrant emphasizes soft, human-centered criteria, whereas the other quadrant emphasizes hard, competitive criteria. Similarly, the upper right quadrant is consistent with the acquisition of new resources (*system resource*) model of effectiveness—i.e., emphasizing growth, innovation, new products, and change criteria—whereas the lower left quadrant emphasizes the *internal processes model*—i.e., error reduction, standardized processes, measurement, and cost control criteria. One quadrant focuses on change, innovation, and new resources, whereas the other emphasizes efficiency, quality control, and permanence.

These competing or opposite criteria in each quadrant give rise to one of the most important features of the Competing Values Framework—the presence and necessity of paradox. Cameron (1986), Weick (1976), Peters and Waterman (1982), and Eisenhart and Wescott (1988) all argued that effectiveness is inherently paradoxical. Effective organizations simultaneously operate in competing quadrants and manifest paradoxical characteristics. For example, my review of several empirical studies led to the conclusion that,

These general findings illustrate the presence of simultaneous opposites in organizations that are highly effective, or that improve in effectiveness, particularly in turbulent conditions... It is not just the presence of mutually exclusive opposites that makes for effectiveness, but it is the creative leaps, the flexibility, and the unity made possible by them that leads to excellence... the presence of creative tension arising from paradoxical attributes helps foster organizational effectiveness. (Cameron, 1986: 549)

In addition to identifying the necessity of paradoxical tensions as a condition for organizational effectiveness, the Competing Values Framework provides several other theoretical predictions about effectiveness. Evidence exists, for example, that effectiveness is higher in organizations when the quadrants in which managerial competencies are strongest match the quadrants in which the organization's culture is dominant. The effectiveness and success of mergers and acquisitions is strongly related to the congruence of the cultural profiles of merging organizations using the competing values quadrants. The financial performance of companies is significantly higher when financial strategies are pursued in each of the four quadrants as opposed to one or two quadrants (which is the most common situation). Effectiveness over the long run is significantly predicted based on the quadrants that become dominant in different stages of an organization's life cycle. Organizational effectiveness is significantly higher when activities related to innovation and creativity are associated with all four quadrants as part of an improvement strategy (for explanations, see Cameron and Quinn, 1999; Cameron, et al., 2005).

15.3 CONCLUSIONS ABOUT EFFECTIVENESS

None of the models of effectiveness has emerged as the universalistic model of choice, of course, although the Competing Values Framework is probably considered to be the most comprehensive. Some writers have became so frustrated by the confusion surrounding effectiveness models, in fact, that they recommended a "moratorium on all studies of organizational effectiveness, books on organizational effectiveness, and chapters on organizational effectiveness" (Goodman, Atkin, and Schoorman, 1983: 4; Hannan and Freeman, 1977).

In response to this confusion and resistance, the literature in organizational studies and the discussions at annual Academy of Management meetings provided a series of suggestions for resolving issues and clarifying approaches (Cameron and Whetten, 1983). The primary objective was to clarify the construct and stimulate additional research. Five conclusions emerged from that literature (see Cameron, 1986).

1. *Despite the ambiguity and confusion surrounding it, the construct of organizational effectiveness is central to the organizational sciences and cannot be ignored in theory and research.* All theories of organizations rely on some conception of the differences between effective performance and ineffective performance. At their core, organizational theories try to explain effective performance. Hence, effectiveness has important *theoretical* relevance. *Empirically,* effectiveness is usually the ultimate dependent variable for organizational research. Relationships between structure and environment, design and innovation, or adaptation and uncertainty, for example, are important because their results lead ultimately to organizational effectiveness. *Pragmatically,* consumers, clients, resource providers, managers, regulators, members, and other stakeholders in organizations are continually faced with the need to make judgments about effectiveness. Obtaining the best value, the best return, or the best outcome depends a great deal on judgments about which organization can perform the most effectively.

2. *Because no conceptualization of an organization is comprehensive, no conceptualization of an effective organization is comprehensive. As the metaphor describing an organization changes, so does the definition or appropriate model of organizational effectiveness.* Many of the scientific breakthroughs of the last century emerged from insight resulting from the use of a new metaphor. Organizational theory advanced, for example, by borrowing the open systems metaphor from biology (e.g., McKelvey, 1982), the social contract metaphor from political science (e.g., Keeley, 1978), the transactions cost metaphor from economics (e.g., Williamson, 1983), the force field metaphor from engineering (e.g., Lewin, 1951, 1997), or the networks metaphor from computer science (e.g., Baker, 2000). Each time a new metaphor is used, certain aspects of organizational phenomena are uncovered that were not evident with other metaphors. In fact, the usefulness of metaphors lies in their possession of some degree of falsehood so that new images and associations emerge. The same is true with conceptions of organizations. As the view changes from an organization being a social contract, for example, to its being an open system, the conceptualization of an *effective* organization changes, and with it the appropriate criteria that indicate successful performance.

Multiple models of organizational effectiveness are products of multiple conceptions of organizations. Since no one conception of organization can be proven to
be better than any other, no model of effectiveness has an advantage over any
other. There is no inherent advantage, for example, in conceiving of an organization as a network of constituencies as opposed to an information processing
entity.

3. *Consensus regarding the best, or sufficient, set of indicators of effectiveness is
impossible to obtain. Criteria are based on the values and preferences of individuals,
and no specifiable construct boundaries exist.* Constructs, by definition, have no
objective referent. They are mental abstractions used by individuals to interpret
reality. Therefore, judgments of effectiveness are based on the values and preferences that individuals hold for an organization. These values and preferences
are often contradictory among different constituencies, and preferences are
difficult for individuals themselves to identify accurately. Several researchers
have concluded that what people say they prefer and what their behavior suggests
they prefer is not always the same (Slovic and Lichtenstein, 1971; Nisbet and
Wilson, 1977; Argyris and Schon, 1978). Moreover, preferences change over
time and vary with changing circumstances, and most importantly, contradictory preferences are held by individuals and pursued by organizations simultaneously. For example, preferences for growth and stability, efficiency and
flexibility, high capital investment and high return to stockholders, autonomy
and control, or a caring climate and aggressive competition, are often simultaneously pursued in organizations, so they must be managed through sequencing
(Cyert and March, 1963), satisficing (Simon, 1948), or incrementalism (Lindblom, 1959).

Of particular concern, however, is that evaluators of effectiveness often select
models and criteria arbitrarily, relying primarily on convenience. A recent review
of the effectiveness literature found that more than 80 percent of the criteria used
in evaluations of effectiveness do not overlap with those in other studies. The
most frequently used criterion is a single, overall rating of effectiveness given by
respondents within the organization. Seldom do evaluators make explicit their
assumptions about why they selected the criteria being used, and few authors
describe any rational consideration of the most appropriate alternative indicators of effectiveness. Because the conceptual boundaries of effectiveness are
unknown, it is often not clear what criteria are *indicators* of effectiveness, what
criteria are *predictors* of effectiveness, and what criteria are *outcomes* of effectiveness. Customer satisfaction, for example, can be any of the three. In short, much
of the literature in which the term effectiveness is used continues to report
careless assessment, not just non-consensual assessment.

4. *Different models of effectiveness are useful for research in different circumstances.
Their usefulness depends on the purposes and constraints placed on the organizational effectiveness investigation.* The circumstances in which each of the popular

models of effectiveness are most likely to be applied (e.g., the goal model is used when goals are specific, measurable, time-bound, overt) are not universal. No model covers all contingencies or applies to all settings. Each has its own focus and strengths. None of the models can be directly substituted for the others in assessments, although combinations of criteria have been found in some studies. Debates about which model of effectiveness is best or right are largely beside the point, therefore, because models are more likely to complement one another than supplant one another. Even the Competing Values Framework, which tries to subsume and organize the other popular models, cannot be claimed to be a universally applicable model for assessing effectiveness.

5. *Organizational effectiveness is mainly a problem-driven construct rather than a theory-driven construct.* As mentioned, because no single model or criterion exists for organizational effectiveness, there cannot be a single theory about effectiveness. This does not imply that multiple theories cannot be developed for certain models of effectiveness. It just argues that predictive variables and relationships relevant to one model may not be applicable to other models. Despite this, the basic problems surrounding organizational effectiveness are not theoretical problems; they are criteria problems. Individuals are constantly faced with the need to make judgments about the effectiveness of organizations, and pragmatic choices are continually made about effectiveness—which school will close, which firm will be awarded a contract, in which company will an investment be made, and so on. The primary task facing any investigator of effectiveness, therefore, lies in determining the appropriate indicators and standards. It is the assessment issue, not the theoretical issue, which dominates concerns of evaluators and managers.

More specifically, indicators of effectiveness selected by researchers are often too narrowly or too broadly defined, or they do not relate to organizational performance at all. Individual or group effectiveness, for instance, is not necessarily the same as organizational effectiveness. Yet, indicators such as personal need satisfaction (e.g., Cummings, 1983), small group cohesion (e.g., Guzzo, 1982), economic welfare (e.g., Nord, 1983), or social justice (e.g., Keeley, 1978), appear in the literature as being indicative of effectiveness of single organizations. Moreover, variables such as organizational architecture, decision processes, culture, job design, quality, customer satisfaction, and environmental responsiveness are equated with effectiveness, but they are as likely to be antecedents or consequences of effectiveness as they are indicators. Even common criteria such as profitability, productivity, or shareholder value are not necessarily synonymous with effectiveness inasmuch as many well-known examples exist of firms with high revenues or increasing stock prices which were found not to be effective (e.g., Enron, Tyco). The key issue surrounding effectiveness, therefore, is usually a practical one: how to identify the appropriate indicators, standards, and measures.

The practical problems associated with effectiveness, in other words, dominate the theoretical concerns, so investigators are more likely to be immersed in assessment and criteria selection issues than in theoretical concerns.

15.4 METHODOLOGICAL CHALLENGES RELATED TO EFFECTIVENESS

Because rigorous effectiveness evaluations are much more complicated than merely using a single, universalistic assessment (e.g., a perceptual judgment of effectiveness) or a single numerical indicator (e.g., profitability) as a proxy for effectiveness, guidelines were created to assist effectiveness researchers in systematically assessing this construct. These guidelines are in the form of seven questions meant to assist researchers in selecting appropriate effectiveness criteria and to help build a set of comparable effectiveness studies (Cameron and Whetten, 1983, 1996). That is, by carefully and systematically selecting effectiveness criteria, comparisons among definitions and approaches to effectiveness are possible, cumulative findings can emerge, and theoretical propositions can begin to be developed.

These seven guidelines should be taken into account in any assessment of organizational effectiveness. That is, every investigator of effectiveness consciously or unconsciously makes a selection regarding these seven questions, and deliberately articulating which choices are made will greatly enhance the probability of comparative research.

1. *What time frame is being employed?* Short-term effects may differ from long-term effects, and different stages in an organization's life cycle may produce different levels of performance. Using short-term criteria, or measuring effectiveness in early stages of development, for example, may lead to very different conclusions than applying long-term criteria or assessing effectiveness over a mature life cycle stage.
2. *What level of analysis is being used?* Effectiveness at different levels of analysis in an organization (e.g., subunit activities, individual behavior, organizational performance) may be incompatible and inconsistent. A subunit may thrive, for example, whereas the broader organization may languish relative to its industry performance.
3. *From whose perspective is effectiveness being judged?* The criteria used by different constituencies to define effectiveness often differ markedly (e.g., customer preferences versus board of directors' mandates) and generally follow

from unique constituency interests. Criteria of effectiveness preferred by different constituencies may be conflicting.

4. *On what domain of activity is the effectiveness judgment being focused?* No assessment can account for everything, and achieving high levels of effectiveness in one domain of activity may militate against effectiveness in another domain. Financial criteria, for example, may be in conflict with employee welfare criteria.

5. *What is the purpose for judging effectiveness?* Changing purposes of an assessment may change the consequences and the criteria that are most relevant. For example, different indicators may be required if the purpose of the assessment is for organizational improvement initiatives as compared to cost cutting or downsizing objectives.

6. *What type of data are being used for judgments of effectiveness?* Official documents, perceptions of organization members, participant observations, or cultural or symbolic artifacts all may produce different conclusions about the effectiveness of an organization. Survey perceptions and objective financial measures, for example, are notoriously weakly correlated.

7. *What is the referent against which effectiveness is judged?* No universal standard exists against which to evaluate performance, and different standards will produce different conclusions about effectiveness. Comparisons to industry averages, for example, may lead to different conclusions than comparisons to past improvement trends, best competitors, or stated goals.

The objective of articulating the five major conclusions about effectiveness and developing the seven methodological guidelines for assessing effectiveness was to address directly the concerns of those who advocate discarding the construct of effectiveness in organizational research. Providing a summary of what is known about effectiveness, it was assumed, would help organizational effectiveness work flourish. The key arguments for pursuing effectiveness research were: First, organizational effectiveness lies at the center of all models and theories of organization. Second, effectiveness is the ultimate dependent variable in organizational studies, and evidence of effective performance is required in most research on organizations. Third, individuals are constantly faced with the need to make judgments about the effectiveness of organizations, and pragmatic choices are continually made about effectiveness. Fourth, consciously addressing the seven assessment guidelines creates parameters that make effectiveness evaluations comparative (Cameron and Whetten, 1996).

Despite this objective, however, scholarly research largely ceased on the topic of organizational effectiveness beginning in the 1990s. From a total of more than twenty articles appearing on the topic in the Academy of Management journals (*Journal, Review, Executive*) and *Administrative Science Quarterly* between 1975 and 1985, only a single article (Tsui, 1990) and no scholarly books appeared after that time. Only one of the thirty-six academic journal articles from the year 2000 to the present time appeared in a mainline organizational studies journal (*Journal of Management Studies*). Moreover, of the 650 plus books with organizational effectiveness in the title on *Amazon.com*, only twenty were published in the last decade, and none of these are scholarly works. Representative titles include, for example: *Ergonomic Design for Organizational Effectiveness, Improving Organizational Effectiveness through Broadbanding, Organizational Effectiveness: The Role of Psychology, Improving Organizational Effectiveness through Transformational Leadership.* Textbooks or consulting treatises dominate the list, and no book claims to make a substantive contribution to the definition or dimensions of organizational effectiveness.

Reasons for the abandonment of effectiveness are difficult to surmise, of course, but at least one major trend in the organizational studies literature may help explain why conceptual and methodological examinations of organizational effectiveness ceased. It is the dramatically intensified emphasis on pragmatics in organizational studies over the past decade. Motivated by escalating cries for relevance in graduate business schools, attacks on scholarly research as lagging practice, aberrant and unethical behavior of major corporations and iconic CEOs, and a continued erosion of confidence in organizations ranging from government to schools, examinations of organizational effectiveness took a decided pivot. Whereas earlier scholarly work focused on appropriate definitions, criteria, and frameworks, scholars more recently have focused on identifying best practices, managerial implications, and practical guidelines (e.g., Collins, 2001; Pfeffer and Sutton, 2000; Weick and Sutcliffe, 2001). Emphasis on definitional and criteria debates has given way to an emphasis on finding appropriate guidelines for managers and leaders—a shift from ends to means.

15.5 A NEW APPROACH TO EFFECTIVENESS: POSITIVE ORGANIZATIONAL SCHOLARSHIP

It must be emphasized that it is only the *concept* of organizational effectiveness that faded, not the need to assess organizational performance, make judgments about excellence, or enhance organizational performance. Effectiveness as a *phenomenon*, in other words, was not abandoned; rather, researchers replaced it with other concepts. One of the most recent and intriguing substitutes for effectiveness research has come from a new movement in the organizational sciences referred to as *Positive Organizational Scholarship*. This new movement contains the promise to breathe life into the topic of effectiveness and lead to new insights about organizational performance.

Positive Organizational Scholarship (POS) is concerned primarily with the study of especially positive outcomes, processes, and attributes of organizations. POS does not represent a single theory, but it focuses on dynamics that are typically described by words such as excellence, thriving, flourishing, abundance, resilience, or virtuousness. POS represents a perspective that includes instrumental concerns but puts an increased emphasis on ideas of "goodness" and positive human potential. It encompasses attention to the enablers (e.g., processes, capabilities, structures, methods), the motivations (e.g., unselfishness, altruism, contribution without regard to self), and the outcomes or effects (e.g., vitality, meaningfulness, exhilaration, high quality relationships) associated with positive performance. POS is distinguished from traditional organizational effectiveness studies in that it seeks to understand what represents and approaches the best of the human condition. In seeking to understand such phenomena, POS has a number of biases. These biases can be understood in terms of each of the three concepts in the label—Positive Organizational Scholarship.

15.5.1 Positive

POS seeks to understand positive states—such as resilience or meaningfulness—as well as the dynamics and outcomes associated with those states—such as positive energy and positive connections. This does not mean that traditional organizational research is accused of focusing on negative or undesirable states, only that especially positive states, dynamics, and outcomes usually receive less attention in traditional organizational studies. POS encompasses the examination of typical patterns of behavior and exchange, but it also tends to emphasize the realization of potential, patterns of excellence, and especially positive deviance from anticipated patterns. POS tends to emphasize the examination of factors that enable positive consequences for individuals, groups, and organizations. More often than not, POS focuses on that which is unexpectedly positive. The interest is in exceptional, virtuous, life-giving, and flourishing phenomena. "*Positive*," in other words, has three general referents: (1) an affirmative bias (away from negative phenomena); (2) an emphasis on goodness, or the best of the human condition; and (3) positive deviance, or extraordinarily successful outcomes. It is this third referent, in particular, that is most relevant to effectiveness research.

15.5.2 Organizational

POS focuses on positive processes and states that occur in association with organizational contexts. It examines positive phenomena within organizations as well as positive organizational contexts themselves. POS draws from the full spectrum of organizational theories to understand, explain, and predict the occurrence, causes, and consequences of positivity. POS expands the boundaries of these theories to make visible positive states, positive processes, and positive relationships that are typically ignored within organizational studies. For example, POS spotlights how virtuousness in organizations is associated with financial performance in the context of downsizing, in contrast to a more typical focus on how organizations try to mitigate the harmful effects of downsizing (Cameron, 2003); or, how organizational practices enable organization members to craft meaningful work through fostering "callings," in contrast to a more typical focus on employee productivity or morale (Wrzesniewski, 2003); or, how the cascading dynamics of empowerment create broader inclusion of stakeholders in public organizations, in contrast to a focus on the political dynamics of stakeholder demands (Feldman and Khademian, 2003); or, how building on strengths produces more positive outcomes in a diverse array of settings such as classroom learning, employee commitment, leadership development, and firm profitability, in contrast to a more typical focus on managing or overcoming weaknesses (Clifton and Harter, 2003). A POS lens is intended to expose new or different mechanisms through which positive organizational dynamics and positive organizational processes produce extraordinarily positive or unexpected outcomes—not merely effective outcomes.

15.5.3 Scholarship

There is no lack of self-help accounts that recommend relatively simple and uncomplicated prescriptions for achieving success, fulfillment, or effectiveness. What is lacking in most of these contributions, however, is empirical credibility and theoretical explanations for how and why the prescriptions work. Further, these more prescriptive accounts do not speak to the contingencies regarding when the directives will produce the desired results and when they won't. Having a foundation in the scientific method is the basis upon which most concepts, relationships, and prescriptions develop staying power. POS does not stand in opposition to the array of self-help publications—many of which recount positive dynamics and outcomes—but it extends beyond them in its focus on developing rigorous, systematic, and theory-based foundations for positive phenomena. POS requires careful definitions of terms, a rationale for prescriptions and recommendations, consistency with scientific procedures in drawing conclusions, and grounding in previous related work. An interest in POS implies a commitment to scholarship.

POS is not value-neutral, of course. It advocates the position that the desire to improve the human condition is universal and that the capacity to do so is latent in almost all systems. The means by which this latent capacity is unleashed and organized, the extent to which human possibilities are enabled, and the extent to which systems produce extraordinarily positive outcomes are of special interest. POS does not exclude phenomena that are typically labeled positive in organizational studies—such as organizational improvement, goal achievement, or making a profit—but it has a bias toward life-giving, generative, and ennobling human conditions. In this way, POS has the potential to breathe life into a waning interest in organizational effectiveness. What had become a mundane and unexciting set of research problems has the potential, through POS, to capture interest and energy again as it relates to organizational performance.

POS is not a new invention, and it recognizes that positive phenomena have been studied in organizational studies for decades. Yet, studies of affirmative, uplifting, and elevating processes and outcomes have not been the norm. They have been overwhelmed in the scholarly literature by non-positive topics. For example, Walsh, Weber, and Margolis (2003) reported that positive terms (e.g., caring, compassion, virtue) have seldom appeared in the business press over the last seventeen years, whereas negatively biased words (e.g., advantage, beat, win) have increased fourfold in the same period. Mayne (1999) found that studies of the relationship between negative phenomena and health outnumbered by 11 to 1 studies of the relationship between positive phenomena and health. Czapinski's (1985) coding of psychology articles found a 2:1 ratio of negative issues to positive or neutral issues. One objective of POS is to redress this bias so that positive phenomena receive their fair share of rigorous and systematic investigation. Up to now, the conscious examination of positive phenomena is vastly under-represented in organizational science.

15.6 A POS Approach to Effectiveness

One way to illustrate the approach taken by POS to effectiveness in organizations is to locate it on a continuum, represented in Figure 15.2. This continuum depicts a state of normal or effect performance in the middle, with a condition of negatively deviant performance on the left and a state of positively deviant performance on the right. Negative and positive deviance refer to aberrations from effective functioning or normality, harmful on one end and virtuous on the other end.

To illustrate, at the *individual* level of analysis, the figure considers physiological and psychological conditions—illness on the left and healthy functioning in the middle (i.e., the absence of illness). On the right side is positive deviance, which

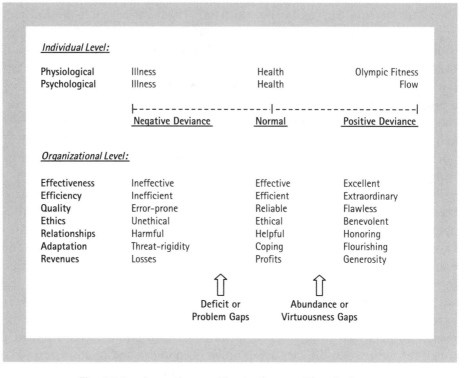

Fig. 15.2   A continuum illustrating positive deviance

may be illustrated by high levels of physical fitness or psychological flow (Csikszentmihalyi, 1990; Fredrickson, 2001; Einsenberg, 1990). At the *organizational* level, the figure portrays conditions ranging from ineffective, inefficient, and error-prone performance on the left side, to effective, efficient, and reliable performance in the middle. On the right side is extraordinarily positive—or virtuous—organizational performance. The extreme right and left points on the continuum are qualitatively distinct from the center point. They do not merely represent a greater or lesser quantity of the middle attributes.

Seligman (2002) reported that more than 99 percent of psychological research in the last fifty years has focused on the left and middle points on the continuum. Similarly, an overwhelming majority of published studies in medical research have focused on the left and middle points (e.g., understanding and treating illness). Most organizational and management research has likewise been conducted on phenomena represented by negative deviance and by phenomena at the middle point. More attention has been paid to solving problems, surmounting obstacles, battling competitors, improving quality, making a profit, motivating employees, or closing deficit gaps than identifying the flourishing and life-giving aspects of organizations and closing abundance gaps (Cameron, Dutton, and Quinn, 2003; Walsh, Weber, and Margolis, 2003). Too little is known, therefore, about the right side of the continuum and the phenomena that represent it. Well-developed concepts do not yet exist to explain the phenomena on the right side of the continuum. A POS approach to effectiveness, therefore, centers on these ill-defined and yet-to-be-investigated phenomena—namely, positive deviance and extraordinary performance.

The traditional construct of effectiveness, consequently, is replaced in POS by constructs such as flourishing, virtuousness, and abundance. These substitute concepts, of course, have frequently been associated with non-scholarly prescriptions or uncritical ecumenicalism (Peterson and Seligman, 2003). Virtuousness, for example, has often been rejected as saccharine, anti-intellectual, or morally dogmatic (Sandage and Hill, 2001). Flourishing and optimism have been interpreted as wishful thinking or naivety (Scheier, Carver, and Bridges, 1994). Prosocial behavior and an abundance approach have been dismissed as disguised and sophisticated motives for personal gain (Cialdini, et al., 1987). On the other hand, some initial POS research has begun to tackle the definition and measurement issues associated with these concepts, and empirical evidence has begun to emerge linking certain organizational dynamics to extraordinarily positive levels of performance.

For example, Spreitzer, et al. (2005) conducted work on the concept of *thriving* in organizations—the achievement of vitality, positive momentum, and learning. This condition stretches beyond mere effectiveness by accounting for especially positive dynamics related to organizational processes and outcomes. Under conditions of thriving, employees reported feeling more vitality, experience more positive emotions, exhibit better physiological and psychological health, and report a sense of flow in their jobs compared to conditions when things are merely functioning "smoothly" or "effectively." Thriving as a construct tends to represent the right end of the continuum in Figure 15.2. Similarly, Cameron and Lavine (2005) analyzed the performance of an organization that was assigned to clean up a nuclear arsenal in Colorado. Such a task had never been accomplished in this country. The U.S. Department of Energy estimated that the project would take more than seventy years and cost at least $36 billion to complete, since more than 100 tons of plutonium and enriched uranium residues had polluted the several-thousand acre site. The company will complete the job, however, fifty-four years early and $30 billion below budget at the end of 2005. An analysis of the enablers and explanatory factors accounting for this extraordinarily positive performance has uncovered new variables and organizational processes not previously associated with organizational effectiveness research.

In addition to positively deviant outcomes, other POS research has focused on previously unexamined positive factors that help explain effectiveness. Losada and Heaphy (2004), for example, reported research in which sixty firms were categorized as high, medium, and low performing based on indicators such as productivity, profitability, and associates' ratings of the effectiveness of the top management team. A senior executive team in each organization was observed for a day as they interacted in a goal setting, budgeting, and strategic planning session. Their communication events (e.g., statements, responses, gestures) were coded by observers. High-performing firms were distinguished significantly from medium- and low-performing firms on the basis of their display of positive communication (i.e., supportive, appreciative, encouraging statements). High-performing firms had a ratio of five positive communication events to every negative event during the observed meetings. Low-performing firms displayed an average of three negative communication events (i.e., disagreeing, criticizing, discouraging statements) for every positive event. An emphasis on positive communication was found overwhelmingly to be the most powerful predictor of especially high firm performance.

Baker, Cross, and Parker (2003) studied social network connections among a variety of firms including financial service, consulting, software, and engineering companies. They measured the usual network connections based on factors such as information exchange and influence. However, using a POS perspective they also added a measure of *positive energy* based on the extent to which people felt positively energized or de-energized when they interacted with each other person. The research found that position in the energy network is four times the predictor of performance as is position in information and influence networks. Those who positively energize others performed better personally and their units performed significantly better than those who resided in the center of information or influence networks. Moreover, high-performing firms had three times as many positive energizing networks as low-performing firms. Positive energy, the study concluded, is the major predictor of high performance.

Cameron (2003) reported two studies in which measures of organizational virtuousness were significantly predictive of organizational performance and recovery from downsizing. One study was conducted in eight independent business units randomly selected within a large corporation in the transportation industry. A second study included a large sample of organizations from sixteen industries (e.g., automotive, consulting, financial services, health care, retail), all of which had recently engaged in downsizing. A survey instrument was completed by a sample of employees in these firms (i.e., across levels and across functions) measuring aspects of organizational virtuousness—*compassion, integrity, forgiveness, trust,* and *optimism.* Organizational performance measures consisted of objective measures of *productivity* (efficiency ratios), *quality* (customer claims), *employee commitment* (voluntary turnover), and *profitability* from company records and from publicly available sources, as well as perceptual measures of *productivity, quality, profitability, customer retention,* and *compensation.* Respondents compared their own firm's performance on these five perceptual outcomes with four benchmarks—their best competitors, past performance, industry average, and stated goals.

Statistical results revealed that, as predicted, when controlling for all other factors, downsizing led to deteriorating organizational performance. However, statistically significant relationships were found between organizational virtuous-ness and objectively measured outcomes (e.g., profitability) and perceptual effec-tiveness (e.g., exceeding best competitors' performance). Organizations scoring higher in virtuousness were more profitable, and, when compared to competitors, industry averages, goals, and past performance, virtuousness also mitigated the negative effects of downsizing. Organizations with higher virtuousness scores had significantly higher objective and perceived performance.

Gittell, Cameron, and Lim (2005) also found a significant relationship between recovery in firms within the U.S. airline industry after the September 11 attacks and the presence of a virtuous culture. Because passenger ridership declined an average of 20 percent during the first year after the tragedy, almost all of the major carriers resorted to layoffs and cutbacks to cope with the financial exigencies. Only two firms ardently refused to lay off employees—Southwest and Alaska—citing virtu-ous motives for their decisions. Despite losing more than $1 million a day, for example, Southwest's CEO stated: "Clearly we can't continue to do this indefinitely, but we are willing to suffer some damage, even to our stock price, to protect the jobs of our people ... We want to show our people that we value them, and we're not going to hurt them just to get a little more money in the short term. Not furloughing people breeds loyalty. It breeds a sense of security. It breeds a sense of trust" (Conlin, 2001).

An analysis of stock price recovery and profitability shows an almost perfect correlation between a carrier's virtuous coping strategy and financial recovery. Airlines such as U.S. Airways and United Airlines violated their labor contracts and refused to provide severance benefits, citing the need to preserve the company's financial base as the reason. Southwest and Alaska, on the other hand, put employ-ees' concerns first and absorbed losses to preserve jobs. Stock price recovery correlated significantly with the number of employees laid off by the airline com-panies—Southwest, Alaska, Northwest, Delta, American, America West, Continen-tal, United, U.S. Airways, in that order—and the extent to which they demonstrated consideration for the human condition in their recovery strategy. Profitability was also strongly correlated across the industry with the firms' approach to the crisis, with Southwest remaining profitable in every quarter—the only U.S. airline com-pany to do so—and U.S. Airways sustaining a loss in every quarter.

One theoretical explanation for the findings summarized in these various studies centers on two key attributes of positive deviance, virtuousness, positive energy, and positive communication: their *amplifying* qualities—which foster escalating positive consequences—and their *buffering* qualities—which protect against nega-tive encroachments. Several writers have examined these qualities (Sutcliffe and Vogus, 2003; Fredrickson, 2003; Dienstbier and Zillig, 2002; Masten and Reed, 2002; Hatch, 1999; Seligman, et al., 1999) demonstrating that when positive devi-ance, virtuousness, positive energy, and positive communication are demonstrated in organizations, and when organizations recognize and legitimize these kinds of dynamics, they become self-reinforcing (i.e., they *amplify* the positive consequences). They also foster resiliency against negative and challenging conditions, and provide a strengthening dynamic that helps systems resist negative consequences (i.e., they *buffer* organizations from deterioration in outcomes) (see Cameron, Bright, and Caza, 2004).

15.7 REVITALIZING INTEREST IN ORGANIZATIONAL EFFECTIVENESS THROUGH POS

An advantage of this new POS approach to effectiveness is that new variables are being uncovered (e.g., positive energy networks) as predictors of performance, and new definitions of effectiveness are being considered (e.g., positive deviance). The abandonment of organizational effectiveness as a topic of investigation occurred because of several factors—the ambiguity of its conceptual boundaries, the difficulties associated with its measurement, and the shift toward pragmatics and away from conceptual debates regarding which effectiveness model was most appropriate. Whereas these concerns will not disappear, the new emphasis by Positive Organizational Scholarship on inherently meaningful and positively uplifting phenomena has the potential to revitalize interest in organizational effectiveness. In place of definitions and models of effectiveness being centered on goal achievement, acquiring resources, avoiding internal strain, satisfying constituencies, or fostering collaboration (all located at the middle point on the continuum in Figure 15.2), POS highlights a completely new set of effectiveness considerations. It emphasizes achieving the best of the human condition, extraordinarily positive performance, and that which elevates and revitalizes human systems (the right side of the continuum in Figure 15.2). Because amplifying and buffering qualities are associated with these new phenomena, the potential exists to resurrect and expand research on organizational effectiveness. They represent outcomes to which individuals and organizations aspire when they are at their very best, they are self-reinforcing, and they lead to stronger and more resilient systems. Hence, by introducing a POS alternative to effectiveness research, researchers may once again become attracted to understanding organizational performance as a phenomenon of interest.

The resurrection of effectiveness research is needed because of the four reasons enumerated earlier: Organizational effectiveness lies at the center of all models and theories of organization; effectiveness is the ultimate dependent variable in organizational studies; individuals are constantly faced with the need to make judgments about the effectiveness of organizations; and addressing assessment guidelines creates comparative evaluations. These reasons remain and are as applicable to POS variables as to the more traditional effectiveness research. Thus, research on positive deviance in effectiveness work should be informed by work already accomplished in the more traditional effectiveness literature. Conceptual clarity is still required, rigorous assessment techniques are still needed, and appropriate frameworks are still necessary.

Whereas some progress is beginning to emerge, questions such as the following are among those requiring attention by the new effectiveness researchers. This list is not comprehensive, of course, but is merely illustrative of the questions associated with a POS approach to effectiveness.

1. *Frameworks*: What are the relationships between traditional models of effectiveness and positive deviance? Can current models be modified to account for positively deviant outcomes (i.e., is a transformed goal model still relevant), or are new models required?
2. *New concepts*: What aspects of individual and organizational phenomena have not been taken into account in explaining performance? What new phenomena are highlighted when positive deviance is considered as the indicator of effectiveness?
3. *Measurement*: How are positively deviant concepts and variables best identified, measured, and explained? What are the key measurable indicators? To what extent are the seven guidelines for effectiveness research helpful when POS phenomena are investigated?
4. *Definitions*: What are the conceptual boundaries and precise definitions of POS concepts such as virtuousness, positive energy, high quality relationships, compassion, flourishing, resiliency, and so on? On what scholarly literature in organizational studies can they build?
5. *Enablers*: What are the key enablers of positive deviance? What attributes of the structures, processes, cultures, leadership behaviors, environments, and/or resources are most conducive to, or resistant of, positive dynamics in organizations?
6. *Causal direction*: What are the causal relationships (directionality) associated with various positive phenomena? Which comes first, for example, virtuousness or high performance in organizations? Separating predictors from effects—and identifying which is which—under conditions of mutual reinforcement, requires clarification.
7. *Level of analysis*: Do positive individual dynamics reproduce themselves in organizations, and vice versa? To what extent does extraordinarily individual performance lead or extraordinary organizational performance, and vice versa?

8. *Time*: How long does it take for positive dynamics to unfold, to be demonstrated, and to produce effects? How quickly can positive deviance occur?

9. *Positive spirals*: How do positive dynamics emerge in self-reinforcing loops? What are the underpinnings of amplifying and buffering effects?

10. *Relations among outcomes*: What is the relationship among points of the positive deviance continuum—e.g., ineffectiveness, effectiveness, excellence? Does positive deviance depend on reaching a state of basic effectiveness, or are the points on the continuum independent of one another?

In sum, the study of organizational effectiveness appears to be on a cusp at the present time. The traditional approach to effectiveness research is on the verge of demise, but a replacement approach may be on the verge of ascendance. On the other hand, organizational studies has a tradition of being caught up in intellectual fads with limited long-term scholarly contribution, so whether the POS approach is a fad or a legitimate supplement to effectiveness research is an open question. The key may not be so much whether POS is a savior of effectiveness as whether a renewed interest in organizational effectiveness can once again be stimulated and sustained. An emphasis on extraordinary positivity may be required to help generate extraordinary interest.

REFERENCES

ARGYRIS, C. (1960). *Interpersonal Competence and Organizational Effectiveness*. Homewood, Ill.: Irwin.

—— and SCHON, D. (1978). *Organizational Learning: A Theory of Action Perspective*. Reading, Mass.: Addison-Wesley Series on Organization Development.

BAKER, W. (2000). *Achieving Success Through Social Capital*. San Francisco: Jossey-Bass.

—— CROSS, R., and PARKER, A. (2003). Energy in organizations. *Sloan Management Review*, July.

BARNARD, C. I. (1938). *The Functions of the Executive*. Cambridge, Mass.: Harvard University Press.

BLUEDORN, A. C. (1980). Cutting the Gordian knot: A critique of the effectiveness tradition in organizational research. *Sociology and Social Research*, 64: 477–496.

BURNS, T., and STALKER, G. M. (1961). *The Management of Innovation*. New York: Barnes and Noble.

CAMERON, K. S. (1984). The effectiveness of ineffectiveness. In B. M. Staw and L. L. Cummings (eds.), *Research in Organizational Behavior*: 6. 276. Greenwich, Conn.: JAI Press.

—— (1986). Effectiveness as paradox: Consensus and conflict in conceptions of organizational effectiveness. *Management Science*, 32: 539–553.

—— (2003). Organizational virtuousness and performance. In Cameron, Dutton, and Quinn (2003: 48–65).

—— Bright, D., and Caza, A. (2004). Exploring the relationships between organizational virtuousness and performance. *American Behavioral Scientist*, 47: 766–790.

—— Dutton, J. E., and Quinn, R. E. (2003). *Positive Organizational Scholarship*. San Francisco: Berrett Koehler.

—— and Lavine, M. (2005). *Making the Impossible Possible: The Case for Positive Deviance in Organizations*. Working paper, Center for Positive Organizational Scholarship, University of Michigan.

—— and Quinn, R. E. (1999). *Diagnosing and Changing Organizational Culture*. Reading, MA: Addison Wesley.

—— —— DeGraff, J., and Thakor, A. (2005). *The Structure of Value*. Center for Positive Organizational Scholarship, University of Michigan.

—— and Whetten, D. A. (1983). *Organizational Effectiveness: A Comparison of Multiple Models*. New York: Academic Press.

—— —— (1996). Organizational effectiveness and quality: The second generation. *Higher Education: Handbook of Theory and Research*, 11: 265–306. New York: Agathon.

Cialdini, R. B., Schaller, M., Houlihan, D., Arps, K., Fultz, J., and Beaman, A. (1987). Empathy based helping: Is it selflessly or selfishly motivated? *Journal of Personality and Social Psychology*, 52: 749–758.

Clifton, D. O., and Harter, J. K. (2003). Investing in strengths. In Cameron, Dutton, and Quinn (2003: 111–121).

Collins, J. (2001). *Good to Great*. Boston, Mass.: HarperCollins.

Conlin, M. (2001). Where layoffs are a last resort. *Business Week*, October 8.

Connolly, T., Conlon, E. J., and Deutsch, S. J. (1980). Organizational effectiveness: A multiple-constituency approach. *Academy of Management Review*, 5: 211–217.

Csikszentmihalyi, M. (1990). *Flow: The Psychology of Optimal Experience*. New York: Harper Perennial.

Cummings, L. L. (1983). Organizational effectiveness and organizational behavior: A critical perspective. In Cameron and Whetten (1983: 187–204).

Cyert, R. M., and March, J. G. (1963). *The Behavioral Theory of the Firm*. Englewood Cliffs, NJ: Prentice Hall.

Czapinski, J. (1985). Negativity bias in psychology: An evaluation of Polish publications. *Polish Psychological Bulletin*, 16: 27–44.

Dienstbier. R. A. and Zillig, L. M. P. (2002). Toughness. In C. R. Snyder and Shane J. Lopez (eds.), *Handbook of Positive Psychology*: 515–527. New York: Oxford University Press.

Eisenberg, E. M. (1990). Jamming: Transcendence through organizing. *Communication Research*, 17: 139–164.

Eisenhart, K. M., and Wescott, B. J. (1988). Paradoxical demands and the creation of excellence: The case of just-in-time manufacturing. In R. E. Quinn and K. S. Cameron (eds.), *Paradox and Transformation*. Boston: Ballinger.

Fredrickson, B. L. (2001). The role of positive emotions in positive psychology: The broaden-and-build theory of positive emotions. *American Psychologist*, 56: 218–226.

—— (2003). Positive emotions and upward spirals in organizations. In Cameron, Dutton, and Quinn (2003: 163–175).

Gittell, J. H., Cameron, K. S., and Lim, S. G. P. (2005). Relationships, layoffs, and organizational resilience. *Academy of Management Executive* (forthcoming).

Goodman, P. S., Atkin, R. S., and Schoorman, D. F. (1983). On the demise of organizational effectiveness studies. In Cameron and Whetten (1983: 163–186).

GUZZO, R. A. (1982). *Improving Group Decision Making in Organizations*. New York: Academic Press.

HANNAN, M. T., and FREEMAN, J. H. (1977). Obstacles to the comparative study of organizational effectiveness. In P. S. Goodman and J. M. Pennings (eds.), *New Perspectives on Organizational Effectiveness*. San Francisco: Jossey-Bass.

HATCH, M. J. (1999). Exploring the empty spaces of organizing: How improvisational jazz helps redescribe organizational structure. *Organizational Studies*, 20: 75–100.

HIRSCH, P. M., and LEVIN, D. Z. (1999). Umbrella advocates versus validity police: A life-cycle model. *Organization Science*, 10(2): 199–213.

KEELEY, M. (1978). A social justice approach to organizational evaluation. *Administrative Science Quarterly*, 22: 272–292.

LAWRENCE, P., and LORSCH, J. (1967). *Organization and Environment*. Cambridge, Mass.: Harvard University Press.

LEWIN, A. Y., and MINTON, J. W. (1986). Determining organizational effectiveness: Another look, and an agenda for research. *Management Science*, 32: 514–538.

LEWIN, K. (1951). *Resolving Social Conflicts*. Washington, DC: American Psychological Association.

—— (1997). *Resolving Social Conflicts: And, Field Theory in Social Science*. Washington, DC: American Psychological Association.

LIKERT, R. (1961). *New Patterns of Management*. New Work: McGraw Hill.

LINDBLOM, C. E. (1959). The science of muddling through. *Public Administration Review*, 20: 79–88.

LOSADA, M., and HEAPHY, E. (2004). The role of positivity and connectivity in the performance of business teams. *American Behavioral Scientist*, 47: 740–765.

McKELVEY, W. (1982). *Organizational Systematics: Taxonomy, Evolution, Classification*. Berkeley, Calif.: University of California Press.

MASTEN, A. S., and REED, M. G. J. (2002). Resilience in development. In C. R. Snyder and Shane J. Lopez (eds.), *Handbook of Positive Psychology*: 74–88. New York: Oxford University Press.

MAYNE, T. T. (1999). Negative effect and health: The importance of being earnest. *Cognition and Emotion*, 13: 601–635.

NADLER, D. A., and TUSHMAN, M. L. (1980). A congruence model for organizational assessment. In E. E. Lawler, D. A. Nadler, and C. Cammann (eds.), *Organizational Assessment*. New York: Wiley.

NISBET, R. E., and WILSON, T. (1977). Telling more than we can know: Verbal reports of mental processes. *Psychological Review*, 143: 231–259.

NORD, W. R. (1983). A political-economic perspective on organizational effectiveness. In Cameron and Whetten (1983: 95–134).

PERROW, C. (1986). *Complex Organizations*. New York: Random House.

PETERS, T., and WATERMAN, R. H. (1982). *In Search of Excellence*. New York: Harper and Row.

PETERSON, C. M., and SELIGMAN, M. E. P. (2003). Positive organizational studies: Lessons from positive psychology. In Cameron, Dutton, and Quinn (2003: 14–27).

PFEFFER, J., and SALANCIK, G. R. (1978). *The External Control of Organizations*. New York: Harper and Row.

—— and SUTTON, R. I. (2000). *The Knowing–Doing Gap: How Smart Companies Turn Knowledge into Action*. Cambridge, Mass.: Harvard Business School.

PRICE, J. L. (1982).The study of organizational effectiveness. *Sociological Quarterly*, 13: 3–15.

PUGH, D. S., HICKSON, D. J., and HININGS, C. R. (1969). An empirical taxonomy of structures in work organizations. *Administrative Science Quarterly*, 14: 115–126.

QUINN, R. E., and ROHRBAUGH, J. (1981). A competing values approach to organizational effectiveness. *Public Productivity Review*, 5: 122–140.

ROETHLISBERGER, F. J., and DICKSON, W. J. (1947). *Management and the Worker*. Cambridge. Mass.: Harvard University Press.

SANDAGE, S. J., and HILL, P. C. (2001). The virtues of positive psychology: The rapprochement and challenges of the affirmative postmodern perspective. *Journal for the Theory of Social Behavior*, 31: 241–260.

SCHEIER, M. F., CARVER, C. S., and BRIDGES, M. W. (1994). Distinguishing optimism from neuroticism (and trait anxiety, self-mastery, and self-esteem): A reevaluation of the Life Orientation Test. *Journal of Personality and Social Psychology*, 67: 1063–1078.

SEASHORE, S. E., and YUCHTMAN, E. (1967). Factorial analysis of organizational performance. *Administrative Science Quarterly*, 12: 377–395.

SELIGMAN, M. E. P. (2002). *Authentic Happiness*. New York: Free Press.

—— SCHULMAN, P., DeRUBEIS, R. J., and HOLLON, S. D. (1999). The prevention of depression and anxiety. *Prevention and Treatment*, 2. http://journals.apa.org/prevention/

SELZNICK, P. (1948). Foundations of a theory of organizations. *American Sociological Review*, 13: 25–35.

SIMON, H. A. (1948). *Models of Man*. New York: Free Press.

—— (1956). *Models of Man*. New York: Wiley.

SLOVIC, P., and LICHTENSTEIN, S. (1971). Comparison of Bayesian and regression approaches to the study of information processing judgment. *Organizational Behavior and Human Performance*, 6: 649–744.

SPREITZER, G., SUTCLIFFE, K., DUTTON, J., SONENSHEIN, S., and GRANT, A. (2005). Thriving at work. *Organizational Science* (forthcoming).

SUTCLIFFE, K. M., and VOGUS, T. J. (2003). Organizing for resilience. In Cameron, Dutton, and Quinn (2003: 94–110).

TSUI, A. S. (1990). A multiple constituency model of effectiveness: Empirical examination at the human resource subunit level. *Administrative Science Quarterly*, 35: 458–483.

VAN DE VEN, A. H., and FERRY, D. L. (1980). *Measuring and Assessing Organizations*. New York: Wiley.

WALSH, J. P., WEBER, K., and MARGOLIS, J. D. (2003). Social issues in management: Our lost cause found. *Journal of Management*, 29: 859–881.

WEBER, M. (1947). *The Theory of Social and Economic Organization*, trans. A. M. Henderson and T. Parsons. New York: Oxford.

WEICK, K. E. (1976). Educational organizations as loosely coupled systems. *Administrative Science Quarterly*, 21: 1–19.

—— and DAFT, R. L. (1983). The effectiveness of interpretation systems. In Cameron and Whetten (1983: 71–94).

—— and SUTCLIFFE, K. M. (2001). *Managing the Unexpected*. San Francisco: Jossey-Bass.

WHETTEN D. A. (2004). *In Search of the 'O' in OMT*. Distinguished Scholar Address, Organization and Management Theory Division, Academy of Management, New Orleans.

WILLIAMSON, O. E. (1983). *Markets and Hierarchies*. New York: Free Press.

WRZESNIEWSKI, A. (2003). Finding positive meaning in work. In Cameron, Dutton, and Quinn (2003: 296–308).

ZAMMUTO, R. F. (1984). A comparison of multiple constituencies models of organizational effectiveness. *Academy of Management Review*, 9: 606–616.

CHAPTER 16

....

MANAGERIAL AND ORGANIZATIONAL COGNITION

ISLANDS OF COHERENCE

....

ANNE S. HUFF

COGNITION is important. Attempts to understand it are rooted most deeply in psychology, a field that takes a major share of the behavioral science pie in most universities, often larger than the other main contenders: sociology and economics. As cognition became a subject of its own in the 1970s and 1980s, it was strongly shaped by the subfield of social psychology, but also by computer and information science, along with many other fields. It was a "golden era" of argument within an arena that all agreed had enormous potential. Part of the assurance of those working in the emerging discipline came from rapid developments in computer science, and the assumption that the human brain functioned in the way a computer (of that time) functioned. Particular attention was given to the mental representations—called frameworks, schemata, schema, and other terms—that facilitate and shape attention, memory, and other cognitive activities (see Hodgkinson and Sparrow, 2002: 21–25 for a brief review).

Although that early wave of enthusiasm has subsided, and the assumed isomorphism between brains and computers has been abandoned, I still strongly believe that

I appreciate comments from Jim Huff, Gabriel Szulanski, and Ken Smith.

understanding cognition is required to understand human affairs. Cognition is especially important to management, which involves the deliberate attempt to influence human behavior and its outcomes (Barnard, 1938). Its place is secured not only by continuing research on organizational processes, but also by the recent appearance of cognitive variables in economic and sociological theories of organization.

The foundation for understanding managerial and organizational cognition (MOC) was laid in the 1980s. *The Thinking Organization* (1986), edited by Sims and Gioia, was an important early landmark that showed how management scholars were applying a cognitive perspective to a broad range of management subjects. I wanted the book I edited, *Mapping Strategic Thought* (1990), to be the next major landmark. It provides a hierarchy for organizing work in the field, and ties that organizing framework to a set of available methodologies. Key concepts from this book and other work I did in the "golden era" of MOC research are summarized in the first part of this chapter. The second part describes how I moved from thinking about cognition as the central aspect of strategic decision making to making cognition the anchor of a broader attempt to understand strategic action. This transition is part of a general shift in strategy and organization theory toward dynamic models. I suggest that we could be entering a new era of enthusiasm for cognitive research because of the requirements of these models.

My research interests and objectives have been informed by others' work, and I am particularly aware of the influence of people at the University of Illinois, one of the important centers of cognitive research (in management and in other fields) in the 1980s. It is not possible to describe MOC in detail in this chapter, but it is interesting to relate a brief summary of MOC to descriptions of scholarly development from the philosophy of science, which I do toward the end of the chapter. That leads to some advice for readers in the conclusion.

16.1 MAPPING STRATEGIC THOUGHT

An influential foundation for much of the research on MOC is Herbert Simon's (1947[1976]) assertion that human rationality (which many equated with "knowledge" or "cognition") is inevitably bounded. He argues that every environment or context, even the relatively impoverished, contains more stimuli than the human observer can recognize or process.[1] Some MOC researchers accept this statement as a useful starting point for distinguishing more or less "accurate" or "useful"

---

[1] Winograd and Flores (1986, 14–26) discuss how Simon's argument affected cognitive science as a whole, especially research on artificial intelligence.

perceptions, and one large area of inquiry involves identification of heuristics and bias in perception and subsequent cognitive operations (see Tenbrunsel, et al., 1996, for a review). A basic assumption underlying this work, consistent with the logical positivist research tradition, is that external observers, if they are careful about their own potential for bias, are able to evaluate performance in perceptual and other cognitive tasks against an accepted standard.

Other researchers find this assumption highly problematic. Social construction-ists (Berger and Luckman, 1967), in particular, assert that environments do not exist independent of actors. Rather, perceptions and subsequent activities of individuals "enact" environment or context. Rationality exists, in the sense that individuals are generally assumed to be doing things that make sense from their point of view, but emotion, conflict and other aspects of life are part of the picture. Researchers are not able to make an independent assessment of this activity; they can only make their own interpretive observations and recognize that their presence plays a part in enacting what they describe.

Making sense of what is happening is not easy from an interpretive point of view, and cognition is not always the leader. Karl Weick (1969, 1995) was an early spokesperson for the difficulty individuals can have in "parsing" stimuli to make sense of themselves and the settings they are in; he suggests that actors (members of organizations and researchers) tend to discover what they know over time. Bill Starbuck (1983, 1993) has also influentially argued that managers and researchers are better advised to look at the action that generates sense, rather than the sense that guides action.

Although a more complicated story could be told, the division just described makes the important point that MOC research can be approached in very different ways, influenced by different assumptions about the world (ontology) and what we can know about it (epistemology).[2] The distinctions are not always finely drawn in this field, but a major bifurcation is between those who assume the researcher can be an independent observer and those who feel that the line between actor and setting is blurred and affected by the observer's own cognitive activity.

16.1.1 Strategic Frames

One of my early papers, "Industry Influences on Strategy Formulation" (Huff, 1982), argued that the industry setting should be expected to have a particularly strong effect on strategists' perception of the environment and their strategic choices. The paper suggests that the activities of firms with quite similar

---

[2] I am encouraged here by Bob De Wit and Ron Meyer (2004) who emphasize paradox as an important tool in advancing strategic thought.

strategies—firms in the same "strategic group" within an industry—are especially influential. The performance of comparable firms is likely to get close attention as evidence about what succeeds in the focal organization's environment. Direct interactions—including meeting at industry associations, cross-company hiring, and selling to the same customers—provide a good deal of this information and increase the probability that similar conclusions and actions persist over time.

J. C. Spender's (1980, 1989) idea that firms tend to follow an industry "recipe" is quoted in this paper, but my primary emphasis is on strategy as a "frame" that aids sensemaking and subsequent decision. Bower and Doz (1979) had said that the central task of the CEO was to "shape the premises of other executives' thoughts." That encouraged me to describe the strategic frame as an arena within which, or around which, others (decision makers within the firm, but also customers, suppliers, etc.) will ideally make their decisions. The strategic frame is expected to evolve over time as experience interacts with initial ideas about how to act effectively. Cataloguing change in these ideas is one way of tracking the move from intended to realized strategy (Mintzberg, 1978).

The industry influences paper came at a time when environmental uncertainty was discussed in quite general ways, and sufficient distinctions were not being made among organizations in different types of environments. I would like to think that it helped increase awareness of larger institutional factors affecting individual cognition and that it described some of the reasons why individuals can come to similar, coordinating conclusions.

In retrospect, however, the industry influences argument can be interpreted as either claiming that certain aspects of an external and independent environment are more understandable if time and place are specified, or as asserting that actors in an "industry," and especially in a strategic group, create an environment that becomes more coherent as participants interact over time. Foreshadowing a conclusion discussed later in this chapter, it seems to me that both observations are interesting, and can be simultaneously useful, even though they may seem logically contradictory. However, the two traditions in MOC research did not merge in this way, but moved in quite separate, non-interacting directions. I think of myself as an interpretivist in this categorization scheme, but I have tried a variety of methods, including a few that make positivist presumptions.

16.1.2 Five Aspects of Framing: Attention, Categorization, Causal Reasoning, Argument, and Schema

Mapping Strategic Thought presents an organizing framework for describing the broad range of cognitive studies that were emerging from various management subfields in the 1980s. It also provides practical instructions for using different mapping methodologies to carry out different kinds of work. The re-use of the word "frame" was deliberate. This edited volume, which includes quite a bit of my own work, was conceived as a strategic frame in itself: a way of potentially creating additional cohesion in a complex arena by encouraging similar actions. The book connects work in strategy and organization theory with similar work in other social sciences to legitimate MOC and to suggest additional lines of inquiry. I wanted to encourage more people to adopt a cognitive perspective. By dividing the book into two, with theoretical articles followed by chapters that outlined the methods involved, I hoped that newcomers would find it easier to become involved.

More practically, the mapping book offered the opportunity to showcase some of the work we were doing at the University of Illinois. We thought that it was difficult to get research from our emerging, relatively unfamiliar area published. Though I now know how widespread this feeling of exclusion is, at the time I simply found it invigorating to stop trying to publish individual articles in favor of putting together a book that presented a significant set of work as part of a larger social science picture.

The book proposes that the most straightforward approach to describing and understanding cognition in organizations is to assume that a) concepts or "ideas" are the critical building block for cognitive activity (like decision making), b) words adequately summarize these ideas, and c) the repeated use of related words, when compared with other word families used less often, is indicative of an idea's cognitive dominance.

Theories that emerge from these assumptions focus on *attention*. One of the first recorded "cognitive studies" was based on these assumptions: it involved a charge of heresy in eighteenth-century Sweden that presented evidence of unacceptable ideas found in hymns sung by the offending group (Woodrum, 1984). In management, Ned Bowman (1976) took an early look at vocabulary in annual reports and concluded that troubled companies seek risk. In my book, Birnbaum and Weiss analyzed interviews with almost 100 industry experts to show how competitive actions systematically vary across industry and technologies.

The methodology used to map word use is very simple. Families of words are typically identified by their entomological roots. The use of any one of these words in a data set, which might be taken from speeches, written documents, interviews or even recorded conversation, is counted as an occurrence of that concept. Perhaps these are clustered by the researcher or someone familiar with the subject into broader themes. The "map" developed for interpretation and analysis is typically a simple chart illustrating relative use of concepts important to the research, perhaps with graphs showing change over time.

For example, in *Mapping Strategic Thought* Karen Fletcher and I (1990) catalogue how presentations to securities analysts from AT&T in the 1980s gradually decrease references to the "telephony" industry and start using "telecommunications" instead. The ultimate substitution and its timing, we argue, is evidence of a cognitive change that was necessary to accepting the consent decree that broke up AT&T's monopoly.

This example immediately suggests a further complexity, however. It is easy to argue that the meaning of a word like "telecommunications" is more than a direct description of what is, the word also has meaning because of what it is not—in this case "telephony." Telephony sounds incredibly quaint in a world of cell-phones with built in cameras, and therefore it is no longer a meaningful opposite for most people who think about telecommunications. Still, the logic is clear: I think of my cell-phone as something that is similar to but not quite like my landline phone. It is also a way of sending a message that might alternatively be sent by fax or e-mail.

A large number of MOC researchers, influenced by Kelly (1955), thought that *categorization* was essential to cognitive activity in organizations, because it is involved in so many important tasks, like positioning products against competitors' products. They also thought that learning could be linked to change in categorization.

Followers of Kelly's personal construct theory developed and tested the repertory grid technique to discover cognitive structures through forced choice comparisons. Management researchers typically offer subjects three stimuli objects with the request to say which two are most similar, and why. A set of descriptive categories used to identify and think about the class of objects is gradually identified through repeated presentation of different triads.

Ronda Reger (1990) used this methodology to identify dimensions of competition among regional bank holding companies headquartered in Chicago for her chapter in the mapping book. The words used as descriptors by individuals were clustered into a smaller number of concepts by industry and academic experts, who made it possible to develop a consensus view of the relative distance between competitors from the data. In overview, the research suggests that actors in the industry thought in terms of clusters of firms with similar strategies. Some economists had identified strategic groups of firms, but their work had been criticized as a mere artifact of data analysis. Evidence that competitors perceived clusters of similar firms is interesting support for the strategic groups idea.

Rhonda and I did additional analysis on the data that suggests cognitive groups can capture a consensus view of strategic trajectories which current economic definitions of strategic groups can not easily capture (Reger and Huff, 1993). But of course, agreement among industry participants can be problematic. One of the most widely cited cognitive studies from the University of Illinois, reported in Porac, Thomas, and Emme (1987) and Porac, Thomas, and Baden-Fuller (1989), shows how a widely shared categorization scheme in the Scottish knitwear industry allowed incumbents to ignore the importance of emerging Asian competitors. Porac and Thomas (1990) suggest that managers tend to think of their own firm as more prototypic than other firms in a competitive setting, which influences how they analyze competitors' choices.

Categorization studies are more difficult to carry out than studies of attention because they highlight a cognitive operation that is generally assumed to precede verbal statement. As a result, researchers interested in categorization must assert more of their own cognitive effort when compared with those interested in attention, and they are likely to use data gathering techniques that are farther from the day-to-day experience of informants. A balancing strength of the repertory grid technique as typically used in management studies, however, is that it captures categories in the words used by the individuals being studied, rather than categories provided by the researcher. This often gives categorization studies face validity, but it must be remembered that the researcher has made an important (and difficult to directly support) assumption that responses to forced choice comparisons draw on understanding that will indeed affect decisions in the organization.

Studies of *causality*, the third approach to cognition covered in my mapping book, typically require even more intervention from the researcher. The assumption is that causal beliefs have particular relevance for managers because they are the basis for assessing past performance and the probable outcome of future courses of action. The chapter that I wrote with Charles Schwenk (1990), another faculty member from the University of Illinois, analyzes maps of causal attribution from speeches made by oil industry executives. To carry out the study we added a few additional conventions to a set of causal categories (positively/ negatively influences, has some effect, has no effect, etc.) used by researchers in political science.

The inter-coder reliability of causal studies using this coding protocol is generally very high. A data set is identified (in our case speeches to securities analysts) and examined sentence by sentence for direct or inferred causal links. Cause and effect chains are then mapped as phrases linked by signed arrows. The method requires interpretive judgments by coders, since speakers often use indirect rhetorical devices to evoke causal claims. Thus, inter-coder reliability is an important source of confidence and requires some training to achieve.

Many cognitive maps drawn by MOC researchers take this causal form. While I argue in *Mapping Strategic Thought* that it is important for MOC as a field to develop multiple mapping approaches, it is reasonable for management researchers to be especially concerned with causality. It is curious, however, that few feedback loops are found in causal maps, and few contradictions (Huff, 1990: 31). One has to wonder whether the method captures the full range of cognition required for strategizing.

Nevertheless, my study with Charles was particularly interesting to me, because it suggests a complexity that previous studies of causal reasoning might have overlooked. Almost all studies of attribution find, as ours did, that individuals claim to cause successful outcomes, but they point to external factors as influential causes of negative outcomes. This is typically seen as a human bias, but we propose an additional explanation that is also consistent with the data. Positive outcomes are the expected result of organizational efforts. Thus, speakers who emphasize the details of a specific execution can reasonably assume (without much conscious thought or reference) that a larger schematic framework has been supported. When things do not go as planned, however, they are pressed to reassess their understanding of the world. Though it makes sense to consider whether managers are evading responsibility by talking about external causes, it also makes sense that negative events lead to reconsidering accepted assumptions, which often will require more external references. This is an interesting cognitive counterpoint to conclusions from a well-established stream of research—one that in my mind illustrates the potential of cognitive studies.

Studies of *argument*, or problem solving, also have great potential. This kind of research focuses on reasoning as a particularly important aspect of cognition. The theoretic assumption is that decisions to act require weighing evidence for and against an action. The evidence that merits thought and discussion is evidence that is inconclusive. In fact, the subject of interest is often not the status of facts but the reasoning underlying the choice and interpretation of facts.

I think this description of argument does a good job of capturing what strategy is about, but it is particularly challenging to study because more researcher intervention is necessary to establish the cognitive aspects of argument than the three approaches already summarized. The researcher interested in argument must worry particularly that his or her assumptions about rationality, learned from childhood, become an inappropriate lens for data collection and analysis. Of course, subjects who come from western cultures are likely to have learned similar conventions of rational argument. The question is whether they are using this structure (if found in the data) as a cognitive processor or a "post-cognitive" representation for political effect.

Attention revealed in word choices, categorization revealed in response to specific stimuli, and even the causal links embedded in language use, are arguably under less conscious control than argument. But in our AT&T study, Karen Fletcher and I (1990) felt that the acceptance of monopoly break-up had to involve a complicated cognitive change that could not be fully captured by changes in attention, categorization, or causal understanding. Though very much aware of the political nature of this event, we suggest that it would be a very difficult cognitive feat for participants to maintain internal and external arguments in a rapidly changing environment—one to assess what was "actually" going on, the other to make the company look good. Though public speaking clearly involves positive presentation of self, we also assert that obviously self-serving pronouncements should be limited when speaking to knowledgeable audiences.

The methodology we use, based on the work of Steven Toulmin (1958) and Toulmin, Ricke, and Janik (1979), divides speeches into "claims"—statements the speaker presents for audience acceptance. The block of text associated with each claim is subdivided into supporting data (which might include underlying arguments about why the data should be taken as evidence), qualifiers and elaborations.

The data showed interesting similarities and differences in argument over time. I believe we found out something important about shifts in cognitive frames when we uncovered a similarity between early arguments against break-up that involved the importance of public service (to those in isolated locations, for example) and later arguments that competition could serve customers by providing a wider range of products and services. Continuity in the idea of service provided a bridge from one strategy to another in our analysis. I now believe that most change efforts have to establish such a bridge.

From a research point of view, however, this and other studies of argument require still more imposition of the researcher's judgment that the other studies just summarized. The mapping method is supported by a formal protocol that is summarized in the book, but inter-coder reliability cannot be expected to be as high as in causal mapping studies. Often texts can be divided in different ways, and each makes some sense. It is harder to provide coders with tie-breaking decision rules. I did not find that problematic, because I was engaged in an interpretive study, not a positivist one.

The fifth and last family of mapping methods covered in *Mapping Strategic Thought* is even most complicated. The researcher assumes that expectations based on previous experience, whether or not recognized by the individual(s) under study, affect cognitive activities. These *schemas* are stored in memory. They not only influence what is perceived, but what is inferred from "filling in the gaps" of received stimuli. The very interesting result is that people often "remember" stimuli that are not in fact part of a specific situation—a famous example come from a laboratory experiment in which subjects recall that pictures of an upscale restaurant include silver candle sticks and other objects commonly found in this kind of establishment, even though they are not in the presented picture.

The knowledge structure assumed to underlie perception, recall and other cognitive activities is worth investigating precisely because it is likely to be unrecognized by the subject (or perhaps the researcher). One particularly interesting finding involves contradiction. Steve Barley (1983) provides an example in his study of funeral homes. When people working in this context were asked to sort words relating to their domain, they revealed "codes" that connected opposites: the chapel is a home, the dead body is asleep, and so on. In the mapping book, Marlene Fiol used semiotics to similarly compare annual reports from medium sized firms in the chemical industry. Her analysis, which is too complicated to quickly summarize here, shows systematic differences between the cognitive structures revealed by firms that were active in joint ventures, and those that were not.

16.2 END OF THE GOLDEN ERA

Jim Walsh made a major contribution to MOC in his 1995 *Organization Science* review of the field. His organizing framework clustered empirical and theoretical work in terms of the level of analysis (individual, group, organization, and industry) and attention to three aspects of knowledge structure (or schema) content: the *representation* of an information environment, the origins or *development* of that representation, and its *use*.

The article had an immediate impact by cataloguing how much effort had been put into representation, using at least seventy-seven different labels (in addition to "schema") to capture the idea that cognition helps structure stimuli from an environment. Walsh quite rightly suggested that the field should narrow its vocabulary, and move on. He also makes the important point that "management researchers have been interested in a set of questions that generally are beyond the scope of basic psychological research" (Walsh, 1995: 282–283), which reinforces my belief that MOC has found a subject of study that requires an independent theoretic agenda and methodological base.

It is a dense and useful survey of the field, still in use by MOC researchers. Ten years later, however, I also see this important paper as the unintentional demarcation of the end of an era. By the time Walsh catalogued over-attention to schema in MOC, the concept had become problematic in cognitive science. New metaphors were being explored: one argument was that an overarching framework is not necessary for purposeful activity by individuals, or even by groups (one compelling argument is that it is possible to model the way birds fly together in a flock using rules of propinquity without assuming that they share a common mental map). Faith in schema as an overarching concept quickly diminished in cognitive science and this and other ideas were explored, and the field seemed to splinter in my reading. But perhaps that reading merely reflected my eroding faith in mental maps as the guiding force of strategy.

MOC research has continued and expanded in each of the areas Walsh identified, however (Naryanan and Kemmerer, 2001), with notable forays into the more complicated terrain our base discipline was beginning to explore (Eden and Spender, 1998). At the same time, it is interesting that cognitive theory is beginning to appear in management research from other disciplinary bases. Cognitive variables in strategy studies written from an economics perspective are of particular interest to me. Though simplistic, from the perspective of research done within the MOC community, these studies indicate that cognition is joining other behavioral sciences as a source for management research.

I am also encouraged by efforts within the MOC community to link cognition to broader agendas. Gerard Hodgkinson, who has done a great deal of work on categorization of competitors (Hodgkinson, 2002), has recently published a book with Paul Sparrow (2002) titled *The Competent Organization*. It appears in a series called "Managing Work and Organizations" at the Open University Press. The title and placement are significant—and a further indication that cognition is increasingly recognized in management research. The first chapter in this book is called "The Cognitive Perspective Comes of Age"—a positive end to the "golden era."

16.3 A COGNITIVELY ANCHORED THEORY OF ACTION

By the time Walsh's 1995 review was published, I had broadened my initial focus on cognition to include social, political, economic, and legal variables in an (overly) ambitious project carried out with my husband, Jim Huff. The new emphasis was on action. More specifically, we wanted to develop a model that could more successfully predict strategic change. It took ten years to work through the project; I call it "overly" ambitious because it was brought to a resting point rather than completed.

In the process, I came to see cognition as more complicated, but less central, than I had before. Though I had "heard" what Karl Weick, Bill Starbuck and others had to say about the necessary connection between thought and action, I understood their message much more completely after the experience of trying to simultaneously think about both cognition and action myself. A critical and practical step forward was to begin thinking about strategic framing as inexorably bound to socio-political interaction (Huff and Pondy, 1985; Huff, 2000).

16.3.1 Cognition, Will, Skill, and Values

Our book, *When Firms Change Direction* (2000) includes inputs from Pam Barr and others from the University of Illinois as well as inputs from authors from the University of Colorado, where we had moved. The book develops a cognitively *anchored* theory of the firm, which means that individual cognition, found at the bottom left corner of the matrix shown in Figure 16.1, triggers and is triggered by a much larger set of things that must be considered by the management researcher.

At the individual level, across the bottom row, the figure suggests that individual action is the result not just of cognition, but also of individual will, skill, and values.

	Signification (Cognition and Social Psychology)	Domination (politics)	Domination (economics and technology)	Legitimation (Law & Sociology)
Industry	**Industry Recipes** Assumptions and procedures for creating and serving markets used by many firms	**Industry Associations & Alliances** Relationships among firms to improve access to resources	**Markets/ Knowledge Generation** Organization of commercial and scientific opportunities	**Regulation** Constrains on behavior via legislation
Firm	**Strategic Frames** Widely accepted ways of defining key problems and tasks	**Leadership** Capacity and authority to organize individual and group activities	**Socio-technical Systems** Equipment & routines for reliably reproducing outcomes	**Contracts, Budgets** Enforceable constrains on access to and use of resources
Group	**"Party Platforms"** Shared problem definitions and preferred solutions	**Coalition** Cooperation to achieve desired outcomes	**Shared Experience & Tools** Increased knowledgeability via formal and informal networks	**Ideology** Shared beliefs about appropriate behavior
Individual	**Cognition** Attention, explanations and expectations based on experience and invention	**Motivation** Energy and will to identify and generate desired outcomes	**Knowledge/Skills** Capacity to execute specified patterns of behavior	**Values** Standards of worth, importance, propriety, etc.
	Communication	*Power*	*Power*	*Sanction*

Fig. 16.1   Individual cognition in a structuration framework

Source: Huff and Huff (2000)

The absence of these concepts in early MOC studies helps explain why attempts to link cognition to action outcomes (like performance) were so often frustrated. In other words, thought (the basic domain of MOC) is necessary to explain both the occurrence and outcome of purposeful action, but it is not sufficient.

Values, which might be included in some definitions of cognition, are treated as a separate concept in this figure because of the connection to regulation at more macro levels of analysis. Those who know structuration theory will recognize that the concept of "legitimization," which influences and is influenced by individual values, comes from Giddens (1984). It is one of three modes of behaviour, along with signification and domination, in which Giddens's core concept, the "duality of structure," can be observed.

16.3.2 Strategic Frames as Rules and Resources

Although structuration is a complicated meta-theory, the duality of structure is relatively straightforward: action or "agency" and "structure" (which Giddens defines as "rules and resources") are recursively bound together. Individuals always have the possibility of acting in unique and individually motivated ways, but as they act, they "instantiate" social rules and resources that can influence the actions of others. Thus, it is highly unlikely that any given action will not reflect in some way, perhaps unknown to the actor or the observer, rules and resources from previous experience.

Cognitive science's roots in social psychology have insured that most researchers understand that individual cognition is influenced by social setting, but structuration theory gave me useful specifics. Whittington's (1992) insightful article on its application to strategic management notes, for example, that even the most creatively destructive entrepreneurial actions tend to draw from rules and resources articulated in other contexts.

Rules, as Giddens describes them, however, are more like the informal rules of children's games than the formal rules of chess. That means acts of agency are not influenced by previous experience in a rigid, completely predictable way. "Resources" include many intangibles as well as tradable goods that also influence acts of agency in incompletely predictable ways.

These ideas can be applied more specifically to the nature of strategic frames. I now understand strategy as a highly distributed effort to make positive change from the perspective of some situated group of actors; it involves thought but centers on action. The strategic frame exists only because, and when, actors draw upon it. It includes ideas for action and references to the resources that might be used in action. The frame is influenced by, and influences in a loose and probabilistic way, not only individual thought, but also individual will, skill, and values. At the same time, more aggregate categories found in Figure 16.1 (like budgets) can contribute to or detract from the strategic arena.

Figure 16.1 is complicated, but it "punctuates" (Weick, 1969) an even more complex reality. We found it an analytic convenience in *When Firms Change Direction*. Any given cell potentially influences, and is potentially influenced by, every other cell. This is not a format for easy empirical analysis, but the book includes studies at each level that draw on a range of methods, including causal mapping, simulation, and quantitative analysis. Our theoretic agenda was to develop a coherent set of explanations about organizational change at multiple levels of analysis.

16.3.3 Stress and Inertia

I will not attempt to summarize a complicated book in this chapter, but do want to raise one additional issue—the interaction of stress and inertia—that is particularly important to understanding the conditions under which individual cognition or related ideas at more aggregate levels of analysis might change. The interaction of stress and inertia is a dynamic that Jim first explored in research on residential mobility as an economic geographer, where inertia has to do with things like neighbourhood friendships, and stress has to do with things like growing families (Huff and Clark, 1978). "Inertia" is basically satisfaction with the outcomes of current ways of doing things. Stress increases if these outcomes significantly deviate from expectations, in either a positive or a negative direction.

Figure 16.2 summarizes how the interaction of these two concepts is expected to affect individual schemas, interpretations shared by a group, firm level strategic frames and industry recipes. We compute the probability of strategic change in terms of this dynamic, but prediction also depends upon the availability of opportunities and other issues we can investigate in some detail in a book length manuscript. In the end, we were very pleased to be able to predict strategic change over 20 years in two industries with models based on these dynamic interactions.

Figure 16.2 shows that I have maintained an interest in the persistent regularities (schemas, frames, etc.) that many cognitive scientists in management and other disciplines have found problematic. This was facilitated by an interesting methodological departure. We started mixing studies with different ontological and

	Inertia	Stress
Industry	Inertia increases as recipes for success diffuse among organizations providing similar goods and services.	Stress increases as maverick and newcomer firms achieve success in the industry by drawing on unfamiliar recipes.
Firm	Inertia increases as use of a strategic frame routinizes practices that allow individuals and groups to come and go without disrupting the status quo.	Stress accumulates if the use of the current strategic frame does not meet the performance expectations of key stakeholders.
Group	Inertia increases as affiliated individuals reinforce confidence in "shared" interpretations and practices.	Stress increases if mavericks, newcomers, or other groups plausibly challenge shared cognition.
Individual	Inertia arises from the reuse of schema available in the social setting and developed from the individual's own experience.	Stress rises if stimuli attracting attention cannot be interpreted by established or invented schematic frameworks.

Fig. 16.2   Stress and inertia influences on cognitive frameworks

Source: Huff and Huff (2000)

epistemological assumptions in our work, and were delighted to find a justifying quote from Karl Weick:

People who study sensemaking oscillate ontologically because that is what helps them understand the actions of people in everyday life who could care less about ontology.... If people have multiple identities and deal with multiple realities, why should we expect them to be ontological purists? To do so is to limit their capability for sensemaking. More likely is the possibility that over time people will act like interpretivists, functionalists, radical humanists, and radical structuralists. (1995: 34–35)

Weick articulates an enormously freeing research position. It helped me see that the crisis I initially felt from the move away from schema theory in cognitive science was less significant than I at first thought. Many alternative research approaches are available, including Weick's own emphasis on sensemaking, for identifying "islands" of relative coherence. However, this "multilectic" (Huff, 1981) view marks a departure from many expectations about theory development and scientific practice.

16.4 LINK TO PHILOSOPHY OF SCIENCE

The editors of this book ask that authors relate their own theory building efforts to accounts from the philosophy of science. I have been particularly influenced by the work of Thomas Kuhn (1970). It seems obvious to me that Kuhn's emphasis on a "paradigm" as an organizing collection of shared assumptions and practices was strongly influenced by emerging cognitive science. Furthermore, I believe widespread references to Kuhn in management studies are due at least in part to familiarity with the idea of schematic frameworks.

Most of the observations in this chapter can be put into a Kuhnian framework: Cognitive science as a field was developing a strong paradigm around schema theory in the 1970s. Work in MOC drew on this source, but was developing its own interests and methods as a subfield in the subsequent decades. The MOC division in the Academy of Management provided an important forum for regular interaction, and usefully promoted both methodological and theoretical discussions. Similar but distinctive meetings were being held in Europe, with enough international travel to enrich the worldwide gene pool of research ideas.

My mapping book was an attempt to contribute to theoretic arguments in this field as well as codify tools and methods. The book was strengthened by knowledge of and discussion of research activities at the University of Illinois, especially in the business school, but also in psychology and other fields. Other strong centers for cognitive research, especially at New York University, Penn State, Cranfield University, Bath, and Strathclyde provided other hospitable climates.

Although all of this is compatible with Kuhn's account of paradigmatic science, the historical development of MOC also refutes some aspects of his account. In particular, the development of theory has been less coherent than a reading of Kuhn might suggest. Many opportunities for sustained conversation, even in the areas of environmental interpretation and competitor analysis where work has been most concentrated, have not fully developed. In part this seems to be due to a strong desire for independence, which decreases desirable cross-citation, and lures many individuals into new directions before they fully develop their current projects. Cumulative activity also seems to be weakened by journals that encourage claims of independent discovery. But neither of these seem to be sufficient explanation.

I have to look beyond the kind of interactions Kuhn describes to understand the field of managerial and organizational cognition. Karl Popper (1970) suggested that scientists are not as bound by paradigms as Kuhn believed, and I agree. I have also argued that the importance of a paradigm (or a schema, or a theoretic frame) is changed, and potentially diminished, once its presence is revealed (Huff, 1981).

Feyerabend (1970, 1978) also reminds us that children have an enormous capacity to change focus and direction, and so do scientists. This analogy finds a strong echo in Giddens's (1984) descriptions of the nature of rules in structuration theory as similar to the rules of children's play. Theorizing that can quickly change focus and direction also fits a contemporary world that most perceive as requiring rapid change. More specifically, the innate human capacity for shifting focus and changing direction is an important reason why we can only experience "islands of coherence" in strategic practice as well as strategy theory.

Conversation in the philosophy of science, as I understand it, also moved away from the island of coherence Kuhn was part of (Suppe, 1979). Toulmin (1972), Toulmin, et al. (1979), and Hull (1988), in particular, argued that science is what scientists do, and recent meetings of philosophers of science (e.g., http://www.temple.edu/psa2004) provide evidence that studies of specific disciplinary practice continues to attract attention. This emphasis on action is similar to the emphasis I reached in my research. It is also similar to the guiding rationale for this book: by asking individuals to reflect on their own practice, the editors are gathering micro-level data to help inform further theorizing.

16.5 CONCLUDING DISCUSSION

To conclude this chapter I will turn to two last requests from the editors of this book. They ask that authors reflect on what has influenced their activities and offer advice to readers interested in developing theory themselves. The following are several suggestions from my experience.

Work on things that interest you. I have always wanted to understand how to make things "better," and strategy has been an excellent base for that effort. In part because of the evolution of cognitive theory, I now understand strategy as a highly distributed effort to make positive change from the perspective of some situated group of actors; it involves thought but centers on action. Whatever your interest as a reader of this chapter, my strongest advice is to find a subject of study that you find as engaging as I find strategy. A great deal of academic work is solitary, even in multi-authored projects, and the successful outcome of that effort cannot be assured. Absorption in the subject of research is a useful anchor.

Perhaps this advice is especially important for interpretivists, and those working in areas of inquiry that are not yet well articulated, but I think that it is more broadly relevant. "Focus on the phenomenon" is basically advice not to be distracted by fame or fortune—it is more energizing to be intrinsically motivated (Deci, 1995). More specifically, as stewards of the field (and we are all stewards), I believe we should recognize our responsibility for output without over-emphasizing it. Today's strong requirements to publish in "A" journals can become an instrumental focus that weakens an essential requirement for theory building—a motivating personal connection to and interest in the subject of study.

Choose to work in the company of engaging people. The ebb and flow of intellectual conversation is significantly affected by employment. For example, I worked as the cook for a wealthy family in my sophomore year of college. Luckily, both husband and wife were excellent cooks already; I improved my week-day skills enormously as their weekend helper. At the end of the year, as a well-meaning and philanthropic gesture, they offered to pay the considerable tuition for my last two years of college and then send me to Europe as a graduation present, just as they had sent their own children. However: the job not only took an enormous amount of time, it kept me far from the university. I am glad that I was able to say no to their generous proposal.

The next year I worked even harder, but as a research assistant. That led to a job for Harold Guetzgow, a well-known political scientist. His research and the people around him were energizing and again I learned a great deal from my job. The point is that intellectual contribution depends upon context. My advice is to walk away from jobs that deplete rather than nourish your intellectual efforts; conversely, seek places where you learn new things.

Focus, but be willing to jump. Of course, relocation is a drastic step, and I have never found the "perfect" situation, although after the fact I see my time at the University of Illinois as very close to the ideal, and my current position looks very promising. It makes sense to find what and who can be interesting where you are before taking Hirschman's (1970) exit option. I have searched for new ideas in every job I have taken, and found them.

In retrospect, however, the attempt to take advantage of local opportunity in a number of different universities spread my list of publications more widely than I now think is strategic. Though I still find the things that I have published interesting, I advise pursing a smaller number of topics more intensely. This may seem like advice for succeeding in a world that so highly values output, but that is not what I mean. It makes intellectual sense to build depth in a few areas of inquiry. Focus increases expertise and allows stronger conversational connections to develop (Huff, 1998). The advice in short: look carefully under the light post of your current work when you search for interesting new projects.

Sustained attention is particularly important in emerging fields of inquiry. It takes a group of people committed to look in the same direction for a new field to develop. Understanding grows as they attend the same conferences, arrange smaller meetings, use the same words, piggyback on each other's ideas, establish web-sites, publish articles on similar topics, arrange special issues that focus public attention on new approaches, and edit books that establish the contours of inquiry.

All of this makes sense, but it is accompanied by a contradictory corollary. The corollary is based on the observation that creative contribution often comes from outside of an area of inquiry. Structuration theory helps explain the reason for success as the transfer of one logic to another sphere of action (Whittington, 1992). Black (1962) more directly argues that all scientific models are metaphors—they generate insight by describing something "as if" it were something else. Thus, an occasional discontinuous step can contribute important new content to theory as well as be personally invigorating.

Every professional move I have made has had that salutary effect. I was thinking in terms of decision making at UCLA, but switched to cognition at the University of Illinois. I learned a lot about entrepreneurship at the University of Colorado, and then broadened my focus to an international level at London Business School. Now at the Technical University of Munich, I am thinking in terms of German competitive advantage and the link between innovation and motivation. In each case, I have refashioned past insights into new forms.

Accept the fact that you cannot orchestrate your impact. Many of the things I tried hardest to arrange did not work out as I anticipated. For example, I chose Wiley as a publisher for *Mapping Strategic Thought* for two primary reasons: it was a strong international publisher, and the editor promised to publish the book for $35 a copy. However, the conditions driving publishing changed by the time I completed the manuscript, and the book ended up retailing for what then seemed like an astronomical sum of $138, effectively precluding purchase by many of the doctoral students I had hoped to attract.

That was very disappointing, and so was the fact that almost immediately after I relinquished the manuscript, I realized that I had not given sufficient attention to the work of people outside of the United States, even though I had overtly chosen a publisher with international reach. I deeply regretted the fact that I had insufficiently grasped an opportunity to contribute to the internationalization of intellectual conversation on MOC just as I was beginning to be more engaged in that conversation.

In retrospect, however, I think that the book had as much impact on doctoral students and an international audience as it did on established scholars in the United States, despite these disappointments. Why? Perhaps because cognition was gaining attention among these two groups just as the book was published. A reviewer of this chapter asked if it did in fact rival Sims and Gioia (1986) or Walsh (1995) in impact. It is impossible for me to answer that question. I know that it had some effect, though I have been surprised that the methodological agenda seems to have been more widely recognized than the attempt I made to categorize alternative approaches to defining cognition. Certainly the publication of this book and other articles led to new opportunities, including the invitation to contribute to this volume. Giddens's (1984) arguments about the close connection between agency and structure are interesting to apply here. My broad response to the reviewer is that my initial act of agency became part of the structural resources available in MOC. Basically, we have to accept that we are temporary custodians for ideas in play. They pass through our hands, are molded in the process, and then we pass them on.

Think about the increasingly complex audience of theoretic development. My reviewer did not ask if *When Firms Change Direction* has had significant impact, nevertheless I will answer that it was a finalist for the Terry Book award, and it too has led to some interesting new conversations. However, but it is far more complex than my first book, and exemplifies in its diversity and relative idiosyncrasy an issue that increasingly challenges effective theorizing in management and the social sciences more generally.

Theoretic conversations are increasingly porous. Cross-field citation is encouraged by growing interdisciplinary contacts in university courses and scholarly meetings, and accelerated by digital search engines. As a result, however, it is much harder for the theorist to establish and maintain an intellectual conversation that can have significant impact.

I spend much of my teaching time these days trying to help people write for scholarly publication. Almost always, a student's initial idea is too diffuse. An early draft often has a title like "Leading multidisciplinary IT teams in a complex global environment: a dynamic perspective." Is this going to be a paper about leadership? Multidisciplinary teams? IT? Complexity? Global Environments? Dynamics? All of these things, and more, are possible. But it is almost impossible to simultaneously advance knowledge in all of these areas in an article, a dissertation or even a book. Even if one could keep the large number of concepts involved in mind, a relevant question would be: who cares? There are few who would find each of these ideas equally compelling.

My point is that our effectiveness as scholars is challenged by a world where scholars read and respond to inputs from so many different disciplines, and think simultaneously about so many different issues. At least two things have to happen to make progress. First, I am convinced by Weick's (1995) argument that it is impossible to make sense of a situation without an identity, so it is important for theorists to decide (and declare) who they are. Second, it is impossible to develop new theory without a sense of where one stands with respect to other scholars. The key task is not just to constrain attention so that a coherent contribution can be made, but also to establish links to other scholars so that collective progress can be made. When I started my career as an academic, I thought that the theorizing burden was on my shoulders, now I know that it is on "our" shoulders—but I have to find "our" in order to proceed.

Institutionalize community. Bill Starbuck and Marlene Fiol took the initiative to organize the first meetings of a cognitive interest group at the Academy of Management. That effort led to the MOC division, which now provides the infrastructure for assembling an annual meeting of research presentations and professional development activities. I have been struck by the importance of this organization for MOC as an emerging field of inquiry as I thought through this chapter. Many people in my cohort have stopped working on managerial and organizational cognition in the last decade; quite a few stopped doing research altogether as they were lured into administration and other activities. Luckily, the routines of the MOC division at the Academy of Management support continuity and the development of new voices that provide new insights into the cognitive aspects of organizing.

Similar institutional support is important within universities. In writing this chapter, I have wondered if *Mapping Strategic Thought* offered a chance for leadership that I should have more clearly recognized and pursued. Looking back, I wish that I had thought about establishing a center for cognitive research in management. It would have given more structure to my work; it also could have facilitated the work of others. Both of the books mentioned in this chapter did those things to some extent, as I intended them to, but I now have a clearer idea of the importance of enduring social organizations for intellectual conversation.

In the last several years, I have given a great deal of attention to building infrastructures for management research. They are particularly necessary in management because the organizations we study are so large in comparison to business schools and the kind of research they can support. It is time for us to increase the scale of our efforts. That is a matter of expanded socio-political organization as well as expanded thought.

Learn from teaching and practice. Karl Weick (1995: 12) perceptively observes that you don't know what you think until you see what you say. The first place I often say something about new ideas is in the classroom. Because I had a young family at the beginning of my career, I chose to do very little consulting, but I did gradually increase my contact with executives through research and teaching.

As I became convinced by methodologies that treat the organizational insider as a research partner (Bartunek and Louis, 1996; Balogun, Huff, and Johnson, 2003), those contacts became increasingly important. I still draw on what I learned from the three school superintendents Lou Pondy and I (Huff and Pondy, 1985; Pondy and Huff, 1988) intensively observed for two years in the 1980s, for example. Their capacity to strategize at multiple levels of analysis encouraged my attempts to theorize in a more complex way. I mention this now, because this chapter on theory building and the influence of other academics did not adequately stress the insights gained from practice.

Contribute to conversations about assessment. I have thought more about contributions *to* practice once I started to worry that the academic study of management is endangered rather than improved by increasing attention to assessment (Huff, 2000). The positive side of the current hyper-attention to journal rankings is that it encourages authors to find a broad audience. One negative is that the audience of top ranked journals is overwhelmingly academic. Further, the early pressure to publish can pervert both individual attention and the development of inquiry.

Individual scholars, especially those without tenure, lose intellectual connection with their work if they feel forced to bow to editorial and reviewer suggestions in order to be published. Narrow definitions of contribution based on appearance in a small list of journals make that almost inevitable, and around the world more and more business schools are adopting these definitions. The consumption of theory also is affected because the number of "top" journals is too small to produce the varied inputs needed to understand the complex and changing world of organizations.

I worry that assessment systems increase the likelihood that publication is branded by journal location rather than being read. Even more problematic is the fact that journal articles alone cannot encompass the complex understanding that complex organizational interactions require. More discussion of these issues is needed. In my opinion we urgently need to invent assessment systems that will foster the requisite variety (Ashby, 1956) demanded by our subject.

Have fun. However, I do not want to end on a pessimistic note. In my current job I am thinking a lot about motivation, and this summer read Linus Torvald's (2001) book *Just for Fun*. Though initiator of Linux, and an important articulator for the open source movement more broadly, he is neither philosopher, psychologist, nor cognitive scientist. When invited to talk on a panel with a group of philosophers, however, Torvald made an observation that seems wise to me. He said that people do what they do for one of three reasons: security, social relationships, or fun. I have been fortunate in a dual career family to not have to worry very much about basic security, and I certainly wish you as reader the same good fortune—it is hard to theorize without security, though of course a few notable exceptions have done so.

With respect to the second motivator, I hope that the impact of social relationships on my intellectual efforts is clear, though I wish I could have mentioned more people whose presence in my life has made an emotional as well as an intellectual difference. The philosophy of science emphasizes that science is intrinsically social, but it could say even more about the importance of interpersonal contact for theory building.

I began this conclusion with something not on Torvald's list: a desire not just to understand, but to make things better. Certainly, this is an important driver of open source, though Torvald's explanation of the open source movement relies on the pleasures of relationship (both close comrades and unknown users) and on his last point: fun. Academic life (as opposed, say, to the undergraduate experience) is not envied by outsiders as a source of fun. Yet, I do what I do because it frequently generates that combination of energy and well being that I think of as fun. That is an excellent summary thought to emphasize in a book focused on the difficult and serious effort of building theory.

REFERENCES

ASHBY, W. R. (1956). *Introduction to Cybernetics*. London: Wiley, ch. 11.

BARLEY, S. R. (1983). Semiotics and the study of occupations and organizational cultures. *Administrative Science Quarterly*, 28: 393–413.

BARNARD, C. I. (1938). *The Functions of the Executive*. Cambridge, Mass.: Harvard University Press.

BALOGUN, J., HUFF, A. S., and JOHNSON, P. (2003). Three responses to the methodological challenges of studying strategizing. *Journal of Management Studies*, 40(1): 197–224.

BARTUNEK, J., and LOUIS, M. (1996). *Insider/Outsider Team Research*, Thousand Oaks, Calif.: Sage.

BERGER, P. L., and LUCKMAN, T. (1967). *The Social Construction of Reality*. New York: Doubleday.

BLACK, M. (1962). *Models and Metaphors*. Ithaca, NY: Cornell University.

BOWER, J. L., and DOZ, Y. (1979). Strategy formulation: a social and political process. In D. E. Schendel and C. W. Hofer (eds.), *Strategic Management*. Boston: Little, Brown.

BOWMAN, E. H. (1976). Strategy and the weather. *Sloan Management Review*, 17(2): 49–62.

DECI, E. L., with FLASTE, R. (1995). *Why We Do What We Do*. London: Penguin.

DE WIT, B., and MEYER, R. (2004). *Strategy: Process, Content, Context*, 3rd edn. London: Thompson.

EDEN, C., and SPENDER, J. C. (eds.) (1998). *Managerial and Organizational Cognition: Theory, Methods and Research*. London: Sage.

FEYERABEND, P. (1970). Consolations for the specialist. In I. Lakatos and A. Musgrave (eds.), *Criticism and the Growth of Knowledge*: 197–230. Cambridge: Cambridge University Press.

—— (1978). *Against Method*. New York: Schoken.

GIDDENS, A. (1984). *The Constitution of Society: Outline of the Theory of Structuration.* Berkeley: University of California Press.

HIRSCHMAN, A. O. (1970). *Exit, Voice and Loyalty.* Cambridge, Mass.: Harvard University Press.

HODGKINSON, G. P. (2002). Comparing managers' mental models of competition: why self-report measures of belief similarity won't do. *Organization Studies,* 23: 63–72.

—— and SPARROW, P. R. (2002). *The Competent Organization.* Buckingham, UK: Open University Press.

—— (1981). Multilectic methods of inquiry. *Human Systems Management,* 2: 83–94.

—— (1982). Industry influences on strategy reformulation. *Strategic Management Journal,* 3: 119–131.

—— (ed.) (1990). *Mapping Strategic Thought.* Chichester: Wiley.

—— (2000). Presidential Address: Changes in Organizational Knowledge Production. *Academy of Management Review,* 25: 2.

—— and FLETCHER, K. E. (1990). Strategy reformulation at AT&T. In A. S. Huff (ed.), *Mapping Strategic Thought.* Chichester: Wiley.

—— and HUFF, J. O., with BARR, P. S. (2000). *When Firms Change Direction.* Oxford: Oxford University Press.

—— and PONDY L. R. (1985). Achieving Routine in Organizational Change. *Journal of Management,* 11(2), 103–116.

—— and SCHWENK, C. R. (1990). Bias and sensemaking in good times and bad. In A. S. Huff (ed.), *Mapping Strategic Thought.* Chichester: Wiley.

HUFF, J. O., and CLARK, W. A. V. (1978). Cumulative stress and cumulative inertia: A behavioral model of the decision to move. *Environmental Planning,* 10(10): 101–119.

HULL, D. (1988). *Science as a Process: An Evolutionary Account of the Social and Conceptual Development of Science.* Chicago: University of Chicago Press.

KELLY, G. (1955). *The Psychology of Personal Constructs,* vols. 1 and 2. New York: Norton.

KUHN, T. S. (1970). *The Structure of Scientific Revolutions.* Chicago: University of Chicago Press.

MINTZBERG, H. (1978). Patterns of strategy formation. *Management Science,* 24: 934–938.

NARYANAN, V. K., and KEMMERER, B. (2001). A Cognitive Perspective on Strategic Management: Contributions, Challenges and Implications. Presentation at the Academy of Management.

PONDY, L. R., and HUFF, A. S. (1988). Budget cutting in Riverside: Emergent policy reframing as a process of conflict minimization. In L. R. Pondy, R. Boland, and H. Thomas (eds.), *Managing Ambiguity and Change:* 177–200. New York: Wiley.

POPPER, K. R. (1970). Normal science and its dangers. In I. Lakatos and A. Musgrave (eds.), *Criticism and the Growth of Knowledge:* 51–58. Cambridge: Cambridge University Press.

PORAC, J. F., and THOMAS, H. (1990). Taxonomic mental models in competitor definitions. *Academy of Management Review,* 15: 224–240.

—— —— and BADEN-FULLER, C. (1989). Competitive groups as cognitive communities: The case of Scottish knitwear manufacturers. *Journal of Management Studies,* 26: 397–416.

—— —— and EMME, B. (1987). Knowing the competition: Mental models of retailing strategies. In Johnson, G. (ed.) *Business Strategy and Retailing:* 55–79. New York: Wiley.

REGER, R. (1990). Managerial thought structures and competitive positioning. In A. S. Huff (ed.), *Mapping Strategic Thought.* Chichester: Wiley.

REGER, R. and HUFF, A. S. (1993). Strategic groups: A cognitive perspective. *Strategic Management Journal*, 14: 103–124.

SIMON, H. A. (1976). *Administrative Behavior*, 3rd edn. New York: Free Press. (Originally published in 1947.)

SIMS, H. P., and GIOIA, D. A. (eds.) (1986). *The Thinking Organization*. San Francisco: Jossey-Bass.

SPENDER, J. C. (1980). Strategy making in business. Unpublished doctoral dissertation. Manchester University, UK.

—— (1989). *Industry recipes: an enquiry into the nature and sources of managerial judgment*. Oxford: Blackwell.

STARBUCK, W. H. (1983). Organizations as action generators. *American Sociological Review*, 48: 91–103.

—— (1993). Strategizing in the real world. *International Journal of Technology Management*, 8: 77–85.

SUPPE, F. (1979). *The Structure of Scientific Theories*. Champaign-Urbana, Ill.: University of Illinois Press.

TENBRUNSEL, A., GALVIN, T. L., NEALE, M., and BAZERMAN, M. (1996). Cognitions in organizations. In S. Clegg, C. Hardy, and W. Nord (eds.), *Handbook of Organization Studies*. London: Sage.

TORVALD, L. (2001). *Just for Fun*. New York: HarperCollins.

TOULMIN, S. (1958). *The Uses of Argument*. Cambridge: Cambridge University Press.

—— (1972). *Human Understanding*, vol. 1. Princeton: Princeton University Press.

—— RIEKE, R., and JANIK, A. (1979). *An Introduction to Reasoning*. New York: Macmillan.

WALSH, J. P. (1995). Managerial and organizational cognition: Notes from a trip down memory lane. *Organization Science*, 6(3): 280–321.

WEICK, K. E. (1969). *The Social Psychology of Organizing*. Reading, Mass.: Addison-Wesley.

—— (1995). *Sensemaking in Organizations*. Thousand Oaks, Calif.: Sage.

WHITTINGTON, R. (1992). Putting Giddens into action: Social systems and managerial agency. *Journal of Management Studies*, 29(4): 693–712.

WINOGRAD, T., and FLORES, F. (1986). *Understanding computers and cognition*. Norwood, NJ: Ablex.

WOODRUM, E. (1984). Mainstreaming content analysis in social science—methodological advantages, obstacles, solutions. *Social Science Research*, 13(1): 1–9.

CHAPTER 17

DEVELOPING THEORY ABOUT THE DEVELOPMENT OF THEORY

HENRY MINTZBERG

I HAVE no clue how I develop theory. I don't think about it; I just try to do it. Indeed, thinking about it could be dangerous:

> The centipede was happy quite
>   Until a toad in fun
> Said, "Pray, which leg goes after which?"
> That worked her mind to such a pitch,
> She lay distracted in a ditch
> Considering how to run.
>
> (Mrs. Edward Craster, 1871)

I have no desire to lay distracted in a ditch considering how to develop theory. Besides, that's the work of cognitive psychologists, who study concept attainment, pattern recognition, and the like, but never really tell us much about how we think. Nonetheless, I'll take the bait, this once, at the request of the editors of this book, because I probably won't get far either.

I want to start with what theory isn't and then go on to what theory development isn't, for me at least, before turning, very tentatively, to what they seem to be.

17.1 WHAT THEORY ISN'T: TRUE

It is important to realize, at the outset, that all theories are false. They are, after all, just words and symbols on pieces of paper, about the reality they purport to describe; they are not that reality. So they simplify it. This means we must choose our theories according to how useful they are, not how true they are. A simple example will explain.

In 1492, we discovered truth. The earth is round, not flat. Or did we? Is it?

To make this discovery, Columbus sailed on the sea. Did the builders of his ships, or at least subsequent ones, correct for the curvature of the sea? I suspect not; to this day, the flat earth theory works perfectly well for the building of ships.

But not for the sailing of ships. Here the round earth theory works much better. Otherwise, we would not have heard from Columbus again. Actually that theory is not true either, as a trip to Switzerland will quickly show. It is no coincidence that it was not a Swiss who came up with the round earth theory. Switzerland is the land of the bumpy earth theory, also quite accurate—there. Finally, even considered overall, say from a satellite, the earth is not round; it bulges at the equator (although what to do with this theory I'm not sure).

If the earth isn't quite round or flat or even even, then how can we expect any other theory to be true? Donald Hebb, the renowned psychologist, resolved this problem quite nicely: "A good theory is one that holds together long enough to get you to a better theory."

But as our examples just made clear, the next theory is often not better so much as more useful for another application. For example, we probably still use Newton's physics far more than that of Einstein. This is what makes fashion in the social sciences so dysfunctional, whether the economists' current obsession with free markets or the psychologists' earlier captivation with behavioralism. So much effort about arm's lengths and salivating dogs. Theory itself may be neutral, but the promotion of any one theory as truth is dogma, and that stops thinking in favor of indoctrination.

So we need all kinds of theories—the more, the better. As researchers, scholars, and teachers, our obligation is to stimulate thinking, and a good way to do that is to offer alternate theories—multiple explanations of the same phenomena. Our students and readers should leave our classrooms and publications pondering, wondering, thinking—not knowing.

17.2 WHAT THEORY DEVELOPMENT ISN'T: OBJECTIVE AND DEDUCTIVE

If theories aren't true, how can they be objective? We make a great fuss about objectivity in science, and research, and in so doing, often confuse its two very different processes. There is the creation of theory, which this book is supposed to be about, and there is the testing of theory. The former relies on the process of induction—from the particular to the general, tangible data to general concepts—while the latter is rooted in deduction—from the general to the particular.

These two processes can certainly feed each other, in fact great scholarship, at least in the hard sciences, goes back and forth between them. But not necessarily by the same person. I'm glad that other people test theory—i.e., do deductive research. That is useful; we need to find out, if not that any particular theory is false (since all are), at least how, why, when, and where it works best, compared with other theories. I just don't believe we need so many people doing that in our field, compared with the few who create interesting theory (for reasons I shall suggest shortly).

As for myself, I have always considered life too short to test theories. It never ceases to amaze me how we tie ourselves in knots testing hypothesis in our field, whether it be "does planning pay?" or "do companies do well by doing good?" Maybe the problem is that our theories are about ourselves, and how can we be objective about that, compared with researchers who study molecules and stones.

What makes me salivate is induction: inventing explanations about things. Not finding them—that's truth; inventing them. We don't discover theory; we create it. And that's great fun; if only more of our doctoral students took the chance. But no, they are taught to be objective, scientific (in the narrow sense of the term), which means no invention please, only deduction. *That* is academically correct.

17.2.1 Popper Research

In the *Strategic Management Journal* a few years ago, its editor wrote in an editorial that "if our field is to continue its growth, and develop important linkages between research and practice, as it must, then we need to improve our research and understand that relevance comes from rigor" (Schendel 1995: 1). This claim itself was not rigorous, since no evidence was presented on its behalf. As usual, it was taken as an article of faith.

Read the "rigorous" literature in our field, and you may come to the opposite conclusion: that this kind of rigor—methodological rigor—gets in the way of relevance. People too concerned about doing their research correctly often fail to do it insightfully.

Of course, intellectual rigor—namely, clear thinking—does not get in the way of relevance. The editor referred to this too in his editorial (as "careful logic"), but what he meant was the following: "Research in this field should not be speculation, opinion, or clever journalism; it should be about producing replicable work from which conclusions can be drawn independently of whoever does the work or applies the work results" (p. 1).

I think of this as bureaucratic research, because it seeks to factor out the human dimension—imagination, insight, discovery. If I study a phenomenon and come up with an interesting theory, is that not rigorous because someone else would not have come up with the same theory? Accept that and you must reject pretty much all theory, from physics to philosophy, because all were idiosyncratic efforts, the inventions of creative minds. ("I'm sorry, Mr. Einstein, but your theory of relativity is speculative, not proven, so we cannot publish it.") Sumantra Ghoshal wrote to the same editor about an article that he had earlier reviewed:

I have seen the article three times... The reviewing process, over these iterations, has changed the flavor of the article significantly. I believe that the new argument... is interesting but unavoidably superficial... Citations and literature linkages have driven out most of the richness and almost all of the speculation that I liked so much in the first draft. While the article perhaps looks more "scholarly," I am not sure who exactly gains from this look... I cannot get over the regret of description, insight and speculation losing out to citation, definition and tightness. (Reprinted in Mintzberg, 2004: 399)

But it does so much of the time, because we confuse rigor with relevance, and deduction with induction. Indeed the proposal I received for this very book did that: "... the process of theory building and testing is objective and enjoys a self-correcting characteristic that is unique to science. Thus the checks and balances involved in the development and testing of theory are so conceived and used that they control and verify knowledge development in an objective manner independent of the scientist." They sure do: that is why we see so little induction in our field, the creation of so little interesting theory.

Karl Popper, whose name a secretary of mine once mistyped as "Propper," wrote a whole book about *The Logic of Scientific Discovery* (1959). In the first four pages (27–30), in a section entitled "The Problem of Induction," he dismissed this process, or more exactly what he called, oxymoronically, "inductive logic." Yet with regard to theory development itself, he came out much as I did above.

The initial stage, the act of conceiving or inventing a theory, seems to me neither to call for logic analysis not to be susceptible of it. The question how it happens that a new idea occurs to a man—whether it is a musical theme, a dramatic conflict, or a scientific theory—may be of great interest to empirical psychology; but it is irrelevant to the logical analysis of scientific knowledge. This latter is concerned not with *questions of fact* (Kant's *quid facti?*), but only with questions of *justification or validity* (Kant's *quid juris?*)... Accordingly,

I shall distinguish sharply between the process of conceiving a new idea, and the methods and results of examining it logically. (Popper, 1959: 31)

Fair enough. But why, when he devoted the rest of his book to "the deductive method of testing" (p. 30), did Popper title his book "The Logic of Scientific *Discovery*"? What discovery is there in deduction? Maybe something about the how, why, when, and where of given theory (as noted earlier), but not the what—not the creation of the theory itself. (Indeed why did Popper call his book *The Logic of Scientific Discovery* when in the passage above he used, more correctly, the phrase "scientific *knowledge*"?) And why have untold numbers of researchers-in-training been given this book to read as if it is science, and research, when it is only one side of these, and the side wholly dependent on the other, which is dismissed with a few words at the beginning? What impression has that left on doctoral students in our fields? (Read the journals.) As Karl Weick (1969: 63) quoted Somerset Maugham, "She plunged into a sea of platitudes, and with the powerful breast stroke of a channel swimmer made her confident way toward the while cliff of the obvious."

Popper devoted his book to deductive research for the purposes of falsifying theories. But as noted earlier, falsification by itself adds nothing; only when it is followed by the creation of new theories or at least the significant adaptation of old ones do we get the necessary insights. As Alfred Hirshman put it, "A model is never defeated by the facts, however damaging, but only by another model."

17.2.2 Qualitative Research?

While on this subject, let me try to clarify another confusion, the use of the terms "quantitative" and "qualitative" when we mean "deductive" and "inductive." It is as if all deduction is quantitative and all induction is qualitative. Not so. Theories can be assessed without numbers (even, dare I say, judgmentally—which, by the way, is what most seven point scales really amount to), just as numbers can be used to induce theories. Indeed, I was invited to contribute to this volume because of an inductive study I did that was loaded with numbers (*The Nature of Managerial Work*, 1973; for a better example, see my paper with Alexandra McHugh, "Strategy Formation in an Adhocracy" (1985), which has often been referred to as qualitative even though it is based on a study of 3000 films tabulated every which way).

This mix-up leaves the impression that "quantitative" research is somehow proper (or Propper)—i.e., "scientific"—even if it contributes no insight, while qualitative research is something to be tolerated at best, and then only when exemplary. This is the double standard that pervades our academic journals to their terrible discredit. It also manifests itself destructively in doctoral courses that teach quantitative methods (mostly statistics) as rites of passages. Those who cannot handle the fancy techniques cannot get the doctoral degree, even though there is all kinds of wonderful research with no numbers. Why not, instead, preclude from doctoral program students incapable of coming up with interesting ideas. Imagine that!

17.3 WHAT THEORY SEEMS TO BE: A CONTINUUM

I have not thought much about what theory is either. I am interested in explanation, and don't much care what it's called, theory or otherwise.

When I think about it, however, I see explanation along a continuum, from lists (categories), to typologies (comprehensive lists), to impressions of relationships among factors (not necessarily "variables": that sounds too reified for many of the factors I work with), to causations between and patterns among these relationships, to fully explanatory models (which interweave all the factors in question).

I think of myself as an obsessive categorizer—I love neat typologies—but I have done my share of trying to develop relationships and models too.

As noted earlier, I am supposed to be using here my research on managerial work, presumably as I first developed it in the 1960s (for 1973). There I described various characteristics of managerial work and a framework of the roles managers seem to perform, as well as discussing variations in managerial work. Much of that was more about lists and typologies, with lots of impressions as well as numbers, than a full-blown model. (Put more exactly, perhaps, the models in that book were its weakest part.) Only much later ("Rounding Out the Manager's Job," 1994), did I come up with more of a model, by using the categories of my earlier work as well as those of other studies.

The theory development of which I am more proud—I see it as my most parsimonious work—is in my book *The Structuring of Organizations* (Mintzberg, 1979a). I described first how organizations function, in terms of five basic parts and five essential mechanisms of coordination. After describing the basic parameters of designing organizations (positions, superstructure, linkages, etc.), and contingency factors influencing that designing (age and size of the organization, complexity and dynamism of its environment, etc.), I wove all this together around a typology of five models: forms, or "configurations" (i.e., patterns) of organizing, each a theory unto itself, with detailed explanations and causations. Only later (1989, Section II) did I weave these different models into a model in its own right, using what I called forces alongside forms, to discuss configuration, combination, conversion, contradiction, and competencies, ending with a life cycle model of organizations.

17.4 WHAT THEORY DEVELOPMENT SEEMS TO BE: UNEXPECTED

We get interesting theory when we let go of all this scientific correctness, or to use a famous phrase, suspend our disbeliefs, and allow our minds to roam freely and creatively—to muse like mad, albeit immersed in an interesting, revealing context. Hans Selye, the great physiologist, captured this sentiment perfectly in quoting one item on a list of "Intellectual Immortalities" put out by a well-known physiology department: "Generalizing beyond one's data." Selye quoted approvingly a commentator who asked whether it would have been more correct for this to read: "*Not* generalizing beyond one's data" (1964: 228). No generalizing beyond the data, no theory. And no theory, no insight. And if no insight, why do research?

Theory is insightful when it surprises, when it allows us to see profoundly, imaginatively, unconventionally into phenomena we thought we understood. To quote Will Henry, "What is research but a blind date with knowledge." No matter how accepted eventually, theory is of no use unless it initially surprises—that is, changes perceptions. (A professor of mine once said that theories go through three stages: first they're wrong; then they're subversive; finally they're obvious.)

All of this is to say that there is a great deal of art and craft in true science. In fact, an obsession with the science, narrowly considered, gets in the way of scientific development. To quote Berger, "In science, as in love, a concentration on technique is likely to lead to impotence" (1963: 13).

17.5 SOME [EMERGING] PROPOSITIONS ABOUT THEORY DEVELOPMENT

So how to do this generalizing beyond the data, this subjective, idiosyncratic musing like mad in order to climb the scale from lists to models? I have no idea what goes on in my head, as I noted earlier, but I can describe, in a series of propositions, some of the things that happen outside of it, up to and after the point where my head takes over. So let's look at what can be articulated, while accepting that this is about a process that is most significantly tacit.

First, I start with an interesting question, not a fancy hypothesis. Hypotheses close me down; questions open me up. I have started with, for example: What do managers do? How do organizations structure themselves? How do strategies form? And now: How can we redress the balance in this economically obsessed world?

I think of this approach as pull, not push, and I believe it key to theory development. Let yourself be pulled by an important concern out there, not pushed by some elegant construct in here. Take your lead from behavior in practice. And ask the big questions. In my experience, the problem in doctoral theses, and subsequent research people do, is not that they bite off more than they can chew, but that they nibble less than they should consume. Or to use another metaphor, I admire researchers who try to build cathedrals, not lay a few bricks. As Fritjds Capra put it in *Turning Point,* "If I ask a particle question, [the electron] will give me a particle answer" (1982: 77).

Second, I need to be stimulated by rich description. There are novelists who sit down with a blank pad and write—management theorists too, I suppose. I can't do that. I need to be stimulated by some body of rich inputs that I see right before me. Tangible data is best—the "thick" description that Clifford Geertz has described—not data all nicely ordered and systematically presented. (Robert Darnton has described Geertz's work as "open-ended, rather than bottom-lined.") And stories are best of all, because while hard data may suggest some relationship, it is this kind of rich description that best helps to explain it. So anecdotal data is not incidental to theory development at all, but an essential part of it.

But this needn't be data *per se.* My favorite among my own books, *The Structuring of Organizations,* was written out of the theories, research findings, and descriptions of others—in other words, it was based mostly on existing literature. But even here, it was the thickest descriptive literature, closest to the data, most notably in Joan Woodward's work (to which I shall return), that helped me most in the development of the theory. Highly structured descriptions, for example based on data collection around a couple of abstract variables, was far less useful. Think of the would-be theorist trying to swim in water as compared with a tank of shredded paper.

Third, and perhaps trickiest of all, I need to bootstrap an outline. That is, I must have an outline to write down my ideas, even if the object of writing down my ideas is to come up with an outline. This is the ultimate problem in creating theory (and, I suspect, doing interesting writing in general).

No matter how we *think* about our theories, ultimately we have to convey them to other people in linear order, and that means mostly in words. Mozart claimed about creating a symphony that the "best of all is the hearing it all at once." (He also wrote about being able to "see the whole of it at a single glance in my mind.") Wow! I wonder what that's like. But even Mozart had to convert it to linear order on paper so that others could play it.

The trouble with linear order, of course, is that the world we are trying to explain does not function in linear order. Now, if I don't start with a blank sheet of paper, but in my case all kinds of little papers scribbled with my notes, about findings and ideas, etc., plus neat sheets of paper printed with the findings and ideas of others, what am I to do with them? How can I order them when I don't have an outline (an order) to begin with? But how can I get an outline if I have no way to code the very inputs to the outline. And if I *do* have an outline, or theory, to begin with, how am I supposed to suspend disbelief to get to a better theory? Theory *is* belief.

There is no solution to this bootstrap problem except, I guess, something equivalent to how you lift yourself up by the bootstraps. A little bit at a time, using whatever you can get a hold of. (Climb on a stone? Tie a rope to a tree?)

Linear outlines are great. I still have the one I finally ended up with for *The Structuring of Organizations*—about 200 pages long! It was so detailed that I wrote the first draft of this 500-page book in three months. I never did such an outline again, and always pay the price. I used much sloppier outlines, and so have had to rewrite and rewrite and rewrite. Very messy to redo an outline in prose! *The Structuring of Organizations* came out faster—at least *once* I had that outline— and far more coherently, or perhaps I should say orderly, than any other book I have written. It literally integrates from the opening dedication to the final sentence. On the other hand, messy can sometimes be better, because it can be richer. To quote Voltaire, "Doubt is not a pleasant state, but certainty is a ridiculous one" (in Seldes, 1983: 713).

Fourth, linearity notwithstanding, I use diagrams of all kinds to express the inter-relationships among the concepts I am dealing with. [Let's stop for a moment and consider what is happening here. I am writing, by hand, for reasons I'll explain in a later point. (See what I mean about linearity. I keep mixing up the order of my points. What a pain. If only, like Mozart, you and I could see the whole of this at a single glance in our minds.) I decided after the last point that I would start each new point on a new page, so I can easily go back and stick in points I hadn't thought about before, that should come between. This may seem like an awfully clever idea—I'm just kidding—but it wasn't really an idea. I happened to start the last point on a new page because the previous one finished at the bottom, and then I thought, hey, that's good, I should do that for all the points. You see, here too I am responding to what I see before me. I do have an outline—some scribbles about various points I want to make, based on having reviewed other papers I wrote about research (Mintzberg, 1973: Appendix C, 1979a, 1982, 1991, 2002, 2004: 250–252, and 1983 with Danny Miller). But I haven't looked at this outline for awhile, because as I got into the first point, all kinds of other points occurred to me. It's the rendering of this on paper that really gets the ideas flowing in my head. Please take this as point #5.]

My work is loaded with diagrams, seeking to express every which way how the ideas I am trying to make come together. Aristotle said that: "The soul...never thinks without a picture" (2001: 594). I try to help my soul think. Years ago, I wrote an autobiographical piece called "Twenty-five Years Later...the Illusive Strategy" (Mintzberg, 1993: see it on www.mintzberg.org) for a collection Art Bedeian put together. In looking over my own publications, tracking my own strategies as patterns in my writings, much like I have tracked the strategies of organizations, I found something interesting: there were distinct periods in the diagrams I did. As in painters' work (e.g., Picasso's "Blue Period"). I used rectangular boxes (flow charts, and like) in my earliest years (as in *The Nature of Managerial Work)*, blobs to depict organizations in the next period (as in *The Structuring of Organizations)*, and then everything went into circles of one kind or another.

These diagrams really help me a great deal: I can see it all at a glance, even if outside my head. But not always into other heads. I have been puzzled to find that some people are puzzled by these diagrams. They don't think in such terms, nor are they even able to *see* it in the work of others. Even many of my own doctoral students, sometimes including the best, when urged by me to express their ideas in diagrammatic form, have not gotten past a 2 × 2 matrix or two. Maybe this has to do with my education as a a mechanical engineer—probably the only thing left of that—or at least my predisposition to do that kind of education, because I like to *see* things altogether, at a single glance, to quote a famous composer.

[Back to what's going on here. As new ideas are coming up, while I am writing down the previous ones like mad (maybe I'm just the medium?), I make little notes in the margins so as not to forget them. Now I am going to go back and look at them. Then I'm going to return to the outline to see if I am remotely on track. I know I am— remotely. But first I should point out that I did not make a note about inserting this italic type in these square brackets, about these going ons here and now (as you are now reading), because it occurred to me to do that just as I started the fourth point (above), and so I did it straight away, although it is only now, in this second of these square brackets, that I realize what I am doing: I am using this *experience itself to figure out how I develop theory (if you can call these musings theory). Got that?! [If the above seems confusing—as I reread it, I can't blame you, so maybe you should reread it too!—then you should be getting an idea of what's really involved in the development of theory.] Think about how much richer is this writing experience itself as the basis for writing this paper than a book I did thirty years ago. How can I theorize about that, as compared with this, which is happening right here and now? What better to theorize about? So I have gone back and changed the title of this paper. It was "Sorry— No Theory for Theory." Now it is "Developing Theory About the Development of Theory."]*

[Now this is interesting. I have just gone back to my notes and found a note about what are the "sources of inputs" for theorizing. It said: "any and all—you never know what will work." Little did I realize how true that would prove to be here: how the best inputs for doing this paper have proved to be doing this paper!]

[Years ago, I heard about a well-known Australian potter approached by a researcher who wanted to study the creative process. He proposed to elicit protocols as the potter worked. But that didn't do it—the potter couldn't verbalize. Then he had a creative idea, consistent with his own creative process. He proposed to make a

thousand pots in succession, each influenced by the last, so that the researcher would have a visual record of the creative process. Nine hundred and ninety nine more articles like this and maybe we'll have an idea of how I develop theory. In the meantime, assuming the tolerance of the publisher will not stretch that far, you have one. [Afterthought: I will not do draft after draft after draft of this paper, as I usually do. Aside from cleaning it up for clarity, somewhat, I want to leave the outline and conceptual points more or less as they developed. What would be the use of showing you only the thousandth article? Too much theory about theory development is already like that—neat rationalizations of a messy process. Here you have the full messiness of the first effort!]]

Sixth [going back to the original outline, which is why this may seem a little disconnected], to develop good theory you have to connect and disconnect. In other words, you have to get as close to the phenomena as possible in digging out the inputs (data, stories, and lots more), but then be able to step back to make something interesting out of them.

Too connected and you risk getting co-opted by the phenomenon—that, to my mind, is why so called "action research" has, with a few notable exceptions, not produced much interesting theory. The researcher cannot have his or her cake (of consulting income) and eat it too (with research publications—practical publications maybe, good research ones rarely). Researchers have to be able to step back.

But too disconnected and you cannot develop interesting theory either. As suggested earlier, the imagination is stimulated by rich description, nuanced exposure: stories and anecdotes are better than measures on seven point scales and the like. If you are going to measure, then measure as much as possible in real terms—close to how things actually happen in the world, for example the time managers actually spend on e-mail instead of the time managers claim they spend on e-mail (unless of course you are studying perceptions). This is what I believe to be the problem hounding economics today. This is one social science where researchers have nowhere to go to observe firsthand the behaviors they seek to describe. So they pile abstraction upon abstraction. (Sure there are fish markets. But ironically, what economists take to be markets today are fundamentally removed from the markets we can all go and see. These are places of community, where economic, social, and cultural factors all converge. The arm's length markets of today's economics overemphasize the economic at the expense of the social and cultural: they are antithetical to communities.)

Do we encourage our researchers to connect every which way? Hardly. In the case of doctoral students, we lock them in libraries for years and then tell them to go find a research topic. The library is the worst place in the world in which to find a research topic. Even students who were once in the world of real things have forgotten what goes on there.

The result is that a great deal of research is pushed by some theoretical construct or angle: game theory, networking concepts, beliefs about corporate social responsibility (yet again), whatever is fashionable in the world of academe. Under the scrutiny of such single lenses, organizations look distorted. Recall the "rule of the tool"—you give a little boy a hammer and everything looks like a nail. Narrow concepts are no better than narrow techniques. Organizations don't need to be hit over the head with either.

Seventh, to connect, you have to keep the research method simple, direct, and straightforward. For example, just go look (while of course recording carefully what you see). As usual, Yogi Berra said it best: "You can observe a lot just by watching." Or in the more somber words of a Russian proverb: "Believe not your own brother—believe, instead, your own blind eye."

The initial supervisor of my doctoral program told me that my thesis should be "elegant". He meant methodologically elegant. I have always prided myself in the inelegance, or at least straightforwardness, of my methodology—I called it "structured observation" (written up in an appendix to *The Nature of Managerial Work*). I sat in managers' offices and wrote down what they did all day. That, I believe, helped me get closer to elegant conclusions.

We are altogether too hung up on fancy methods in our field, and in much of the social sciences in general. All too often they lead to banal results, significant only in the statistical sense of the word. Elegant means often get in the way of elegant ends. People intent on being correct often go astray. What, for example, is the problem with a sample of one, at least for induction? Piaget studied his own children; a physicist once split a single atom. Who cares, if the results are insightful. Alternatively, what is more boring than a bunch of academics arguing about statistical tests? Sure we need to get them right. But let's not confound them, as did Popper, with scientific discovery.

Eighth, researching is detective work: you have to dig, dig, dig, for every scrap of information you can get. Don't forget about that "you never know."

Ninth, take prolific notes. [I realize now that from the sixth point I have changed the sentence construction, to a more declarative form. But that just reveals point #10 (not in my notes): At early stages, keep it messy. This paper, as noted, is at an early stage!] I write down everything I can think of. When I am working on something, I have little scraps of paper coming out my ears. About anything, everything. Sometimes one is just a better way to word a particular idea I already recorded in another. In preparing for what I call my "Smith and Marx" pamphlet, there are ideas I have probably written down fifteen different times. Not because I forget the earlier versions: only because I think I have expressed it better each time. *[Which reminds me—bear in mind point #11 (not in my notes either), that it is not only having the ideas that make a successful theory but also expressing them engagingly. William Schultz has made the engaging point that if you can't express your idea without jargon, maybe you don't quite have it: "When I look over the books I have written, I know exactly which parts I understood and which parts I did not understand when I wrote them down. The poorly understood parts sound scientific. When I barely understood something, I kept it in scientific jargon. When I really comprehended it, I was able to explain it to anyone in language they understood . . . Understanding evolves through three phases: simplistic, complex, and profoundly simple."]*

Twelfth, when possible as I go along I code the notes in terms of the outline. That is why I need the outline in advance of the writing. What can I possibly do with thousands of uncoded notes? Indeed, how could I even come up with these notes unless I have the sense of an outline? So I need the outline to think the thoughts and get the codes. But only after I have the thoughts can I really do the outline, and so the codes. This means I have to recycle back repeatedly to redo and flesh out whatever outline I do have, in order to enhance the codes and so to recode what has been coded. Got that?

Hopefully many of the codes stay the same—otherwise I can be at this for years. (Look for Smith and Marx in 2020. I did the first draft almost ten years ago!) All of this effort is to get everything in linear order, to get all those notes in one sequence, or at least in many little coded piles that are in one sequence. Then I can pull the piles out one by one, in order, to do sub-outlines of each section and then write. But what if in the thirty-second pile I pull out a note that should change the first thirty-one? Should I go on? Many people, I suspect, do. I also suspect you never heard of most of them. And that brings me to the most important point of all. If you can only retain one message from this paper, this is it!

Thirteenth, cherish anomalies. If you wish to get tenure within, say, fifteen years, you may be reluctant to constantly be recoding all your notes, let alone rewriting written text. But on some codes you must be in no hurry to close.

You are not going to make the great breakthrough from the note that fits. As you order the notes, it is of course quite nice when things fall into place. You proceed happily; parsimony is in your grasp, maybe tenure too. Also, perhaps, banality. And then comes this nasty note: some observation, idea, or example that simply refuses to fit. Weak theorists, I believe, throw such notes away. They don't wish to deal with the ambiguity. They want it all to be neat.

Keep these notes. Cherish them. Repeatedly return to them. Ask why? Why? Why? Be a bulldog *(really point #14).* Never give up trying to figure out what they mean. If you can come to grips with the anomaly, you may have something big. The poet W. B. Yeats captured this sentiment perfectly: "We made out of our quarrels with others rhetoric, but out of our quarrels with ourselves poetry" (1969: 331). Make poetry!

Anomalies are important because, to continue the text but not strictly the point, *fifteenth, everything depends on the creative leap. And sixteenth, that can be trivial.* So Fleming saw mold in parts of his sample. Big deal. Later he went back and found thirty-one footnotes (if I remember correctly some forgotten source) in the reports of other studies that experienced similar problems. For those researchers, it certainly was no big deal. They went on. Fleming stopped. Who knows what happened to the rest of his study, or all of theirs, but history records what happened to Fleming's digression: we got penicillin, and eventually antibiotics in general.

What you set out to do doesn't matter; it's what you end up doing. Many of the best theses I have supervised ended up surprising their authors, and me. That is why I am not enamored of highly detailed research plans that leave no room for surprises. Back to Hans Selye for another wonderful quote, in remarks to the Canadian Senate on Science Policy: "I doubt that Fleming could have obtained a grant for the discovery of penicillin on that basis because he could not have said, 'I propose to have an accident in a culture so that it will be spoiled by a mould falling on it, and I propose to recognize the possibility of extracting an antibiotic from this mould.' "

I get a great kick out of the fact that many of my doctoral students defend their thesis proposals well into their empirical work. After all, how can they know what they will do until they do it? I'm waiting for someone to defend the proposal in the morning and the dissertation in the afternoon!

Was Fleming a genius because of his insight? I'll bet many of those thirty-one other researchers were considered geniuses (then if not now). We have altogether too many geniuses in research and not enough ordinary, open minds.

I believe that there are not creative people in this world so much as blocked people. After all, every one of us has wild and wooly dreams. Only after we wake up do most of us stop being creative. (That is why the best of creativity so often happens at the interface, just as we wake up, when our more visually inclined right hemisphere, where dreaming activity occurs, connects with our more analytically inclined left, where speech takes place. That is when we are best able to connect those Mozart-like images with the linear order of words. To repeat, to be creative is not just to have the idea but also to express it.)

As the day unfolds, we hit the world as it is—fighting traffic to work, meeting an agitated boss, getting Propperian reviews of our latest journal submission—and that's the end of creativity. We get careful, or scared, either way blocked: we become *correct*. So much for those dreams.

I don't consider myself particularly creative. I certainly do badly in all those Mickey Mouse tests for creativity—like "Come up with 32 ways to ..." See. I can't even invent one. On the other hand, I don't scare easily, not about ideas. Plus, I have been lucky enough to fall into academic life, which is supposed to be about ideas, and at McGill, in Canada, which are particularly tolerant places. (I was on sabbatical in France when the dean called to say I got tenure. I didn't even know I was being considered! Times have changed, even at McGill.) So I have been able to respond to what I see before me—let it speak to me. The world is so rich and varied, that if you see it as it is, you are bound to appear creative. (And by the way I don't take seriously people who tell me that I am courageous. It doesn't take much courage to write words down on pieces of paper (unless, of course, you live in mortal fear that the Propperians will reject you). Yet, I am amazed at how many colleagues are just plain scared to be different. That is not a good trait in an academic.)

My one hero in this world is the little boy in that Hans Christian Andersen story. Not because he *said* that the emperor was wearing no clothes: that was the easy part. Because he *saw* it. Amidst all those people who wouldn't let themselves see it, because they were afraid, he was open.

Fear is antithetical to theory development—fear of being different, fear of standing out, fear of not belonging, fear of being wrong, or subversive (if not obvious). Yet we have built fear into the whole process by which we do and assess research, especially in the tenure process. Open the journals and read the results.

I don't much care for regular doctoral students, the ones who have always done everything correctly—gotten the right grades, moved smoothly up some hierarchy, etc.—always as expected. As Paul Shepheard put it in *What is Architecture*, "The mainstream is a current too strong to think in." I cherish the ones who did the unexpected. (I should add that I have always prided myself in never having had a doctoral student who replicated any of my own research. If they couldn't break out on their own in their dissertation, when would they ever be able to do so? You can see the list of their topics in my C.V. on www.mintzberg.org.)

In other words, I prefer a bit of quirkiness in my doctoral students, which reflects no fear of being different. (Not too quirky, mind you: they still need the capability to get into the world and observe it firsthand, close-up.) Any kind of "correctness," even being a self-proclaimed "contrarian," impedes openness. In research, we have enough of people who see things as most everyone does; we desperately need ones prepared to step back and see the obvious as no-one else has. "Dare to be naïve," said Buckminster Fuller.

Theory development is really about discovering patterns *[let's make this point 17]*, recognizing similarities in things that appear dissimilar to others, i.e., making unexpected connections. Theory is about connections, and the more, and the more interesting, the better.

In my first study, my doctoral research, I found that managers got interrupted a lot. That their work was largely oral. That they spent a lot of time in lateral relationships. I just wrote it down. All this had to be patently obvious to anyone who ever spent time in a managerial office, behind the desk or in front of it. (It is our great discredit that too few scholars of "management" ever did, or do.) These findings just didn't jive with the then (and largely still) prevalent view of managerial work, dating back to Henri Fayol's book (1916 [1984]): "planning, organizing, coordinating, and controlling." (Four words for controlling.) Where are the lateral relations here? What room does this leave for interruption? Sure managers control (this is our flat earth theory), but they do much that is evidentially quite different. I just wrote it down, and so managed to parlay some rather obvious observations about the emperor (not being naked so much as attired in a different suit) into an academic reputation. Lucky me. Not so difficult. Nobody ever said: "Are you kidding?" Somebody at least should have said: "They must all have been kidding for fifty years," at least for what they failed to see. (Back to that emperor again— I guess you don't mess with people in uniforms.)

When I wrote *The Structuring of Organizations*, just about the best research I read for it was that by Joan Woodward (*Industrial Organization: Theory and Practice*, 1965). But I couldn't reconcile her findings about process industries with my outline to that point. Without thinking about anomalies, etc., I just kept coming back to my notes about this. When it finally hit me, when I figured out how to reconcile her description of the structures used in highly automated industries with my description of "adhocracy," or project organization, used in fields like R&D and consulting, I had a breakthrough for my own framework. I realized that Woodward was in effect describing post-bureaucratic processes, ones that were so formalized, so perfectly machine bureaucratic, that they no longer needed human beings. That freed up the human beings to design and maintain the equipment, working in project teams, much like in those other fields. So beyond machine bureaucracy was adhocracy.

Eighteenth, once you have all those notes coded, and those anomalies messily set aside, you have to weave it all together. My example above about Woodward, and the story of Fleming, may have left one wrong impression, at least for the social sciences. It is rarely *the* insight that makes for an interesting theory. That usually comes from the weaving together of many insights, many creative leaps, most small and perhaps a few big. It's all in the weaving. And that comes, for me at least, in the writing, whether of the text itself (as I hope you have been able to see here) or of the detailed outline. And this leads, for me at least, to the *nineteenth point: clear the decks of technology: write, literally.*

Nothing impedes integrating more than that damn keyboard. It pushes everything away. It's just you and all those keys, etc.; everything else, all those glorious notes you may or may not have written, all those anomalies you should be cherishing, are pushed aside—you can barely find them.

There are apparently great poets who just wrote down their great poems. They could have used a keyboard. It all flowed out of their heads. But what about the poet who revised his great poem ninety-one times before he got it right? In those days, he had to use a flat desk. Would he have come up with that poem on a slanted keyboard and a vertical screen?

I write on a flat desk [*as I am doing now*] with my papers around me. I can pull them in every which way. I am comfortable with a keyboard (as a student, I was Sports Editor of the McGill Daily, although reporting on a hockey game is admittedly different from coming up with a theory). I even used word processing before almost anyone else, because a professor at McGill had a very early system. (That nearly drove us mad—for example, we had to correct from the end in!) But then, as now, I *write* and my P.A. types (now Santa, a gift from that other Santa). Indeed, I correct too on paper, still needing to spread out—and Santa retypes.

Shall we ever understand what damage the keyboard has done to theory development?

And finally, twentieth (as mentioned already), *iterate, iterate, iterate.* I write draft after draft after draft. I keep correcting, fixing, adjusting, reconceiving, changing, until it all feels right (for then; as noted about my work on managerial work, I came back to it later, seventeen years later—see my 1991 article "Managerial Work: Forty Years Later"). I am simply my own harshest critic. Nobody tears my work apart like I do. Too bad you can't see the thousand of pages of rewrites of my latest book, *Managers not MBAs.* It is 462 pages long, and every part of it was redone at least five times. One very long chapter, which was eventually split into four chapters (3–6), was redone at least nine times. I just kept coming back until it felt right.

But not here. It feels right to keep this messy, like theory development itself, so as better to make my points. The first of a thousand articles, the rest never to be written.

So, do twenty points on theory development a theory of theory development make? And am I describing the flat earth of theory development, or the round earth, or the vertical face of some mountain that I am taking to be the whole earth? Who cares. If you have learned something helpful, that is what matters.

And if you haven't, then at least I leave you with a testable hypothesis. Right here. If theory creation really is replicable, then the author of another chapter of this book must have come up with the same theory about theory development. (Unless, of course, mine is not true.) So go test that hypothesis, all you Propperians.

References

ARISTOTLE (2001). *The Basic works of Aristotle,* trans. J. A. Smith. New York: Modern Library.

BERGER, P. L. (1963). *Invitation to Sociology: A Humanistic Perspective.* Harmondsworth: Penguin Books.

CAPRA, F. (1982). *The Turning Point: Science, Society, and the Rising Culture.* New York: Simon and Schuster.

FAYOL, H. (1984). *General and Industrial Management* (first pub. 1916), rev. edn., trans. I. Gray. New York: Institute of Electrical and Electronics Engineers.

—— and MINTZBERG, H. (1983). The case for configuration. In G. Morgan (ed.), *Beyond Method: Strategies for Social Research* : 57–73. Beverly Hills, Calif: Sage.

MINTZBERG, H. (1973). *The Nature of Managerial Work.* New York: Harper and Row.

—— (1979*a*). *The Structuring of Organizations: A Synthesis of the Research.* Englewood Cliffs, NJ: Prentice-Hall.

—— (1982). If you are not serving Bill and Barbara, then you're not serving leadership. In J. G. Hunt, U. Sekaran, and C. Schriesheim (eds.), *Leadership, beyond Establishment Views*: 239–259. Carbondale, Ill.: Southern Illinois University Press.

MINTZBERG, H. (1991). Managerial work: Forty years later. In S. Carlson (ed.), *Executive Behaviour*. Uppsala, Stockholm: Upsaliensis Academiae.

—— (1993). Twenty-five years later... The illusive strategy. In H. I. Ansoff and A. G. Bedeian (eds.), *Management Laureates: A Collection of Autobiographical Essays*: 2. 323–374. Greenwich, Conn.: JAI Press.

—— (1994). Rounding out the manager's job. *Sloan Management Review*, 36(1): 11–26.

—— (2002). Researching the researching of walking. *Journal of Management Inquiry*, 11(4): 426–428.

—— (2004). *Managers not MBAs: A Hard Look at the Soft Practice of Managing and Management Development*. San Francisco: Berrett-Koehler.

—— and MCHUGH, A. (1985). Strategy formation in an adhocracy. *Administrative Science Quarterly*, 30(2): 160–197.

POPPER, K. R. (1959). *The Logic of Scientific Discovery*. New York: Basic Books.

SCHENDEL, D. (1995). Notes from the editor-in-chief. *Strategic Management Journal*, 13(3): 1–2.

SELYE, H. (1964). *From Dream to Discovery: On Being a Scientist*. New York: McGraw Hill.

SELDES, G. (1983). *The Great Quotations*. Secaucus, NJ: Citadel Press.

WEICK, K. E. (1969). *The Social Psychology of Organizing*. Reading, Mass.: Addison-Wesley.

YEATS, W. B. (1969). *Mythologies*. New York: Collier Books.

....

CHAPTER 18

MANAGING ORGANIZATIONAL KNOWLEDGE

THEORETICAL AND METHODOLOGICAL FOUNDATIONS

....

IKUJIRO NONAKA

It has been more than ten years since a series of papers on knowledge creation was published (Nonaka, 1991, 1994; Nonaka and Takeuchi, 1995), and we have seen a significant amount of publication concerning knowledge in the management science field since then. As one of the most important resources for a firm, knowledge has been researched and discussed in every aspect of management science, such as strategy, marketing, accounting, organizational science, organizational learning, and economics.

In spite of all these proliferating discussions about knowledge, we cannot say that we have acquired enough understanding about it and how knowledge is created and used. Part of the difficulty in establishing a knowledge-creating theory is that

The author wishes to thank Ryoko Toyama and Vesa Peltokorpi for their invaluable help in writing this chapter.

knowledge cannot be dealt solely with the positivism that has been the philosophical foundation of economics and management science. We need to look into other ontological and epistemological paradigms to really understand the nature of knowledge and how organizations deal with knowledge.

Management science, like other fields in social science, has been trying to emulate natural science. For that, consciously or subconsciously, positivism has been selected as a dominant paradigm on which management science is based. Although its limitations have been suggested even for natural science, not to mention social science, positivism has given researchers a certain "scientific" way to perceive the world with its naturalistic subject–object separations, persuasion of rational causal relationships among objects, and persuasion of generality and replicability of the findings. It is based on the belief that objective "facts" and universal rules concerning how these facts are connected can be found. In management science, an organization has been viewed as an information-processing machine, and students in this field have been told to separate factual premises from value premises for management to become science (Simon, 1945).

As a doctoral student at the University of California, Berkeley, I was of course influenced by such a view of an organization. I studied marketing under Francisco Nicosia, whose major contribution was the conceptualization of consumer decision processes from the perspective of information processing. My interest shifted from marketing to organization science after I took a sequence of three sociology courses from Neil Smelser's theoretical viewpoint and Arthur Stinchcomb's methodological viewpoint, where I learned that we had to construct our own social theory.

My main research focus back then was the contingency theory, in which an organization is viewed as an entity to adapt to the environment with requisite variety (Nonaka and Nicosia, 1979). In such a view, an organization tries to process the information as efficiently as possible according to the complexity of the environment. However, as I continued to study the innovation process of Japanese firms together with my colleagues, Hirotaka Takeuchi and Kenichi Imai, I started to feel that we could not explain the complex process of innovation with the information-processing model. These firms were not merely adapting to the environment, but were actively changing itself and the environment through their innovation (Nonaka and Takeuchi, 1986).

So I proposed the concept of "information creation" (Nonaka, 1985, 1988*a*, 1988*b*). In it, a firm is viewed as an entity to intentionally evolve through information creation. Instead of trying to reach an equilibrium point by reducing uncertainty as the contingency theory suggested, an organization sometimes amplifies uncertainty and variety to create new solutions.

However, I could not be satisfied with the concept of information creation. In almost all the innovation processes we studied, we found strong beliefs or wills among those who were involved in the innovation. To deal with such beliefs and wills, we could not ignore people's value system, which Simon insisted we researchers have to carefully remove from our research. That was when I realized that we need the theory of knowledge creation, not just information creation.

In this chapter, I will try to revisit and propose further developments in the theory and methodology to research the complex process of knowledge being created organizationally. Based on epistemology and ontology, the theory tries to incorporate values, contexts, and power, and capture the dynamic process of knowledge being created to adapt to the environment and change the environment in return. Different from the long tradition of epistemology, which has interpreted the issue of subjectivity as one of knowing the "truth" beyond one's subjectivity, the theory of knowledge creation views subjectivity as being based on the values and contexts of those who see truth. It also has to be based on another branch of philosophy, that is, ontology. The ontology here is not just about "whether it exists or not," but about "for what it exists." As Flyvbjerg (2001) suggested, we cannot ignore such issues as values, contexts, and power when we conduct research in social science.

For that, this chapter first examines the interlocking ontological and epistemological assumptions of the knowledge/truth, human agents, organizations, and environment. The assumptions of positivism, which we inherited from natural science, will be contrasted with those of another philosophical paradigm, phenomenology. While positivism separates objectivity from subjectivity to create objective knowledge through formal logic, phenomenology views phenomena in non-dualistic terms and treats objectivity and subjectivity are inseparable as they are interlined in time-space (Husserl, 1931; Heidegger, 1962). While the goal for the positivism-based research is to describe the world objectively, phenomenological research seeks to discover the meanings through the eyes of the embedded actors. In the phenomenological view, all knowing is at one level subjective since it is always related to, and constructed by, the person engaged in knowing. This perspective maintains that social sciences are essentially dialectic as they are concerned with the life-world of embedded but intentional human agents.

However, the goal of this chapter is not to argue which paradigm is a better choice to research the process of knowledge creation. Rather than the "either–or" choices, complex social phenomena can be effectively described based on non-dualistic and pluralistic "both-and" methodology of Hegelian synthesis of theme and anti-theme. This chapter lays out the various philosophical paradigms such as phenomenology, idealism, rationalism, and pragmatism, and shows how they are synthesized to constitute the theory and methodology of knowledge creation. This chapter also discusses the issue of leadership as the force to push forward a knowledge-creating process.

18.1 KNOWLEDGE/TRUTH

Knowledge has been traditionally defined as "justified true belief." A fundamental issue in various streams of epistemology is how one can justify one's subjective belief as objective "truth." In other words, the issue is whether human beings can ever achieve any form of knowledge that is independent of their own subjective construction since they are the agents through which knowledge is perceived or experienced (Morgan and Smircich, 1980). While the ontological position of positivism as the world as concrete structures supports objective knowledge, the phenomenological philosophers see part of the world inherently subjective.

The Cartesian split and power of reasoning supports the view of objective knowledge and truth in positivism. John Locke, among the others, maintained that human knowledge is an inner mental presentation (or mirror image) of the outside world that can be explained in linguistic signs and mathematics through reasoning. All things beyond the thought/senses consequently do not exist and/or are irrelevant. Loosely following this conceptualization, traditional economic and psychological theories are limited to objective knowledge, which can be processed through formal logic and tested empirically. The advantage of this mono-dimensional notion of knowledge is that it allows scholars further to claim that all genuine human knowledge is contained within the boundaries of science.

In contrast, for phenomenological philosophers knowledge is subjective, context-specific, bodily, relative, and interpretational (Heidegger, 1962; Husserl, 1970, 1977; Merleau-Ponty, 1962). They rather uniformly claim that the mental and the physical worlds evolve in a dialectic joint advent. As meanings emerge through experiences, the primacy is paid on subjective tacit knowledge over objective prepositional knowledge. Practical knowledge is often prioritized over theoretical knowledge (Hayek, 1945; Polanyi, 1952, 1966). Tacit knowledge, accumulated in dialectic individual–environment interaction, is very difficult to articulate (Polanyi, 1952, 1966). Husserl (1977) believed in attaining true knowledge through "epoche" or "bracketing," that is, seeing things as they are and grasping them through a kind of direct insight. Pure phenomenological experience is even claimed to precede cognition (Nishida, 1970).

The identified wide and fundamental ontological and epistemological differences in positivism and phenomenology create methodological challenges. It can be claimed that the positivist dominance has limited comprehensive context-specific discussions on knowledge in management science. This problem was already noticed by Edith Penrose (1959) who argued that the relative negligence was the result of the difficulties involved in taking knowledge into account. This is because positivist epistemology is based on the assumption that lived experiences can be linguistically carved up and conventionally portioned into preexistent conceptual categories for the purposes of systematic analysis and causal attribution. In effect, positivism-based social science tries to freeze-frame the dynamic and living social world into a preexisting static structure.

In contrast to the context-free positivist mirror image of human mind and the environment, the knowledge-creating theory is rooted on the belief that knowledge inherently includes human values and ideals. The knowledge creation process cannot be captured solely as a normative causal model because human values and ideals are subjective and the concept of truth depends on values, ideals, and contexts.

However, the knowledge-creating theory does not view knowledge as solely subjective. It treats knowledge creation as a continuous process in which subjective tacit knowledge and objective explicit knowledge are converted into each other (Nonaka, 1991, 1994; Nonaka and Takeuchi, 1995). The boundaries between explicit and tacit knowledge are porous as all knowledge and action is rooted in the tacit component (Tsoukas, 1996). Tacit knowledge, in turn, is built partly on the existing explicit knowledge since tacit knowledge is acquired through experiences and observations in the physical world.

Viewing the knowledge-creating process as the conversion process between tacit and explicit knowledge means that it is viewed as the social process of validating truth (Nonaka, 1994; Nonaka and Takeuchi, 1995). Contemporary philosophers claim that group validation produces knowledge that is not private and subjective (Rorty, 1979). As long as the knowledge stays tacit and subjective, it can be acquired only through direct sensory experience, and cannot go beyond one's own values, ideals, and contexts. In such a case, it is hard to create new knowledge or achieve universality of knowledge. Through the knowledge conversion process, called SECI process, a personal subjective knowledge is validated socially and synthesized with others' knowledge so that knowledge keeps expanding (Nonaka and Takeuchi, 1995).

Unlike positivism, the knowledge-creating theory does not treat knowledge as something absolute and infallible. The truth can be claimed to be incomplete as any current state of knowledge is fallible and influenced by historical factors such as ideologies, values, and interests of collectives. The knowledge-creating theory views knowledge and truth as the result of a permanent and unfinished questioning of the present. While absolute truth may not be achieved, the knowledge validation leads to ever more true and fewer false consequences, increasing plausibility. The pragmatic solution is to accept collectively "objectified" knowledge as the "truth" because it works in a certain time and context. Hence, knowledge-creating theory defines knowledge as a dynamic process of justifying personal belief towards the "truth."

18.1.1 Human Agents

The nature of human agents differs in the positivist and phenomenological philosophies. The subject–object dualism enables *a priori* notions of human behavior to be dominant in positivism. Emphasizing rationality, positivism views human agents as separable parts, which operate the same as the parts in unison. Human behavior is consequently reduced to nothing but reactive "stimulus-action" loops, explicable solely by scientific laws. This makes human agents products of the external forces in the environment to which they are exposed (Morgan and Smircich, 1980). The static and atomistic nature of humans and their environmental linkage is apparent in neoclassical economics that deny/exclude individual differences in values, moral, experience, and choice. Indeed, the British empiricist, David Hume, argued that our belief in such a thing as personal identity is not justified since any individual is just a collection of perceptions, not values.

The human agents in phenomenology act as parts of an integrated system. It is human nature to be practically involved in a complex world rather than rationally involved with a conceptually simplified world. Being thrown into the world (Heidegger, 1962), humans exhibit subjective goal-seeking behavior in their everyday experiences, orientations, and actions through which human agents pursue their interests and affairs. The process of social changes is explained by human intentionalities, which are embedded in the categories of perception and basic orientation to the world. Intentionality such as beliefs, wants, and desires can be understood as something that people attribute to other people (Dennett, 1987), or through *noema* (what of the experience) and *noesis* (the way in which the what is experienced) (Husserl, 1970).

The phenomenological and pragmatic notions of irregularity in human rational action complicate model building in social sciences. This is because there are realms of being and reality constituted through different kinds of founding acts. As humans tend not to function like machines in a rule-governed manner, causalities cannot accurately capture complex social phenomena, such as knowledge creation. The positivism-based management science has tried to deal with such irregularity due to bounded rationality and opportunism of human beings by treating humans as unreliable parts of an information-processing machine and researching how such a machine can be fine-tuned to function rationally.

On the other hand, the theory of knowledge creation is based on the assumption that humans are not just imperfect parts of such an information-processing machine, but are existences who have a potential to grow together through the process of knowledge creation. Instead of being static, human nature and action evolve through environmental dialectics (Heidegger, 1962; Merleau-Ponty, 1962). An individual transcends him/herself through knowledge creation (Nonaka, Toyama, and Konno, 2000; Nonaka and Toyama, 2003). In organizational knowledge-creating process, individuals interact with each other to transcend their own boundaries, and as a result, change themselves, others, the organization, and the environment. Creating knowledge *organizationally* does not just mean organizational members supplementing each other to overcome an individual's bounded rationality.

The transcendental nature of human agents takes place through dialectics between individual mind and collective intersubjectivity. While human agents are social, individual mind is idiosyncratic due to unique experiences and interpretations. The knowledge-creating process of socially validating personal subjective knowledge is the process of synthesizing such social and idiosyncratic nature of human agents.

18.1.2 Organizations

Following the bipolarity of positivism and phenomenology, social institutions can be explained either as the deterministic "positivist machines" or as the phenomenological "transcendental organisms." The objective approach in social sciences presents the positivist organizational machines are homogeneous entities existing for some predetermined purpose. As their primary function in the neoclassical economics was to convert inputs to outputs, the conversion process itself and the managerial decision making are taken as given and common to all the players. The bounded-rationality concept in behavioral economics enabled scholars to conceptualize social institutions as aggregated entities in which individuals act with incomplete knowledge/information (Simon, 1945). The reality is cut into pieces of information that are small and simple enough to be processed by one person, and organizations are information-processing machines that are made of imperfect parts, that are, human beings.

Organizations as phenomenological "transcendental organisms" are allowed to have distinctive histories, mental models, and other emerging collective characteristics. Human agents in phenomenological organizations live as parts of interrelated systems constructed through individual and collective action. People and the physical and social artifacts they create are fundamentally different from the physical reality examined by natural science. In addition to their objective properties, organizations present different subjective meanings to people based on their networked relations, reputation, and values. The tacit meanings are acquired and constructed through experiences and networks of recurrent and recursive conversations between individuals and groups of individuals (Mingers, 2001). The interactions within the company in terms of norms and values are also based on collectively negotiated behavioral expectations and inter-subjective meanings.

The knowledge-creating theory does not view an organization as mere objective economic structure as positivist-based economics and management science does. It does not view an organization as a mere collection of social processes of meaning creation as phenomenological philosophers suggest. Instead, the knowledge-creating theory views an organization as an organic configuration of ba (roughly means "place"). Ba is a foundation of knowledge-creating activity, where dialectic dialogues and practices take place.

The concept of ba was first sought out to explain the energy that continuously drives the SECI process. Philosophers have discussed the importance of place in human cognition and action, from Plato's place for a genesis of existence "Chora," Aristotle's "Topos," to Heidegger's place for human existence "Ort." However, we realized that it was not just a physical place but a meaning space that is required for SECI process to take place. Based on the concept that was originally proposed by the Japanese philosopher Kitaro Nishida (1921, 1970), we defined ba in knowledge-creating theory as a shared context in motion, in which knowledge is shared, created, and utilized. As has been discussed, knowledge is context-specific, and therefore, needs a physical context, or situated action (Suchman, 1987), for it to be created. When individuals empathize with shared contexts, their subjective knowledge is shared and socially justified to acquire objectivity and expand.

The essence of ba is the contexts and the meanings that are shared and created through interactions that occur at a specific time and space, rather than a space itself. The Japanese word, ba, means not just a physical space, but also a specific time and space, or relationships of those who are at the specific time and space. Ba can emerge in individuals, working groups, project teams, informal circles, temporary meetings, virtual space such as e-mail groups, and at the front-line contact with the customer. Participants of ba bring in their own contexts to share, and create new meanings through interactions, since context is in interactions, rather than in one's cognition (Ueno, 2000).

Ba is defined as a shared context in motion since it is constantly moving. Through interactions with others and the environment, both the contexts of ba and participants grow. New knowledge is created through such changes in meanings and contexts.

To participate in ba means to get involved and transcend one's own limited perspective. Nishida states that the essence of ba is "nothingness." It does not mean that nothing exists at ba. It means that at ba, one exists in the relationship with others, instead of as an atomistic and absolute "self." At ba, one can be open to others by losing oneself, that is, the preconceived notion of what is absolute truth for oneself. The relationship here is an "I–Thou" relationship, instead of "I–It" relationship. The "I–Thou" relationship is a direct, highly personal relationship in which one opens oneself to others to reach out to them, while the "I–It" relationship is impersonal and remote (Buber, 1923). Through such a relationship, one can see oneself in relation to others, and can accept others' views and values so that subjective views are understood and shared. As has been argued, knowledge creation needs subjectivity to be shared and to interact with others' subjectivity. Hence, ba supports such sharing and synthesizing of subjectivity. For that, ba needs to have a permeable boundary so that it can accept necessary contexts. Ba also needs participants with multi-viewpoints and backgrounds so that they can bring in various contexts, which are shared through dialogues and practices.

Ba does not necessarily mean one meeting or one project. Ba is connected to each other through interactions among participants. Hence, in the theory of the knowledge-creating firm, a firm can be viewed as an organic configuration of multi-layered ba.

A view of an organization as an organic configuration of multi-layered ba synthesizes the views of an organization both as an economic structure and as meaning-creating processes. Such a view helps to solve the paradox to explain structures suited for both routine and non-routine tasks (Thompson, 1967). The organizational structure of a firm defines the interactions within the firm in terms of formally defined command and information. However, such interactions are only a part of interactions to create knowledge. As the social collectives through "ba" are conceptualized more as flow of meanings (insiders' view) than as static entities (outsiders' view), the context-specific truth opens to embedded actors. The meanings emerge and evolve through intersubjectivity and dialectic environmental interaction. An organization, therefore, can be seen partly as organic meaning networks. While the hierarchies on the objective side determine the objective allocation of resources and formal power, social interaction patterns enable actors to locate and utilize knowledge.

As the organic configuration of the "ba" permeates beyond the economic boundaries of the firm, the non-dualistic perception challenges the positivist boundary assumptions. Tangible resources enable a clear separation between "in here" and "out there" in the positivist theories. The boundaries are frequently determined simply by ownership (Arrow, 1974) based on the economic perception of organizations as objective measurable entities. However, the boundary setting becomes far more complicated when an organization is viewed as an organic configuration of multi-layered ba, which has an emergent and intersubjective nature. Knowledge is created through interactions, and interactions cannot be owned even by those who are in such interactions. While firms can be explained as acquiring knowledge through contractual arrangement (Williamson, 1975), value of the acquired knowledge and its interrelated significance goes well beyond the context-free objective boundaries. As a consequence, the subjective "out there" might be vital for the economic performance "in here" and cannot be objectively separated when describing the existence and functioning of an organization.

18.1.3 Environment

The positivist and phenomenological philosophers tend to agree that human agents and organizations do not exist in environmental isolation. However, they differ in their views of the mechanisms and nature of the interactions between agents and the environment. The positivists treat the environment as atomized objects existing independently outside of human agents, while phenomenologists describe relationship between agents and their environment holistically and inter-dependently.

The goal of positivism is to decompose the environment into manageable parts in order to explain the causal relationships among the parts. By doing so, re-searchers seek to generate universal knowledge allowing manipulation of organ-izational and environmental variables. For example, the positioning school emphasizes the analysis of the environment so that a company can take an advantageous position over competitors (Porter, 1980). In such a view, competitors and the environment are perceived as mechanistic entities moving in predeter-mined law. With such atomization of the environmental objects, the external world can be described with great precision. However, the precision comes with a potential risk of overlooking the importance of the human world and the meaning of the environment to each of the embedded human actors.

In contrast, the strategic rules are emergent in the phenomenological world because what the environment means to actors is context dependent. In the process all things exist as a part of the whole rather than disconnected and separate entities. This essentially means that humans and companies are parts of interlinked totality, which influences their present existence and future possibilities. This existence and these possibilities, in turn, are subject to their history, i.e., accumulated experi-ences. Instead of looking at the environment objectively, managers are thrown into strategic decision making as a way of life.

The focus of knowledge-creating theory is the dialectical evolution of the social world through interactions between human agents and the environment. Human agents create knowledge when they find new opportunities through environmental interaction, and the environment changes through knowledge creation. The coex-istence connotes to agent–environment dialectics (Nonaka and Toyama, 2002, 2003; Nonaka, Peltokorpi, and Tomae, forthcoming). The theory is holistic as the objects and subjects are inseparable, existing as the totality of human-being-in-the-world (Heidegger, 1962). The organization and environment should, thus, be understood to evolve together rather as separate entities. The constant accumula-tion and processing of knowledge helps firms to redefine their visions, dialogues, and practices, which in turn impact the environment through their new or improved services/products.

18.2 METHODOLOGICAL CONSIDERATIONS

18.2.1 Process (SECI)

As has been argued, knowledge is created through the continuous conversion of subjective tacit knowledge and objective explicit knowledge as shown in Figure 18.1. Instead of adopting a purely objective approach to knowledge, the knowledge conversion process utilizes insights from several philosophical schools. Figure 18.2 shows the philosophical backgrounds of the methodologies used in each of the four modes of the knowledge conversion process.

Knowledge creation starts with the *Socialization*, which is the process of converting new tacit knowledge through shared experiences in day-to-day social interaction. In the socialization process, the phenomenological method of seeing things as they are is effective. Knowledge creation includes the elements of phenomenology, idealism, rationalism, and pragmatism. The dialectic process starts with the attachment to the environment through which actors are able to acquire tacit knowledge. The phenomenological and Eastern philosophical concepts of temporary suspension of all personal biases, beliefs, preconceptions, or assumptions enable pure experience (Nishida, 1921; Husserl, 1931), through which tacit knowledge, which is difficult to formalize and often time- and space-specific, can be acquired and shared. By discarding preconceived notions and "living in" or "indwelling" the world, individuals accumulate and share tacit knowledge about the world that surrounds them. The concept of life-world enables to overcome the positivist actor–environment dichotomy (Heidegger, 1962). For example, one can accumulate the tacit knowledge about the customers through his/her own experience as a customer. One can share the tacit knowledge of customers, suppliers, and even competitors by empathizing them through shared experience. Here, individuals embrace contradictions rather than confront them (Nonaka and Toyama, 2003; Varela and Shear, 1999). This enables actors to absorb the knowledge in their social environment through action and perception.

Such tacit knowledge is articulated into objective explicit knowledge through *Externalization*, a dialectic process in thought. Tacit knowledge is made explicit so that it can be shared by others to become the basis of new knowledge such as concepts, figures, and written documents. The philosophical foundation of the externalization process is idealism, since tacit knowledge is articulated by pursuing the essence of one's subjective experience to realize one's ideal. Here, dialogue is an effective method to articulate one's tacit knowledge and share the articulated knowledge with others. People tend to argue in conversations for their case through logic and try to change the opinions of other people. In contrast, dialogues

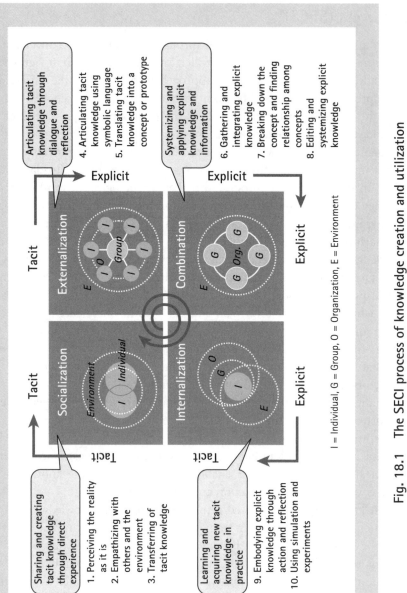

Fig. 18.1   The SECI process of knowledge creation and utilization

Adapted from Nonaka and Takeuchi (1995).

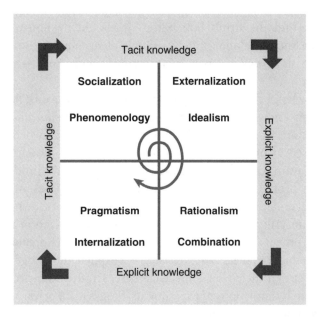

Fig. 18.2   Underlying philosophical methodologies of SECI

are based on active listening and on being open to change opinions. In order to externalize deeper layers of subjective tacit knowledge in social space, abduction or retroduction is effective rather than induction or deduction. The sequential use of metaphor, analogy, and model is a basic method in abduction (Lawson, 1997). It is critical here to understand that actors seek to detach themselves from routines to pursue ideals by actively exposing them in a context that enables them to see the inherent contradiction between the reality and ideal; a sequential use of the methods of abduction and retroduction are effective (Lawson, 1997).

Explicit knowledge is collected from inside or outside the organization and then combined, edited, and processed to form a more complex and systematic set of explicit knowledge through the *Combination* process. The new explicit knowledge is then disseminated among the members of the organization. The combination mode of knowledge conversion can also include the "breakdown" of concepts. Breaking down a concept such as a corporate vision into operationalized business or product concepts also creates systemic, explicit knowledge. Here, contradictions are solved through logic rather than synthesized. Rationalism is an effective method to combine, edit, and break down explicit knowledge. The externalized tacit knowledge is systemized, validated, and crystallized during the combination phase in explicit forms for collective awareness and practical usage. The process also includes monitoring, testing, and refining to fit the created knowledge with the existing reality. Knowledge combination and distribution can be facilitated by information technology, division of labor, and hierarchy. A creative use of computerized networks and large-scale databases helps to transfer explicit knowledge within and beyond the firm's boundaries. It should be noted, however, that information technology alone is rarely a source of sustainable competitive advantage because it plays only one part in knowledge management and can be fairly easily replicated.

Explicit knowledge created and shared throughout an organization is then converted into tacit knowledge by individuals through *Internalization*, a process of dialectic in action. This stage can be understood as praxis where knowledge is applied and used in practical situations and becomes the base for new routines (Nonaka and Toyama, 2003). Thus, explicit knowledge, such as product concepts or manufacturing procedures, has to be actualized through action, practice, and reflection so that it can really become knowledge of one's own. For example, training programs can help trainees to understand an organization and themselves. By reading documents or manuals about their jobs and the organization, and by reflecting upon them, trainees can internalize the explicit knowledge written in such documents to enrich their tacit knowledge base. Explicit knowledge can also be embodied through simulations or experiments. Pragmatism of learning-by-doing is an effective method to test, modify, and embody the explicit knowledge as one's own tacit knowledge. Internalized knowledge affects both individuals and the environment, as it changes the action of individuals and how they view the environment. The synthesis of individuals and the environment occurs at this level as well.

It is important to note that the movement through the four modes of knowledge conversion forms a *spiral*, not a circle. In the spiral of knowledge creation, the interaction between tacit and explicit knowledge is amplified through the four modes of knowledge conversion. The spiral becomes larger in scale as it moves up the ontological levels. Knowledge created through the SECI process can trigger a new spiral of knowledge creation, expanding horizontally and vertically as it moves through communities of interaction that transcend sectional, departmental, divisional, and even organizational boundaries. Knowledge can be transferred beyond organizational boundaries, and knowledge from different organizations interacts to create new knowledge (Badaracco, 1991; Wikstrom and Normann, 1994; Nonaka and Takeuchi, 1995; Inkpen, 1996). Through dynamic interaction among individuals and between individuals and the environment, knowledge created by the organization can trigger the mobilization of knowledge held by outside constituents such as consumers, affiliated companies, universities, or distributors. For example, an innovative new manufacturing process may bring about changes in the suppliers' manufacturing process, which in turn can trigger a new round of product and process innovation at the organization. Another example is the articulation of tacit knowledge possessed by customers that they themselves have not been able to articulate. A product works as the trigger for eliciting tacit knowledge when customers give meaning to the product by purchasing, adapting, using, or not purchasing it. It can also trigger changes in customers in terms of their worldview, and eventually reconstruct the environment. Their actions are then reflected in the innovative process of the organization and start a new spiral of knowledge creation. Organizational knowledge creation is a never-ending process that upgrades itself continuously.

As has been noted, knowledge creation is a self-transcending process, in which one reaches out beyond the boundaries of one's own existence (Jantsch, 1980) so that subjective views are socially justified in order to acquire objectivity. In socialization, self-transcendence is fundamental because tacit knowledge can only be shared through direct experiences, which go beyond individuals. For example, in the socialization process people empathize with their colleagues and customers, which diminishes barriers between individuals. Basically, frequent physical interaction and perception help individuals to create shared mental presentations and routines. In externalization, an individual transcends the inner and outer boundaries of the self by committing to the group and becoming one with it. Here, the sum of the individuals' intentions and ideas fuse and become integrated with the group's mental world. This stage is integral because the externalization of knowledge often helps people to see that the same phenomena can be viewed in many different and contrasting ways. In combination, new knowledge generated through externalization transcends the group to be combined. In internalization, individuals reflect upon themselves by putting themselves in the context of newly acquired knowledge and the environment where the knowledge should be utilized. This again requires self-transcendence.

18.2.2 Synthesis through Leadership

Then, what drives such a continuous process of knowledge creation? Schumpeter argued that innovations are brought by leaders with entrepreneurship. However, Schumpeter considered leadership as something for elites, and therefore, entrepreneurship was viewed as a matter of individuals' disposition in the end (Peukert, 2003).

However, the leadership in a knowledge-creating firm is based on more flexible distributed leadership, rather than leadership as a fixed control mechanism. Since knowledge is created through dynamic interactions among individuals and between individuals and the environment, leadership in a knowledge-creating firm is required to be improvisational. It also requires active commitment from all the members of the organization, not just from a few elites. In a knowledge-creating firm, planning and implementation of strategy is integrated through the interaction between subjectivities and objectivities, instead of being separated as suggested by existing theories of strategy and organization.

It does not mean that everyone starts creating knowledge immediately. For knowledge leadership to work, the mechanism of middle-up-down is a key

(Nonaka, 1988*b*). In such a process, middle managers break down the knowledge vision into concrete concepts or plans, build ba, and lead dialogues and practices to facilitate the SECI process. Middle managers can also function as tipping points in small-world network to connect previously unconnected ba to set off innovation (Gladwell, 2000; Watts, 2003).

The issue of leadership is closely related with the issue of power. However, power here does not necessarily mean legitimate power, which stems from hierarchical position. Knowledge itself can be a source of power, and therefore, can exist outside the hierarchy of the organization. Knowledge as a source of power also means that it is fragile and needs careful treatment. The human attractiveness of a leader, which depends on his/her values and views of the world, often affects the efficiency and effectiveness of the knowledge-creating process more than what kind of legitimate power s/he exercises. Research indicates that effective leaders have a capability for synthesizing contradictions through understanding that contradictory ideas are a way of life. They energize the emotional and spiritual resources of the organization.

Leadership plays various roles in knowledge-creating process such as providing a knowledge vision, developing and promoting sharing of knowledge assets, creating, energizing, and connecting ba, and enabling and promoting the continuous spiral of knowledge creation. This chapter focuses on the leadership role in providing knowledge vision and ba.

18.2.3 Knowledge Vision

Leaders synthesize the ontology and epistemology of knowledge creation through knowledge vision. Knowledge vision, determining collective ideal mission and domain, is rooted in the essential question of "for what do we exist?" Knowledge vision is a value-driven articulation of an idealistic praxis for the organization. Knowledge visions materialize as a set of shared beliefs about how to act and interact to attain some determined idealized future state, giving the firm a focus on the knowledge to be created that goes beyond the existing boundaries of the products, the organizational structure, and the markets. The possibilities of attaining the future praxis are manifested at each organizational level by answering to a living question of "what can we do?" (Heidegger, 1962). Through personal aspirations and collective sense making, leaders develop a mental image of a possible and desirable future state of the organization in order to choose a direction. The consequent mental and behavioral patterns linked to the knowledge vision occur both at the implicit and explicit levels, and gives a direction to the knowledge spiral.

While it always refers to future, it ties the past experiences in the present action. According to Martin Heidegger (1962), the most important dimension of temporality is future because it presents the potentiality-for-being. In a similar way, knowledge vision forms a nexus between the past, present, and future.

Knowledge vision inspires the intellectual passion of organizational members so that they are encouraged to "reach further" to create knowledge that cross the existing boundary of product, organization, market, or technological limit. As Rescher wrote, "Oprimal results are often attainable only by trying for too much—by reaching beyond the limits of the possible. Man is a dual citizen of the realms of reality and possibility" (Rescher, 1987: 143).

Knowledge vision also defines a consistent value system to evaluate and justify the knowledge created in the organization. As stated, when knowledge is created out of individual subjective knowledge for an organization, it needs a social process of justifying knowledge. For that, the organization needs a value system to define what is truth, goodness, and beauty for it. Therefore, knowledge vision needs to be based on an absolute value, which goes beyond the Wall Street values of winning the competition and maximizing a profit, for the existence of the organization.

18.2.4 Building, Energizing, and Connecting Ba

Ba can be built intentionally, or created spontaneously. Leaders can facilitate ba building by providing physical space such as meeting rooms, cyber space such as a computer network, or mental space such as common goals, and promote inter- actions among participants at such a space. Forming a task force is a typical example of intentional building of ba. To build ba, leaders also have to choose the right mix of people to participate, who can bring various contexts to share. It is also important for managers to "find" and utilize spontaneously formed ba, which changes or disappears very quickly. Hence, leaders have to read the situation in terms of how members of the organization are interacting with each other and with outside environments in order to quickly capture the naturally emerging ba, as well as to form ba effectively.

However, building and finding ba is not enough for a firm to manage the dynamic knowledge-creating process. Ba should be "energized" to give energy and quality to the SECI process. For that, leaders have to supply necessary conditions such as autonomy, creative chaos, redundancy, requisite variety, love, care, trust, and commitment.

Further, various ba are connected with each other to form a greater ba. For that, leaders have to facilitate the interactions among various ba, and among the participants, based on the knowledge vision. In many cases, the relationships among ba are not predetermined. Which ba should be connected in which way is often unclear. Therefore, leaders have to read the situation to connect various ba, as the relationships among them unfold.

Ba needs a certain boundary so that a meaningful shared context can emerge. Therefore, leaders should protect ba from the contexts outside so that it can grow its own context, especially when the ba is trying to create the kind of knowledge that is not part of the organization's current norm. At the same time, the boundary of ba should be open so that it can be connected with other ba. It is often difficult for participants of ba to see and accept the need to bring in different contexts from the one shared in ba, it is an important task for a leader who is outside the ba to find and build the connection among various ba. Legitimate power can be effectively used to protect the boundary (cocooning) and keep the boundary open.

18.3 CONCLUSION

This chapter argues that building the theory of knowledge creation needs to an epistemological and ontological discussion, instead of just relying on a positivist approach, which has been the implicit paradigm of social science. The positivist rationality has become identified with analytical thinking that focuses on generating and testing hypotheses through formal logic. While providing a clear guideline for theory building and empirical examinations, it poses problems for the investigation of complex and dynamic social phenomena, such as knowledge creation. In positivist-based research, knowledge is still often treated as an exogenous variable or distraction against linear economic rationale. The relative lack of alternative conceptualization has meant that management science has slowly been detached from the surrounding societal reality. The understanding of social systems cannot be based entirely on natural scientific facts.

This chapter proposed a framework to capture such a dynamic process of knowledge creation, with the concepts of SECI process, ba, and knowledge leadership to deal with the issues of contexts, values, ideals, and power. Since knowledge emerges out of subjective views of the world, it probably cannot be reached by one and only one absolute "truth." Hence, our view of knowledge is pragmatic, in the sense that it is temporally regarded as "truth" as long as it is practical to those who use it. However, the knowledge-creating process is idealistic at the same time, since knowledge is created through the social justification process, which relentlessly pursues the truth that may never be reached. We can say that the theory of knowledge creation is based on the idealistic pragmatism, which synthesizes the rational pursuit of appropriate ends, whose appropriateness are determined by ideals (Rescher, 2003).

The ontological and epistemological tenets in this chapter are the first steps towards establishing a more comprehensive explanation of knowledge in management science. It still needs further conceptual and theoretical development, especially, the issue of power in organizations. We also need more empirical research combining qualitative and quantitative methodologies (Nonaka, et al., 1994). In contrast to seeking to provide any finite solutions, I hope this chapter opens a lively discussion on the role of knowledge in social sciences and management science in particular.

References

ARROW, K. J. (1974). *The Limits of Organization*. New York, W. W. Norton.

BADARACCO, J. L., Jr. (1991). *The Knowledge Link: How Firms Compete Through Strategic Alliances*. Boston: Harvard Business School Press.

BUBER, M. (1923). *I and Thou*. New York: Charles Scriber's Sons.

DENNETT, D. C. (1987). *The Intentional Stance*. Cambridge, Mass.: MIT Press.

FLYVBJERG, B. (2001). *Making Social Science Matter: Why Social Science Fails and How it Can Succeed Again*. Cambridge: Cambridge University Press.

GLADWELL, M. M. (2000). *The Tipping Point: How Little Things Can Make a Big Difference*. Boston: Wheeler.

HAYEK, F. A. (1945). The use of knowledge in society. In F. A. Hayek (ed.), *Individualism and Economic Order*. Chicago: University of Chicago Press.

HEIDEGGER, M. (1962). *Being and Time*. New York: Harper and Row.

HUSSERL, E. (1931). *Ideas: General Introduction to Pure Phenomenology*, trans. W. R. Boyce Gibson. New York: Macmillan.

—— (1970). *The Crisis of European Sciences and Transcendental Phenomenology*. Northwestern University Press, Evanston. (First pub. 1954.)

—— (1977). *Cartesian Meditations*. The Hague: Martinus Nijhoff.

INKPEN, A. C. (1996). Creating knowledge through collaboration. *California Management Review*, 39(1): 123–140.

JANTSCH, E. (1980). *The Self-Organizing Universe*. Oxford: Pergamon Press.

LAWSON, T. (1997). *Economics and Reality*. New York: Routledge.

MERLEAU-PONTY, M. (1962). *Phenomenology of Perception*. London: Routledge.

MINGERS, J. (2001). Combining IS research methods: Towards a pluralistic methodology, *Information Systems Research*, 12(3): 240–259.

MORGAN, G., and SMIRCHICH, L. (1980). The case for qualitative research. *The Academy of Management Review*, 5(4): 491–500.

NISHIDA, K. (1921, 1990). *An Inquiry into the Good*, trans. M. Abe and C. Ives. New Haven: Yale University Press.

—— (1970). *Fundamental Problems of Philosophy: The World of Action and the Dialectical World*. Tokyo: Sophia University.

NONAKA, I. (1985). *Kigyou Sinkaron: Jouhou Souzou no Management (The Theory of Evolving Firms: Management of Information Creation)*, Tokyo: Nihon Keizai Shinbunsya (in Japanese).

NONAKA, I. (1988a). Creating organizational order out of chaos: Self-renewal in Japanese firms, *California Management Review*, 30(3): 57–73.

—— (1988b). Toward middle-up-down management: Accelerating information creation, *Sloan Management Review*, 29(3): 9–18.

—— (1991). The knowledge-creating company. *Harvard Business Review*, Nov.–Dec.: 96–104.

—— (1994). A dynamic theory of organizational knowledge creation. *Organizational Science*, 5(1): 14–37.

—— BYOSIERE, P., BORUCHI, C., and KONNO, N. (1994). Organizational knowledge creation theory: A first comprehensive test. *International Business Review*, 3(4): 337–351.

—— and NICOSIA, F. M. (1979). Marketing management, its environment, and information processing: A problem in organizational design. *Journal of Business Research*, 7(4): 277–300.

—— PELTOKORPI, V., and TOMAE, H. (forthcoming), Strategic knowledge creation: The case of Hamamatsu photonics. *International Journal of Technology Management*.

—— and TAKEUCHI, H. (1986). The new new product development game. *Harvard Business Review*, Jan.–Feb.: 137–146.

—— —— (1995). *The Knowledge-Creating Company: How Japanese Companies Create the Dynamics of Innovation*. New York: Oxford University Press.

—— and TOYAMA, R. (2002). Firm as a dialectic being: Toward the dynamic theory of the firm. *Industrial and Corporate Change*, 11: 995–1109.

—— —— (2003). The knowledge-creating theory revisited: Knowledge creation as a synthesizing process. *Knowledge Management Research & Practice*, 1(1): 2–10.

—— —— and KONNO, N. (2000). SECI, Ba and leadership: A unified model of dynamic knowledge creation. *Long Range Planning*, 33: 1–31.

PENROSE, E. T. (1959). *The Theory of the Growth of the Firm*. New York: Wiley.

PEUKERT, H. (2003). The missing chapter in Schumpeter's *The Theory of Economic Development*. In J. Backhaus (ed.), *Joseph Alois Schumpeter*: 221–231. Berlin: Springer.

POLANYI, M. (1952). *Personal Knowledge*. Chicago: University of Chicago Press.

—— (1966). *The Tacit Dimension*. Garden City, NY: Doubleday.

PORTER, M. E. (1980). *Competitive Strategy: Techniques for Analyzing Industries and Competitors*. New York: Free Press.

RESCHER, N. (1987). *Ethical Idealism: An Inquiry into the Nature and Function of Ideals*. London: University of California Press.

—— (2003). *Rationality in pragmatic perspective*. Lewiston, NY: Edwin Mellen Press.

SIMON, H. (1945). *Administrative Behavior*. New York: McMillan.

SUCHMAN, L. (1987). *Plans and Situated Actions: The Problem of Human–Machine Communication*. New York: Cambridge University Press.

THOMPSON, J. (1967). *Organizations in Action*. New York: McGraw Hill.

TSOUKAS, H. (1996). The firm as a distributed knowledge system: A constructionist approach. *Strategic Management Journal*, 17(Winter Special Issue): 11–25.

UENO, N. (2000). *Interaction*. Tokyo: Daishukan Shoin.

VARELA, F., and SHEAR, J. (1999). First-person accounts: Why, what, and how. In F. Varela and J. Shear (eds.), *The View from Within: First Person Approaches to the Study of Consciousness*. Thorverton: Imprint Academic.

WATTS, D. J. (2003). *Six Degrees: The Science of a Connected Age.* New York: W. W. Norton.

WIKSTROM, S., and NORMANN, R. (1994). *Knowledge and Value: A New Perspective on Corporate Transformation.* London: Routledge.

WILLIAMSON, O. (1975). *Markets and Hierarchies.* New York: Free Press.

··

CHAPTER 19

THE EXPERIENCE
OF THEORIZING

SENSEMAKING AS TOPIC
AND RESOURCE

··

KARL E. WEICK

THE experience of theorizing is much like the experience of sensemaking. Both consist of actions that are explicative, evocative, equivocality reducing, exegetical, transient, narrative, embedded in paradigms, and meaningful. It is this correspondence that supplies both the topic and the resources for this chapter. And it is respect for this correspondence that is characteristic of the actual process of theory development that will be described. This correspondence is noteworthy since it is often neglected in polished prescriptions for steps to follow when trying to develop theory (e.g., Donaldson, 2003). The result of this neglect is theories that have less impact than they could have because authors hold back from digging deeper into their own experience and intuitions for ideas that matter. I discuss these issues in the following manner. First, I discuss the phenomenon of sensemaking, sampling heavily some properties that have a direct bearing on theory development. Second, I reverse the emphasis and take a closer look at the nature of the theorizing that

I am grateful to Kathleen Sutcliffe for comments on a preliminary version of this chapter and to Lance Sandelands, Hari Tsoukas, Barbara Czarniawska, John Van Maanen, David Whetten, Reuben McDaniel and Jeffrey Pfeffer for helping me to gain a better understanding of theorizing.

drives the ongoing elaboration of ideas about sensemaking. Third, these discussions of sensemaking and theorizing are converted into guidelines for theory development.

19.1 ON SENSEMAKING

Sensemaking, viewed as central both to the process of theorizing and to the conduct of everyday organizational life, is a sprawling collection of ongoing interpretive actions. To define this "sprawl" is to walk a thin line between trying to put plausible boundaries around a diverse set of actions that seem to cohere, while also trying to include enough properties so that the coherence is seen as distinctive and significant but something less than the totality of the human condition. This bounding is a crucial move in theory construction. It starts early, but it never stops. Theorizing involves continuously resetting the boundaries of the phenomenon and continuously rejustifying what has newly been included and excluded. In theorizing, as in everyday life, meanings always seem to become clear a little too late. Accounts, cognitions, and categories all lie in the path of earlier action, which means that definitions and theories tend to be retrospective summaries of ongoing inquiring rather than definitive constraints on future inquiring. These complications are evident in efforts to define sensemaking.

Some portraits of sensemaking suggest that it resembles an evolutionary process of blind variation and selective retention. "An evolutionary epistemology is implicit in organizational sensemaking, which consists of retrospective interpretations built during interaction" (Weick 1995b: 67). Here we see sensemaking being aligned with the insight that "a system can respond adaptively to its environment by mimicking inside itself the basic dynamics of evolutionary processes" (Warglien, 2002: 110), an insight that is tied directly to theory development when theorizing is described as "disciplined imagination" (Weick, 1989).

Some portraits of sensemaking suggest that it consists of activities that construct reality. For example the concept of sensemaking

focuses attention upon the idea that reality of everyday life must be seen as an ongoing "accomplishment", which takes particular shape and form as individuals attempt to create order and make retrospective sense of the situations in which they find themselves ... The sensemaking metaphor encourages an analytical focus upon the processes through which individuals create and use symbols; it focuses attention upon the study of symbolic processes through which reality is created and sustained. Individuals are not seen as living *in*, and acting out their lives in relation *to*, a wider reality, so much as creating and sustaining images of a wider reality, in part to rationalize what they are doing. They realize their reality, by "reading into" their situation patterns of significant meaning. (Morgan, Frost, and Pondy, 1983: 24)

Here, we see even more clearly the affinity between theorizing and sensemaking. When people make sense in any setting they use symbols to make meaning, remain sensitive to changes in ongoing events, and locate recurrent patterns that establish order in those changes.

Still other portraits of sensemaking emphasize its close ties to surprise and that which is equivocal (e.g., Mills, 2003: 35). For example, Magala (1997: 324) suggests that sensemaking means basically "inventing a new meaning (interpretation) for something that has already occurred during the organizing process, *but does not yet have a name* (italics in original), has never been recognized as a separate autonomous process, object, event." Naming, interpreting, and inventing meanings are actions that lie at the core of theorizing. When this theorizing is directed at the phenomenon of organizational sensemaking theorists ask the question, "How does something come to be an event for organizational members?" When organizational actors face similar contexts of surprise and equivocality, they ask an equivalent question, "What's the story here?" Their sensemaking doesn't stop when they get an answer because all they've done so far is bring an event into existence. They face the further question, "If that's the story, what should we do?" Now the problem is to bring a meaning into existence, a meaning that will stabilize continued acting but remain sensitive to the continuing flow of potentially new stories.

There are some portraits of sensemaking that are mischievous and can be misleading. For example, there is mischief in the title of my 1995 book that summarizes key ideas about sensemaking (Weick, 1995b). The book is titled *Sensemaking in Organizations*, which implies that if sensemaking stops the organization goes on. It doesn't. That's the point of the article on the collapse of sensemaking at Mann Gulch (Weick, 1993a). As sensemaking began to deteriorate so too did the organization of the firefighting crew. Weakening of one weakened the other. Sensemaking and organizing have been described as mutually constitutive almost from the beginning (e.g., Weick, 1969). But as my own lapse makes clear, that unity is easy to forget.

And speaking of unity, there is further mischief in the innocent punctuation mark called a hyphen. Hyphens are used to signify that two separate words such as sense-making, are to be read as a compounded single unit. I hyphenated sense-making in 1979, but dropped the hyphen in favor of the single word sensemaking in 1995. Why? The hyphenated word sense-making is still read as a compound process, assembled from at least two parts that remain parts with no clear rules for their assembling. If you do away with the hyphen then you do away with such distracting issues as what is sensing, what is making, and how and under what conditions do the two combine? Those are not my issues. Instead, I want to understand how the conditions of interdependency associated with organizing affect how people deal with situations where there are too many or too few meanings. When people encounter such situations, they are already engaged in "absorbed coping" or as Heidegger called it, a *ready-to-hand* mode of engagement. Their actions are not compounds. Instead, people are aware of the world holistically as a network of interrelated projects, possible tasks, and "thwarted potentialities" (Packer, 1985: 1083. If an ongoing project is interrupted, then experience changes into an *unready-to-hand* mode, but it still isn't a compound. "Particular aspects of the whole situation stand out but only against a background provided by the project we are engaged in and the interests and involvements guiding it" (Packer, 1985: 1084). What persists despite these interruptions are projects and routines for explaining, interpreting, and recovery (Weick, Sutcliffe, and Obstfeld, 1999). Compounds do not appear until people adopt a *present-at-hand* detached mode of engagement. To hyphenate sensemaking as it weaves in and out of everyday life is to carve that process at places other than at its joints.

Diverse as these portraits are they share a presumption that sensemaking is a complex process (Patriotta, 2003; Mills, 2003) involving evolution (Campbell, 1965; Warglien, 2002), interpretations (Lant, 2002), action (Laroche, 1995), and interaction (Taylor and Van Every, 2000). We can keep all of these in play if, for the duration of this chapter, we define sensemaking as the ongoing retrospective development of plausible images that rationalize what people are doing. This definition reminds us that retrospect, plausibility, images, reasons, identity, and most of all ongoing action are crucial in sensemaking, as they are also in theory development.

Sensemaking is defined not just by words that summarize its properties but also by its outcroppings. Any theorizing is dependent on the quality and extent of the details that ground it. To ground sensemaking is to study, for example, people such as incident commanders who have to size up chaotic streams of events. "By definition an emergency or crisis occurs suddenly and unpredictably; these incidents are characterized by their unfamiliarity, scale, and speed of escalation... The challenge for the incident commander is to continually make sense of the unexpected and often dynamic situation in order to deploy the available resources most efficiently" (Flin, 1996: 105). Problems in incident command, as in theory development, may occur when people neglect seven properties that have an important effect on sensemaking (Weick, 1995b: 17–62. These seven include (1) social context, (2) identity, (3) retrospect, (4) salient cues, (5) ongoing projects, (6) plausibility, and (7) enactment. These seven can be retained by means of the acronym, SIR COPE. They are important because they affect the extent to which people will update and develop their sense of the situation. These properties, in other words, have an effect on the willingness of people to disengage from their initial story and adopt a newer story that is more sensitive to the particulars of the present context. Faced with a confused world, a world not unlike that which puzzles the theorist, it is important not to view this confusion solely as a problem in decision making.

The necessity for moving beyond decision making is made clear by the late Paul Gleason, reputed to be one of the five best wildland firefighters in the world. Gleason said that when fighting fires, he was in a more mindful position as leader if he viewed his efforts at leadership as sensemaking rather than decision making. In his words, "If I make a decision it is a possession, I take pride in it, I tend to defend it and not listen to those who question it. If I make sense, then this is more dynamic and I listen and I can change it. A decision is something you polish. Sensemaking is a direction for the next period" (Personal communication, June 13, 1995). When Gleason perceives himself as making a decision, he reports that he postpones action so he can get the decision "right" and that after he makes the decision, he finds himself defending it rather than revising it to suit changing circumstances. Both polishing and defending eat up valuable time and encourage blind spots. If, instead, Gleason sees himself as making sense of an unfolding fire, then he gives his crew a direction for some indefinite period, a direction that by definition is dynamic, open to revision at any time, self-correcting, responsive, with its rationale being transparent.

Similar agility in theorizing occurs when that activity is also treated as a direction that is subject to revision, rather than as a decision that invokes selective attention in the service of justification. Other things being equal sensemaking is more fruitful in a context that allows for more interactions, clearer identities, more use of elapsed action as a guide, unobstructed access to a wider range of cues, closer attention to the ways in which the ongoing situation is changing, the replacement of less plausible stories of what is happening with those that incorporate even more observations than the stories they replace, and deeper acceptance of the reality that people act while thinking, which means they don't reach single decision points so much as they shape what they will next think about, act upon, and bring into existence.

My own grounding of the phenomenon of sensemaking sprawls almost as much as do my accounts of what is a common pattern across those outcroppings. Among the outcroppings of sensemaking that I have tried to understand are college students making sense of unexpected reward contingencies (Weick, 1964; Weick and Prestholdt, 1968), jazz musicians making sense of new music and imperfect performance (Weick, Gilfillan, and Keith, 1973; Weick, 1995a), soldiers trying to make sense of chaotic battlefields (Weick, 1985), air traffic controllers trying to make sense of a non-standard communiqué from a moving aircraft (Weick, 1990), therapy patients trying to make sense of unwelcome overtures from therapists (Weick, 1992b), smokejumpers making sense of a small fire that suddenly turns explosive (Weick, 1993a), flight operations personnel on an aircraft carrier trying to make sense of communiqués from pilots in trouble (Weick and Roberts, 1993), firefighters trying to make sense of the frightening order to drop their tools and run (Weick, 1996a, 2001), and medical practitioners trying to make sense of unexpected adverse medical events (Weick, 2002; Weick and Sutcliffe, 2003).

Some of these examples are more compelling than others. That has a subtle effect on theorizing. A compelling example animates the theorist to dig into that example deeply. But the resulting explanation tends to contract and to fit the example more tightly but everything else more loosely. Given the impossibility of drafting explanations that are simultaneously general, accurate, and simple (Thorngate, 1976) and given the probability that a compelling example compels one toward accuracy, the result is either an accurate explanation that struggles to be general and loses all hope of simplicity or an accurate explanation that struggles for simplicity and loses all hope of generality. In the case of the Mann Gulch disaster, arguably the most compelling instance of sensemaking I've worked with, there is an interesting twist in the fact that some readers see it is a blend of generality and accuracy and other readers see it as a blend of generality and simplicity. Mann Gulch is accurate–general when read as "a general theory of how organizations unravel, what the social conditions of such unraveling are, and how organizations can be made more resilient" (Dougherty, 2002: 852). Mann Gulch is accurate–simple when read as a depiction of leadership in a disintegrating organization that proposes four ways in which organizations can be made less vulnerable to interruptions in sensemaking (Gililand and Day, 2000: 335).

There are two lessons here with respect to outcroppings and theorizing. First, no one theorist can have it all, "all" being an explanation that is general, accurate, and simple. To develop a theory that falls short on one of these three dimensions is not a sign of incompetence but a sign of the intransigence of the task itself. Second, what is impossible for one theorist is often possible for a collection of theorists. A set of people, each with a different pattern of tradeoffs, can spread the weaknesses among them and collectively triangulate a set of ideas that survives as a robust general, simple, accurate account.

Hypothetically, a single theorist could do the same thing by drafting multiple versions of an explanation, each version trying to implement a different set of tradeoffs. I suspect this solution may be more common than we expect. Over the course of a career, people may start with accurate explanations. They know one thing really well, the object that was studied for their dissertation research. They move from this accurate explanation to efforts to generalize it, which means that their explanations grow more complex and less simple. As they continue to work with complex general explanations, they begin to see themes and patterns that are key triggers, drivers, and moments that were hard to see in all the general complexity. Once they articulate some of these simplicities they may then return to the place from which they started, and now actually see it for the first time. Whether the lone theorist moves from accurate to general to simple, or from accurate to simple to general, it is likely that the progression will be one that moves from superficial simplicity through confused complexity to profound simplicity (Schutz, 1979: 68–69). The trick is not to get cocky with one's superficial simplicities or disheartened by one's confused complexity.

Additional insight into the process of theory development viewed as an instance of sensemaking are found if we take a closer look at talking in order to think, and retrospecting elapsed experience.

19.1.1 Seeing What I Say

The signature of sensemaking theory is a question: "how can I know what I think until I see what I say?" People talk and examine their talk to see what they are thinking and what their talk might mean. The words they use in talking, the paradigms they impose while seeing, the images they carry forward from earlier episodes of sensemaking, all influence meaning. These words and paradigms are socialized and shaped by culture, institutions, projects, habits, assumptions, and identity. That doesn't exclude much. The surprise, therefore, is the stubbornness with which a handful of meanings often persist and produce fixation, confirmation bias, selective perception, and the dogmatic true believer. Clearly, seeing what I say is neither as open-ended nor as creative as we might hope for. Organizations count on that very stability and inertia but theorists renounce it. They do so in ways such as writing *in order to* think, experimenting with different ways of seeing, and most of all by trying different words when they say things.

Vocabulary and the deployment of words are a big deal in my view of sensemaking (e.g., Weick, 1995a: ch. 5) and in my work as a theorist (see discussion of theory as glossing in Weick, 1981). For example, the phrase "cognitive dissonance" (Festinger, 1957) was a new term in 1957, it resonated in its joint emphasis on cognition and interruption, and it has been sufficiently foundational to serve as a part of my saying ever since (e.g., Weick, 1995b: 11–13). My attempt to theorize the interconnection between organizing and sensemaking is summarized in a list of thirty-six terms (Weick, 1979: 241) that define the results of the interconnecting. The list serves to introduce novel distinctions, form the beginnings of a language to say and see organizing, and to link sensemaking to other literatures. To theorize about organizing is partly to craft a vocabulary and a grammar for organizational description. When that grammar is imposed on events, one's thinking tends to be channeled in directions that embody the relationships highlighted in the language of the theory. Thus, people who talk the language of organizing, literally talk organization into existence. In doing so they are thereby enabled to think for the moment as if organizing mattered in ways defined in the theory. That thinking may prove useful. It may not. But that's no different than the outcome of any episode of sensemaking.

In my own theorizing I often try to say things without using the verb form "to be." This tactic, known as e-prime (Kellogg, 1987), means that I'm not allowed to say "Reuben *is* a formidable competitor." Instead, I'm forced to be explicit about the actions that went into the prohibited summary judgment. Now I say things like, "Reuben works with smaller margins, gets new products to market faster, does more manufacturing offshore, provides larger kickbacks, etc". When I'm forced to forego the verb form "to be" I pay more attention to particulars, context, and the situation. I also tend to see more clearly what I am not in a position to say. If I say that Reuben operates on smaller margins, that may or may not mean that he is a competitor. It all depends on other explicit descriptions about how he behaves.

The larger point about e-prime is that it helps the theorist move closer to the territory that is being mapped. Part of my fascination with "saying" is summarized in one of Robert Irwin's favorite maxims: "to see is to forget the name of the thing one sees" (Weschler, 1982: 203). In Irwin's view sensemaking starts with perception of undifferentiated sensations. These sensations gradually take on meaning when they are named, systematized, and formalized. Essentially, when people engage in sensemaking, they invoke more and more abstractions, which means they move farther and farther away from their initial impressions. This transformation is necessary in order to share and coordinate perceptions, but people pay a price for it. As social complexity increases, people shift from perceptually based knowing to categorically based knowing in the interest of coordination (Baron and Misovich, 1999). As demands for coordination increase, concepts become simpler and more general in the interest of transmission. While these changes facilitate coordination, they do so at the potential cost of greater intellectual and emotional distance from the phenomena picked up by direct perception.

Thus, in a reversal of Robert Irwin's maxim, people who succeed at coordination may fail at perception. They fail because they remember the name but not the substance of the originating experience. This means that whenever events occur that are beyond the reach of the labels that people do share, they will be the *last* to know about those events. If a coordinated group seldom reworks its labels, then there is a higher probability that it will be overwhelmed by changes that have been incubating unnoticed. That's what happened when NASA engineers kept labeling the burn marks on O-rings, "within mission parameters" (Vaughan, 1996) and when, more recently, they labeled repeated foam shedding on the Columbia shuttle as an "in family" event meaning that it was well understood (Gehman, 2003). It wasn't. Coordinated theorizing can produce similar lapses in accuracy as has been argued by Weick (1983) and Campbell (1979) in discussions of a cohesion–accuracy tradeoff in communities of scholars. Research groups that are more cohesive and tightly knit tend to develop less adequate theories than do those groups that are more loosely coupled. Tight coupling tends to produce more redundancy and more internal dependencies among sensors, which means that the sensors register less of what is being observed (Heider, 1959).

19.1.2 Retrospecting Elapsed Experience

Seeing what I say is not just an issue of words, conversation, and grammar. It is also an issue of retrospect. My focus on retrospect is part of a more pervasive tendency to be interested in reactive phenomena, literally phenomena where the action is less internally motivated and more a response or reaction to actions and contexts that originate elsewhere. People often enact their environments as we saw earlier. But what is crucial is that we also note that this means that they are the authors of that which constrains them. A pervasive focus on reactive phenomena is evident in my work on disasters, resilience, improvisation, recovery, adaptation, retrospect, firefighting. For example, consider the question, "What will be the next AIDS?" That's not a question that interests me. What interests me is the impossibility of answering it and how people cope with that impossibility.

You can't do much until the first wave of human infection occurs. You can't prevent the next epidemic. Furthermore, signs get buried among other diseases. If you find a new virus, you don't know whether it is significant or not until a human episode occurs. The trouble is that by the time you do establish that it is significant, the virus has already settled into hosts, reservoirs, and vectors and is being amplified. Edwin Kilbourne, a microbiologist at Mt. Sinai hospital states the reactive quality of diagnosis: "I think in a sense we have to be prepared to do what the Centers for Disease Control does so very well, and that is *put out fire....* It's not intellectually very satisfying to wait to react to a situation, but I think there's only so much preliminary planning you can do. I think the preliminary planning has to focus on what you do when the emergency happens: Is your fire company well drilled? Are they ready to act, or are they sitting around the station house for months." (Henig, 1993: 193–194)

The picture is one of perennially playing catch up. Geertz is sensitive to the reactive quality of living when he comments on "The after-the-fact, ex post, life-trailing nature of consciousness generally—occurrence first, formulation later on.... [Theorists make] a continual effort to devise systems of discourse that can keep up, more or less, with what, perhaps, is going on" (Geertz, 1995: 19).

There is a clear tension here, one that is prevalent in theorizing. When we look back over outcomes or data to see how they cohere and what they might mean, we are often looking at outcomes that were enacted by our own efforts (Weick, 2003a). Thus, retrospect and agency coexist, but it is often hard to reconcile proactive enactment and reactive retrospect. Furthermore, it is hard to separate that which we are able to will and enact from that which we can't. In my own writing I tend to overattribute agency rather than underestimate it. Institutionalists and critical theorists tend to roll their eyes when I depict organizational actors as people who invent, improvise, create, conceive, enact, construct, transform, originate, make, and generate small wins that have large consequences. These attributions of agency obviously are overdetermined. They stem from such things as my fascination with small structures that have large consequences (Weick, 1993b), socialization into macro psychology and social psychology, efforts to offset an INTJ Myers-Briggs bias in my own sensemaking (Weick, 1992*a*), skepticism that a linear stimulus–response unit of analysis is useful theorizing (Dewey, 1998), and equal skepticism that the monolith of "the" external environment is any more useful as a construct to explain human functioning.

One way to convert all of this into a lesson for theorizing is to borrow Adam Phillips' counsel to those who craft psychoanalytic theory and apply it to organizational studies. Phillips said that psychoanalysis "does not need any more abstruse or sentimental abstractions—any new paradigms or radical revisions—it just needs more good sentences" (Phillips, 2001: xvi). Later on in his book, he cites just such a good sentence crafted by Leslie Farber. I quote this sentence for two reasons. First, it shows how words can bracket and improve thinking. Second, the content of this quotation is a perfect description of existence that is simultaneously enactive and reactive. The sentence is a welcome caution when I'm tempted to be carried away by enactive imagery. People have a

recurring temptation to apply the will...to those portions of life that not only will not comply, but that will become distorted under such coercion. Let me give a few examples: I can will knowledge, but not wisdom; going to bed, but not sleeping; eating but not hunger; meekness, but not humility; scrupulosity but not virtue; self-assertion or bravado, but not courage; lust, but not love; commiseration, but not sympathy; congratulations, but not admiration; religiosity, but not faith; reading, but not understanding...I can will speech or silence, but not conversation. (Phillips, 2001: 318–319)

19.1.3 Sensemaking as Zeitgeist

All theorizing begins somewhere, but since living is ongoing and overdetermined with people being thrown into events that are already underway, the nomination of beginnings and formative influences can seldom be stated with any certainty. But what is certain is that theorizing reflects the times, even if the theorist is the last person to notice this. Let me illustrate that by discussing a comment about the "origins" of sensemaking that took me by complete surprise. Everything that I've said about sensemaking bears an imprint of contemporary western society and its values. We all know that the times influence our inquiries, although some acknowledge this more readily than others (Kenneth Gergen has been remarkably lucid on this point. The idea of sensemaking certainly reflects the times. The idea has a historical, generational legacy but I didn't spot it, Magala did (1997). He argued that two core ideas in sensemaking are the idea that each individual sensemaker is a "parliament of selves" (individuals have multiple identities) and that organizations are "negotiation parlors" where diverse views are reviewed. When combined, these two ideas allow "for a more egalitarian approach toward organizational processes and for a more democratic review of subjective meanings and intersubjective negotiation procedures than would otherwise be the case" (Magala, 1997: 333). The historical generational twist to this condensed core is that

Weick's concept of organizing as sensemaking [drafted in the late 1960s and published in 1969] can thus be considered a theoretical equivalent of the political anti-authoritarian movements of protest of the late sixties and early seventies (very much as Hegel's philosophy of history was a theoretical equivalent of the political experiences labeled "the French Revolution")... One wonders if a public debate with Weick, Cohn-Bendit, and Wallerstein on the one hand, and Fukuyama, Senge, Porter on the other might reveal this hidden "cluster" of generational experiences of protest as a major dividing line in modern social science. (Magala, 1997: 333)

While the ideas of sensemaking have previously been situated in terms of prominent social science theories of the 1960s such as cognitive dissonance theory and ethnomethodology (Weick 1995b: 10–12) and prominent philosophical positions such as pragmatism and existentialism, Magala's speculation is the first time that ideas about sensemaking have been situated in larger cultural and societal forces. Magala argues that experiences of the 1960s such as Vietnam produced a changed concept of agency and a less authoritarian approach to generating a larger variety of choices in formulating organizational alternatives. These shifts refocused attention away from decisions (e.g. should we increase troop strength in Vietnam) toward the "background and software of choices" (Magala, 1997: 333) (e.g., how did it come to pass that we find ourselves in a position where troop strength is a matter we feel needs to be decided. One version of Magala's "software of choices" is the phenomenon of sensemaking, which occurs when agents, acting as parliaments of selves, interact in "negotiation parlors" to generate courses of collective action.

Positioned this way, sensemaking is not just an individual-level, subjective phenomenon that is naive about the conflict-laden, power-driven, interest-derived character of the organized "real" world. Instead, sensemaking, like all social science positions, is a situated description in social science terminology of less visible context-sensitive dynamics in social life. In many ways, translating those dynamics into the language of sensemaking was and remains an affirmation that small interventions can have larger consequences. That translation may endure. What is more likely to change are ideas about just what happens during those formative moments of intervention.

To take a closer look at just how such changes in ideas materialize, we turn to the topic of theorizing.

19.2 ON THEORIZING

So far sensemaking has been figure and theorizing has been ground. In this section we reverse that relationship and focus on the qualities of theory that were implicit in the preceding analysis. The implications for theory and the activity of theorizing are subtle and not nearly as tidy or simple as one would hope.

The meaning of "theory" that best fits the preceding discussion is Reber's statement that theory is "a general principle or a collection of interrelated general principles that is put forward as an explanation of a set of known facts and empirical findings...(T)he term is "awarded to almost any honest attempt to provide an explanation of some body of fact or data" (Reber, 1995: 793–794).

This definition fits what I've said so far in several ways. It doesn't talk about axioms, theorems, or variables. These characteristics are commonly mentioned in the canon of theory construction though they are rare in actual theory building. For example, despite all the talk about "variables" in theory development, the claim that the universe can be abstracted into variables that can be meaningfully manipulated at the behest of the actor is shaky (Guba, 1990: 373). Variables are not the only medium that conveys an explanation. Relevant media also include "principles," connected ideas, images, patterns, metaphors, even allegories (Van Maanen, 1995).

The "known facts" and "empirical findings" that theories "explain" can precede theory construction or follow it. The fact that theory construction is a form of retrospective sensemaking, does not decouple it from facts. Rather, it means that facticity is often an achievement. Having first said something, theorists discover what they have been thinking about when they look more closely at that talk. A close look at the talk often suggests that the talk is about examples, experiences, and stories that had previously been understood though not articulated. The talk enacts facts because it makes that understanding visible, explicit, and available for reflective thinking, but the talk doesn't create the understanding. Instead, it articulates the understanding by converting "know how" into "know that." Sensemaking, with its insistence on retrospective sensemaking, is a valuable standpoint for theorizing because it preserves the proper order for understanding and explanation (understanding precedes explanation: Sandelands, 1990: 241–247). It reminds the investigator to keep saying and writing so that he or she can have something to see in order then to think theoretically.

When theorizing is portrayed this way, what now becomes much more important are "stop rules." Continuous saying and thinking sooner or later articulates an explanation that matters in a seriously plausible way. But how does one spot that moment? If people stumble onto theory when they see what they say, how do they know that they have found theory rather than nonsense? Again, there are no hard and fast rules. But any of the following help:

1. Someone tells them that they have a theory.
2. The saying resembles other theories that they've seen.
3. The saying explains events not used in its construction.
4. The saying depicts abstract, conceptual, generalizable patterns.

5. The saying fits one of Merton's four categories of approximations to theory (see below)
6. The saying is a useful guide to what one can expect to see in a future event.
7. The saying serves as a higher order frame for a lower order cue to which it can be connected.
8. The author claims that it is a theory and others subject that claim to their own truth tests.
9. The author ignores the question "is it a theory or not" and simply uses it.

This is not as haphazard as it sounds. Instead, these stop rules for theory simply recognize that theories are coherent orientations to events, sets of abstractions, consensually validated explanations and embodiments of aphoristic thinking.

Reber's definition is also intriguing because it talks about theory as a label that is "*awarded*" to almost any *honest* attempt at explanation. Here we get a hint that theory is a continuum and an approximation. The image of theory as continuum comes from Runkel.

Theory belongs to the family of words that includes *guess, speculation, supposition, conjecture, proposition, hypothesis, conception, explanation, model*. The dictionaries permit us to use *theory* for anything from "guess" to a system of assumptions... (Social scientists) will naturally want to underpin their *theories* with more empirical data than they need for a *speculation*. They will naturally want a *theory* to incorporate more than one *hypothesis*. We plead only that they do not save *theory* to label their ultimate triumph, but use it as well to label their interim struggles. (Runkel and Runkel, 1984: 130)

As we have seen, most products that are labeled theory actually approximate theory. Robert Merton (1967: 143–149) was sensitive to this point and suggested that there were at least four ways in which theory was approximated. These were (1) general orientation in which broad frameworks specify types of variables people should take into account without any specification of relationships among these variables (e.g., Scott, 1998 analyzes rational, natural, and open systems); (2) analysis of concepts in which concepts are specified but not interrelated (Perrow, 1984 analyzes the concept of normal accident); (3) post factum interpretation in which ad hoc hypotheses are derived from a single observation, with no effort to explore new observations or alternative explanations (e.g., Weick, 1990 analyzes behavioral regression in the Tenerife air disaster); and (4) empirical generalization in which an isolated proposition summarizes the relationship between two variables, but further interrelations are not attempted (e.g., Pfeffer and Salancik, 1977) analyze how power flows to those who reduce significant uncertainties.

Reber's use of the phrase "any *honest* attempt at explanation" deserves comment because it underscores the social dimension of theory development. This dimension was mentioned earlier in the discussion of cohesion–accuracy tradeoffs. Implicit in that earlier discussion was the issue of assigning relative weights to one's personal experience and to reports on the experience of others (e.g., models, vicarious learning, social influence). The question is what weights do people give to their own vs. others' perceptions when these modes are in conflict and need to be combined in a net decision about inclusions, exclusions, and connections in theory construction? Donald Campbell calls this question "the rationality aspect of the conformity problem." He means that in many instances, "so-called conformity behavior is an intelligent part of a rational search for valid knowledge about a fallibly and indirectly known world rather than merely an interest in being like other persons whether or not they are correct" (Campbell, 1961: 108). Campbell later notes that "collective knowledge is maximized when each person so behaves as to be in his turn a valid dependable model for others. Each acts as both model and observer" (p. 123). This means that for collectively valid theory construction, one must both report honestly so that others can depend on his/her report, and also be respectful of others' reports as a source of information about the world. While doing this one must also reconcile these often disparate inputs in a manner that maintains self-respect, preserves credibility, and enables triangulation that produces valid perception, effective performance, and group survival.

It is the centrality of trustworthiness in the theorizing process that lies behind our insistence that experience and intuitions be treated as valued inputs. People trust first-hand experience, and if they are to be trustworthy contributors to theory development, they need to build on that experience. Dennis Gioia's (1992) development of script theory based on his experience as Ford's recall coordinator at the time of the Pinto fires, is the best example I know of on this point. Whatever one's reaction to Gioia's analysis or to his actions as recall coordinator, no one questions the account of the experience. Gioia acts like a trustworthy informant, others trust his account and provide their own truthworthy accounts, and differences of opinion are met with neither rejection nor surrender.

A pragmatic sense of what I mean by theory is also implied in my other writing about theory. For example, in the paper "Amendments to organizational theorizing" (Weick, 1974) the tacit message is that theory work consists of continuous theorizing that amends existing work. The message of this essay is compact and unconventional: "if you want to improve organizational theory, quit studying organizations" (p. 487). The argument is that organizational functioning is opaque, and equivalent functioning elsewhere is less opaque (e.g., collective sensemaking in a fire crew of strangers. Said differently, the advice is to theorize about units and events that you can understand. Once you understand, summarize that understanding in mechanisms, and generalize (perhaps shamelessly) those mechanisms to other settings. That's what people do in everyday sensemaking when they extract lessons from a vivid experience, and then treat subsequent experiences as moments of recognition.

The "Amendment" essay is also representative of another crucial point in theory development. There is a fragmentary quality to this essay in the sense that theorists are urged to pay closer attention to such diverse settings as everyday events, everyday places, everyday questions, micro-organizations, and absurd organizations, as well as to such diverse objects as escalators, car radios, memorials, bribes, auctions, graphics of life histories, bands, and banks. That assortment looks a lot like a garage sale or an arcade (Benjamin, 1999). But there is more going on here than merely constructing a scrapbook using whatever is at hand. Exhibits that seem to be fragments, may nevertheless be connected since they were collected and positioned by a single intelligence. The connections may be elusive, they may stretch the categories one has ready-to-hand, but those connections don't disappear. Instead, they are there waiting to be written into existence as principles and explanations. Loosely connected fragments, you will recall, are good media capable of registering subtle complex events.

My other discussions of theory suggest that the theorizing associated with sensemaking is middle range theory that glosses and integrates the work of predecessors, in ways that are intended to have impact on practice (Weick, 2003*b*). This is a fairly standard litany in discussions of theory development. But my point is that these are portions of that litany, which are readily practiced, at least in my case.

It is challenging and precarious to try turning the complexity of sensemaking and theorizing into a set of guidelines for practice. To further complicate matters, my experience is that whenever I craft what seem like concrete guidelines to me, those same guidelines seem like incomprehensible "road kill" to others (see Weick, 1996*b*, where a student at the University of Utah described running into my work as similar to running into something on the road at night: "you know you hit something but you don't know what the hell it was!" With that truth in advertising disclaimer in place, here are ways to approach the form of sensemaking called theory development more mindfully and more richly:

1. View theorizing, as a direction to update, not a decision to polish. Since fixation slows updating, hold ideas lightly and be prepared to drop tools that foster fixation.
2. Keep talking and keep variety in your talk to encourage updating and enrichment. Theorizing is as much about authoring an environment as it is about discovering a ready-made structure.
3. Get off your analytic hands and do something. You won't know what you've understood until you do something and draw inferences from what you do and say. Theorists act their way into meaningful categories.
4. Treat boundaries of your phenomenon as transient limits that are subject to rejustification and redefinition.
5. It's okay to interpret, to make it up as you go along, to be in the dark until it is too late, to second guess, and to feel thrown, because those are givens of the human condition that aren't suspended just because you're doing theory.
6. Pay close attention to surprise, interruption, and breakdown because these are your best opportunities for sensemaking and theorizing.

7. Engage in truth-making rather than truth-seeking since truth is something one authors, imposes, and negotiates rather than discovers.
8. Mimic processes of evolution in your theorizing.
9. Name phenomena with care and forget the names you inherit so that you can see the referent more richly.
10. Design the context for theoretical sensemaking so that it provides the supports for sensemaking that are summarized in the acronym SIR COPE.
11. Craft your explanations with different tradeoffs among generality, simplicity, and accuracy.
12. Moderate your demands that people agree with your definitions so that they register more nuances in the phenomenon being conceptualized.
13. Theorize about what you already understand by saying aloud your stream of consciousness, and then seeing what you already knew. There's your theory.
14. Aim for good sentences.

These guidelines don't sound much like the usual fare in a methods cookbook. Can they really help a beleaguered doctoral student writing endless dissertation proposals in his or her head, an anxious un-tenured researcher searching for impact, a confirmed positivist searching for certainty, or a frustrated author poised over a revise and resubmit? That's for them to decide. The above has worked for me, a judgment that may be specific to the topic on which I have worked, sensemaking. That judgment is also silent about a million other moments that probably were worked out by and worked into my continuous theorizing. Nevertheless, if readers see what I have said as a way of working that holds possibilities for renewal somewhere down the line, if readers cherry-picked these ideas anew at different career milestones, if readers used these ideas merely as a foil to contrast and sharpen other ideas that they really believed and wanted to convey, if the spirit of independent breaching displayed here informed identities being developed elsewhere, if somewhere in here there was a phrase or a reference that triggered a thought, if anything like these possibilities materialized, then this nudge to better theory development would have worked. And besides, since all I can do is control inputs rather than outcomes, this is the best I can do anyway.

19.3 CONCLUSION

If nothing else, this chapter should have made clear that organizational theorizing and sensemaking are a lot more complicated than simply putting variables together. That's not surprising since organization itself is elusive. Organization never actually exists as an identifiable entity. What exists instead is organizing, "an ongoing process of mediation in which the objective world where we live and interact both frames what we do and supplies us with the material for our own reconstruction of it. What we think of as organization is what is left over as a trace or memory of yesterday's organizing . . . (B)y the time we recognize the organization it is no longer there. What is there is our transformation of it; what makes it recognizable—re-cognizable—is precisely its no longer existing" (Taylor and Van Every, 2000: 163). When researchers quiz participants about the organization, its norms, or its culture, the participants' have in mind yesterday's organization and their experience of it. However, that organization no longer exists. Yesterday's organizing, viewed in hindsight, is all the tangible social reality we're likely to have to live with and theorize about.

When people theorize about any facet of organizing, including sensemaking, they focus on conceptual properties that are thought to be crucial. While their conclusions could be called "findings," that label fits only in the sense that when investigators look for something like the deployment of retrospect, or the reconciliation of competing frames, or the responses to ambiguity, they are more or less surprised by what they "find" given what they were looking for. Surprise under these conditions amounts to soft falsification, since the theory-based hunches were found to be insufficient rather than wrong. Steady cumulating of highlighted cases whose insufficiencies are heterogeneous can lead to growing confidence that sensemaking is a viable moment in organizational life. Sooner or later (and sometimes never) the case for sensemaking as an economical, useful set of ideas feels persuasive. Validity under these conditions boils down as much to a matter of feeling and intuition as it does to a matter of apprehension. What makes that feeling matter is that it is shared. Shared feeling is a form of "consensual validation," which, as Ruth Munroe puts it, amounts to "common sense of a high order—the things people agree upon because their common sensual apparatus and deeply common interpersonal experiences make them seem objectively so" (Weick, 1979: 3). Theorizing and sensemaking both have a big dose of higher order common sense when done right. And to do sensemaking and theorizing "right" means to appreciate their affinity.

References

Baron, R. M., and Misovich, S. J. (1999). On the relationship between social and cognitive modes of organization. In S. Chaiken and Y. Trope (eds.), *Dual-Process Theories in Social Psychology*: 586–605. New York: Guilford.

Benjamin, W. (1999). *The Arcades Project*. Cambridge, Mass.: Belknap Press.

Campbell, D. T. (1961). Conformity in psychology's theories of acquired behavioral dispositions. In I. A. Berg and B. M. Bass (eds.), *Conformity and Deviation*: 101–142. New York: Harper.

—— (1965). Variation and selective retention in socio-cultural evolution. In H. R. Barringer, G. I. Blanksten, and R. Mack (eds.), *Social Change in Developing Areas*: 19–49. Cambridge, Mass.: Schenkman.

—— (1979). A tribal model of the social system vehicle carrying scientific knowledge. *Knowledge: Creation, Diffusion, Utilization*, 1(2): 181–201.

DEWEY, J. (1998). The reflex arc concept in psychology. In L. A. Hickman and T. M. Alexander (eds.), *The Essential Dewey: Ethics, Logic, Psychology*, vol. 2: 3–10. Bloomington, Indiana: Indiana University Press.

DONALDSON, L. (2003). Organization theory as positive science. In H. Tsoukas and C. Knudsen (eds.), *The Oxford Handbook of Organization Theory*: 39–62. Oxford: Oxford University Press.

DOUGHERTY, D. (2002). Grounded theory research methods. In J. A. C. Baum (ed.), *The Blackwell Companion to Organizations*: 849–866. Oxford: Blackwell.

FESTINGER, L. (1957). *A Theory of Cognitive Dissonance*. Stanford: Stanford University Press.

FLIN, R. H. (1996). *Sitting in the Hot Seat: Leaders and Teams for Critical Incident Management*. New York: John Wiley.

GEERTZ, C. (1995). *After the Fact*. Cambridge, Mass.: Harvard University.

GEHMAN Jr., H. W. (2003). *Columbia Accident Investigation Board: Report, Volume One*. Washington, DC: U.S. Government.

GILILAND, S. W., and DAY, D. V. (2000). Business management. In F. T. Durso (ed.), *Handbook of Applied Cognition*: 315–342. New York: Wiley.

GIOIA, D. A. (1992). Pinto fires and personal ethics: A script analysis of missed opportunities. *Journal of Business Ethics*, 11: 379–389.

GUBA, E. G. (1990). *The Paradigm Dialog*. Newbury Park, Calif.: Sage.

HEIDER, F. (1959). On perception and event structure and the psychological environment. *Psychological Issues*, 1(3): 1–124.

HENIG, R. M. (1993). *A Dancing Matrix: How Science Confronts Emerging Viruses*. New York: Vintage.

KELLOGG, E. W. (1987). Speaking in e-prime: An experimental method for integrating general semantics into daily life. *ETC*, 44(2): 118–128.

LANT, T. K. (2002). Organizational cognition and interpretation. In J. A. C. Baum (ed.), *The Blackwell Companion to Organizations*: 344–362. Oxford: Blackwell.

LAROCHE, H. (1995). From decision to action in organizations' decision-making as a social representation. *Organization Science*, 6(1): 62–75.

MAGALA, S. J. (1997). The making and unmaking of sense. *Organization Studies*, 18(2): 317–338.

MERTON, R. K. (1967). *On Theoretical Sociology*. New York: Free Press.

MILLS, J. H. (2003). *Making Sense of Organizational Change*. New York: Routledge.

MORGAN, G., FROST, P. M., and PONDY, L. R. (1983). Organizational symbolism. In L. R. Pondy, P. J. Frost, G. Morgan, and T. C. Dandridge (eds.), *Organizational Symbolism*: 3–35. Greenwich, Conn.: JAI.

PACKER, M. J. (1985). Hermeneutic inquiry in the study of human conduct. *American Psychologist*, 40: 1081–1093.

PATRIOTTA, G. (2003). Sensemaking on the shop floor: Narratives of knowledge in organizations. *Journal of Management Studies*, 40(2): 349–376.

PERROW, C. (1984). *Normal Accidents*. New York: Basic.

PFEFFER, J., and SALANCIK, G. R. (1977). Organizational design: The case for a coalition model of organizations. *Organizational Dynamics*, Autumn.

PHILLIPS, A. (2001). *Promises, Promises.* New York: Basic.

REBER, A. S. (1995). *Dictionary of Psychology*, 2nd edn., London: Penguin.

RUNKEL, P. J., and RUNKEL, M. (1984). *A Guide to Usage for Writers and Students in the Social Sciences.* Totowa, NJ: Rowman and Allanheld.

SANDELANDS, L. E. (1990). What is so practical about theory? Lewin revisited. *Journal for the Theory of Social Behaviour*, 20: 235–262.

SCHUTZ, W. (1979). *Profound Simplicity.* New York: Bantam.

SCOTT, W. R. (1998). *Organizations: Rational, Natural, and Open Systems*, 4th ed. Upper Saddle River, NJ: Prentice-Hall.

TAYLOR, J. R., and VAN EVERY, E. J. (2000). *The Emergent Organization: Communication as its Site and Surface.* Mahwah, NJ: Erlbaum.

THORNGATE, W. (1976). Possible limits on a science of social behavior. In L. H. Strickland, F. E. Aboud, and K. J. Gergen (eds.), *Social Psychology in Transition*: 121–139. New York: Plenum.

VAN MAANEN, J. (1995). Style as theory. *Organization Science*, 6: 133–143.

VAUGHAN, D. (1996). *The Challenger Launch Decision: Risky Technology, Culture and Deviance at NASA.* Chicago, Ill.: University of Chicago Press.

WARGLIEN, M. (2002). Intraorganizational evolution. In J. A. C. Baum (ed.), *The Blackwell Companion to* Organizations: 98–118. Oxford: Blackwell.

WEICK, K. E. (1964). The reduction of cognitive dissonance through task enhancement and effort expenditure. *Journal of Abnormal and Social Psychology*, 68: 533–539.

—— (1969). *Social Psychology of Organizing.* Reading, Mass.: Addison-Wesley.

—— (1974). Amendments to organizational theorizing. *Journal of Academy of Management*, 17: 487–502.

—— (1979). *The Social Psychology of Organizing*, 2nd edn., Reading, Mass.: Addison-Wesley.

—— (1981). Psychology as gloss. In R. Kasschau and C. N. Cofer (eds.), *Psychology's Second Century*: 110–132. New York: Praeger.

—— (1983). Contradictions in a community of scholars: The cohesion-accuracy tradeoff. *The Review of Higher Education*, 6(4): 253–267.

—— (1985). A stress analysis of future battlefields. In J. G. Hunt (ed.), *Leadership and Future Battlefields*: 32–46. Washington, D.C.: Pergamon-Brassey's.

—— (1989). Theory construction as disciplined imagination. *Academy of Management Review*, 14: 516–531.

—— (1990). The vulnerable system: Analysis of the Tenerife air disaster. *Journal of Management*, 16: 571–593.

—— (1992a). Agenda setting in organizational behavior: A theory-focused approach. *Journal of Management Inquiry*, 1(3): 171–182.

—— (1992b). The management of closeness in Jungian training societies: An organizational analysis. In H. A. Wilmer (ed.), *Closeness*: 181–202. Denver: Shambala.

—— (1993a). The collapse of sensemaking in organizations: The Mann Gulch disaster. *Administrative Science Quarterly*, 38: 628–652.

—— (1993b). Sensemaking in organizations: Small structures with large consequences. In J. K. Murnighan (ed.), *Social Psychology in Organizations: Advances in Theory and Research*: 10–37. Englewood Cliffs, NJ: Prentice-Hall.

—— (1995a). Creativity and the aesthetics of imperfection. In C. M. Ford, and D. Gioia (eds.), *Creative Action in Organizations*: 187–192. Newbury Park, Calif.: Sage.

—— (1995b). *Sensemaking in Organizations*. Thousand Oaks, Calif.: Sage.

—— (1996a). Drop your tools: An allegory for organizational studies. *Administrative Science Quarterly*, 41(2): 301–313.

—— (1996b). Speaking to practice: The scholarship of integration. *Journal of Management Inquiry*, 5: 251–258.

—— (2001). Tool retention and fatalities in wildland fire settings: Conceptualizing the naturalistic. In E. Salas and G. Klein (eds.), *Linking Expertise and Naturalistic Decision Making*: 321–336. Mahwah, NJ: Erlbaum.

—— (2002). The reduction of medical errors through mindful interdependence. In M. Rosenthal and K. M. Sutcliffe (eds.), *What Do We Know about Medical Mistakes?* 177–199. San Francisco: Jossey-Bass.

—— (2003a). Enacting an environment: The infrastructure of organizing. In R. Westwood and S. Clegg (eds.), *Debating Organization*: 183–207. Oxford: Oxford University Press.

—— (2003b). Theory and practice in the real world. In H. Tsoukas and C. Knudsen (eds.), *The Oxford Handbook of Organization Theory*: 453–475. New York: Oxford University Press.

—— GILFILLAN, D. P., and KEITH, T. (1973). The effect of composer credibility on orchestra performance. *Sociometry*, 36: 435–462.

—— and PRESTHOLDT, P. (1968). The realignment of discrepant reinforcement value. *Journal of Personality and Social Psychology*, 8: 180–187.

—— and ROBERTS, K. H. (1993). Collective mind in organizations: Heedful interrelating on flight decks. *Administrative Science Quarterly*, 38: 357–381.

—— and SUTCLIFFE, K. M. (2003). Hospitals as cultures of entrapment: A re-analysis of the Bristol Royal Infirmary. *California Management Review*, 45(2): 73–84.

—— —— and OBSTFELD, D. (1999). Organizing for high reliability: Processes of collective mindfulness. In B. Staw and R. Sutton (eds.), *Research in Organizational Behavior*: 21. 81–123. Greenwich, Conn.: JAI.

WESCHLER, L. (1982). *Seeing is forgetting the name of the thing one sees: A life of contemporary artist Robert Irwin*. Berkeley, Calif.: University of California Press.

PART III

ENVIRONMENTAL
CONTINGENCIES
AND
ORGANIZATIONS

....

THE
DEVELOPMENT
OF STAKEHOLDER
THEORY

AN IDIOSYNCRATIC
APPROACH

....

R. EDWARD FREEMAN

20.1 INTRODUCTION

....

THE purpose of this chapter is to trace the development of what has come to be known as "stakeholder theory." I intend to accomplish this in a manner that could be called "autobiographical" or "idiosyncratic" because I want to illustrate a philosophical point about the general issue of "theory development" and the importance of a role for "the author." To claim that "the author" has an important role in the development of management theory is neither to promote the self-importance of particular individuals nor to deny the role of inter-subjective agreement that is so vital in science. Rather it is to claim that contextual factors and serendipity can be crucial in process of theory development.

In section 20.2 I shall offer a brief explanation of my interest in stakeholder theory. In particular I focus on the contextual factors around my eventual publication of *Strategic Management: A Stakeholder Approach* in 1984. Section 20.3 is a brief summary of that book and an assessment of its strengths, weaknesses, and an analysis of some "misinterpretations" that have led to what we now know of as "stakeholder theory". Section 20.4 is my assessment of the current state of the art of "stakeholder theory" and some suggestions for the future development of the theory.[1]

20.2 STAKEHOLDER THEORY: MY EARLY INVOLVEMENT

After studying philosophy and mathematics at Duke University and graduate study in philosophy at Washington University in St. Louis, I accepted an appointment on the research staff at the Wharton School, University of Pennsylvania with a group called the Busch Center, run by Russell Ackoff, acknowledged as a pioneer in Operations Research and Systems Theory.[2] After working at the Busch Center on several projects for a few months, I moved to a new splinter group started by James R. Emshoff, a former student of Ackoff. This new group was called "the Wharton Applied Research Center," and its mission was to serve as "Wharton's window to the world," a kind of real-world consulting arm that would combine research staff, students, and Wharton faculty. We organized this new center much like a traditional consulting firm, by projects and by "development areas" which were conceptual spaces where we wanted to develop both expertise and new clients to try out our ideas.[3]

The stakeholder concept was very much in the air at the Busch Center. Ackoff had written about the idea, extensively in *Redesigning the Future*.[4] And, the idea was the centerpiece of several projects underway at the Center. In particular, the

---

[1] Recently I have written about the development of stakeholder theory and its current "state of the art" in a number of places. Cf. "The Stakeholder Approach Revisited," *Zeitschrift für Wirtschafts- und Unternehmensethik*, forthcoming. Freeman and J. McVea, "Stakeholder Theory: The State of the Art," in Hitt, Freeman, and Harrison (eds.) *The Blackwell Handbook of Strategic Management*, Oxford: Blackwell Publishing, 2001; and Freeman, McVea, Wicks, and Parmar, "Stakeholder Theory: The State of the Art and Future Perspectives," *Politeia*, Anno XX, No. 74, 2004. I am grateful to editors, publishers, and co-authors for permission to recast and reuse some of the material in these works.

[2] To illustrate what I said earlier about the role of serendipity, I would never have accepted an appointment at Wharton, indeed I didn't even know what or where Wharton was, but for the fact that my girlfriend, Maureen Wellen, now wife of 25+ years was going to graduate school in fine arts at Pennsylvania.

[3] See James R. Emshoff—Busch Center paper.

[4] Ackoff, 1974. To further the story begun in n. 2 above, I originally got an interview at Wharton because Professor Richard Rudner's son, an anthropology student at Penn, knew people at the Busch Center, and Rudner knew that Ackoff had a philosophy degree. (Rudner was on my dissertation

Scientific Communication and Technology Transfer project funded by the National Science Foundation, as a kind of Library of the Future design project, used the idea of getting stakeholder input into radical system redesign. More relevant to business, the idea had been used in assessing the strategic direction of a large Mexican brewer, which was dealing with its government and other key stakeholders. However, most of the uses of the idea at that time were as a way to organize thinking about the external environment, or in thinking about system design.

Around the same time Ian Mitroff was visiting at the Busch Center and he and Emshoff and Richard Mason were working on Strategic Assumptions Analysis, a project in which the stakeholder idea was used to organize the assumptions that executives made about their external environment. This use of the stakeholder idea as an organizing concept was consistent with the original use at Stanford Research Institute where it evolved under the leadership of Robert Stewart, Marion Doscher, Igor Ansoff, Eric Rhenman, and others as a way of organizing the "environmental scan" that SRI published.

There was little in the way of a "management approach" that could help executives actually make decisions, other than at a very high level. Around this same time Emshoff and Ackoff organized a "faculty seminar" around "what are we to make of this stakeholder idea." Eric Trist, Howard Perlmutter (management), Alan Shipiro (finance), and a few others attended. I was a very junior person and listened intently to these senior people discuss how they interpreted the stakeholder idea. There seemed to me to be a common thread in the seminar, and that was the reluctance of any of these management thinkers to talk about issues of values, ethics, or justice. I remember vividly, someone drawing a stakeholder "wheel and spoke" map on the board, throwing their hands up in the air and claiming "Well, that's a normative problem of distributive justice, and we can't say anything about that." As a philosopher, I was fairly naive. I had not yet experienced the fanatical concern with "method" and "positive" and "empirical" that so defines most business school intellectuals. I remember thinking, "Well, I can certainly say something about normative and justice issues."

Emshoff encouraged me to begin exploring these ideas and writing about them, and we prepared a working paper, entitled "Stakeholder Management," that we sent out to a mailing list of companies and people. At some point in 1977, some executives from the Human Resources Department at AT&T came to the Applied Research Center to discuss our developing a portion of a four-week seminar for their "leaders of the future." They had done a survey of their Bell System officers and "how to manage the external environment" ranked high on the list of skills needed by the leaders of the future. While Emshoff and I were novices at executive

committee.) What none of us knew was that Ackoff was in a period of reasonable hostility towards academic philosophers. But, none of this mattered since he was out of the country when I interviewed and left these hiring decisions to others.

education, we believed that we had something to offer on the basis of our thinking about how the stakeholder idea could anchor an approach to managerial decision making. Ram Charan from Northwestern at the time, Fred Sturdivant from Ohio State, and Mel Horwitch from Harvard were also working with AT&T on this project and we designed a one-week course that was aimed at sensitizing managers to the need to deal with stakeholders; giving them some tools and techniques for tasks like prioritizing stakeholders; and putting them into a decision making simulation where they had to confront live strategic issues of importance to the company. We involved a number of actual stakeholders in the training, and over time, we created a very successful experience.

We developed these ideas in two papers. The first was a conceptual paper laying out the argument for why managers needed an active managerial approach for thinking about stakeholders. We defined "stakeholder" in a broad strategic sense as "any group or individual that can affect or is affected by the achievement of a corporation's purpose." While this definition has been the subject of much debate in the ensuing years, the basic idea was quite simple. We were taking the viewpoint of the executive and our claim was that if a group or individual could affect the firm (or be affected by it, and reciprocate) then executives should worry about that group in the sense that it needed an explicit strategy for dealing with that stakeholder.

We developed some of the techniques of "stakeholder management," as we began to call it, in a paper for a volume of applications of management science. In "Stakeholder Management: A Case Study of the U.S. Brewers and the Container Issue," we looked at our ongoing work with the United States Brewers Association and their struggle over what to do about taxes, recycling, and regulation of beverage containers. At that time, we were enamored of the promise of applying management science techniques to more accurately allocate resources among stakeholders, a view which I now believe to be deeply wrongheaded and mistaken. But, we did develop a useful way of thinking about stakeholder behavior in terms of thinking through concrete actual behavior, cooperative potential, and competitive threat for each stakeholder group.

During the same time, we developed a managerial version of the same material published in *The Wharton Magazine*, entitled pretentiously, "Who's Butting Into Your Business." This was an attempt to show managers that stakeholders had at least "managerial legitimacy," i.e., that from a strategic standpoint executives needed to put explicit strategies into place. We drew from our clinical experiences with the Bell companies, since we began to do many consulting/applied research projects after our successful seminars in the late 1970s. And, Ram Charan and I published a paper called "Negotiating with Stakeholders" in a magazine put out by AMACOM that focused on what we had learned about the negotiation process with a variety of stakeholder groups.

The burning questions, which I had during this time, were pretty straightforward: (1) Could I develop a method for executives to strategically manage stakeholder relationships as a routine ongoing part of their day to day activities? (2) Could strategic management as a discipline be recast along stakeholder lines, rather than the six tasks of Schendel and Hofer? And, (3) Why was any of this thinking controversial, since it seemed like complete "common sense" to me?

In 1980, serendipity again entered the equation. My brother was killed in a car accident, and like many when faced with such a personal loss, I was "forced" to think about what I really wanted to do with my life. Did I want to continue to do consulting (with teaching being a part-time assignment), or did I want to commit to actually trying to answer these "burning questions," and trying to live a more scholarly life? I chose the academic route and was fortunate to be offered a position as Assistant Professor in the Management Department at Wharton. I set myself the rather clear task of working out the stakeholder approach to strategy in a book, and to write as many scholarly articles as I could to develop the ideas.

It was really here that I entered the academic world of management theory. While I was not completely ignorant of management theory, I had no systematic knowledge of any of the subfields. I began to read widely in strategy, organization theory, management history, systems theory and a burgeoning literature on corporate social responsibility. It was here that I encountered what I knew to be philosophically outdated ideas of "theory," "evidence", the "normative–prescriptive" distinction, the "fact–value" distinction, and a whole host of ideas around methodology that took me back to the positivists of the 1920s in philosophy.

Essentially I ignored all these "rules and methods for research." I knew that I was dealing with a real problem, "How can executives make better decisions in a world with multiple stakeholder demands?" And, I knew that I was getting the clinical experience with my consulting projects with real executives dealing with this real problem. So, I decided to build from my experiences into more general ideas about how to systematize the stakeholder approach.

For instance, when I worked with companies whose executives were trying to deal with critical stakeholders by changing their entire points of view about the company, the idea arose that perhaps it would be more fruitful to work on small behavioral changes, rather than large attitude changes. When a company expert guaranteed that he knew what a particular stakeholder group wanted from the company, and it turned out to be wrong, I began to question the idea that structuring a team of stakeholder experts was necessarily the best way to run a strategic planning process. The clinical lessons were countless. Unfortunately (but maybe fortunately), I didn't know anything about qualitative research or grounded theory or some of the other ways to dress up intelligent observation into scientific clothes. I was stuck with the role models like Graham Allison's *Essence of Decision*; Selznick's book on the TVA; Freud's clinical studies; and other more classic works of "social science."

I also began to get involved in the management academic community through the Academy of Management. Jim Post of Boston University had invited me to give a talk to the Social Issues in Management Division in 1980 in Detroit. Even though I knew little about this group, I agreed because I had read Post's book with Lee Preston, and knew that it was an important book. I gave a paper on the idea of stakeholder management, which argued that this was a better unit of analysis than an "issue." I remember the paper as being controversial and there being lots of heated discussion—so much so that I was reminded of philosophy meetings. Clearly I had found an intellectual home, even if I was unsure of why anything I had said was controversial.

During this time, I began to work with Professor William Evan, a distinguished sociologist at Penn. I was very flattered when Evan called me one day and asked to meet to discuss the stakeholder idea. Evan saw this project as a way to democratize the large corporation. Even though he was an impeccable empirical researcher, he immediately saw the normative implications of coming to see business as "serving stakeholders." We began to meet weekly and talk about how to do the "next project" after *Strategic Management: A Stakeholder Approach*, even though that project wasn't yet finished. We began an empirical study aimed at seeing how Chief Executive Officers made trade-offs among stakeholders and we began to plan a book that would deal with the normative implications of reconceptualizing the corporate governance debate in stakeholder terms. While we never finished the book, we did complete a number of essays, one of which is reprinted countless times in business ethics textbooks. What I learned from Bill Evan was invaluable: to be the philosopher that I was, rather than some positivist version of a social scientist. Evan gave me the courage to tackle the normative dimension, in an intellectual atmosphere, the modern twentieth-century Business School that had disdain for such analysis.

In summary, I spent most of my time from 1978 until 1983 teaching executives and working with them to develop very practical ways of understanding how they could be more effective in the relationships with key stakeholders. In the summer of 1982, I sat down at my home in Princeton Junction, New Jersey and drafted the initial manuscript of *Strategic Management: A Stakeholder Approach*. I tried to set forth a method or set of methods/techniques for executives to use to better understand how to manage key stakeholder relationships. In addition, I wanted to track down the origins of the stakeholder idea, and give credit to its originators and the people whose work I had found so useful.

20.3 STRATEGIC MANAGEMENT: A STAKEHOLDER APPROACH. AN ASSESSMENT

I am not sure what to make of what is now called "stakeholder theory." I was never certain that my book contained a "theory" as it is understood by the management thinkers represented in this volume. I recently listened to a panel at the Academy of Management debate whether stakeholder theory was "a theory," "a framework," or "a paradigm." As a pragmatist, these questions do not seem very interesting to me. I have come to believe that whatever the academic verdict is on what is now called stakeholder theory, at least from a "managerial point of view" it is simply "a good idea that is useful to executives and stakeholders." At the time of writing the book, I was less interested in "theory development" than in trying to say something systematic about what worked.

Strategic Management contains an underlying narrative or story about how to be a more effective executive. The "evidence" for this approach was the conversations that I had had with literally thousands of executives over the previous seven years, plus the countless stories in the business press about good and bad stakeholder management, plus my own clinical experience with a number of clients.

The point of the book was and remains very clear to me—how could executives and academics think about strategy or strategic management if they took the stakeholder concept seriously, or as the basic unit of analysis of whatever framework they applied? The basic insight was to suggest that a more useful unit of analysis for thinking about strategy was the stakeholder relationship, rather than the tasks of "formulating, implementing, evaluating, etc." or the idea of "industry," or the other myriad ideas of the times. I took this to be a matter of common sense and practicality, rather than some deep academic insight. The executives that I was working with found thinking about stakeholder relationships very helpful for dealing with the kinds of change that was confronting their corporations.

The approach of the book was modeled after what I took to be some of the best writing I had encountered that tried to interweave clinical cases and facts with the development of insights and ideas. So, I relied on the "clinical cases" I had worked on with a number of companies over these years, as well as my reading of the business press, case studies written by others, and my conversations with other people (experts) worried about the same phenomena. Again, I was trained as a philosopher, so what was important to me was the overall logic of the argument. I found the insistence by some colleagues on empirical methods and an obsession with "methodology" to be highly amusing and full of logic mistakes. Surely the insights of thinkers like Freud or Harry Levinson in management, or Graham Allison in politics, did not become questionable because of their methods, but because of their logic. The obsession with what Richard Rorty has called "methodolatry" continues even in this world of critical studies, post-modernism, pragmatism, and other assorted post-positivist justifications of intellectual activity. I confess to paying no attention to methods. Perhaps if I had kept careful notes, interview transcripts, had a panel of experts sort all of the "data," I could have gained even more insight into the phenomena of businesses trying to deal with stakeholder relationships. However, I thought that all of this stuff was just silly window dressing. I never had interest in the question, "Are you doing something that is descriptive of the way companies act, or are you prescribing how they should act, or are you suggesting that if they act in this way it will lead to these results?" Donaldson and Preston (1995) have suggested that stakeholder theory can be separated into descriptive, prescriptive, and instrumental categories. I thought I was doing all three and that any good theory or narrative ought to do all three. In short the stakeholder approach has always been what Donaldson and Preston have called "managerial." There is more than adequate philosophical justification for such an approach and Andy Wicks and I (1998) have tried to set forth such a pragmatist "methodology."

I would summarize *Strategic Management: A Stakeholder Approach* in the following logical schemata:

1. No matter what you stand for, no matter what your ultimate purpose may be, you must take into account the effects of your actions on others, as well as their potential effects on you.
2. Doing so means you have to understand stakeholder behaviors, values, and backgrounds/contexts including the societal context. To be successful over time it will be better to have a clear answer to the question "what do we stand for."
3. There are some focal points that can serve as answers to the question "what do we stand for" or Enterprise Strategy. (The book laid out a typology which no one ever took seriously.)
4. We need to understand how stakeholder relationships work at three levels of analysis: the Rational or "organization as a whole"; the Process, or standard operating procedures; and the transactional, or day to day bargaining. (These levels are just the three levels in Graham Allison's *Missiles of October*.)
5. We can apply these ideas to think through new structures, processes, and business functions, and we can especially rethink how the strategic planning process works to take stakeholders into account.
6. Stakeholder interests need to be balanced over time.

There are a number of implications of this argument. If it is correct, then the idea of "corporate social responsibility" is probably superfluous. Since stakeholders are defined widely and their concerns are integrated into the business processes, there is simply no need for a separate CSR approach. Social Issues Management or "issue" is simply the wrong unit of analysis. Groups and individuals behave, not issues. Issues emerge through the behavior and interaction of stakeholders, therefore "stakeholders" is a more fundamental and useful unit of analysis. Finally, the major implication of this argument, which cannot be overemphasized today given the development of stakeholder theory, is that "stakeholders are about the business, and the business is about the stakeholders."

During the ensuing twenty years, I have continued to try and work out the implications of this basic argument, concentrating on more of the ethical and normative aspects of the stakeholder approach, while steadfastly maintaining that the normative–descriptive distinction is not hard and fast. In 1983, I moved to the

University of Minnesota with the explicit understanding that I would be teaching more Ph.D. students, and more ethics. At Wharton, I had taught primarily Business Policy and Principles of Management. I had the opportunity to immerse myself in the business ethics literature, and to try and contribute to it. On reflection, given the split or separation between "business" and "ethics," this may have been a mistake, as it led to many misinterpretations of the basic argument.

Once again serendipity played a large part in the decision. My wife was working for a consulting firm and traveling extensively. We were commuting three hours a day (when everything worked), and the chance to both have jobs in Minneapolis meant that we could actually spend a lot of time together. As a result of our decision, "stakeholder theory" became more embedded in "business ethics" than it did in strategic management.

In 1986, we decided to move to Virginia and the Darden School, together with our 9-month-old son. My charge at Darden was to help build the research capability of the school and the Olsson Center which had been founded in 1967. Again this personal move can be seen as helping to influence the interpretation of "stakeholder theory" as belonging more to ethics than to management.[5] For the last eighteen years I have had the privilege to work with lots of colleagues at Darden in an environment that is much more like the one at the Wharton Applied Research Center. Darden is very "business oriented," and the basic argument of "stakeholder theory" that it is about helping executives make better decisions, has found a friendlier home.

To answer some of the more obvious misinterpretations, at least from my point of view Robert Phillips, Andrew Wicks, and I (2003) have published a paper entitled "What Stakeholder Theory is Not." Some of the more obvious misinterpretations are: (1) Stakeholders are critics and other non-business entities; (2) there is a conflict between shareholders and the other stakeholders; and (3) the stakeholder concept can and should be used to formulate a new, non-shareholder theory of the firm. Obviously (1) completely cuts against both the actual formulation of the theory and the spirit in which it was developed. Andrew Wicks, Bidhan Parmar, and I (2004) have recently offered a rebuttal of (2), since shareholders are stakeholders, and the whole point is that stakeholder interests have to move in the same general direction over time. (3) is a trickier matter, and I have published a number of papers in which it seems I am claiming that there is one univalent "stakeholder theory" that will work for all businesses. However, I believe that it is more useful to consider "stakeholder theory" as a genre (Freeman, 1994). There may be many particular "stakeholder narratives," and indeed that is the original insight behind

---

[5] Serendipity played a large role here. We were unsure about moving to Virginia, and were having fairly intense discussions about it. My wife's career had stalled unless she was willing to move, and I was unsatisfied at Minnesota. Literally, one day we looked out the back window, saw the station wagon, which quickly became a symbol of suburban middle age, and decided that we needed some new challenges. So, we moved on to Charlottesville and the University of Virginia.

"enterprise strategy." Surely there are lots of ways to run a firm. All of these ways have to ultimately generate profits and satisfy some set of stakeholders, but context and other factors may well determine which kind of narrative works best.

While I believe that much of the basic logic of the book is still valid, especially if the misinterpretations are clarified, there are several obvious weaknesses in it. First of all much of the language of the book is couched in the idiom of strategic planning in general, and Vancil and Lorange's (1975) version of strategic planning in particular. Lorange was at Wharton at the time and I was heavily influenced by his ideas. Therefore, there is far too much "process-speak" and far too much "consultant-speak," both of which have served as a barrier to understanding the basic idea. Second, the book was overly analytical. Henry Mintzberg seems never to tire of repeating the criticism that I seem to believe that if we draw the stakeholder maps accurately enough, and model and predict their behavior, we can cast out uncertainty from the strategic thinking process. While this was never my aim, I do understand how Mintzberg and others read this into the work. I simply wanted to suggest that we could think about stakeholders systematically. Obviously, there are limits to our ability to analyze, and just as obviously we can use analysis to hide behind, rather than for going out and actively creating capabilities for dealing with stakeholders. Again, part of this weakness, I believe, comes from the reliance on the strategic planning literature of the time. Third, there is a tension in the writing of the book between "managerial thinking" and "academic thinking." I believe that chapter two could only be interesting to academics, and that chapters five and six could only be interesting to executives who were trying to "do it." I'm afraid that this tension served neither audience very well. Fourth, I have come to believe that questions of purpose, values, ethics, and other elements of which I crudely follow- ing Drucker and Schendel and Hofer, called "enterprise strategy," are far more important than I originally anticipated. Strategic management as a field universally ignored these issues for years, and many continue to do so today. Once I came to see this as perhaps the most important part of the book, I undertook to write what I hoped was a sequel to the book with Daniel R. Gilbert, Jr. (1988), entitled *Corporate Strategy and the Search for Ethics.*[6] Unfortunately, almost no one reads or refers to that book today. Fifth, there was a missing level of analysis. I said virtually nothing about how business or capitalism would look if we began to understand it as consisting of "creating value for stakeholders." Sixth, there is too much concern with structure in the book. While I still find some of the insights about corporate governance interesting, the chapters on recasting the functions of

---

[6] Again the role of serendipity emerged. While I was at Minnesota, Dan Gilbert was a doctoral student. I sat in on one of his classes to assess his teaching, and the class I chose was one in which he was using my book, and arguing to the students that I was a Utilitarian. As an ardent Rawlsian, at the time, I was appalled, and determined to fix this inadequacy in the book, so we began to work on *Corporate Strategy and the Search for Ethics.* There are many classes I could have picked to sit in and there were many other topics in the class.

business along stakeholder lines were misguided. The underlying issue is the separation of business and ethics in the foundational disciplines of business, not the practical organization and working of these disciplines. I'm certain there are even more flaws, bad writing, mistakes, and bad ideas in the book, but these are at least some of the major weaknesses from my point of view.

Since I am currently engaged in the process of rewriting *Strategic Management: A Stakeholder Approach*, I want to suggest what my current thinking is, and how I'm going about this new project. First of all there will be two books, both of them will be written by a team consisting of myself, Jeffrey Harrison, Robert Phillips, and Andrew Wicks. The initial book is tentatively titled, *Managing for Stakeholders: Business in the 21st Century* (Freeman, et al., forthcoming). It is written purely for managers and executives. There will be no academic arguments, not much discussion of the finer points of how stakeholders are defined, and no mention of most of the literature and debates that have developed over the last twenty years. The basic argument remains intact except that, given the changes wrought by globalization, information technology, and the recent ethics related scandals, there is more urgency in adopting a stakeholder approach to value creation and trade (our name for "business"). We spend a fair amount of time laying out the argument that concern for stakeholders is just what the business is about. We suggest that there is a "stakeholder mind-set" that consists of a number of key principles that more clearly guide the implementation of stakeholder thinking. We connect the stakeholder idea to ethics and values very explicitly, by suggesting that one of the key questions of enterprise strategy is: How does your firm make each stakeholder better off, and what are you doing to improve any tradeoffs that may exist between stakeholders? We distill the process and techniques of the earlier book and our experiences over the last twenty years, into eight techniques for creating value for stakeholders. Then, we end with an explicit call for "ethical leadership" that is required by the stakeholder mind-set. We are hoping to include an appendix with FAQs that will prevent a number of the misinterpretations of the first book. The second book is tentatively titled, *Stakeholder Theory: The State of the Art* (Freeman, et al., forthcoming). We plan for this book to be "everything a doctoral student ever wants to know about stakeholder theory." We will cover a number of disciplines, from law to marketing, including some outside the mainstream of business such as healthcare and public administration. We plan both to summarize and evaluate the research that has been done, and to suggest what some interesting avenues of research might be. I want to emphasize, as I tried to do in my earlier book, that the thinking on which these books are based has been done by many people, academics and executives alike, over many years. What we are trying to do is to distill this thinking into a useful form, and in doing so continue in the spirit of the early founders of the idea. With that in mind, I want to set forth some of the developments by a host of scholars who have taken the stakeholder concept and placed it squarely in the mainstream of management thinking, though I want to caution that this section is very abbreviated and incomplete.

20.4 STAKEHOLDER THEORY: THE CURRENT LANDSCAPE AND FUTURE DIRECTIONS

Since 1984, academic interest in a stakeholder approach has both grown and broadened. Indeed, the number of citations using the word stakeholder has increased enormously as suggested by Donaldson and Preston (1995). Most of the research on the stakeholder concept has taken place in four sub-fields: (1) normative theories of business; (2) corporate governance and organizational theory; (3) corporate social responsibility and performance; and (4) strategic management.[7]

20.4.1 A Stakeholder Approach to Normative Theories of Business

This approach emphasizes the importance of investing in the relationships with those who have a stake in the firm. The stability of these relationships depends on the sharing of, at least, a core of principles or values. Thus, stakeholder theory allows managers to incorporate personal values into the formulation and implementation of strategic plans. An example of this is the concept of an enterprise strategy. An enterprise strategy (Schendel and Hofer, 1979, building on Drucker) describes the relationship between the firm and society by answering the question "What do we stand for?" In its original form a stakeholder approach emphasized the importance of developing an enterprise strategy, while leaving open the question of which type of values are the most appropriate.

It is very easy to misinterpret the foregoing analysis as yet another call for corporate social responsibility or business ethics. While these issues are important in their own right, enterprise level strategy is a different concept. We need to worry about the enterprise level strategy for the simple fact that corporate survival depends in part on there being some "fit" between the values of the corporation and its managers, the expectations of stakeholders in the firm and the societal issues which will determine the ability of the firm to sell its products. (Freeman, 1984: 107)

However, the illustration that values are an essential ingredient to strategic management has, indeed, set in train an inquiry into the normative roots of stakeholder theory.

The question this research stream is trying to answer is: "Above and beyond the consequences of stakeholder management, is there a fundamental moral

---

[7] Portions of this section are from R. Edward Freeman and John McVea, "Stakeholder Theory: The State of the Art," in M. Hitt, E. Freeman, and J. Harrison (eds.), *The Blackwell Handbook of Strategic Management*, Oxford: Blackwell Publishing, 2001. I am grateful to my co-author and my co-editors and publishers for permission to include this material here.

requirement to adopt this style of management?" Various attempts have been made to ground stakeholder management in a broad range of philosophical foundations. Evan and Freeman (1993) developed a justification of a stakeholder approach based on Kantian principles. In its simplest form this approach argued that we are required to treat people "as ends unto themselves." This framework has been further developed by Norman Bowie (1999) into a fully fledged ethical theory of business. From a different perspective Phillips (1997) has grounded a stakeholder approach in the principle of fairness. Others (Wicks, Freeman, and Gilbert, 1994; Burton and Dunn, 1996) have tried to justify a stakeholder approach through the ethics of care. Finally, Donaldson and Dunfee (1999) have developed a justification for a stakeholder approach that is based on social contract theory.

Recently, Kochan and Rubenstein (2000) have developed a normative stakeholder theory based on an extensive study of the Saturn automotive manufacturer. In this study they try and answer the question: "Why should stakeholder models be given serious consideration at this moment in history?" Stakeholder firms will only be sustainable when leaders' incentives encourage responsiveness to stakeholders and when stakeholder legitimacy can overcome society's skeptical ideological legacy towards stakeholder management.

20.4.2 A Stakeholder Approach to Corporate Governance and Organizational Theory

This stream of research has grown out of the contrast between the traditional view that it is the fiduciary duty of management to protect the interests of the shareholder and the stakeholder view that management should make decisions for the benefit of all stakeholders. Williamson (1984) used a transaction cost framework to show that shareholders deserved special consideration over other stakeholders because of "asset specificity." Freeman and Evan (1990) have argued, to the contrary, that Williamson's approach to corporate governance can indeed be used to explain all stakeholders' relationships. Many other stakeholders have stakes that are, to a degree, firm specific. Furthermore, shareholders have a more liquid market (the stock market) for exit than most other stakeholders. Thus, asset specificity alone does not grant a prime responsibility towards stockholders at the expense of all others.

Goodpaster (1991) outlined an apparent paradox that accompanies the stakeholder approach. Management appears to have a contractual duty to manage the firm in the interests of the stockholders and at the same time management seems to have a moral duty to take other stakeholders into account. This stakeholder paradox has been attacked by Boatright (1994) and Marens and Wicks (1999) and defended by Goodpaster and Holloran (1994). Others have explored the legal standing of the fiduciary duty of management towards stockholders (Orts, 1997; Blair, 1995). Many of these debates are ongoing, with some advocating fundamental changes to corporate governance and with others rejecting the relevance of the whole debate to a stakeholder approach.

There have also been a number of attempts to expand stakeholder theory into what Jones (1995) has referred to as a "central paradigm" that links together theories such as agency theory, transactions costs, and contracts theory into a coherent whole (Jones, 1995; Clarkson, 1995). From this perspective stakeholder theory can be used as a counterpoint to traditional shareholder-based theory. While it is generally accepted that stakeholder theory could constitute good management practice, its main value for these theorists is to expose the traditional model as being morally untenable or at least too accommodating to immoral behavior. More recently Jones and Wicks (1999) have explicitly tried to pull together diverging research streams in their paper "Convergent Stakeholder Theory."

20.4.3 A Stakeholder Approach to Social Responsibility and Social Performance

A significant area of interests for theorists of social responsibility has been the definition of legitimate stakeholders. It has been stated that "one glaring short-coming is the problem of stakeholder identity. That is, that the theory is often unable to distinguish those individuals and groups that are stakeholders from those that are not" (Phillips and Reichart, 1998). Mitchell, Agle, and Wood (1997) addressed this issue by developing a framework for stakeholder identification. Using qualitative criteria of power, legitimacy and urgency, they develop what they refer to as "the principle of who and what really counts." This line of research is particularly relevant in areas such as the environment and grassroots political activism. The critical question is whether there is such a thing as an illegitimate stakeholder, and if so how legitimacy should be defined. Agle, Mitchell, and Sonnenfeld (1999) have taken an opposite approach. Rather than try and theoret-ically define stakeholder legitimacy, they have conducted an empirical study to identify which stakeholders managers actually consider to be legitimate.

A large body of research has been carried out in order to test the "instrumental" claim that managing for stakeholders is just good management practice. This claim infers that firms that practice stakeholder management would outperform firms that do not practice stakeholder management. Wood (1995) pointed out that causality is complex and that the relationship between corporate social perform-ance (CSP) and financial performance is ambiguous. Graves and Waddock (1990) have demonstrated the growth in importance of institutional stakeholders over the last twenty years. On further investigation they found that firms that demonstrated a high level of corporate social performance (CSP) tends to lead to an increase in the number of institutions that invest in the stock (Graves and Waddock, 1994).

A range of recent studies have been carried out using new data and techniques to try and shed light on the links between stakeholder management and social and financial performance (Berman, et al. (1999), Harrison and Fiet (1999), Luoma and Goodstein (1999). At a more practitioner level, Ogden and Watson (1999) have carried out a detailed case study into corporate and stakeholder management in the UK water industry. At present, most conclusions in this area are somewhat tentative as the precision of techniques and data sources continue to be developed.

20.4.4 A Stakeholder Approach to Strategic Management

Harrison and St. John (1994) have been the leaders in developing an integrated approach with many of the conceptual frameworks of mainstream strategy theory, a task which I quickly abandoned after publishing my 1984 book.

Harrison and St. John are able to combine traditional and stakeholder approaches because they use the stakeholder approach as an overarching framework within which traditional approaches can operate as strategic tools. For example, they divide the environment into the operating environment and the broader environment. Within the operating environment, the "resource-based view of the firm" can operate as a useful framework to study the relationships of internal stakeholders such as management and employees. Equally, Porter's five-force model (Porter, 1998) can be used to shed light on the relationships of many external stakeholders such as competitors and suppliers. However, strategic management does not stop at this analytical/descriptive phase. Prioritizing stakeholders is more than a complex task of assessing the strength of their stake on the basis of economic or political power. The values and the enterprise strategy of a firm may dictate priorities for particular partnerships and discourage others. Thus, a stakeholder approach allows management to infuse traditional strategic analysis with the values and direction that are unique to that organization.

20.5 CONCLUSION

There are many promising developments in stakeholder theory. The purpose of this section is to set forth a few of these ideas and point the reader to this emerging literature. Sandra Waddock and a number of colleagues have used the stakeholder idea as one of the conceptual centerpieces for their work on corporate citizenship, and have been involved with a number of NGOs, such as the United Nations, to develop a consensus around a set of stakeholder principles that corporations could adopt voluntarily. A compendium of essays, *Understanding Stakeholder Thinking* (Andriof, et al., 2002) is a good starting point for this very promising work. Jeanne Liedtka, Laura Dunham, and I have suggested that citizenship may well be a problematic concept if it is restricted to an analysis of the "community" stakeholder, and Waddock may well offer a way out of this morass. "Community" may well by the "soft underbelly" of stakeholder theory since it is very difficult to pin down a meaning in today's world which is nearly absent of a "sense of place" (Dunham, Liedtka, and Freeman, 2005).

Andrew Wicks and Bidhan Parmar have suggested that one of the central tasks of both stakeholder theory and business ethics is to put "business" and "ethics" together in a coherent and practical way (Wicks, Freeman, and Parmar, 2004). Kirsten Martin has suggested that the separation of business and ethics which is so central to the stakeholder debate needs to be expanded to take the role of technology into account in an explicit manner (Martin and Freeman, forthcoming). Venkataraman (2002) has argued that thinking about entrepreneurship would hasten this combination, strengthening both stakeholder theory and entrepreneurship as important fields of inquiry.

Open questions remain. For instance:

1. Is there a useful typology of enterprise strategy or answers to questions of purpose?
2. How can we understand the relationship between fine-grained narratives of how firms create value for stakeholders, and the idea of stakeholder theory as a genre or set of loosely connected narratives?
3. If we understand business, broadly, as "creating value for stakeholders" what are the appropriate background disciplines? And, in particular what are the connections between the traditional "social sciences" and "humanities"?
4. How can the traditional disciplines of business such as marketing and finance develop conceptual schemes that do not separate "business" from "ethics" and can the stakeholder concept be useful in developing these schemes?
5. If we understand "business," broadly, as "creating value for stakeholders," under what conditions is value creation stable over time?
6. Can we take as the foundational question of political philosophy, "how is value creation and trade sustainable over time" rather than "how is the state justified"?

I am certain that there are many additional research questions, and many more people working on these questions than I have mentioned here. I hope this paper has clarified some of my own writing in the stakeholder area, and provoked others to respond.

If I try to summarize the lessons for management theorists of the development of stakeholder theory they would be four. First, don't underestimate the role of serendipity and context. My role would have been very different, indeed probably nonexistent, if a few key life events had unfolded differently. Second, don't underestimate the contributions of others. Really, my own contribution has been to try and synthesize the contributions of many others. I am always amused and somewhat horrified when I'm at a conference and am introduced as the "father of stakeholder theory." Many others did far more work, and more important work than I did, and that continues today as stakeholder theory unfolds in a number of fields. Third, pay attention to the real world of what managers, executives, and stakeholders are doing and saying. Our role as intellectuals is to interpret what is going on, and to give better, more coherent accounts of management practice, so that ultimately we can improve how we create value for each other, and how we live. That, I believe is a kind of pragmatist's credo. Finally, surely the author has a role in management theory. Overemphasis on reviews, reviewers, revisions, and the socialization of the paper-writing process can lead to a kind of collective group think. I believe that I could not have published the work in *Strategic Management: A Stakeholder Approach* as a set of A-journal articles. By publishing a book, I managed to create a voice, building heavily on the voices of others that could express a point of view. I believe that in today's business school world, that is much more difficult, and that we need to return to a more ancient idea of the author in management theory.

REFERENCES

ACKOFF, R. (1974). *Redesigning the Future*. Hoboken, NJ: John Wiley and Sons.

ANDRIOF, J., WADDOCK, S., HUSTED, B., and RAHMAN, S. S. (eds.) (2002). *Unfolding Stakeholder Thinking*. Sheffield, UK: Greenleaf Publishing.

AGLE, B., MITCHELL, R., and SONNENFELD, J. A. (1999). "Who matters to CEOs? An investigation of stakeholder attributes and salience, corporate performance, and CEO values." *Academy of Management Journal*, 42(5): 507–525.

BERMAN, S., WICKS, A. C., KOTHA, S., and JONES, T. (1999). "Does stakeholder orientation matter: An empirical examination of the relationship between stakeholder management models and firm financial performance." *Academy of Management Journal*, 42: 488–506.

BLAIR, M. (1995). "Whose interests should be served?" In M. Clarkson (ed.), *Ownership and Control: Rethinking Corporate Governance for the Twenty First Century*: 202–234. Washington, DC: The Brookings Institution.

BOATRIGHT, J. (1994). "Fiduciary duties and the shareholder–management relation: Or, what's so special about shareholders?" *Business Ethics Quarterly*, 4: 393–407.

BOWIE, N. (1999). *Business Ethics: A Kantian Perspective*. Oxford: Blackwell.

BURTON, B. K., and DUNN, C. P. (1996). "Collaborative control and the commons: Safeguarding employee rights." *Business Ethics Quarterly*, 6: 277–288.

CLARKSON, M. (1995). "A stakeholder framework for analyzing and evaluating corporate social performance." *Academy of Management Review*, 20: 92–117.

DONALDSON, T., and DUNFEE, T. (1999). *Ties That Bind: A Social Contracts Approach to Business Ethics*. Boston: Harvard Business School Press.

—— and PRESTON, L. (1995). "The stakeholder theory of the corporation: Concepts, evidence, and implications." *Academy of Management Review*, 20: 65–91.

DUNHAM, L., LIEDTKA, J., and FREEMAN, R. E. (2005). "Enhancing stakeholder practice: A particularized exploration of community." *Business Ethics Quarterly* (forthcoming).

EVAN, W., and FREEMAN, R. E. (1993). "A stakeholder theory of the modern corporation: Kantian capitalism." In T. Beauchamp and N. Bowie (eds.), *Ethical Theory and Business*. Englewood Cliffs: Prentice Hall.

FREEMAN, R. E. (1984). *Strategic Management: A Stakeholder Approach*. Boston: Pitman.

—— (1994). "The politics of stakeholder theory." *Business Ethics Quarterly*. Vol. 4(4).

—— and EVAN, W. (1990). "Corporate governance: A stakeholder interpretation." *The Journal of Behavioral Economics*, 19(4), pp. 337–359.

—— and McVEA, J. (2001). "Stakeholder theory: The state of the art." In M. A. Hitt, R. E. Freeman, and J. Harrison (eds.), *The Blackwell Handbook of Strategic Management*. Oxford: Blackwell.

—— WICKS, A. C., and PARMAR, B. (2004). "Stakeholder theory: The state of the art and future perspectives." *Politeia*, Anno XX, No. 74.

—— HARRISON, J., PHILLPS, R., and WICKS, A. C. (forthcoming). *Stakeholder Theory: Business in the 21st Century*.

—— —— —— —— (forthcoming). *Stakeholder Theory: The State of the Art*.

GOODPASTER, K. (1991). "Business ethics and stakeholder analysis." *Business Ethics Quarterly*, 1: 53–73.

—— and HOLLORAN, T. (1994). "In defense of a paradox." *Business Ethics Quarterly*, 4: 423–430.

GRAVES, S., and WADDOCK, S. (1990). "Institutional ownership and control: Implications for long-term corporate performance." *Academy of Management Executive*, 37: 1034–1046.

—— —— (1994). "Institutional owners and corporate social performance." *Academy of Management Journal*, 37(4): 1034.

HARRISON, J., and FIET, J. O. (1999). "New CEOs pursue their own self-interests by sacrificing stakeholder values." *Journal of Business Ethics*, 19: 301–308.

—— and St. JOHN, C. (1994). *Strategic Management of Organizations and Stakeholders*. St. Paul: West Publishing.

JONES, T. (1995). "Instrumental stakeholder theory: A synthesis of ethics and economics." *Academy of Management Review*, 20: 92–117.

—— and WICKS, A. C. (1999). "Convergent stakeholder theory." *Academy of Management Review*. 24: 206–221.

KOCHAN, T., and RUBENSTEIN, S. (2000). "Towards a stakeholder theory of the firm: The Saturn partnership." *Organizational Science*, 11(4): 367–386.

LUOMA, P., and GOODSTEIN, J. (1999). "Stakeholders and corporate boards: Institutional influences on board composition and structure." *Academy of Management Journal*, 42: 553–563.

MARENS, R., and WICKS, A. C. (1999). "Getting real: Stakeholder theory, managerial practice, and the general irrelevance of fiduciary duties owed to shareholders." *Business Ethics Quarterly*, 9(2): 273–293.

MARTIN, K., and FREEMAN, R. E. (forthcoming). "The separation of technology and ethics in business ethics." *Journal of Business Ethics.*

MITCHELL, R. K., AGLE, B. R., and WOOD, D. J. (1997). "Toward a theory of stakeholder identification and salience: Defining the principle of who and what really counts." *Academy of Management Review*, 22: 853–886.

OGDEN, S., and WATSON, R. (1999). "Corporate performance and stakeholder management: Balancing shareholder and customer interests in the U.K. privatized water industry." *Academy of Management Journal*, 42: 526–538.

ORTS, E. (1997). "A North American legal perspective on stakeholder management theory." In F. Patfield (ed.), *Perspectives on Company Law*: 2. 165–179.

PHILLIPS, R. (1997). "Stakeholder theory and a principle of fairness." *Business Ethics Quarterly*, 7: 51–66.

—— and REICHART, J. (1998). "The environment as a stakeholder: A fairness-based approach." *Journal of Business Ethics*. 23(2), 185–197.

—— FREEMAN, R. E. and WICKS, A. C. (2003). "What stakeholder theory is not." *Business Ethics Quarterly*, 13(4): 479–502.

PORTER, M. (1998). *Competitive Advantage*. New York: The Free Press.

SCHENDEL, D., and HOFER, C. (eds.) (1979). *Strategic Management: A New View of Business Policy and Planning*. Boston: Little Brown.

VANCIL, R. F., and LORANGE, P. (1975). "Strategic Planning in Diversified Companies." *Harvard Business Review*, 53(1): 81–91.

VENKATARAMAN, S. (2002). "Stakeholder equilibration and the entrepreneurial process." In R. E. Freeman and S. Venkataraman (eds.), *The Ruffin Series #3, Ethics and Entrepreneurship*: 45–57. Charlottesville, Va.: Philosophy Documentation Center.

WICKS, A. C., FREEMAN, R. E., and GILBERT, D. (1994). "A feminist reinterpretation of the stakeholder concept." *Business Ethics Quarterly*, 4: 475–497.

—— —— (1998). "Organization studies and the new pragmatism: Positivism, anti-positivism, and the search for ethics." *Organization Science*. 9(2): 123–140.

—— —— and PARMAR, B. (2004). "The corporate objective revisited." *Organization Science*. 15(3): 364–369.

WILLIAMSON, O. (1984). *The Economic Institutions of Capitalism*. New York: Free Press.

WOOD, D. (1995). "The Fortune database as a CSP measure." *Business and Society*, 24(2), 1997–1999.

···

DEVELOPING RESOURCE DEPENDENCE THEORY

HOW THEORY IS AFFECTED BY ITS ENVIRONMENT

··

JEFFREY PFEFFER

RESOURCE dependence theory was developed in the 1970s at a time when there was a proliferation of important theories dealing with the relationship of organizations to their environments. As Davis (2003: 5) noted, it is somewhat remarkable that a single four-year period saw the major foundational statements of transaction cost economics (Williamson, 1975), the agency theory of the firm (Jensen and Meckling, 1976), organizational ecology (Hannan and Freeman, 1977), the new institutional theory of organizations (Meyer and Rowan, 1977), and resource dependence theory (Pfeffer and Salancik, 1978). In some sense, however, it was actually not surprising that there was a plethora of theory development at that time. Each of these theories arose in response to the perceived need for a theoretical approach that treated the relationship between organizations and their environments. In a research context in which the idea of organizations as open systems was increasingly recognized (e.g., Katz and Kahn, 1966; Yuchtman and Seashore, 1967; Terreberry, 1968; Lawrence and Lorsch, 1967) and in which there were few existing well-developed theoretical approaches available to analyze the relationship between organizations and their environments, a perceived need for theory produced a corresponding supply of relevant theoretical approaches. Resource dependence was one such approach.

Demand for theory—in the sense of there being important aspects of organizations or significant organizational phenomena unexplored or unaccounted for—is not the only reason or stimulus for theory development. There are also numerous reasons why people might want to *supply* new theory, regardless of the need. Career issues loom large in this regard. It is not only a source of prestige to develop some widely accepted and cited theoretical perspective. The conventions of publishing in the organization sciences make new theoretical development, at least to some degree, a virtual sine qua non for getting into print. And many doctoral students in the organization sciences are encouraged to do original work and develop ideas that break new theoretical ground to launch their careers. There seems to be less emphasis on doing research that promulgates new theory or terminology in the physical sciences or even in psychology, where continuing the empirical exploration of an existing theoretical paradigm seems somehow more acceptable.

It is certainly true that developing good theory is important for the progress of any science or social science, and that would obviously include the field of organization studies as well. Nonetheless, I begin my discussion of the development of resource dependence theory by noting that I am not sure we should be encouraging the development of *more* new and different theory at this stage in the evolution of organization science. As Mone and McKinley (1993) have so eloquently argued, there is a premium in organization studies for uniqueness. This has led to a seeking after theoretical novelty for its own sake and has resulted in people labeling the same concepts or basic ideas with different terms, as well as developing new ideas and theories without very much consideration of the existing conceptual terrain. The consequence has been a profusion of ideas, conceptual frameworks, and theories that have surprisingly little contact with each other in an increasingly differentiated intellectual landscape. As noted previously (Pfeffer, 1993, 1997), I would encourage those who seek to advance organization science to think hard about the desirability of developing yet more new theory, conceptual frameworks, and terminology, as contrasted with the task of refining existing theories and, even more importantly, testing theories and their predictions against each other as a way of seeing what works and what doesn't.

Contrast the situation in organization studies with that in economics, where there is not only a higher level of paradigmatic consensus (Lodahl and Gordon, 1972) but also a much more parsimonious set of axioms and theoretical principles—a fact that may both help to account for the greater level of consensus and also be a consequence of that greater level of agreement. To the extent that there is a market for ideas and organization studies competes in that marketplace with other social sciences, something that I believe to be unarguably true, and particularly to the extent that the field seeks to influence social and organizational policy, the profusion of our theoretical wares may actually lead to a competitive disadvantage.

The seemingly counterintuitive idea that more options or choices may be harmful is an insight that should be familiar to those who have followed the recent social psychological research on the sometimes negative consequences of having more alternatives (e.g., Iyengar and Lepper, 2000; Iyengar and Jiang, 2004). That research shows that, unlike common sense expectations and the predictions of the economics of choice, consumer welfare can be impeded when the number of options becomes excessive, as decision makers may be immobilized or over-whelmed by the task of choosing. One might make a parallel argument in the research context, and note that a profusion of conceptual models, terms, and theoretical perspectives may not only confuse graduate students trying to decide what research avenues to pursue but even bedevil more advanced scholars trying to determine how to frame and situate their work. Too much choice of theoretical perspectives, terms, and concepts can lead to risk aversion in the choice of research topics (following the logic of Iyengar and Jiang, 2004), less satisfaction with the research process, and even less likelihood of choosing research topics in the first place (following the logic of Iyengar and Lepper, 2000).

My colleague, Dale Miller, argues that what we need is a systematic effort to discover a set of primitive first principles that most if not all organization scholars can agree on, and then begin the task of building integrated models of organizational behavior relying on those first principles and their logical derivations. This effort to develop logically integrated theory from first principles is precisely the path that population ecology has been pursuing (e.g., Peli, Polos, and Hannan, 2000), particularly with the recent increased emphasis on formal deduction and logic. Davis and Marquis (forthcoming) have commented on the distinctiveness of the research effort in population ecology: With the notable exception of population ecologists, macro-organizational scholars since 1990 have largely abandoned the idea of cumulative work within a particular paradigm. The existence of a logical structure, consistent set of measures, terms, and theoretical constructs, and theoretical consensus may be part of the reason that population ecology continues to have influence on the field of organization studies that far surpasses either the number of its practitioners or, for that matter, its practical or possibly even theoretical utility.

Nonetheless, for those seeking to build organization theory, the history of resource dependence offers some instructive lessons on both what to do and, I believe, some lessons on what not to do and also perhaps what else to do, to cause a theory to thrive in the marketplace of ideas. So, the following is offered in the spirit of learning from experience, at least as that experience is imperfectly apprehended by one of the developers of the resource dependence perspective.

21.1 THE BASIC TENETS AND ORIGINS OF RESOURCE DEPENDENCE THEORY

Resource dependence theory, like virtually all of the other theoretical ideas with which I am associated—for example, organizational demography (Pfeffer, 1983), social information processing (Salancik and Pfeffer, 1978), or power in organizations (Pfeffer and Salancik, 1974; Pfeffer, 1992)—began with the observation of a phenomenon and a search for an explanation of that phenomenon in the existing literature. When it was the case that currently available theoretical perspectives either did not adequately explain the phenomenon or address it at all, this absence of a relevant literature led to formulating and then testing a theoretical approach that might explain the observed phenomenon more effectively.

This emphasis on phenomenon-driven theory development is an approach that Mintzberg (2004: 401), among others, has also advocated: Good research is deeply grounded in the phenomenon it seeks to describe. And problem-driven work, distinguished by its orientation toward explaining events in the world (Davis and Marquis, forthcoming: 8) has been argued to provide a useful focus for research efforts in a complex, rapidly changing environment that begs for explanation and understanding.

Phenomenon- or problem-driven research connects theory with the world it is ostensibly about. It is a way of doing theory development that places a premium on the close observation of the organizational world and then confronting those observations with existing theoretical perspectives, and vice versa. Although there are no systematic data on this point that I know of, I believe that it is the close observation of phenomena coupled with a deep knowledge of the literature that together aid in the development of innovative and important theory.

So, the observation that sparked the development of organizational demography was that at the business school at the University of Illinois, assistant professors had a lot of influence in the governance process while at the University of California at Berkeley they had almost none. Why might this be? It turns out that Illinois, because of its recent growth, was filled with people who had come to the university very recently, while Berkeley had a much more senior faculty. That observation led to a search for relevant literature and other examples of the effects of age and tenure distributions on organizations, and sparked subsequent empirical research on the importance of demographic distributions on organizational processes.

The research on power arose from the observation that even though the Management Department and the School of Business at Illinois were taking on the teaching of more and more students in an effort to grow the number of faculty positions, the incremental resources obtained seemed to be much smaller than the increases in the workload, calling into question the idea of an enrollment economy.

Instead, powerful departments obtained a higher proportion of budgetary resources (Pfeffer and Salancik, 1974) and were more able to turn workload and academic prestige into faculty positions. At that time, existing theories of power mostly examined the bases of individual power and did not speak to the interaction of subunits and departments, which was obviously where a lot of internal power dynamics occurred. And, as yet one more example, social information processing arose from the observation that what constituted good teaching was very much socially constructed, and the further observation that people doing relatively boring and seemingly routine jobs—at least as assessed by the typical job design dimensions—did not invariably perceive their jobs as either routine or boring.

In the case of resource dependence, the observation that sparked the development of the theory was the varying organizational reactions to the pressure in the late 1960s and early 1970s to end employment discrimination against women and minorities and to, instead, take affirmative action to incorporate these previously excluded groups. Organizations varied significantly in terms of their responses and responsiveness not only to these, and for that matter, other external pressures from the government but also in their responses to other external groups. That raised the question of why.

At the time, many of the major theoretical perspectives now taken for granted—such as population ecology, institutional theory, and transaction cost economics—had yet to appear on the scene. The dominant explanation for variation in organizational behavior lodged the causal mechanism in the values and actions of organizational leaders (Pfeffer, 1977) or in other internal organizational dynamics such as motivation and group processes. The study of interorganizational behavior was nascent. In spite of all of the subsequent theoretical and empirical work, writing that locates explanations for organizational phenomena in considerations of the social context, something that characterizes much of the research by myself and Salancik (e.g., Weick, 1996), remains relatively rare. For instance, Khurana's (2002) recent book describing the search for corporate saviors nicely illustrates how little things have changed, at least in the world of practice, in the ensuing decades, with a continued emphasis on single individuals as being the explanation for organizational performance.

But to Salancik and me, an explanation emphasizing the unconstrained choices of individual leaders did not seem correct. In the first place, this story did not correspond to the casual observation that companies that seemed to be more closely tied in their business to various levels of government seemed to be the most responsive to government pressure. In the second place, an explanation for organizational behavior as emanating from the values and beliefs of senior leaders would imply more variability over time in that behavior than seemed to be the case, because decisions would result from apparently random accession of people with varying ideologies and political beliefs into leadership roles.

In building a theory to address the questions of organizational responses to external pressures and how organizations attempted to manage those constraints, resource dependence drew on a number of well-established theoretical ideas. There were existing models of power (e.g., Emerson, 1962; Blau, 1964) that conceptualized power as the obverse of dependence in a bilateral relationship. So, resource dependence sought to take those models of power and dependence and translate them to a more macro level of analysis. Thompson (1967) had written about the organizational imperative to attempt to buffer the technical core from external shocks so that internal processes could proceed in a more efficient and less disrupted fashion. Consequently, resource dependence sought to explore not only how power and dependence affected organizational choices but also how, in the spirit of Thompson, organizations might seek to buffer themselves from the consequences of this dependence and interdependence, so as to obtain more autonomy.

Open systems ideas emphasized that organizations imported inputs from the environment—inputs such as people and raw materials—and then after some internal transformation, delivered some good or service back into the environment to acquire more resources to continue the process of exchange. The idea of inputs and outputs and the importance of transactions with external agents in the environment therefore assumed a prominent place in resource dependence theory. What resource dependence mostly did was put these existing ideas together and showed how they might account for a number of phenomena of interest including patterns of mergers (Pfeffer, 1972*b*), joint ventures (Pfeffer and Nowak, 1976), and board of director interlocks (Pfeffer, 1973), as well as some aspects of internal organizational dynamics such as executive succession and even the specific decisions organizations made. Resource dependence represented an effort to see how much of the empirical regularity observable in the world of organizations and their environments could be accounted for by a single, reasonably inclusive, approach.

21.1.1 Fundamental Theoretical Ideas

The most central idea of resource dependence was that organizations, as open systems, had to both obtain resources and, after some transformation, deliver the goods or services thereby produced to some customers broadly defined that would then provide the money to permit the organization to acquire more inputs and continue the cycle. In order to survive, something it was assumed organizations and their members sought as a goal, organizations had to be effective. But effectiveness was defined not simply in terms of efficiency or profitability but by an organization's ability to satisfy the demands of those external entities on which it depended (Pfeffer and Salancik, 1978: 3). As long as an organization could attract sufficient resources from the environment to continue to acquire the inputs necessary for survival, the organization was, by definition, at least minimally effective. It was, therefore, quite possible to observe organizations that were always in some sense failing but survived because they were able, through political or other means, to obtain sufficient resources to continue (e.g., Meyer and Zucker, 1989).

Because the organization necessarily transacted with external actors in the acquisition of inputs and the disposal of outputs, the interdependence created by and through such tractions was, *potentially*, a source of power and its obverse, constraint. To the extent that the external environment was highly concentrated so a focal organization had few alternative sources for some necessary input, and to the extent the dependence on the particular resource obtained from a concentrated source was high, the focal organization would be more constrained and prone to accede to the demands of those powerful external actors. External constraints, if exercised by actors with sufficient power, affected internal organizational decisions as well as organizational profitability (e.g., Burt, 1983). The ability of Burt (1983) to analyze variation in profits by considering not internal factors of production or management or traditional measures of industry concentration but rather the pattern of relations among sectors in the economy using measures of constraint and its obverse, autonomy, was a remarkable contribution to the literature on industry structure and strategy.

21.1.2 Early Empirical Research

The early strategy for the empirical development of resource dependence theory was influenced by the ideas of Eugene Webb, someone who had influenced the intellectual development of both myself as a doctoral student at Stanford (Webb was on my thesis committee) and Salancik, whom Webb had taught in the journalism program at Northwestern. Webb was a co-author of the book *Unobtrusive Measures* (Webb, et al., 1966) that argued, among other things, that almost no single empirical study could completely address all theoretical issues. Therefore, one viable research strategy for developing and testing theory was to derive as many empirical implications or outcroppings of a theory as possible and then try to test as many of these empirical predictions as possible over time. To the extent that one was able to accumulate a greater number of empirical results consistent with some theoretical perspective, one could have greater confidence in the validity of that particular theoretical approach.

So, to examine how resource dependence affected organizational decisions, one empirical study used survey data to show how the extent to which Israeli firms depended on the government for sales and for financing affected their expressed willingness to invest in development areas being promoted by the government (Pfeffer and Salancik, 1978: 54–56). Another study by Salancik (1979) examined companies' response to affirmative action using a field stimulation methodology in which firms were queried in the guise of getting information to furnish to female MBA graduates. For large visible firms that did not control the production of the items being purchased by the government (they were dependent on the government but the government was not dependent on them), the correlation between their level of sales to the government and their responsiveness to the inquiry about affirmative action was .84. For smaller, less visible firms that controlled the production of items purchased by the government, there was actually a negative relationship between the proportion of sales to the government and the firms' responsiveness to the inquiry.

The problem organizations faced in making decisions under environmental constraint was not just that this limited the autonomy of management, although it certainly did that. A bigger problem was that demands from various environmental actors were often inconsistent (Friedlander and Pickle, 1968), a fact that left organizations seeking to meet the demands of those on whom they were dependent in a quandary about what to do. In response to both of these issues—a search for autonomy and buffering per the arguments of Thompson (1967) and the accompanying certainty and predictability that such autonomy provided, as well as an attempt to deal with conflicting demands—resource dependence argued that organizations would attempt to manage their environments and attempt to construct them to make them more beneficent.

This led, logically, to empirical research that traced the relationship between patterns of resource dependence and actions that organizations might undertake to manage that interdependence. Thus, for example, organizations might attempt to co-opt those entities on which they depended through, for instance, placing representatives from these potent external actors on their boards of directors (Pfeffer and Salancik, 1978: ch. 7), merge or create joint ventures to absorb either totally or partially the source of interdependence, or try, through legislation or other government action, to obtain autonomy through regulation or the legal system. Organizations might also try to persuade powerful external actors that they were meeting their demands, potentially through the symbolic actions so nicely described in the early writings of institutional theory (Meyer and Rowan, 1977).

The empirical tests of these ideas were reasonably straightforward. With respect to mergers, the original data (Pfeffer, 1972b) and a subsequent replication (Finkelstein, 1997) showed that merger patterns tended to follow patterns of transactions interdependence: the higher the proportion of transactions a given industry sector did with another industry sector, the higher the proportion of mergers occurred between the two sectors, even after controlling for alternative explanations such as the relative profitability of the sectors and the number of firms—potential merger partners—in the industry. In a similar fashion, the composition of boards of directors tended to follow patterns of resource dependence (e.g., Pfeffer, 1972a, 1973).

The final major point of resource dependence theory was to connect organization–environment interactions with internal organizational dynamics. Specifically, Pfeffer and Salancik (1978: ch. 9) noted that those internal subunits that could best cope with managing the constraints and contingencies emanating from the environment would, over time, come to have more power inside the organization. This argument was similar in spirit to that developed by Hickson, et al. (1971; see also Hinings, et al., 1974) with one relatively small difference: Hickson and colleagues argued that power accrued to those inside the organization that could best cope with uncertainty, whereas resource dependence argued that power accrued to those units that could most successfully deal with one quite specific source of uncertainty, the provision of resources.

One way in which this internal subunit power would be manifest was in the backgrounds and origins of those acceding to chief executive positions. So, for instance, as the contingencies faced by electric utilities changed from technical issues of power plant design and operation to finance and interaction with increasingly potent regulators, the background of utility executives changed from engineering to law and business (Pfeffer, 1992). As hospitals became less dependent on doctors to supply patients and more dependent on both the government and large insurers and health maintenance organizations to pay from them, the background of hospital administrators would shift from being physicians to those with experience in contracting and accounting, who could better cope with the new environmental demands. Thornton's (2004) study of the changing dynamics in the academic publishing industry, with the shift in concern from quality books to profits, traces how this change in the environment produced changes in leadership succession dynamics.

As should be clear from the foregoing, resource dependence theory as originally conceived was broad in scope, seeking to account for external influences on organizational decisions, a variety of organizational efforts to preserve decision autonomy by attempting to mitigate external constraint, and how both external constraints and efforts to operate in an environment of interdependence might affect internal organizational dynamics, particularly power dynamics such as which subunits would come to have the most power. As should be also clear, the theory built on a number of prominent ideas particularly from the sociology of organizations literature. If resource dependence made a contribution to organization theory, it was primarily by bringing a lot of theoretical ideas together in a comprehensive framework, by forcefully arguing for the importance of understanding the effect of the environment as a means of understanding organizations, and by arguing for the importance of the material conditions of organizational transactions with the environment.

21.2 THE SOCIAL CONTEXT OF THEORY DEVELOPMENT

To understand the development of resource dependence, or for that matter, the origins and evolution of any other theory, it is useful to understand something about the place and time of the theory's development. As Davis (2003: 6) has noted, organizations were powerful social actors throughout the 1950s, 1960s, and 1970s and there was a growing realization that we lived in organizational society, so that to understand society and economic institutions, understanding organizations was important. Moreover, in the corporate economy of the United States, "firms had increased in size and scope... corporate ownership had grown increasingly dispersed among atomized shareholders, leaving corporate managers the undisputed masters of their domains and bureaucratic processes... had rendered these large firms relatively inert." The theories that developed reflected the organizational landscape at the time when they arose.

In addition, the late 1960s and the 1970s, when much of the original conceptual and empirical work on the theory was done, was a time of political ferment in the United States. The Vietnam War, the presidency of Lyndon Johnson, the master politician (e.g., Caro, 1982, 1990) and then Richard Nixon with the Watergate scandal, and the poor economy suffering from inflation and stagnant growth made issues of power and politics and conflict salient. Politics and social issues were very much on the front burner. It was a former doctoral student and colleague, Richard Harrison, who first pointed out to me how much of the theoretical work developed during that time reflected, in sometimes quite direct ways, the world outside the academy.

So, for instance, Barry Staw's work on escalating commitment (Staw, 1976) drew directly on George Ball's prescient comments on the ease of getting into Vietnam and the difficulty of getting out, and how decisions, once made, would tend to cause their own justification by investing more even if, or perhaps particularly if, the initial decisions seemed flawed. Staw's (1974) thesis, a field test of insufficient justification ideas, drew on the draft lottery as a naturally occurring field experiment and his interest in how one's fortunes in that lottery affected attitudes towards ROTC. Women's entry into and then difficulty in the labor market stimulated work on discrimination in its many forms (e.g., Bielby and Baron, 1986). Walsh, Weber, and Margolis (2003) have empirically shown how in the field of organization studies, interest in social welfare and outcomes other than economic performance, at least as reflected in publication in management journals, peaked in the 1970s and has subsequently declined dramatically. Their data are consistent with the observation that the period of the 1970s was a time of social activism and a heightened concern with social issues.

As already noted, resource dependence theory arose out of an interest in how organizations influenced other organizations (e.g., Salancik, 1979) and the responses of the organizations that were subject to that influence. So, in a very direct way resource dependence arose as a way of understanding a major set of actions going on at the time—organizations on the one hand attempting to get others to do their bidding and, on the other hand, other organizations trying to figure out ways to resist the external pressure. But resource dependence is a theory of those times in an even more fundamental way. Resource dependence is a theory about power, developed in a time in which power, including the power of organizations and institutions, was very much a subject of attention. The theory focused on interorganizational power—for instance, how the power of social agencies affected their ability to obtain resources from United Funds (Pfeffer and Leong, 1977). And it focused on how power dynamics in the environment affected things such as subunit power and executive succession inside organizations.

Another important contextual factor affecting the development of resource dependence theory was the co-location at the University of Illinois of Gerald Salancik, Barry Staw, and myself. The management department was very much trying to grow and gain status, but was not one of the most prestigious business departments at that time. Consequently, junior faculty were actually more able to take intellectual risks, including the risk of developing new theory, because there was nothing to lose.

Salancik, a social psychologist from Yale, and I had complementary work styles—I tended to be organized and not lose materials and he was sometimes disorganized but always free-thinking and creative. But we shared very similar theoretical orientations, including an emphasis on situationism, a love of learning from observation, and an interest in asking provocative questions. We also shared a personal liking and respect, which made it perfectly possible and acceptable for one to obliterate the other's writing in a new draft without provoking ego defensiveness. The goal was to come up with the best account possible with the most compelling writing, and credit and authorship were of lesser importance. In many respects, the complementary skills, overlapping theoretical perspectives, and style of interpersonal interaction between Salancik and myself have recently been reproduced in my collaboration with Robert Sutton (Pfeffer and Sutton, 1999). In each instance, the focus on the final product, the willingness to take on popular ideas, and a desire to develop ideas that are both original but also speak to real phenomena with the potential of actually influencing policy and practice may have collectively contributed to the quality of the final research products.

Because theory is context dependent in its development, there is always the risk that theories can become irrelevant as contexts change. Davis (e.g., 2003: 10) has argued that resource dependence was one of a set of sociological theories about firms and environments [that] increasingly described a world of large, vertically integrated, relatively autonomous corporations that no longer existed. As I will argue presently, I believe that claim, particularly as an explanation for the relative disappearance of empirical work on resource dependence theory, is not correct, as Davis's own data convincingly demonstrate. But Davis is correct in his observation that the environment has changed. However, what has changed is not so much an environment that makes resource dependence or other theories developed at that time more or less correct, but rather an environment that makes some ideas more and other ideas less accepted and used in building theory. Power is one of those ideas that seems to have, at least temporarily, fallen out of fashion.

21.3 Refinement Through Contrast

To reprise a familiar refrain, the field of organization studies misses out on an important opportunity for theory development by its tendency to not counterpose theories and their predictions. As Mackenzie and House (1978) have argued, all theories eventually fail, at least under some conditions. Therefore, theory development should be about finding out the conditions under which theories are true and the conditions under which they are false, and this can be accomplished best by stretching theories to their limits. It can also be accomplished by comparing theories one to the other. Such comparisons do more than just determining which theory is superior, at least in a given prediction domain. The rigor of theoretical comparison forces more precision in the argument and thereby enhances the development and elaboration of the theories being compared.

Because resource dependence was developed and its initial empirical work largely completed before the emergence of alternative theoretical perspectives on organizations and environments, the early work on resource dependence sought to use economics as the comparison theory. That choice seemed particularly appropriate because economics dealt explicitly with some of the same dependent variables, such as mergers, and at a deeper level, because the emphasis of economics on efficiency as an explanation contrasted nicely with resource dependence's reliance on power (Williamson and Ouchi, 1981).

The analysis of patterns of mergers found that there was, overall, no correlation with the proportion of mergers made with a given industry and the profitability of that industry (Pfeffer and Salancik, 1978: 118). This result shows that it is not the case the profitable industries necessarily attract more acquisition activity, a prediction that would be consistent with the economic idea that profits encourage new entry, including entry accomplished through mergers. Instead, considerations of uncertainty reduction—both reducing competitive uncertainty and transactional uncertainty—were more successful in accounting for patterns of both horizontal and vertical merger behavior than measures of profits. This finding, by the way, foreshadows the subsequent empirical work demonstrating how most mergers destroy shareholder value. Even though there has been evidence for decades that mergers, presumably an important form of economic activity, are unrelated or negatively related to corporate profitability, economic theories of mergers have persistent appeal.

The comparison of predictions from different theories evident in this particular research on mergers is remarkably rare. In subsequent years there have been few if any attempts to test the predictions of the various theories of organization–environment relations against each other. This is unfortunate. The null hypothesis of no relationship is in many instances a weak alternative to a theory's predictions. A more robust test would be exploring the extent to which a given theory's accounts not only do better than chance but also do better than alternative conceptualizations in understanding the phenomena being investigated.

21.4 Success and Setbacks of Resource Dependence Theory

The history of the evolution of resource dependence ideas from their original publication in the 1970s to the present is instructive. The original formulations actually had quite precise and clearly falsifiable predictions about many discrete aspects of interorganizational behavior. So, for instance, there were quite detailed predictions about which forms of interdependence would be more important for explaining interorganizational behavior under different circumstances:

To the extent that the organization operates in a relatively concentrated environment, we argue that its interdependence with suppliers of input will be relatively more important and problematic than its interdependence with customers [because it has more power with respect to customers because of the high level of industry concentration which means that its customers have few alternatives]. Consequently, we predict that there will be a higher correlation between merger activities and purchase interdependence the higher the concentration of the organization's economic environment. (Pfeffer and Salancik, 1978: 121)

In a similar fashion, specific predictions were made concerning the conditions that would promote mergers made for diversification. And because mergers to absorb interdependence had to, of necessity, be with firms that could reduce that interdependence while there was a wider range of targets for diversification, the prediction, confirmed by the data, was that profitability would explain more about targets for diversification than for mergers made to absorb transactional interdependence.

Burt (1980, 1983) subsequently operationalized resource dependence ideas in explicitly network terms, providing particular specificity to the idea of constraint. Burt's research found that constraint predicted profit margins and that patterns of constraint also predicted the occurrence of actions or strategies to mitigate that constraint, such as merger and co-optation.

Although there was a flurry of empirical activity directly exploring some of the core ideas of the theory, the subsequent history of resource dependence is consistent with its ideas being used more as a metaphor or general theoretical orientation rather than testing very precise, falsifiable, predictions and estimating parameters for theoretical models (Pfeffer, 2003). In part, this was because the two primary originators of the theory each went on to do research on other topics, moving to explore and develop additional avenues of inquiry rather than remaining focused just on the elaboration and testing of resource dependence ideas. And, in part, this was because once articulated and in the presence of some promising early empirical work, resource dependence theory appeared to be both intuitively correct and complete enough to not warrant a lot of additional testing and development.

One sees this phenomenon in many other topic domains as well, with the ironic consequence that the more successful the theory initially seems to be, the less subsequent work that theory sometimes receives. If competition makes a theory stronger by mobilizing research on the theory, an absence of competition and corresponding research effort hinders a theory's evolution and, over time, the extent to which it is actually incorporated into new empirical research. Along these lines, Barry Staw has commented to me that although there are many alternative explanations, conditions under which it might hold more or less strongly, and other elaborations possible to understand processes of escalating commitment, the work of more precisely specifying and elaborating ideas of escalating commitment remains largely undone. Commitment was demonstrated, there was a sound explanation, and given the field's interest in novelty, in part because journals, their protestations to the contrary, really do not readily publish replications and refinements as much as they do new and different ideas, there was really little incentive for people to continue developing data and ideas about escalating commitment.

So, in some sense, resource dependence was quite successful as a theory in the social sciences. By the summer of 2004, *The External Control of Organizations*, the most customary citation for the theory had received 2,655 citations. And of that total number, some 54 percent had been received in the most recent ten-year period, indicating that even though the book was now more than 25 years old, it was still being regularly cited.

Moreover, resource dependence ideas and subjects continued to form the conceptual foundation for some ongoing empirical research programs. For instance,

Beckman, Haunschild, and Phillips (2004) empirically explored the choice of alliance and interlock partners. They noted that some theories posited stability in the social structure, maintaining the firms formed linkages with past exchange partners. Other theories emphasized change in social structure, with companies building linkages to new partners. Their work sought to resolve this theoretical tension by arguing that the type of linkages formed depended on the type of uncertainty the firms faced—firm-level or market-level. Firm-level uncertainty produced the formation of new ties, while industry-level uncertainty tended to lead companies to strengthen existing affiliations. Gulati and Gargiulo's (1999) study of alliances in three industries and nine countries concluded that resource interdependence predicted patterns of alliance formation.

Kim, Hoskisson, and Wan (2004) explored the effect of power-dependence relations in Japanese keiretsu on performance and strategy. Their study found that powerful firms were able to place an emphasis on growth and international diversification while less powerful keiretsu members were compelled to emphasize profitability and were subject to strong monitoring. Christensen's study of why market leaders often failed to innovate also emphasized the constraint of external organizations, in particular, existing customers. A firm's scope for strategic change is strongly bounded by the interests of external entities (customers, in this study) who provide the resources the firm needs to survive (Christensen and Bower, 1996: 212).

Schuler, Rehbein, and Cramer (2002: 668), analyzing the political activities of firms, found that companies that relied heavily on government contracts lobbied and contributed to campaigns to maintain close ties with the policy makers responsible for their livelihoods. Thornton and Ocasio (1999) noted that as the higher education publishing industry morphed from one concerned about books and their quality to one more concerned about financial results, the determinants of senior executive succession changed as one might expect.

In short, as this brief, selective overview of a few studies suggest, the basic predictions of resource dependence theory in terms of responses to dependence, the effect of environmental dependence on succession, and the effects of dependence on decisions—in this instance, to forgo new technologies to serve existing customers—continue to be empirically examined and often supported.

But there is some bad news as well for resource dependence theory. Particularly with respect to the study of corporate interlocks, challenging alternative views of the determinants and role of board interlocks have arisen and recent data are inconsistent with resource dependence predictions. Palmer (1983) noted that if corporate interlocks were made to co-opt interdependence, ties should be reconstituted when they are broken, but there is evidence that this is not very often the case. Palmer viewed corporate ties not as binding organizations to each other but, instead, as a forum for the capitalist class to come together. Friedland and Palmer (1984) also argued that resource dependence, along with most other organization theory, ignored geography, and there was an effect of geographic propinquity—friendship networks determined by common place—that loomed large in understanding corporate board composition. Davis (1996) noted that by 1994, an examination of the patterns of interlocks observed among the largest U.S. firms—not just industrial firms but financial institutions and service companies as well—revealed no evidence of horizontal interlocks and almost no interlocking between firms and either customers or buyers. He also found little support for the idea of banks as being central to interlock networks. In a study of mergers updating the original work, Finkelstein (1997), using more sophisticated measures and less aggregated data, found that the original predictions of resource dependence in explaining patterns of merger activity were replicated, although the results were not as strong.

But the main challenge to resource dependence has come not because it has been tested and found empirically wanting, or because it has been difficult to operationalize or to specify empirical tests. Instead, the problem has been that resource dependence has been declared irrelevant. Death by fiat, rather than death—or even modification—by empirical test. Carroll (2002: 3), for instance, made two claims in arguing that resource dependence is virtually dead. The first is that much of the empirical research in institutional theory is indistinguishable from that of resource dependence theory. And the second is that transaction cost economics has subsumed resource dependence theory (does that mean, by logical implication, that transaction costs theory has also subsumed institutional theory?)

Davis (2003) has argued that resource dependence theory no longer stimulates a lot of empirical research because the theory describes a world—large, powerful organizations with autonomy—that no longer exists in an economy where shareholders rule supreme and companies have become smaller and more focused. Davis's argument, however, is inconsistent with Finkelstein's (1997) finding that the strength of the effects predicted by resource dependence have not diminished over time and, if anything, are stronger when examining mergers in more recent periods. His argument is also actually inconsistent with his own data and assertions.

Although there is some evidence that economic concentration has not continued to increase and may have declined a little and there have been changes in the extent of conglomeration and vertical integration, Davis (see also Davis, 1996; Davis and Marquis, forthcoming) has actually documented in great detail not the decline in organizational autonomy and power but rather its obverse. Multinational companies are, in some instances, larger than most nations and in many instances exist outside of the control of governments. Companies operating across boundaries constitute problematic targets for government regulation as locales compete for jobs and tax revenues. Companies—he uses General Electric and Westinghouse as examples—are free to virtually completely reinvent themselves, shedding old businesses and acquiring new ones. Companies are also free to shed their employees and to avoid unionization and, using a number of strategies nicely described by Davis, even avoid taxation. The increase in global trade has made it possible for companies to avoid dependence on suppliers because they have numerous sources for producing the items they intend to sell, and indeed, find it easier to exert power over those in the supply chain than to exert power over manufacturing executives within their own boundaries.

It is important to note that nowhere in the original formulation of resource dependence was there any claim that corporations were free from constraint and completely autonomous. Nor was it argued that the environment would remain the same over time, and that, therefore, there would not be change in patterns of dependence and constraint and, consequently, differences in how corporations responded to those changes in the power dynamics in their environments. Indeed, resource dependence theory was formulated precisely to assess both the effects of constraints on corporate decision making and organizational responses to those constraints. Institutional investors and their power as constraining organizational action, and organizational responses to those investors, would fall squarely within the topic domain of resource dependence. So would organizations' increasing ability to shape the laws and regulations that govern their activities and those of their competitors.

There is also the issue that institutional theory and resource dependence share many perspectives and predictions in common. In fact, Pfeffer and Salancik (1978) argued that legitimacy was an important resource necessary for organizational survival and acquired in much the same way as other resources, through alliances with legitimate social actors (Dowling and Pfeffer, 1975), through political actions, and possibly even through mergers. There are, of course, differences between the two theories, not only in the level of analysis—institutional theory tends to focus more on fields whereas resource dependence focuses more on the focal organization—but also in the explicit attention to power dynamics. Institutional theory has tended to take rules and norms as givens, whereas resource dependence sees the institutional structure itself as the result of an interplay between contending and competing organizational interests.

Nonetheless, the lesson for those building theories, should they want their theories to persist, is clear. As Ronald Burt once commented, theoretical success or dominance, certainly in social science, requires armies of acolytes to not only push the empirical and theoretical development of the theory but, perhaps as importantly, to continue its promulgation and rise to its defense. Here, again, there are many lessons to be learned from population ecology and its relative success. Neither Salancik nor I, nor Burt for that matter, have had legions of doctoral students nor did our taste run to indoctrinating the students we trained into some sort of orthodoxy or filial loyalty. Many of my students wrote on completely nonrelated topics and one, Davis, has turned out to be one of resource dependence's critics.

21.5 THE POLITICS OF THEORY IN THE SOCIAL SCIENCES

....

There are, I believe, many misconceptions about theory and theory development in the organization and social sciences, particularly on the part of younger scholars. In concluding this discussion of the development and evolution of resource dependence theory, it is useful to both review these beliefs and see how they play out in understanding the growth and development of resource dependence.

The first, most strongly held, and possibly most harmful mistaken belief is that theories succeed or fail, prevail or fall into disuse, primarily, and some would maintain exclusively, on the basis of their ability to explain or predict the behavior that is the focus of the theory. Moreover, there is a belief that a theory's success in prediction and explanation is particularly important in explaining its success if there are competitive theories covering the same dependent variables. This belief is erroneous in at least two ways.

First of all, as argued elsewhere (Ferraro, Pfeffer, and Sutton, 2005), theories may create the environment they predict, thereby becoming true by construction rather than because they were originally veridical with the world they sought to explain. To the extent people believe in a particular theory, they may create institutional arrangements based on the theory that thereby bring the theory into reality through these practices and institutional structures. To the extent people hold a theory as true, they will act on the basis of the theory and expect others to act on that basis also, creating a normative environment in which it becomes difficult to not behave on the basis of the theory because to do so would violate some implicit or explicit expectations for behavior. And to the extent that people adhere to a theory and therefore use language derived from and consistent with the theory, the theory can become true because language primes both what we see and how we apprehend the world around us, so that talking using the terminology of a particular theory also makes the theory become true.

Second, the philosophy of science notwithstanding, theories are quite capable of surviving disconfirming evidence. Behavioral decision theory and its numerous empirical tests have shown that many of the most fundamental axioms of choice and decision that underlie economics are demonstrably false (e.g., Bazerman, forthcoming), but economics is scarcely withering away. Nor are the specific portions of economic theory predicated on assumptions that have been shown to be false necessarily any less believed or used. A similar situation is true in finance, where assumptions of capital market efficiency and the instantaneous diffusion of relevant information, so that a security's market price presumably incorporates all relevant information available at the time, have withstood numerous empirical and theoretical attacks. To take a case closer to organization studies, the reliance on and belief in the efficacy of extrinsic incentives and monetary rewards persists not only in the lay community but in the scholarly literature as well. So, Heath's (1999) insightful study of what he terms an extrinsic incentives bias is as relevant to the domain of scholars as it is to practicing managers and lay people.

What this means for resource dependence theory is that to the extent that claims that it is virtually dead (Carroll, 2002) are true and that it has been subsumed by transactions cost theory, this state of affairs may say less than one might expect about the comparative empirical success or theoretical coherence of transactions cost theory. As David and Han (2004: 39) summarized in their review of sixty-three articles empirically examining transaction cost economics, "we...found considerable disagreement on how to operationalize some of TCE's central constructs and propositions, and relatively low levels of empirical support in other core areas." Instead, the comment about the relative position of resource dependence and transactions cost theory may say more about the politics of social science and the fact that power is currently out of vogue and efficiency and environmental determinism such as that propounded by population ecology and other perspectives reifying an impersonal environment, with all of their conservative implications, is currently more in favor.

Documenting the rise in theories that eschew considerations of power, or often, even people, and the consequences of these theories for the form of theorizing that occurs in the organization sciences is something well beyond the scope of this paper, requiring literally a book. Let me briefly note that there has been a rise in a conservative brand of economics eschewing mixed economies, regulation, and intervention in markets. As Kuttner (1996: 33) so nicely put it, in the 1950s, Milton Friedman was dismissed as a curiosity. By the 1980s, Friedman and several of his followers had won the Nobel prize. This new economics has come to dominate curricula and analysis in numerous social sciences (Bernstein, 2001) such as political science (Green and Shapiro, 1994), law (Posner, 2003), and some branches of sociology (e.g., Coleman, 1993).

Any theory, including the economics of impersonal markets, that eschews political explanations and instead relies on impersonal mechanisms such as market competition or its related cousin, natural selection, is attractive for its benign view of how to theoretically deal with problems of social order, coordination, and control. As Granovetter (1985: 484) has written:

It has long been recognized that the idealized markets...have survived intellectual attack in part because self-regulating...structures are politically attractive to many...Competition determines the terms of trade in a way that individual traders cannot manipulate...social relations and their details thus become frictional matters.

As shown in several analyses (e.g., Kuttner, 1996; Blyth, 2002), the rise of a more conservative social science has been helped along by funding from conservative foundations. That social science theory reflects the political milieu of the times seems both unsurprising and not controversial. After all, theories depend on ideas and support and both of these come from the environment.

Second, the ability of a theory to grow and prosper depends importantly both on the willingness and ability of its proponents to attract allies—mostly, by the way, through the ability to offer resources of research support and favorable publication and career outcomes. Collins (2004: 560) nicely described the process:

Indeed... what appears to be an altruistic search for a truthful rendering of the management process might, in fact, be better understood as a war for the monopoly of management studies... Latour [1987] argues that academics... inscribe rather than merely reflect the nature of reality. Indeed, Latour warns us that scientists—like Balkan politicians—must enroll others in their programmes and must protect these manifestos from cross-border incursions if they are to acquire and retain a loyal following.

The irony for the development and persistence of resource dependence theory is delicious. A theory with power as one of its most important components, propounded by two people who went on to do numerous empirical studies of power and to teach courses on power in organizations (Pfeffer, 1992), has been handicapped in the contest with other theories of organization and environment because it failed to have proponents with the sufficient will or skill to spend a lot of time enlisting allies (and punishing opponents).

Of course, just as Barley and Kunda (1992) have shown for logics of managerial control, theoretical ideas also have ebbs and flows. It is not so much that truth triumphs, although one might hope for that. It is rather that ideas very much have currency. As this chapter is being written, economic approaches to organizational analysis have come under some modest amount of increasing attack (e.g., Ghoshal and Moran, 1996; Ghoshal, forthcoming; Ferraro, Pfeffer, and Sutton, 2005). Organization theories such as population ecology that leave human agency, including power, out of organization studies are also being challenged, on the one hand, by those that argue that organization studies has an obligation to the profession, management, and administration, it ostensibly serves to provide guidance, and on the other hand, by some (e.g., Podolny, Khurana, and Hill-Popper, forthcoming) who note that the current disdain for theories of action and disgust with concepts such as leadership are fundamentally untrue to and at odds with the history of organizational sociology (e.g., Selznick, 1957).

The lessons of all of this for those doing theory seem clear, particularly in hindsight. It is helpful to have good theory, where good is defined using the conventional scientific criteria. It is even better to have a theory that has some advantage in its parsimony, its conceptual clarity, its intuitive appeal, and its ability to account for phenomena over its competitors. But it is by far best of all to have a theory that, in its fundamental assumptions, is in tune with the times and the political ideas currently in vogue. Unfortunately for aspiring scholars, predicting cycles of ideas is a tricky business, made more so by the fact that there is surprisingly little self-reflective empirical examination of the rise and fall of such ideas and their impact on social science and particularly little empirical study of theory development and evolution in the organization sciences. In the end, the success or problems of resource dependence theory at any particular point in time can, appropriately, be productively analyzed by the ideas of resource dependence theory itself.

References

BARLEY, S., and KUNDA, G. (1992). Design and devotion: Surges of rational and normative ideologies of control in managerial discourse. *Administrative Science Quarterly*, 37: 363–399.

BAZERMAN, M. H. (forthcoming). Conducting influential research: The need for prescriptive implications. *Academy of Management Review*.

BECKMAN, C. M., HAUNSCHILD, P. R., and PHILLIPS, D. J. (2004). Friends or strangers? Firm-specific uncertainty, market uncertainty, and network partner selection. *Strategic Management Journal*, 15: 259–275.

BERNSTEIN, M. (2001). *A Perilous Progress: Economists and Public Purpose in Twentieth Century America*. Princeton: Princeton University Press.

BIELBY, W. T., and BARON, J. N. (1986). Men and women at work: Sex segregation and statistical discrimination. *American Journal of Sociology*, 91: 759–799.

BLAU, P. M. (1964). *Exchange and Power in Social Life*. New York: Wiley.

BLYTH, M. (2002). *Great Transformations: Economic Ideas and Institutional Change in the Twentieth Century*. New York: Cambridge University Press.

BURT, R. S. (1980). Autonomy in a social topology. *American Journal of Sociology*, 85: 892–925.

—— (1983). *Corporate Profits and Co-optation*. New York: Academic Press.

CARO, R. A. (1982). *The Path to Power*. New York: Knopf.

—— (1990). *Means of Ascent*. New York: Knopf.

CARROLL, G. R. (2002). Williamson and organizational sociology. Presentation at a conference to celebrate the 70th birthday of Oliver Williamson. Berkeley, Calif.: October, 2002.

CHRISTENSEN, C. M., and BOWER, J. J. (1996). Customer power, strategic investment, and the failure of leading firms. *Strategic Management Journal*, 17: 197–218.

COLEMAN, J. S. (1993). The rational reconstruction of society. *American Sociological Review*, 58: 1–15.

COLLINS, D. (2004). Who put the con in consultancy? Fads, recipes, and "vodka margarine." *Human Relations*, 57: 553–572.

DAVID, R. J., and HAN, S. (2004). A systematic assessment of the empirical support for transaction cost economics. *Strategic Management Journal*, 25: 39–58.

DAVIS, G. F. (1996). The significance of board interlocks for corporate governance. *Corporate Governance*, 4: 154–159.

—— (2003). Firms and environments. In N. Smelser and R. Swedberg (eds.), *Handbook of Economic Sociology*, 2nd edn., October 9, 2003 (forthcoming).

—— and MARQUIS, C. (forthcoming). Prospects for organization theory in the early 21st century: Institutional fields and mechanisms. *Organization Science*.

DOWLING, J., and PFEFFER, J. (1975). Organizational legitimacy: Social values and organizational behavior. *Pacific Sociological Review*, 18: 122–136.

EMERSON, R. M. (1962). Power-dependence relations. *American Sociological Review*, 27: 31–41.

FERRARO, F., PFEFFER, J., and SUTTON, R. I. (2005). Economic language and assumptions: How theories can become self-fulfilling. *Academy of Management Review*, 30: 32–35.

FINKELSTEIN, S. (1997). Interindustry merger patterns and resource dependence: A replication and extension of Pfeffer 1972. *Strategic Management Journal*, 18: 787–810.

FRIEDLAND, R., and PALMER, D. (1984). Park Place and Main Street: Business and the urban power structure. *Annual Review of Sociology*, 10: 393–416.

FRIEDLANDER, F., and PICKLE, H. (1968). Components of effectiveness in small organizations. *Administrative Science Quarterly*, 13: 289–304.

GHOSHAL, S. (forthcoming). Bad management theories are destroying good management practice. *Academy of Management Learning and Education.*

—— and MORAN, P. (1996). Bad for practice: A critique of the transaction cost theory. *Academy of Management Review*, 21: 13–47.

GRANOVETTER, M. (1985). Economic action and social structure: The problem of embeddedness. *American Journal of Sociology*, 91: 481–510.

GREEN, D. P., and SHAPIRO, I. (1994). *Pathologies of Rational Choice Theory: A Critique of Applications in Political Science.* New Haven: Yale University Press.

GULATI, R., and GARGIULO, M. (1999). Where do interorganizational networks come from? *American Journal of Sociology*, 104: 1439–1493.

HANNAN, M. T., and FREEMAN, J. (1977). The population ecology of organizations. *American Journal of Sociology*, 82: 929–964.

HEATH, C. (1999). On the social psychology of agency relationships: Lay theories of motivation overemphasize extrinsic incentives. *Organizational Behavior and Human Decision Processes*, 78: 25–62.

HICKSON, D. J., HININGS, C. R., LEE, C. A., SCHNECK, R. E., and PENNINGS, J. M. (1971). A strategic contingencies' theory of intraorganizational power. *Administrative Science Quarterly*, 16: 216–229.

HININGS, C. R., HICKSON, D. J., PENNINGS, J. M., and SCHNECK, R. E. (1974). Structural conditions of intraorganizational power. *Administrative Science Quarterly*, 19: 22–44.

IYENGAR, S. S., and JIANG, W. (2004). Choosing not to choose: The effect of more choices on retirement savings decisions. Unpublished thesis. New York: Columbia Business School.

—— and LEPPER, M. R. (2000). When choice is demotivating: Can one desire too much of a good thing? *Journal of Personality and Social Psychology*, 79: 995–1006.

JENSEN, M. C., and MECKLING, W. H. (1976). Theory of the firm: Managerial behavior, agency costs, and ownership structure. *Journal of Financial Economics*, 3: 305–360.

KATZ, D., and KAHN, R. (1966). *The Social Psychology of Organizations.* New York: Wiley.

KHURANA, R. (2002). *Searching for a Corporate Savior.* Princeton: Princeton University Press.

KIM, H., HOSKISSON, R. E., and WAN, W. P. (2004). Power dependence, diversification strategy, and performance in keiretsu member firms. *Strategic Management Journal*, 25: 613–636.

KUTTNER, R. (1996). *Everything for Sale: The Virtues and Limitations of Markets.* Chicago: University of Chicago Press.

LATOUR, B. (1987). *Science in Action*. Cambridge, Mass.: Harvard University Press.

LAWRENCE, P., and LORSCH, J. (1967). *Organizations and Environments*. Boston: Harvard University Press.

LODAHL, J. B., and GORDON, G. (1972). The structure of scientific fields and the functioning of university graduate departments. *American Sociological Review*, 37: 57–72.

MACKENZIE, K. D., and HOUSE, R. (1978). Paradigm development in the social sciences: A proposed research strategy. *Academy of Management Review*, 3: 7–23.

MEYER, J. W., and ROWAN, B. (1977). Institutionalized organizations: Formal structure as myth and ceremony. *American Journal of Sociology*, 83: 340–363.

MEYER, M. W., and ZUCKER, L. (1989). *Permanently Failing Organizations*. Newbury Park, Calif.: Sage.

MINTZBERG, H. (2004). *Managers Not MBAs*. San Francisco: Berrett-Koehler.

MONE, M. A., and McKINLEY, W. (1993). The uniqueness value and its consequences for organization studies. *Journal of Management Inquiry*, 2: 284–296.

PALMER, D. (1983). Broken ties: Interlocking directorates and intercorporate coordination. *Administrative Science Quarterly*, 28: 40–55.

PELI, G. L., POLOS, L., and HANNAN, M. T. (2000). Back to inertia: Theoretical implications of alternative styles of logical formalization. *Sociological Theory*, 18: 195–215.

PFEFFER, J. (1972a). Size and composition of corporate boards of directors: The organization and its environment. *Administrative Science Quarterly*, 17: 218–228.

—— (1972b). Merger as a response to organizational interdependence. *Administrative Science Quarterly*, 17: 382–394.

—— (1973). Size, composition, and function of hospital boards of directors. *Administrative Science Quarterly*, 18: 349–364.

—— (1977). The ambiguity of leadership. *Academy of Management Review*, 2: 104–112.

—— (1983). Organizational demography. In L. L. Cummings and B. M. Staw (eds.), *Research in Organizational Behavior*: 5. 299–357. Greenwich, Conn.: JAI Press.

—— (1992). *Managing with Power: Politics and Influence in Organizations*. Boston: Harvard Business School Press.

—— (1993). Barriers to the advance of organizational science: Paradigm development as a dependent variable. *Academy of Management Review*, 18: 599–620.

—— (1997). *New Directions for Organization Theory: Problems and Prospects*. New York: Oxford University Press.

—— (2003). Introduction to the classic edition. *The External Control of Organizations: A Resource Dependence Perspective*: xi–xxix. Stanford, Calif.: Stanford University Press.

—— and LEONG, A. (1977). Resource allocations in United Funds: Examination of power and dependence. *Social Forces*, 55: 775–790.

—— and NOWAK, P. D. (1976). Joint ventures and interorganizational interdependence. *Administrative Science Quarterly*, 21: 398–418.

—— and SALANCIK, G. R. (1974). Organizational decision making as a political process: The case of a university budget. *Administrative Science Quarterly*, 19: 135–151.

—— —— (1978). *The External Control of Organizations: A Resource Dependence Perspective*. New York: Harper and Row.

—— and SUTTON, R. I. (1999). *The Knowing–Doing Gap*. Boston: Harvard Business School Press.

PODOLNY, J., KHURANA, R., and HILL-POPPER, M. (forthcoming). Revisiting meaning of leadership. *Research in Organizational Behavior*.

POSNER, R. A. (2003). *Economic Analysis of Law*, 6th edn., Aspen: Law and Business.

SALANCIK, G. R. (1979). Interorganizational dependence and responsiveness to affirmative action: The case of women and defense contractors. *Academy of Management Journal*, 22: 375–394.

—— and PFEFFER, J. (1978). A social information processing approach to job attitudes and task design. *Administrative Science Quarterly*, 23: 224–253.

SCHULER, D. A., REHBEIN, K., and CRAMER, R. D. (2002). Pursuing strategic advantage through political means: A multivariate approach. *Academy of Management Journal*, 45: 659–672.

SELZNICK, P. (1957). *Leadership in Administration*. Evanston, Ill.: Row, Peterson.

STAW, B. M. (1974). Attitudinal and behavioral consequences of changing a major organizational reward: A natural field experiment. *Journal of Personality and Social Psychology*, 29: 742–751.

—— (1976). Knee-deep in the big muddy: A study of escalating commitment to a chosen course of action. *Organizational Behavior and Human Performance*, 16: 27–44.

TERREBERRY, S. (1968). The evolution of organizational environments. *Administrative Science Quarterly*, 12: 590–613.

THOMPSON, J. D. (1967). *Organizations in Action*. New York: McGraw-Hill.

THORNTON, P. H. (2004). *Markets from Culture: Institutional Logics and Organizational Decisions in Higher Education Publishing*. Stanford, Calif.: Stanford University Press.

—— and OCASIO, W. (1999). Institutional logics and the historical contingency of power in organizations: Executive succession in the higher education publishing industry, 1958–1990. *American Journal of Sociology*, 105: 801–843.

WALSH, J. P., WEBER, K., and MARGOLIS, J. (2003). Social issues and management: Our lost cause found. *Journal of Management*, 29: 859–881.

WEBB, E. J., CAMPBELL, D. T., SCHWARTZ, R. D., and SECHREST, L. B. (1966). *Unobtrusive Measures: Nonreactive Research in the Social Sciences*. Chicago: Rand McNally.

WEICK, K. E. (1996). An appreciation of social context: One legacy of Gerald Salancik. *Administrative Science Quarterly*, 41: 563–573.

WILLIAMSON, O. E. (1975). *Markets and Hierarchies: Analysis and Antitrust Implications*. New York: Free Press.

—— and OUCHI, W. G. (1981). The markets and hierarchies program of research: Origins, implications, and prospects. In A. H. Van de Ven and W. F. Joyce (eds.), *Perspectives on Organizational Design and Behavior*: 347–370. New York: John Wiley.

YUCHTMAN, E., and SEASHORE, S. E. (1967). A system resource approach to organizational effectiveness. *American Sociological Review*, 73: 261–272.

CHAPTER 22

INSTITUTIONAL THEORY

CONTRIBUTING TO A THEORETICAL RESEARCH PROGRAM

W. RICHARD SCOTT

INSTITUTIONAL theory attends to the deeper and more resilient aspects of social structure. It considers the processes by which structures, including schemas, rules, norms, and routines, become established as authoritative guidelines for social behavior. It inquires into how these elements are created, diffused, adopted, and adapted over space and time; and how they fall into decline and disuse. Although the ostensible subject is stability and order in social life, students of institutions must perforce attend not just to consensus and conformity but to conflict and change in social structures (Scott, 2004b).

The roots of institutional theory run richly through the formative years of the social sciences, enlisting and incorporating the creative insights of scholars ranging from Marx and Weber, Cooley and Mead, to Veblen and Commons. Much of this work, carried out at the end of the nineteenth and beginning of the twentieth centuries, was submerged under the onslaught of neoclassical theory in economics, behavioralism in political science, and positivism in sociology, but has experienced a remarkable renaissance in our own time. (For reviews of early institutional theory, see Bill and Hardgrave, 1981; Hodgson, 1994; Scott, 1995, 2001.)

Contemporary institutional theory has captured the attention of a wide range of scholars across the social sciences and is employed to examine systems ranging from micro interpersonal interactions to macro global frameworks. Although the presence of institutional scholars in many disciplines provides important opportunities for exchange and cross-fertilization, an astonishing variety of approaches and sometimes, conflicting assumptions limits scholarly discourse.

Given the complexity and variety of the current scene, I restrict attention in this chapter to more recent institutional work carried out by organizational sociologists and management scholars. And, within this realm, I concentrate on macro perspectives, examining the structure of wider environments and their effects on organizational forms and processes. (For a related approach, with emphasis on the micro-foundations of institutional theory, see Zucker and Darby, Ch. 25, this volume. For closely related chapters employing transaction cost economic and evolutionary economic approaches, see Williamson, Ch. 23, this volume and Winter, Ch. 24, this volume.) Taken in its entirety, I believe that this body of work constitutes an impressive example of a "cumulative theoretical research program" (Berger and Zelditch, 1993) that has grown and matured over the course of its development. To understand, interpret, and advance this program has been central to my own intellectual agenda during the past three decades.

22.1 Building a Theoretical Argument

22.1.1 Early Insights

At the University of Chicago where I completed my doctorate degree, I studied and worked with Everett C. Hughes as well as with Peter M. Blau. Hughes first directed my attention to the institutional structures surrounding and supporting work activities, in particular to the role of unions and professional associations in shaping occupations and organizations (Hughes, 1958). Although my dissertation provided data to support the examination of the contextual effects of organizations on work groups (Blau and Scott, 1962/2003), its principal theoretical focus was on the tensions arising between professional employees and bureaucratic rules and hierarchial supervision (Scott, 1965, 1966). I viewed this topic then and now as an important instance illustrating two competing visions—today, I would say alternative "institutional logics"—as to how best to rationalize a set of activities.

I pursued my interest in competing conceptions of appropriate work structure with colleagues at Stanford during the 1960s in an examination of organizational authority systems (Dornbusch and Scott, 1975). In studies of a variety of organizations, we examined discrepancies between preferred and actual authority systems as well as between workers with varying degrees of power to enforce their preferences. I concluded that work arrangements are not preordained by natural economic laws, but are shaped as well by cultural, social, and political processes.

22.1.2 A Bolder Conception

However, it was not until my collaborative work with John W. Meyer, together with colleagues in the School of Education at Stanford during the 1970s, that I began to recognize the larger sense in which institutional forces shape organizational systems. Our early research designs were drawn from the then-reining paradigm, contingency theory (Lawrence and Lorsch, 1967; Thompson, 1967/2003), as we examined the effects of employing more complex instructional methods ("technologies") on classroom and school structure (Cohen et al., 1979). But trying to learn from the data, we recognized the limitations of existing theories and began to entertain alternative explanations for sources of structuring. Drawing on the insights of the early social theorists, Durkheim (1912/1961) and Weber (1924/1968), as well as the ideas of Berger and Luckmann (1967), Meyer (1970) suggested that much social order is a product of social norms and rules that constitute particular types of actors and specify ways in which they can take action. Such behaviors are not so much socially influenced as socially constructed.

These arguments were elaborated and applied by Meyer, me, and a number of collaborators to the analysis of educational systems (Meyer, 1977; Meyer and Rowan, 1977; Meyer et al., 1978, 1988; Meyer and Scott, 1983; Meyer, Scott, and Deal, 1981), but quickly generalized to apply to the full range of organizations. Consistent with conventional accounts, organizations were recognized to be "rationalized" systems—sets of roles and associated activities laid out to reflect means-ends relationships oriented to the pursuit of specified goals. The key insight, however, was the recognition that models of rationality are themselves cultural systems, constructed to represent appropriate methods for pursuing purposes. A wide variety of institutional systems have existed over space and time, providing diverse guidelines for social behavior, many of which sanction quite arbitrary behavior; but the modern world is dominated by systems embracing rationality and these, in turn, support the proliferation of organizations. Norms of rationality play a causal role in the creation of formal organizations (Meyer and Rowan, 1977).

Many of the models giving rise to organizations are based on "rationalized myths"—rule-like systems that "depend for their efficacy—for their reality, on the fact that they are widely shared, or have been promulgated by individuals or groups that have been granted the right to determine such matters" (Scott, 1983: 14). The models provide templates for the design of organizational structures: "the positions, policies, programs, and procedures of modern organizations" (Meyer and Rowan, 1977: 343). These models exert their power, not via their effect on the task activities of organizational participants—work activities are often decoupled from rule systems or from the accounts depicting them—but on stakeholders and audiences external to the organization. Their adoption by the organization garners social legitimacy.

22.1.3 An East-Coast Variant

While these ideas were under development at Stanford, across the country at Yale University, two other sociologists, Paul M. DiMaggio and Walter W. Powell, were developing their own variant of institutional theory. Drawing on network arguments, both connectedness and structural equivalence (White, Boorman, and Breiger, 1976), DiMaggio and Powell provided a related explanation to account for processes that "make organizations more similar without necessarily making them more efficient" (1983: 147). Whereas the Stanford models privileged widely shared symbolic models, DiMaggio and Powell stressed the importance of palpable network connections that transmitted coercive or normative pressures from institutional agents, such as the state and professional bodies, or mimetic influences stemming from similar or related organizations.

At about the same time, researchers on both coasts recognized the value of concentrating attention on more delimited sets of organizations. Whereas early formulations (e.g., Meyer and Rowan, 1977) advanced arguments applicable to all organizations, DiMaggio and Powell's (1983) concept of "organizational field" (influenced by Bourdieu's (1977) notion of "social field") and Meyer's and my (Scott and Meyer, 1983) concept of "societal sector" (influenced by the work of public policy analysts and community ecologists) simultaneously recognized that both cultural and network systems gave rise to a socially constructed arena within which diverse, interdependent organizations carry out specialized functions. It is within such fields that institutional forces have their strongest effects and, hence, are most readily examined.

Early empirical work centered around three themes: factors affecting the diffusion of institutional forms (Tolbert and Zucker, 1983; Hinings and Greenwood, 1988; Dobbin et al., 1988; Meyer et al., 1988), the disruptive effects of conflicted or fragmented institutional environments on organizational forms (Meyer, Scott, and Strang, 1987; Powell, 1988), and the processes at work in constructing the rules and logics unpinning an organizational field (DiMaggio, 1983; Leblebici and

Salancik, 1982). Arguments were not only being crafted but, increasingly, confronted with data. Institutional theory had reached the stage of a promising adolescent (Scott, 1987).

22.2 CONSTRUCTING A COMPREHENSIVE FRAMEWORK

I was invited to spend the academic year 1989–1990 as a Fellow at the Center for Advanced Study in the Social and Behavioral Sciences, a national center, albeit located on the outskirts of Stanford University. This year-long fellowship, enjoyed in the company of more than fifty other scholars, is quite rightly prized and has proved beneficial to many in their intellectual pursuits. Having spent my previous years furiously teaching, researching, and writing (as well as administering departments and programs), I elected to spend the bulk of my fellowship year reading. I knew that institutional theory had multiple roots and was being pursued in varied ways across the social sciences. I wanted to find out if there were commonalities among these approaches, and determine whether institutional theory could be contained within a comprehensive conceptual framework. That year I worked to steep myself in the wide-ranging literature of institutional theory, including older and more recent versions as pursued by economists, political scientists, and sociologists.

Attempting to bring some coherence to the enterprise, the approach I adopted was to construct what Tilly (1984: 81) terms an "encompassing" framework, that incorporates related but different concepts and arguments and locates them within a broader theoretical system. I postulated that institutions are variously comprised of "cultural-cognitive, normative and regulative elements that, together with associated activities and resources, provide stability and meaning to social life" (Scott, 2001: 48; see also, Scott, 1995: 33). Although institutional scholars vary in the relative emphasis they place on these elements and in the levels of analysis at which they work, all recognize the common theme that social behavior and associated resources are anchored in rule systems and cultural schema. Relational and material features of social structures are constituted, empowered and constrained by the virtual elements, which they, in turn produce and reproduce (Giddens, 1979; Sewell, 1992).

As summarized in Table 22.1, the pillars framework asserts that institutions are made up of diverse elements that differ in a number of important ways. They posit different bases of order and compliance, varying mechanisms and logics, diverse empirical indicators, and alternative rationales for establishing legitimacy claims.

Table 22.1 Three pillars of institutions

	Regulative	Normative	Cultural-Cognitive
Basis of compliance	Expedience	Social obligation	Taken-for-grantedness Shared understanding
Basis of order	Regulative rules	Binding expectations	Constitutive schema
Mechanisms	Coercive	Normative	Mimetic
Logic	Instrumentality	Appropriateness	Orthodoxy
Indicators	Rules	Certification	Common beliefs
	Laws	Accreditation	Shared logics of action
	Sanctions		
Basis of legitimacy	Legally sanctioned	Morally governed	Comprehensible Recognizable Culturally supported

Source: Scott, 2001: 52, Table 3.1.

Although all institutions are composed of various combinations of elements, they vary among themselves and over time in which elements are dominant. Different theorists also tend to privilege one or another class of elements. Thus, most economists and rational choice theorists stress regulative elements (e.g., Moe, 1984; Williamson, 1975; North, 1990); early sociologists favored normative elements (Hughes, 1939; Parsons, 1934/1990; Selznick, 1949); and more recent organizational sociologists and cultural anthropologists emphasize cultural-cognitive elements (e.g., Zucker, 1977; DiMaggio and Powell, 1991; Douglas, 1986; see also Scott, 2001: 83–88).

The framework outlined in Table 22.1 is not a theory, but a conceptual schema. It depicts and differentiates among three complexes of ideas, each of which provide the ingredients for an alternative conception of and explanation for institutions. The framework attempts to capture both the commonality and the diversity of theorizing about institutions, past and present. It suggests not simply that theories differ, but indicates how they differ. It does not provide an integrated theory of institutions but points out directions for pursuing such a theory. It is intended to better enable us to compare and contrast the diverse conceptions of institutional theory advanced, as well as to identify the varying levels at which these arguments are being pursued.

While my own theorizing and research has emphasized the cultural-cognitive elements as a basis for institutional analysis, I see great value in work favoring the regulative or the normative approaches. Indeed, much of the research in which I have participated considers the impact of governmental organizations, legislation, and court decisions—all primarily regulative agents—on the structure and activities of organizations. And I continue to be impressed by—and to study—the power of normative agents, such as professional associations, in shaping organizational forms and processes. All three elements are at work, albeit in varying ways, to stabilize social behavior—from pair-wise interactions to world-wide systems.

22.3 SHAPING AND CORRECTING THE AGENDA

Arguments and approaches devised during the formative period when institutional theory was being revived and constructively connected to organizations, roughly 1975–1985, have continued to affect the development of the field. We should never underestimate the power of foundational works in shaping the course of subsequent developments in a social arena. Many social phenomena, including social theory, exhibit path-dependent effects. While most of the effects have been salutary some, in my view, were not. I consider three areas where reconsideration and corrections were called for, and, to a considerable extent, have occurred. (See also, Scott, forthcoming.)

22.3.1 Toward More Interactive Models

Too much early theorizing and research on institutions posited "top-down" models of social influence. Scholars examined the various ways in which rules, norms, and shared beliefs impacted organizational forms. Such a focus is understandable since a necessary condition for calling attention to the importance of institutions is to demonstrate their influence on organizations. However, the language used was predominantly that of "institutional effects," as if a given set of environmental forces was able to exert influence in a unilateral manner on compliant organizations. Two corrections were required, and both are now well underway.

First, we needed to recognize that institutional environments are not monolithic, but often varied and conflicted. Authoritative bodies may diverge—indeed, in liberal states, they are often designed to do so, providing "checks and balances"—and schemas and models may compete. The elements of institutions—regulative, normative, cultural-cognitive—may not be aligned, and one may undermine the effects of the other. The boundaries of organizational fields are often vague or weak, allowing alternative logics to penetrate and support divergent models of behavior. Suppressed groups and interests may mobilize and successfully promote new models of structure and repertoires of acting. Some of the most interesting work of the past two decades has helped to unpack the multiplicity of institutional arrangements, both between and within a given field, examining the intersection of structures, and documenting the transposability of schemas, as actors and ideas flow across field boundaries (Friedland and Alford, 1991; Sewell, 1992). Empirical studies of these processes range from examining the effects of the fragmentation of U.S. state structures (Meyer, Scott, and Strang, 1987; Abzug and Mezias, 1993); to competition among alternative professional models (DiMaggio, 1991); to conflicts between faltering and emergent regimes, e.g., the rise of market models in socialist states (Campbell and Pedersen, 1996; Stark, 1996). Clearly, competing rules or schema open up possibilities for choice and bargaining among subordinate actors.

Second, while recognizing that actors are institutionally constructed, it is essential to affirm their (varying) potential for reconstructing the rules, norms, and beliefs that guide—but do not determine—their actions. Barley's (1986) influential study of the variable response of actors in hospitals to the introduction of (presumably determinant) technologies, helped to open the door for the consideration of power exercised by "subjects," and was reinforced by DiMaggio's (1988) essay calling for the reintroduction of "agency"—the capacity to "make a difference" in one's situation—into institutional theorizing. Gradually, the language began to shift from discussions of institutional "effects" to institutional "processes"; and theorists began to craft recursive models, recognizing "bottom-up" modes of influence, to supplement or replace prevailing top-down models (Scott, 1995, 2001).

The introduction of agentic actors was required at multiple levels. Rather than positing the presence of "widely shared" belief systems or norms, it was important to specify who—which actors—held the beliefs or were enforcing the norms. Similarly, as noted, analysts needed to recognize that actors subject to institutional influences are capable of responding in a variety of ways. The latter effort was reinforced and advanced by Oliver (1991), who recognized the value of linking resource-dependence arguments with institutional models. She suggested that organizations, and their leaders, might not simply respond to institutional demands with passive compliance (as suggested by prevailing theories) but could employ a range of "strategic" responses—reactions that included acquiesce, but included as well, compromise, avoidance, defiance, and manipulation. Amidst the rush by analysts to embrace strategic arguments, Goodrick and Salancik (1996), introduced an appropriate, cautionary note to the effect that well-established beliefs and standards do not countenance strategic responses. Still, a probably salutary effect of Oliver's initiative was to help restore institutional arguments to favor within professional schools. (Professional schools have little use for theories that deny or severely constrain the ability of organizational managers to affect the environments in which their organizations function.)

Of course, the two corrective arguments interact. A more conflicted or ambiguous environment allows for greater opportunity for strategic and agentic behavior. In addition, recognition of agency at multiple levels encourages attention to the variety of interactive processes at work between actors within organizational fields as they engage in interpretation, sense-making, translation, and negotiation activities (Edelman, 1992; Dobbin, et al., 1993; Weick, 1995).

In these developments, institutional theory mirrors trends generally present in theorizing about social structure and action from the classical to contemporary theorists (Alexander, 1983). Interactive and recursive models increasingly have replaced one-way, determinist arguments. In my view, the work of Giddens (1979, 1984) has been particularly helpful to latter-day social scientists in developing a more balanced conception of the relation between freedom and order.

22.3.2 Conditionalizing De-coupling

The Stanford camp's initial theoretical formulation proposed that the formal structures produced in response to institutional demands are routinely decoupled from technical work processes (Meyer and Rowan, 1977; Meyer, Scott, and Deal, 1981). While the notion of "loose coupling" among structural elements has a long and rich history in organization studies (Weick, 1976; Scott 2003b: 88–89), decoupling carried stronger intellectual and affective baggage, striking many critics as connoting deception, duplicity, and merely "ceremonial" conformity (e.g., Perrow, 1985; Hall, 1992).

An enduring truth associated with the original argument is that modern organization structures are a product not only of coordinative demands imposed by complex technologies but also of rationalized norms legitimizing adoption of appropriate structural models. Indeed, these can be viewed as two quasi-independent sources of structures, in the absence of which, organizing efforts are crippled (Scott and Meyer, 1983). Additionally, each source is associated with a different layer of structure. Following Parsons (1960) and Thompson (1967/2003), I argued that technical forces primarily shape the "core" functions, including work units and coordinative arrangements, while institutional forces shape the more "peripheral" structures, such as managerial and governance systems (Scott, 1981b: 2003b: chs. 10–11). Organizations reflect, and their participants must work to reconcile, two somewhat independent sources of structuring.

That being said, I believe our early arguments regarding the extent and degree of decoupling were overstated. While organizations can and do decouple work activities from accounting, control, and other review systems, the extent to which this occurs varies greatly, both over time and among organizations. Some institutional requirements are strongly backed by authoritative agents or by effective surveillance systems and sanctions. Others receive sympathetic responses from organizational participants in positions to implement them. Indeed, some tap into—and/or construct—the basic premises and organizing logics employed by key organizational players. Response will also vary depending on which elements are predominant: regulative systems, that depend more on external controls—surveillance and sanctioning—are more likely to elicit strategic responses. Indeed, research has shown that compliance to regulations varies as a function of the resources devoted to enforcement (Mezias, 1995). Normative elements, which rely more on internalization processes, are less likely to induce only lip service or resistant responses; and as for cultural-cognitive elements, which rest on more deeply set beliefs and assumptions, strategic responses are, for many, literally "unthinkable." In this vein, for many institutional theorists, "to *be* institutional, structure must generate action" (Tolbert and Zucker, 1996: 179).

Westphal and Zajac (1994) conducted a model empirical investigation examining not only the extent, but the causes, of decoupling in organizations. They studied the behavior of 570 of the largest U.S. corporations over two decades during the period when many such firms were adopting long-term incentive plans, attempting to better align incentives for executives with stockholders' interests. Following the lead of many earlier studies of the diffusion of structural models and procedures, they sought to identify organizational characteristics associated with adoption, both early and late, and non-adoption. However, rather than assuming decoupling, they assessed the extent to which organizations actually implemented changes in executive compensation programs. Finding such variation, they sought to examine which organizational characteristics predicted the extent of implementation observed. Decoupling was not treated as a (likely) response to pressures from the institutional environment. Rather, it was treated as a variable—a response that differed among organizations and that, in turn, was in need of being explained. They found both similar and divergent factors to account for adoption and implementation: for example, CEO influence was positively associated both with adoption and with *non*-implementation; while firm performance was negatively associated with adoption but not correlated with implementation.

22.3.3 Reconsidering Rationality

The classic founding statements linking organizations with latter-day versions of institutional theory struck a common chord in contrasting institutional with rational or efficiency-based arguments. Thus, according to Meyer and Rowan (1977: 355): "Formal structures that celebrate institutionalized myths differ from structures that act efficiently... Categorical rules conflict with the logic of efficiency." DiMaggio and Powell (1983: 147) concur, asserting that institutions produce structural change "as a result of processes that make organizations more similar without necessarily making them more efficient." These and related arguments focusing on "myths," "ceremonial behavior," and mindless conformity, placed sociological institutionalists in danger of focusing exclusively on the irrational and the superficial aspects of organization.

In collaborative work appearing at about the same time (Scott and Meyer, 1983), I worked with Meyer to introduce the intermediate argument noted above, that rational (or technical) performance pressures are not necessarily opposed but somewhat orthogonal to institutional forces—each a source of expanding rationalized structural arrangements. We asserted that *all* organizations confront both types of pressure, although the strength of these forces varies across organizational sectors. Thus, educational organizations are typically subject to stronger institutional than technical pressures, whereas the reverse is the case for many industrial concerns. Other organizations, such as banks and nuclear power plants, confront strong pressures of both types, effects that produce quite complex structures; while a final group of organizations, such as child care centers in the U.S., lack strong technical and institutional pressures (and supports), and so tend to be weak and unstable.

A broader, and more satisfactory, interpretation of the relation between rational and institutional forces began to appear during the 1990s, as the ideas of a number of scholars independently converged toward a new formulation. A conception emerged of the role of institutional arrangements in constructing rationality, not just in the absence of effective instrumentalities, but as a framework for defining and supporting the full range of means–ends chains. A concern with effectiveness, efficiency and other types of performance measures does not exist in a vacuum but requires the creation of distinctions, criteria, common definitions and understandings—all institutional constructions. The broader cultural-cognitive, normative and regulatory aspects of institutions shape the nature of competition and of markets, as well as the meanings of effective performance and efficient operation (Fligstein, 1990; Orrù, Biggart, and Hamilton, 1991; Powell, 1991; Whitley, 1992). In sum, institutional frameworks bound and define rational arguments and approaches.

It remains true, however, that within these broader frameworks other types of institutional provisions may support the creation of structures that are more attuned to insuring accountability, gaining legitimacy, and securing social fitness than to directly improving the quality or quantity of products and services. Such requirements, while not directed related to core technologies, can nevertheless make important contributions to organizations adopting them, increasing recognizability, acceptability, and reputation. Institutions are varied in their effects as well as in the levels at which they operate.

In addition to reorienting the relation between rational and institutional arguments, many contemporary scholars are working to broaden the conception of rationality. To supplement and amend narrow utilitarian arguments, they propose to recognize the rationality that resides in rule-following, procedural, and normatively oriented behavior (Langlois, 1986; March and Olsen, 1989; DiMaggio and Powell, 1991; Scott, 2001). Much wisdom is instantiated in conventions, habits, and rules. Instrumental logics must be supplemented with social intelligence.

The problems posed by the persistence of errors associated with the founding period of an intellectual perspective are not unique to institutional theory. It is all too common that errors present at the origins prove difficult to correct. They seem to be built-in to the fabric of the enterprise. And, it takes considerable energy and, even, courage to confront them. But, I think, this is one of the important roles of empirical research in building theory. When predictions are confounded by findings, it suggests the need to re-examine premises and assumptions, as well as propositions and logic. Empirical research does not just test arguments; it provides the bases for reformulating them, sometimes in quite basic ways.

22.4 BROADENING THE AGENDA FOR STUDYING INSTITUTIONAL CHANGE PROCESSES

22.4.1 Convergent and Disruptive Change

In an important sense, a concern with institutional change has been present in both the theoretical and empirical agenda of institutional theorists from the beginning of the modern period. However, virtually all early work focused on "convergent" change—explanations for and evidence of increasing similarity among organizational structures and processes. Because of the prevailing emphasis on top-down models, it was presumed that institutional arguments were primarily of use to explain increased conformity to a given rule or model. Increasing isomorphism was taken to be the central indicator that institutional processes were at work (Scott, 2001). Thus, early theory and research focused on the diffusion of existing institutional models (e.g., Tolbert and Zucker, 1983; Baron, Dobbin, and Jennings, 1986). Such a focus, of course, excludes crucial phases in the institutionalization process (Tolbert and Zucker, 1996), which has, necessarily, a beginning and an end as well as a middle.

22.4.2 Origins and Endings

This focus on the middle moment was soon supplemented by attention to the origins of institutional models. In his influential analysis of the formative stages of "high culture" organizations (art museums), DiMaggio (1991) examined the often contentious processes at work as actors advocated alternative models around which to organize. DiMaggio wisely observed that lack of attention to such early structuration processes

provides a one-sided vision of institutional change that emphasizes taken-for-granted, nondirectional, nonconflictual evolution at the expense of intentional (if bounded rational), directive and conflict-laden processes that define fields and set them upon trajectories that eventually appear as "natural" developments to participants and observers alike. (1991: 268)

A growing number of investigators have recognized the advantages of adopting institutional arguments to examine the origins of new types of organizations—new models or archetypes for organizing—and, relatedly, new organizational fields or industries (Aldrich and Fiol, 1994; Dezalay and Garth, 1996; Greenwood and Hinings, 1993; Suchman, 1995; Ventresca and Porac, 2003). This interest connects productively to the ongoing work of organizational ecologists who, like early institutional theorists have focused more attention on the diffusion of successful forms than on the origin of forms, thereby adding a population genetics (the creation of new forms) to a population ecology (competition among existing forms) (Baum, 1996; Suchman, 2004). It also has begun to usefully engage institutionalists with the valuable work of political scientists, sociologists, and social movement theorists who have specialized in studying contending interests, the emergence of suppressed groups, and the development of novel models of organizing and repertories of action (Clemens and Cook, 1999; Clemens and Minkoff, 2004; Davis, et al., 2004).

Current research efforts have begun to fill in the third, missing phase of the arc of institutionalization, examining the onset of deinstitutionalization and the collapse of structures and routines. Zucker (1988) has long insisted that institutional persistence is not the rule, but the exception. Like all systems, institutional arrangements are subject to entropic forces, and require the continuing input of energy and resources to prevent decay and decline. Organizational forms and fields erode as well as emerge. It is instructive to observe both the beginning and the end since in both the construction and deconstruction phases, conflict and agency are likely to be more visible.

Along with others, I have devoted considerable effort in recent years to examining the processes involved when once-stable institutional arrangements are challenged, undermined, and, gradually, replaced with different beliefs, rules, and models. For a recent study, my colleagues and I selected as our subject the field of health care delivery services in the U.S. during the second half of the twentieth century because this arena, once so stable, has undergone considerable transformation during recent decades (Scott, et al., 2000; Scott, 2004a). In tracking institutional change empirically, we found it advisable to focus on three measurable components—*types of actors* or organizing models (a combination of cultural-cognitive and normative elements), *institutional logics* (primarily cultural-cognitive elements) and *governance structures* (a combination of regulative and normative elements). Charting systematic change over several decades in the types and numbers of actors (individual roles, organizational forms and their interrelations), in the nature of institutional logics (the organizing principles that provide work guidelines to participants (Friedland and Alford, 1991)), and in the governance structures (the private and public controls utilized in overseeing a field), provided a revealing class of indicators for depicting institutional change.

Like other comparable studies (e.g., Campbell and Pedersen, 1996; Holm, 1995; Stark, 1996; Thornton, 2004), we found deinstitutionalization and reconstructive processes to be fueled by both exogenous and endogenous forces, and reconstruction to reflect both novel elements—newly invented or imported from outside the field—and new combinations of existing elements. And, like these studies, we found evidence that ideas and other types of conceptual models increasingly are carried not only across sector or field, but also across national boundaries (Dacin, Goodstein, and Scott, 2002). During the current time, for example, neo-liberal logics are penetrating domains (e.g., professional, public, and nonprofit) formerly insulated from market and managerial logics (Campbell and Pedersen, 2001).

These and related studies suggest that the major contributions of institutional theory to organizational studies may still lie ahead. Institutional concepts and arguments seem ready-made to address the complex processes now unfolding as inhabitants of our planet become more interdependent.

22.5 Onward and Upward

22.5.1 Expanding Facets and Levels

I have long argued that the most important intellectual revolution shaping contemporary organizational studies has been the introduction of open systems models (Scott 2003b, 2004c). A growing recognition of the pervasive importance of the wider environment for the structure and functioning of organizations has progressed since the early 1960s and continues to this moment. Three somewhat distinct developments may be distinguished. First, there has been a growing awareness of the multiple and varied facets of the environment, as an early recognition of technical features and material resources expanded to include political and relational interdependencies, then moved to incorporate symbolic and cultural features. Second, the levels at which units of analysis are defined have expanded from the *individual* or *group* within an organization, to the *organization* itself, to the organizational *set* (a system of actors linked by the exchange of commodities and services), to the organization *population* (the aggregate of organizations carrying on similar functions and hence competing for the same resources), to the organization *field* (an interdependent collection of similar and dissimilar organizations operating in the same domain).

22.5.2 Non-local Knowledge

Third, and less widely recognized, today's organizations are more open to and affected by non-local events and ideas. Because of changes in information technology as well as the increasing mobility of capital, labor, ideologies, beliefs, consumer preferences, and fads, the environment is permeated by multiple and diverse messages. Nations and peoples long buffered from competing models and alternative logics are now routinely confronted by challenges to their indigenous institutions from ideas carried by multiple carriers including immigrants, the mass media, consultants, and the Internet (Appadurai, 1996; Sahlin-Andersson and Engwall, 2002; Scott, 2003*a*).

A single organization is now more likely to operate simultaneously in numerous institutional environments, as does the multinational corporation (Westney, 1993; Nohria and Ghoshal, 1997). And, without leaving home, organizations are bombarded by "foreign" actors, beliefs, and practices. Both allies and foes in Europe were confronted by and strongly encouraged to adopt U.S. business models as they rebuilt their economies after World War II with the assistance of the American Marshall plan (Djelic, 1998). Innovators like Demming, unable to gain a hearing in the U.S., traveled to Japan where his ideas were welcomed and adopted, and the resulting success of these models carried them back to the U.S., where organizations were pressured to join the "quality revolution" (Cole and Scott, 2000). Organizations increasingly form joint ventures to construct complex projects—dams, underground transit systems, skyscrapers—working in combination with foreign partners on alien soil and becoming, thereby, subject to multiple, possible conflicting, layers of cultural, regulative, and normative prescriptions (Levitt and Scott, 2004). What body of ideas or research is better constituted to confront these types of problems than institutional theory?

However, the utility of the theory is not confined to the organizational level. Important changes are also underway at national, transnational, and global levels, and institutional theory is well positioned to assist scholars in characterizing and explaining these changes. My colleague, John Meyer and his associates, along with others, have productively employed institutional theory to examine the distinctive properties and dynamics of the nation-state (Meyer, et al., 1997; Thomas, et al.,

1987). And increasing attention is now being directed to structures and processes at the transnational and/or global level, as growing numbers of inter-governmental arrangements (treaties, commissions), international non-governmental organizations (INGOs), and international professional bodies compete for attention and influence in every conceivable arena (Boli and Thomas, 1999; Djelic and Quack, 2003). Institution-building is proceeding apace at the global level. Since centralized power and authority are still lacking at these supra-national levels, cultural-cognitive and normative modes of influence—"soft power"—are the weapons of choice. For example, professional groups are likely to promote the development of "standards"—normative guidelines carrying moral but not coercive backing (Brunsson and Jacobsson, 2000); and non-governmental groups are likely to propose cultural-cognitive distinctions combined with moral principles to exert individuals, organizations, and nation-states to exhibit "progress" along a wide range of proposed indicators. In sum, a growing array of institutions will continue to play an influential role in social life and furnish an increasingly rich and challenging environment for individual organization and systems of organizations. And, consequently, institutional theory appears well positioned to help us make sense of and, perhaps, help us to better guide the course of these important developments.

22.6 COMMENTS ON PERSONAL CONTRIBUTION

The editors have encouraged each of us to say a few words about what we see as our own distinctive contribution to the development and understanding of the theory under review. Before doing so, I would like to state for the record that institutional theory and, indeed, most compelling theoretical programs of which I have knowledge, are much more accurately portrayed as collective rather than individual projects. Science is, by its nature, a social activity, advanced by both cooperative and competitive processes. (My favorite definition of science is that of a community of "organized skepticism.") While individuals have insights, "it takes a village" or, better, an "invisible college" to develop, evaluate, elaborate, and exploit a fledging idea. I have been educated—informed, enlightened, criticized, and corrected—by my "colleagues", ranging from Max Weber, whose portrait hangs on my office wall, to contemporaries, with whom I interact in seminar rooms and conferences, through their publications, blind reviews and e-mail, to students, who ask innocent, profound questions, raise challenging counter-examples, search out new types of data, and suggest new applications.

As I have tried to make clear, I make no claims to be the originator of institutional theory or, indeed, to count myself among its most innovative progenitors (whether in the nineneenth or twentieth centuries). Rather, I would describe my particular contributions by noting four of the roles or functions I have performed: as connecter, codifier, carrier, and contributing researcher.

As *connecter,* I have worked to link the broad world of institutional theory with the interests and agenda of organization theorists and analysts. In my earlier work, I emphasized the effects of institutions on the structure and function of organizations; and in later work, I have been attentive to the more active roles that organizations play as incubator, co-producer, interpreter, and carrier of institutional schemas and routines. Within organization studies, I see and have attempted to cultivate connections between institutional theory and such diverse areas as: strategy, entrepreneurship, health care management, human resources, international management, management history, organizational cognition, organization structure and change, organizations and the natural environment, and public and nonprofit forms. Beyond the field of organizational studies, I have worked to develop and demonstrate the connections between institutional theory and closely related areas of study, such as law and society (Scott, 1994), policy analysis (Scott, 2002), and social movements (McAdam and Scott, 2005).

In the role of *codifier,* as previously discussed, I have summarized, organized, and distilled the manifold conceptions and arguments of a range of institutional theorists into a more comprehensive framework, in an attempt to foster their comparison, cross-stimulation, and, perhaps eventually, integration. My Pillars framework is not assumed to be the last word, but is intended as a useful step in encouraging scholars to contribute to the cumulative growth of the theoretical program. It also advances the concerns of *connecting* varying brands of institutional theory—transaction cost, evolutionary economics, historical institutionalism, ethnomethology, organization culture and identity, population ecology, and both traditional—and neo-institutional sociological—so that each is seen as a part of a larger tapestry (Scott and Meyer, 1994; Scott, 1995, 2001).

As *carrier,* I have been active in communicating institutional conceptions and approaches to a wider audience. I have done this through my research, lectures, teaching, and especially, my textbooks. In terms of texts, I wrote the book *Institutions and Organizations* (1995, 2001) in an effort to clearly communicate institutional arguments relating to organizations to as wide an audience as possible. I endeavored in this book to trace the unfolding history of the development of institutional theory and research, but also to point out areas that had been neglected, arenas of controversy, and needed research. In my general organizations text, *Organizations: Rational, Natural and Open Systems* (Scott, 2003b), as new editions have appeared, I have devoted an ever larger portion of it to institutional arguments and ideas. Now in its fifth edition, this general survey of theory and scholarship affords me the opportunity to describe how institutional theory's assumptions and arguments complement, compete with, and connect to other theoretical traditions.

As *contributing researcher*, I have worked to show the relevance of institutional theory as an approach to analyzing a number of diverse sectors and organization fields, beginning with public education in collaborative studies with Meyer and others as previously described, then extending to mental health (Scott and Black, 1986), services for the aging (Scott, 1981a), medical care (Alexander and Scott, 1984; Ruef and Scott, 1998), training programs in firms and agencies (Scott and Meyer, 1991; Monahan, Meyer, and Scott, 1994), and human resource programs, as we examined the diffusion of equal opportunity and other labor protections in firms and public organizations (Dobbin, et al., 1988, 1993; Sutton, et al., 1994).

In selecting topics for research, I have attempted to be governed more by theoretical criteria than by applied concerns, focusing more attention on the longer-term goal of improving the general explanatory framework (independent variables) and arguments than on the short-term concern of solving specific problems (dependent variables). Hence, in early work with Meyer, we focused analytic attention on situations in which institutional regimes were conflicting and/or ambiguous. I selected sectors or fields for study because they represented differing values on independent variables—for example, being poorly bounded and institutionally underdeveloped (e.g., mental health), or undergoing rapid change and destructuration processes (e.g., medical care in the U.S. (Scott, et al., 2000)). And, in recent studies, I have consciously attempted to bridge and integrate various levels of analysis (Scott, 1993; Scott, et al., 2000).

In sum, I have sought and pursued numerous paths in attempting to advance institutional theory. The development of a theoretical research program, like the building of a great cathedral, requires long periods of time, the extensive expenditure of resources, and a highly diverse pool of labor, involving different expertise, skills, and work routines. Each of us must wrestle with two related but different questions: "What is the best thing to do?" and "What do I do best?"

22.7 CONCLUDING COMMENT

As I have tried to suggest, institutional theory has a long past and a promising future. It is not a fly-by-night theory that is here today and gone tomorrow. It is not a boutique theory in which some academic entrepreneur declares his or her theory to explain a disproportionate proportion of the variance in some specific dependent variable or in some limited domain of social behavior. It is broadly positioned to help us confront important and enduring questions, including the bases of organizational similarity and differentiation, the relation between structure and behavior, the role of symbols in social life, the relation between ideas and interests, and the tensions between freedom and order.

Of particular importance for the future health of organization studies, institutional theory encourages scholars to take a longer and a broader perspective in crafting testable arguments. An embarrassingly large proportion of our theoretical conceptions and empirical findings has been constructed by U.S. scholars based on data collected from U.S. organizations operating during the past few decades. Institutional theory can do much to overcome this regional, temporal bias as it fosters a rich combination of historical and comparative research, and supports this effort by providing conceptual tools to encompass and interpret the extraordinary variety of organizations over time and space.

REFERENCES

ABZUG, R., and MEZIAS, S. J. (1993). The fragmented state and due process protections in organizations: The case of comparable worth. *Organization Science*, 4: 433–53.

ALDRICH, H. E., and FIOL, E. M. (1994). Fools rush in? The institutional context of industry creation. *Academy of Management Review*, 19: 645–70.

ALEXANDER, J. C. (1983). *Theoretical Logic in Sociology*, vols. 1–4. Berkeley: University of California Press.

—— and SCOTT, W. R. (1984). The impact of regulation on the administrative structure of hospitals. *Hospitals and Health Services Administration*, 29(May/June): 71–85.

APPADURAI, A. (1996). *Modernity and Large: Cultural Dimensions of Globalization*. Minneapolis: University of Minnesota Press.

BARLEY, S. R. (1986). Technology as an occasion for structuring: Evidence from observations of CT scanners and the social order of radiology departments. *Administrative Science Quarterly*, 31: 78–108.

BARON, J. N., DOBBIN, F. R., and JENNINGS, P. D. (1986). War and peace: The evolution of modern personnel administration in U.S. industry. *American Journal of Sociology*, 92: 350–83.

BAUM, J. A. C. (1996). Organizational ecology. In S. R. Clegg, C. Hardy, and W. R. Nord (eds.), *Handbook of Organization Studies*: 77–114. London: Sage.

BERGER, J., and ZELDITCH, M., Jr. (eds.) (1993). *Theoretical Research Programs: Studies in the Growth of Theory*. Stanford, Calif.: Stanford University Press.

BERGER, P. K, and LUCKMANN, T. (1967). *The Social Construction of Reality*. New York: Doubleday.

BILL, J. A., and HARDGRAVE, R. L., Jr. (1981). *Comparative Politics: The Quest for Theory*. Washington, DC: Bell and Howell, University Press of America.

BLAU, P. M., and SCOTT, W. R. (1962). *Formal Organizations: A Comparative Approach.* San Francisco: Chandler. Reprinted as a Stanford Business Classic by Stanford University Press, 2003.

BOURDIEU, P. (1977). *Outline of A Theory of Practice.* Cambridge: Cambridge University Press.

BRUNSSON, N., and JACOBSSON, B. (eds.) (2000). *A World of Standards.* Oxford: Oxford University Press.

BOLI, J., and THOMAS, G. M. (eds.) (1999). *Constructing World Culture: International Nongovernmental Organizations since 1875.* Stanford, Calif.: Stanford University Press.

CAMPBELL, J. L., and PEDERSEN, O. K. (eds.) (1996). *Legacies of Change: Transformations of Postcommunist European Economies.* New York: Aldine de Gruyter.

—— —— (eds.) (2001). *The Rise of Neoliberalism and Institutional Analysis.* Princeton: Princeton University Press.

CLEMENS, E. S., and COOK, J. M. (1999). Politics and institutionalism: Explaining durability and change. *Annual Review of Sociology,* 25: 441–66.

—— and MINKOFF, D. C. (2004). Beyond the iron law: Rethinking the place of organizations in social movement research. In D. A. Snow, S. A. Soule, and H. Kriesi (eds.), *The Blackwell Companion to Social Movements:* 155–70. Oxford: Blackwell.

COHEN, E. G., MEYER, J. W., SCOTT, W. R., and DEAL, T. E. (1979). Technology and teaming in the elementary school. *Sociology of Education,* 52: 20–33.

COLE, R. E., and SCOTT, W. R. (eds.) (2000). *The Quality Movement and Organization Theory.* Thousand Oaks, Calif.: Sage.

DACIN, M. T., GOODSTEIN, J., and SCOTT, W. R. (2002). Institutional theory and institutional change: Introduction to the special research forum. *Academy of Management Journal,* 45: 45–54.

DAVIS, G. F., McADAM, D., SCOTT, W. D., and ZALD, M. N. (eds.) (2004). *Social Movements and Organization Theory.* New York: Cambridge University Press.

DEZALAY, Y., and GARTH, B. G. (1996). *Dealing in Virtue: International Commercial Arbitration and the Construction of a Transnational Legal Order.* Chicago: University of Chicago Press.

DiMAGGIO, P. J. (1983). State expansion and organization fields. In R. H. Hall and R. E. Quinn (eds.), *Organization Theory and Public Policy:* 147–61. Beverly Hills, Calif.: Sage.

—— (1988). Interest and agency in institutional theory. In L. G. Zucker (ed.), *Institutional patterns and organizations: Culture and environment:* 3–21. Cambridge, Mass.: Ballinger.

—— (1991). Constructing an organizational field as a professional project: U.S. art museums, 1920–1940. In W. W. Powell and P. J. DiMaggio (eds.), *The New Institutionalism in Organizational Analysis:* 267–92. Chicago: University of Chicago Press.

—— and POWELL, W. W. (1983). The iron cage revisited: Institutional isomorphism and collective rationality in organizational fields. *American Sociological Review,* 48: 147–60.

—— —— (1991). Introduction. In W. W. Powell and P. J. DiMaggio (eds.), *The New Institutionalism in Organizational Analysis:* 1–38. Chicago: University of Chicago Press.

DJELIC, M.-L. (1998). *Exporting the American Model.* New York: Oxford University Press.

—— and QUACK, S. (eds.) (2003). *Globalization and Institutions: Redefining the Rules of the Economic Game.* Cheltenham: Edward Elgar.

DOBBIN, F. R., EDELMAN, L., MEYER, J. W., SCOTT, W. R., and SWIDLER, A. (1988). The expansion of due process in organizations. In L. G. Zucker (ed.), *Institutional Patterns and Organizations: Culture and Environment*: 71–98. Cambridge, Mass.: Ballinger.

—— SUTTON, J. R., MEYER, J. W., and SCOTT, W. R. (1993). Equal opportunity law and the construction of internal labor markets. *American Journal of Sociology*, 99: 396–427.

DORNBUSCH, S. M., and SCOTT, W. R. (with the assistance of B. C. Busching and J. D. Laing) (1975). *Evaluation and the Exercise of Authority*. San Francisco: Jossey-Bass.

DOUGLAS, M. (1986). *How Institutions Think*. Syracuse, NY: Syracuse University Press.

DURKHEIM, E. (1912/1961). *The Elementary Forms of Religious Life*. New York: Collier.

EDELMAN, L. B. (1992). Legal ambiguity and symbolic structures: Organizational mediation of civil rights. *American Journal of Sociology*, 95: 1401–1440.

FLIGSTEIN, N. (1990). *The Transformation of Corporate Control*. Cambridge, Mass.: Harvard University Press.

FRIEDLAND, R., and ALFORD, R. R. (1991). Bringing society back in: Symbols, practices, and institutional contradictions. In W. W. Powell and P. J. DiMaggio (eds.), *The New Institutionalism in Organizational Analysis*: 232–263. Chicago: University of Chicago Press.

GIDDENS, A. (1979). *Central Problems in Social Theory: Action, Structure, and Contradiction in Social Analysis*. Berkeley, Calif.: University of California Press.

—— (1984). *The Constitution of Society*. Berkeley, Calif.: University of California Press.

GOODRICK, E., and SALANCIK, G. R. (1996). Organizational discretion in responding to institutional practices: Hospitals and Cesarean births. *Administrative Science Quarterly*, 41: 1–28.

GREENWOOD, R., and HININGS, C. R. (1993). Understanding strategic change: The contribution of archetypes. *Academy of Management Journal*, 37: 467–498.

HALL, R. H. (1992). Taking things a bit too far: Some problems with emergent institutional theory. In K. Kelley (ed.), *Issues, Theory, and Research in Industrial Organizational Psychology*: 71–87, Amsterdam: Elsevier.

HININGS, B., and GREENWOOD, R. (1988). The normative prescription of organizations. In L. G. Zucker (ed.), *Institutional Patterns and Organizations: Culture and Environment*: 53–70. Cambridge, Mass.: Ballinger.

HODGSON, G. M. (1994). The return of institutional economics. In N. J. Smelser and R. Swedberg (eds.), *The Handbook of Economic Sociology*: 58–76. Princeton and New York: Princeton University Press and Russell Sage Foundation.

HOLM, P. (1995). The dynamics of institutionalism: Transformation processes in Norwegian fisheries. *Administrative Science Quarterly*, 40: 398–422.

HUGHES, E. C. (1939). Institutions. In R. E. Park (ed.), *An Outline of the Principles of Sociology*: 281–330. New York: Barnes and Noble.

—— (1958). *Men and their Work*. Glencoe, Ill.: Free Press.

LANGLOIS, R. N. (ed.) (1986). *Economics as a Process: Essays in the New Institutional Economics*. New York: Cambridge University Press.

LAWRENCE, P. R., and LORSCH, J. W. (1967). *Organization and Environment: Managing Differentiation and Integration*. Boston: Graduate School of Business Administration, Harvard University.

LEBLEBICI, H., and SALANCIK, G. (1982). Stability in interorganizational exchanges: Rule-making processes of the Chicago Board of Trade. *Administrative Science Quarterly*, 27: 227–242.

LEVITT, R. E., and SCOTT, W. R. (2004). Understanding and mitigating the effects of conflicting institutions on global projects. Unpublished paper, Department of Civil Engineering, Stanford University.

McADAM, D., and SCOTT, W. R. (2005). Organizations and movements. In G. Davis, D. McAdam, W. R. Scott, and M. Zald (eds.), *Social Movements and Organization Theory*. New York: Cambridge University Press (forthcoming).

MARCH, J. G., and OLSEN, J. P. (1989). *Rediscovering Institutions: The Organizational Basis of Politics*. New York: Free Press.

MEYER, J. W. (1970). Institutionalization. Unpublished paper, Department of Sociology, Stanford University.

—— (1977). The effects of education as an institution. *American Journal of Sociology*, 83: 55–77.

—— BOLI, J., THOMAS, G. M., and RAMIREZ, F. O. (1997). World society and the nation state. *American Journal of Sociology*, 103: 144–181.

—— and ROWAN, B. (1977). Institutionalized organizations: Formal structure as myth and ceremony. *American Journal of Sociology*, 83: 340–363.

—— and SCOTT, W. R. (1983). *Organizational Environments: Ritual and Rationality*. Beverly Hills, Calif.: Sage.

—— —— COLE, S., and INTILI, J.-A. K. (1978). Instructional dissensus and institutional consensus in schools. In M. W. Meyer (ed.), *Environments and Organizations*: 290–305. San Francisco: Jossey-Bass.

—— —— and DEAL, T. E. (1981). Institutional and technical sources of organizational structure: Explaining the structure of educational organizations. In H. D. Stein (ed.), *Organization and the Human Services*: 151–178. Philadelphia: Temple University Press.

—— —— and STRANG, D. (1987). Centralization, fragmentation, and school district complexity. *Administrative Science Quarterly*, 32: 186–201.

—— —— —— and CREIGHTON, A. L. (1988). Bureaucratization without centralization: Changes in the organizational system of U.S. public education, 1940–80. In L. G. Zucker (ed.), *Institutional Patterns and Organizations: Culture and Environment*: 139–167. Cambridge, Mass.: Ballinger.

MEZIAS, S. J. (1995). Using institutional theory to understand for-profit sectors: The case of financial reporting standards. In W. R. Scott and S. Christensen (eds.), *The Institutional Construction of Organizations: International and Longitudinal Studies*: 164–196. Thousand Oaks, Calif.: Sage.

MOE, T. M. (1984). The new economics of organization. *American Journal of Political Science*, 28: 739–777.

MONAHAN, S. E., MEYER, J. W., and SCOTT, W. R. (1994). Employee training: The expansion of organizational citizenship. In W. R. Scott and J. W. Meyer (eds.), *Institutional Environments and Organizations: Structural Complexity and Individualism*: 255–271. Thousand Oaks, Calif.: Sage.

NOHRIA, N., and GHOSHAL, S. (1997). *The Differentiated Network: Organizing Multinational Corporations for Value Creation*. San Francisco: Jossey-Bass.

NORTH, D. C. (1990). *Institutions, Institutional Change and Economic Performance*. Cambridge: Cambridge University Press.

OLIVER, C. (1991). Strategic responses to institutional processes. *Academy of Management Review*, 16: 145–179.

Orrù, M., Biggart, N. W., and Hamilton, G. G. (1991). Organizational isomorphism in East Asia. In W. W. Powell and P. J. DiMaggio (eds.), *The New Institutionalism in Organizational Analysis*: 361–389. Chicago: University of Chicago Press.

Parsons, T. (1934/1990). Prolegomena to a theory of social institutions. *American Sociological Review*, 55: 319–339.

—— (1960). *Structure and Process in Modern Societies*. Glencoe, Ill.: Free Press.

Perrow, C. (1985). Review essay: Overboard with myth and symbols. *American Journal of Sociology*, 91: 151–155.

Powell, W. W. (1988). Institutional effects on organizational structure and performance. In L. G. Zucker (ed.), *Institutional Patterns and Organizations: Culture and Environment*: 115–136. Cambridge, Mass.: Ballinger.

—— (1991). Expanding the scope of institutional analysis. In W. W. Powell and P. J. DiMaggio (eds.), *The New Institutionalism in Organizational Analysis*: 183–203. Chicago: University of Chicago Press.

Ruef, M., and Scott, W. R. (1998). A multidimensional model of organizational legitimacy: Hospital survival in changing institutional environments. *Administrative Science Quarterly*, 43: 877–904.

Sahlin-Andersson, K., and Engwall, L. (eds.) (2002). *The Expansion of Management Knowledge: Carriers, Flows and Sources*. Stanford, Calif.: Stanford University Press.

Scott, W. R. (1965). Reactions to supervision in a heteronomous professional organization. *Administrative Science Quarterly*, 10: 65–81.

—— (1966). Professionals in bureaucracies—areas of conflict. In H. M. Vollmer and D. L. Mills (eds.), *Professionalization*: 265–275. Englewood Cliffs, NJ: Prentice Hall.

—— 1981*a*. Reform movements and organizations: The case of aging. In J. G. March (ed.), *Aging: Social Change*: 331–345. New York: Academic Press.

—— 1981*b*. *Organizations: Rational, natural and open systems*. Englewod Cliffs, NJ: Prentice Hall.

—— (1983). Introduction: From technology to environment. In J. W. Meyer and W. R. Scott (eds.), *Organizational Environments: Ritual and Rationality*: 13–17. Beverly Hills, Calif.: Sage.

—— (1987). The adolescence of institutional theory. *Administrative Science Quarterly*, 32: 493–511.

—— (1993). The organization of medical care services: Toward an integrated theoretical model. *Medical Care Review*, 50: 271–302.

—— (1994). Law and organizations. In S. B. Sitkin and R. J. Bies (eds.), *The Legalistic Organization*: 3–18. Newbury Park, Calif.: Sage.

—— (1995). *Institutions and Organizations*. Thousand Oaks, Calif.: Sage.

—— (2001). *Institutions and Organizations*, 2nd edn., Thousand Oaks, Calif.: Sage.

—— (2002). Organizations and the natural environment: Evolving models. In A. Hoffman and M. Ventresca (eds.), *Organizations, Policy, and the Natural Environment: Institutional and Strategic Perspectives*: 453–464. Stanford, Calif.: Stanford University Press.

—— (2003*a*). Institutional carriers: Reviewing modes of transporting ideas over time and space and considering their consequences. *Industrial and Corporate Change*, 12: 879–894.

—— (2003*b*). *Organizations: Rational, Natural and Open Systems*, 5th edn., Upper Saddle River, NJ: Prentice-Hall.

—— (2004a). Competing logics in health care: Professional, state, and managerial. In F. Dobbin (ed.), *The Sociology of the Economy*: 276–287. New York: Russell Sage Foundation.

—— (2004b). Institutional theory. In G. Ritzer (ed.), *Encyclopedia of Social Theory*: 408–414. Thousand Oaks, Calif.: Sage.

—— (2004c). Reflections on a half-century of organizational sociology. *Annual Review of Sociology*, 30: 1–21.

—— (forthcoming). Approaching adulthood: The maturing of institutional theory. *Theory and Society*.

—— and BLACK, B. L. (ed.) (1986). *The Organization of Mental Health Services: Societal and Community Systems*. Beverly Hills, Calif.: Sage.

—— and MEYER, J. W. (1983). The organization of societal sectors. In J. W. Meyer and W. R. Scott (eds.), *Organizational Environments: Ritual and Rationality*: 129–153. Beverly Hills, CA: Sage.

—— —— (1991). The rise of training programs in firms and agencies: An institutional perspective. In B. M. Staw and L. L. Cummings (eds.), *Research in Organizational Behavior*: 13: 297–326. Greenwich, Conn.: JAI Press.

—— —— (1994). *Institutional Environments and Organizations: Structural Complexity and Individualism*. Thousand Oaks, Calif.: Sage.

—— RUEF, M., MENDEL, P. J., and CARONNA, C. A. (2000). *Institutional Change and Healthcare Organizations: From Professional Dominance to Managed Care*. Chicago: University of Chicago Press.

SELZNICK, P. (1949). *TVA and the Grass Roots*. Berkeley, Calif.: University of California Press.

SEWELL, W. H., Jr. (1992). A theory of structure: Duality, agency, and transformation. *American Journal of Sociology*, 98: 1–29.

STARK, D. (1996). Recombinant property in East European capitalism. *American Journal of Sociology*, 101: 993–1027.

SUCHMAN, M. C. (1995). Localism and globalism in institutional analysis: The emergence of contractual norms in venture finance. In W. R. Scott and S. Christensen (eds.), *The Institutional Construction of Organizations: International and Longitudinal Studies*: 39–63. Thousand Oaks, Calif.: Sage.

—— (2004). Constructed ecologies: Reproduction and structuration in emerging organizational communities. In W. W. Powell and D. L. Jones (eds.), *How Institutions Change*. Chicago: University of Chicago Press.

SUTTON, J., DOBBIN, F., MEYER, J. W., and SCOTT, W. R. (1994). Legalization of the workplace. *American Journal of Sociology*, 99: 944–971.

THOMAS, G. M., MEYER, J. W., RAMIREZ, F. O., and BOLI, J. (eds.) (1987). *Institutional Structure: Constituting State, Society, and the Individual*. Newbury Park, Calif.: Sage.

THOMPSON, J. W. (1967/2003). *Organizations in Action*. New York: McGraw Hill. Reprinted New Brunswick, NJ: Transaction Publishers.

THORNTON, P. H. (2004). *Markets from Culture: Institutional Logics and Organizational Decisions in Higher Education Publishing*. Stanford, Calif.: Stanford University Press.

TILLY, C. (1984). *Big Structures, Large Processes, Huge Comparisons*. New York: Russell Sage Foundation.

TOLBERT, P. S., and ZUCKER, L. G. (1983). Institutional sources of change in the formal structure of organizations: The diffusion of civil service reform, 1880–1935. *Administrative Science Quarterly*, 30: 22–39.

TOLBERT, P. S., and ZUCKER, L. G. (1996). The institutionalization of institutional theory. In S. R. Clegg, C. Hardy, and W. R. Nord (eds.), *Handbook of Organization Studies*: 175–190. Thousand Oaks, Calif.: Sage.

VENTRESCA, M. J., and PORAC, J. (eds.) (2003). *Constructing Industries and Markets*. London: Elsevier Science.

WEBER, M. (1924/1968). *Economy and Society: An Interpretive Sociology*, 2 vols., eds. G. Roth and C. Wittich. New York: Bedminister Press.

WEICK, K. (1976). Educational organizations as loosely-coupled systems. *Administrative Science Quarterly*, 21: 1–19.

—— (1995). *Sensemaking in Organizations*. Thousand Oaks, Calif.: Sage.

WESTNEY, D. E. (1993). Institutional theory and the multinational corporation. In S. Ghoshal and D. E. Westney (eds.), *Organization Theory and the Multinational Corporation*: 53–76. New York: St. Martin's.

WESTPHAL, J., and ZAJAC, E. J. (1994). Substance and symbolism in CEOs' long-term incentive plans. *Administrative Science Quarterly*, 39: 367–390.

WHITE, H. C., BOORMAN, S. A., and BREIGER, R. L. (1976). Social structure from multiple networks. I: Blockmodels of roles and positions. *American Journal of Sociology*, 81: 730–780.

WHITLEY, R. (1992). The social construction of organizations and markets: The comparative analysis of business recipes. In M. Reed and M. Hughes (eds.), *Rethinking Organizations: New Directions in Organization Theory and Analysis*: 120–143. Newbury Park, Calif.: Sage.

WILLIAMSON, O. E. (1975). *Markets and Hierarchies: Analysis and Antitrust Implications*. New York: Free Press.

ZUCKER, L. G. (1977). The role of institutionalization in cultural persistence. *American Journal of Sociology*, 42: 726–743.

—— (1988). Where do institutional patterns come from? Organizations as actors in social systems. In L. G. Zucker (ed.), *Institutional Patterns and Organizations: Culture and Environment*: 23–49. Cambridge, Mass.: Ballinger.

CHAPTER 23

....

TRANSACTION COST ECONOMICS

THE PROCESS OF THEORY DEVELOPMENT

....

OLIVER E. WILLIAMSON

TRANSACTION cost economics is an interdisciplinary research project in which law, economics, and organization theory are joined (Williamson, 1985). Although the operationalization of transaction cost economics began in the 1970s and has continued to develop in conceptual, theoretical, empirical, and public policy respects since, many of the key ideas out of which transaction cost economics (TCE) works have their origins in path-breaking contributions in law, economics, and organization theory from the 1930s. It was not, however, obvious how these key ideas were related, much less how they could be fruitfully combined. Two follow-on developments—the interdisciplinary program for doing social science research that took shape at the Graduate School of Industrial Administration (GSIA) at Carnegie-Mellon University during the late 1950s and early 1960s; and new developments in the market failure literature during the 1960s—were needed to set the stage.[1]

The author is Professor of the Graduate School and Edgar F. Kaiser Professor of Business, Economics, and Law, University of California, Berkeley. Comments invited: owilliam@haas.berkeley.edu
[1] The operationalization of TCE is the result of the concerted effort of many contributors. A selection of some of the more influential articles can be found in Williamson and Masten, *Transaction Cost Economics*, Vols. I and II (1995). Also see Claude Menard (2005).

As for my own involvement, I seriously doubt that I would have perceived the research opportunity presented by TCE but for my training in the Ph.D. program at GSIA (from 1960 to 1963).[2] More than such training, however, would be needed. My teaching, research, and public policy experience during the decade of the 1960s all served to alert me to the research needs and opportunities posed by TCE.

This chapter is organized in seven parts. Section 23.1 describes seminal contributions from the 1930s. Follow-on developments in the 1960s are examined in 23.2. My training, teaching, research, and involvement with public policy during the decade of the 1960s are sketched in 23.3. The foregoing led into what, for me, was a transformative research project: my paper on "The Vertical Integration of Production: Market Failure Considerations" (1971), which is described in 23.4. Some reflections on TCE as it has evolved since are set out in 23.5. I discuss the "Carnegie Triple"—be disciplined; be interdisciplinary; have an active mind—in 23.6. Concluding remarks follow.

23.1 KEY CONTRIBUTIONS FROM LAW, ECONOMICS, AND ORGANIZATION THEORY IN THE 1930S[3]

23.1.1 Economics

Both John R. Commons (1932) and Ronald Coase (1937) advanced key economic ideas. Commons was the older of the two and had a wider vision of the need to move beyond orthodoxy. Possibly, however, because he operated at such a high level of generability and his message was obscure even to sympathetic readers, his ideas were less influential to TCE than were those of Coase, who focused on a crucial lapse of logic in the orthodox theory of firm and market organization.

23.1.1.1 *Commons*

Commons had an abiding interest in going concerns. As against the preoccupation of orthodoxy with the resource allocation paradigm and simple market exchange

[2] For an autobiographical sketch of earlier events and people that were influential to my training and intellectual development, see Williamson (1995). Although good instincts helped me to make the "right choices" at critical forks in the road, I also had the benefit of a number of exceptional advisors and teachers—and fortunately often had the good sense to listen.

[3] This section and the next are based on my forthcoming article on "The Economics of Governance" (in the May 2005 issue of the American Economic Review).

(Reder, 1999), Commons examined economics in contractual terms, whereupon he formulated the problem of economic organization as follows: "the ultimate unit of activity...must contain in itself the three principles of conflict, mutuality, and order. This unit is a transaction" (Commons, 1932: 4). He, furthermore, recommended that "theories of economics center on transactions and working rules, on problems of organization, and on the...[ways] the organization of activity is... stabilized" (1950: 21).

Not only was Commons ahead of his time in proposing a contractual approach to economic organization in which the transaction is made the unit of analysis, but his focus on the triple of conflict, mutuality, and order prefigured the concept of governance. More generally, he was among the first to view organization—as both problem and solution—as a fit subject for economic analysis. Neither Commons nor his students and colleagues, however, made a concerted effort to breathe operational content into these ideas. Instead, the older style of institutional economics of which he was a part ran itself into the sand.

23.1.1.2 *Coase*

Coase's pathbreaking paper on "The Nature of the Firm" (1937) is the first and arguably the most important of his challenges to orthodoxy. His training in business administration and his field work on vertical integration contributed to his skepticism with orthodox treatments of firm and market organization (Coase, 1988).

Coase's 1937 article confronted orthodox economics with a logical lapse. Thus, whereas orthodoxy took the distribution of economic activity as between firm and market organization as given, whereupon attention was focused on "the economic system as being coordinated by the price mechanism" (1937: 387), firm and market are properly regarded as "*alternative* methods of coordinating production" (1937: 388; emphasis added). Rather than take the distribution of economic activity as given, this should be derived. The 1937 paper thus took as its purpose "to bridge *what appears to be a gap in economic theory*...We have to explain the basis on which, *in practice*, this choice between alternatives is effected" (Coase, 1937: 389; emphasis added). And he nominated transaction costs as the gap-closing concept.

23.1.2 Organization Theory

Chester Barnard's extraordinary insights into the mechanisms of and purposes served by internal economic organization were based not on his academic training but on his business experience. His book, *The Functions of the Executive* (1938), not only broke new ground but entertained the ambition that a "science of organization" was in prospect (1938: 290).

Of the series of key insights that I associate with Barnard (Williamson, 1990), the two that are most important to TCE are (1) his argument that adaptation is the central problem of economic organization and (2) his emphasis on cooperative adaptations within firms that are accomplished in a "conscious, deliberate, purposeful" way through administration (1938: 4, 6, 73).

Interestingly, Friedrich Hayek would also advance the argument that adaptation is the central problem of economic organization. Yet there were differences. Hayek, as an economist, focused on the adaptations of economic actors who adjusted spontaneously to changes in the market, mainly as signaled by changes in relative prices: Upon looking "at the price system as ... a mechanism for communicating information," the marvel of the market resides in "how little the individual participants need to know to be able to take the right action" (Hayek, 1945: 526–527). By contrast, Barnard featured coordinated adaptation among economic actors working through administration (hierarchy). The latter, to repeat, is accomplished not spontaneously but in a "conscious, deliberate, purposeful" way (1938: 4). Because a high performance economic system must have the capacity to make adaptations of both kinds, a role for both markets and hierarchies resides therein.[4]

23.1.3 Law

The fiction that contracts are well defined and costlessly enforced by well-informed courts is an analytical convenience for both law and economics. This fiction of legal centralism was nevertheless disputed by Karl Llewellyn in 1931 who perceived the need to move beyond a legal rules conception of contract and introduced the idea of contract as framework. As Llewellyn put it, the "major importance of legal contract is to provide ... a framework which never accurately reflects real working relations, but which provides a rough indication around which such relations vary, an occasional guide in cases of doubt, and a norm of ultimate appeal when the relations cease in fact to work" (1931: 736–737). The object of contract, so construed, was not to be legalistic but to get the job done.

To be sure, recourse to the courts for purposes of ultimate appeal is important in that it serves to delimit threat positions. But the key idea is this: the legalistic view of contract that applies to simple transactions needs to make way for a more flexible and managerial conception of contract as contractual complexities build up. As against the convenient notion of one all-purpose law of contract (singular),

---

[4] To be sure, Barnard's focus was entirely on internal organization (rather than with comparative economic organization, markets, and hierarchies. He is nonetheless to be credited both with deep insights into the formal and informal mechanisms of internal organization and in perceiving that organization was not merely important but that social scientists should aspire to the development of a science of organization.

the need for contract laws (plural) is introduced. Such contract law differences are not incidental but are important in distinguishing among alternative modes of governance (Williamson, 1991).

Taken together, I associate the following combined insights with the foregoing: (1) organization is important and should be made susceptible to analysis; (2) cooperative adaptation in support ongoing economic relations is important; (3) a contractual/transactional approach to economic organization holds out promise; and (4) much of the action resides in the microanalytics. Albeit related key ideas, the several contributors were operating independently of one another and the complementarities went unnoticed.[5]

23.2 FOLLOW-ON DEVELOPMENTS IN THE 1960S

These good ideas remained fallow for most of the next thirty-five years.[6] Follow-on developments in the organization theory and market failure literatures from the late 1950s into the 1960s would also be needed. Carnegie was especially important to the former while positive transaction costs were central to the latter.

23.2.1 Interdisciplinary Social Science

Economics and the contiguous social sciences, especially economics and sociology, mainly went their own ways during the 1940s and 1950s. Thus, Paul Samuelson (1947) distinguished economics and sociology in terms of their rationality orientations, with rationality being the domain of economics and nonrationality being relegated to sociology. James Duesenberry subsequently quipped (1960) that economics was preoccupied with how individuals made choices, whereas sociology maintained that individuals did not have any choices to make. Herbert Simon saw it otherwise.

---

[5] The exception is Commons. Barnard makes reference to Commons's use of the term "strategic factors" (1938: 202–205); and Llewellyn was inspired by the idea of going concern (Scott, 2002: 1027–1028).

[6] As Coase would observe (1972: 69), his 1937 paper on "The Nature of the Firm" was much cited but little used as of 1972.

Simon received his Ph.D. from the University of Chicago in 1942 in political science. In addition to his "excellent training in political science," Simon also had a "solid foundation in economics... [and] had made a modest beginning in mathematics," as a result of which he was prepared to do "teaching and research in administration, economics, and even operations research" (Simon, 1991: 85)—and much more. Indeed, Simon was to become an interdisciplinary social scientist without compare. He combined extraordinary intelligence with energy, a curious mind, and the ability to address whatever subject to which he applied himself—be it in political science, economics, sociology, organization theory, statistics, philosophy, cognitive science, and the list goes on—*on its own terms*.

Simon had the benefit of Barnard's *Functions of the Executive* to work off in producing his own book on *Administrative Behavior* (Simon, 1947). Using Barnard's earlier book as a framework, Simon set out to develop more relevant concepts and a more precise vocabulary (1957a: xlv). Among the important contributions that Simon has made to organization theory are bounded rationality,[7] a focus on processes (of which search is one), a formal theory of employment relation, the architecture of complexity, and sub-goal pursuit.

As Simon would subsequently observe, bounded rationality would become his lodestar (1991: 86). More generally, Simon advised social scientists that "the way in which human actors were described was consequential: Nothing is more fundamental in setting our research agenda and informing our research methods than our view of the nature of the human beings whose behavior we are studying" (1985: 303).

Simon joined the faculty of the Graduate School of Industrial Administration at Carnegie-Mellon in 1949. This was an important move for Simon and for the small band of colleagues at GSIA who would go on to revolutionize business education.[8] Interdisciplinary social science teaching and research would flourish.

To be sure, economics was then and is now the gold standard for rigor in the social sciences. But the GSIA faculty aspired to rigor more generally and was not intimidated by disciplinary boundaries. Instead, if and as the issues crossed disciplinary boundaries, so should the student of economic organization. It was my privilege to have been a part of this project. Jacques Dreze speaks for me and,

---

[7] Bounded rationality implies neither non-rationality nor irrationality. Rather, "bounded rationality is behavior that is intendedly rational but only limitedly so" (Simon, 1957a: xxiv). So construed, bounded rationality takes exception with the analytically convenient assumption of hyper-rationality but does not preclude a predominantly rational approach to the study of complex economic organization.

[8] Studies by the Ford Foundation (Gordon and Howell, 1958) and the Carnegie Foundation (Pierson, 1959) speak to the languid status of business education in the 1950s. But whereas most of business education was fragmented and lacking in rigor, the faculty at GSIA perceived a need for a scientific approach to the study of business administration and progressively worked up a three-part program—combining economics, organization theory, and operations research. Both the Ford and Carnegie Foundation reports featured GSIA in describing the promise for the future.

I believe, for many others by summarizing his Carnegie experience as follows: "Never since have I experienced such intellectual excitement" (1995: 123).

23.2.2 New Developments in the Market Failure Literature

The market failure literature developed rapidly in the post-World War II era. Of the many important contributions to this literature, the two to which I call special attention are papers by Coase (1960) and Arrow (1969). Both illustrate why zero transaction cost reasoning is bankrupt.

Upon reformulating the tort problem (or, more generally, the externality problem) in contractual terms, Coase showed in his 1960 paper on "The Problem of Social Cost" that the externality problem vanished if the logic of zero transaction costs was taken to completion. As Coase put it in his Nobel Prize lecture (1992: 717; emphasis added):

Pigou's conclusion and that of most economists using standard economic theory was ... that some kind of government action (usually the imposition of taxes) was required to restrain those whose actions had harmful effects on others (often termed negative externalities. What I showed ... was that *in a regime of zero transaction costs, an assumption of standard economic theory*, negotiations between the parties would lead to those arrangements being made which would maximize wealth and this irrespective of the initial assignment of property rights.

Plainly, provision for positive transaction costs would thereafter have to be made if externalities, and the study of complex contracting more generally, were to be accurately described and assessed.

Arrow's examination of "The Organization of Economic Activity: Issues Pertinent to the Choice of Market versus Non-market Allocation" (1969) likewise made a prominent place for transaction costs, both in general and with reference to vertical integration. The general argument is this (Arrow, 1969: 48):

I contend that market failure is a more general condition than externality; and both differ from increasing returns in a basic sense, since market failures in general and externalities in particular are relative to the mode of economic organization, while increasing returns are essentially a technological phenomenon.

Current writing has helped to bring out the point that market failure is not absolute; it is better to consider a broader category, that of transaction costs, which in general impede and in particular cases completely block the formation of markets .... [T]ransaction costs are the costs of running the economic system.

Organizational considerations now take their place alongside technology, which had previously been treated as determinative. Upon recognizing that organization matters, transaction cost differences, as between internal organization and market exchange (where both are regarded as alternative modes of contracting), now make their appearance. Arrow's remarks about vertical integration are especially pertinent: "An incentive for vertical integration is replacement of the costs of buying and selling on the market by the costs of intra-firm transfers; the existence of vertical integration may suggest that *the costs of operating competitive markets are not zero, as is usually assumed by our theoretical analysis*" (1969: 48; emphasis added).

The stage was set, as it were, for the concerted study of positive transaction costs.

23.3 MY RELATION TO THE ENTERPRISE

By 1970, TCE was an idea whose time had come. The good ideas of the 1930s in combination with the successes of interdisciplinary social science at Carnegie and the reinterpretation of market failures in positive transaction cost terms (by Coase and Arrow) in the 1960s all served to prepare the ground. I describe here what I regard as critical events in the 1960s—in my training, teaching, research, and public policy experience—that presented the following research challenge: find a way to reformulate the vertical integration problem in transaction cost terms.

23.3.1 Training

I mention above and have elsewhere related my experience as a student in the Ph.D. program in the Graduate School of Industrial Administration at Carnegie from 1960–1963.[9] The approach to research, as I learned it at Carnegie, was this: be disciplined; be interdisciplinary; have an active mind. Being disciplined meant to think of and conduct yourself as a scientist. Being interdisciplinary entailed addressing problems on their own terms, crossing disciplinary boundaries if and as the problems had an interdisciplinary character. Having an active mind entailed being alert to research opportunities, which were then examined not by forcing these into orthodox boxes but by asking the question, "What is going on here?" Carnegie was an exhilarating experience in interdisciplinary social science.

---

[9] See Williamson (1996, 2004).

23.3.2 Teaching and Research at Berkeley

My first academic appointment upon graduation from Carnegie was in the economics department at the University of California, Berkeley. Both the chair of the department, Aaron Gordon, and the chair of the recruiting committee, Andreas Papandreou, had written on the modern corporation along lines that I addressed in my dissertation, *The Economics of Discretionary Behavior: Managerial Objectives in a Theory of the Firm* (1964). Also, my paper on "Selling Expense as a Barrier to Entry" (1963) was of interest to Joe Bain, who was the senior person in the field of industrial organization. So even though I had taken no courses and read no texts on industrial organization before being hired as the junior person in this field in Berkeley economics, I plainly shared interests with faculty who were key to the hiring process.

Inasmuch as the field of industrial organization was in disarray in the 1960s, my lack of IO training had the redeeming advantage that I was, as it were, free to choose. Thus although it was judicious for me to choose Bain's book, *Industrial Organization* (1959) as the text for the undergraduate course in industrial organization, which I did, it was also natural for me to supplement my teaching of IO by drawing upon organizational ideas from Carnegie that deviated from the prevailing views of firms and markets. Rather, therefore, than rely entirely on the neoclassical theory of the firm as a production function (which is a technological construction), I also saw opportunities to introduce the argument that the organization of firms mattered and was potentially susceptible to analysis. My subsequent reading of Alfred Chandler's (1962) interpretation of the reorganization of the modern corporation from a centralized (unitary form) to a decentralized (multi-divisional form), with economizing purpose and effect, would further buttress my predilections to examine economic organization in a combined economics and organization theory way.

In addition to teaching intermediate micro and macro theory, I also inherited a graduate course on "The Pricing of Public Services" that had been designed by Julius Margolis and was open for the asking when Margolis moved from Berkeley to Stanford. The course included a lot of applied welfare economics, cost-benefit analysis, some economics of property rights, collective choice, and the like. Material that I learned and taught for this course would have a lasting impact on my research and teaching.

My nonstandard training at Carnegie notwithstanding, much of my early research—on the theory of the firm (e.g., "Hierarchical Control and Optimum Firm Size" (1967)), applied welfare economics (e.g., "Peak Load Pricing and Optimal Capacity Under Indivisibility Constraints" (1966)), and industrial organization (e.g., "Wage Rates as a Barrier to Entry: The Pennington Case in Perspective" (1968))—largely employed neoclassical apparatus. My research strategy at the time was to (1) identify and motivate an interesting researchable issue, (2) develop a simple mathematical model and work out the economic ramifications, and (3) find some data that are pertinent thereto and perform empirical tests. I used neoclassical apparatus because that seemed to get the job done. An unanticipated benefit from addressing these and other issues in an orthodox way is that this served to credentialize me as a journeyman, which would stand me in good stead when I departed from orthodoxy to address problems in the new domain of transaction cost economics.

23.3.3 Antitrust Experience

I left Berkeley to accept an appointment as a non-tenured associate professor of economics at the University of Pennsylvania in 1965. Again, my main field was industrial organization. Almarin Philips, the senior person in the field, was generous in sharing it and I was periodically teaching the graduate IO class shortly thereafter.

I received a telephone call from Carl Kaysen, who was IO specialist at Harvard, late in the spring of 1966, asking if I would be interested in serving as the Special Economic Assistant to Donald Turner. Turner had co-authored the book *Antitrust Policy: An Economic and Legal Analysis* (1959) with Kaysen and was named head of the Antitrust Division of the U.S. Department of Justice in 1965. He brought extraordinary credentials to the job: a Ph.D. in economics from Harvard, a law degree from Yale, clerked for the Supreme Court, and worked for Wilmer Cutler in Washington before taking a position on the Harvard Law School faculty as a specialist in antitrust. I was thrilled at the prospect. The chair of the Economics Department at Penn, Irving Kravis, instantly agreed. So Dolores and I and our three children (soon to be joined by the birth of twins) went to Washington in August 1966.

Working with Turner, his first assistant Edwin Zimmerman (from Stanford), and the members of the newly formed Evaluation Group (mainly recent graduates from Harvard and Stanford law schools) together with Stephen Breyer (Turner's special legal assistant) and Richard Posner (in the Solicitor General's office) was heady stuff. I participated, in varying degrees, in over thirty cases during the ensuing year and got to see how antitrust enforcement at its best functioned. Yet, I also witnessed first-hand the sometimes primitive and wrong-headed conceptual foundations out of which antitrust enforcement worked. As interpreted through the lens of the neoclassical theory of the firm as production function, both the Chicago School (by appealing to price discrimination) and the Harvard School (by appealing to barriers to entry) explained deviations from simple market exchange by invoking monopoly.[10]

---

[10] As George Stigler put it, "Monopoly is a devious thing...A firm cannot practice price discrimination in the stages in which it does not operate" (Stigler, 1951: 138). Purportedly, vertical integration loses its innocence if there is appreciable monopoly control at even one stage of the production

The suspicion that monopoly purposes were lurking behind all nonstandard or unfamiliar contractual practices and organizational structures culminated in the inhospitality tradition, according to which customer and territorial restrictions were interpreted not hospitably in the common law tradition, but inhospitably in the tradition of antitrust.[11] The prevailing state of affairs was described by Coase as follows (1972: 67):

One important result of this preoccupation with the monopoly problem is that if an economist finds something—a business practice of one sort or another—that he does not understand, he looks for a monopoly explanation. And as in this field we are very ignorant, the number of understandable practices tends to be very large, and the reliance on a monopoly explanation, frequent.

Persuaded as I was that this readiness to ascribe monopoly purpose to non-standard and unfamiliar forms of contract and organization was often mistaken (partly because the requisite preconditions needed to support monopoly purpose were frequently lacking, but also because, as a student of Carnegie, I had acquired an understanding and respect for the economic benefits that accrued to organiza-tion), I found myself in opposition to the economic arguments that were being made to support several of the cases that were in progress within the Antitrust Division. Among these was the Schwinn case (which involved franchise restrictions on the resale of Schwinn bicycles by Schwinn franchisees.

As described elsewhere, the brief by the government for the Schwinn case was egregiously flawed (Williamson, 1985: 183–189). Fortunately, the Supreme Court's decision to uphold the government's fanciful arguments (which featured antisocial abuse and conceded no contractual benefits to Schwinn's vertical market restric-tions) would be reversed ten years later in the GTE Sylvania case—as a growing appreciation for non-technological benefits had begun to set in. Merger litigation was also in a state of disarray. As Justice Stewart put it in his dissenting opinion in 1966, "the sole consistency that I can find in [merger] litigation under Section 7 [is that] the Government always wins."[12] Public policy toward business was careening out of control.

Antitrust enforcement, moreover, was not alone. Lacking an appropriate lens for examining the strengths and weaknesses of all modes of organization, government included, in a symmetrical way, much of public policy analysis suffered from

process, where monopoly power was ascribed to a 20 percent market share (Stigler, 1955: 224). Working out of the structure–conduct–performance setup, Joe Bain also advanced a market power explanation for vertical integration: because the cases of clear economies of integration generally involve a "*physical or technical* integration" of successive stages of production or distribution, the purpose served by integration that lacks such a technological justification "is evidently the increase of the market power of the firms involved" (1968: 381; emphasis added).

[11] The Statement was made by the then head of the Antitrust Division, Donald Turner. See Stanley Robinson, 1968, N.Y. State Bar Association, Antitrust Symposium, p. 29.

[12] *United States v. Von's Grocery Co.*, U 384 U.S. 270 (1966) (Stewart J. dissenting).

serious conceptual deficiencies. The time was ripe for examining the inner workings of firms, and of markets, and of government bureaus through the lens of contract in which transaction costs were featured (Dixit, 1996: 9).

23.3.4 Teaching and Research at Penn

The years 1967–1970 were the transition years for me. Teaching, again, would play an important role in my research. Dismayed as I was, by the upside-down economics that I had observed in the Antitrust Division, I resolved to study the issues of vertical integration and vertical market restrictions when I returned to Penn in 1967 and organized a graduate seminar on vertical firm and market relations for that purpose. We went through the economics literature exhaustively. Although much of it was interesting and some of it excellent (as Lionel McKenzie's classic article on "Ideal Output and the Interdependence of Firms" (1951)), the literature worked entirely out of a price theoretic setup, as a consequence of which possible efficiency benefits of a contractual/organizational kind were ignored or suppressed.[13]

I was satisfied at the end of this course that I had a good understanding of the limited and convoluted state of the literature. But here as elsewhere it does not suffice to be a critic. It takes a theory to beat a theory, and I did not see my way through the thicket to pull a systematic rival theory together.

Then another lucky thing happened. Julius Margolis, whom I had known from Berkeley, was named the first dean of the new School of Public and Urban Policy at the University of Pennsylvania in 1969. Jules asked me to participate in the Ph.D. program at SPUP and teach a two-semester sequence in organization theory. Having benefited from the organization theory courses that I had taken at Carnegie (from Richard Cyert, James March, and Herbert Simon), I was persuaded that the subject was both interesting and important. So I agreed with alacrity.

The two-semester sequence in organization theory that I prepared drew extensively on my background at Carnegie together with related work in sociology, some of the economics of property rights literature, parts of the managerial discretion literature, and especially parts of the market failure literature. The classes were small and the discussions were intense as the students and I struggled to bring a combined economics and organization theory approach to each of the topics. Recurring features that seemed to hold promise were: (1) the attributes of human

[13] Actually, Michael Riordan and I worked up a neoclassical variant of the TCE tradeoffs by introducing additional revenue and cost features into a production function setup (Riordan and Williamson, 1985). The basic TCE logic had previously been worked out elsewhere, however. We merely translated this into an orthodox optimization problem.

actors; (2) differential transaction costs; and (3) a contractual approach to the issues.

23.4 THE PARADIGM PROBLEM: VERTICAL INTEGRATION

Vertical integration was the obvious project to bring transaction cost reasoning to bear. This for several reasons: (1) it was the issue on which Coase had focused in 1937; (2) interim neoclassical treatments had brought scant relief; (3) Arrow had expressly described vertical integration as a response to market failures in a positive transaction cost world; (4) public policy toward business in this area was deeply confused; and (5) my training, teaching, and research of a combined economics and organizational kind provided me with an obvious entrée. Indeed, if ever there was a research topic to which I brought (what for me was) a prepared mind, vertical integration was it.

Inasmuch as I had been invited to give a paper at the session on "Responses to Market Imperfection" at the meetings of the American Economic Association in January 1971, I decided to examine the possibility that vertical integration could be, indeed should be, interpreted as a response to "market imperfections" of a positive transaction cost kind. My paper, "The Vertical Integration of Production: Market Failure Considerations" (1971) was the result.

This paper moved away from the resource allocation tradition (the science of choice) into what would later be described as the science of contract (Buchanan, 2001). A whole host of new concepts and analytical tools attended the effort. Key concepts that the 1971 paper introduced in re-examining the make-or-buy decision in comparative contractual terms, with emphasis on positive transaction costs, include the following:

1. *Human Actors.* The key attributes of human actors on which I rely are bounded rationality and opportunism. Whereas Simon held that the chief lesson of bounded rationality (especially in the context of search behavior) was to supplant maximizing by "satisficing"—of finding a course of action that is "good enough" (Simon, 1957*b*: 204–205), the main lesson of bounded rationality in the context of contract is different: *all complex contracts are unavoidably incomplete.* At the time (1971), and to some degree even today, many economists were uneasy with (and some dismissive of) the idea of incomplete contracts.

Opportunism is an encompassing concept and introduces strategic issues that had been ignored by neoclassical economists from 1870 to 1970 (Makowski and

Ostroy, 2001: 482–483, 490–491). Moral hazard, adverse selection, and the defection hazards to which incomplete long-term contracts are subject would all vanish but for opportunism (in that contract as mere promise, unsupported by credible commitments, would then suffice).[14]

In combination with transaction attributes that are responsible for contractual complications (see below), bounded rationality and opportunism turn out to have pervasive ramifications for the study of contract and organization.

2. *Adaptation to Uncertainty/Governance.* I argue that problems of contracting under fully stationary conditions are uninteresting: "Only when the need to make unprogrammed adaptations is introduced does the market versus internal organization issue become engaging" (1971: 123). Because the firm "possesses coordinating potential that sometimes transcends that of the market" (1971: 112), the firm is more than a production function for transforming inputs into outputs according to the laws of technology. It is also a governance structure. By comparison with the market, the firm had additional access to fiat for dispute resolution and for the exercise command and control more generally.[15] Disturbances for which coordinated adaptation is needed to restore efficiency are thus ones for which hierarchy enjoys advantages over simple market exchange, *ceteris paribus.*

3. *Asset Specificity.* I argue that outsourcing can "pose problems...if either (1) efficient supply requires investment in special-purpose, long-life equipment, or (2) the winner of the original contract acquires a cost advantage, say by reason of first mover advantages (such as unique location or learning, including the acquisition of undisclosed or proprietary technical and managerial procedures and task-specific labor skills)" (1971: 116). Such problems are uncovered by examining the contracting process in an intertemporal way and by recognizing that asset specificity (of physical and human asset kinds) gives rise to bilateral dependency. What would subsequently be described as the Fundamental Transformation, whereby a large numbers supply condition at the outset would be transformed into a small numbers exchange relation during contract implementation and at the contract renewal interval was plainly contemplated. Transactions for which bilateral dependency was in prospect would thus pose the aforementioned need for coordinated adaptation when incomplete contracts are subject to disturbances. Vertical integration will thus arise to promote efficient adaptation in these circumstances.

4. *Discrete Structural Differences.* Firm and market organization differ not merely in degree but also differ in kind: "The properties of the firm that commend internal organization as a market substitute...fall into three categories: incentives,

---

[14] For a discussion of contract as promise, see Williamson (1985: 65–67).

[15] The famous paper by Armen Alchian and Harold Demsetz (1972), which was published a year and a half later, was dismissive of fiat differences between firm and market.

controls, and what may be referred to broadly as 'inherent structural advantages' " (1971: 113).[16] This, however, varies with the transaction, in that the advantages of markets in relation to firms are also attributable to incentive, control, and contract law differences. Which governance structure is best depends on whether the adaptive needs of transactions are primarily of the autonomous kind (in which case the market is favored) or of a cooperative kind (where hierarchy enjoys the advantage. Because the added bureaucratic burdens of hierarchy are always a deterrent, hierarchy is reserved for "complex" transactions.

5. *Remediableness.* I expressly eschew comparison with hypothetical ideals in favor of comparisons with feasible alternatives, all of which are flawed: "What are referred to here as market failures are failures only in the limited sense that they involve transaction costs that can be attenuated by substituting internal organization for market exchange" (1971: 114). This relates to arguments made earlier by Coase (1964) and Harold Demsetz (1969) and prefigures the remediableness criterion (Williamson, 1996).

The upshot is that examining the make-or-buy decision from a combined economics and organization theory perspective in which (1) attention is focused on transaction cost economizing, (2) human actors are described in a more veridical way, (3) intertemporal process transformations are taken into account, and (4) locating the analytical action in the details of transactions on one hand and governance structures on the other yields a new understanding of and predictions about vertical integration.[17] More generally, the seeds for a predictive theory of economic organization were at hand. Upon sowing them, germination awaits.

23.5 SOME PERSPECTIVES

I successively discuss the core hypothesis out of which TCE works (the discriminating alignment hypothesis), applications of TCE reasoning to additional phenomena (which are interpreted as variations upon the paradigm problem), and possible misconceptions about TCE.

---

[16] The "property rights theory of the firm" (Grossman and Hart, 1986) assumes away all of these differences.

[17] To be sure, this short 1971 paper could not do it all. I nonetheless identified many of the critical issues that would prove crucial to the transaction cost economics and located the study of governance in the very center of the TCE research agenda. The paper also makes evident that the prior literature on vertical integration dealt only with special cases and/or worked out of a truncated logic.

23.5.1 The Rudiments

Reduced to its rudiments, TCE is the very essence of simplicity:

1. If some transactions are simple and others are complex, then the attributes of transactions that are responsible for these differences must be named and their ramifications set out. TCE responds by naming asset specificity (which can take a variety of forms), uncertainty, and frequency as three of the critical dimensions for describing transactions.
2. If the comparative efficacy of different modes of organization (market, hybrid, hierarchy, public bureau, etc.) differ, then the critical attributes with respect to which governance structures differ need to be named and the internally consistent syndromes of attributes that define viable modes need to be worked out.
3. A predictive theory of economic organization resides in the discriminating alignment hypothesis: transactions, which differ in their attributes, are aligned with governance structures, which differ in their costs and competencies, so as to effect a (mainly) transaction cost economizing result.

Operationalizing TCE in this way would prove crucial to its subsequent development.

23.5.2 Subsequent Developments

My claim of a "prepared mind" notwithstanding, "The Vertical Integration of Production" was a difficult paper for me to write. But it was also rewarding. Albeit focused on intermediate product market contracting, I knew, by the time that the paper was completed, that the approach had application to other commercial contracting relations—although I did not appreciate that a new comparative contractual approach to the economics of organization, transaction cost economics, was so near in prospect.

One obvious application was to labor market contracting, where the issue of credible contracting between employer and employees was posed. Rather than view the collective organization of labor in monopoly terms, I inquired instead into when the collective organization of labor could serve to infuse order, thereby to mitigate costly conflicts and realize mutual gains. The answer closely tracked the logic of vertical integration: as the degree of bilateral dependency built up, both employer and employee had stronger interests in crafting governance structures that permitted them to work through contractual conflicts and differences, thereby to preserve continuity, rather than allow a costly impasse or contractual breakdown to occur. The collective organization of labor (unions) into which governance mechanisms have been crafted (of which grievance mechanisms and arbitration are examples) is, thus, indicated as the condition of bilateral dependency (firm-specific human capital) increases.

This is not to say that unions will arise only for efficiency reasons. The argument, rather, is that collective organization can serve continuity purposes (of a governance kind) as well as monopoly purposes (of a price theoretic kind. The difference between these two is that much more fully elaborated union governance measures will be designed to support efficiency purposes (mutual gain) than will be observed for mere monopoly.

Indeed, variations on the efficient governance theme proliferate—with applications to vertical market restrictions, oligopoly, franchising, regulation/deregulation, corporate governance, finance, final product markets, public bureaus, and the list goes on.[18] TCE, moreover, has had numerous public policy ramifications[19] and has generated considerable interest among empirically minded students of firm and market organization—especially among economists (in industrial organization and other applied micro fields), business school faculty (in strategy, organizational behavior, marketing, finance, and operations), and among law, sociology, and political science faculties.[20] TCE has helped to shape and encourage research in both the economics of organization (Mahoney, 2004) and the New Institutional Economics (Williamson, 2000; Menard, 2005).

23.5.3 Misconceptions?

The New Institutional Economics, of which TCE is a part, has been described by Victor Nee and Paul Ingram as follows (1998: 20):

[18] Many of these are worked out in three of my books: *Markets and Hierarchies* (1975), *The Economic Institutions of Capitalism* (1985), and *The Mechanisms of Governance* (1996). More generally, see the collection of articles in *Transaction Cost Economics*, vols. 1 and 2 (Williamson and Masten, 1995) and the more recent collection of articles in the *International Library of the New Institutional Economics*, 6 vols., ed. Claude Menard (2005).

[19] Public policy applications to antitrust and regulation have been followed by public policy applications more generally. As Avinash Dixit observes (1996: 9): "[T]he neoclassical theory of production and supply viewed the firm as a profit-maximizing black box. While some useful insights follow from this, it leaves some very important gaps in our understanding and gives us some very misleading ideas about the possibilities of beneficial policy intervention. Economists studying business and industrial organization have long recognized the inadequacy of the neoclassical view of the firm and have developed richer paradigms and models based on the concepts of various kinds of transaction costs. Policy analysis ... stands to benefit from ... opening the black box and examining the actual workings of the mechanism inside."

[20] As Scott Masten observes, "surveys of the empirical transaction cost literature attest ... [that] the theory and evidence have displayed remarkable congruity" (1995: xi–xii). The most recent such survey records that published empirical studies of TCE number more than 600 through the year 2000 and that exponential growth is observed over the interval 1980–2000 (Boerner and Macher, 2002). To be sure, TCE will benefit from more and better empirical testing. As compared with other theories of firm and market organization, however, TCE is an empirical success story.

Ronald Coase's seminal essays, "The Nature of the Firm" (1937) and "The Problem of Social Cost" (1960) introduced the core concepts of the new institutional economics... Rather than aligning themselves with the earlier American institutionalists... new institutionalists in economics have instead positioned themselves as direct heirs of Adam Smith by incorporating the behavioral assumptions of microeconomics into a choice-within-institutional-constraints framework of empirical analysis. As Coase (1984: 230) succinctly put it, "What distinguished modern institutional economists is not that they speak about institutions...but that they use standard economic theory to analyze the workings of these institutions and to discover the part they play in the operation of the economy."

I partly concur but also dissent from this description.

1. I agree that Coase's two essays are seminal. His imprint is unmistakable. But other core concepts—by Commons, Barnard, Llewellyn, Simon, and Arrow—go unmentioned. Of these, I would especially call attention to the Commons Triple of conflict, mutuality, and order, which prefigures the concept of governance—in that governance is the means by which to infuse *order*, thereby to *mitigate* conflict and realize *mutual gains*. There is no more basic recurrent theme.

2. Adam Smith is always a good name. Incorporating the behavioral assumptions of microeconomics is not, however, what the NIE/TCE enterprise is all about. Assumptions of maximization and simple self-interest seeking are *obstacles* to the crucial concepts of incomplete contracts and strategic behavior—which arise because of bounds on rationality and opportunism, respectfully. But for bounds on rationality and opportunism, problems of governance evaporate.

3. I am at a loss to understand what Coase means by saying that NIE economists use standard economic theory. Sometimes, to be sure. But doing TCE is largely accomplished by moving from the orthodox lens of choice (the resource allocation paradigm) to use the lens of contract. As Arrow observes, "the work of Williamson and others of the New Institutional Economics movement...does not consist of giving new answers to the traditional questions of economics—resource allocation and degree of utilization. Rather it consists of answering new questions...[and] brings sharper nanoeconomic... reasoning to bear than has been customary" (1987: 734). The resulting departures from standard economic theory are fundamental (Kreps, 1990, 1999).

4. I concur that an understanding of institutions and the part they play in the operation of the economy is central to the New Institutional Economics enterprise.

On my reading, the Nee and Ingram summary starts and ends well but otherwise sows confusion.

23.6 LESSONS OF THE CARNEGIE TRIPLE

My experience with TCE is that it has been a demanding and rewarding research enterprise. It does not, to be sure, inform everything. Any issue, however, that arises as or can be reconceptualized as a contracting problem can be examined to advantage in transaction cost economizing terms. That covers a lot of territory, much of it yet to be visited. TCE, moreover, will benefit from further work of conceptual and theoretical kinds. Accordingly, TCE should be regarded as a work-in-progress to which young scholars with interdisciplinary interests are invited to participate.

The Carnegie Triple—be disciplined; be interdisciplinary; have an active mind—has a good deal to recommend it for those who would respond to this challenge.

23.6.1 Be Disciplined

Promising new concepts and would-be theories proliferate. Being disciplined will be promoted by subscribing to Robert Solow's three precepts for doing good economic theory: keep it simple; get it right; make it plausible (2001: 111).

Keeping it simple is made necessary by "the very complexity of real life" (Solow, 2001: 111). The need is to focus on first order effects—of which economizing on transaction costs is arguably one. But there is also a concern that oversimplifications will lose contact with the phenomenon in question. Tensions between the precept to keep it simple and to make it plausible are thus posed.

Getting it right entails working through the logic—in words, diagrams, or mathematics (Solow, 2001: 112), possibly all three. For TCE this entails working through the logic of discriminating alignment with the use of close comparative institutional reasoning of a microanalytic kind—examples being the Fundamental Transformation and asking and answering the question, Why can't a large (composite) firm do everything that a collection of small firms can do and more?[21]

Making it plausible means eschewing fanciful constructions, the effect of which is to lose contact with the phenomenon.

To this list of precepts, moreover, I would add a further requirement: ask all would-be theories of economic organization to make predictions and submit these

---

[21] As developed elsewhere, I address this question by postulating two mechanisms, replication and selective intervention, which, if they could be implemented, would imply that a bigger, composite firm is never worse and usually better than a collection of small firms. The impossibility of combining replication with selective intervention leads into the important but elusive issues of bureaucracy (Williamson, 1985: ch. 6).

to empirical testing. The object of this requirement is to sort the sheep from the goats.

This is especially important in an interdisciplinary arena such as the economics of organization where the practice of spinning new theories, many of which purport to be dynamic or Knightian or are otherwise "more relevant," is widespread. Although the protagonists of such theories sometimes back off when the logic is shown to be incomplete or defective, others respond that their theory is saved by its "relevance" and that beauty is in the eye of the beholder.

Confronted with a proliferation of would-be theories, what to do? Nicholas Georgescu-Roegen, who pronounced that "the purpose of science is not prediction, but knowledge for its own sake" yet held that prediction is "the touchstone of scientific knowledge" (1971: 37), seems to me to have it exactly right. My suggestion, therefore, is that all theories be asked to stand up and be counted—by which I mean derive predictions and submit them to the data.

Some will observe that new theories deserve a grace period. I agree, but with the stipulation that later, if not sooner, would-be theories should show their hand or fold.

23.6.2 Be Interdisciplinary

If and as problems are interdisciplinary by nature, in that they do not fall neatly within a single discipline, social scientists are encouraged to cross disciplinary boundaries. To be sure, that comes at a cost. Some social scientists will leave such problems for others and work on problems within their home discipline. I have no problem with that. What I find deeply problematic, however, is the *emasculation of an inherently interdisciplinary problem by suppressing key interdisciplinary features.*

Inasmuch, however, as acceptable and unacceptable simplifications can be disputed, I revert to the hard-headed criterion advanced above: derive refutable implications and submit these to the data.

23.6.3 Have an Active Mind

Roy D'Andrade's discussion of different scientific research traditions (1986) distinguishes between authoritative and inquiring research orientations. Whereas the former is characterized by an advanced state of development, is self-confident, and declares that "This is the law here," the latter is more tentative, pluralist, and exploratory and poses the question, "What is going on here?" The latter favors bottom-up constructions.

To be sure, few economists have no curiosity whatsoever with the phenomena. The readiness, however, to impose preconceptions—rather than to get close to the phenomena by asking and attempting to answer the question, "What is going on here?"—is nevertheless widespread, as John McMillan noted in contrasting his research strategy and that of others (2002: 225; emphasis added):

To answer any question about the economy, you need some good theory to organize your thoughts and some facts to ensure that they are on target. You have to look and see *how things actually work or do not work*. That might seem so trite as not to be worth saying, but assertions about economic matters that are based more on preconceptions than on the specifics of the situation are still regrettably common.

Those who have an abiding interest in economic organization are thus advised to combine detailed knowledge of the phenomena, to which to "look and see" contributions of organization theorists are frequently pertinent, *with a focused lens*—although some, myself included, would put this last in the plural, in that a deeper understanding of complex phenomena will often benefit from the application of several focused lenses, some of which may be rival but others complementary. Having an active mind is facilitated by a willingness to entertain the possibility that the emperor should periodically visit his tailor.

Conceptual, theoretical, public policy, and empirical research opportunities await those who can bring detailed knowledge of the relevant phenomena to bear.

23.7 CONCLUDING REMARKS

Although I have emphasized aspects of TCE in which I have had a direct involvement, TCE is the product of many contributors—including my teachers, contemporaries, students, and colleagues. Also, I have "met" many scholars that influenced my research in my capacity as editor of the *Bell Journal of Economics* and the *Journal of Law, Economics, and Organization*, through my involvement in the International Society for the New Institutional Economics, at conferences and workshops that I have given and attended, in published articles and books, and in e-mail correspondence.

I trust that it is evident from the odyssey that I have described that working on TCE has given me a lot of satisfaction—although there have also been many struggles and dead-ends along the way. I also take satisfaction that TCE is a work-in-progress. As in the past, my conjecture is that it will continue to develop in a modest, slow, molecular, definitive way.

References

ALCHIAN, A., and DEMSETZ, H. (1972). Production, information costs, and economic organization. *American Economic Review*, 62: 777–795.

ARROW, K. (1969). The organization of economic activity: Issues pertinent to the choice of market versus nonmarket allocation. In *The Analysis and Evaluation of Public Expenditure: The PPB System*: 1. 39–73. U.S. Joint Economic Committee, 91st Congress, 1st Session. Washington, DC: U.S. Government Printing Office.

—— (1987). Reflections on the Essays. In G. Feiwel (ed.), *Arrow and the Foundations of the Theory of Economic Policy*: 727–734: New York: NYU Press.

BAIN, J. (1959). *Industrial Organization*. New York: John Wiley.

—— (1968). *Industrial Organization*. 2nd edn., New York: John Wiley.

BARNARD, C. (1938). *The Functions of the Executive*. Cambridge, Mass.: Harvard University Press.

BOERNER, C., and MACHER, J. (2002). Transaction cost economics: An assessment of empirical research in the social sciences. Unpublished manuscript.

BUCHANAN, J. (2001). Game theory, mathematics, and economics. *Journal of Economic Methodology*, 8: 27–32.

CHANDLER, A. (1962). *Strategy and Structure*. New York: Doubleday and Co.

COASE, R. (1937). The nature of the firm. *Economica*, ns 4: 386–405.

—— (1960). The problem of social cost. *Journal of Law and Economics*, 3: 1–44.

—— (1964). The regulated industries: Discussion. *American Economic Review*, 54: 194–197.

—— (1972). Industrial organization: A proposal for research. In V. R. Fuchs (ed.), *Policy Issues and Research Opportunities in Industrial Organization*: 59–73. New York: National Bureau of Economic Research.

—— (1984). The new institutional economics. *Journal of Institutional and Theoretical Economics*, 140: 229–231.

—— (1988). *The Firm, the Market, and the Law*. Chicago: University of Chicago Press.

—— (1992). The institutional structure of production. *American Economic Review*, 82: 713–719.

COMMONS, J. (1932). The problem of correlating law, economics, and ethics. *Wisconsin Law Review*, 8: 3–26.

—— (1950). *The Economics of Collective Action*. Madison: University of Wisconsin Press.

D'ANDRADE, R. (1986). Three scientific world views and the covering law model. In D. W. Fiske and R. A. Schweder (eds.), *Metatheory in Social Science: Pluralisms and Subjectivities*. Chicago: University of Chicago Press.

DEMSETZ, H. (1969). Information and efficiency: Another viewpoint. *Journal of Law and Economics*, 12: 1–22.

DIXIT, A. (1996). *The Making of Economic Policy: A Transaction Cost Politics Perspective*. Cambridge, Mass.: MIT Press.

DREZE, J. (1995). Forty years of public economics: A personal perspective. *The Journal of Economic Perspectives*, 9: 111–130.

DUESENBERRY, J. (1960). An economic analysis of fertility: Comment. In *Demographic and Economic Change in Developed Countries*, National Bureau of Economic Research. Princeton: Princeton University Press.

GEORGESCU-ROEGEN, N. (1971). *The Entropy Law and Economic Process*. Cambridge, Mass.: Harvard University Press.

GORDON, R., and HOWELL, J. (1958). *Higher Education for Business*. New York: Columbia University Press.

GROSSMAN, S., and HART, O. (1986). The costs and benefits of ownership: A theory of vertical and lateral integration. *Journal of Political Economy*. 94: 691–719.

HAYEK, F. (1945). The use of knowledge in society. *American Economic Review*, 35: 519–530.

KAYSEN, C., and TURNER, D. (1959). *Antitrust Policy: An Economic and Legal Analysis*. Cambridge, Mass.: Harvard University Press.

KREPS, D. (1990). Corporate culture and economic theory. In J. Alt and K. Shepsle (eds.), *Perspectives on Positive Political Economy*: 90–143. New York: Cambridge University Press.

—— (1999). Markets and hierarchies and (mathematical) economic theory. In G. Carroll and D. Teece (eds.), *Firms, Markets, and Hierarchies*. New York: Oxford University Press.

LLEWELLYN, K. N. (1931). What price contract? An essay in perspective. *Yale Law Journal*, 40: 704–751.

MAHONEY, J. (2004). *The Economic Foundations of Strategy*. Thousand Oaks, Calif.: Sage Publications.

MAKOWSKI, L., and OSTROY, J. (2001). Perfect competition and the creativity of the market. *Journal of Economic Literature*, 32(2): 479–535.

MASTEN, S. (1995). Introduction to vol. 2. In O. Williamson and S. Masten (eds.), *Transaction Cost Economics*. Aldershot: Edward Elgar.

McKENZIE, L. (1951). Ideal output and the interdependence of firms. *Economic Journal*, 61: 785–803.

McMILLAN, J. (2002). *Reinventing the Bazaar: A Natural History of Markets*. New York: W. W. Norton.

MENARD, C. (ed.) (2005). *International Library of the New Institutional Economics*. Northampton, Mass.: Edward Elgar.

NEE, V., and INGRAM, P. (1998). Embeddedness and beyond: Institutions, exchange and social structure. In M. Brinton and V. Nee (eds.), *The New Institutionalism in Sociology*: 19–45. New York: Russell Sage Foundation.

PIERSON, F. (1959). *The Education of American Businessmen*. New York: McGraw Hill.

REDER, M. (1999). *The Culture of a Controversial Science*. Chicago: University of Chicago Press.

RIORDAN, M., and WILLIAMSON, O. (1985). Asset specificity and economic organization. *International Journal of Industrial Organization*, 3: 365–378.

SAMUELSON, P. (1947). *Foundations of Economic Analysis*. Cambridge, Mass.: Harvard University Press.

SCOTT, W. R. (2002). *Institutions and Organizations*. 2nd edn., Thousand Oaks, Calif.: Sage Publications.

SIMON, H. (1947). *Administrative Behavior*. New York: Macmillan.

—— (1957a). *Administrative Behavior*. 2nd edn., New York: Macmillan.

—— (1957b). *Models of Man*. New York: John Wiley and Sons.

—— (1985). Human nature in politics: A dialogue of psychology with political science. *American Political Science Review*, 79: 293–304.

—— (1991). Organizations and markets. *Journal of Economic Perspectives*, 5: 25–44.

SOLOW, R. (2001). A native informant speaks. *Journal of Economic Methodology*, 8: 111–112.

STIGLER, G. (1951). The division of labor is limited by the extent of the market. *Journal of Political Economy*, 59: 185–193.

STIGLER, G. (1955). Mergers and preventive antitrust policy. *University of Pennsylvania Law Review*, 104: 176–185.

WILLIAMSON, O. (1963). Selling expense as a barrier to entry. *Quarterly Journal of Economics*, 77: 112–128.

—— (1964). *The Economics of Discretionary Behavior: Managerial Objectives in a Theory of the Firm.* Englewood Cliffs, NJ: Prentice-Hall.

—— (1966). Peak load pricing and optimal capacity under indivisibility constraints. *American Economic Review*, 56: 810–827.

—— (1967). Hierarchical control and optimum firm size. *Journal of Political Economy*, 75: 123–138.

—— (1968). Wage rates as a barrier to entry: The Pennington Case in perspective. *Quarterly Journal of Economics*, 82: 85–116.

—— (1971). The vertical integration of production: Market failure considerations. *American Economic Review*, 61: 112–123.

—— (1975). *Markets and Hierarchies: Analysis and Antitrust Implications.* New York: Free Press.

—— (1985). *The Economic Institutions of Capitalism.* New York: Free Press.

—— (1990). Chester Barnard and the incipient science of organization. In O. E. Williamson (ed.), *Organization Theory: From Chester Barnard to the Present and Beyond*: 172–206: New York: Oxford University Press.

—— (1991). Comparative economic organization: The analysis of discrete structural alternatives. *Administrative Science Quarterly*, 36: 269–296.

—— (1995). Economic institutions and development: A view from the bottom. Unpublished manuscript, University of California, Berkeley.

—— (1996). *The Mechanisms of Governance.* New York: Oxford University Press.

—— (2000). The new institutional economics: Taking stock, looking ahead. *Journal of Economic Literature*, 38: 595–613.

—— (2004). Herbert Simon and organization theory: Lessons for the theory of the firm. In M. Augier and J. March (eds.), *Essays in Honor of Herbert Simon.* Cambridge, Mass.: MIT Press.

—— (2005). The economics of governance. *American Economic Review*, May (forthcoming).

—— and MASTEN, S. (1995). *Transaction Cost Economics*, vols. 1 and 2. Aldershot: Edward Elgar.

....

CHAPTER 24

DEVELOPING EVOLUTIONARY THEORY FOR ECONOMICS AND MANAGEMENT

....

SIDNEY G. WINTER

24.1 INTRODUCTION

....

IN the spring of 1959, chance events led me to read a 1950 paper by Armen Alchian, entitled "Uncertainty, Evolution and Economic Theory" (Alchian, 1950). At the time, I was trying to do a dissertation featuring an empirical analysis of the determinants of corporate spending on research and development. R&D had become quite a hot topic in applied economics after the mid-1950s. The theoretical framework that I had planned to use in this investigation was a model based on the familiar concept of the profit-maximizing firm, a core theoretical commitment of mainstream economics then and now. But, at the time of the fortuitous encounter with the Alchian paper, I had become concerned that my model of profit-maximizing R&D spending related to a decision situation that did not actually exist, at least not in any form resembling the context-free one that the model addressed.

Reading Alchian, I saw that an evolutionary approach on the theoretical front might offer a promising way to address satisfactorily a set of otherwise bothersome facts: (1) business discourse on R&D intensity seemed to be anchored on some notion of an appropriate R&D-to-sales ratio; (2) firm R&D decisions of any particular year were strongly shaped and constrained by decisions and their consequences from previous years; (3) incremental changes in policy nevertheless occurred, and had in fact accumulated over time into a pattern of significant and persistent *inter-industry* differences in R&D intensity; and (4) sustained pressures from the economic and technological environment seemed to play a shaping role in the emergence of those inter-industry differences. Such was the starting point of my long odyssey with evolutionary thinking.

That personal journey is now half way through its fifth decade. More than three decades have passed since Richard Nelson and I published our first collaborative papers on evolutionary economics, and more than two since we presented a major statement of our theory in *An Evolutionary Theory of Economic Change* (Nelson and Winter, 1982a). Needless to say, there have been a number of significant twists and turns along the way. In particular, the opportunity to present this chapter in a volume devoted to management theory reflects developments that certainly were not anticipated in the early stages. From its original status as a possible solution to my specific problem with R&D spending, the evolutionary approach quickly became the basis of an attempt at major reform in *economic* theory. That it remained, though the scope became even broader, as the collaboration with Nelson began. A contribution to *management* theory was not on the program.

Nevertheless, the logic of the connection to management is clear enough. As my subsequent discussion here explains, one of the key advantages of the evolutionary approach is that it offers liberation from overly stylized theoretical accounts of business behavior. Alternatively, one might say that the evolutionary approach embraces the realities of business decision making rather than shrinking defensively from them (exactly the choice posed in my encounter with the question of R&D spending). It, thereby, makes room for managers in the economic account of business behavior, and at the same time offers a style of economic thinking that is more interesting and potentially helpful to managers. In both directions of that traffic, the words "technology," "organization," and "change" are prominent, along with "management" and "evolution." A considerable portion of this promise has been realized, thanks in great part to the number of other scholars who have shared this vision, or pieces of it, and sought to bring it to realization. Major opportunities still lie before us.

In the remainder of this chapter, I continue the story from the beginnings just described. My chosen structure is quasi-chronological, addressing major substantive areas in roughly the historical order in which they presented themselves to me. Since things didn't actually develop in such discrete stages, there is a good deal of chronological disorder in the resulting picture.

The basic issues raised at the very beginning are as alive as they ever were. In particular, the realism-scorning methodological position that Milton Friedman staked out (Friedman, 1953) remains, in practice, a core commitment of the economics discipline today, even if the actual citations to that essay are less commonly encountered than they once were. That commitment is, in turn, a major source of frustration to anyone who looks to mainstream economics in the reasonable hope that it might offer substantial help with the task of understanding how firm behavior shapes the economic system, or how managers shape firm behavior, or how technology and economic growth are shaping the future of the planet. The following section (24.2) explores these basic issues, as consequential substantively as they are methodologically fundamental, which were focal in the early stages of my own work on the evolutionary approach. I turn next (24.3) to the links between the evolutionary theory and the direct study of business behavior— as specifically represented by work in the Carnegie School tradition of Herbert Simon, James March, and Richard Cyert. Section 24.4 then introduces the connections to technical change, and hence to economic growth and development. That inquiry points to still broader issues about how one thinks of the role of knowledge in productive activity, addressed in Section 24.5. The penultimate section (24.6) discusses some of the key empirical issues—those that are in dispute with mainstream economics or with other prominent schools of thought, and those that are key simply because of their central place in the evolutionary argument. Finally, Section 24.7 argues that the evolutionary approach offers a style for doing economic theory that has a good fit to the needs of the management discipline.

24.2 "REALISM," MAXIMIZATION, AND THE THEORY OF THE FIRM

The Friedman paper mentioned above soon supplanted the Alchian paper as the main focus of my early thinking about economic evolution, but Alchian's work remained a fundamental guide in one key respect. Alchian had proposed a *reconstruction* of economic theory on evolutionary principles, and plausibly sketched some key elements of such a program. That idea appealed to me, but it certainly was not what Friedman was up to.[1]

---

[1] An argument that Friedman's evolutionary insights *should* imply reconstruction was actually made by Tjalling Koopmans, a much-admired mathematical economist who was a professor of mine at Yale (Koopmans, 1957: 140–141). I do not recall reading that passage in Koopmans before I read Alchian—but I might not have reacted, even if I did.

Friedman's essay, "The Methodology of Positive Economics," appeared as the first chapter of his *Essays in Positive Economics* (Friedman, 1953). In large part, it was Friedman's response to a lively scholarly controversy about the profit maximization assumption that had emerged in the 1940s. The critics complained that the assumption was not realistic, and some of them cited evidence from close-in observation of business behavior to back their claims.[2] Friedman argued that the critics suffered from a simplistic understanding of what "realism" meant in science. He also put forward arguments about why profit maximization might be a "fruitful hypothesis" in spite of apparent conflicts with direct observation—scorning the latter with the comment "A fundamental hypothesis of science is that appearances are deceptive" (p. 33). One of his supportive arguments for profit maximization as a scientific hypothesis was an evolutionary "natural selection" argument that concluded with these words:

The process of "natural selection" thus helps to validate the hypothesis—or rather, given natural selection, acceptance of the hypothesis can be based largely on the judgment that it summarizes appropriately the conditions for survival. (1953: 22)

The critical assessment of this proposition—which I have come to call "the Friedman conjecture"—became the central theme of my dissertation research, at a rather late stage in the year that I was supposedly devoting to the dissertation. The study of corporate R&D spending was never completed; the theoretical puzzle it presented was recast as an example of a much larger puzzle about the general representation of business behavior in economic theory, and about profit maximization in particular. The topics of R&D and technological change were set aside, but the early concern with these issues was a portent of things to come in the development of evolutionary economics.

As Friedman's essay explained quite well, every science faces the challenge of finding ways to makes its theoretical concepts operational, thus building a bridge from a theory to a set of facts that might be expected to throw light on the merit of the theory. Just how this "light-throwing" works is not obvious. It is actually a deep and sometimes contentious issue, though elementary accounts of the scientific method often posit a simple and reassuring answer. One particular puzzle concerns the appropriateness of leaving a theoretical term without any direct empirical reference of its own, so that it serves only as a convenient place-holder in a longer argument that engages observable reality at some distant point. Friedman's position was that the notion of "profit maximization" in economic theory was a theoretical term of this kind: what the theory says, per Friedman, is that firms behave *as if* they maximize profits. Hence, mounting an effort to examine firm decision making at close range is simply misguided (as economic science), because economic theory makes no real prediction as to what you should expect to find.

---

[2] A good example is Gordon (1948), which cites a lot of the other relevant work.

Friedman suggested that other processes—such as "natural selection" or tacit skill—might create the observable consequences of profit maximization.[3] This could be happening even if the maximization itself—in the sense of clear object-ives, explicit calculation and careful comparison of alternatives—were not only unobservable, but absent. He also expressed skepticism about the possibility of discovering how business decisions are made through observation or interviews, suggesting that respondents might dissemble in some way or perhaps were actually not consciously aware of the mental processes involved (the tacit skill point). For example,

the billiard player, if asked how he decides where to hit the ball, may say that he "just figures it out but then also rubs a rabbit's foot just to make sure; and the businessman may well say that he prices at average cost, with of course some minor deviations when the market makes it necessary. The one statement is about as helpful as the other, and neither is a relevant test of the associated (maximization) hypothesis. (Friedman, 1953: 22)

This skepticism about the value of direct observation of firms is by no means peculiar to Friedman, or to those who are explicitly committed to something like his methodological outlook. It remains a broadly held attitude in the economics discipline, though perhaps not so broadly as when Friedman wrote. Anyone who undertakes a direct approach to studying firm behavior is sure to encounter it, sooner rather than later, when discussing the project with economists.[4] To be clear, there certainly is merit in warning against the possibility that respondents are dissembling, or reporting socially approved motivations and procedures, or exer-cising tacit skills that they cannot explicate effectively. These points are familiar and accepted in social science research, and for that matter are widely relevant in everyday life. What is distinctive about the response often encountered from economists is its extreme and unqualified nature. Instead of being the beginning of a discussion of how likely it actually is, given the actual context, that the results are tainted in these ways, it tends to be offered as the end of the discussion—both for the present and the foreseeable future.

The methodological issues surrounding profit maximization have rough paral-lels in other sciences. The case of the neutrino is a classic of the type. When originally proposed, the new particle appeared to be nothing more than an *ex post* adjustment to prevailing physical theory to protect it from apparently disconfirm-ing observations. Even the proposer, Wolfgang Pauli, referred to the proposal as a "desperate expedient." As a patch to the theory, the neutrino seemed to have the disturbing property that it was apparently impossible to check its validity, since the assumed properties of zero mass and zero charge posed a major obstacle to

---

[3] Friedman did not use the terminology of "tacit skill," but it seems fully appropriate in retrospect.

[4] For a recent example, see Truman Bewley's discussion of these attitudes, which he encountered in connection with his interview-based study of why firms don't cut wages in recession (Bewley, 1999: esp. 8–16). More generally, see also Schwartz (1998).

observation. Thus, paralleling the case of "as if" profit maximization, the proposed patch was put forward in a context of cogent reasoning as to why it was impossible to check on its validity. Physicists and philosophers debated the legitimacy of the neutrino patch for some decades—after which the question faded, as first indirect and then relatively direct confirming evidence was developed.

Closer to home (i.e., management theory), a similar dispute exists concerning concepts of "legitimation" and "legitimacy" in organizational ecology. Given the unquestioned success in accumulating a mass of indirect statistical evidence (said to be) indicative of a significant role for legitimacy in the evolution of organizational populations, is it reasonable to ask for new kinds of measurements that would go more directly to the concept of legitimacy as that concept is understood in sociology, or even more broadly? Perhaps, but perhaps not. (See (Hannan and Carroll, 1995), accusing critics (Baum and Powell, 1995) of "cheap talk.")

When a mechanism or entity featured in a theory is declared "off limits" to observation, suspicions generally arise that this declaration might be nothing more than a convenient device to protect against some unwelcome observations that might be considered threatening to the theory. Such devices are objectionable on the ground that continuing recourse to them would ultimately deprive the theory of all empirical content, turning it into a mere tautology. There are also, however, reasonable grounds for tolerating the use of such *ad hoc* and *ex post* adjustments, at least on an occasional and temporary basis. First, given that theories typically have nothing very sharp to say about the appropriate steps for making them operational, it is clear that any *specific* method of observation generally lacks a clear, theoretically grounded claim to appropriateness. Apparent trouble for the theory could therefore represent nothing more than an empirical technique that is flawed in the sense (at least) that it is not precisely what the theory requires. Second, it is hardly plausible to suggest that a useful and broadly accurate theory should be abandoned merely because it conflicts with some particular observations, especially if no viable alternative theory is available at the moment. The second point is plainly supported by the first; it would be particularly short-sighted to let a useful theory fall victim to bad or irrelevant observations. Friedman's essay involves both of these general points. His argument, however, seems to go far beyond objecting to the relevance of some actual observations of firm decision making, and perhaps extends even to the extreme claim that no *conceivable* direct observations of firm decision making could legitimately cast doubt on the maximization hypothesis.

The deep issues involved here have long received great attention in the philosophy of science (consider, for example, Popper, 1959; Kuhn, 1970; Quine, 1961; Lakatos, 1970). In the substantial economics literature on these matters, much of the discussion has focused on the Friedman essay specifically—and has had the peculiar feature of making little reference to the broader discussion while at the same time making considerable use of examples from physical theory. The particularly valuable contributions, in my view, include Massey (1965) and Blaug

(1980). My own comments on the methodological issues have largely been incidental to discussion of the theory of the firm (see in particular Winter, 1964*a*, 1975, 1986*a*, 1986*b*, 1987). It is not my purpose here to further explore the general methodological questions.

In the interest of clarity, however, I should declare where I stand on the specific issue of profit maximization. It does seem clear to me that the idea of "as if" maximization, along with its associated constellation of highly skeptical attitudes regarding the value of direct observation, is basically a defensive maneuver that serves to protect a seriously flawed theory. In my view, the theory thus defended is not actually supported by any compelling evidence—although, as I discuss below, understanding why the allegedly supporting evidence is not probative does require a careful parsing of the issues at stake. Since business decisions are manifestly a key part of the functioning of the economic system, the strong disciplinary commitment to analyzing them on the basis of mistaken theoretical premises is a large obstacle to scientific progress. This assessment of mine is hardly idiosyncratic. It is widely shared among social scientists and business people, whose work often leads them much closer to business decision making than most academic economists ever get.[5] Like many of these other observers from outside of mainstream economics, I seem to encounter evidence of the negative consequences quite frequently.

The parsing of the issues begins with considering the relevance of the mass of statistical evidence that supports the qualitative predictions of standard economic theory—"supply curves are upward sloping" is the prototype here. This sort of evidence does not actually discriminate between the profit maximization hypothesis and plausible alternative behaviors. Indeed, this in a sense was Friedman's point—some things do indeed happen "as if" there were profit maximization, thereby producing a spurious impression of true maximization at work. Not all things happen that way, however. Empirical discrimination between (true, causally fundamental) maximization and the alternatives is generally quite possible, with details depending on the precise formulations that we are talking about on both sides. (Of course, the really obvious opportunity for such discrimination lies in—direct observation of decision making!) The second key point is to recognize that the dispute is not about the motivational claim that business firms and individuals are often, or generally, "trying to make money." That claim has, by itself, no

---

[5] Criticism of the profit maximization assumption, or of rational choice models more broadly, is a perennial feature of economic discourse. Since I began my own engagement with these issues, particularly influential academic criticism has come from psychologists such as Amos Tversky, Daniel Kahneman, Paul Slovic, George Lowenstein, and Robyn Dawes. Among economists who have taken some part of the criticism seriously (although not identifying fully with the evolutionary view), prominent names include George Akerlof, John Conlisk, Richard Day, David Laibson, Roy Radner, Robert Shiller, and Richard Thaler. The rationality of *organizational* behavior has received little attention from these authors, however. Most of the attention has gone to individual behavior, or to market phenomena that directly reflect it. Schwartz (1998) is a useful and wide-ranging survey of the literature.

empirical content. If, for example, this "trying" is afflicted with a lot of randomness and erratic adherence to superstitious belief (as Friedman also suggested), the logic by which the usual qualitative predictions might somehow follow has not been adduced. Acknowledging that other motivations might also be at work will generally make this impasse worse.

The point that requires emphasis here is that the characteristic predictions of mainstream theory are not the implications of the motivational assumption alone, but of that assumption plus constant constraints (opportunity sets) plus true maximization—the actors consistently get it right! That last is the claim that is centrally at issue.[6]

To conclude the parsing, I note that critics like myself do not have to burden ourselves with the extreme claim that nothing resembling true maximization is ever found in business behavior. Due partly to the normative role of standard economics, but probably more to the practical value of operations research, that claim is far from correct. There is some tendency for real actors to enact the theories that economists have about them, or at least to try to. A complete picture has to include this piece, and evolutionary economics does include it. The contextual factors that favor the appearance of these pockets of "true maximization" are an interesting object of study. One key practical consideration obviously plays a major role in setting a favorable context: the data required for a systematic comparison of alternative policies are actually available. Beyond that, it does not seem that the context is typically ruled by narrowly economic considerations. As a result, such studies require the tools of sociology as much as those of economics (see, e.g., Beunza and Stark, 2004).

If it were possible to address the economics of the firm and industry in a way that avoided fundamental commitment to fictions about decision making, would that be desirable? The discussion above only sketches some of the relevant points. It suggests, contrary to Friedman's classic argument, that the answer should be in the affirmative. But is it in fact possible? Somewhat paradoxically, Friedman's case for "as if" maximization contains key elements of a program that dispenses with maximization (as a *fundamental* postulate) altogether.[7] Those elements, however, are plainly insufficient to define the needed program. A commitment to greater "realism" clearly entails a more substantial concern with characterizing reality. But, what is that reality?

---

[6] The theory of rational choice says that actors do not make *ex ante* mistakes, but it can readily acknowledge the reality of *ex post* mistakes. To fend off a reply along this line, we have to begin by accepting one point about "they always get it right": it does depend what you mean by "it." Addressing this qualification in a careful way makes the necessary argument longer, but does not basically change the conclusion: to the extent that the theory has predictive content, its predictions derive in crucial part from the assumption that the actors get it right.

[7] Displacing maximization from the foundations of the theory does not mean discarding it entirely from the theoretical tool box. Some discussion of Friedman, featuring the term "instrumentalism," essentially frames the dispute as being about the tool box, not the theory (see Boland, 1979) In my

24.3 FROM THE "FRIEDMAN CONJECTURE" TO THE "CARNEGIE SCHOOL"

24.3.1 Defining the Stakes

Neither in management nor in public policy analysis is there real interest in discussing whether business decisions deviate *by minor amounts* from norms of perfection, such as those that theoretical economics conventionally offers. Also, in neither of those scholarly communities could you round up a patient audience for an argument that the important deficiencies in decision making are primarily attributable to *a widespread deficiency of myopic greed*. Rather, there is a broad consensus that levels of myopic greed tend to be on the high side—assuredly from the public policy viewpoint, but, in many cases, even from the viewpoint of the long-term self-interest of the actor. Combining these two observations, we reach a conclusion that can be expressed in terms of the familiar "money left on the table" metaphor: it is not small change that we are talking about here, and evidently the real money must be hidden under the tablecloth or somewhere. For, at least in the historical and cultural circumstances of advanced economies today, we simply do not put much credence in the suggestion that serious money is sitting there unclaimed on the table, in full view. Consequential decision making failures involve substantial stakes, and a satisfying explanation for such failures includes an account of the sources of flawed perception on the part of decision makers—not an assumption of willful indifference to large stakes.

The practical questions thus delimited are, unfortunately, difficult ones. In particular, an adequate assessment of what might be obscuring the decision makers' view (playing the role of the tablecloth) would have to take into account a wide range of considerations that have been identified and discussed in social science literature, from individual-level cognitive limitations through social pressures in groups to system-level coordination issues. These various failure mechanisms fall within the domains of different social science disciplines, and also cut across them. In short, the practical questions do not constitute practical objectives for research, at least in any direct, near-term sense. More limited objectives are needed, ones that can be pursued via identifiable research approaches.

---

view, a theory involves commitments about the nature of reality that go beyond specific considerations of instrumental effectiveness. A good "engineering approximation" (for a particular context) may be a very poor theory (in general). (See Friedman, 1953: 17–19 on how bodies fall "as if" in a vacuum.) A good theory suggests useful advice about engineering approximations, and a good theory of the firm would illuminate when profit maximization is a reasonable working assumption and when not.

24.3.2 The Friedman Conjecture

Theoretical analysis of the Friedman conjecture is one such approach. Essentially, the question is whether money will be left on the table in the long run if it is being pursued by profit-seeking firms with plausible, though typically not optimal, policies. In its basic form, such analysis first posits a situation in which it is logically possible for business firms to get the right answers to their decision problems, for at least there *is* a right answer. (Without this very substantial assumption, the Friedman conjecture is dead on arrival as a matter of strict logic.) The second constituent of the analysis is some postulated set of possible behavior patterns for firms, such that at least some of these patterns are not comprehensively optimal. That is, contrary to the standard assumptions of economics, not all firms are necessarily getting the right answer all the time. (Without this assumption, the conclusion "firms maximize profits" is the trivial result of the familiar postulate, requiring no evolutionary logic or process to establish it.) The final constituent is a characterization of the dynamic process by which firms interact competitively, determining their survival and growth. With the details of a hypothetical context thus specified, the problem of such analysis is to characterize how the dynamic process turns out, and whether this outcome is consistent with Friedman's conjecture of "as if" profit maximization.

To consider a simple example,[8] suppose all firms in an industry base their capacity investment decisions on a firm-specific, aspiration-level rate of return that (for some firms at least) is higher than the market cost of capital they all face. This behavior does not automatically align with maximization of profit (or, here, net present value), since it can imply leaving money on the table in the form of positive NPV investments that are passed up. To this modestly non-standard behavioral assumption add the standard ingredients of an economic model of a competitive industry, and let the situation unfold over time. If firms are otherwise identical, this situation is essentially a long-run competition in which the lowest aspiration-level rate of return wins.

This outcome scores as a partial victory for the Friedman conjecture, in the sense that the industry-level outcome is the standard long run competitive outcome provided *some* firms aspire only to cover the cost of capital.[9] The assumption "all firms maximize profits" has thus been effectively weakened to "some firms maximize profit," and the remainder of the work has been done by the evolutionary process, producing an outcome "as if all firms maximize profits." It is only a *partial*

[8] Even this example is not as simple as it is here pretended to be, for the sake of brevity. (For more painstaking discussion of this kind of exercise see Winter, 1964a, 1971, 1987, 1990; Hodgson, 1994; Nelson and Winter 1982a: ch. 6.)

[9] There is a cluster of complications here around the issue of whether firms act strictly as "price-takers" or can perceive their market power and act accordingly. Allowing for these does not change the moral of the story any, so I ignore them and rely on the standard logic of competition.

victory because, first, we do need the "some firms" assumption. Without it the same model can just as well illustrate the point that the evolutionary process may deliver non-standard outcomes. Second, it is a *long-run* outcome; it takes time for evolution to do its work. This raises the question: suppose exogenous change occurs intermittently, do we have to wait for a new evolutionary process to do its work every time the game is changed? Or is there basically only one competition in spite of the changes? In this model there is only one, but this is not a general result.[10] Finally, there is a crucial, understated assumption of *stability* implicit in the behavior patterns assumed. The aspiration-level rate-of-return is a durable "quasi-genetic trait."

The example just discussed illustrates the general flavor of the analysis that appeared in my early dissertation-based article (Winter, 1964a). Its focal concern is with the logic of the Friedman conjecture. It shows on the one hand that it is possible to spell out a logical basis that converts Friedman's intuition into a theorem. On the other hand, the "audit" provided by this explicit formal modeling points out considerations that limit the real significance of the result. While the considerations identified above are relevant to a broad range of such models, there are other important ones that are not in view because of the simplicity of the example—e.g., issues involving exit and entry processes, or the consequences of multi- rather than single-dimensional heterogeneity in the "genetic" attributes of firms, or the implications of search processes that modify those attributes over time. The latter considerations also interact with the former, creating a complex variety of specific situations and corresponding answers regarding the conjecture. Finally, there is the very important and general "rules vs. actions" problem. An evolutionary contest among firms whose actions are rule-based cannot test the optimality of the responses the rules offer in environments that never appear, or appear rarely, in the course of the contest. Hence, even a result that confirms the Friedman conjecture with respect to *actions* in the long run cannot possibly confirm it with respect to *rules* (Winter, 1964a).

What there is to be learned from this type of inquiry cannot be learned from studying any single model, and consists largely in a sharpened understanding of the range of relevant mechanisms and their interactions, plus an enhanced appreciation that the real import of the conclusions depends on quantitative aspects that the qualitative analysis suppresses.

As the above summary suggests, my early work on the Friedman conjecture did not involve a serious attempt to answer the question about the reality of firm decision making—beyond the clear reality of "not nearly as perfect as usually assumed in economics." The subsequent development of evolutionary economics

---

[10]   That is, given a common environment and firms that are all identical except in aspirations and scale (capacity), the growth rates of firms are always ranked inversely to the aspiration-level rates of return, regardless of what else may be affecting them in the common environment.

involved downplaying the Friedman conjecture as a focal issue and, instead, turning up the light on reality. Substantial illumination was drawn from several different sources, of which a key one was the behavioral theory of the firm.

24.3.3 Behavioralism

At the time, I was beginning my dissertation research, the "Carnegie School" was reaching an advanced stage of development in Pittsburgh. Herbert Simon's famous article on satisficing, "A Behavioral Model of Rational Choice," had appeared in 1955 (Simon, 1955), and I had had the good fortune to encounter it in graduate school.[11] The classic *Organizations* volume by Simon and James March appeared in 1958 (March and Simon, 1958). Much of the research that in 1963 appeared as the Richard Cyert and James March book, *A Behavioral Theory of the Firm* (Cyert and March, 1963), was under way and was beginning to appear in working paper form. What the Carnegie scholars had to say about firm behavior was partly familiar, being in some ways parallel to what had been said earlier by the economists who criticized the orthodoxy in the theory of the firm. These were the very critics to whom Friedman responded in his essay, and I was well aware of their work. In retrospect, it may appear that even at that early stage there was an evident opportunity to use an evolutionary approach to build on and complement the "micro-foundations" of firm behavior contributed by the Carnegie School.

In fact, that did not happen—at the time. There was some cross-fertilization, and some sense of encouragement (at least in the Carnegie-to-Winter direction), but not much. The "behavioral theory of the firm" was not easy to absorb, especially in its unfinished form. It involved novel theory, novel research techniques (especially computer simulation) and novel-seeming blind spots (especially, an apparent indifference to the role of markets as understood by economists).

When the Cyert and March book appeared in 1963, I was invited to review it for the *American Economic Review* (Winter, 1964b). In the course of reading the book and preparing the review, I was able to see the Carnegie work as a *program* for the first time—and to see it as complementary to the evolutionary approach, as suggested above. My review noted that the authors seemed content to regard firm behavior as a significant scientific problem in its own right, and willing therefore to set aside the task of predicting market phenomena—and suggested that this should not be the permanent state of affairs:

---

[11] I doubt that Simon's article ever made an appearance on many reading lists for economics courses, and certainly not by 1957. But it was on the list for Jacob Marschak's seminar on Economics of Information and Organization, which I took at Yale in that year. Even the title of Marschak's seminar now seems quite remarkable, given the date.

Also, it is to be hoped that someone will eventually accept the challenge of attempting to provide a better definition of the relationship between the behavioral theory and the traditional theory than is provided by the assertion that the two theories are concerned with different problems....

... the consistency of the behavioral theory with the more persuasive portion of the *empirical evidence* for the traditional theory has yet to be determined. Investigation of the relationship between the two theories will probably involve closer attention to the circumstances that determine when the profit goal is evoked and when profit aspirations adjust upward, as well as to the ways in which competition may force an approach to profit maximization by firms whose decision processes are governed in the short run by crude rule-of-thumb decision rules. (Winter, 1964b: 147; emphasis in original)

Although it was not fully spelled out in my review, any more than in the book itself, I could see that the Cyert and March book suggested the possibility of a new division of scientific labor. Firm behavior could be regarded as a subject matter in its own right, which on the face of it appeared to involve aspects appropriately studied in psychology, sociology, organizational behavior, engineering, operations research, management, finance, accounting, marketing, and perhaps other disciplines as well, in addition to economics. The primary role of economics was not to strive for imperial control over these other intellectual domains, and certainly not to ignore them, but to point out the systemic and long-run implications of whatever firm-level truths might be brought forward, from whatever source. This role is especially suitable for economists insofar as those implications are largely the result of firms interacting through markets. At the same time, operations research and the business-oriented disciplines might reasonably concern themselves (at least in part) with how existing modes of business behavior might realistically be improved—and that, too, is not the central role of economics. This vision of the appropriate division of labor represents my present view.

Given this view of the general relationship of economics to business behavior, one can identify specific analytical tasks of the following kind. Take any empirical pattern of business behavior that has been identified and alleged to be a general phenomenon, and analyze its survival prospects in an evolutionary contest among similar firms. Such analysis begins by positing that the identified pattern is widespread, but acknowledging also that market discipline generally provides real constraint in the long run. The required analysis is particularly feasible and informative if the "identified pattern" involves some relatively simple rule-governed behavior. As previously noted, the claim that behavior often takes that form was a prominent part of the behavioralist position, and in fact the specific example of mark-up pricing behavior had been prominent in the whole controversy about profit maximization since before World War II (Hall and Hitch, 1939). Recall also that my own early work on corporate R&D spending involved the puzzle presented by precisely this sort of observation: the research-to-sales ratio functions as a decision rule. There was (and remains), a substantial backlog of such generalizations about behavior patterns to which the proposed type of analysis is relevant.

The task of such analysis is to determine whether, or under what conditions, the identified pattern can survive the constraints imposed by market discipline in the long run—especially if its practitioners are challenged by otherwise similar firms who behave, in this particular domain, according to plausible rules that are seemingly more "rational." It can happen that such an analysis yields the conclusion "under no conditions," i.e., that the behavior pattern is inevitably selected against in the long run. This implies either that the pattern is in fact a temporary aberration, or the pattern itself has been mis-characterized, or the force of market discipline has been overstated.

More often, the conclusions have a different tendency, suggesting that there are particular environments where the observed pattern might be viable. Consider the following general pattern, for which specific examples are easily found: firms are lavish in their use of input X; they essentially behave as if it were free. In an environment where input X is indeed (approximately) free, this behavior imposes a negligible burden. It cannot be competed out of existence by rivals who are more circumspect in the use of X, unless these rivals tend also to be otherwise advantaged. (What will happen if the price of X increases dramatically, so that its cost share is no longer trivial? The rules vs. actions problem arises here: is there an underlying behavioral rule connecting the use of X to its price? Evolutionary processes do not guarantee that.)

If being "more circumspect" itself entails a modest cost, these rivals may in fact be *dis*advantaged—providing an instance of the general proposition, "it doesn't pay to pay attention to things that don't matter." This proposition provides a ready interpretation of much behavior that appears, in the logic of its *form*, to defy considerations of efficiency or cost (e.g., leaving the office supplies cabinet unlocked). It redirects attention to the substantive consequences—particularly those bearing on organizational growth and survival.

Thus, the work at Carnegie provided important support for the notion that parts of business behavior are based on simple rules. This provided some specific fodder for theoretical analysis in the evolutionary style, somewhat paralleling the logical analysis of the Friedman conjecture but having a more explicit grounding in behavioral reality. More importantly, it also underscored the point that a firm-level, empirically-based component of the theory was needed to complement the predominantly long-run, system-level insights of the evolutionary approach. Indeed, such a component was not only needed, but at least to some extent the Carnegie work had made it available. "Simple rules" were, of course, only part of the Carnegie story. For example, the concepts of "problemistic search" and "quasi-resolution of conflict" effected permanent changes in the lenses through which I, and many others, viewed business behavior. Above all, the concept of satisficing behavior became a tool of pervasive relevance to evolutionary thinking about organizations.

Simon's development of satisficing placed the concept in the context of costly search of some set of potential problem solutions. It was quite clear that the problems he had in mind were the sorts of problems that economists typically considered, and analyzed with the familiar tools of mathematical optimization. Satisficing was a theory of bounded rationality, put forward as a contrast with full optimization. As Simon subsequently explained, it was a theory about searching a haystack for "a needle sharp enough to sew with (satisficing)" as opposed to "the sharpest needle in the haystack (optimization)" (Simon, 1987: 244). Considerations of cost and feasibility decree that search should stop before the true optimum is found.[12] In the appendix to the 1955 article, Simon supported this view by establishing it as the conclusion of a meta-level optimization of the search process itself.[13]

As adapted to evolutionary thinking about organizations, satisficing is not so much about stopping search as about starting it. Also, it is not so much about finding a "solution" that can be definitively scored according to some criterion, but about finding a way of doing things that at least promises to be superior to an existing way that is perceived to be inadequate (results are below aspiration). This evolutionary twist on satisficing joins it to the concept of problemistic search— search motivated by the appearance of a problem, and conducted in a way that is in some sense local to the problem.[14]

Thus adapted, the satisficing concept suggests that the power of economic evolution is enhanced by powerful mechanism that is notably lacking in biological evolution: a source of endogenous control on the mutation rate. When things are going well, satisficing favors behavioral stability. When they are going poorly, the satisficing trigger produces search for superior alternatives. The specific consequences of this asymmetric search propensity depend on how "well" and "poorly" are defined by the aspiration level adjustment mechanism, on the way the competitive context affects aspirations, on the nature of the space that is searched, and on the quality of the test that determines whether the status quo is rejected in favor of a newly identified alternative. In general, however, satisficing produces a powerful net force for "improvement" in an absolute sense—upward motion on the same scale on which aspiration level floats as a moving target. It does so even if the search itself is totally uninformed as to which alternatives deserve examination. To appreciate the potential economic significance of this idea, think of that scale as labeled "productivity."

---

[12] One can only marvel at the "pointedness" of Simon's little example: the legendary quasi-impossibility of finding a needle in a haystack, the manifest idiocy of continuing such a difficult search once "a needle sharp enough to sew with" is found.

[13] In my view, the appendix muddled the message of a great paper in an unfortunate way. It did accurately reflect an important fact about Simon: he was a rationalist. In this sense, the appendix was a characteristic move, having a certain "boundedly, yet more rational than thou" aspect to it.

[14] Similar "twists" have been made by others (see Winter (2000) for discussion).

I pursued this line of thinking in my 1971 paper, "Satisficing, Selection and the Innovating Remnant" (Winter, 1971). The paper built explicitly on the portrayal of business behavior in the Cyert and March volume, invoked satisficing in the manner just described, and proposed innovative entry and the stick of competition as the mechanisms that tended to drive firms below their aspiration levels whenever their achievements could somehow be improved upon. These elements were built into a mathematical model that was structured as a Markov process in a set of "industry states"—a scheme that has many advantages and that was employed in much subsequent work.

Unfortunately, I made a serious strategic blunder: the featured result of the paper was a new proof of the Friedman conjecture. I somehow imagined that this result, with its required stringent assumptions out in the open and (to my mind) virtually begging to be rejected, might provide a bridge that cautious researchers could use to cross from mainstream economics to an evolutionary vantage point. I tried to facilitate this in a later section of the paper, by using the same basic apparatus to sketch a model of continuing progressive change, in a Schumpeterian spirit. The ploy didn't work; most economist readers seem instead to have taken comfort in the fact that the Friedman conjecture could actually be proved. My hopes were naive, and they were not realized. I should have known better. Certainly, I was by that time well aware that assessing the Friedman conjecture was not where the real promise of evolutionary thinking lay. There were more important questions to address.

24.4 TECHNOLOGY AND ECONOMIC GROWTH

At the end of 1959, I joined the staff of the RAND Corporation. This was a good move from several points of view, but particularly because it made me Dick Nelson's colleague. At that stage, I had done considerable work on my new, theoretical dissertation focused on the Friedman conjecture. It was far from complete, however. At RAND, I had the benefit of Dick's remarkable intellectual enthusiasm and high-quality feedback (for which, after a few decades of this sort of thing, a multitude of scholars are in his debt). Over the ensuing nine years, we shared a total of about four years at RAND in two different episodes, and were also together for a brief period in Washington, on the staff of the Council of Economic Advisers. Only in a rather modest fraction of that total time were we doing things that turned out to contribute significantly to the development of evolutionary economics. What we did do counted for a lot. By the end of that period, and largely due to Dick's influence, the questions at the top of the agenda for evolutionary economics had to do with the sources of economic progress, at the level of firms, industries, and national economies.

When I arrived at RAND, Dick had been involved for some time with the research program on R&D management and technological change, centered in the economics department and headed by Burton Klein. He had published a classic paper on "The Simple Economics of Basic Scientific Research" (Nelson, 1959b), and a valuable survey article on the economics of invention (Nelson, 1959a), and had conducted a penetrating case study of the invention of the transistor (ultimately published as (Nelson, 1962)). These interests in technology were joined to an existing and more basic interest in the causes of long-term economic growth. His dissertation (published as (Nelson, 1956) dealt theoretically with how overpopulation can bar the appearance of cumulative economic growth (in the sense of rising real incomes per capita).

In Dick's view (then and now), technological advance has been the key driving force of economic growth. The advance of technology, however, involves interaction with other mechanisms and domains—among them the advance of scientific knowledge, capital accumulation, processes of market competition, and the development of institutions for education and research. For the most part, these processes have played out over the past few centuries within the broad historical frame of "capitalism"—by which is meant, not the pure market economy of the economics textbooks, but the much more complex and diverse institutional phenomenon seen in modern history, complete with kings, presidents, congressional committees, military establishments, wars, academies, bureaucracies, pressure groups, pension systems, government-funded think tanks, and so on.

This is not a particularly radical perspective. The number of people who would accept it, at least as a plausible first approximation, is undoubtedly much larger than the number who have let the research priorities of an entire career be governed by a determination to illuminate these issues. Dick Nelson is in the latter camp; he has followed such a path. To do that requires a great dedication to the proposition that economic growth is centrally important to the human enterprise, the insight and flexibility to keep locating each season's main chance for improved understanding, and the determination to pursue that main chance wherever it leads—even if it leads across disciplinary boundaries that others are disposed to regard as sacrosanct.

24.4.1 Decisions in unfamiliar contexts

Under Burt Klein's leadership, Dick and others in the RAND group probed deeply into the decision making that went on in the course of R&D activities (or "invention").[15] Such inquiry reveals quite a different face of the problems of rational choice than is presented in the familiar arenas of the "profit maximization" discussion, such as the pricing of goods for retail sale. In the R&D context, there is a very real possibility that currently unimagined alternatives will appear down the road. In fact, this possibility is recognized and hoped for (impasse will yield to "Aha!"), deliberately sought (e.g., "brainstorming") and sometimes feared ("all this work will be for nothing"). Knightian uncertainty prevails; objective probabilities are not known. While rational choice theories direct the individual actor toward the use of subjective probabilities in such circumstances, there are actually many relevant actors, and the subjective probabilities are often a highly contentious subject for them. "Contentious" tends to mean that opinions correlate mysteriously with perceived interests and also with background experience, and that "political" influence processes of some kind will be a factor in the resolution. All alternatives, whether foreseen in general terms or not, get fully spelled out only in the course of a lengthy sequential design process. Uncertainty about how the next attempted stage will play out therefore tends to forestall effective planning and preparation for later stages—and also makes the current evaluation of future promise more problematic. Only by going forward is it possible to learn what the options are for going further forward. Throughout this design process, there is a dialectical dance between "feasibility" and "desirability," such that proximate objectives co-evolve with the technical achievements.

With respect to these features, R&D management presents particularly vivid examples of the general problems of making decisions in a highly unfamiliar context. A lot of the key things that happen in the course of an R&D project are happening for the first time ever. The *ex ante* uncertainty about such things does not relate just to *whether they will happen*, it relates to *what they are*—because they haven't been seen before.

The notion that actors can optimize their behavior is in a different kind of trouble in such unfamiliar situations than it is in familiar ones, and it is worse trouble. This trouble is not a matter of motivation, or of calculating ability, or of training in decision analysis. It is about whether a set of decision alternatives can reasonably be said to exist at all. After all, the essence of optimization is a thorough surveying of a set of alternatives, accompanied by consistent application of decision criteria. In the probing of an unfamiliar context, the typical situation is that the only alternatives actually available for surveying are a collection of first steps in various divergent directions. The further steps are largely hidden, and so are the reachable end states, or outcomes, and the steps in between. Whether a situation of this type can be satisfactorily represented by some formal theory of rational choice is not really the point, though I personally am skeptical. The real

---

[15] While most of the work of the others had to do with military R&D, Dick addressed broader issues in the economics of technological change, as suggested by the list of publications above.

point is that it is very difficult to imagine that such a theory could be given any empirical traction, for either descriptive or prescriptive purposes. This is because so few of the facts that matter are available *ex ante* to guide decisions; they emerge as the *product* of decisions.

I was not quick to absorb the research implications of this. Perhaps because I still hadn't fully shed that portion of my training as an economist, I was still disposed to rely on a scale anchored by a notional "right answer" when thinking about decision making and its possible shortcomings. This is often helpful, but it is sometimes a digression, or even a form of procrastination. (One of the points the RAND group made about the conduct of military R&D was that there was a tendency for planning to drive out doing, for discussions of feasibility to pre-empt the testing of feasibility (Klein, 1962).) The less familiar the context, the more rapid and fundamental the change that is going on, the less helpful it is to get hung up in the quest for the right answer. Through exposure to the work of the RAND group, and particularly through interactions with Dick, I gradually came to understand and accept this viewpoint. I also came to understand that behind the leadership of Burt Klein one could discern the shadow of another leader, now departed from the scene. That was Joseph Schumpeter, who had said rather similar things many years before.

Carrying out a new plan and acting according to a customary one are things as different as making a road and walking along it. (Schumpeter, 1934: 85)

Also,

The assumption that conduct is prompt and rational is in all cases a fiction. But it proves to be sufficiently near to reality, *if things have had time to hammer logic into men.* Where this has happened, and within the limits in which it has happened, one may rest content with this fiction and build theories upon it...Outside of these limits our fiction loses its closeness to reality.... To cling to it there also...is to hide an essential thing...(Schumpeter, 1934: 80, emphasis added)

Klein had been a student of Schumpeter at Harvard.

24.4.2 Innovative Competition

Schumpeter's fame derives from his emphasis on innovation as the driving force of capitalist development. More broadly, he stands out among the great economic thinkers because his theoretical approach to capitalism was fundamentally historical—it is a *theory of economic change*, as experienced historically. At RAND, Dick Nelson and I became increasingly aware that we were following Schumpeter's path, and increasingly appreciative of how valuable the master's guidance actually was. He seemed to have a lot of the big things right, though he fortunately left a lot for others to do, and at least a few things for others to straighten out. As the outlines of our joint research program began to emerge at the end of the 1960s, the term "neo-Schumpeterian" came to be one of the ways we described it.

Although most of Schumpeter's ideas had been largely forgotten in mainstream economics, there was one area where his ideas—or at least an idea named for him—continued to guide research. The question was, what structural conditions are favorable to strong innovative performance in an industry? A possible answer to that was dubbed the "Schumpeterian hypothesis." In its simplest form, the answer offered was, "oligopoly, relatively tight oligopoly." That is, innovative performance is enhanced when a small number of large firms are vigorously competing with each other in the domain of new process and (particularly) product development, even while likely sustaining a mutually supportive relationship in the domain of price competition. Schumpeter's name was attached to this hypothesis because it was claimed to be the main message of a few pages in his *Capitalism, Socialism and Democracy* (Schumpeter, 1950). There are some eloquent words in that passage, including the following very pointed ones:

The introduction of new methods of production and new commodities is hardly conceivable with perfect—and perfectly prompt—competition from the start. (Schumpeter, 1950: 105)

He meant, presumably, the costs of the innovation can never be recovered under those perfectly competitive conditions. That by itself is an important, and valid, comment about the theoretical "ideal" of perfect competition. The passage as a whole is, however, quite complex, evoking a number of different considerations. Whether it is reasonable to say that it all adds up to "the Schumpeterian hypothesis," as known in the literature, is far from clear.

In any case, the industrial organization literature that explored the hypothesis empirically was not very well disciplined, either with respect to theoretical grounding or (in many cases) econometric technique. Nelson and I set out to do something about the theoretical grounding, based on conversations between us going back to the RAND days. We produced three papers, which ultimately were the basis of the section of our book titled "Schumpeterian Competition." Our approach combined many of the elements identified above. In retrospect, when one considers all the "heresy" that was explicit or implicit in our approach, it is remarkable and also reassuring that we did manage to place the key paper in the *American Economic Review* (Nelson and Winter, 1982*b*).

We found a number of interesting things. Perhaps most interesting, we discovered quite unexpectedly the phenomenon known informally as "the monster imitator." While Schumpeter's remarks about informational scale economies favoring innovation were on target, he failed to point out that the same economies favor the large, technically competent imitator. Such a firm avoids the cost burdens of innovation and simply gobbles up what innovators elsewhere have made available. That behavior shifts the innovation incentives adversely for other firms, and can be very destructive to the industry's innovation performance.

This result suggested the importance of taking a second, long look at any dominant firm that touts itself as a fountain of innovation. In the time of the paper, the plausible target for that long look was IBM. Today, it would probably be Microsoft. The question is, are these firms really the fountains of innovation they claim to be? Or is it their actual virtue that they quickly make the innovations of others widely available, while at the same time depressing the incentives for further innovation?

24.5 From Skills to Routines and Capabilities

24.5.1 The Limitations of Production Theory

An economist who takes a close look at production activity and its supporting technologies is likely to suffer a form of dissonance quite akin to the effects of a close look at business decision making. The fundamental constructs used to describe technological possibilities in mainstream theory, the production function or production set, do not seem to be much in evidence. To be sure, there are inputs and outputs, and "ways of doing things" that convert the former into the latter. Also, contrary to some heterodox arguments that have at times been advanced in economics, there is often a lot of flexibility in these ways of doing things, and this flexibility is sometimes used to respond to changing prices. This degree of correspondence to reality is not, however, enough to support the validity of the familiar constructs—any more than "firms try to make money" is enough to support the theoretical reliance on true profit maximization. The commitments of mainstream production theory go well beyond the realistic points noted; they envisage a set of alternative methods, all equally available, that can be comprehensively surveyed for the best ones, and that stays constant long enough so that multiple choices from the same set can be scrutinized for their mutual consistency. If there is real predictive power in this theory, it derives crucially from this constellation of assumptions. Needless to say, the close parallels between these remarks and the corresponding ones about maximization are no accident. The elements are intertwined in the mainstream theory of the firm, and evolutionary economists argue that they are even more intertwined in reality.

There is to my knowledge no paper about the "as if" theory of production that parallels Friedman on profit maximization,[16] but there certainly could be. A world without production functions can mimic a world with true production functions at its causal foundations. One of the first major accomplishments of the Nelson–Winter collaboration was to illustrate this point with respect to the analysis of aggregate data on U.S. economic growth (Nelson and Winter, 1973, 1974; Nelson, Winter, and Schuette, 1976). This type of analysis can be extended in several directions; we sketched the mathematical framework of one such extension in our book (Nelson and Winter, 1982a: 175–184). While it may well be true that some econometricians have managed to estimate true short-run production functions, we would argue that most of the econometric work on production (especially long-run production functions) is more likely capturing the effects of mechanisms that merely mimic the real thing.

What is it that distinguishes the "as if" mimics from the real thing? In general, we proposed that statistical analysis based on data from a large number of firms, or aggregate data, tends to misinterpret the variation in the data in a way that considerably overstates the flexibility of production at the firm level. In our models, a key feature is that firms always have a "status quo" technique (or set of routines). While they can change that technique, the effective opportunities for doing so are much less rich than the amount of cross-sectional variation would suggest. We believe that this is true in reality as well as in our models. The inflexibility reflects the fact that firms are committed to their ways of doing things in ways that are hard to capture fully in standard economic data, and for reasons that are not reflected in the standard economic analysis of choice of technique. In evolutionary theory, those reasons are a prominent part of the story, as I now discuss.

24.5.2 Probing Productive Knowledge

Our conversations in the mid-1960s were much concerned with trying to understand technology and production, the role of knowledge in these, and the ways in which all of this might be represented effectively for theoretical purposes. The "theoretical purposes" we had in mind did not, however, have to do with improving the static theory of production, or its econometric implementation. Rather, they had to do with the treatment of technological change, with how technology relates to scientific understanding and other forms of knowledge, and what considerations limit the extent to which methods can travel from firm to firm and nation to nation (see Nelson, 1968). At the time, the economics discipline was

---

[16] There is, however, an important article by McFadden, containing theorems that can usefully be read as explicating one form of "as if" production theory (McFadden, 1969).

fascinated by neoclassical growth theory, a body of thought in which the production function apparatus was sacrosanct. Technical change was central to the subject but was introduced in an abstract, analytically convenient way that kept the production function center stage, but thereby produced a picture that was very hard to connect to any specific technology or change process that one might study. We shared an interest both in getting a clear view of the limitations of the neoclassical approach and in trying to find a better path.

Without ever really defining this as a project in its own right, we had a number of conversations that involved trying to re-think the whole problem at a very micro level. This effort drew particularly on Dick's broad understanding of technology, but it also involved a lot of discussion of a class of examples that were more micro and much more accessible than the ones encountered in prior research: cake recipes. This somewhat whimsical line of inquiry rested on the serious premise that, at the level of abstraction we were trying for, one account of a way of doing something is pretty much like another.[17] We might as well think about one that was easy to understand. More accurately, it *seemed* to be easy to understand. It turned out that there is a great deal to understand, and some part of that total problem remains at the top of my research agenda today.

There was one thing that came to light very quickly, however: there is an important contrast between a cake recipe and a cake production function. The former is actually useful in baking a cake, while the latter is not—though it would be useful for the preparatory shopping trip, where you acquire the needed inputs. This can be turned into a puzzle about economic theory. How is it possible to get along with a characterization of the knowledge used in production that leaves out the crucial procedural knowledge from the recipe and deals only in the list of ingredients?[18] This, on reflection, is quite possible provided (1) only input and outflows are considered interesting, not methods, (2) the set of possible input-output flows is given and constant. Under those assumptions, the "interesting" behavior of a cost-minimizing baker is predictable, given the appropriate price list.

Assumption (1) provides a disputable answer to another long-standing question about the scope of economics. But even if (1) is considered acceptable, taken by itself, assumption (2) imposes a crucial limitation on standard economic analysis. It cannot cope with change, because the baker's capacity to deal with a new recipe cannot be determined simply by examining the new list of ingredients. Rather, it is necessary to know something about the baker's command of productive *proced-ures*. (Note the connection to the statistical discussion above: ignoring the know-ledge-of-procedures constraint biases analysis in the direction of overstating

[17] The influence of this "cake paradigm" was seen in Nelson's published work at an early stage. (See Nelson, et al., 1967: 99–100.)

[18] There is side-exercise involved in expanding the list of ingredients of a typical recipe into an input list of the kind used in economic theory, but this is a minor technical point.

flexibility.) There is a moral to this little story that seemed compelling to us then and seems so now: if we're ever going to get serious about understanding technological change as a phenomenon of advancing knowledge, the production function has to go.[19]

The second major point that emerges is, the account of procedures given by a recipe relies on words. Words are not procedures. It is not the word "stir" that stirs the batter, nor the words "until smooth" that provides an effective smoothness test. If, therefore, you want to understand how these productive events actually happen, you need to look behind the words and ask how effective connections between the words and the procedures got created. At that point, you are suddenly and painfully deprived of the cheerful illusion that you were finally closing in on the knowledge aspect of this familiar productive activity. It turns out that you need, at a minimum, to know how language works, and how psychomotor skill works. These requirements present an overwhelmingly large and discouraging agenda. One might reasonably have concluded that the "cake paradigm" exercise, while stimulating, had reached a dead end.

24.5.3 Tacit knowledge

Somehow, the thinking of the chemist-philosopher Michael Polanyi came along to rescue us (Polanyi, 1964). I cannot entirely recall how that happened, and some of what I do recall ranges too far afield to include here. Let it just be said that we somewhat fortuitously stumbled into Polanyi's footsteps, just as we had previously stumbled into Schumpeter's. Perhaps surprisingly, those two paths are not that far apart.

Reading Polanyi made it clear that the difficulties we had encountered were on the one hand common ones, and on the other very deep philosophically. If you try to plumb the depths of human knowledge, and the sources of human commitment to beliefs, you will eventually run out of rope. Polanyi accepts this conclusion and takes it in a constructive direction, showing by example that understanding can move forward nevertheless. In Polanyi's famous phrase, "we know more than we can tell" (Polanyi 1966: 4). The term "tacit knowledge" labels this circumstance. Sometimes the knower's incapacities can be at least partly remedied by an external observer, as Polanyi's discussion illustrates. Often they cannot, if only because some of the parts that resist articulation involve mechanisms that are not well understood by contemporary science.

---

[19] It has to be discarded as a *fundamental commitment*, as the theory's single accepted way of characterizing technological possibilities, though of course it remains welcome as part of the tool kit.

What was most directly relevant in Polanyi's work was his analysis of skill, a large portion of which we imported directly into our own. Polanyi observes that the "aim of a skilled performance is achieved by the observance of a set of rules which are not known as such to the person following them" (Polanyi, 1964: 49). So much for trying to spell out the procedures that are involved in baking a cake; the skilled baker will likely not be able to tell us. (Again, it is sometimes the case that external observers can helpfully fill in things of which the knower/producer is unaware, but the scope of that is limited.) The depth to which a way of doing things can effectively be explicated is limited by the encounter with human skill. When the probe reaches that level, the inquiry is in deep trouble—for reasons that Polanyi explicates with great clarity.

Is "tacit knowledge" then, another name for "deep trouble"? Some critics argue that Polanyi labeled a problem but did not solve it. If the "problem" is to achieve ever-deeper understanding of a particular procedure, this observation is quite correct. However, Polanyi's discussion is radically more helpful than merely putting up a sign with "Road Closed" at the bottom of the canyon. His sign actually reads "Road Closed: DETOUR." In particular, one part of the detour goes toward the question of how tacit knowledge is created, and how it can be *transferred* or *reproduced* without being *articulated*. These things surely happen every day, and on a massive scale. Fortunately, what blocks the depth of our understanding does not block production, and that fact itself becomes the new target of understanding.

24.5.4 Routines and Capabilities

Reflect on some highly skilled performer that you have read about or perhaps personally observed—be it a gymnast, a pianist, a medical diagnostician, a scientist, or a CEO. Did you say to yourself, "What a beautiful example of the universal human capacity for mutually consistent decisions"? Did you say, "Isn't it remarkable what a boundedly rational individual can do by following a few simple rules"? Or did you perhaps say something like, "Awesome!"?

Skill provides a compelling model of effective behavior that is different, and deeply different, from what we are told either by theories of rational decision or by behavioral theories featuring "bounded rationality." As far as I can see, the latter theories do not lead one to expect that the word "awesome" will ever be needed to describe human behavior. The former leads you to expect the awesome powers of explicit calculation displayed by a supercomputer—but that (putting aside the illuminating exception of calculating prodigies) is one particular kind of awesomeness that human behavior rarely displays. Thus, these two very impressive intellectual camps both seem to be missing something quite important about human behavior—that it can indeed be awesome, but is rarely so in the supercomputer style.

At least in the case of psychomotor skills, like those of the gymnast and the pianist, it is quite clear that coordination is of the essence, a major part of what makes the performance impressive. The overall "production" has a lot of visible segments, which may be impressive in themselves, but the totality is particularly impressive because the segments flow together with such flawless coherence. Perhaps coordination is of the essence in the other cases too, but it is hidden from us.

Organizations, too, can be awesome. For example, the safety record of U.S. scheduled airlines is awesome. The achievement of high yields in a process as sensitive as semiconductor production is awesome. In these examples, the awesome performance is actually the joint product of a large number of organizations and, of course, the (skilled) individuals who comprise them. Again, it is clear that coordination is of the essence. To understand how knowledge shapes productive activity, you have to understand coordination above all. At the individual level, the kind of knowledge that underlies impressive coordinated performance goes by the name of skill, and it is the fruit of long practice, attended by much trial-and-error effort. What do you call that knowledge in organizations, and where does it come from? We chose to call it "organizational routines," and to attribute it broadly to the same source.

It is certainly not possible here to probe the limits and nuances of the notion of organizational routine. The phenomenon poses deep puzzles, as skill does, and besides that the substantial literature of the subject has taken the concept in different directions, which are not necessarily mutually consistent. The treatment in our 1982 book was itself less than consistent (see Cohen, et al., 1996; Hodgson, 2003).

I feature here the interpretation that is central to our book: "organizational routines are multi-person skills." To explain its origin, I point to the latent tension between the "Carnegie" discussion in Section 24.3 above and the subsequent discussion of technology. The problem is, it doesn't seem plausible that those Carnegie-type organizations could do the impressive things in the technological realm that organizations actually do accomplish—and accomplish through attendant impressive things in the realm of organization. This tension, which was a major concern from the start, we subsequently dubbed "the competence puzzle" (Nelson and Winter, 2002). How can organizations, with their numerous well-known flaws, display such extraordinary competence? To solve this puzzle, we drew on the skill model, with attendant insights from Polanyi, to modify the picture that the Carnegie school had bequeathed to us. The resulting picture is a good deal richer, and it admits the "awesome" aspects of organizational performance alongside the "simple rules" aspect, not to mention the "how could they be so stupid" aspect. These diverse aspects are effectively blended in the concept of routines as multi-person skills, as is beautifully explicated and, in a sense, proved in a key paper by Cohen and Bacdayan (1994).

There are low levels of skill as well as high ones, occasionally giving rise to laughably poor performances. The same is true for routines. Some organizational routines are more like bad habits than skills—but bad habits are a familiar type of imperfection in individual skills as well. For both skills and routines, there are subtle hazards of inflexibility associated with being too good at the wrong thing, being caught in a "competency trap." In both individuals and organizations, practiced skills and routines have to be complemented by deliberate but unpracticed adjustments. Individuals often do not improvise well, and there are good reasons to think that organizations might be distinctively worse in this respect. Organizations are in this sense more heavily dependent on their routines than individuals are on their skills.

Some have argued that the word "routine" has too many negative connotations, and that if we had wanted to "sell" our skill-like concept we should have chosen some other term for it. One answer to that is that we would thereby give up the nice catch-phrase "routines as genes," which concisely summarize the point that routines are, in our theory, a key source of the continuity in behavior that is required if "ways of doing things" are to be shaped by a truly evolutionary process. A more responsive answer is to point to the term *capabilities*. The original title of the Nelson and Winter book, carried by the draft we circulated for comment, was "An Evolutionary Theory of Economic Capabilities and Behavior." Prodded by the publisher, we agreed to a shorter title for the book. But "Organizational Capabilities and Behavior" did remain as the title of chapter 5, the "routines" chapter.[20]

Cake-making *capabilities* are what a bakery needs to make cakes. They combine knowledge, particularly in the form of individual skills and organizational routines, with the sorts of inputs recognized in the economic theory of production. Since many of those "inputs" participate in the storage and reproduction of the required knowledge, they are not really the same entities featured in standard economic theory. The knowledge we can identify in skills and routines cannot, however, be the whole story about the knowledge that makes cake production happen—because, as Polanyi explained, the "whole story" is forever beyond our reach.

24.5.5 Sources of Routines and Technologies

The discussion of routines in the 1982 book said quite a lot about what they were like and why they were important, but very little about where they came from. This

---

[20] We had used the term "capabilities" in the title of the first paper of our evolutionary collaboration (Nelson and Winter, 1973). As far as I recall, we were unaware at that time of the use of the term in the fine paper of Richardson (1972). Since the term was used in a similar sense in military circles, it may be that our RAND experience had something to do with it.

was not because the latter question was considered uninteresting. It was because we thought it would be very difficult to address it well, and we did not want to hold up the completion of the book while we made the attempt.

A good deal can now be said about this subject. On the theoretical front, much insight has been derived from work that joins the familiar idea that organizations engage in "local search" to a particular characterization of the space that is searched—a characterization provided by the "NK modeling" technique. As shown by Levinthal (Levinthal, 1997), this combination readily produces a picture that displays key elements of the picture needed in this foundational part of the theory. Here is just a part of that picture. In a population of new organizations occupying a common environment, you will see the development of systematic ways of doing things. Different organizations will generally develop *different* ways of doing things, because of the path dependence that arises from local search that has diverse starting points, and has random elements along the way. The amount of diversity that survives depends on the amount of interaction among policy dimensions, which determines the complexity of the overall problem and thereby determines the "ruggedness" of the landscape searched—the number of local peaks. Significant differences will persist, not merely in ways of doing things, but in performance (fitness).

Although this is all demonstrated at the level of abstract theoretical parable, it is evidently a very powerful parable. It conveys a vision of the key mechanisms that far transcends the particular mathematical form in which they are represented, and thereby suggests that there is probably a wide range of alternative approaches to the same substantive ends—now that we have the idea. For extensions and applications of this approach to management problems, see, for example, Gavetti and Levinthal (2000); Rivkin (2000, 2001); Rivkin and Siggelkow (2003).

There was more in the 1982 book about where technologies come from. Here the major conceptual point is that it is far from correct to think of new methods as arising from sources that are beyond the reach of economic incentives or are intrinsically very difficult to predict (e.g., creativity, basic science). While these characteristics are certainly present some of the time, it is reasonable to argue that these cases are the exception to the rule. The rule is that the new emerges from the old, and it does so in ways that are strongly patterned by economic incentives, by intrinsic features of the technologies themselves, and by the specific investments of business firms that are trying to make it happen.

In the book, we discussed a number of these patterning aspects. Following a lead provided by Rosenberg (1969), we emphasized particularly the phenomenon of "natural trajectories"—a sustained path of improvement in a technology that is generated by the repeated invocation of the same problem-solving approaches or "technological paradigm." The miniaturization trajectory in semiconductor devices is a particularly compelling and important example (see Dosi, 1982). The idea of a trajectory is closely related to the idea of "dynamic capabilities" in the strategic management literature (Teece, Pisano, and Shuen, 1997). For example, Intel's dynamic capabilities are the package of routines and resources that have allowed it, in particular, to pursue the miniaturization trajectory effectively. Among many other works that pursue various aspects of the phenomenon—the patterned way in which new technology emerges—see Malerba (1985), Levinthal (1998), and Murmann (2003); and for related discussion that places more emphasis on routines and organization than technology, see Winter and Szulanski (2001) and Zollo and Winter (2002).

24.6 A SAMPLING OF EMPIRICS

The range of empirical topics touched upon in the discussion to this point is so wide that it is clearly impossible to do more than mention a few significant examples. Under many important headings, we would acknowledge that there is a great dearth of empirical work that is directly relevant to the evolutionary economics program that Dick Nelson and I put forward. In large part this is because economists, especially American economists, have not been much interested in the propositions of evolutionary economics, whether for the purpose of developing theory, testing hypotheses or attempting refutation. Much of this missing work is of a kind that *should* be done by economists, either for reasons of characteristic skills or typical interests. Elsewhere—in both a geographical and a disciplinary sense—the situation tends to be much better.[21] As is discussed below, there are even areas where fortune has truly smiled, giving us supportive, interested colleagues in relevant areas where we did not provide much leadership.

There is one fundamentally important area where we would argue that empirical dearth vs. plenty may lie in the eye of the beholder—and we see plenty. This is the question of the general character of firm decision processes. Because of the peculiar cast given to the whole discussion by the influence of Friedman's methodological stance, it is unclear who is supposed to be persuading whom about what. Are we called upon to mount a case that our account of firm behavior is considerably more

---

[21] There is a formidable list of scholars who deserve mention and citation for their efforts to further the evolutionary program, or at least their willingness to take it seriously. They must be thanked collectively, for to actually give that recognition in this already-long paper, with its already-voluminous references, is quite impractical. Many of these people are found at the bi-annual meetings of the International J. A. Schumpeter society. For specific indications of the reception of the 1982 book see Freeman and Pavitt (2002), Dosi (2002), and Dosi, Malerba, and Teece (2003), the papers in those journal issues. See also the introductory essay in Giovanni Dosi's collected papers (Dosi, 2000).

realistic overall than the optimization model favored in mainstream economics? Such a case does not call for new empirical research, it calls for a gigantic survey article. That evidence has long been abundant, and more comes in every day[22]— but of course it doesn't come from mainstream economics.

The fact is, nobody has ever taken the stance that evolutionary economics is inferior to the mainstream brand in terms of its general conformity to the result of direct observation of business behavior. We take it, therefore, that virtually every-one agrees that we win that contest—which is hardly a surprise, since the need to win it was a key premise of our undertaking and a matter of indifference on the other side. If dramatic new facts about business behavior were to become firmly established, showing evident discord with our prevailing generalizations, would we fold the evolutionary tent and steal away? No, we would make the necessary adjustments and carry on. The premise is that it is the task of economics to *accommodate* the realities of behavior and determine the implications—not to commit to an econo-centric view of behavior that has to shelter itself from the facts that the rest of the scientific and practical world turns up.

The real question is whether economics can effectively be done in the style that we favor. It is in the worthy cause of doing economics effectively that the Friedman-influenced mainstream asserts its scientific right to hide from inconvenient facts (or, from their viewpoint, "irrelevant details"). We, on the contrary, argue that economics can be done effectively without such hiding, and have tried to illustrate the point. Of course, the discipline's territory is so vast that we can barely provide scattered hints relative to the total, and such hints need not be persuasive on the large point even if considered meritorious on small ones.

Somewhat narrower aspects of the evolutionary proposal present some of the same framing problems posed by the broad characterization of business decision making. Overall, there is abundant evidence, but only a small portion of it was produced with the evolutionary economics agenda directly in view. Here again it is often hard to be sure regarding who needs to be persuaded of what. For example, are organizational routines and capabilities features of reality; do they tend to be firm-specific in significant ways, and do they actually persist for extended periods? Many people do not need persuading, but anybody who does could consult, e.g. Usselman (1993), Helfat (1994a, 1994b), Klepper and Simons (2000a), plus the many empirical studies in, or cited in, Dosi, Nelson, and Winter (2000) and Helfat (2003). What about the proposition that durable firm attributes have a powerful shaping effect on the course of competition? If you doubt that, you should examine the "entrants vs. incumbents" literature (including, e.g., Tushman and Anderson, 1986; Henderson and Clark, 1990; Tripsas, 1997; Tripsas and Gavetti, 2000). What about the suggestions that organizational knowledge is not the transparent, trans-

---

[22] For some recent, quite striking evidence see Starbuck and Mezias (2003), and the papers, including mine, commenting thereon.

ferable, readily exploited asset that standard production theory pretends it to be? (See Kogut and Zander, 1992; Szulanski, 1996.)

There is one important subject that Nelson and I did not address explicitly in our book, and which is obviously of central importance in the evolutionary scheme. This is the subject of industry evolution—the evolutionary patterns that characterize the development of an industry or product market over time. The industry evolution perspective teaches lessons of great importance for economic policy, particularly the point that industry structure has to be understood in historical context. I belatedly turned to the theory of this subject in my 1984 paper (Winter, 1984). Already at that point, my article shows, the influence of Steven Klepper's empiricism was being felt—the paper that ultimately appeared as Klepper and Graddy (1990) was available to me in working paper form. Klepper's subsequent work (including among many others Klepper, 1996, 1997; Klepper and Simons, 2000a, 2000b; Klepper and Sleeper, 2000) has documented the pervasive patterns and greatly advanced theoretical understanding of them. Although Klepper's way of characterizing firm behavior in the short run leans in the orthodox direction, his dynamics are more in the evolutionary spirit. In any case, the empirical evidence he presents is both valuable and generally supportive. A great many scholars have done related empirical work. Meanwhile, the theory of industry evolution has been further addressed in an empirically grounded way with the methods of "history friendly" simulation (see Malerba, et al., 1999; Malerba, et al., 2001).

I conclude this sampler by addressing the linked topics of firm size and firm growth. These two present, respectively, an evident success of evolutionary theory and a currently significant refutation hazard.

A striking fact about the category "business firms" is the extraordinary magnitude of the size discrepancies among the examples in that category. A conservative statement about the magnitude of that discrepancy, top to down, would be a factor of about 100,000. At the high end, there are firms near the top of the Fortune 500, at annual sales above 10^{11} dollars. At the low end, the question arises as to what attributes are required for membership in the "firm" category—for example, does a business conducted by a single individual, part-time, from home qualify? To be very conservative about that point, I put the lower end at annual sales of 10^6 dollars; one obviously could argue for a much lower figure. This factor of 100,000 is a large number, an in-your-face feature of economic reality that might seem to call for explanation. What is there to say?[23]

Evolutionary theory says that it is the product of long-extended processes of cumulative growth (and consolidation). It says that most firms start quite small

---

[23] Our emphasis on being guided by the realities of firm size and industrial structure is one of the key differences between the Nelson–Winter brand of evolutionism and that of the organizational ecologists. See Winter (1990a) for further discussion.

and grow large because of their success. It notes that particularly rapid firm growth often attends the birth of an industry, or of a new specialized niche within an industry, and that this is all part of the evolutionary struggle among ways of doing things. These patterns arise quite naturally in evolutionary models, as has now been demonstrated innumerable times. Just how much of the pattern is an "assumption" of the model and how much a derived "prediction" varies from model to model, but in any case assumptions *are* predictions (predictions with short derivations, as many of Friedman's critics have pointed out). Along with the major phenomenon of large size discrepancies, these models typically predict many other patterns that are found in the turbulent competitive processes of reality. Presumably, a critic replying to this point might claim that the possibility of deriving realistic patterns from realistic processes is "obvious" and hence not a significant accomplishment of the theory. Should we conclude then that this part of reality is legitimately ignored? Should the academic discussions of generic "firms" go on indefinitely while almost always maintaining a discrete silence about the factor of 100,000? What do other theories have to say?

Evolutionary theory says, to understand firm size, look at firm growth. Here there appears to be some trouble for the theory. The highly skewed size distributions of business firm have long been explained by a variety of models of cumulative random growth. That by itself is not trouble; what evolutionary theory offers is an improvement on these models that identifies significant exogenous features of the context in which growth takes place (Nelson and Winter, 1978). There clearly is trouble, however, if the specification of the stochastic process involves too austere a version of "randomness"—a version that would seem to rule out the systematic long-term consequences of firm attributes that are featured in evolutionary theory.

That this is in fact the case has been argued forcefully by Paul Geroski (Geroski, 2000) In particular, he claims, the strict "Gibrat specification" fits the growth data quite well. This is a statistical model in which random shocks to the log of firm size are distributed identically and independently across firms and time (annual data). Geroski does not target evolutionary economics specifically; he correctly points out that any theory or argument featuring persistent firm traits (e.g., capabilities) is in some trouble here. Indeed, the broad consensus about what business firms mean in the economic system might be considered to be in trouble.

The sorting out of these theoretical and econometric issues has barely begun (but see, e.g., Bottazzi, et al., 2001). There are lines of possible reply to Geroski that would dispose of the apparent threat to fundamental commitments of evolutionary theory—but whether those replies are empirically credible remains to be seen. So, for the moment, it is possible only to conclude here with two items of good news: (1) there is an exciting research agenda here; (2) there is no merit in the occasional claims that evolutionary theory is not seriously exposed to refutation.

24.7 EVOLUTIONARY ECONOMICS
AND MANAGEMENT

....

Economics needs to take large firms very seriously because of their major influence on the system as a whole. Taking large firms seriously means taking managers seriously, because managers make real choices under real uncertainty. In organizational economics, there are valiant efforts to take managers seriously within the familiar frame of rational choice modeling (Gibbons, 2003). Such efforts, while capable of generating useful insight at the micro level, have limited power to address the evolution of the context, capturing the larger scale interactions in the system. For that purpose, the familiar story of profit maximizing firms and (even) competitive markets provides the backdrop for the analysis, as it does elsewhere in the discipline, for want of anything better (or so it is claimed).

In management, the need to take managers seriously does not require an argument, and is not limited to accounting for the influence of large firms. A possibly more serious question is, does management need to take economics seriously? While a lot of useful work under the broad rubric of management probably does *not* need to take economics seriously, there are areas where economic principles are fundamental to the problems addressed. Strategic management is the obvious case. Like mainstream economics, evolutionary theory illuminates the workings of competition in the marketplace, through which firms influence each others' profitability as well as their prospects for growth and survival. Unlike mainstream economics, its illumination of those "workings" falls directly on the dynamic processes of competition, and not just on equilibrium outcomes or tendencies. Also unlike mainstream economics, its image of a population of firms is an image of *heterogeneous* firms, differing in their ways of doing things and also in size—with the size differences produced endogenously as a consequence of those idiosyncrasies.

Indeed, thanks to the complementary theoretical work in organizational learning and the partial filling of the major gap concerning industry evolution, it should now be within reach to produce a comprehensive model of the creation and evolution of an industry—a sort of "Big Bang" model for an industrial universe. Such a model would map the entry processes, the learning processes, the market competition processes, the differential growth and survival, and the appearance of concentrated structure—all within a frame that represented and controlled the key exogenous forces and structural determinants, but none of the details. It could even extend to the significant problems relating to the determination of industry and firm boundaries, since evolutionary forces are at work there as well (Langlois, 1991; Jacobides and Winter, 2005). Such a model would rest on a layered structure of theoretical commitments about key processes—commitments that have already been identified and debated, and of course can be debated further. Implemented as a simulation model, it would produce a realistic picture of an industry that responded in systematic ways to differences in the exogenous conditions. It might misrepresent reality, not merely because of the necessarily abstract character of theory, but because it failed to capture significant patterns in the reality. And if it did misrepresent reality in significant ways, that discrepancy would be ascertainable. In short, it would have content.

Most fundamentally from the viewpoint of management theory, evolutionary theory invites detailed attention to individual firms and the problems they face in dealing with competitive environments.[24] It does not merely accept, but *urges*, that inquiry extend to the inner workings of firms. It offers the investigator suggestions about what to look for—especially if the inquiry is one that includes a concern with how that firm fits and fares in the larger system. It also urges, however, that an open mind about the nature of decision processes found in firms will prove more useful than a closed one.

REFERENCES

ALCHIAN, A. (1950). Uncertainty, evolution and economic theory. *Journal of Political Economy* 58: 211–222.

BAUM, J. A. C., and POWELL, W. W. (1995). Cultivating an institutional ecology of organizations: Comment on Hannan, Carroll, Dundon and Torres. *American Sociological Review*, 60: 529–538.

BEUNZA, D., and STARK, D. (2004). Tools of the trade: the socio-technology of arbitrage in a Wall Street trading firm. *Industrial and Corporate Change*, 13: 369–400.

BEWLEY, T. F. (1999). *Why Wages Don't Fall During a Recession*. Cambridge, Mass.: Harvard University Press.

BLAUG, M. (1980). *The Methodology of Economics, Or How Economists Explain*. Cambridge: Cambridge University Press.

BOLAND, L. A. (1979). A critique of Friedman's critics. *Journal of Economic Literature*, 17: 503–522.

BOTTAZZI, G., DOSI, G., LIPPI, M., PAMMOLLI, F., and RICCABONI, M. (2001). Innovation and corporate growth in the evolution of the drug industry. *International Journal of Industrial Organization*, 19: 1161–1187.

COHEN, M. and BACDAYAN, P. (1994). Organizational routines are stored as procedural memory. *Organization Science*, 5: 554–568.

—— BURKHART, R., DOSI, G., EGIDI, M., MARENGO, L., WARGLIEN, M., and WINTER, S. (1996). Routines and other recurring action patterns of organizations: Contemporary research issues. *Industrial and Corporate Change*, 5: 653–698.

CYERT, R. M., and MARCH, J. G. (1963). *A Behavioral Theory of the Firm*. Englewood Cliffs, NJ: Prentice-Hall.

---

[24] In this connection, see Gavetti and Levinthal (forthcoming) for an encouraging assessment.

DOSI, G. (1982). Technological paradigms and technological trajectories. *Research Policy*, 11: 147–162.

—— (2000). *Innovation, Organization and Economic Dynamics, Selected Essays*. Cheltenham: Elgar.

—— (2002). Interpreting industrial dynamics twenty years after and Nelson and Winter's Evolutionary Theory of Economic Change: a preface. *Industrial and Corporate Change*, 11: 619–622.

—— NELSON, R. R., and WINTER, S. G. (2000). *The Nature and Dynamics of Organizational Capabilities*. Oxford: Oxford University Press.

—— MALERBA, F., and TEECE, D. (2003). Twenty years after Nelson and Winter's *An Evolutionary Theory of Economic Change*: a preface on knowledge, the nature of organizations and the patterns of organizational changes. *Industrial and Corporate Change*, 12: 147–148.

FREEMAN, C., and PAVITT, K. (2002). Editorial. Special Issue "Nelson + Winter + 20". *Research Policy*, 31: 1221–1226.

FRIEDMAN, M. (1953). The methodology of positive economics. *The Methodology of Positive Economics*. Chicago: University of Chicago Press.

GAVETTI, G., and LEVINTHAL, D. (2000). Looking forward and looking backward: Cognitive and experiential search. *Administrative Science Quarterly*, 45(1): 113–137.

—— —— (forthcoming). The strategy field from the perspective of management science: Divergent strands and possible integration. *Management Science*.

GEROSKI, P. (2000). The growth of firms in theory and practice. In N. Foss and V. Mahnke (eds.), *Competence, Governance and Entrepreneurship*: 168–186. Oxford: Oxford University Press.

GIBBONS, R. (2003). Team theory, garbage cans and real organizations: some history and prospects of economic research on decision making in organizations. *Industrial and Corporate Change*, 12: 753–787.

GORDON, R. A. (1948). Short period price determination in theory and practice. *American Economic Review*, 38: 265–288.

HALL, R. L., and HITCH, C. J. (1939). Price theory and business behavior. *Oxford Economic Papers*, 2: 12–45.

HANNAN, M. T., and CARROLL, G. R. (1995). Theory building and cheap talk about legitimation: reply to Baum and Powell. *American Sociological Review*, 60: 539–544.

HELFAT, C. E. (1994a). Evolutionary trajectories in petroleum firm R&D. *Management Science*, 40: 1720–1747.

—— (1994b). Firm-specificity in corporate applied R&D. *Organization Science*, 5: 173–184.

—— (ed.) (2003). *The SMS Blackwell Handbook of Organizational Capabilities: Emergence, Development and Change*. Oxford: Blackwell.

HENDERSON, R., and CLARK, K. (1990). Architectural innovation: The reconfiguration of existing product technologies and the failure of established firms. *Administrative Science Quarterly*, 35: 9–30.

HODGSON, G. (1994). Optimization and evolution: Winter's critique of Friedman revisited. *Cambridge Journal of Economics*, 18: 413–430.

—— (2003). The mystery of the routine: The Darwinian destiny of An Evolutonary Theory of Economic Change. *Revue Economique*, 54: 355–384.

JACOBIDES, M. G., and WINTER, S. G. (2005). The coevolution of capabilities and transaction costs: Explaining the institutional structure of production. *Strategic Management Journal*, 26: 395–413.

KLEIN, B. H. (1962). The decision making problem in development. In R. R. Nelson (ed.), *The Rate and Direction of Inventive Activity.* Princeton: Princeton University Press.

KLEPPER, S. (1996). Entry, exit, growth and innovation over the product life cycle. *American Economic Review*, 86: 562–583.

—— (1997). Industry life cycles. *Industrial and Corporate Change*, 6: 145–181.

—— and GRADDY, E. (1990). The evolution of industries and the determinants of market structure. *RAND Journal of Economics*, 21: 27–44.

—— and SIMONS, K. L. (2000a). Dominance by birthright: entry of prior radio producers and competitive ramifications in the U.S. television receiver industry. *Strategic Management Journal*, 21: 997–1016.

—— —— (2000b). The making of an ologopoly: firm survival and technological change in the evolution of the U.S. tire industry. *Journal of Political Economy*, 108: 728–760.

—— and SLEEPER, S. (2000). Entry by Spinoffs. Pittsburgh, Working paper, Carnegie Mellon University.

KOGUT, B., and ZANDER, U. (1992). Knowledge of the firm, combinative capabilities, and the replication of technology. *Organization Science*, 3: 383–397.

KOOPMANS, T. C. (1957). *Three Essays on the State of Economic Science.* New York: McGraw-Hill.

KUHN, T. S. (1970). *The Structure of Scientific Revolutions*, 2nd edn., Chicago: University of Chicago Press.

LAKATOS, I. (1970). Falsification and the methodology of scientific research programmes. In I. Lakatos and R. Musgrave (eds.), *Criticism and the Growth of Knowledge.* Cambridge: Cambridge University Press.

LANGLOIS, R. (1991). Transaction cost economics in real time. *Industrial and Corporate Change*, 1: 99–127.

LEVINTHAL, D. (1997). Adaptation on rugged landscapes. *Management Science*, 43: 934–950.

—— (1998). The slow pace of rapid technological change: Gradualism and punctuation in technological change. *Industrial and Corporate Change*, 7(2): 217–247.

McFADDEN, D. (1969). A simple remark on the second best Pareto optimallity of market equilibria. *Journal of Economic Theory*, 1: 26–38.

MALERBA, F. (1985). *The Semiconductor Business.* Madison: University of Wisconsin Press.

—— NELSON, R., ORSENIGO, L., and WINTER, S. G. (1999). History-friendly models of industry evolution: The computer industry. *Industrial and Corporate Change*, 8: 1–36.

—— —— —— —— (2001). Competition and industrial policies in a history friendly model of the evolution of the computer industry. *International Journal of Industrial Organization*, 19: 635–664.

MARCH, J. G., and SIMON, H. A. (1958). *Organizations.* New York: Wiley.

MASSEY, G. J. (1965). Professor Samuelson on theory and realism: comment. *American Economic Review*, 55: 1155–1163.

MURMANN, J. P. (2003). *Knowledge and Competitive Advantage: The Coevolution of Firms, Technology and National Institutions.* Cambridge: Cambridge University Press.

NELSON, R. R. (1956). A theory of the low-level equilibrium trap in underdeveloped economies. *American Economic Review*, 46: 894–908.

—— (1959a). The economics of invention: A survey of the literature. *Journal of Business*, 32: 101–127.

—— (1959b). The simple economics of basic scientific research. *Journal of Political Economy*, 67: 297–306.

—— (1962). The link between science and invention: The case of the transistor. In R. R. Nelson (ed.), *The Rate and Direction of Inventive Activity*: 549–583. Princeton: Princeton University Press.

—— (1968). A diffusion model of international productivity differences in manufacturing industry. *American Economic Review* 58: 1219–1248.

—— PECK, M. J., and KALACHEK, E. D. (1967). *Technology, Economic Growth and Public Policy*. Washington, D.C: Brookings Institution.

—— and WINTER, S. G. (1973). Toward an evolutionary theory of economic capabilities. *American Economic Review*, 63(May): 440–449.

—— —— (1974). Neoclassical vs. evolutionary theories of economic growth: Critique and prospectus. *Economic Journal*, 84: 886–905.

—— —— (1978). Forces generating and limiting concentration under Schumpeterian competition. *The Bell Journal of Economics*, 9: 524–548.

—— —— (1982a). *An Evolutionary Theory of Economic Change*. Cambridge, Mass.: Harvard University Press.

—— —— (1982b). The Schumpeterian trade-off revisited. *American Economic Review*, 72(March): 114–132.

—— —— (2002). Evolutionary theorizing in economics. *Journal of Economic Perspectives*, 16: 23–46.

—— —— and SCHUETTE, H. L. (1976). Technical change in an evolutionary model. *Quarterly Journal of Economics*, 90: 90–118.

POLANYI, M. (1964). *Personal Knowledge: Towards a Post-Critical Philosophy*. New York: Harper and Row.

—— (1966). *The Tacit Dimension*. Garden City, NY: Doubleday.

POPPER, K. (1959). *The Logic of Scientific Discovery*. New York: Basic Books.

QUINE, W. V. O. (1961) *From a Logical Point of View: Logico-Philosophical Essays*, 2nd edn. New York: Harper Torchbooks.

RICHARDSON, G. B. (1972). The organisation of industry. *Economic Journal*, 82: 883–896.

RIVKIN, J. W. (2000). Imitation of complex strategies. *Management Science*, 46: 824–844.

—— (2001). Reproducing knowledge: Replication without imitation at moderate complexity. *Organization Science*, 12: 274–293.

—— and SIGGELKOW, N. (2003). Balancing search and stability: Interdependencies among elements of organizational design. *Management Science*, 49: 290–311.

ROSENBERG, N. (1969). The direction of technological change: Inducement mechanisms and focusing devices. *Economic Development and Cultural Change*, 18: 1–24.

SCHUMPETER, J. (1934). *The Theory of Economic Development*. Cambridge, Mass.: Harvard University Press.

—— (1950). *Capitalism, Socialism and Democracy*. New York: Harper and Row.

SCHWARTZ, H. (1998). *Rationality Gone Awry?* Westport, Conn.: Prager.

SIMON, H. A. (1955). A behavioral model of rational choice. *Quarterly Journal of Economics*, 69: 99–118.

—— (1987). Satisficing. *The New Palgrave: A Dictionary of Economics*, vol. 4, eds. J. Eatwell, M. Millgate, and P. Newman. New York, Stockton Press: 243–245.

STARBUCK, W. H., and MEZIAS, J. M. (2003). Studying the accuracy of managers' perceptions: A research odyssey. *British Journal of Management*, 14: 3–17.

SZULANSKI, G. (1996). Exploring internal stickiness: Impediments to the transfer of best practice within the firm. *Strategic Management Journal*, 17: 27–43.

TEECE, D., PISANO, G., and SHUEN, A. (1997). Dynamic capabilities and strategic management. *Strategic Management Journal*, 18(7): 509–533.

TRIPSAS, M. (1997). Unraveling the process of creative destruction: Complementary assets and incumbent survival in the typesetter industry. *Stratetgic Management Journal*, 18 (Special issue, Summer): 119–142.

—— and GAVETTI, G. (2000). Capabilities, cognition, and inertia: Evidence from digital imaging. *Strategic Management Journal*, 21: 1147–1161.

TUSHMAN, M., and ANDERSON, P. (1986). Technological discontinuities and organization environments. *Administrative Science Quarterly*, 31: 439–465.

USSELMAN, S. W. (1993). IBM and its imitators: organizational capabilities and the emergence of the international computer industry. *Business and Economic History*, 22: 1–35.

WINTER, S. G. (1964a). Economic "natural selection" and the theory of the firm. *Yale Economic Essays*, 4: 225–272.

—— (1964b). Review of "A Behavioral Theory of the Firm". *American Economic Review*, 54: 144–148.

—— (1971). Satisficing, selection and the innovating remnant. *Quarterly Journal of Economics*, 85: 237–261.

—— (1975). Optimization and evolution in the theory of the firm. In R. H. Day and T. Groves (eds.), *Adaptive Economic Models*: 73–118. New York: Academic Press.

—— (1984). Schumpeterian competition in alternative technological regimes. *Journal of Economic Behavior and Organization*, 5: 287–320.

—— (1986a). Comments on Arrow and on Lucas. *Journal of Business*, 59(4, Part 2): S427–S434.

—— (1986b). The research program of the behavioral theory of the firm: orthodox critique and evolutionary perspective. In B. Gilad and S. Kaish (eds.), *Handbook of Behavioral Economics, A: Behavioral Microeconomics*: 151–188. Greenwich, Conn.: JAI Press.

—— (1987). Competition and selection. In J. Eatwell, M. Milgate, and P. Newman (eds.), *The New Palgrave: A Dictionary of Economics*: 1. 545–548. New York: Stockton Press.

—— (1990). Survival, selection and inheritance in evolutonary theories of organization. In J. V. Singh (ed.), *Organizational Evolution: New Directions*. Newbury Park, Calif.: Sage Publications.

—— (2000). The satisficing principle in capability learning. *Strategic Management Journal*, 21 (special issue): 981–996.

—— and SZULANSKI, G. (2001). Replication as strategy. *Organization Science*, 12: 730–743.

ZOLLO, M., and WINTER, S. G. (2002). Deliberate learning and the evolution of dynamic capabilities. *Organization Science*, 13: 339–351.

....

CHAPTER 25

AN EVOLUTIONARY APPROACH TO INSTITUTIONS AND SOCIAL CONSTRUCTION

PROCESS AND STRUCTURE

....

LYNNE G. ZUCKER

MICHAEL R. DARBY

BUILDING blocks of institutional theory come from a variety of different sources. Some are concerned with development of the core theory itself, with structure or processes, while others are related to developing plausible measurement strategies. Much of the process of institutionalization is tacit and not open to direct measurement. Thus, indirect indicators of the social construction processes have been used.

The authors acknowledge support for this chapter from the National Science Foundation (grant number SES 0304727) and from the University of California's Industry-University Cooperative Research Program.

Among them are outcomes, from social influence to firm success, and indicators of the nature and amount of the process and its change over time including language and classification change. Social construction does not just build new social structure, it fundamentally changes cognitive conceptions and frames through which we view many aspects of social and economic life (DiMaggio, 1997).

The more cognitive, information-based form of institutional theory that we have been involved in developing fits with both an economic approach (information, expectations, incentives) and a phenomenological approach (cognitive, tacit knowledge, social construction). Working across sociology and economic discipline lines has helped to make the underlying concepts and theory more explicit by borrowing concepts and theories across the disciplines. It is our goal in this chapter to make our integration of the economic and phenomenological approaches more codified, and to advance the integration.

Over the last three decades, institutional theory has become one of the central approaches to understanding the fundamental building blocks of organizations and societies. Critical turning points in institutional theory are well known, but we will briefly summarize them here. The early work quickly divided into a more macro set of approaches (Meyer and Rowan, 1977), and micro set of approaches to institutions and to the process of institutionalization (Zucker, 1977, 1983), and an approach that straddled the two (DiMaggio and Powell, 1983). While different streams of theorizing fed in to each of the approaches, much of the empirical work done under the umbrella of the various approaches often overlapped by emphasizing concepts, and related measures, that appear in most institutional formulations. Good roadmaps can be found in reviews of institutional theory, most of which also evaluate the research and define new pathways for exploration (Meyer, 2002; Scott, 1987, 1995; Tolbert and Zucker, 1996; Zucker, 1987).

Section 25.1 lays out fundamental elements for a theory of institution building and institutionalization. Section 25.2 examines markets for information, particularly for the kind of information which forms and transforms industries. We show how organizational and professional boundaries slow the diffusion of valuable information in Section 25.3. Section 25.4 examines the creation and transmission of tacit knowledge in metamorphic growth, when the value is high, with particular focus on the variation-generating part of the change process, including combination and permutation of existing templates and invention of new templates. Section 25.5 lays out a formal model of the construction of trust-producing social structure, explicitly tying the process and structure approaches together in a way that passes initial empirical tests. We conclude with our views on the construction of theory (Section 25.6), arguing that institutional theory has attained sufficient maturity to warrant more formal models, codification of tacit concepts and relations, rigorous test, and evaluation of the theory in light of the evidence.

25.1 THE FUNDAMENTALS

Central puzzles in a theory of institution-building and institutionalization include explaining how action reinforces (maintains) or alters structure. Structure alone cannot explain the living, changing role that institutions play, since it is human agency that must actualize/act out that structure. Personal motivation to use or build structure comes from two main sources: Expectations, including knowledge of the expectations of others or "background expectancies" that define the situation (Garfinkel, 1964, 1967: ch. 2), and expected incentives, both self-identified and vicarious learning based on other's observed success. For the purposes of our argument here, information and knowledge are equivalent.

Figure 25.1 lists the main defining elements of process-based and structure-based institutional theory. In our thinking, these two approaches are not different pillars, but rather different stages of the same underlying social construction of institutions. Please also refer to W. Richard Scott in Chapter 22 of this book who provides a very insightful review of institutional theory that arose at Stanford during the time I was writing my dissertation, working primarily with my dissertation chair, Morris Zelditch, Jr., and John Meyer (see Zucker, 1977, 1974).

Process-based theory stresses action and differentiates kinds of actions that lead to institution building and divergent structures (and de-institutionalization with disappearance of structures), while structure-based theory stresses the outcome of action in the form of resilient structures, in codified norms, values, regulations, and laws, and in the development of some structures with widespread, overarching relevance. In practice, the actual theorizing and research largely ignores this artificial process/structure boundary and writes right across it, though one's work tends to belong more to process and social construction or more to social structure and widespread framing of action. We use this distinction here as an artifice to help describe the two ends of a mutual set of concerns.

Following Berger and Luckmann (1966), institutional structure is the sedimentation or outcome of the process of institutionalization. The twin aspects of institution place limits on each other: (1) the available set of processes of institutionalization makes some institutions possible to construct at a given time, and other institutions impossible; (2) the existing set of institutions, as a whole or individually depending on their degree of integration, constrain the kinds of processes that can be used to construct new institutions.

Focus on action/process, however, also means that the person and the group or organization that he/she mobilizes is central to the theory. The defining role of one or a few actors is central, and the *natural excludability* that is inherent in tacit knowledge provides a basis for supernormal returns, competition, and differentiation, and success (Michael R. Darby developed the concept of natural excludability; see Zucker and Darby, 1996, and especially Darby and Zucker, 2003). Our approach

Defining Elements	PROCESS-BASED THEORY	STRUCTURE-BASED THEORY
Initial assumptions	Cognitive, expectations, incentives Legitimate: reciprocal expectations/content	Norms, values, moral, legal system External authority, connect to norms/rules
Central problems	Change, maintenance, resistance-to-change	Stability; isomorphism, world convergence
Social construction	Emergence of new: tacit to codified*	Coercive, regulatory, normative: replication
Main source	Entrepreneurial invention,* mobilization Background expectancies→context	Societal leitmotif: rationalization project External authority, legal, normative
Scope/level	Localized initially, relevance: bottom→up*	Widespread, de-coupled, roughly top→down
Institutional change	New social/tech invention, sudden redefinition*	Incremental change; convergence
Means and Outcomes		
Transmission	Social fact, impersonal and objectified, success	Material resources, power asymmetries
Core logics	Natural excludability* and legitimation	Demand for a good function of others' demand
Content/context	Actions as information, social facts Tacit to codified Combine endowed, new social structure*	Normative, regulative, coercive Codified rules, legal or moral World/subsystem convergence along leitmotif
Value/cost	Markets for information	Selection based on common values
Highly institutional	Taken-for-granted, social fact/information Social relations more impersonal, exterior Formal organizations as social context	Resilient structures, legitimate or rule-governed Social relations stable, based on history Organization and occupation templates, not efficiency
Knowledge economy	Professional networks dominate organizations	Science widespread as part of rationalization project

Fig. 25.1 Institutional theory approaches

Note: *Defining role of one or few actors: Charismatic leadership, resource mobilization, elites building new "high culture," and discovering scientists/inventors founding new companies and transmitting tacit knowledge that increases company success. Refer to text.

to tracing the effects of natural excludability has focused primarily on discovering scientists/inventors, their organizational and institutional context, including founding of new companies, and their role in transmission of tacit knowledge about discoveries that increase success of those companies in biotechnology and nanotechnology (Zucker, Darby, and Brewer, 1998; Darby and Zucker, 2005*a*, 2005*b*; Zucker, Darby, and Armstrong, 1998, 2002).[1]

Professionals as the holders of knowledge is also a central theme in several other approaches, though these approaches generally leave aside the questions of any returns to that knowledge. Professionals have recently been identified as among the more important definers and diffusers of new "cultural" information in the form of at least fads and fashions, providing an organizing and legitimating vision applied recently to innovation in information technology (Greenwood, Suddaby, and Hinings, 2002; DiMaggio, 1991). The cascades model provides a more general approach to modeling these phenomena and identifying implications for fragility and transmission of error (Bikhchandani, Hirshleifer, and Welch, 1992).[2]

25.2 MARKETS FOR INFORMATION

Our argument starts from the classic Stigler (1961) observation that information is a valuable and costly resource and that individuals are thus motivated to adopt strategies such as search, that weighs the expected costs and benefits of acquiring information. For example, if individuals' search involves unique goods, then costs of search are sufficiently high that transactions are commonly localized as a device for identifying potential buyers and sellers. Stigler pointed out that medieval markets were an example of actual localization; advertising is an example of a "virtually" localized market.

A profession (or craft) is another mechanism of "virtual" localization to the degree that members' knowledge base is a prerequisite to obtaining and using the new information; in some cases, this virtual aspect is coupled with geographic localization, as concentration of a discipline is thought to yield a "critical mass" of

---

[1] In structure-based theory, external logics imply a person's demand for a good being a function of others' demand for that good (see esp. Becker, 1991), and that process leads to widespread, bandwagon diffusion of demand for certain goods, sometimes defined as "taste."

[2] Other important approaches include: charismatic authority (Weber, 1947: 328); resource mobilization by leaders of social movements (McCarthy and Zald, 1977); small groups of elites mobilizing resources to build new "high culture" arts organizations in Boston (DiMaggio, 1982*a*, 1982*b*). These also largely leave aside questions of returns.

professionals who gain through interaction with each other. The size and geographic distribution of that knowledge base determines the extent and concentration of initial demand for the new knowledge. For example, University of California, San Francisco, with its critical mass of molecular biologists, played a central role in the biotechnology revolution and commercialization.

Professions are transparently involved in determining the "social distribution of knowledge" (Schutz, 1962: 149). Whether or not this is a deliberate attempt to decrease supply is not germane to our argument here. More relevant are the implications for balkanization of knowledge. Various structures create knowledge boundaries that limit its spread; we will discuss organizations as a case in point below.

25.2.1 Tacit Knowledge and Natural Excludability

We now turn to our work in the past ten years or so on breakthrough discoveries in science and their commercialization. Breakthrough discoveries are characterized by natural excludability due to the tacit nature of the underlying knowledge held by the discovering scientist(s). To the extent that the knowledge is both scarce and tacit, it constitutes intellectual human capital retained by the discovering scientists and therefore they become the main resource around which firms are built or transformed (Zucker, Darby, and Brewer, 1998; Zucker, Darby, and Armstrong, 1998, 2002). Hence, tacit knowledge can be viewed as at least partially rivalrous and excludable information and thus "appropriable" as long as it remains difficult (or impossible) to learn it. This has a number of important implications:

* Diffusion occurs slowly, from one of the discoverers to his/her research team. Tacit knowledge, not yet codified, is transmitted best at the lab bench. From 1969 to the end of our data set in 1992, 81 percent of new authors reporting genetic-sequence discoveries for the first time were writing as co-authors with previously published discoverers (Zucker, Darby, and Torero, 2002: 632–633).

* The discovery is not alienable from the scientists as long as it remains tacit. The tacit knowledge is part of their intellectual human capital. This human capital earns supranormal returns to investment until the diffusion level drives the return to that knowledge down to the cost of learning it from others.

As tacit knowledge becomes increasingly codified—or translated into "recipe knowledge" as Schutz (1962) terms it—tacitness decreases and knowledge transfer is easier. But significant barriers may stand in the way of codification. Relevance between old and new knowledge can be difficult to determine (Schutz, 1970), increasing the demand for social construction of new codes, formulae, and machines such as gene splicers for biotechnology and scanning probe microscopes for nanotechnology.

Paradoxically, once the value is known:

- If the value is low relative to alternative uses of scientific talent, then there are few incentives to codify it. Low value knowledge tends to be highly perishable, and without codification disappears, leaving little or no citation trail.
- If it is high, those few scientists who hold the new knowledge will have to weigh returns to codification against returns to time invested in scientific research, a tradeoff that pits knowledge transfer against knowledge creation.
    - Hence, the average scientific discovery is never codified, and valuable discoveries experience a significant codification lag that tends to increase with their value.
    - Encoding valuable discoveries in a machine is significantly more likely than other forms of codification, under the condition that the machine directly contributes to good science (e.g., speed, accuracy), even for those who already know the techniques. Returns to use of these machines are not only scientific; equipment manufacturers are a separate industry providing incentives for invention and improvement.

Under conditions of natural excludability when knowledge is embodied in the discoverer, it is transferred slowly only by learning-by-doing-with. Even if the university is assigned a patent to the discovery most of the value accrues to the discoverers since without their cooperation the patent cannot be used. Our fieldwork for biotechnology and more general studies by Jensen and Thursby (2001) and Thursby and Thursby (2002) support the natural excludability hypothesis. For example, in the Jensen and Thursby (2001: 243) survey of Technology Transfer Office managers, "For 71 percent of the inventions licensed, respondents claim that successful commercialization requires cooperation by the inventor and licensee in further development."

25.3 SOCIAL BOUNDARIES: ORGANIZATIONS AND PROFESSIONS AS INFORMATION ENVELOPES

Trust is extraordinarily important in communicating early discoveries in any scientific area, but especially so in biotechnology and nanotechnology because of their high scientific and commercial value. The resulting intense competition produces an information dilemma, with contradictory incentives to communicate the new knowledge and to withhold it (Schneider and Brewer, 1987).[3] In brief, if a scientist communicates usable information about a new discovery, the benefits associated with exclusive access to that information are compromised. But withholding information about the new discovery may slow progress in the field as a whole. Partial solutions to this dilemma have been achieved by requiring deposits of the genetic materials upon patenting and in some cases upon publication and by the importance placed on priority of publication for professional recognition.

Information dilemmas, usually couched as conflict between individual self-interest and group interest, can be resolved by relying on close-knit collaborations, sharply limiting with whom the new discovery is shared. While the information is not shared with the field as a whole, it is shared with a group of collaborators that tends to grow over time. The information boundaries that these collaboration structures define determine the extent of diffusion of the new discovery. Because organizations have both established internal exchange relations and enforcement mechanisms, we expect that trust among members of the same organization will be significantly higher than trust between members of different organizations, and thus that organizational boundaries are efficient *information envelopes*. In general, the higher the value of the intellectual human capital, the more likely organizational boundaries are used to limit its diffusion.

Thus, we can extend our argument one step further, to the effects of organizational boundaries on diffusion of information. If trust is produced, and information flow is in fact restricted along organizational lines, then diffusion should slow differentially. Specifically, within a geographic area, the higher the proportion of same organization pairs of co-authors, the less information should diffuse within that area. We report a full model in Zucker, et al. (1996) that explains nearly all of the variation in diffusion to new co-authors of scientific articles between geographic areas, with significant amounts explained by variables related to value of intellectual human capital and the resultant patterns of collaboration within or between organizations.

Table 25.1, Panels A and B, provides a summary of the within-organization and cross-organization patterns of co-authoring on and citations to scientific articles in biotechnology (Table 25.1 combines Tables 6.3 and 6.5, with some additional calculations added to Table 6.3, from Zucker, et al., 1996). In the top half of the

---

[3] Very little research has examined trust production in organizational settings; most has focused on the effects of trust once it exists. Brewer and Silver (1978) found that ingroup members were rated as more trustworthy, honest, and cooperative than their outgroup counterparts. Some laboratory research on small groups, simulating organizations, has found that members of the same organization are more likely to communicate freely with each other, assuming that reciprocity of communication is more likely (Schneider and Brewer, 1987; Kramer and Brewer, 1984). But this increased communication occurs only when individuals believe that the benefits are going exclusively to members of their own group (Dawes, Van de Kragt, and Orbell, 1988).

Table 25.1 Collaborating pairs for genetic discoveries

	Organization Type		
	University	Firm	Research Institute
Panel A - Counts of Collaboration Pairs			
Collaborations within same org. type:			
Same org. for both authors	2,747	346	532
Different orgs. for the authors	771	17	141
Collaborations across org. type:			
Other author from University		302	420
Other author from Firm	302		111
Other author from Research Inst.	420	111	
Total collaboration pairs	4,240	776	1,204
Within same organization	65%	45%	44%
Across different organizations:	35%	55%	56%
Different orgs. of same org. type	18%	2%	12%
Orgs. of different org. type	17%	53%	44%
Other author at a university	18%	39%	35%
Panel B - Citation Rates by Collaboration Pairs			
Collaborations within same org. type:			
Same org. for both authors	17.64	69.57	18.03
Different orgs. for the authors	29.01	64.18	26.54
Collaborations across org. type:			
Other author from University		49.53	22.00
Other author from Firm	49.53		95.60
Other author from Research Inst.	22.00	95.60	

Source: Zucker, et al. (1996).

table, Panel A, it shows that over 75 percent of collaborations with the same type of organization occur within the organizational boundaries, increasing to 95 percent for firms. Firm scientists very rarely coauthor with scientists at other firms. Most collaboration outside the boundaries of the same organization takes place between university scientists and other scientists located in research institutes and firms. Since universities are the "source," that is the location of many of the initial discoveries and talent; it is not surprising that both firms and research institutes collaborate frequently with scientists in universities. Overall, our findings counter assumptions about the open structure of scientific discovery across different universities.

Transaction-cost economics provides an alternative—possibly complementary—explanation to protection of valuable intellectual capital for the high frequency of collaborations inside organizational boundaries (Williamson, 1979, 1991).

Generally, both protection is lower and *other* transaction costs are higher for collaborations across organizational boundaries, as compared to within one's own organization. Therefore, all else equal, transactions across organizational boundaries should occur only when there are sufficient benefits to offset the additional costs involved. Looking again at Panel A of Table 25.1, it appears that the reward/cost ratio of transacting with organizations of the same type seldom make it worthwhile. This is especially so for firms, with very rare collaboration with other firms, perhaps in part because of problems concerning property rights that don't emerge when firms collaborate with scientists at universities or research institutes.

But if we examine the average benefits of collaborations in terms of citations that the research receives, occurring within or across organizational boundaries as shown in the bottom half of Table 25.1, Panel B, the data appear to support the hypothesis that transaction costs (including distrust) increase in inter-organizational collaborations: For authors from the same type of organizations, collaborations across organizational boundaries are more highly cited than for those within the same organization, significantly so for universities and research institutes. Interestingly, there is a much greater apparent citation payoff for scientists from universities and research institutes who collaborate with those from firms, consistent with the hypothesis that the difference in cultures further reduces trust, but also possibly due to selection of the best academic scientists for collaborations by the generally more highly cited firm scientists (some empirical support for selection as a significant factor is provided in Zucker, Darby, and Armstrong, 1998 and in Zucker, Darby, and Torero, 2002). Our innovation above is that we can use indicators of the value of the information produced to identify collaborations for which reduced trust has a greater impact on the total transaction costs.

Our results summarized above suggest both restriction of ties and careful, strategic selection of them. In contrast, Powell, Koput, and Smith-Doerr (1996) reported rich networks connected for learning among organizations in the bio-technology domain. The rich multiconnectivity and diversity of networks is even more apparent in a later report by Powell and his team (Powell, et al., 2004). Network connections tend to be to partners who are more broadly linked, and to newcomers who are sponsored by nodes in the network.

In part, these different stories of ties and how they play out in biotechnology is due to our central focus on success of firms, compared to the Powell team's omission of success variables. But also our focus has been primarily on the role of the individual top scientist, while the Powell team focuses on the organization and all of its network connections. When our research team has also looked at the organization level, the use of the network connections for learning is also one of our main conclusions (Liebeskind, et al., 1996). Field work has suggested to our team that strategic decisions, or more precisely the technical advice that leads to them, are being made by the key scientists, with the other parts of the network emerging as a consequence of these decisions. There are clearly some interesting causal issues to resolve. Taking the full series of research findings into account poses interesting questions for both research teams.

25.4 FUNDAMENTAL PROCESSES AND OUTCOMES

25.4.1 Transmission of Tacit Knowledge

There is a large literature on knowledge and learning that focuses on codified knowledge, and that lies outside our purview. For reasons discussed above, there may be a substantial lag until the breakthrough knowledge is sufficiently codified to be transmitted via a textbook or lecture. The greater the discontinuity, the more difficult it is to anchor in prior systems of knowledge and the more opportunities it is likely to offer, increasing incentives to enter.

There are four aspects of transmission that offer insights for a process-based institutional theory:

- Which individuals serve as the *transmission agents*?
- What varieties are there of *transmission process* and *transmission content*?
- What is the *transmission quantity*?
- What is the *transmission impact*?

Using a variety of empirical contexts, our emphasis has been on transmission agents, process, and impact, with some measurement of transmission quantity.

25.4.2 Knowledge Transmission by Academic Scientists

The breakthrough discoveries with significant tacit knowledge are being made primarily by the top bioscientists in biotechnology (for the U.S. see Zucker, Darby, and Brewer, 1998; for Japan, see Darby and Zucker, 2001) and the top nanoscientists in nanotechnology (for the U.S., see Darby and Zucker, 2005a). When and where these scientists are actively publishing predicts when and where firms working in the corresponding technology area are born for both biotech and nanotech. This provides evidence of geographic localization of knowledge, as expected with interpersonal transmission required to learn tacit knowledge, in this case best done by working together at the lab bench.

Zucker, Darby, and Armstrong (1998, 2002) and Zucker and Darby (2001) show for California, the U.S., and Japan, respectively, that university effects on nearby firm R&D productivity are highly concentrated in those specific firms with bench–science working relationships with top academic scientists and practically absent otherwise. We identify these academic–firm links by the academic scientist publishing a journal article that also has one or more firm-affiliated authors.[4]

Figure 25.2 reports the strong estimated effects on company research productivity in biotechnology of these linked articles, either via "star" scientists who discovered over forty genetic sequences or via a scientist from one of the top 112

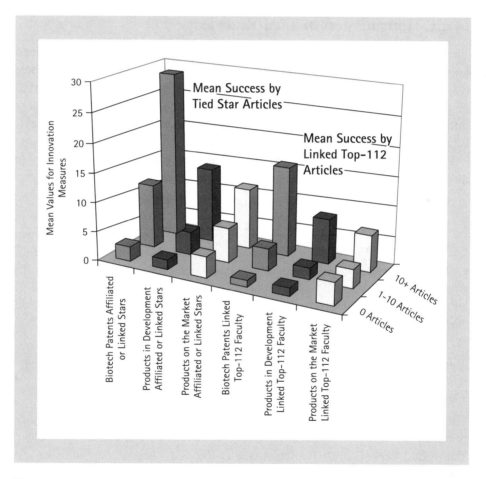

Fig. 25.2 Biotech firms are more successful if tied to star scientists or if linked to top-research-university faculty

---

[4] Publications involving scientists at two firms are extremely rare. Further, the scientists practice serial monogamy: usually writing with only one firm during his or her career and, in the alternative, writing with only one firm at a time.

universities in the U.S (Zucker, Darby, and Armstrong, 2002: fig. 2a). The link itself is measuring the work connection at the lab bench, but we add weighting by the number of articles to measure the magnitude of effort impact. The weighting produces stronger effects, generally significant compared to the link alone, suggesting that transmission occurs through the work effort and close contact, not just reciprocal knowledge of each other.

Fieldwork, supported by analysis of the timing of the academic scientists' first articles with a firm and its founding, indicates that these academic-firm co-publishing relationships most often connote that the academic scientist was a firm founder or at least presently has a significant financial interest in the firm in the U.S. Indeed, Herbert Boyer of the Cohen–Boyer team which discovered recombinant-RNA or genetic engineering and entrepreneur Robert Swanson founded the first of the new biotech firms that has also become one of the most successful, Genentech.

25.4.3 New Organizational Forms Generated by Metamorphic Progress

Most firms achieve perfective progress, incrementally improving commodities or productivity. But technological progress is concentrated in a few firms achieving metamorphic progress (Darby and Zucker, 2003): forming or transforming industries with technological breakthroughs (e.g., biotechnology, lasers, semiconductors, nanotechnology). Unless congruent with incumbents' science and technology base, metamorphic progress promotes entry.

The process underlying metamorphic economic growth is defined by the introduction of a new "breakthrough" technology which either eliminates the ability of firms practicing the old technology to survive or which creates an entirely new industry. If the technological breakthrough relies on the same scientific and engineering base as the previous technology incumbent firms are generally strengthened as they readily convert to the new technology ("competence-enhancing," see Tushman and Anderson, 1986).

Metamorphic progress can be expected both to promote entry, arising almost always from outside the industry(ies) to which it will be applied, and to generate new organizational forms (Darby and Zucker, 2003; Romanelli, 1991). Here, we define organizational form not in terms of specific attributes of organizations, but instead in terms of commonality of basic processes and shared fates: Organizations that are born and die, and grow/decline in number and in size, as a function of the same set of fundamentals constitute an organizational form.

When and where top scientists are actively publishing—different scientists for different high technology areas—predicts where and when firms are born in the specific new technology area. The number of joint research articles these same top scientists write with firm scientists is the central factor in determining the success of the firm in the relevant high technology area, not just in terms of patents, employment, and products as we reviewed earlier, but also in terms of rounds of venture capital, time to IPO, size of initial offering, and valuation of publicly traded firms (Darby, Liu, and Zucker, 2003; Darby and Zucker, 2005b).

Table 25.2 shows the relationship between co-publishing links to top scientists and employment growth: Ranking firms by their linked articles up to 1989 does about as well as ranking by 1989 employment in Table 25.2, second column, at predicting the 1989–1994 employment increase. Put another way, an investor who restricted his or her biotech portfolio at the end of 1989 to only the 22.7 percent of firms with any linked firm–research university core biotech publications or the 10.9 percent with more than one or two of these would include all of the top ten firms and nearly all of the successful, but not quite "home-run," firms. The message of these simple correlations holds up in the context of poison regressions that allow for other determinants.

Table 25.2 Relation of employment in new biotech firms to links to high science

	Number of Firms	Employment in 1989	Employment Change 1989–94	Core Links[a] to Top-112 Universities	Other Links[b] to Top-112 Universities
By 1989 Employment:					
Top Decile	21	53.8%	53.2%	76.4%	79.4%
Next Decile	21	15.0%	9.4%	6.2%	4.0%
Bottom 80%	169	31.2%	37.4%	17.4%	16.6%
Totals	211	100.0%	100.0%	100.0%	100.0%
By Core Links					
Top Decile	21	48.7%	53.4%	94.0%	81.5%
Next Decile	21	7.1%	4.6%	5.1%	7.7%
Bottom 80%	169	44.2%	42.0%	0.9%	10.7%
Totals	211	100.0%	100.0%	100.0%	100.0%

Notes: a. Core links: count of articles through 1989 directly related to biotechnology, indexed by the Institute of Scientific Information, with at least one author affiliated with the firm, and at least one author affiliated with a top 112 U.S. research university.
　　　b. Other links: count of articles through 1989 not directly related to biotechnology, indexed by the Institute of Scientific Information, with at least one author affiliated with the firm, and at least one author affiliated with a top 112 U.S. research university.
Source: Calculations of the authors for the biotech-using firms which disclosed employment for 1989 and 1994 and were formed after 1975 in the Zucker, Darby, and Armstrong (2002) database.

During the initial period of growth, with high rates of birth, it will often not be possible to tell if the end point will be a new industry or simply a small group of similar companies forming around an expected opportunity that may or may not materialize. However, there is a tendency for a bandwagon effect to develop upon some good news. The evidence of success must be clear, but can come in a variety of forms. In the case of biotech, Genentech's very successful IPO in 1981, following the U.S. Supreme Court decision to allow "patenting life," and Genentech's collaborative agreement in 1983 with Eli Lilly to market rDNA insulin ("human insulin") are generally recognized as key turning points in the biotechnology industry as a whole. Humulin has remained in the top ten biotech drugs; in 2001, it was the fifth largest selling biotechnology drug at $1.1 billion (Standard and Poor's 2002 Biotechnology, as reported in Powell, et al., 2004).

The bandwagon effect that builds on this success is driven, or at least enhanced, by rhetoric, framing, and an organizing vision (Green, 2004; Swanson and Ramiller, 1997). These processes focus attention on potential benefits of the new organizational form, providing "rhetorical justifications" or a frame "to make sense of the innovation." More generally, the new process and structure may be framed in terms of emergent cognitive legitimacy and buttressed by rhetoric that mobilizes forces for change (Tolbert and Zucker, 1983, 1996), or as relevant to external, already constructed, legitimate authority (Walker, Thomas, and Zelditch, 1986). These mechanisms and actions can provide a basis for resource mobilization that generally involves both drawing in new resources and redirecting resources that had previously been allocated elsewhere, including human activity and labor (McCarthy and Zald, 1977).

To apply this view to an emerging technology area, in nanotechnology there is much rhetoric, a reasonably clear organizing vision, extensive resource mobilization in terms of research funding (Roco, 2004), and also some venture capital activity (Forman, 2004). There are successful products, such as nano-coatings and other nanomaterials, already on the market but not yet a home-run success story similar to Genentech's humulin that provides expectational guidelines for extraordinary long-run payoff of the breakthrough scientific discoveries.

In this section, we have considered primarily the variation-generating part of the change process, including combination and permutation of existing templates and invention of new templates. We have not explicitly considered variation-constraining processes that also lead to new organizational forms, such as isomorphism and competition. As has been shown repeatedly, institutional structure can be both more varied or isomorphic, more differentiated or homogeneous depending on the specific context of action (Haunschild and Miner, 1997; Brubaker, 1994).

25.5 SOCIAL GOODS PRODUCING SOCIAL STRUCTURE

Social structure can be designed to produce specific social goods, including knowledge, trust, formal rules, and commitment or loyalty. We are interested in two major determinants of trust-producing social structure: group identity, shared characteristics, and administrative rules that exist prior to beginning a new scientific collaboration, or the *endowed supply* of trust-producing structure, and the characteristics of each collaboration such as the expected value of the science that increase or decrease the demand for trust-producing structure within the collaboration. Together, the endowed supply of and demand for trust-producing social structure, along with the cost of creating any additional forms of that structure, determine the amount of social construction of trust that will occur during the course of the collaboration. Thus, social construction explicitly links structure and process.

Our model combines central concepts from the sociological literature on institutions, especially the identification of factors creating the endowed supply of trust, and basic concepts of price theory drawn from the economic literature to explicate the conditions under which new construction of trust-producing social structure will occur, to predict the amount of trust that will be constructed, and to explore the mechanisms of social construction. We develop a general model that we believe applies to the construction of social structure and institutions more generally, but we draw our examples from trust-producing structure.

Figure 25.3 provides some examples of endowment and demand, and the social construction process in teams, with some generalization to other settings. The basic outline of the components involved first emerged in an attempt to understand societal processes of production of trust (Zucker, 1986), and helped to define and generalize our approach.[5]

The model of trust-producing social structure was initially developed to explain some social construction we observed in "Big Science" teams in the context of an American Institute of Physics project (Zucker and Darby, 1995). Figures 25.4 and 25.5 summarize our analysis of how much trust-producing social structure would

---

[5] At the societal level, initial endowment included characteristic-based trust or process-based trust; specific to person or one exchange. Demand to generalize beyond this trust-producing social structure derived from high rates of immigration and internal migration, and also widespread business instability. Institutional trust generalized trust producing social structure too difficult to bridge exchanges: across group boundaries under conditions of significant social distance, across geographic distance, and involving non-separable elements, so that one failure implies more. Institutional trust-producing social structure was constructed in the late 1800s through the 1900s by: (1) spread of the rational bureaucratic form; (2) professional credentialing; (3) growth of the service economy, including financial services and government; and (4) regulation and legislation.

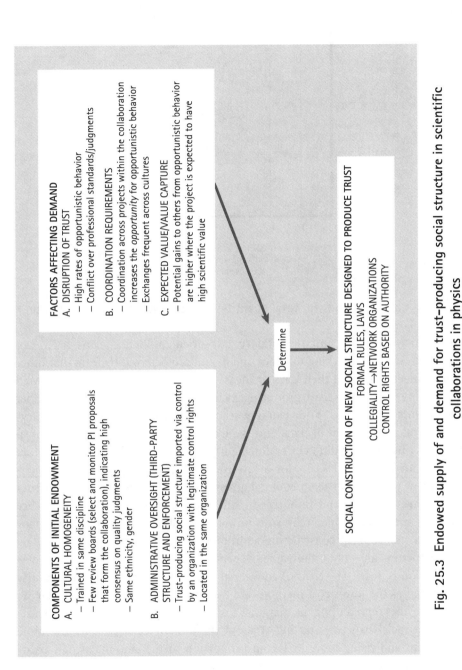

COMPONENTS OF INITIAL ENDOWMENT
A. CULTURAL HOMOGENEITY
    – Trained in same discipline
    – Few review boards (select and monitor PI proposals
      that form the collaboration), indicating high
      consensus on quality judgments
    – Same ethnicity, gender

B. ADMINISTRATIVE OVERSIGHT (THIRD-PARTY
    STRUCTURE AND ENFORCEMENT)
    – Trust-producing social structure imported via control
      by an organization with legitimate control rights
    – Located in the same organization

FACTORS AFFECTING DEMAND
A. DISRUPTION OF TRUST
    – High rates of opportunistic behavior
    – Conflict over professional standards/judgments

B. COORDINATION REQUIREMENTS
    – Coordination across projects within the collaboration
      increases the opportunity for opportunistic behavior
    – Exchanges frequent across cultures

C. EXPECTED VALUE/VALUE CAPTURE
    – Potential gains to others from opportunistic behavior
      are higher where the project is expected to have
      high scientific value

Determine

SOCIAL CONSTRUCTION OF NEW SOCIAL STRUCTURE DESIGNED TO PRODUCE TRUST
FORMAL RULES, LAWS
COLLEGIALITY→NETWORK ORGANIZATIONS
CONTROL RIGHTS BASED ON AUTHORITY

Fig. 25.3 Endowed supply of and demand for trust-producing social structure in scientific
collaborations in physics

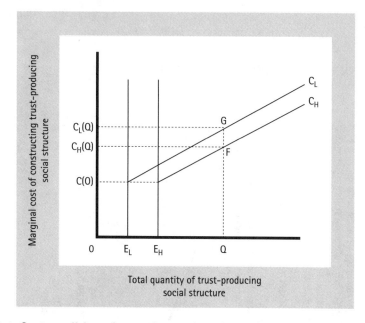

Fig. 25.4 Cost conditions for total quantity of trust–producing social structure

be constructed by large, interdisciplinary, task-oriented science teams which can accomplish more by working together openly but are deterred by fears that other team members will steal their data or ideas. These teams were initially endowed with varying amounts of trust-producing social structure according to the number of disciplines represented, prior working relationships, extent of funding-agency-imposed rules on control of data, and the like. We represent these differences in Figure 25.4 by drawing different endowments of trust-producing social structure coming into the project as E_L for a low-endowment team and E_H for a high-endowment team. Either team could augment their trust-producing social structure by investing time and resources in rulemaking, more frequent face-to-face meetings, and creating hierarchy with power to resolve disputes. Wherever they start from, the costs of constructing additional units of ad-hoc trust-producing social structure are about the same, depending primarily on how much new construction is done. The costs of additional ad-hoc units rises with the quantity constructed as the lower cost methods are used first. This is illustrated in Figure 25.4 by the lines representing the marginal cost (the cost of one more unit) of trust-producing social structure starting at about the same level at each team's initial endowment and rising more or less in proportion to the amount of new trust-producing social structure which is constructed.

To produce any total amount Q of trust-producing social structure—both endowed and newly constructed—the low-endowment teams are at a double cost advantage: Not only do they have the cost of catching up to the starting point for the high-endowment team, they also face higher costs for additional units between

E_H and Q since they have already picked their lower-hanging fruit while moving from E_L to E_H. We argue that the *value* of an additional unit of trust-producing social structure will generally decline as its total quantity increases, since the most important impediments to collaboration are eliminated first and each additional unit adds less to the ability of the team to achieve its goals. This declining value of additional units of trust-producing social structure is illustrated by the downward sloping line D in Figure 25.5.

Whenever the value of an additional unit of trust-producing social structure is greater than its cost, the team is more likely to engage in further construction than when the reverse is true. This model makes the following, empirically testable prediction: Teams which start out with more trust-producing social structure will end up with more of it in total, but will construct less new trust-producing social structure than will teams with low initial endowments. This prediction is conditioned upon the teams placing similar values on accomplishing their goals. If the low-endowment team placed sufficiently higher values on the ends facilitated by trust, they could invest in enough new construction to overcome the endowment advantage of the other team. On the other hand, if the high-endowment team instead placed enough higher value on its goals, then it could end up constructing more new trust-producing social structure than the low-endowment team. What makes the model interesting is that there are cases in which we can quantify not only differences in initial endowments but also in the value of working together and thus make nuanced predictions of the total and newly constructed amounts of trust-producing social structure.

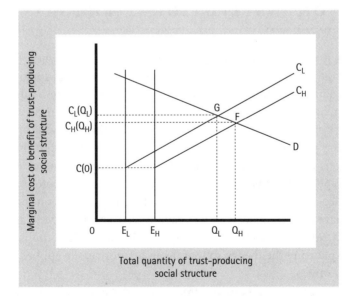

Fig. 25.5 Equilibrium social structures with different endowments of trust-producing social structure

In Zucker and Darby (1995), we find that higher demand for trust and lower initial endowments of trust-producing social structure both significantly increase construction of trust-producing social structure. We find suggestive evidence that this social construction actually results in production of higher valued science.

A number of research projects have been motivated by endowed and socially constructed culture/knowledge. Results from two that overlap substantially with our model will help to generalize it. Tolbert (1988) indexed amount of endowed culture in law firms by the percentage of members coming from the same law school, and found in multiple regression that law firms with higher educational homogeneity had fewer formal socialization practices: formal review, training, feedback. Formal socialization was increased with increasing growth of the firm. Smith, Collins, and Clark (2005) find that pre-existing (endowed) knowledge (education level, work experience, functional heterogeneity) and organization climate for risk-taking increase the development of new knowledge (through combination and exchange, including network structure), while the amount of newly created knowledge alone significantly increases the rate of new products and services produced in high technology firms.

25.6 SOME FURTHER THOUGHTS
ON INSTITUTIONAL THEORY

A theory is in many ways like a living tree. It grows according to where the nutrients and sun are the best, and in the process sometimes grows odd-looking branches and may be quite unbalanced in its growth in the sense that one side of the tree grows more than the other. Many people work at developing a theory, and not all use the same approach. One's own ideas change over time, as well.

A rewarding part of theory construction is the flash of insight one gets from putting various pieces of mosaic or puzzle together, when you see relationships among concepts and measures that were not open to you before. Figure 25.6 outlines one conception of how theory is developed, a conception that feels right to us as we have tried to make tacit ideas about institutional process and structure more explicit. At the bottom of the figure, we briefly outline the basics for the process of explicating the theory so that it can be more easily applied and further developed by others.

Like a giant sequoia (or an organization), a theory can live a long time, and every once in a while it is a good idea to prune the branches and perhaps clear out some of the surrounding growth that obstructs light or takes nutrients. Constructing

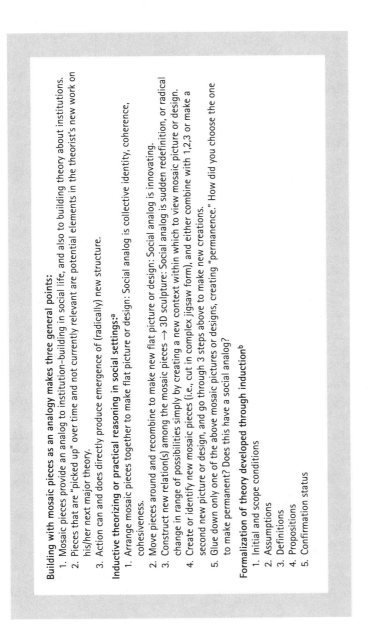

Building with mosaic pieces as an analogy makes three general points:

1. Mosaic pieces provide an analog to institution-building in social life, and also to building theory about institutions.
2. Pieces that are "picked up" over time and not currently relevant elements in the theorist's new work on his/her next major theory.
3. Action can and does directly produce emergence of (radically) new structure.

Inductive theorizing or practical reasoning in social settings:[a]

1. Arrange mosaic pieces together to make flat picture or design: Social analog is collective identity, coherence, cohesiveness.
2. Move pieces around and recombine to make new flat picture or design: Social analog is innovating.
3. Construct new relation(s) among the mosaic pieces → 3D sculpture: Social analog is sudden redefinition, or radical change in range of possibilities simply by creating a new context within which to view mosaic picture or design.
4. Create or identify new mosaic pieces (i.e., cut in complex jigsaw form), and either combine with 1,2,3 or make a second new picture or design, and go through 3 steps above to make new creations.
5. Glue down only one of the above mosaic pictures or designs, creating "permanence." How did you choose the one to make permanent? Does this have a social analog?

Formalization of theory developed through induction[b]

1. Initial and scope conditions
2. Assumptions
3. Definitions
4. Propositions
5. Confirmation status

Fig. 25.6 Institutional tool kits: Mosaic pieces as illustration of inductive theorizing and formalization

Notes: a. Suggested by Weick (1989: 528).
b. See Cohen (1988) on theory formalization.

theory is much like social construction: it is inherently a social process, and also often has significant tacit components. The most difficult work a theorist does is to codify some of the tacit components, but this work can also be very rewarding, since implications of the theory, like the flash of insight mentioned above, suddenly become visible and codified in a way that makes them more accessible to you, as well as to others (Cohen, 1988; Berger, et al., 1962). It is at this point in the process, the formalization and codification of the theory and not the early, more tacit development, where the normative accounts of theory construction best hold.

Theories, or more commonly empirical generalizations or theoretical approaches, sometimes take hold in a way that makes it difficult to take negative evidence into account. Examples abound, with perhaps the most famous the Pygmalion Effect (Rosenthal and Jacobson, 1968).[6] Thus, a more systematic approach to determining confirmation status of a theory is essential. Institutional theory is past its adolescence (Scott, 1987), and ready for more systematic formalization and test.

REFERENCES

BECKER, G. S. (1991). A note on restaurant pricing and other examples of social influences on price. *Journal of Political Economy*, 99: 1109–1116.

BERGER, J., COHEN, B. P., SNELL, J. L., and ZELDITCH, M., Jr. (1962). *Types of Formalization in Small Group Research*. Boston: Houghton Mifflin.

BERGER, P. L., and LUCKMANN, T. (1966). *The Social Construction of Reality: A Treatise in the Sociology of Knowledge*, New York: Doubleday.

BIKHCHANDANI, S., HIRSHLEIFER, D., and WELCH, I. (1992). A theory of fads, fashion, custom, and cultural change as informational cascades. *Journal of Political Economy*, 100: 992–1026.

BREWER, M. B., and SILVER, M. (1978). Ingroup bias as a function of task characteristics. *European Journal of Social Psychology*, 8: 393–400.

BRUBAKER, R. (1994). Nationhood and the national question in the Soviet Union and post-Soviet Eurasia: An institutionalist account. *Theory and Society*, 23: 47–78.

COHEN, B. P. (1988). *Developing Sociological Knowledge*. 2nd edn., Belmont, Calif.: Wadsworth Publishing.

DARBY, M. R., and ZUCKER, L. G. (2001). Change or die: The adoption of biotechnology in the Japanese and U.S. pharmaceutical industries. *Comparative Studies of Technological Evolution*, 7: 85–125.

---

[6] This is contested terrain with strong critiques of Rosenthal and Jacobson's research being followed by research that disconfirmed their findings on expectation effects, followed by a flood of research that provided confirming evidence some of the time and disconfirming evidence relatively less often. For a summary of the controversy and findings, see Miller and Turnbull (1986).

—— —— (2003). Growing by leaps and inches: creative destruction, real cost reduction, and inching up. *Economic Inquiry*, 41: 1–19.

—— —— (2005*a*). Grilichesian breakthroughs: Inventions of methods of inventing in nanotechnology and biotechnology, *Annales d'Economie et Statistique* (forthcoming).

—— —— (2005*b*). Going public when you can in biotechnology. In N. Lamoreaux and K. Sokoloff (eds.), *The Financing of Innovation in Historical Perspective*, New York: Social Science Research Council (forthcoming).

—— Liu, Q., and Zucker, L. G. (2004). High stakes in high technology: High-tech market values as options. *Economic Inquiry*, 42: 351–369.

Dawes, R. M., Van de Kragt, A. J. C., and Orbell, J. (1988). Not me or thee but we: The importance of group identity in eliciting cooperation in dilemma situations: Experimental manipulations. *Acta Psychologica*, 68: 83–97.

DiMaggio, P. J. (1982*a*). Cultural entrepreneurship in nineteenth-century Boston. Part I: The creation of an organizational base for high culture in America. *Media, Culture and Society*, 4 (Winter): 33–50.

—— (1982*b*). Cultural entrepreneurship in nineteenth-century Boston. Part II: The classification and framing of American art. *Media, Culture and Society*, 4(Autumn): 303–321.

—— (1991). Constructing an organizational field as a professional project: U.S. art museums, 1920–1940. In W. W. Powell and P. J. DiMaggio (eds.), *The New Institutionalism in Organizational Analysis*, Chicago: University of Chicago Press.

—— (1997). Culture and cognition. *Annual Review of Sociology*, 23: 263–287.

—— and Powell, W. W. (1983). The iron cage revisited: Institutional isomorphism and collective rationality in organizational fields, *American Sociological Review*, 48: 147–160.

Forman, D. (2004). Nanotech rides a rising tide: Venture cash flows into more mature startups as Wall Street prepares to float some shares. *Small Times*, 4(2): 18–21.

Garfinkel, H. (1964). Studies of the routine grounds of everyday activities. *Social Problems*, 11: 225–250.

—— (1967). *Studies in Ethnomethodology*. Englewood Cliffs, NJ: Prentice-Hall.

Green, S. E., Jr. (2004). A rhetorical theory of diffusion. *Academy of Management Review*, 29: 653–669.

Greenwood, R., Suddaby, R., and Hinings, C. R. (2002). Theorizing change: The role of professional associations in the transformation of institutionalized fields. *Academy of Management Journal*, 45: 58–80.

Haunschild, P., and Miner, A. S. (1997). Modes of interorganizational imitation: The effects of outcome salience and uncertainty. *Administrative Science Quarterly*, 42: 472–499.

Jensen, R. A., and Thursby, M. C. (2001). Proofs and prototypes for sale: The tale of university licensing. *American Economic Review*, 91(1): 240–259.

Kramer, R. M., and Brewer, M. B. (1984). Effects of group identity on resource use in a simulated commons dilemma. *Journal of Personality and Social Psychology*, 46: 1044–1056.

Liebeskind, J. P., Oliver, A. L., Zucker, L. G., and Brewer, M. B. (1996) Social networks, learning, and flexibility: Sourcing scientific knowledge in new biotechnology firms. *Organization Science*, 7: 428–443.

McCarthy, J. D., and Zald, M. N. (1977). Resource mobilization and social movements: A partial theory. *American Journal of Sociology*, 82: 1212–1241.

Meyer, J. W. (2002). Globalization, national culture, and the future of the world polity. *Hong Kong Journal of Sociology*, 3: 1–18.

MEYER, J. W. and ROWAN, B. (1977). Institutionalized organizations: Formal structure as myth and ceremony. *American Journal of Sociology*, 83: 340–363.

MILLER, D. T., and TURNBULL, W. (1986). Expectancies and interpersonal processes. *Annual Review of Psychology*, 37: 233–256.

POWELL, W. W., KOPUT, K., and SMITH-DOERR, L. (1996). Inter-organizational collaboration and the locus of innovation: Networks of learning in biotechnology. *Administrative Science Quarterly*, 41: 116–145.

—— WHITE, D. R., KOPUT, K. W., and OWEN-SMITH, J. (2004). Network dynamics and field evolution: The growth of inter-organizational collaboration in the life sciences. *American Journal of Sociology* (forthcoming).

ROCO, M. C. (2004). Nanoscale Science and Engineering at NSF: paper presented at the 2004 Nanoscale Science and Technology Grantee Conference, National Science Foundation, Arlington, Va., December 13–15.

ROMANELLI, E. (1991). The evolution of new organizational forms. *Annual Review of Sociology*, 17: 79–103.

ROSENTHAL, R., and JACOBSON, L. (1968). *Pygmalion in the Classroom*. New York: Holt, Rinehart and Winston.

SCHNEIDER, S. K., and BREWER, M. B. (1987). Effects of group composition on contributions to a public good. Unpublished manuscript, UCLA Psychology Department.

SCHUTZ, A. (1962) *Collected Papers*, vol. 1: *The Problem of Social Reality*, ed. M. Natanson. The Hague: Martinus Nijhoff.

—— (1970). *Reflections on the Problem of Relevance*. New Haven: Yale University Press.

SCOTT, W. R. (1987). The adolescence of institutional theory. *Administrative Science Quarterly*, 32: 493–511.

—— (1995). *Institutions and Organizations*. Foundations for Organizational Science, Thousand Oaks, Calif: Sage.

SMITH, K. G., COLLINS, C. J., and CLARK, K. D. (2005). Existing knowledge, knowledge creation capability and the rate of new product introduction in high technology firms. *Academy of Management Journal* (forthcoming).

STIGLER, G. J. (1961). The economics of information. *Journal of Political Economy*, 69: 213–225.

SWANSON, E. B., and RAMILLER, N. C. (1997). The organizing vision in information systems innovation. *Organization Science*, 8: 458–474.

THURSBY, J. G., and THURSBY, M. (2002). Who is selling the ivory tower? Sources of growth in university licensing. *Management Science*, 48: 90–104.

TOLBERT, P. S. (1988). Institutional sources of organizational culture in major law firms. In Lynne G. Zucker (ed.), *Institutional Patterns and Organizations: Culture and Environment*. Cambridge, Mass.: Ballinger Publishing Company.

—— and ZUCKER, L. G. (1983). Institutional sources of change in the formal structure of organizations: The diffusion of civil service reform, 1880–1935. *Administrative Science Quarterly*, 28: 22–39.

—— —— (1996), The institutionalization of institutional theory. In S. R. Clegg, C. Hardy, and W. R. Nord (eds.), *Handbook of Organization Studies*, London: Sage.

TUSHMAN, M. L., and ANDERSON, P. (1986). Technological discontinuities and organizational environments. *Administrative Science Quarterly*, 31(1): 439–465.

WALKER, H. A., THOMAS, G. M., and ZELDITCH, M., Jr. (1986). Legitimation, endorsement, and stability. *Social Forces*, 64: 620–643.

WEBER, M. (1947). *The Theory of Social and Economic Organization*, trans. from the 1924 German edn. by A. M. Henderson and T. Parsons, ed. and introd. by T. Parsons, New York: Free Press of Glencoe.

WEICK, K. E. (1989). Theory construction as disciplined imagination. *Academy of Management Review*, 14: 516–531.

WILLIAMSON, O. E. (1979). Transaction-cost economics: The governance of contractual relations. *Journal of Law and Economics*, 22: 233–261.

—— (1991). Comparative economic organization: The analysis of discrete structural alternatives. *Administrative Science Quarterly*, 36: 269–296.

ZUCKER, L. G. (1974). An Experimental Investigation of the Role of Institutionalization in the Persistence of Cultural Meaning. Ph.D. dissertation, Stanford University.

—— (1977). The role of institutionalization in cultural persistence. *American Sociological Review*, 42: 726–743.

—— (1983). Organizations as institutions. *Research in the Sociology of Organizations*, 2: 1–47.

—— (1986). Production of trust: Institutional sources of economic structure, 1840–1920. *Research in Organizational Behavior*, 8: 53–111.

—— (1987). Institutional theories of organization. *Annual Review of Sociology*, 13: 443–464.

—— and DARBY, M. R. (1995). Sociological analysis of multi-institutional collaborations in space science and geophysics. In J. Warnow-Blewett, A. J. Capitos, J. Genuth, and S. R. Weart (eds.), *AIP Study of Multi-Institutional Collaborations, Phase II: Space Science and Geophysics. Report No. 2: Documenting Collaborations in Space Science and Geophysics.* College Park, Md.: American Institute of Physics.

—— —— (1996). Star scientists and institutional transformation: Patterns of invention and innovation in the formation of the biotechnology industry. *Proceedings of the National Academy of Sciences*, November 12, 93: 12,709–12,716.

—— —— (2001). Capturing technological opportunity via Japan's star scientists: Evidence from Japanese firms' biotech patents and products. *Journal of Technology Transfer*, 26: 37–58.

—— —— and ARMSTRONG, J. (1998). Geographically localized knowledge: Spillovers or markets? *Economic Inquiry*, 36: 65–86.

—— —— —— (2002). Commercializing knowledge: University science, knowledge capture, and firm performance in biotechnology. *Management Science*, 48: 138–153.

—— —— and BREWER, M. B. (1998). Intellectual human capital and the birth of U.S. biotechnology enterprises. *American Economic Review*, 88: 290–306.

—— —— —— and PENG, Y. (1996). Collaboration structure and information dilemmas in biotechnology: Organizational boundaries as trust production. In R. M. Kramer and T. R. Tyler (eds.), *Trust in Organizations*, Thousand Oaks, Calif.: Sage.

—— —— and TORERO, M. (2002). Labor mobility from academe to commerce. *Journal of Labor Economics*, 20: 629–660.

··

CHAPTER 26

EPILOGUE

LEARNING HOW TO DEVELOP THEORY FROM THE MASTERS

··

KEN G. SMITH

MICHAEL A. HITT

> Without creative personalities able to think and judge independ-
> ently, the upward development of society is as unthinkable as the
> development of the individual personality without the nourishing
> soil of the community.
>
> (Albert Einstein)

THE purpose of this book is to help us learn how some of the greatest minds in management and organization research developed their ideas and theories. We believe that the best way to learn how to develop theory is by studying the masters who have developed important management theories. For the most part, the process of theory development is causally ambiguous, involving tacit knowledge and difficult-to-observe processes. Although well intentioned, prior literature on theory development has often been produced by scholars with limited experience in developing prominent theory. Such scholars are like lifeguards, outside of the swimming pool, attempting to teach someone to swim with commands: breathe, move your arms, kick your feet, etc. The parallel in theory development are

We thank Qing Cao and Mike Pfarrer for their comments on an earlier draft of this chapter.

commands such as: identify variables, state relationships, and clarify boundary conditions.

Our approach was to ask those in the pool, and perhaps the better swimmers, to reflect on the processes. Thus, we invited a group of scholars to describe how they developed their important theories. Our hypothesis was that we could learn more from those who actually know how to swim. Indeed, in this volume we observe the personal and professional struggles of these scholars, many in career-long pursuits to create, develop, and advance their theories.

The contribution of this set of authors to the scholarship and profession of management has been immense. For example, the average number of citations to their work, per author, is an extraordinary 4,900 citations and the median is around 3,600.[1] Our label for these authors as the "Great Minds of Management" seems most appropriate.

In this chapter, we attempt to summarize the common wisdom and riches provided by the different chapters. Although each chapter is different in terms of content, style, and approach, some common themes could be identified. In particular, we focus on the processes, roles, and characteristics involved in theory development.

26.1 THE PROCESS OF THEORY DEVELOPMENT

The various processes our scholars used to develop their theories are complex and unique to each scholar. Yet, we were able to discern four separate stages: Tension, Search, Elaboration, and Proclamation. Although we describe these as four separate linear stages, for many of our scholars the stages overlapped and often they moved back and forth through the stages as they developed their ideas.

26.1.1 Tension/Phenomena

The starting point for many of our scholars was a conflict or dissonance between the scholars' firmly embedded viewpoint about management, organizations, and

---

[1] Citations for this group of authors are a dynamic estimate. It is an estimate because some of these authors have made multiple contributions while in this volume they focus on a specific theory. Moreover, the citation count changes quite rapidly given the importance of their theories.

nature of the world, and an observation of phenomena that contradicted this viewpoint. These phenomena included contradictory research findings, faulty assumptions in an existing line of research or business behavior, or events that required additional or even a different explanation. Generally, these conflicts created tension for the scholars, which motivated them to resolve the tension. Hambrick notes, "My sense is that those who have a knack for developing theories are astute observers of phenomena; they detect puzzles in those phenomena; and they then start thinking about ways to solve the puzzles...puzzles trigger theory development."

We observe two related sources of tension explained by the scholars. First, a tension might exist between the assumptions of existing theories or explanations, and the scholars' own personal viewpoint. Locke and Latham and Bandura, for example, were motivated to develop their theories of goal setting and social cognition because of their belief that existing behavioral theories of human behavior, which assumed limited volition to individuals, were inaccurate. Similarly, Pfeffer was motivated to develop resource dependence theory by a belief that existing organizational theories gave too much explanatory power to the organizational leaders and that the environment likely plays a more important role. Barney was motivated to develop resource-based theory to resolve conflict about different world-views on the value of inequality. Nonaka proposed a theory of knowledge creation because of his dissatisfaction with the theory of information creation. He also expressed frustration with the dominance of positivism in management research. Winter describes how the motivation for an evolutionary theory of the firm came from the tension between "profit maximization" ideas in economics and behavioral viewpoints of the firm from the Carnegie School.

The second source of tension was created by specific research results or observations of actual managerial/organizational behavior that violated the researchers' viewpoint. That is, our scholars were also motivated by conflicting data. We use the word "data" in a very broad sense to include "highly structured descriptions" (Mintzberg), "real phenomena" (Pfeffer), and results of formal positivist research studies. As an example of this tension, Beach and Mitchell sought to develop image theory because the results of their studies suggested that probabilistic decision theory played a limited role in decision making. Scott concluded from his research on authority systems that work structures are not determined by economic laws but from social and political processes. Rousseau developed social contract theory, in part, because of employee consequences during the 1980s of corporate downsizing, buyouts, and restructuring. Porter, Steers, and Mowday began their study of organizational commitment because of the disparity between extreme political change and social activism during the 1960s and 1970s and the tranquility and unchanging nature of organizational life. Staw was motivated to study the escalation of commitment from his observations of the U.S. Government's difficulty getting out of the Vietnam War in the 1970s. Hambrick posited upper echelon theory in response to *Fortune*'s listing of demographic data for the CEOs of *Fortune* 500 companies. He recognized that they were publishing these data precisely because CEOs matter. Argyris's work on learning theory was borne out of his observations that individuals created policies that were later counterproductive and that they experienced difficulties in changing these policies, despite their dysfunction. Huff suggests that when focusing on real phenomena, a scholar is more intrinsically motivated.

Violation of viewpoints motivates the scholars to "correct" the explanation. The motivation to remove the tension or dissonance was extremely strong for virtually all of our authors. Perhaps, this is because their deep-seated beliefs were questioned. For example, many of our scholars, Bandura, Barney, Freeman, Frese, Huff, Latham, Locke, Rousseau, Staw, Weick, Williamson, and others have spent much of their careers in development of their theories.

26.1.2 Search

Levitt and March (1988) suggest that search is motivated to solve problems. Tension and dissonance led our masters to search for potential answers in order to reduce or eliminate the tension they experienced. The answers in this case involve the initial framework of their original theory. We label this phase "search" because there had to be exploration and discovery to develop the framework of the proposed theory. That is, the new theory is a consequence of the tension and search for answers.

Interestingly, our scholars were not highly explicit about the search processes or search behaviors they used other than to recognize that the search process occurred. Bandura notes, "Discontent with adequacy of existing theoretical explanations provides the impetus to search for conceptual schemes that can offer better explanations." Vroom describes how he was "searching for a dissertation topic" when he obtained an insight for expectancy theory. Rousseau describes the search process: "Observe and listen to people in the workplace, do lots of reading, and talk with other colleagues to figure out the way forward." Mintzberg argues, "We get interesting theory when we let go of all this scientific correctness, or to use a famous phrase, suspend our beliefs, and allow our minds to roam freely and creatively." We suspect that the search process is not independent of the tension that created it. They likely occur almost simultaneously and the tension continues until the framework for the new theory is developed. In fact, some tension is likely to exist until others in the field embrace the new theory. That said, we infer different patterns of search based on career paths of our scholars, and the colleagues with whom they interacted. Thus, their career orientations and their collegial relationships interacted with their individual training and experiences (knowledge stocks) to produce the new theory.

Most of our scholars describe how their career paths and trajectories influenced the development of their theory. Barney for example, talks about the move from Yale to UCLA and the intellectual environment at UCLA that inspired his original conception of the resource-based view. Victor Vroom describes his journey from Concordia University, to McGill University, to the University of Michigan, and then to the University of Pennsylvania in his pursuit to reconcile industrial psychology with psychology. Ed Freeman describes his travels from the Wharton School to the University of Minnesota and then to the University of Virginia to explore and establish stakeholder theory. Mike Frese suggests that his socialization and training in Germany interacted with his first job at the University of Pennsylvania to affect his thinking on individual personal initiative. Anne Huff describes the evolution of her research on management and organizational cognition from her early days at Illinois, to Colorado, and then on to the London Business School. Oliver Williamson explains how moves from Carnegie Mellon to the University of California at Berkeley to the University of Pennsylvania and then for a brief stay in the Antitrust Division of the U.S. Department of Justice influenced his work on transaction cost economics. Winter describes how evolutionary theory was derived through his journey from Yale to Michigan and then to Berkeley. He also worked at the RAND Corporation, the General Accounting Office, and the Council of Economic Advisers.[2]

As part of the search process, scholars often engage in discourse and interaction with other scholars to further develop their ideas. The role of others, especially close colleagues, appears to be a highly important part of the search process and the evolution of the theoretical ideas. Oldham and Hackman suggest that the intellectual culture at Yale during the 1970s, including scholars such as Clay Alderfer, Chris Argyris, Tim Hall, Ed Lawler, Ben Schneider, and others provided great stimulus for the theory on job design. Porter, Steers, and Mowday point to how their friendships with John Van Maanen, Joseph Champoux, William Crampon, Robert Dubin, and Harold Angle at University of California, Irvine, facilitated their work on organizational commitment. Williamson describes how Herbert Simon provided intellectual excitement at Carnegie Mellon to Williamson's ideas on transaction cost economics. Scott discusses how his work with Everett C. Hughes, Peter Blau, and John Meyer affected his views of institutional theory in his early years at Stanford. Pfeffer gives credit for the development of resource dependence theory to his co-location with Gerald Salancik and Barry Staw at the University of Illinois. Folger begins his chapter on "Fairness and Beyond" noting: "Like the Realtor's 'location, location, location' mantra, surely (sic the mantra) 'colleagues, colleagues,

---

[2] Clearly not all of our scholars moved around. Specifically, Albert Bandura, Ed Locke, Don Hambrick, Richard Scott, and Greg Oldham spent most of their careers at one school.

colleagues' is key to research and theory building." Bandura describes how career paths lead to many co-authors. He suggests that these seemingly chance encounters along life's pathways can have profound affects on career trajectories.

At least five other examples of collegial relationships are worthy of special note in our volume. Specifically, Beach and Mitchell have been working and writing together in the area of image theory for over twenty-five years, and Locke and Latham have collaborated on goal setting theory for nearly thirty years. Moreover, Pfeffer describes how Salancik and he complemented one another to develop resource dependence, and Oldham and Hackman suggest that the differences in their backgrounds promoted their theory of job enrichment. Winter also describes how his association with Dick Nelson facilitated their joint work on an evolutionary theory of the firm. In these cases, authors worked jointly to develop their theory.

How do the search processes, especially career paths (locations) and collegue-ship (interaction) affect theory development? We agree with Mintzberg that developing new theory is a creative act. Koestler, in his book *The Act of Creation* (1964), introduced the term bisociation to refer to the creative process through which two seemingly unrelated matrices of thought are combined to form a novel outcome. He argued that the results from bisociation are more radically creative than those resulting from routine, logical, and single dimension thought. According to Koestler, the creative act does not result from fashioning some creative product from out of nowhere. Rather, "it uncovers, selects, re-shuffles, combines, synthesizes already existing facts, ideas, faculties, [and] skills" (Koestler, 1964: 120). In our view, the search process, including different locations and different colleagues, expose the searcher to new and seemingly unrelated matrices of thought and ideas that when combined lead to the development of new theory. Zucker and Darby capture this aspect of theory development: "A rewarding part of theory construction is the flash of insight one gets from putting various pieces of mosaic or puzzle together, when you see relationships among concepts and measures that were not open to you before" (p. 567). Nahapiet and Ghoshal's (1998) ideas on intellectual capital also capture this process. Specifically, they suggest that new knowledge is likely to be created when there is greater interaction and exchange.

Authors such as Freeman, Bandura, Huff, and Rousseau suggest the search process often includes significant serendipity or chance. While serendipity may play some role, our masters still were able to purposively create new knowledge or theory as a result of this process. So far, we have only discussed search in terms of location and relationships. However, it is also evident that the effect of location and interactions with others is moderated by the masters' backgrounds, especially their educations and experiences at different institutions.

The backgrounds of our authors in terms of education/training are fascinating. Table 26.1 reports where the scholars obtained their Ph.D. degrees. Most of our scholars were trained at Division 1 Research Schools such as Ohio State, Michigan, UCLA, and many at elite private universities, including Cornell, Yale, and North-

Table 26.1 Authors and their School of Ph.D.

Name	Ph.D.	Name	Ph.D.
Argyris	Cornell	Mowday	UC-Irvine
Bandura	Iowa	Nonaka	UC-Berkeley
Barney	Yale	Oldham	Yale
Beach	Colorado	Pfeffer	Stanford
Cameron	Yale	Porter	Yale
Folger	UNC-Chapel Hill	Rousseau	UC-Berkeley
Freeman	Washington University	Scott	Chicago
Frese	Tech. Univ. of Berlin	Staw	Northwestern
Hackman	Illinois	Steers	UC-Irvine
Hambrick	Penn State	Vroom	Michigan
Huff	Northwestern	Weick	Ohio State
Latham	Akron	Williamson	Carnegie-Mellon
Locke	Cornell	Winter	Yale
Mintzberg	MIT	Zucker	Stanford
Mitchell	Illinois		

western. A number of our scholars explain how their training prepared them for the development of their theory. For example, Rousseau describes how her training in sociology and clinical psychology helped her understand social contracts. Barney discusses the importance of sociology training while he was at Yale. He concludes that his education in sociology allowed him to ask big questions in turn suggesting that, "there is at least a chance that some bigger answers might emerge." Williamson identifies his training at Carnegie and his exposure to Herbert Simon as uniquely preparing him to develop his theory. Indeed, a number of our scholars make connections to Herbert Simon.

We have described the search process whereby our scholars were motivated to reduce or remove the tension that originally prompted the search. We focused on physical locations and interpersonal interactions, which combine with individual training to lead to the development of important new theory. Next, we examine how our scholars elaborated or expanded their initial ideas.

26.1.3 Elaboration/Research

The process by which scholars research and expand their ideas characterizes the elaboration stage of theory development. The process of elaboration is broadly described by our authors as detective work, induction, sensemaking, and research. Weick describes this stage of theory development as a:

sprawling collection of ongoing interpretive actions. To define this "sprawl" is to walk a thin line between trying to put plausible boundaries around a diverse set of actions that seem to cohere while also trying to include enough properties so that the coherence is seen as distinctive and significant but something less than the totality of the human condition.

Bandura also captures this part of the process: "Initial formulations prompt lines of experimentation that help improve the theory. Successive theoretical refinements bring one closer to understanding the phenomena of interest." Oldham and Hackman note:

We suspect that no theory, and certainly not ours, emerges all at once in a flash of insight. Instead, theory development can seem as if it is an endless iterative process, moving back and forth between choice of variables and specification of the links among them, hoping that eventually the small, grudgingly achieved advances will outnumber the forced retreats.

Locke and Latham are more specific in discussions of their means of elaboration in their goal setting research:

by doing many experiments over a long period of time, by showing that our experiments worked and thereby getting other researchers interested in goal setting research, by coming at the subject of goal setting from many different angles, by examining failures and trying to identify their causes, by resolving contractions and paradoxes, by integrating valid ideas from other developing theories, by responding to criticism that seemed to have merit and refuting those that did not, by asking ourselves critical questions and by keeping an open mind.

Zucker and Darby use the metaphor of a growing tree to portray the process of theory development: "It grows according to where the nutrients and sun are best, and in the process sometimes grows odd-looking branches and may be quite unbalanced in its growth in the sense that one side of the tree grows more than the other. Many people work at developing a theory, and not all use the same approach". Rousseau suggests that three specific mechanisms (four distinct sets of actions) helped her elaborate psychological contract theory: spending time in organizations, writing two books, and producing a series of research projects. In some cases, this process of elaboration is of a shorter-term nature and in others it is a career-long endeavor. For the most part, elaboration involves a rather long period of time, although not necessarily a whole career.

We observe that elaboration occurs in different ways based on the level of theoretical abstraction. In particular, when the theoretical concepts are closer to measurement, elaboration tends follow the scientific model of quantitative research. In such cases, other researchers and scholars may join in the elaboration process. In contrast, the more removed the concepts in the theory are from measurement, elaboration tends to follow a path of description, diagrams, and more qualitative research. Frese makes a distinction between grand theories and mid-level theories that somewhat capture the differences in abstraction we describe here.

A number of authors talk about theory development at an abstract level. For example, Mintzberg observes,

My favorite among my own books, *The Structuring of Organizations*, was written out of the theories, research findings, and descriptions of others . . . Highly structured descriptions, for examples based on data collection around a couple of abstract variables, were far less useful. Think of the would-be theorist trying to swim in water as compared with a tank of shredded paper.

Later he notes, "I must have an outline to write down my ideas, even if the object of writing down my ideas is to come up with an outline. This is the ultimate problem in creating theory." Our scholars talk about the need to draw abstract pictures and diagrams. For example, Rousseau suggests that heuristics such as "diagrams, continua, NXN tables, etc." are an important aid to theory development. William- son similarly observes, "Getting it right entails working through the logic—in words, diagrams, or mathematics, possibly all three". Mintzberg reflects, "My work is loaded with diagrams, seeking to express every which way how the ideas I am trying to make come together."

Barney discusses the abstract nature of the resource-based view. He notes that his framework was never intended for empirical testing but was designed to "lead scholars to think about the attributes, and that through that effort, empirical implications of resource-based logic could be developed." Pfeffer suggests that for the resource dependence theory, "Although there was a flurry of empirical activity directly exploring some of the core ideas of the theory, the subsequent history of resource dependence is consistent with its ideas being used more as a metaphor or general theoretical orientation rather than testing very precise fal- sifiable, predictions." Scott describes how institutional theory was being elaborated on both the east and west coasts of the U.S., when he put forth a conceptual schema that might capture the common ideas and thus yield an integrated theory.

We also observe that when theory is defined at a less abstract level, elaboration tends to follow the more normal science routine. For example, Hambrick describes how after the publication in the *Academy of Management Review* of Upper Echelon Theory, which contains concepts of demography and firm performance for which measures could be readily obtained, empirical evidence quickly mounted to sup- port the view. Porter, Steers, and Mowday capture the elaboration of organizational commitment research:

In the thirty years or so since work on the concept of organizational commitment first began, numerous studies have been conducted that shed light on the relevance of employee attitudes toward the overall organization. In general, the predictions made as a result of our initial work concerning performance, turnover, attendance, and extra-role behavior have been supported. This support comes from several meta-analyses of hundreds of studies and the results are robust with respect to the different measures of affective commitment that have been used.

Argyris used a variety of field methods, including observations, tape recordings, and interviews, to study and explicate single loop learning theory. However, such methods were more difficult to use with the more abstract double loop learning theory. Beach and Mitchell describe the decade of quantitative research at University of Arizona and University of Washington that followed the introduction of image theory. These authors explain how they focused on elaborating the screening mechanisms in image theory rather than images because these mechanisms were easier to study. Cameron and colleagues' work on the competing value framework for organizational effectiveness allowed them to empirically integrate a variety of different models and assumptions in prior research on effectiveness. Frese describes how elaboration moves from the empirical testing of less risky to more risky hypotheses. This process allowed him to identify the boundary conditions of his theory of personal initiative.

We conclude that the purpose underlying the theory is important to the way that it evolves. For example, Williamson suggests that a good theory is one that can be tested. Mintzberg, on the other hand, observes that a good theory is a bridge that leads to another theory. Barney also suggest that a good theory is one that produces debate and discussion. The idea that theory can serve multiple purposes, from sensemaking to empirical testing, has not been well acknowledged in the literature.

For some of our scholars, the processes of search and elaboration worked as a combined stage. For example, Staw employed lab, field, and archival studies at both the individual and organizational level of analysis to elaborate his ideas on escalation of commitment. He describes how a theory of escalation of commitment theory emerged from three decades of research involving multiple samples and research designs. Weick, Mintzberg, and Locke and Latham similarly describe the search and elaboration process in developing their theories.

26.1.4 Proclamation/Presentation

The final phase of theory development is presenting the model and research to the various and appropriate constituencies. Although the presentation of one's ideas or theory might seem relatively straightforward, our scholars generally struggled to get their new ideas accepted, especially in the top academic journals. Perhaps, because their ideas were new or the theory too encompassing, several of our scholars had to write a book to present their works.

The proclamation of the theories can occur in many ways, but two alternatives are more common. First, there can be a series of both conceptual and empirical articles that often incrementally build on each other or independently add to the theoretical knowledge. Usually after the quantity of this work passes a critical threshold, it is summarized in a book in order to create a "gestalt" framework and to enhance the coherence of the theory. For example, Locke and Latham summarized over twenty-five years of studies in their 1990 book on goal setting. Similarly, Finkelstein and Hambrick (1996) summarized and elaborated ten years of research in their book, *Strategic Leadership*. Beach and Mitchell (1996) published a number of papers on image theory and summarized this work in an edited volume on Image Theory.

A significantly different alternative is where the theory is explained in a book without a series of journal articles appearing beforehand or as a means of integrating series of disparate research. For example, Anne Huff summarized the key ideas on the management cognition in the *Mapping of Strategic Thought*. Vroom (1964), at 28 years old, published a 150-page monograph, *Work and Motivation*. He notes, "When I now look back at that proposed monograph, I see it as amazingly presumptuous." Much of Williamson's (1975) reasoning on the boundaries of firms was published in his book *Markets and Hierarchies: Analysis and Antitrust Implications*. Scott's (1995) book *Institutions and Organizations* summarizes and integrates a wide variety of work on institutional theory with the goal of theoretical integration. Cameron and Whetten's (1983) book *Organizational Effectiveness: A Comparison of Multiple Models* allowed the authors to put together in one model a variety of different models of effectiveness.

As noted previously, a number of our scholars express concern and some scorn for the academic publishing process that repeatedly rejected much of their work. Barney notes that his seminal paper was rejected multiple times before he accepted his own paper for publication in a special issue of the *Journal of Management* that he was editing. Interestingly, this paper has been cited more than 1,200 times to date and the number of citations to it grows on a continuous basis. Frese claims that "some of my empirical articles that I am most proud of have been the most difficult to publish. My hunch is that they break with the typical approach to doing things." Bandura contends that theory building is "not for the thin-skinned. Theorists must be prepared to see their conceptions and empirical findings challenged, misconstrued or caricatured, sometimes with ad hominem embellishments." Mintzberg goes further, suggesting that developers of theory must not be afraid to experience "fear of being different, fear of standing out, fear of not belonging, fear of being wrong, or subversive (if not obvious). Yet we have built fear into the whole process by which we do and access research especially in the tenure process. Open the journals and read the results." Huff suggests that our profession's strong emphasis on publishing in top journals "weakens an essential requirement of theory building." Rousseau describes how she struggled publishing her early work: "The need to legitimate the study of the psychological contract was something I keenly felt, and absent an early hit in an established journal, I pursued an incremental strategy. This is a case of loving the goals you are near when you aren't near the goals you love." These concerns and comments by our scholars are consonant with statements made by some previous Nobel prize winners who explained that they experienced difficulties in publishing their work or in gaining acceptance by colleagues of their early ideas that eventually led to the advances recognized by the Nobel prize. It is likely that the novelty of our scholars' ideas and the fact that they represent big issues made it difficult for journals to evaluate their contribution.

Clearly, not all of our scholars faced the same difficulty publishing their works. For example, Winter expresses surprise that he and Nelson's first paper focusing on evolutionary theory was published in *American Economic Review.*

26.2 RESEARCHER ROLES

In this next section, we discuss the different roles researchers can play in developing their theories. Importantly, not all of our scholars played all of the roles. We draw heavily on Richard Scott's chapter on institutional theory. Scott argues that development of institutional theory has been a collective effort involving multiple scholars. Clearly, other authors in this volume make this same point. Drawing from Scott, we identify five different roles that scholars can play in theory development: creator, codifier, carrier, researcher, and advocate. Some of our scholars played all of these roles, while others engaged in a more limited set of roles.

1. *Creator.* Mintzberg's chapter emphasizes the role of "imagination, insight and discovery" in theory development. He argues that theory is of little use unless it surprises and changes perceptions. Locke and Latham also point to the important role of discovery based on observation. Using the works of the authors published in this volume, we derived and have attempted to explain the process by which theories are created: tension, search, elaboration, and proclamation.

Our selection of scholars to participate in this volume was with the intent of including the people who created the theories. Still, the initial origins of some of theories preceded the work of our masters. For example, although Williamson elaborated transaction costs economics, the original ideas came from Coase (1937), just as the origins of institutional theory came before Scott's work. In contrast, Freeman is largely credited with creating stakeholder theory, and Hambrick with the creation of upper echelon theory, but efforts to elaborate these theories involved many other scholars.

It is uncommon for doctoral programs and new faculty, particularly in the U.S., to place a heavy emphasis on the role of creativity in theory development or scholarship. Moreover, the short-term nature of the tenure process often drives scholars to make safer choices in the research questions that they pursue and the methods used in pursuing them. This process largely excludes innovation as an option. Yet, given the importance of new theory to the management field and our profession, we should think more about how to inspire greater innovation and creativity in our scholarship. In addition, there seems to be some sentiment among our scholars that many of our best journals are not tolerant of new ideas.

2. *Codifier.* The codifier role is that of summarizing, organizing, and distributing key arguments into a comprehensive framework (Scott, Ch. 22, this volume). Virtually all of our authors engaged in the codifier role. The codifier role appears to be part of the elaboration process and the proclamation process. According to Scott, an important dimension of this role is differentiating and positioning the theory in the context of other perhaps competing theories. This role is also dynamic in the sense that the codifier must periodically update the theory. It is doubtful that a theory can be advanced without codification of its key concepts and boundaries. However, it is likely that the greater the level of abstraction in the theory, the more difficult will be the codification. For example, the key constructs in the resource-based view have been difficult to operationalize, perhaps because of a lack of codification.

Perhaps, if scholars focused more strongly on the purpose of theory, they would be better prepared to know how it should be codified. The process of codification and elaboration may vary depending on the goal of the theory.

3. *Carrier.* The carrier role involves the process of communicating the concepts and approaches of the theory to a wider audience (Scott, this volume). As we have noted, the product of this behavior was often a book or seminal article. The carrier role is probably most apparent in the proclamation stage. All of our scholars were carriers to the extent that they published their works for dissemination to a larger audience. Many of our authors emphasize the importance of words and precision in elaborating their theories.

Like other aspects of the theory development process, the role of diagrams and modeling perhaps requires more emphasis in doctoral training and among new faculty. Especially with more abstract theory, the use of metaphors, rich description, and clear language may be the most important part of the theory development process.

4. *Researcher.* The research role involves demonstrating the relevance of a particular theory by analyzing, predicting, and testing the theory with a variety of samples and contexts (Scott, this volume). As our authors point out, such research can be inductive as well as deductive. It can involve laboratory or field settings and qualitative or quantitative methods. In general, the value of a theory is enhanced to the extent that it is examined and tested using many different samples and contexts and different methods as well. In some way, all of our scholars engaged in the researcher role.

5. *Advocate*. The final role our scholars played in the development of their theory was as an advocate. In other words, they played an important role defending and promulgating their theory. Many of our scholars discuss the market for ideas suggesting that theoretical explanations come in and out of vogue as new theories emerge and diffuse. Although the market for ideas cannot be controlled, some people have more legitimacy than others. As a whole, the great minds are capable of managing the evolution of their theories—perhaps, they accomplish this by engaging in all of the roles identified above. Because they hold a deep knowledge and perspective of their theory, they are in the best position to serve as advocates. Kim Cameron's reconceptualization of organizational effectiveness into positive organizational effectiveness is one example of the role of a scholar as an advocate for his/her theory over time.

26.3 Characteristics of the Researcher that Drive the Process

In this final section, we briefly review some of the common individual characteristics of our scholars that affected the process of theory development. Our group of scholars stand out in the passion they bring to their theory, their persistence in the face of failure, their focused discipline, and their interest on big ideas that matter to managers and organizations. Because we believe these points are obvious from the actual chapters, here, we focus primarily on why these characteristics are important to the process.

1. *Passion*. One cannot read the chapters in this book and not be moved by the authors' passion for their ideas and subjects. This passion is evident in several ways. For example, it is evident in the excitement they express when they are searching for answers, the enthusiasm and high level of motivation they bring to the process of elaboration, and the persistence they demonstrate in proclaiming their ideas. They demonstrate a strong confidence in their theory and ideas. As the various chapters suggest, theory development is difficult, hard work, with an uncertain outcome. The scholars in this volume appear to thrive in this type of environment. Indeed, they describe their work as exciting, fun, and fulfilling.

2. *Persistence*. Developing theory is not for the faint hearted. Indeed, searching for effective answers, elaborating proposed solutions and presenting new ideas to the academic community involves many high-risk activities. For example, a group of scholars may question the value of the theory when it is first presented, reviewers

and editors may reject the first manuscript at a top journal, or the theory might be attacked from the authors of a competing theory. It would seem that the passion and love for what they do, knowledge about their theories, and confidence in their ideas allow our scholars to persist in the face of these threats. Indeed, our scholars are unique because of their ability to overcome adversity and not accept failure. There is probably a strong correlation between their advocacy of the theory and the ultimate evaluation and contribution of it.

3. *Discipline.* Our scholars also express a certain discipline in their manner of and commitment to their work. This discipline can be observed in the long hours they spend crafting their theory, the focused nature of their work over very long periods of time, and in the quality and rigor of the theory they present. Behind this disciplined approach is likely a core set of values. These values are evident when the initial tension is identified, in the comprehensive manner by which they search for answers, and in the coherent way in which they elaborate their ideas. In fact, our scholars are uniformly predictable in their pursuit of excellence.

4. *Big Ideas.* Another characteristic that is prominent among our scholars is their focus on big ideas. Repeatedly, they express scorn for small ideas and ideas that are not based on real phenomena. They search for and encourage doctoral students and colleagues who ask important research questions. Critically, they cope effectively with ambiguity and are capable of working with questions that don't require immediate answers. They seem to thrive trying to answer important questions. It is, perhaps, because their ideas are so big, that many of our scholars have spent their entire research careers developing and elaborating their theories. Figure 26.1 summarizes our conclusions about the theory development process.

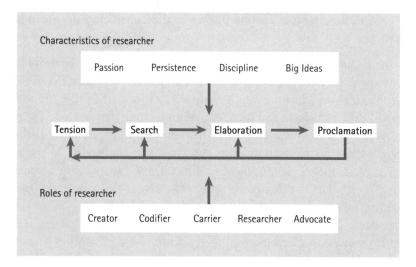

Fig. 26.1 The process of theory development

26.4 Conclusion

We were inspired to develop this book by our observation that there is a substantial amount of variation in viewpoints among scholars about what good theory is and how it should be developed. As former editors of two major journals that demand theory development (*Academy of Management Review* and the *Academy of Management Journal*), we also wanted to learn more about how good theory can be developed. We specifically were interested in determining if there is an identifiable path to theory development, agreement among scholars in how it should be developed, and if our gatekeepers could explicate how to evaluate new theory.

Our conclusion from reading the wonderful chapters in this book is that theory development is a demanding process, not to be taken lightly. Moreover, the development of a significant new theory does not occur often. Although more good theories will always be desirable and important in advancing our understanding of management and organizations, development of such theory is unlikely to be achieved fully through our scholarly journals or in the short term. However, by recognizing that development of good theory requires significant investments, often is long term in nature, fraught with failure, sequential in process, but exhilarating work, we can better prepare our students and new management faculty for this endeavor.

Accordingly, this book provides a realistic preview into how theory is developed. With this preview, we hope that more scholars will be better prepared to develop new theory. We hope that by understanding the different processes, roles, and characteristics, it will inspire and help more of us to advance theory and our profession. We admire and thank our authors for showing us the way! We hope that more in our profession can have as much fun and excitement as the "great minds" who contributed to this volume.

> Your faith is what you believe, not what you know
> (John Lancaster Spalding)

References

BEACH, L. R., and MITCHELL, T. R. (1996). Image theory, the unifying perspective. In L. R. Beach (ed.), *Decision Making in the Work Place: A Unified Perspective*: 1–20. Mahwah, NM: Erlbaum.

CAMERON, K. S., and WHETTEN, D. A. (1983) *Organizational Effectiveness: A Comparison of Multiple Models*. New York: Academic Press.

COASE, R. H. (1937). The nature of the firm. *Economica*, 4(16): 386–405.

FINKELSTEIN, S., and HAMBRICK, D. C. (1996). *Strategic Leadership: Top Executives and their Effects on Organizations*. Minneapolis/St Paul: West Publishing.

KOESTLER, A. (1964). *The Act of Creation*. New York: Macmillan.

LEVITT, B., and MARCH, J. (1988). Organizational learning. *Annual Review of Sociology*, 14: 319–340.

NAHAPIET, J., and GHOSHAL, S. (1998). Social capital, intellectual capital, and the organizational advantage. *Academy of Management Review*, 23: 242–266.

SCOTT, W. R. (1995). *Institutions and Organizations*. Thousand Oaks, Calif.: Sage.

VROOM, V. H. (1964). *Work and Motivation*, New York: Wiley.

WILLIAMSON, O. (1975). *Markets and Hierarchies: Analysis and Antitrust Implications*. New York: Free Press.

Index

ABB 277
abductive logic 63
accountability 68–9
  moral accountability 72–6
Ackoff, R.L. 274, 418–19
action production 262–7
  Model I theory-in-use 264–6
  Model II theory-in-use 266–7, 274
    moving toward 267–72
  single and double-loop learning 262–4, 271–2
actions 519
action theory 84–5, 86, 104
  cognitively anchored theory 341–5
  planning 99–101
  see also action production
Adams, J.S. 56–7, 67
adaptation 498
  economic organization and 488
adaptation level effects 72
adoption decisions 45, 46
affective commitment 176
agency 9–10, 69–70, 343, 467–8
  exercise of agency through self-regulation 16–22
  focal agents 70
  moral agency 21–2
  nature of human agents 377–9
  triadic model 26–8
Agle, B. 430
Alaska Airlines 323
Alchian, Armen 509–10
Alderfer, Clay 286
Allen, N.J. 174, 181
American Pulpwood Association 133
Amit, Raffi 293–4
amplifying qualities 323–4
Anderson, J. 12, 199
antitrust enforcement 494–5
Anton, Ron 197
Aquino, Karl 197
argument 338–9
Argyris, Chris 162, 195, 308
Arrow, K. 491–2, 502
Atiyah, Patrick S. 196–7, 205
Atkinson, J. 139, 242, 246
attention 335–6

Ba 380–1
  building, energizing, and connecting 389–90
Bacdayan, P. 534
Baden-Fuller, C. 336
Bain, Joe 493
Baker, W. 322
Balkin, D.B. 119
Bandura, Albert 134, 139
Bantel, K.A. 118
Barbosa, Ricardo 116
Barley, Steve 339, 455, 467
Barnard, C. 195, 306, 487–8
Barsade, Sigal 230
Bateman, T.S. 96
Baum, J.R. 117
Bazerman, Max 197, 198
Beach, H.D. 133
Becker, H.S. 175
Beckman, C.M. 450
behavioral decision theory 453
behavioral integration 120–2
behavioralism 10–11, 520–1
behavioral theory of the firm 520
Benson, Lehman 48–9
Berger, P.L. 549
Bergmann, Gustav 247
Bernoulli, Daniel 38
Berra, Yogi 366
Bies, Bob 66, 67–8, 198
big questions 300
biotechnology 554–61
Birley, S. 117–18
Bissell, Byron 48
Black, M. 348
Black, Sylvia 116
Blaug, M. 514–15
Blau, Peter M. 461
Blood, Milt 191–2
Bluedorn, A.C. 307
Bobocel, Ramona 80
Bodo doll study 15
Boorman, Scott 285
bounded rationality 497
Bower, J.L. 334
Bowie, Norman 428

Breyer, Stephen 494
Brickman, Phil 56, 63
Brighton, William 218
Brockner, Joel 219
buffering qualities 323–4
Burns, T. 306
Burt, Ronald S. 442, 449, 452
business behavior 521–2

Calder, Bobby J. 216
Campbell, Donald 406
Canadair 241–2
Cannella, Bert 116
capabilities 535
    dynamic capabilities 536–7
capitalism 525
Cappelli, P. 174, 185–6
careerism 201
Carnegie School 110, 520
Carpenter, M.A. 118
Carroll, G.R. 451
Cartright, Don 242, 244
categorization 336–7
causal analysis 23–4
causality 337–8
causal relationships 146
Chaganti, R. 117
chance events 18–20
Chandler, Alfred 493
Charan, Ram 420
choice set 42
Cho, Theresa 116
Christensen, C.M. 450
Christiensen-Szalanski, Jay 41–2, 47
Clark, Margaret 199
Coase, Ronald 486, 487, 491, 495, 502
cognition 331–2
    see also managerial and organizational
        cognition (MOC)
cognitive behaviorist theory 84–5
cognitive determinants 24
cognitive dissonance 63, 400
cognitively anchored theory of action 341–5
Cohen, M. 534
collaborations 554, 556
Collins, D. 455
Collins, J. 186
commitment 175
    affective commitment 176
    goal commitment 137–9
    see also escalation of commitment;
        organizational commitment
Commons, John R. 486–7
compatibility test 46–7
Conlon, E.J. 308
Conner, Kate 295

Connolly, T. 308
contingency theory 374
contracts 488–9
    see also psychological contract theory
control theory 143
Cook, Tom 64
Corbin, A.K. 196
corporate governance, stakeholder
        approach 429–30
corporate social performance (CSP) 430–1
Cramer, R.D. 450
Crant, J.M. 96
critical incident technique 60
Cronbach, Lee 243, 246
Crosby, Faye 64
Cross, R. 322
cultural influences 27–8, 85–6
    changing culture 277
    error management culture 89–90
Cummings, Larry 199, 200
Cyert, Richard 520–1
Czapinski, J. 319

Dabos, Guillermo 207, 208
D'Andrade, Roy 504
D'Aveni, Richard 116
David, R.J. 454
Davis, G.F. 438, 445, 446–7, 451–2
Day, D.V. 117
Dearborn, DeWitt 114–15
decision making 36–51, 537–8
    adoption decisions 45, 46
    framing the decision 46
    gamble analogy 38–40
    Image Theory 36, 43–50
    mechanisms 46–7
    normative model 38
    participation in (pdm) 137–9
    principles 42, 44
    progress decisions 45, 46
    in unfamiliar contexts 525–6
decoupling 468–9
defensive routines 275–6
DeHoyos, Genevieve 283
Demsetz, Harold 290, 291
deonance 77, 79
Deonance Theory (DT) 78–80
deprivation:
    perceived legitimacy of deprivations 66
    relative 56
Descartes 144
Deutsch, S.J. 308
diagrams 363–4
Dickson, W.J. 306
DiMaggio, Paul M. 463, 467, 469, 471–2
Dino, R.N. 121

discretion 118–20
discriminating alignment hypothesis 500
dissatisfaction 70–1
  goals and 129–30
dissonance theory 217
distributive justice 73
Dollard, J. 11
Donaldson, G. 39
Donaldson, T. 424, 429
double-loop learning 262–4, 271–2
Doz, Y. 334
Dreze, Jacques 490–1
Droge, C. 117
duality of structure 342–3
dual knowledge system 12
Dubin, Robert 1–2, 175
Duesenberry, James 489
Duke, James 283
Dunegan, Ken 49
Dunfee, T. 429
Dunham, Laura 432
Durkheim, Emile 284
dynamic capabilities 536–7

economic growth, technology and 524–9, 559–60
economics 486–7, 541
education level, innovation relationship 117–18
Edwards, Ward 38
efficacy beliefs 28
Einstein, Albert 144
employee absenteeism, organizational
  commitment and 183–4
employment contract see Psychological Contract
  Theory
Emshoff, James R. 418, 419–20
enterprise strategy 426, 428
entrepreneurship 98–101
environment 18, 453
  knowledge creation 382
  organizational effectiveness and 306–7
  personal initiative and 96–7
  resource-dependence theory and 444, 446–7
environmental scanning 114
e-prime 400–1
equity 56–7
Erez, Miriam 136, 138
error management 87–90
  function of error culture in
    organizations 89–90
  training 87–9
escalation of commitment 215–36, 445
  origins of theory 215–22
    initial research findings 218–19
    limiting conditions 220
    subsequent research 220–2
  toward an organizational theory 222–33

alternative paths to understanding 231–2
  falsifiability 228–9
  field studies 229–31
  learning from controversy 232–3
  modifications to the theory 227–8
  see also commitment; organizational
    commitment
Etzioni, Amatai 173–4
Evanisko, M.J. 117
Evan, William 422
evolutionary theory 509–42
  behavioralism 520–1
  defining the stakes 517
  empirics 537–40
  Friedman conjecture 512, 518–20
  production theory limitations 529–30
  productive knowledge 530–2
  profit maximization 512–4, 515–6, 518–9
  routines and capabilities 533–5
  sources of routines and technologies 535–7
  tacit knowledge 532–3
  technology and economic growth 524–9
    decisions in unfamiliar contexts 525–7
    innovative competition 527–8
executive compensation, discretion and 119–20
expectancy theory (ET) 36–7, 139, 239–40,
  247–56
  limitations of 37–41
  motivation and 247–55
    fitting the theory to the data 249–51
    reprise 253–5
    self analysis 251–2
experienced meaningfulness 153, 154
experienced responsibility 154
explicit knowledge 377, 383–6
Expo, British Columbia 223–5
extra-role behavior, organizational commitment
  and 184

fairness theory (FT) 68–78
  conditions 70–4
  conduct and 74–6
  key variables 69–70
  limitations and boundary conditions 76–8
Falzer, Paul 49
feedback:
  negative feedback 136
  role in goal setting theory 136
Festinger, L. 61–3
Feyerabend, P. 346
Fiedler, Fred 41, 157
Finkelstein, Syd 112, 116, 118–20, 451
Fiol, Marlene 339, 350
firm growth 539–40
Fischhoff, B. 38
Flanagan, J.C. 60

Fleishman, Ed 134
Fleming, Alexander 367–8
Fletcher, Karen 335–6, 338
focal agents 70
force 248
Ford Foundation 246
fortuitous influences 18–20
Frank, Linda 160
French, Jack 242, 244
Friedland, R. 450–1
Friedman conjecture 512, 518–20, 524
Friedman, Milton 511–13, 516
Frost, P.M. 396
F-scale 244
functional analysis 23–4
fundamental transformation 498

Galileo 144
gamble analogy 38–40
Garcia, John 30
Gargiulo, M. 450
Garland, Howard 139, 140
Geertz, Clifford 362, 402
Geletkanycz, Marta 116, 118
Genetech 559, 561
Georgescu-Roegen, Nicholas 504
Gergen, Kenneth 403
Germany:
    error intolerance 87
    reunification 91–2
    scientific culture 85–6
Geroski, Paul 540
Ghiselli, Ed 192
Giddens, A. 342, 343, 346, 349, 468
Gilbert, Daniel R., Jr. 426
Gilliland, Stephen 48–9
Gioia, Dennis 407
Gittell, J.H. 323
Gleason, Paul 398
globalization 474–5
goals 129–30
    achievement, organizational effectiveness
        and 307, 309
    in decision making 44–5
    goal conflict 136
    learning goals 141–2
    mediators of goal effects 129, 141
    moderators of goal effects 129
    performance and 139–40
    proximal goals 142
    satisfaction and 129–30, 140
    see also goal setting theory
goal setting theory 128–43
    differentiation of goal attributes 135–6
    discovering goal mechanisms 136–7
    expectancy and performance issues 139–40

failures 140
feedback role 136
field studies 135
genesis 130–5
getting goal commitment 137–9
goal conflict 136
need for knowledge, skill or task
        strategies 141–2
performance satisfaction 140
see also goals
Goetein, B. 38
Gomez-Mejia, L.R. 119
Goodpaster, K. 429
Goodrick, E. 467
Gordon, Aaron 493
Gouldner, Alvin 173, 175
Gouldner, H.P. 175
Govindarajan, V. 115
grand theories 85–6, 103–4
Granovetter, M. 454
Graves, S. 430–1
great companies 186
Greif, Siegfried 85
Griffin, R.W. 167, 293
growth:
    economic, technology and 524–9
    of firms 539–40
Growth Need Strength (GNS) 155
Grusky, O. 176
Guetzgow, Harold 347
guided mastery 23–5
Gulati, R. 450
Gupta, A.K. 115

Hacker, W. 84
Han, S. 454
Hansen, Mark 297
Harrison, Jeffrey 427, 431
Harrison, Richard 445
Haunschild, P.R. 450
Hayek, Friedrich 488
health care delivery services, US 472–3
Heaphy, E. 321–2
Heath, C. 454
Hebb, Donald 241, 246, 247
Heckler, Sue 48
Heidegger, Martin 388–9
Heider, F. 79
Helson, H. 55
Hennigan, Karen 64
Herrnstein, Richard 131
Hershey, J.C. 38
Herzberg, Frederick 132, 166
Hickson, D.J. 444
high theory 283
Hirschman, A.O. 57

Hoang, Ha 230
Hodgkinson, Gerard 340–1
Hofstede, G. 85
Hollenbeck, J.R. 139
Horwitch, Mel 420
Hoskisson, R.E. 450
House, R. 447
Ho, Violet 207
Hughes, Everett C. 461
Hulin, Chuck 192
Hull, D. 346
human relations model of organizational
        effectiveness 308, 309
Hume, David 378

ideological referents 72
Ierardi, Gordon 252
image theory 36, 43–50
    Arizona research 48–9
    Washington research 49–50
individual differences 163, 167–8
individual–organization linkages project 175
industrial psychology 241–5
inequality:
    between firms 281, 290
    in society 281–2, 285, 295
    theory of 282
    see also resource-based theory
inequity 56
    see also equity
inertia 344
    stress interaction 343–5
information:
    creation of 374–5
    filtering process 112–14
    markets for 551–3
    organizational boundaries 553–7
Ingram, Paul 501, 502
initiative see personal initiative (PI)
innovation 374–5
    culture of 277
    education relationship 117–18
innovative competition 527–9
institutionalization 549–51
institutional theory 460–78, 547–9, 566–8
    conditionalizing decoupling 468–9
    early insights 461–2
    expanding facets and levels 473–4
    framework 464–6
    institutional change processes 471–3
        convergent and disruptive change 471
        origins and endings 471–3
    non-local knowledge 474–5
    personal contribution to 475–7
    process-based theory 549
    reconsidering rationality 469–71

structure-based theory 549
    toward more interactive models 466–8
    see also social construction
interactional justice 75–6
interdisciplinary social science 489–91
internal congruence model of organizational
        effectiveness 308, 309
intervention, role of 273–4
Irwin, Robert 401
issues 424

Janson, Bob 152, 159–60
Jensen, M.C. 120, 290
JetBlue 186–7
job characteristics theory (JCT) 152–68
    controversies 165–8
        individual differences 167–8
        job perceptions 166–7
        motivating potential 168
    development of 156–64
        external impetus 159–60
        relevant preparation 156–8
        robust personal relationship 158–9
        supportive context 160–1
    early success of 164–5
    iterative process 161–4
        core job characteristics 162
        individual differences 163
        outcome variables 162
        psychological states 162
        subsequent developments 163–4
    overview 152–6
job diagnostic survey (JDS) 155–6, 160, 165, 166
job performance, see performance
Job Rating Form (JRF) 155–6, 166–7
Johns, G. 195
Jones, T. 430
justice 55, 69
    distributive justice 73
    interactional justice 75–6
    procedural justice 75–6
    see also fairness theory (FT)
justification 66–8
    in escalation of commitment 222

Kahneman, Danny 39, 63–5
Kahn, Robert 244
Kanfer, Frederick 195, 203
Kanter, R.M. 175–6, 286
Katz, Daniel 242
Kaysen, Carl 494
Kelley, H.H. 55
Kelly, G. 336
Kemosabe effects 80
Kets de Vries, M.F.R. 115
Khurana, R. 440

Kimberly, J.R. 117, 286
Kim, H. 450
Klein, Burton 525, 527
Klein, H.J. 139
Klepper, Steven 539
knowledge 376–82
    explicit knowledge 377, 383–6
    non-local knowledge 474–5
    objective knowledge 376–7
    productive knowledge 530–2
    subjective knowledge 376–7
    tacit knowledge 376–7, 383, 532–3, 552–3
        natural excludability 552–3
        transmission of 557
    transmission by academic scientists 557–9
knowledge creation theory 373–5, 377
    building, energizing, and connecting
            Ba 389–90
    environment and 382
    human agents 377–9
    knowledge vision 388–9
    organizations and 379–81
    SECI process 383–7
        combination 385–6
        externalization 383–5
        internalization 386
        socialization 383
    synthesis through leadership 387–8
knowledge of results 154, 155
Kochan, T. 429
Koput, Ken 230, 557
Kraatz, Matt 201
Kuhn, Thomas 345–6
Kunda, G. 455
Kunz, Philip 283
Kuttner, R. 454

Lavelle, Jim 78
Lawler, Ed 157–8, 161, 162
Lawrence, P.R. 162
leadership:
    knowledge creation and 387–8
    knowledge vision 388–9
    style of 243–4
learned helplessness theory 84–5
learning:
    goals 141–2
    single and double-loop learning 262–4, 271–2
Lee, Tom 49–50
legitimacy 514
    of deprivations 66
Levinson, Harry 195
Lewin, A. 292, 307–8
Lewin, Kurt 2, 58, 84, 103, 247, 248, 276
Liedtka, Jeanne 432
Likert, Rensis 242, 308

Lind, Alan 57
Litschert, R.J. 117
Llewellyn, Karl 488
Locke, John 376
Long Island Lighting Corporation 227–8
Lopez, S.J. 276
Lorange, P. 426
Lord, R.G. 117
Lorsch, J.W. 39
Losada, M. 321–2
Lubatkin, M.H. 121
Luckmann, T. 549

3M 277
McAllister, Dan 42
McClelland, David 130–1
Mace, C.A. 131
McGrath, Joe 157
Mackenzie, K.D. 447
McKinley, W. 437
McMillan, John 505
Macneil, Ian 196, 198
Magala, S.J. 396, 403–4
Maier, Norman 242–3, 246
management 541
    practice, theory development and 299
management theory 420
managerial discretion 118–20
managerial and organizational cognition
            (MOC) 332
    mapping strategic thought 332.339
        argument 338–9
        attention 335–6
        categorization 336–7
        causality 337–8
        schema 339, 340
        strategic frames 333–4
Mann Gulch 396, 399
March, James 520–1
Margolis, Julius D. 319, 445, 493, 496
market failure literature 491–2
Marquis, C. 438
Martin, Kirsten 432
Mason, Phyllis 111–12, 114
Mason, Richard 419
Massey, G.J. 514–5
Mathieu, J.E. 181–2, 183–4
Mayne, T.T. 319
Meckling, W.H. 290
Meichenbaum, D. 14
Meredith, Bill 192
mergers, profitability and 447–8
Messick, David 199
metamorphic progress 559–61
Meyer, John W. 462, 469, 470, 474–5, 477
Meyer, J.P. 174, 181, 185, 187

mid-range theories 85–6
Miles, Bob 286
Miller, D. 115, 117, 438
Miller, N.E. 11
Minton, J.W. 307–8
Mintzberg, H. 38, 42
Mitchell, R. 430
Mitroff, Ian 419
modeling:
    misconceptions about 13–14
    social modeling 10–12
    symbolic modeling 14–16
Mone, M.A. 437
monster imitator 528–9
moral accountability 72–6
moral agency 21–2
Morgan, G. 396
Morgenstern, O. 38
Morris, Tony 157
motivating potential score (MPS) 155, 168
motivation 246
    definition 247
    expectancy theory 247–55
        fitting the theory to the data 249–51
        self analysis 251–2
Murphy, K.J. 120

Nadler, D.A. 307–8
Napier, N.K. 119–20
natural trajectories 536
need for independence 244
Nee, Victor 501, 502
negative feedback 88
Nelson, Kim 48
Nelson, Richard 510, 524–31
networks 556
new institutional economics 501–2
Newton, Isaac 144
Nicholson, N. 195
Nicosia, Francisco 374
Nishida, Kitaro 380
NK modeling technique 536
Norburn, D. 117–18
Notz, Bill 216

observational learning 11
Ocasio, W. 450
Ogden, S. 431
Oliver, C. 467
Olson, Mancur 284
open systems models 473
opportunism 497–8
Ordonez, Lisa 48
organizational commitment 171–87
    consequences of 180–4, 187
        employee absenteeism 183–4

employee turnover 183
        extra-role behavior 184
        job performance 181–3
    definition 175–7
    development of 177–80
        anticipation stage 178–9
        entrenchment stage 180
        initiation stage 179
    early research 172–4
    future directions 184–7
    UCI individual–organization linkages
        project 175
    see also commitment; escalation of
        commitment
Organizational Commitment Questionnaire
    (OCQ) 177
organizational effectiveness 304–26
    competing values framework 308–10
    conclusions about 310–14
    demise of 315–16
    foundations of 305–7
    indicators of, problems with 313
    methodological challenges 314–16
    models of 307–10
        bureaucratic model 305–6
        contingency model 306–7
        goal achievement model 307, 309
        human relations model 308, 309
        internal congruence model 308, 309
        resource dependence model 307, 309
        strategic constituencies model 308, 309
    positive organizational scholarship (POS) as
        new approach 316–26
    revitalizing interest 324–6
organizational routines 533–5
    sources of 535–7
organizational virtuousness 322–3
organizations 379–81
    decoupling 468–9
    as information envelopes 553–7
    knowledge creation 380–1
    new forms generated by metamorphic
        progress 559–61
    as rationalized systems 462–3
    stakeholder approach 429–30
    structural differences 498–9
    see also institutional theory
organization theory 287
    contribution to transaction cost
        economics 487–8
Ouchi, Bill 287–8, 289
outsourcing 498

Palmer, D. 450–1
Pan American Airlines 225
Papandreou, Andreas 493

Parks, Judi Maclean 199, 207
Parmar, Bidhan 432
participation in decision making (pdm)
     137–9
Peak, Helen 242, 246, 248
Pearce, Jone 167
Penrose, Edith 376
performance:
    goal difficulty relationship 139–40
    organizational commitment 181–3
    personal initiative relationships 97–8
    social performance, stakeholder
         approach 430–1
persistence 92–3
personal agency 9–10
    exercise of agency through self-regulation 16–23
    triadic model 26–8
personal initiative (PI) 91–8
    antecedents and consequences of 93–7
         environmental supports 96–7
         knowledge, skills, ability (KSA) 96
         orientations 94–6
         personality factors 96
    aspects of 92–3
    concept of 92
    effects on the environment 97
    facets of 93
    performance and 97–8
    planning relationship 100
    training program 101–2
personality 26
    personal initiative and 96
Peteraf, Margie 293–4
Peters, T. 38–9
Pfeffer, Jeff 166, 182–3, 186, 307
phenomenology 375, 439
    environment interactions 382
    human agents 377–9
    knowledge 376–7
    organizations 379–81
Phillips, Adam 403
Phillips, Almarin 494
Phillips, D.J. 450
Phillips, Robert 427, 429
philosophy of science 345–6
plan adoption 45
planning 99–101
    personal initiative relationship 100
pointer knowledge 198
Polanyi, Michael 532–3, 534
Pondy, L.R. 396
Popper, K.R. 2, 89, 143, 346, 358–9
Porac, J.F. 336–7
Porter, Lyman 162
Porter, Michael 290–1, 431
positive energy 322

positive organizational scholarship
     (POS) 316–26
    organizational effectiveness approach 319–24
    revitalizing interest in organizational
         effectiveness 324–6
positivism 374, 375
    environment interactions 382
    human agents 377–9
    knowledge 376–7
    organizations 379–81
Posner, Richard 494
Post, Jim 421
Potter, Richard 48
Powell, Walter W. 463, 469, 556
Powers, W.T. 21
Prahalad, C.K. 295
Prentiss, Don 199
Preston, L. 424
Price, J.L. 307
principles 42, 44
proactivity 92
    training 102
procedural justice 75–6
process control 57
production theory, limitations 529–30
professions 551–2
    as information envelopes 553–7
profitability test 46–7
profit maximization 512–14, 515–16, 518–19
progress decisions 45, 46
prospect theory 39, 255
proximal goals 142
psychodynamic theory 22–4
psychological contract theory 190–209
    boundary conditions 208
    dynamic properties 194, 206
    emerging and future developments 208–9
    idiosyncratic deals 207
    mutuality aspects 194, 206, 208
    overview 193–207
    roots 191–3
    violation 202–3
    zone of negotiability 206
psychological distance 248
psychological safety 158
publication process 30–1
Purdy, Ken 152, 159–60
Puto, Chris 48

Quinn, R.E. 308

Rajagopalan, N. 119
Ramaswamy, K. 117
Rand, Ayn 131, 132
rationality 462, 469–71
    bounded rationality 497

realism 512
Reber, A.S. 405, 406–7
Rediker, Kenneth 42–3
referent-cognitions theory (RCT) 63–8
    simulation heuristic 64–5
Reger, Ronda 336
Rehbein, K. 450
relative deprivation 55–6
    perceived legitimacy of deprivations 66
research and development (R and D)
        activity 509–11
    management 525–6
researcher characteristics 585–6
resiliency 24
resource-based logic 295
resource-based theory:
    background 283–4
    developing the resource-based view 291–4
    finding the question 284–91
    retrospection and generalization 294–6
    see also resource dependence theory
resource dependence theory 436–56
    early empirical research 442–4
    fundamental theoretical ideas 441–2
    organizational effectiveness model 307, 309
    origins 439–41
    refinement through contrast 447–8
    social context of theory development 445–7
    success and setbacks 448–52
    see also resource-based theory
retrospect 402–3
Richards, Max 110–11
Richmond, Sandra 48
Roberts, Karlene 192
Robinson, Sandra 201–3
Roethlisberger, F.J. 306
Rohrbaugh, J. 308
Roloff, Mike 198
Ronan, Bill 133
Rosenfield, David 67
Ross, Jerry 223, 225, 227
Rotter, J.B. 84
routines 533–5
    sources of 535–7
Rowan, B. 469
Rowland, Ken 216
R-R psychology 243
Rubenstein, S. 429
Rubin, Jeffrey 219
rules 343, 520
Rumelt, Dick 290, 292, 295
Ryan, Art 131

Sabido, Miguel 15–16
sacred values 80
St John, C. 431

Salancik, Gerry 166, 307, 442–3, 446, 467
Sambharya, R. 117
Samuelson, Paul 489
Sanders, W.G. 118
satisfaction, goals and 129–30, 140
satisficing 520, 522–4
Schalk, Rene 206
schema 339, 340
Schepers, Don 48
Schuler, D.A. 450
Schumpeterian hypothesis 528
Schumpeter, Joseph 527–8
Schwenk, Charles 337
Schwinn antitrust case 495
Seashore, Stan 244, 307
SECI process 377, 383–7
    combination 385–6
    externalization 383–5
    internalization 386
    socialization 383
self-efficacy 25–6, 27
    efficacy beliefs 28
    in goal setting theory 139–40
self-esteem 26
self-regulation 16–23
    guided mastery 23–5
self-starting 92
Seligman, M. 84, 320
Selye, Hans 361, 368
Selznick, P. 39, 306
Semmer, Norbert 85
sensemaking 394, 395–404, 409
    retrospecting elapsed experience 402–3
    seeing what I say 400–1
    as Zeitgeist 403–4
Shapira, Z. 38
Shartle, Carroll 242
Shaw, J.B. 167
shift work 244–5
Shoemaker, P.G.H. 38
Shoreham nuclear power plant, Long
        Island 227–8
Simon, Herbert 114–15, 211, 255, 306, 332, 489–90,
        497, 520, 523
Simonton, D.K. 58
Simsek, Z. 121
simulation heuristic 64–5
single-loop learning 262–3
Skinner, B.F. 16–17
Smith, Adam 502
Smith-Doerr, L. 556
Smith, Jim F. 42
Smith, M. 119–20
Smith, Pat 131
Snyder, C.R. 276
social boundaries 553–7

social cognitive theory 9, 15–29
  agentic perspective 9–10
  cultural influences 27–8
  guided mastery 23–5
  self-efficacy 25–6
  self-regulatory capabilities 16–22
  social modeling centrality 10–12
social construction 547–8
  knowledge transmission 557–9
  markets for information 551–3
    tacit knowledge and natural
      excludability 552–3
  metamorphic progress 559–62
  social boundaries 553–7
  social goods producing social structure 562–6
  see also institutional theory
social diffusion model 15, 16
social information processing 440
social issues management 424
social labeling practices 24
social network theory 15, 285
social performance, stakeholder approach 430–1
social responsibility, stakeholder approach 430–1
social structure 562–6
sociology 284–5
Solow, Robert 503
Sonnenfeld, J.A. 430
Sorenson, Don 283
Southwest Airlines 186, 323
Sparrow, Paul 341
Spender, J.C. 334
Spreitzer, G. 321
S-R psychology 243
stakeholders 420, 424
stakeholder theory 417–33
  assessment of 422–7
  early involvement 418–22
  misinterpretations 425–6
  subfields 428–31
    corporate governance and organizational
      theory 429–30
    normative theories of business 428–9
    social responsibility and social
      performance 430–1
    strategic management 431
Stalker, G.M. 30
Starbuck, Bill 333, 350
Staw, Barry 445, 446
Stevens, Cynthia 48
strategic constituencies model 308, 309
strategic frames 333–4
  as rules and resources 343
strategic management, stakeholder approach 431
strategic planning 426
strategic thought mapping 332–9
  argument 338–9

attention 335–6
categorization 336–7
causality 337–8
schemas 339
strategic frames 333–4
strategy selection model 41–3, 47
stress 344
  inertia interaction 343–5
structuration 343
Stucker, Kristin 116
Sturdivant, Fred 420
subjective expected utility (SEU) 36–7
  limitations of 37–41
Sutton, Robert 446
symbolic modeling 14–16

tacit knowledge 376–7, 383, 532–3, 552–3
  natural excludability 552–3
  transmission of 557
technology:
  economic growth 524–9, 559–61
  production 530–2
  sources of 535–7
Tegar, Allen 219
Tetlock, P.E. 74, 79–80
theorizing 395, 404–9
  see also sensemaking; theory development
theory 283–4
  as a continuum 360
  definition 405, 406
  high theory 283
  nature of 356
  politics of 453–6
theory of action *see* action production; action
    theory
theory development 361–71, 572–3
  advice 123–4, 209–10, 233–5, 346–52
  anomalies, importance of 367
  asking questions 300, 361–2
  colleagues and friends, role of 300–1
  connecting and disconnecting 365–6
  critical incident 60–3
  description 362
  diagrams, role of 363–4
  inductive approach 143–7, 357–60
    data gathering 144–5
    differentiating 145
    identifying causal relationships 146
    integrating 145
    keeping theories open-ended 146–7
    taking time 146
  literature role 296–7
  management practice 299
  outlining ideas 362–3
  process of 1–4, 28–31, 58–63, 573–83
    elaboration/research 578–81

proclamation/presentation 581–3
  search 575–9
  tension/phenomena 573–5
reasons for 437–8
reflection on experience 58–9
research roles 357–9, 583–5
  advocate 585
  carrier 584
  codifier 584
  creator 583–4
  empirical research 297–8
  intervention 273–4
  keeping it simple 366
  qualitative and quantitative
    research 359–60
  researcher 584
social context 445–7
starting with the dependent variable 59–60
taking initiatives 272–3
taking notes 366–7
unexpected nature of 361
see also theorizing
Thibaut, John W. 55, 56, 58
Thomas, A.S. 117
Thomas, H. 336–7
Thompson, J.D. 441
Thorndike, E.L. 11
Thornton, P.H. 444, 450
thriving 321
time management 102
Torvald, Linus 351
Toulmin, Steven 338–9, 346
Toulouse, J.M. 115
training:
  error management 87–9
  personal initiative 101–2
transaction cost economics (TCE) 289, 429, 454,
    485–505, 555–6
  antitrust experience 494–6
  applications to additional phenomena 500–1
  background training 492
  developments in the 1960s 489–92
    interdisciplinary social science 489–91
    market failure literature 491–2
  key contributions 486–9
    economics 486–7
    law 488–9
    organization theory 487–8
  lessons 503–5
    be disciplined 503–4
    be interdisciplinary 504
    have an active mind 504–5
  misconceptions 501–2
  rudiments 500
  teaching and research:
    Berkeley 493–4

Penn 496–7
  vertical integration problem 497–9
'Trapped Administrator' experiment 220–1
trust 553–4
trustworthiness 406
truth 376, 377
  see also knowledge
Tsui, A.S. 308
Turner, A.N. 162
Turner, Donald 494
Tushman, M.L. 307–8
Tversky, A. 39
Tyler, Tom 66, 67, 198–9

Ulich, Eberhard 85
Umphress, Elizabeth 80
unfairness 69
  see also Fairness Theory (FT)
unfolding model 49
United Airlines 323
United Parcel Service 243–4
upper echelons theory 109–24
  foundational evidence 114–15
  frustrations 122–3
  initial presentation 111–14
  origins 109–11
  reinforcing evidence 115–18
  theoretical refinements 118–22
    behavioral integration 120–2
    managerial discretion 118–20
U.S. Airways 323
US Brewers Association 420

Valery, P. 191
values 342
Van de Ven, Andy 2
Veiga, J.F. 121
Venkataraman, S. 432
VIE theory see expectancy theory (ET)
Vietnam War 216–18, 445
virtuousness 321, 322–3
Viteles, Maurice 244
voice 57
Volpert, Walter 85
Von Neumann, J. 38

Waddock, S. 430–1, 432
Waller, Bill 42
Wally, S. 117
Walsh, J.P. 319, 340, 445
Walsh, Kenneth 48
Walters, Roy 166
Wan, W.P. 450
Watson, J.B. 11
Watson, R. 431
Weatherly, Kris 48

Webb, Eugene 442
Weber, K. 319, 445
Weber, M. 305
Webster, Edward 241
Weick, Karl 56, 333, 345, 350
Weiss, H.M. 167
Wensley, Robin 290
Wernerfelt, Birger 292
Westphal, J. 469
Wexley, Ken 133–4
Whetton, David 208
White, John 30
Whittington, R. 343
Whyte, William 172, 276
Wicks, Andy 424, 425, 427, 430, 432

Wiersema, M.F. 118
Williams, C.R. 139
Williamson, O. 288, 289, 429
Wilson, Edmund O. 203
Wood, D. 430
Woodward, Joan 370

Yuchtman, E. 307
Yukl, Gary 133–4

Zajac, D.M. 181–2, 183–4
Zajac, E. 199, 469
Zimmerman, Edwin 494
zone of negotiability 206
Zucker, L.G. 472